P. T. BARNUM

P. T. BARNUM

The Legend and the Man

A. H. SAXON

COLUMBIA UNIVERSITY PRESS
NEW YORK

COLUMBIA UNIVERSITY PRESS
New York   Chichester, West Sussex
Copyright © 1989 A. H. Saxon
All rights reserved

LIBRARY OF CONGRESS CATALOGING-IN-PUBLICATION DATA

Saxon, A. H.
  P.T. Barnum : the legend and the man / A. H. Saxon.
    p.   cm.
  Bibliography: p.
  Includes index.
  ISBN 0-231-05686-9 (alk. paper)   ISBN 0-231-05687-7 (pbk.)
  1. Barnum, P. T. (Phineas Taylor), 1810–1891.
  2. Circus owners—United States—Biography.
  I. Title.
GV1811.B3S29 1989
791.3'092—dc20
[8]
                                                        89-982
                                                          CIP

Book design by Jennifer Dossin

PRINTED IN THE UNITED STATES OF AMERICA

c 10 9 8 7 6 5 4 3 2 1
p 10 9 8 7 6 5 4 3 2 1

TO

"Charity" Gail,
without whom "Phineas" is nothing

CONTENTS

ILLUSTRATIONS

Figures

Joice Heth, the 161-year-old "nurse" of George Washington. From a rare bill announcing an 1835 appearance by her in Bridgeport. Somers Historical Society, Somers, New York.

Signor Vivalla, Barnum's early juggling sensation. From an 1836 bill advertising performances by him in Bridgeport. Somers Historical Society, Somers, New York.

The American Museum as it appeared c. 1850. Lithograph by Brown and Severin, printed by G. W. Lewis III. Barnum Museum, Bridgeport, Connecticut.

The "Happy Family" at the American Museum. From Barnum's *Illustrated News* of 28 May 1853.

An interior view of the American Museum. From *Gleason's Pictorial Drawing-Room Companion*, 29 January 1853.

The "What Is It?" Number 12 in the series Barnum's Gallery of Wonders, published by Currier & Ives. Shelburne Museum, Shelburne, Vermont.

Anna Swan, Barnum's "Nova Scotia Giantess." From the original glass negative by Matthew Brady in the Meserve Collection at the National Portrait Gallery, Smithsonian Institution, Washington, D.C.

The Lucasie family of albinos. From the original glass negative by Matthew Brady in the Meserve Collection at the National Portrait Gallery, Smithsonian Institution, Washington, D.C.

A "leopard child." From the original glass negative by Matthew Brady in the Meserve Collection at the National Portrait Gallery, Smithsonian Institution, Washington, D.C.

Zalumma Agra, the famous "Circassian Girl." From the original glass negative by Matthew Brady in the Meserve Collection at the National Portrait Gallery, Smithsonian Institution, Washington, D.C.

The "Lecture Room" at the first American Museum. From *Gleason's Pictorial Drawing-Room Companion*, 29 January 1853.

The architect's drawing for Barnum's proposed new museum in New York City. From *Harper's Weekly*, 17 July 1880.

The "Fejee Mermaid." From the first edition of Barnum's autobiography.

Barnum as he appeared in 1844. Lithograph by Day and Haghe of London after a portrait by Charles Baugniet. Barnum Museum, Bridgeport, Connecticut.

Tom Thumb's equipage standing outside London's Egyptian Hall. Engraving from *Tallis' Illustrated London*. Collection of Leslie P. Symington.

Following page 210

Tom Thumb as Napoleon. Carte de visite dating from the 1860s. Barnum Museum, Bridgeport, Connecticut.

Professor Faber's celebrated talking machine. From *Illustrated History of Wild Animals and Other Curiosities Contained in P. T. Barnum's Great Traveling World's Fair, Museum, Menagerie, Polytechnic Institute, and International Zoological Garden*, 1874.

Iranistan, Barnum's oriental mansion modeled on the Royal Pavilion at Brighton, England. Lithograph by F. D'Avignon, 1850. Private Collection.

Oil portrait of Barnum's daughters by Frederick Spencer, 1847. Barnum Museum, Bridgeport, Connecticut.

Jenny Lind and her conductor, Julius Benedict, and baritone lead, Giovanni Belletti. Lithographed music cover by Sarony, 1850. Private Collection.

The tent used for Barnum's "Asiatic Caravan" of 1851–54. Private Collection.

A five-dollar note for the Pequonnock Bank of Bridgeport. Bridgeport Public Library, Historical Collections.

"The Fairy Wedding." Carte de visite by Matthew Brady. Bridgeport Public Library, Historical Collections.

General and Mrs. Tom Thumb with their "baby." Carte de visite by Matthew Brady. Bridgeport Public Library, Historical Collections.

Waldemere, Barnum's first mansion on the edge of Seaside Park. Colored lithograph. Bridgeport Public Library, Historical Collections.

Captain Djordji Costentenus, the famous tattooed man. Small colored lithograph by H. A. Thomas of New York. Bridgeport Public Library, Historical Collections.

"Ye Kind-hearted Man." Henry Bergh, the founder and first president of the Society for the Prevention of Cruelty to Animals. Small colored print by Tobin of New York. Private Collection.

"The Greatest Show on Earth" as it appeared in 1873. Circus World Museum, Baraboo, Wisconsin.

Charity Barnum in later life. Carte de visite. Barnum Museum, Bridgeport, Connecticut.

The interior of Barnum's Roman Hippodrome in New York. Private Collection.

Nancy Fish, Barnum's second wife. Imperial-sized photograph by Farini of Bridgeport. Private Collection.

The Barnum family monument in Bridgeport's Mountain Grove Cemetery. Photograph by the author.

Thomas Ball's marble bust of Barnum, dating from 1883–84. Tufts University Archives and Special Collections.

The sculptor Thomas Ball with his monumental statue of Barnum. Fred D. Pfening III Collection.

"The Perennial P. T.—The Man the Children Love." From the *New York Daily Graphic*, 23 March 1889.

Following page 306

Barnum and his partner James A. Bailey. Colored cover of the program for a later visit by their show to London's Olympia. Bridgeport Public Library, Historical Collections.

Barnum in his phaeton. Barnum Museum, Bridgeport, Connecticut.

The Bridgeport winter quarters. Illustration in the 1888 juvenile *P. T. Barnum's Circus*, after a lithograph by the Strobridge Company of Cincinnati. Bridgeport Public Library, Historical Collections.

A blessed event at winter quarters. Colored lithographic poster by the Strobridge Company of Cincinnati, 1882. Bridgeport Public Library, Historical Collections.

"The Frog and the Ox." An 1880s colored lithographic poster by the Strobridge Company of Cincinnati. Bridgeport Public Library, Historical Collections.

Scenes from the life of Jumbo. Bridgeport Public Library, Historical Collections.

Barnum and his fellow humbug Jumbo. Cartoon by Thomas Nast in *Harper's Weekly* of 15 April 1882.

"Jumbo at the Bar" and "Jumbo Aesthetic." Two trade cards published around the time of the elephant's arrival in New York. Private Collection.

P. T. BARNUM

PROLOGUE

THE PRESENT BOOK is not meant to be "definitive," nor is it intended as a bi-ography in the popular, anecdotal sense. The life of P. T. Barnum was so packed with incident that the first would be impossible to achieve within the limits of the author's remaining lifetime or his publisher's patience; while examples of the second have been written by several others, most notably by the irre-pressible showman himself, so that by now the broad outline of his public career is familiar, or at least accessible, to all. So, too, is the popular concep-tion of his character: "Prince of Humbugs," as he proudly proclaimed himself early in his career, following a succession of spectacular frauds he foisted upon his gullible patrons; a ceaseless blower of his own horn and an unscrupulous manipulator of public opinion; a heartless addict of practical jokes, sparing neither enemies nor family and friends, which he then delighted in rehearsing over again in print; a hypocrite and perennial cynic, whose one memorable pronouncement on the human condition is supposed to have been "There's a sucker born every minute." One remembers him also, of course, as a circus proprietor and the founder, in late life, of "The Greatest Show on Earth." Yet even here he has typically been denied credit for any contribution beyond the investment of his money and loan of his name, with all of the actual work and innovations being attributed to his self-effacing partners, who supposedly looked upon their blustering colleague as a minor nuisance. It is hardly surprising to find him casually dismissed in one recent circus history as "a man with too much contempt for the public to devote his life to putting on a show of real skill and merit."[1]

His reputation has hardly been any higher abroad. In England, which he visited frequently from 1844 onward, he is most often recalled as the impudent Yankee who insinuated himself and his "dwarf" Tom Thumb into the presence of the young Queen Victoria, and who later returned to raid the Regent's Park Zoo, wresting from the English their favorite "pet," the huge African elephant Jumbo. In France, where he also sojourned with his "man in miniature," the writer Barbey d'Aurevilly has sarcastically characterized him as an "American humbug . . . a great Bible thumper who lies in his advertisements with the pure, tranquil conscience of a Quaker, and who is always ready to lift up to God his innocent hands, filthy from lucre taken in at the box office."[2] Char-latan, con artist, master of (to use the cliché currently favored by journalists writing about him) "hype"—the image persists and in the present century has been further expanded to include his depiction as a lout in a movie featuring the blowsy Wallace Beery in the title role.[3] More recently, he has been portrayed in a popular Broadway musical as a youthful manager and performer in his own circus, and as the passionate lover of the "divine" Jenny Lind—a titillating hint of human frailty that, predictably, has been avidly seized upon by at least one other author.[4] Meanwhile, a French *danseuse* pirouettes onto the scene; rumors of an illegitimate son (or was it a daughter?) inexorably follow; the septuagenarian showman is reported to have been an "old devil" among the unprotected females in his circus. And to crown it all, if one may believe a story that began in his day and has been elaborated on in our own, he was also responsible for the assassination of Jumbo—the gentlest, mightiest, most noble-hearted beast that ever lived!

Among those who have written most thoughtfully about Barnum, even his staunchest supporters have had little success in dispelling these notions. Their grip on the popular imagination is indeed tenacious. By now he has attained the status of an American folk hero—more accurately, anti-hero—whose reputed deeds are no more to be doubted than those of a Davy Crockett or Paul Bunyan. If one cannot unequivocally assign particular acts or sayings to him, it suffices that they be something Barnum *might* have done or said. Nor is this "generic" portrait by any means an invention of the twentieth century. As Barnum himself early came to realize and sometimes regret, the responsibility for its creation was in large part his own. Had the notorious first edition of his autobiography been delayed by two or three years, to the period when his world seemed in hopeless disarray and most people believed he would never recover from the stunning bankruptcy that had overtaken him, it would undoubtedly have been a far different book. But coming as it did in late 1854—when its middle-aged author was still flush with fame and fortune from his recent tour with Jenny Lind, supremely confident in his position as proprietor of the renowned American Museum, a burgeoning real-estate magnate in his adopted city of Bridgeport, Connecticut, where he occupied a mansion fit for an oriental potentate—his book was bound to display a certain amount of classic hubris. Worse yet, in addition to detailing and openly crowing over its author's involvement in such patent frauds as the Fejee Mermaid and "Colonel Frémont's Woolly Horse," the autobiography confirmed what many had suspected all along: that even such "legitimate" enterprises as Barnum's management of Jenny Lind had been so tainted by his questionable publicity practices that they, too, might justifiably be cited as evidence for his preeminence in the realm of "humbug."

The result of this indiscreet publication was that for the remaining nearly forty years of his life friends and foes alike gleefully taunted him with "Joice Heth," the "Fejee Mermaid," and all the other youthful escapades he had so candidly acknowledged in his book. He so firmly established his claim to the title "Prince of Humbugs" in that work that no one ever let him forget it. Thereafter, no matter how altruistic his actions might be, his motives were certain to be suspect. Whenever he succeeded at one of his schemes, many persons automatically assumed he had done so through trickery or fraud.

Whenever he failed or met with some reversal in his life, he was surely getting just what he deserved. Yet even here, some people cautioned, it was advisable to remain on one's guard, since the wily showman's failures and disappointments might themselves be deceptions, planned with some ultimate profit in view! To be sure, in his public utterances Barnum usually laughed at such notions, professed not to care what his detractors said about him, even lent his support to some of the more outrageous tales. He was like the man, he was fond of remarking, who would "rather be kicked than not noticed at all." But in private it was sometimes a different matter, especially when, for one reason or another, he was attempting to put off the "showman" and don some other role—be it preacher, politician, or philanthropist—a metamorphosis that, needless to say, never quite succeeded. As he complained to a friend in 1865, while he was serving in the Connecticut legislature and boldly speaking out in favor of enfranchising the state's Negroes, "For 30 years I have *striven* to *do good*, but (foolishly) stuck my worst side outside, until half the Christian community got to believe that I wore horns & hoofs."[5]

He became, then, a legend in his time and continues so in our own; and one objective of this book is the exploration of the frequent antagonism between the Barnum of popular imagination, the wearer of "horns & hoofs," and Barnum as he really was or wished to be. For it is important to understand at the outset that Barnum was both philosophically and theologically a meliorist, and that far from conceding, as did many of his contemporaries, that individual character was relentlessly fixed, he firmly believed in its perfectibility—an evolutionary process that, if not completed to everyone's satisfaction in the present world, might proceed at a more leisurely pace in the next. And within the grand, all-encompassing legend of Barnum himself are several others that will bear investigation: the legend of Jenny Lind, for example, which, if not entirely of Barnum's creation, was certainly brought to its pitch by him; and the more poignant one of little Charley Stratton, promoted to "General" at the precocious age of four.

While not so thematic as the above, a second, closely related goal of the present work is the exploration of several aspects of Barnum's private life that have been either barely mentioned or totally ignored by his previous biographers. Indeed, so elusive has this life proven to date that a number of writers have concluded there was no such thing as a "private" Barnum—that like the attractions in his celebrated museum, he was himself always on show and possessed no more depth, self-awareness, or sensitivity than one finds displayed in his autobiography. Several twentieth-century authors, admittedly, have attempted to shed light on his personal affairs, and even the Freudians have had their say.[6] But the general impression remains that there was never that much to probe in the first place, or that if something deeper did exist at one time, it is now beyond recovery. As Constance Rourke so fatalistically summarized the situation in a well-known essay on Barnum in her *Trumpets of Jubilee*,

In Barnum's long career remain innumerable small alleys or byways which it might be amusing or instructive for the humble student of character to follow. But such delights are forever barred: the regions which Barnum traversed were too obscure for easy penetration after the long lapse of years; his life was most often interwoven with mean or humble lives, which have left behind them no trace. And strangely enough, almost nothing substantial about him emerges from the ruck of contemporary evidence; scarcely another figure of equal proportions has left so little behind him by way of personal print.

And behind the smile that Barnum always took care to present to his public, she goes on to suggest, there was neither a private life nor a personal character.[7] Nearly half a century after the above was written, the historian Neil Harris addressed the subject in much the same terms: "Barnum was a public man who kept his privacy. Indeed, one is not even sure that he had a notion of privacy, so completely did he define his own needs and reactions in public terms. His inner life, if it existed, was carefully shielded."[8] Compare these opinions with the intriguing statement by an anonymous writer, who as early as 1851 had the following to say in the *Trumpet and Universalist Magazine*:

> Mr. Barnum's life has been written in a dozen languages. They are all mere pictures of his external individuality. His REAL life—his inner and personal identity—remains yet to be edited, and when it is, take our word for it, it will be a psychological curiosity, a novelty of more thoughtful value to the student of human nature, than anything we have yet had published in the field of metaphysical philosophy.[9]

———◆———

AS THE FOLLOWING journey down the "small alleys or byways" of Barnum's life is to a considerable extent a personal one, the author here takes the opportunity to address the reader *in propria persona*. Many years ago, upon first moving into the Bridgeport area, I found myself in a minor dilemma. I had already attained some reputation as a historian of popular entertainments, particularly of the circus, and had recently begun a biography of a famous English equestrian and circus manager that was to occupy me for the next five years. Yet here I now was, almost literally in the backyard of the "world's greatest showman," who until then had possessed only casual interest for me. Friends and colleagues soon began asking if I had any plans to write about Barnum, to which I invariably answered "no."

I had read the notorious autobiography, of course, together with several studies by twentieth-century biographers, and these had convinced me there was little left to do. They also convinced me that if Barnum was not quite so bad as some of the swindlers in our own day, he was hardly the sort I wished to spend my time writing about, for I continued to share the popular conception of him as lying in wait for that "sucker born every minute."[10] I soon discovered that nearly all my neighbors were of the same opinion. No matter where I went in Bridgeport and its vicinity, no matter whom I talked to—or so it seemed—everyone had some favorite story to tell about the great "P. T."

I noticed, too, that while these stories were almost always of a comic nature, their narrators generally maintained a studied reserve, as though wishing me to understand that *they* did not approve of such carryings-on.

I still recall with infinite pleasure, for example, the tale one lifelong resident told me concerning Barnum's acquisition of Bridgeport's old Division Street Cemetery for real-estate development. This particular maneuver, which took place in the 1870s and involved the transferring of remains from a run-down cemetery near the center of town to the more recently established Mountain Grove Cemetery to the west of the city, outraged several of Bridgeport's leading families. There were a number of compelling reasons for the move, however; and much of the contemporary criticism leveled against Barnum, as I subsequently learned, was politically motivated and downright unfair. Still, the person in charge of the actual removal of the corpses (he was a local butcher, incidentally) does not appear to have been overly conscientious in the performance of his duty—and to continue with the story as it was told to me, it was not long until horrified citizens were being treated to the spectacle of open carts, piled high with coffins, rolling along in broad daylight; and of these coffins falling off, breaking open, and scattering decomposing bodies over the elm-lined streets of Bridgeport; so that by the time they finally did arrive at Mountain Grove Cemetery, the remains were so hopelessly mixed up that there could be no guarantee they were being deposited in the proper graves. "And then," said my informant, looking me straight in the eye and without the faintest trace of expression on her face, "do you know what Barnum did? He used the old headstones to pave his driveway!"

As this story illustrates all too well, one can never go wrong by refusing to give Barnum the benefit of the doubt. No matter how outrageous or improbable the tale may be, one is certain to encounter people who are prepared to swear to it, or at least to concede that "it sounds like something old Barnum would do." While I was sitting at my desk to record the above anecdote, word was brought to me of a local band director who was refusing to let his musicians participate in Bridgeport's annual Barnum Festival. His reason? He did not wish to commemorate the person who so callously referred to his fellow human beings as "suckers"! In the stagnant atmosphere of the showman's favorite city, nearly a century after his death, it sometimes seems as though he had driven along Main Street only yesterday.

The stories continued to accumulate, and I soon found myself in almost daily contact with places, institutions, and even a few individuals associated with Barnum. I became acquainted with several of his descendants, among them his last surviving great-grandchild, the late Mrs. Mildred Breul, who as an infant had been dandled on the showman's knee and whose mind—sharp as a pin at the age of ninety—was a veritable storehouse of anecdotes about her ancestor. My travels in the area sometimes took me to Bethel, where curiosity finally got the better of me and I more or less invited myself in to inspect the house in which Barnum was born; and where I also, after several false leads, even managed to locate and visit the fabled "Ivy Island" of the autobiography—an expedition from which, like its onetime owner, I very nearly did not return. Inevitably, my attention was drawn to Bridgeport's other famous resident, Charles Sherwood Stratton, otherwise known as "General Tom Thumb," whose wife's autobiography I eventually edited. And I was soon thoroughly familiar with the holdings of the Barnum Museum and the Historical Collections department of the Bridgeport Public Library, which between them possess the greatest trove anywhere of materials relating to Barnum and his illustrious midget.

As I examined the mass of Barnum memorabilia that came my way—the clothes he wore, the furnishings from his homes, the photographs, letters, diaries, and other manuscripts that were shown to me—I began to wonder if a reassessment might not be in order. Might there have been a "private" Barnum after all? Could it be that previous biographers, working from the assumption there was nothing deep or complex in his character, had been betrayed by a fundamental error? With as yet no firm opinion of my own on the subject, I began to collect systematically copies of all Barnum manuscripts I could learn about. The letters in particular—often quite funny, nearly always informative, attesting to their author's wide range of activities and personal acquaintances—struck me as being of potential interest to others; and in time, having finally completed my biography of that English equestrian, I selected from the over 3000 I had seen to date some 300 for publication. While this work was still in progress, I was invited to lead a seminar on Barnum at Yale University; and shortly thereafter a fellowship from the John Simon Guggenheim Memorial Foundation enabled me to round out my research by personally visiting a number of collections and to reexamine at leisure materials closer to home. By then, obviously, my initial resolve to have nothing to do with the "Prince of Humbugs" had been totally overwhelmed.

For I had finally discovered what I considered to be the key to the mystery— namely, that for all the candor and damaging revelations contained in his autobiography, Barnum was, paradoxically, very much a "private" person. Owing to propriety or to other reasons he deemed equally valid, he deliberately chose not to tell the whole story in his book. He barely mentions his religion in that work, for example; yet, strange as it may seem, he was for most of his life profoundly influenced by religious convictions. Nor—aside from chronicling their births, marriages, and deaths—has he much to say about his immediate family, including his first wife and companion of forty-four years, the elusive Charity, about whom so little is known even among her descendants. Barnum's critics have frequently cited the lack of truly personal information in his autobiography as further evidence of his shallowness and heartlessness, and many of his contemporaries were of the same opinion. My own favorite comment on this topic is a parody entitled *Auto-Biography of Barnum; or, The Opening of the Oyster*, published in Danbury only two years before the showman's death. "According to the best authority I had a father," the book begins, "but no matter about him; and a mother, but that's of no consequence."[11]

Because the autobiography is so candid and seemingly exhaustive a narrative, because it does reveal so much that is less than admirable in Barnum's professional career, readers are apt to come away from it with a feeling of satiety and the impression that very little remains to be learned about the man himself. Yet as Barnum emphatically wrote to his confidential secretary toward the end of his life, "My private personal affairs I always have kept distinct from *business. . . . Business* considerations should *never* be mixed up with other affairs."[12] And in the same way that he kept his personal life separate from his business transactions, so Barnum kept the former discreetly veiled from the readers of his autobiography—a work that, properly understood, is primarily a record of his chief, lifelong business of showman, and that might therefore have been more accurately titled "The *Public* Life of P. T. Barnum."[13]

Where, then, does one go to find the "private" Barnum? To the thousands of extant letters, for a start, especially those he wrote to family and close friends, although even the more mundane ones relating to his business affairs are sometimes not without interest to the experienced eye. Further clues are to be found in a variety of other manuscripts: his daughter Caroline's diaries; the great ledger or "Salmagundi" book and the office diary of his secretary Henry E. Bowser, who kept track of his employer's activities during the last decade of his life; Barnum's own memorandum and address books; numerous contracts and land records; court, municipal, and church archives; etc., etc. All these sources I have patiently sifted, together with the showman's publications and those of others, besides which I believe I may safely claim to possess a "feel" for the subject, developed through the long-standing associations mentioned above. Since the new information here presented is nearly always of a factual, documented nature, I doubt if it will occasion much controversy in itself. But the overall portrait that emerges in the following pages—of a Barnum who was not only a legend in his time but also often an unwilling prisoner of that legend; of a deeply religious man who experienced at mid-life a chastening moral regeneration—is essentially my own interpretation, presented in what I trust is an objective, unbiased manner. I readily confess I could not have devoted so much of my own life to this biography did I not feel some sympathy, even admiration, for the showman. Yet I also feel no need to canonize him, and the portrait, as will be noted, is not always painted in the most flattering colors. If the result of my labor is the acceptance of Barnum as a more plausible human being, if the reader agrees there was more to him than the "Connecticut Yankee" we have had in abundance till now, I shall be content with even this modest achievement.

Fairfield, Connecticut
5 July 1988

I

A Life in Progress

"Blackwood," who a few years since sneeringly asked "Who reads an American book?" now seems to have answered the question.
Barnum to the Reverend Thomas Whittemore, 13 March 1855

IN MID-DECEMBER of 1854, in time for the lucrative holiday trade, the New York firm of J. S. Redfield published a strangely disquieting book, dedicated, its writer cockily proclaimed, to "the universal Yankee nation, of which I am proud to be one."[1] Despite his comparative youth of forty-four years, the gray-eyed author whose likeness gazed so candidly at the reader from the book's engraved frontispiece had long been a familiar figure on both sides of the Atlantic. Of medium height, inclining to portliness, his once luxurious curly black hair beginning to gray and recede from his forehead, he could already look back on an eventful life such as few men of twice his age had experienced.[2] Merchant, lottery agent, boardinghouse proprietor; journalist, newspaper editor, publisher; bank president, agriculturist, land developer—these were but a few of the activities that had engaged his restless attention till now. All were subsidiary, however, to his one true vocation, which he had "fallen" into at the age of twenty-five and had gained for him almost overnight the "notoriety" he so ardently desired. Riches beyond his wildest dreams he had also amassed, as had several others fortunate enough to share in the benefits of his peculiar Midas touch. In America, where he had visited nearly every town of any size east of the Mississippi, he could boast of having been personally acquainted with each successive President from Andrew Jackson on. Abroad, where he had met on easy terms with the great Duke of Wellington, he had stood, and even sat, in the presence of Europe's proudest monarchs.

It came as no surprise to his contemporaries, therefore, that Phineas Taylor Barnum, occupation showman, should decide to publish his autobiography. Indeed, coming so closely on the heels of his spectacularly successful management of Jenny Lind's American tour, the time was probably as propitious for such a work as it would ever be. Nor, one assumes, were there too many raised eyebrows when the exuberant author of *The Life of P. T. Barnum, Written by Himself*, seeking to publicize his book in advance, requested his former brothers of the "Order Editorial" to inform their readers that "fifty-seven different publishers have applied for the chance of publishing it. Such is the *fact*—and if it wasn't, why still it ain't a bad announcement."[3] Although there were subsequent reports in the press of a committee of "respectable booksellers" meeting to examine bids for the book and awarding it to Redfield, it seems obvious Barnum had come to terms with his publisher sometime previous to these events.[4] The actual contract, however, which called for delivery of the completed manuscript no later than the following day, was not signed until 27 October 1854. In addition to binding Redfield to bring out the work on good paper and in good muslin covers, and to advertise the book "in a most liberal manner," this document secured to the author the copyright in his own name and the handsome royalty of 30 percent on the retail copy price of $1.25.[5] Julius Starr Redfield, incidentally, was no stranger to Barnum. He had previously served on the committee established to award a prize of $200 for the best ode to be sung by Jenny Lind upon her debut in this country, and he also attended the same New York City church as did Barnum.

Almost simultaneously with the American edition, which was sold throughout the country by subscription agents, the autobiography was issued in three authorized, differently priced editions by Sampson Low of London. It was quickly pirated by several other English publishers, and translations were shortly available in France, Germany, Sweden, and Holland.[6] Thousands of American and European readers were soon engrossed in reading the *Life*, whose author, in the 404 pages of the original edition, seemed so recklessly to have bared his soul. Approximately a third of the book was devoted to his first twenty-four years in Bethel, Connecticut, where Barnum's well-off maternal grandfather, Phineas Taylor, was both the local squire and the leading practical joker. His namesake lost no time in proving himself a worthy scion in the latter category; and indeed this portion of the book contained so many instances of ingeniously contrived, carefully incubated jokes—of the related sharp trading practices for which the New England region had long been proverbial, of one Yankee gleefully "coming it over" another native or some credulous outsider who had haplessly wandered into the village—that its author was himself finally moved to offer a halfhearted apology for devoting so much space to them. But as he immediately went on to point out, "I was born and reared in an atmosphere of merriment; my natural bias was developed and strengthened by the associations of my youth; and I feel myself entitled to record the sayings and doings of the wags and eccentricities of Bethel, because they partly explain the causes which have made me what I am."[7]

The "eccentricities" were continued in later chapters, as the author related how he was launched upon his career as a showman through his acquisition of a blind, decrepit, but garrulous black slave woman named Joice Heth, whom he confidently exhibited as the 161-year-old "nurse" of George Washington; and by his engagement of a little-known Italian juggler and spinner of plates, whom he rechristened "Signor Vivalla" and profitably brought to the public's notice through fake competitions with an out-of-work circus performer. After further adventures on the road with the circus company of Aaron Turner and a small troupe of his own, and a number of business speculations that ended disastrously, he managed to acquire—largely through "brass," for he had no money—the lease on the old American Museum near New York's city hall, together with an option to buy its collections within a stated period of time. This proved to be a major turning point in his career, for immediately upon taking possession of the property toward the end of 1841, he so unsparingly devoted his time and energy to the Museum that almost overnight it was raised from its former soporific state to that of one of the country's premier amusement attractions. Besides plowing back all his first year's profits into schemes to publicize and improve the Museum, the manager was soon engaged in another hoax of Joice Heth-like, but considerably more scandalous, proportions: the touring exhibit known as the "Fejee Mermaid," which prospective patrons were encouraged to believe was the beautiful, bare-breasted creature of legend and mythology, but which, as they discovered after paying their quarters at the door, looked more like the hideous, dessicated head and torso of a monkey joined to the body of a fish. As indeed it was.

While the uproar over this fraud was continuing, the showman paid a visit to his half-brother in nearby Bridgeport and there discovered another irresistible opportunity in a four-year-old perfectly formed midget named Charles Sherwood Stratton. Following a brief period of tutelage by Barnum himself— who bestowed upon him the resounding name "General Tom Thumb," changed his nationality to English, and added seven years to his age so that patrons might have no doubts "that he was *really a dwarf*"—little Charley made his debut on the stage of the American Museum and proved an even greater attraction than his teacher had anticipated. As the money continued to pour into his bulging pockets, Barnum sent the boy on a tour of the States; then, in early 1844, set out with him on a three-year progress through Europe, where he also engaged in several other speculations, wrote a series of one hundred articles on his impressions of the Old World and its denizens for publication in the *New York Atlas*, and busily acquired exhibits and performers for his museum back home. To ensure the "General's" favorable reception before the European public, Barnum first drew the British aristocracy and their Queen into his net, with the latter, obviously a delighted spectator, inviting the showman and his protégé on three separate occasions to Buckingham Palace. Similar triumphs were thereafter a matter of course in other nations; and the furor to see the famous "man in miniature" continued unabated when, in February of 1847, Barnum and Tom Thumb finally returned to America and, following a brief vacation, started out on a grand tour of the United States and Cuba.

Meanwhile, the showman had been expending part of his wealth to buy up other museums and collections around the nation, and his proclivity for hoaxes had remained undiminished. When Colonel John C. Frémont was reported to have been temporarily lost during one of his expeditions in the Rocky Mountains, and public excitement was at its height over this event, Barnum used the occasion to bring forth and exhibit a curly haired horse he had kept in hiding since purchasing it in Cincinnati while on tour with Tom Thumb. "Col. Frémont's Nondescript or Woolly Horse," as this animal was now called, was said to have been captured by the intrepid explorer and sent east. Advertised as being "extremely complex" and "made up of the Elephant, Deer, Horse,

Buffalo, Camel, and Sheep," it could easily bound, the public was further as-sured, twelve or fifteen feet into the air. When the exhibit was finally taken to Washington, Senator Thomas Hart Benton, Frémont's father-in-law, protested the imposition and had Barnum's agent arrested for taking twenty-five cents from him under false pretences. But as Frémont had inconsiderately never written to Benton to say he had *not* captured a woolly horse, the complaint was thrown out of court, and the ruckus only served to increase the number of people willing to pay to see it. The public, as Barnum crowed ecstatically, was "absolutely famishing" for something associated with Frémont. "They were ravenous. They could have swallowed any thing, and like a good genius, I threw them, not a 'bone,' but a regular tit-bit, a bon-bon—and they swallowed it at a single gulp!"[8]

A few months later he was offering fabulous—some said ruinous—terms to bring to America the great Jenny Lind, whom he candidly admitted to having never heard sing. Despite some unpleasantness that developed between the manager and several of the singer's "advisers," and the cancellation of their contract some two-thirds of the way through the tour, this, too, proved a huge financial success for everyone concerned. The receipts for each concert were scrupulously recorded in the autobiography for all to see, as were Barnum's own gross receipts—some $535,000—after paying Lind her share. Since his rupture with the "Swedish Nightingale" in June of 1851, he had sent another singer, Catharine Hayes, on a tour of California; published a pamphlet on tem-perance and the liquor business; been a founding co-partner in the *Illustrated News*, a New York weekly patterned on the famous *Illustrated London News*; been the American agent for a fire "annihilator" that failed to put out a fire at a public demonstration; briefly served as president of the ill-fated New York Crystal Palace Company, whose own building (of iron, no less) also went up in flames a few years later; and engaged in any number of other entertainment and commercial ventures. Mention was also made of his busy activities in Con-necticut, where he had moved into a showy mansion named "Iranistan" in the fall of 1848 and become one of the principal developers of the area known as East Bridgeport.

In the book's concluding pages the author presented what he considered to be a telling defense of popular entertainments and the rather inconsistent role he had played in them. "The great defect in our American civilization," he wrote, "is a severe and drudging practicalness—a practicalness which is not commendable, because it loses sight of the true aims of life, and concentrates itself upon dry and technical ideas of duty, and upon a sordid love of acqui-sition." Through ministering to the recreational needs of his countrymen, he had certainly made money beyond his most sanguine expectations. But he had also, he thought he might reasonably claim, "been a public benefactor, to an extreme seldom paralleled in the histories of professed and professional phi-lanthropists." His museums and traveling exhibitions had been a means of in-structing the masses; while "for the elevation and refinement of musical taste in this country," he modestly continued, "it will not be denied that I have done more than any man living. By bringing Jenny Lind to the United States, I inaugurated a new era in the most beautiful and humanizing of all the fine arts, and gave to the cultivated and wealthy as well as to the middling classes a larger measure of enjoyment than has ever been derived from the enterprise of any other single individual." If his chief purpose in all these enterprises had been to make money, if he had occasionally stretched truth a bit in advertising one of his attractions, still, he had never actually cheated anyone and had always given his customers at least their money's worth. "And I should like to see the moralist or the Christian," he concluded on a challenging note, "who thinks my patron would have done as well with his money at the drinking den or any of the alternative places of buying entertainment."[9]

———◆———

AT TIMES reading almost like a picaresque novel, at others like a strange medley of jokes, anecdotes, and homilies (for the author, in the best Horatian tradition, had not neglected to blend the instructive with the amusing and to point an occasional moral)—such, briefly summarized, was the *Life of P. T. Barnum* that burst so provocatively upon the world during the winter of 1854–55. So much has been made in the past of the hostile reactions that greeted the book that one easily forgets the many favorable reviews it received. Barnum himself boasted, in a letter of 13 March 1855, that his publisher had already received clippings of more than one thousand such notices from American papers alone, and he cited the review in the *Springfield* (Massachusetts) *Republican* as a fair example:

> THE MORAL OF BARNUM'S BOOK. If this book be not *superficially* read, it is easy to see that, under a cloak of fun, jokes and good humor, the author intends to teach and press home the lesson that mere humbugs and deceptions generally fail, and that money acquired in immoral occupations takes to itself wings and flies away, while permanent wealth is only to be obtained and enjoyed from sources of real merit and substantial worth. Thus he shows . . . his "humbugs" were no source of direct profit to him, but were used merely as advertisements, to attract public attention to himself, and to gain public support for his real and substantial exhibitions, such as his Museum, Tom Thumb in England, and Jenny Lind.
>
> His advice to young men . . . as well as his rules for success in business . . . his temperance maxims . . . and the retrospective view of his life . . . all go to show that Barnum is not a believer in Humbugs, either as a principle or as a mere policy. . . . Indeed, he lays down the most substantial moral principles as the only ground-work on which reliance can be placed, in order to secure competence and happiness. The text of his book proves what his preface promises, viz.: that while many of his adventures produce harmless laughter, they will be found to convey a good practical lesson.[10]

Louis Gaylord Clark, editor of the *Knickerbocker Magazine*, although not so impressed by the book's "moral" content, wished there were more "humbugs" like Barnum in the world. Whatever the public may have thought of Joice Heth and the Fejee Mermaid, there was certainly no denying that they had benefited from the "attractive amusement and valuable information" the showman had so generously furnished at his American Museum; while "but for *his* liberal enterprise . . . we never should have the remembered delight of having heard the world-renowned Swede." The author's personal frugality, assiduity, and faithful adherence to temperance principles were all worthy of emulation; and the book itself—"full of fun," "clever and various," "simply, unaffectedly written"—was destined to have at least a *tolerable* sale, since the editor had learned orders were already upon the publisher's books for over ninety thousand copies.[11]

As might be expected, there was much puffing of the book among the author's journalist friends; and within this category, strange as it may seem, may be included an anonymous burlesque published by the New York firm of P. F. Harris with an 1855 imprint. *The Autobiography of Petite Bunkum, the Showman; Showing His Birth, Education, and Bringing Up; His Astonishing Adventures by Sea and Land; His Connection with Tom Thumb, Judy Heath, the Woolly Horse, the Fudge Mermaid, and the Swedish Nightingale . . . Written by Himself* is itself a frequently amusing work, whose contents, within its restricted range of sixty-four pages, often parallel those of Barnum's own book. Tom Thumb here becomes an incorrigible rowdy, however, who hectors his father and impresario, attempts to run off with a voluptuous English countess, and disgraces himself and his manager by getting drunk while they are dining at the palace with Victoria. "Judy Heath" is attached to her glass as well, and gives her manager a black eye when he refuses to buy her another half-pint of whiskey. The fun at the expense of Barnum's well-known teetotalism is patent enough, although the author is careful to treat the "Swedish Nightingale" with appropriate respect. Further satire is directed at the menagerie and "Happy Family" in Barnum's museum, his failed fire annihilator and association with the New York Crystal Palace, and numerous other topics discussed in the autobiography. But the ridicule never descends to invective or scurrility, and at the end of the narrative the editor himself steps forward to explain that the book's purpose is simply to playfully lampoon Barnum, whom he personally likes, and whose *forthcoming* autobiography is bound to be a huge success, for "everybody must and will read Barnum's book!" It was the sort of publicity the showman loved to receive and that he was quite capable of getting up on his own. And since the burlesque's contents follow so closely those of the autobiography, it seems more than likely he had some hand in it, if only to the extent of supplying its anonymous author with a précis of his own "forthcoming" book.

Although the physician Thomas Low Nichols, who set down his recollections of American life in the early nineteenth century, was of the opinion that "Barnum's autobiography was no severe shock to the conscience of New England,"[12] there were those among his contemporaries who clearly thought otherwise. One of the oddest—yet, in terms of its writer's thinking, most revealing—notices of the autobiography appeared in the March 1855 issue of the *Harvard Magazine*. The anonymous critic confessed to having been amused by many of the anecdotes in the early part of the book, but immediately explained that this feeling was "against our will, and only makes us feel a deeper contempt for that which caused it." Not since Rousseau and his *Confessions*, he continued, had anyone "dared with such deliberate effrontery to insult the world by offering to its inspection so unblushing a record of moral obliquity." But what the reviewer most objected to was not that Barnum had been guilty of so many dishonest tricks but that, rending asunder the "sacred veil which conceals private life," he had actually chosen to acknowledge them. "Excess of candor is a fault of which it is seldom necessary to complain. But Mr. Barnum has carried his frankness too far. It is his very sincerity which makes his book so bad."

The more stodgy among New Englanders were not the only ones to profess outrage over the showman's candid revelations. Old Englanders were shortly venting theirs as well, especially after reading how the Yankee humbug had so expertly taken in themselves and their queen. The hostile reactions of British reviewers have often been catalogued by previous biographers.[13] Here a single example will suffice, that of the critic for the powerful *Blackwood's Edinburgh Magazine*, a journal that wielded considerable influence in this country as well, owing to the publication in New York of an American edition. In the course of a long and by no means unperceptive article that appeared in the February 1855 issue, this reviewer also railed against Barnum's self-complacency, but at least had the satisfaction of announcing to his British readers that "Mr. Phineas Taylor Barnum is, we are thankful to say, not a native of this country." If one could believe Barnum, the critic continued, referring to the chapters dealing with the author's boyhood, Connecticut was a "mere colony of sharpers" in which every man, woman, and child lived but to "outwit, overreach, and defraud their neighbors," while in America itself it would seem that "it is better to be accounted a clever rascal than an honest man." Far from being ashamed of his conduct, Barnum was positively proud of it; and his book, the critic complained, "inspired us with nothing but sensations of disgust for the frauds which it narrates, amazement at its audacity, loathing for its hypocrisy, abhorrence for the moral obliquity which it betrays, and sincere pity for the wretched man who compiled it. He has left nothing for his worst enemy to do; for he has fairly gibbeted himself. No unclean bird of prey, nailed ignominiously to the door of a barn, can present a more humiliating spectacle than Phineas Taylor Barnum, as he appears in his Autobiography."

While it is often claimed Barnum never responded to these attacks on his character and conduct—that he really did not care what critics said about him or his book—he did indeed make one indignant reply. Significantly, it was to a review that appeared in a denominational journal. On 10 March 1855 the *Trumpet and Universalist Magazine*, the leading weekly of the Universalist Church in America, carried a notice of the book by one signing himself "Beta." The critic, who casually admitted to having "barely glanced at" the autobiography, was particularly exercised over the fact that Barnum was himself a Universalist, a connection that was "anything but creditable to our denomination," and had had the effrontery to mention in his book his "extreme intimacy" with several prominent Universalist clergymen. The reviewer then proceeded to quote long extracts from *Blackwood's*—so that readers, as he wrote, might "know in what estimation he [Barnum] is held by the public"—and as a final insult, picking up on and italicizing *Blackwood's* remark about the "wretched man who compiled it," insinuated that someone other than Barnum had written the book and expressed the pious hope that "no additional *Universalist*" had been employed in its making.

This was clearly too much to bear, and on 13 March Barnum sat down to compose a long letter to the journal's editor, the Reverend Thomas Whittemore, who obligingly published it in the 24 March issue. Had "Beta's" been a "fair and manly review," Barnum wrote, "I should have allowed it to pass without any reply; but as it is evidently a malicious attack on others besides myself, I beg your indulgence for enough room in your columns to expose the venom of the writer." It was simply not true that he had anywhere in his book stated that he was a Universalist, or that, in mentioning the favors he had received at various times from three close friends among the Universalist ministry, he had given their denominational affiliation. "Were 'Beta's' real name before your readers," he continued, "few of them would doubt the personal malignity of this cowardly assault, not only on myself, but also on one or more of the distinguished clergymen I have mentioned as among my friends. I happen to know him, and he has long been aware of my opinion of him, for I am no 'backbiter' and have never hesitated publicly to express that opinion, nor to give my reasons for it; hence his personal spite." The false construction put on *Blackwood's* remark about the "wretched man who compiled" the book was one more instance of "Beta's" hypocrisy and wicked purpose in writing his review; and here the nettled writer launched into an earnest defense of his book against this and several other charges that had been made in *Blackwood's* and elsewhere:

> I will here say to all honest men in the plainest English that my Auto-biography is exactly what it professes to be, "The Life of P. T. Barnum, Written by Himself." In any and every sense of authorship, it is wholly *my own*, and I hope everybody who reads it, or reviews it, will make the best or the worst of it on my exclusive responsibility. I profess to be something of a judge of human nature, and I aver positively that the book has been received just about as I anticipated. I would not this day change a line or word in the entire volume were I to re-write it. I did not expect a fair criticism from personal enemies, fools, bigots, or knaves. I expected a diversity of opinion among honest critics, and I willingly bow to their decisions pro and con. I am as thankful to those who honestly blame the book as I am to those who praise it.
>
> "Blackwood," who a few years since sneeringly asked "Who reads an American book?" now seems to have answered the question. But he is evidently so bitter and lop-sided that his review destroys its intended effect with all who think for themselves, for whoever reads my book will be convinced that "the devil is not so black as he has been painted" by

"Blackwood." I feel certain that if my salvation depended on my personal merits, I should have no better chance than multitudes of others, including some preachers; but I solemnly declare that I would rather the reviewers would make me out to be worse than I am, than to stand before the world as a white-washed sepulchre.

I am perfectly sensible that there are some things in my Autobiography which may honestly be objected to. Some people pronounce merry stories frivolous, and others denounce practical jokes as being scandalous, and such things will not be found in the lives of such people; but it happens that I was writing the Life of P. T. Barnum, who was born and trained in an atmosphere of merriment, and the nature of my pursuits only deepened the color of the Ethiopian's skin. I am too great a judge of theatrical effect to omit the part of Hamlet in the play of Hamlet, yet in the faithful narrative of my show-business I have not attempted to justify my stretching of the cords of morality (for this would be indefensible), and any appearance of rejoicing in the success of some of my schemes which may have been considered questionable must be ascribed in a good measure, or a bad measure, to my inborn and life-long love of a practical joke and my professional life as a Showman. It is not a vindication but a fact, that men as politicians, sectarians, and lawyers frequently do what they would *not* do as *men*; and the same I suppose is true generally of caterers for public amusement. I do not defend what I here speak of, but I think it is hardly fair to make fish of a lawyer and flesh of a showman.

"Blackwood" hopes that my book will have "the effect of opening the eyes of the public" to the tricks of trade in the show-business; and so do I, with all my heart. It is precisely the effect I intended to produce, and I said so in very plain words. My exposure of the secret machinery of showmen and the swindles of lotteries ought to be taken into account in estimating the moral tendency of my book, and this has been done by a host of honest and reputable critics. Besides this, I made the fact prominent as a lesson against resorting to "humbug" that nearly all my schemes, up to December, 1841, ended in disaster and reduced myself and family to the pinching income of $4 per week. The fortune I have acquired in the last thirteen years was accumulated almost wholly from enterprises which were undoubtedly legitimate: the American Museum, which is the largest and most complete "Curiosity Shop" on this continent; the Exhibition of Tom Thumb, who is the most remarkable dwarf the world has ever seen; and Jenny Lind.

May I not also be allowed to allude to my earnest devotion to the cause of Tee-total-ism, to Agriculture, and to other subjects which do not strike against anybody's conscience? I only ask the acknowledgement that there are some *good* streaks in me and in my book, for I do not admire the doctrine of total depravity, although I am devoutly thankful that my opinions on this tenet were firmly grounded before I made the acquaintance of "Beta."

Following some additional remarks on the writer's association with Universalism and his opinion of "Beta," the letter concluded by calling attention to the many favorable notices the book had received and by quoting, as an offset to *Blackwood's*, the review that had appeared in the *Springfield Republican*.

Aside from its value as an expression of the author's feelings about some of the invective that had been heaped upon his autobiography—and as an answer, in particular, to the devastating, frequently quoted attack by the critic for *Blackwood's*—Barnum's letter to the Reverend Mr. Whittemore addresses another matter that has often engaged his biographers' attention: Did he really write the book himself? Charles Godfrey Leland, who was on the staff of Barnum's *Illustrated News* for a time in 1853, later reported in his own autobiography that Barnum once asked him to write his "life," but that he shrank from the idea of being identified with such a work. In retrospect, he thought he might as well have complied with the showman's request, for he believed "Dr. Griswold performed the task, and the public never knew or cared anything about it."[14] Dr. Rufus Griswold, described elsewhere by Leland as "one of the most irritable and vindictive men I ever met," had been hired as the paper's chief editor—a post he did not remain at very long, however.[15] A great literary pundit and the editor of numerous anthologies, today he is primarily remembered as the literary executor and defamer of Poe.

There is no more reason to doubt Leland's statement that Barnum once asked him to write his life than Barnum's own unequivocal assertion that his book, "in any and every sense of authorship . . . is wholly *my own*." Throughout his career Barnum frequently employed others to write descriptions of his exhibits, biographies of his freaks, guidebooks to his museums, etc. Usually in pamphlet form, they were both a profitable source of supplementary income and a good way to advertise his attractions. By early 1853, when Leland was working for him on the *Illustrated News* and curiosity about Barnum was at its height, there was clearly a ready market for such a work on the showman himself. The two men obviously got on well together, and after Leland had succeeded to the erratic Griswold's position, Barnum often dropped by to share with him a new joke and to assist on the paper's humor column. "We two had 'beautiful times' over that column," Leland wrote, "for there was a great deal of 'boy' still left in Barnum. . . . How we would sit and mutually and admiringly read to one another our beautiful 'good things,' the world forgetting, by the world forgot!"[16] The showman was often reminded of funny incidents and characters in his own life during these mirthful sessions. Under such congenial circumstances, it would hardly be surprising if he did ask his witty companion to write his biography.

But Leland did not write Barnum's "life," of course. Nor did Rufus Griswold or any other "ghost." Amidst the rush of all his other activities, it is easy to forget how fluent, prolific a writer Barnum was. By the time his autobiography appeared in 1854, he had already been a practicing journalist for several years. From 1831 to 1834, as proprietor of the weekly *Herald of Freedom* in his hometown of Bethel, he had written much of the editorial matter for that paper.

His series of one hundred letters to the *New York Atlas*, written in the 1840s while he was abroad with Tom Thumb, would in themselves constitute a fair-sized book. Innumerable advertisements, newspaper puffs, and pamphlets had also flowed from his pen; and as Leland testifies in the above account, he still liked to keep a finger in while proprietor of the *Illustrated News*, stealing time from his museum and other enterprises in order to assist and encourage his fledgling editor, who seems to have often complained of being overworked and underpaid. His correspondence as well—both business and personal—was always of astonishing proportions.

In addition, he was what might be termed an "economical" writer, in the sense that once having committed some amusing story or trenchant observation to paper, he was by no means reluctant to reuse it in his later writings. Much of the material in his letters to the *Atlas* and in the autobiography, as he occasionally informs readers of both, was drawn from a now lost diary he kept; and the genesis of other passages in his writings may sometimes be found in his personal letters. When he came to write the chapter in his autobiography that recounts his first European tour, he often copied out verbatim his earlier *Atlas* articles. A portion of what he did not lift from this source for the first edition of his book eventually appeared in later editions; while material that was deleted from the same edition might well turn up elsewhere, in magazine articles, for example, or his *Funny Stories*, a potpourri of jokes and anecdotes that appeared simultaneously in England and America in 1890. Contracts, newspaper clippings, letters by himself and others, speeches, "Rules for Success in Business," etc. were also freely incorporated into his narrative, so that, to some degree, the book may indeed be described as a "compilation." But with the exception of occasional communications from others, the style throughout the autobiography is incontestably his own, and there can be no reasonable doubt that Barnum was its sole and only begetter.

Thanks to the letters he wrote around this time, one can also trace Barnum's germinating thoughts and preparations for his book. Biographies and memoirs of entertainers made for popular reading in the nineteenth century, and the showman had himself been the subject of several biographical sketches in newspapers and periodicals since his early days at the American Museum. No doubt he had been contemplating something more substantial since the completion of his tour with Jenny Lind; but the catalyst came in 1853 when the famous western theatrical impresario Sol Smith, recently retired to his home in St. Louis, was trying mightily to find a publisher for his latest volume of memoirs. Barnum generously offered to be of assistance in the East, and from late 1853 into early 1854 tried unsuccessfully to interest various New York publishers in the work. In the midst of these negotiations, writing to Smith on 19 December 1853 to signal the transfer of the manuscript to another publisher, he informed his friend that "I think of writing my life this winter. What do you think about its taking?"[17] When Smith replied encouragingly, Barnum thanked him for his good opinion about "taking my life," but wasn't yet certain he could find the time to do it.[18] By the following August, however, he was hard at work and, as he informed another friend, the writer Bayard Taylor, had laid aside other projects in order to finish with the manuscript by November.[19] A few days later, seeking some information for his chapter on Joice Heth, he was writing to Moses S. Beach of the *New York Sun* for copies of advertisements and notices that had appeared in that paper.[20] Around the same time he was also besieging Moses Kimball of the Boston Museum, his co-conspirator in the Fejee Mermaid affair, for further information on the history of that intriguing object.[21] There are extant several other letters containing similar requests, from which it seems safe to infer that the writer was also actively engaged in the necessary research for his book. And here it may be noted that—with a few notable and deliberate exceptions that will be discussed below—whenever Barnum gives a date or place, quotes a newspaper notice, a contract or some other document, or relates a story capable of verification, almost invariably he is accurate.

———◆———

DISTRIBUTED throughout the United States by Redfield's subscription agents, published abroad in various translations as well as its authorized and pirated English editions, for fifteen years *The Life of P. T. Barnum, Written by Himself* seemed to represent its author's final word on the subject. Meanwhile, to the no small satisfaction of those who had been so outraged by his candid revelations, within barely a year of the book's publication Barnum had plummeted into the chastening fire of bankruptcy court. He had taken Tom Thumb abroad again while recovering from this disgrace; had returned to resume his position as a leading citizen of Connecticut, where he made some stir in its legislature; and had twice seen his American Museum burn down. Following the second conflagration of this famous institution, he had decided to take his friend Horace Greeley's advice to "go a-fishing" and had retired to his town house on New York's Fifth Avenue, still spending the warmer months in Connecticut, however. But time, as he was shortly complaining, hung heavy on his hands, and none of his old friends seemed willing to drop their work to "play" with him. As an antidote to such unaccustomed inactivity, he was soon at work on a new edition of the autobiography. "My *life* is dragging slowly so far as writing it is concerned," he wrote to the Universalist editor George H. Emerson on 23 May 1868.[22] A year later he had made sufficient progress to send off his account of Tom Thumb's courtship and marriage for advance publication in *Packard's Monthly Magazine*, but had still not completed the manuscript. He was in "no sort of hurry about publishing," he wrote to Whitelaw Reid, then chief editor of Greeley's *New York Tribune*, and would wait until he had removed to Bridgeport for the summer and again felt like "scribbling" before finishing it. Reid had consented to advise him on the manuscript, and "if you have a leisure day or week or more to spend with me on the seashore (L.I. Sound) at Bridgeport, say in July, I will be glad to have you come & do so & we can soon see what is needful to be done & what it is worth. I will speak to nobody else about it till you have seen the MS."[23] By the following September the book was in press, and Barnum was typically signaling its imminent appearance to his former brothers of the "Order Editorial," assuring them they would find it "unobjectionable."[24]

Struggles and Triumphs; or, Forty Years' Recollections of P. T. Barnum, Written by Himself, as the new edition was titled, was published by J. B. Burr of Hartford in 1869, with Sampson Low once more the official English publisher. Sold again through subscription agents, the book made substantial demands on its readers, running as it did to nearly 800 octavo pages. No one seems to have complained, however; nor was the book savaged by critics as its predecessor had been. The new edition, as its author observed, represented a "maturer" review of his career as a showman—and indeed, a number of writers, citing the excising or toning down of some of the material that appeared in the earlier book, have suggested it was more than that.[25] Certainly there are a number of notable abridgments and changes in the later edition, possibly made upon Reid's advice. But if (to give a frequently cited example) Barnum no longer felt compelled to inform his readers how he had lied about Tom Thumb's age and nationality, he now gave them a long, hilarious account of his famous midget's wooing of Lavinia Warren, including such highlights as a fight between the General and his rival, the midget Commodore Nutt, in the dressing room of the American Museum; and a blow-by-blow description of the scene (observed by "a couple of mischievous young ladies," or so Barnum claimed) wherein Tom proposed to Lavinia, whose acceptance of her suitor was followed by "a sound of something very much like the popping of several corks from as many beer bottles."[26] Although the showman assures us he first read this indiscreet account to the parties concerned, asking them if they had any corrections to make, it is significant that in her own autobiography, which is otherwise so heavily indebted to Barnum's book, Lavinia makes no mention of it.

Within the greater length of the new edition, too, Barnum was free to expand on several of the earlier topics. He reprinted more of his *Atlas* material concerning his first European tour with Tom Thumb; devoted a separate chapter to his stormy, often savage relations with James Gordon Bennett, still living, still a powerful foe at the time; and was considerably more candid about Jenny Lind and her meddling "advisers," chief among them the lawyer John Jay, whom he now named for the first time. That his deleting or "expurgating" earlier material was not always so calculatedly self-serving as is sometimes assumed is strikingly illustrated by one example that has tarnished his reputation to the present day. In telling the story of Joice Heth in the first edition of his autobiography, Barnum writes of his determination to "purchase" her from R. W. Lindsay, who had himself acquired Heth from John S. Bowling of Kentucky, and of his eventually becoming her "owner" and "proprietor." These statements have been accepted at face value by more than one twentieth-century biographer or editor who ought to have known better, including George S. Bryan, surely one of the most knowledgeable about the various editions of the autobiography, who casually shrugged off the subject with the observation that "those were slavery days."[27] It is true that later in his book, while reporting another encounter with Lindsay, Barnum does write of having "hired"

Heth from him; but this statement (equally imprecise in any case) seems to have been overlooked.

Curiously enough, almost immediately after making these damaging statements, Barnum reproduces, in the first edition of the autobiography for all to see, the actual agreement between him and Lindsay. This is a faithful transcription of the document now in the Boston Public Library, in addition to which the original agreement between Lindsay and Bowling is also extant.[28] Both prove conclusively that neither Lindsay nor Barnum ever "owned" Joice Heth, but were merely the purchasers of the *right to exhibit her* for a stipulated period of time. Lindsay had originally contracted with Bowling on 10 June 1835 for a twelve-month period, and Barnum simply purchased from him the remaining ten months of his agreement. Had Joice Heth not died during the winter of 1835–36, she might very well have been returned to her real master and owner, John S. Bowling, the following summer. For all his outspokenness on behalf of civil rights for blacks, Barnum never cleared up this ambiguity in later editions of the autobiography. And in fact he made matters worse by deleting, after the 1855 edition, the agreement between him and Lindsay. Many of his contemporaries thought of and openly referred to him as the onetime owner of Heth. Was he really so oblivious to their opinion? Was the matter of so trifling importance to him that he never felt it worth correcting? Or was there some other, deeper reason for this strange omission: some shameful episode in his past, perhaps, for which he now sought to atone by letting matters stand as they were?

There are several other interesting lacunae and contradictions in the 780 pages of the 1869 edition—but again, insofar as the work was a chronicle of the *public* life of P. T. Barnum, it remained surprisingly comprehensive, with all the more notorious frauds and humbugs, at least in broad outline, intact. But the real "life" was hardly at an end, of course, and in late 1870 the sixty-year-old author joined the managers William C. Coup and Dan Castello to form a new enterprise: the first of the combined circus, menagerie, and museum companies that were to occupy so much of his attention for the next twenty years. One of his own contractual duties in all these shows was to write about and publicize them whenever he could, and the autobiography offered a superb means of doing so. In March 1871, a month before "P. T. Barnum's Museum, Menagerie, and Circus" opened for the first time in Brooklyn, the copyright of *Struggles and Triumphs* was assigned by Burr to Barnum.[29] Thereafter, brought up to date by annual appendices or supplementary chapters that narrated the progress of his shows as well as the author's own latest adventures, the autobiography went through an astonishing number of "editions" and variations. Indeed, the subject of the continuing evolution of Barnum's book becomes from this point on a bibliographer's nightmare, further complicated by the showman's grandiloquently announcing in the 1880s that anyone who wished to was free to publish his own edition.

The appendices themselves were often published separately, in order to publicize the circus in advance among editors and journalists, but were paginated so that they might also be bound in with the preceding edition, originally the

1869 one, even though they might be set in different-sized type. One such "Appendix IV," for example—bound in paper wrappers, published by Warren, Johnson & Co. of Buffalo in 1874, and paginated 849–864—includes a "Notice to Editors" on the inside front cover offering passes to the circus and a complete copy of the book, and requesting that reviews of the present gift be sent to the publishers.[30] But in truth even this practice does not satisfactorily explain all the book's permutations, for as the hero of *Struggles and Triumphs* steadily marched on to "Fifty," then "Sixty Years' Recollections," changes were made in both the appendices and the main body of the text; and from time to time the former, after further modification, were absorbed into the latter, making room for their inevitable successors. When stricken by his final illness in 1890, Barnum was considering what he would write for the latest of these additions about his visit to England with his circus during the preceding winter. Unable, for once, to favor his readers with his own description of such marvelous proceedings, on his deathbed he exacted from his wife the promise to do the job for him, and to throw in for good measure an account of his last days and funeral. Nancy Barnum obediently, if somewhat reluctantly, honored his request; and in her separately published, appropriately titled *The Last Chapter* the great arc of its subject's life, literally from cradle to grave, was finally completed.[31]

The separate editions were printed on fine and cheap grades of paper, sometimes "extra-illustrated," in large and small type, with the latter used for generous runs of tens of thousands of copies that were hawked along the route of the circus, often with a free ticket to the show thrown in. There were "author's" editions to distinguish those by publishers with whom Barnum made specific arrangements to issue the work; and in 1876, after five appendices had been added to the 1869 edition, the first drastic abridgment appeared, set in small type and reduced to 314 pages, although deluxe copies of the unabridged edition continued to be published until well into the 1880s. Thereafter, new chapters and occasional appendices were generally brief. The 1889 edition, considered by some to be a third major state of the autobiography, is in fact merely a continuation of the earlier abridgment, primarily of interest for Barnum's later contributions to the ongoing story, including a final appendix he wrote in September of that year. Meanwhile, in response to the author's announcement that anyone might publish his life without fee, the book was also issued under different titles. When the New York firm of G. W. Dillingham published it in 1888 as *How I Made Millions*, profusely illustrated and priced at only twenty-five cents, even Barnum could not help being impressed. Writing to his circus partner James A. Bailey in the midst of the season, he pointed out that at a wholesale cost of twelve and one-half cents, thousands of copies "could be worked off at a profit—but the *real big profit* would be in future *harvests* that the reading of the book would produce."[32]

Barnum once boasted that over a million copies of his autobiography had been sold during his lifetime, and his estimate was probably a conservative one. So many circus patrons carried copies away with them that it sometimes looked as if they were coming from a prayer meeting. Some fanatics made a point of buying each successive edition of the book, as religiously as they did the *Farmer's Almanac*. Nor did the flood of editions cease with its author's death. Shortly thereafter the journalist and would-be poet Joel Benton rushed into print, over his own name, what purported to be a *Life of Hon. Phineas T. Barnum*. In reality, it was little more than the autobiography all over again, with Barnum's first-person narrative imaginatively transposed into the third-person singular.[33] At this writing two abridged, very imperfect American editions of the autobiography are still being sold, and a new French translation is about to appear. Taking all the foreign editions into account, the book has probably never been out of print.

Its influence on readers is more difficult to ascertain, although at one time nearly everyone in America and Britain had read or at least heard about it. The English manufacturer John Fish, the father of Barnum's second wife, attributed his rise from laborer to prosperous industrialist to his having read and studied the first edition of the autobiography; and certainly there were many people—despite all the fuming by the moralists—who considered it a near perfect *vade mecum* for those seeking to get on in the world. The book has even been praised as literature, most notably by the eminent critic Ludwig Lewisohn, who spent much of his career battling the "genteel tradition" and false standards of excellence in American letters. "Only one Yankee of a humbler stripe wrote a book in the high days of the New England pseudo-classics which also belongs to the folk-literature of America," he wrote in his *Expression in America*, published in 1932. "That book was, of course, the autobiography of Phineas T. Barnum." As a young boy who had recently arrived on these shores, Lewisohn first encountered *The Life of P. T. Barnum, Written by Himself* on a Charleston bookstall in the 1890s. The boy read the book

with a severe absorption and in the course of the next few years returned to it again and again and carried throughout many succeeding years with him a hundred images and incidents from that homespun narrative which communicated somehow the very tone and taste and tang of American life. And it was not long before the boy was astonished that [*sic*] he was told and taught concerning a hundred books that seemed empty and artificial and meaningless and never heard anyone mention the book of which the reality and concreteness had so absorbed him for reasons that he could in those years not have explained. But he learned those reasons later and with him his whole generation learned them. . . . Barnum, rogue and vulgarian, wrote out what he thought and saw and dreamed and knew.

Americans, Lewisohn concluded on a prematurely optimistic note, were at last beginning to recognize Barnum's book as "literature" and many of his contemporaries' polite, sentimental works as "trash," because "only today does the genteel tradition show signs of loosening its long grip upon our civilization and our life."[34]

———◆———

ALTHOUGH BARNUM himself never made any claims for his autobiography as "literature," the book did become one of the great, abiding passions of his life. For a total of some twenty-five years he busied himself with the writing, revising, and updating of it. It was superb publicity for himself and his various enterprises. More than this, unlike the transitory nature of those same enterprises—of wealth and possessions, of life itself—it was something neither time nor accident could obliterate. And it was in the autobiography, above all else, that he consciously sought to erect a lasting monument to his fame. Were it not for the autobiography, one might reasonably ask, how much would we really know about its blandly smiling author? Virtually nothing about his first thirty years, including the extent of his involvement with Joice Heth. We would recognize him as the museum and circus proprietor, of course, and as the manager of Tom Thumb and Jenny Lind. But we would know little about *how* he managed them—and it was in management above all, combined with his masterful understanding of human nature and publicity, that Barnum truly excelled. Without the evidence of the autobiography, too, few people today would probably be willing to accord him the reputation of the world's, or even America's, greatest showman. It was a reputation of which he was exceedingly jealous, and which he vigorously fought to maintain to the very end of his life. And since it was only to be expected that even the final moments and funeral of so significant a personage would be of avid interest to the grieving public, his desire to have his widow complete the story is readily understood.

That the story did not universally please its readers—that the "monument" contributed more than anything else to the legend enveloping its author, falsely coloring our overall impression of him to the present day—was perhaps inevitable, even desirable. Had the autobiography not been so shocking to Barnum's contemporaries, had it been written instead in the "genteel" tradition so abhorred by Ludwig Lewisohn, its author would hardly interest us. In terms of its lively style, subject matter, and sheer entertainment value, the 1855 edition of Barnum's life deserves to rank among the classics in its genre. And despite all the revisions and attenuating of the more scandalous episodes in the 1869 and later editions, when its author was patently more concerned with projecting an image of himself as a public benefactor and respectable purveyor of wholesome, instructive amusement, there is evidence that the original version remained his personal favorite. Certainly Barnum never repudiated or apologized for it. As late as the year of his death, by which time it had long been out of print and the plates destroyed, the white-haired showman was still handing out to a few select friends inscribed, leather-bound copies of *The Life of P. T. Barnum, Written by Himself.*

II

Bethel

A joke was never given up in Bethel until the very end of it was unravelled.

Autobiography

DANBURY, in western Connecticut, is one of those places only a native can fully appreciate. Lying but a few miles over the New York border, amidst the rolling hills that merge with the Berkshires and the Taconic Mountains to the north and west, the city is largely an unrestricted jumble of uninspiring shops, light industrial plants, and decaying housing—the latest manifestations of the spoliation that began in the nineteenth century, when the fine homes and luxuriant elms that once lined its main streets were removed to make way for brick storefronts and telegraph poles. The town was established in 1685, in what was then a wilderness, by a small band of settlers who had purchased the land from the Indians the year before and who moved with their families from Norwalk, Connecticut, some twenty miles to the south on Long Island Sound.[1] Among the original eight proprietors was one Thomas Barnum, from whom, at least until the end of the last century, all those bearing the same name in America are believed to be descended. Earlier records of him are found in Norwalk and neighboring Fairfield, Connecticut; and according to an incomplete family history begun by his showman descendant in 1882, he arrived in New York from England when he was around twelve years old and "like other adventurous persons in those days, having no money to pay his passage, he was set up at auction and bid off by the man who would accept his labor for the smallest space of time, as payment for his passage money." By the time of his death on 26 December 1695, Thomas Barnum had sired at least five sons and as many daughters, whose numerous descendants, besides populating Danbury and its vicinity, eventually fanned out over most of the nation.[2]

As the little settlement continued to prosper, and fear of Indian raids, "painters" (panthers), and other calamities began to diminish, its inhabitants ventured into neighboring areas. Some three miles to the southeast, below East Swamp and just beyond the area known as Grassy Plain, they soon founded the village of Bethel, whose outlying districts—Plumtrees, Wildcat, Wolfpits, Stony Hill—were named after their more prominent natural features. By 1759 the village had grown to the extent that its citizens were granted the right to form their own ecclesiastical society, although it continued to be a part of Danbury until 1855, when it was finally incorporated as a separate town. When Barnum later conferred, as the occasion might move him, the honor of being his birthplace alternately upon Bethel and Danbury, he was, strictly speaking, within his rights.

Among the village's earliest inhabitants was Ephraim Barnum, a farmer grandson of the original Thomas. One of his sons, Ephraim 2d, served as a captain during the Revolutionary War, and among his many offspring (he married three times) was a son named Philo, born on 4 April 1778, whose mother, Rachel Starr Beebe, had been the widow of Jonathan Beebe of Danbury. Philo himself was twice married and fathered five children by each of his wives, the second of whom was Irena (for that is how the name was spelled) Taylor, who was born on 7 October 1784. She was the daughter of Phineas Taylor, another Revolutionary War veteran and one of the village's leading citizens, and his first wife, Molly Sherwood. When Irena and Philo's first child was born on 5 July 1810, they named him after Irena's delighted father. The boy was never given the opportunity to glory in his biblical name, however, but was always referred to by his parents and elders, and later by his own family, as "Taylor." To his boyhood chums he was known as "Tale."

At the time of "Taylor's" birth Danbury and Bethel were centers of thriving hat and comb industries, although agriculture still played a necessary part in their inhabitants' survival. Communication with the outside world was sporadic at best, with newspapers arriving but once a week, and a journey to the distant metropolis of New York—or "York," as it was called—was looked upon as a great adventure. Philo Barnum himself, his son liked to boast in later life whenever he was in an egalitarian mood, was a tailor; and no doubt he, like many of his neighbors, made part of his income from this useful trade. But he also kept the village tavern and a livery stable, ran a freight service between Danbury and Norwalk, at one time was partner in a country store into which he put young Taylor as clerk, and still found time to do his share of farming.

No matter what the occupation in those days, they all seem to have had an abundance of land. Besides the place where one practiced his business or trade—be it in factory, shop, country store, or inn—there was, to begin with, the "homestead" itself, with its adjacent kitchen garden, barn, and outbuildings. Pasturage was necessary for one's horses, cows, and sheep, of course, and fields for the hay and fodder that were to sustain them through the long winters. Flax might also be grown to supply the spinning wheels, rye or wheat for bread, and corn for the hogs, which were allowed to run loose in the village streets. One also needed a plentiful supply of firewood, to be sure, so a piece of woodland would be added to these holdings. If one were fortunate enough to own a hillside with a spring upon it, water might be piped directly to the kitchen or springhouse, thereby obviating the need for a well. Philo Barnum, although of relatively modest means, possessed his share of such real estate; and his father-in-law Phineas Taylor, who sustained a comfortable life-style while carefully selling land piece by piece according to his neighbors' needs, was in the eighteenth century one of Bethel's principal landowners. As late as his death in 1837, he still owned considerable property in the village, with his daughter Irena alone receiving as her share of his estate no less than nine different parcels of land, amounting in all to sixty-three acres.[3]

Barnum himself, in a speech he delivered in 1881 on the occasion of his presenting to his "native" town a singularly inappropriate fountain with a baroque triton atop it, recalled what life was like in those self-sufficient days. It was surprising how much he could remember, he said, as he described the physical discomfort of alternately sweltering and shivering through the long Sundays at the local church, and suffering under the ferule in the old schoolhouse. The women of the town hatcheled the flax and carded the wool, spinning and weaving it into fabrics to clothe the entire family. "The same good mothers did the knitting, darning, mending, washing, ironing, cooking, soap and candle making, picked the geese, milked the cows, made butter and cheese, and did many other things for the support of the family." Houses were lighted by tallow candles, and in summer nearly all went to bed as soon as it grew dark in order to conserve these precious objects. Children ate their meals from wooden trenchers, until in time an extravagant streak crept in and the trenchers were discarded for pewter plates and lead spoons. Food consisted largely of boiled and baked beans, coarse rye bread, applesauce, and hasty pudding in milk, although the elder members of the family regularly ate meat and several times a week all partook of "pot luck," a medley of corned beef, salt pork, and vegetables boiled together in the same big pot. Peddlers brought fish and clams from the coast, and once a week the town's only butcher offered what he then had on hand. Usually it was only a single kind of meat, and "probably he did not have beef oftener than once a month."

The town's elders still spoke of Indian ravages and the burning of Danbury by the British when he was a child, and among his earliest memories was that of seeing the local militia put through daily drill during the War of 1812. Carriages and wagons were but few in town, and the men used to travel on horseback with their grain and other burdens in bags, at other times with their wives and sweethearts riding behind them on pillions. When one of the wealthier citizens covered the bare floor in his bedroom with a small piece of carpet, the town was abuzz over such ostentation for weeks. Hard cider and rum were consumed by everyone, the clergy not excepted, even during working hours, and the slightest occasion was made the excuse for treating or being treated. "The public whipping-post and imprisonment for debt both flourished in Bethel in my youthful days. Suicides were buried at cross-roads."[4]

In the same speech Barnum referred to the "old-fashioned house on Elm Street, where the great elm tree now stands," as his place of birth. As the present-day visitor travels down the road from the east leading to the center of town, he can still see the house standing on an embankment to the right, although one would hardly recognize it from Barnum's description. The original plain "saltbox" structure has been extensively remodeled and today presents a decidedly Georgian facade to the world. The great elm that once grew before its front door and was a local landmark has long since disappeared, having been chopped down at the end of the last century to accommodate a now defunct trolley line. Even the name of the street has been changed—not, strangely enough, to that of Bethel's most famous native, but to that of the person who once assisted him in managing the American Museum, John Greenwood Jr., who was born in England, did not come to this country until he was twenty years old, and died in Germany while inconspicuously serving there as a consular official.[5]

If one continues down Greenwood Avenue a short distance and turns right onto Chestnut Street, one is only a block from the Congregational Church and what was originally the village center. Almost diagonally across from the church, situated at number 4 Chestnut Street, is another large house dating from the eighteenth century. Presently divided into apartments, it was for many years the village inn and presumably the same tavern Philo Barnum, and later his widow, once kept. The church or "meeting house" itself is the third structure to occupy the site and too recent for the period under discussion. Within the green repose of its neatly kept graveyard, however, one may read another chapter in the village's history. The roughhewn headstones of the early settlers are largely gone or indecipherable by now, but among those of their descendants one notices a profusion of certain names that recur throughout Barnum's own history: Taylor, Benedict, Hickok, Ferry, Starr, Seelye, Hoyt, and Judd, together with a considerable number of Barnums, of course. The bones of Barnum's grandparents are here, as are those of Philo Barnum and his first wife, Polly Fairchild. The same familiar names continue in the more recently established municipal cemetery a few blocks south, where Irena Barnum is buried only a few feet from Deacon Seth Seelye, who once haled her editor-son into court for libel. For all their once vehemently held opinions on such momentous topics as religion and politics, their long forgotten rivalries and differences, they were nearly all related in one way or another—with Taylors marrying Seelyes, Seelyes marrying Barnums, Barnums marrying Benedicts and Taylors, et sequitur—so that the village custom, in Barnum's day, of indiscriminately addressing one's elders as "Uncle" and "Aunt" often had more than quaintness to recommend it.

———◆———

"PHINEAS TAYLOR was my maternal grandfather," Barnum writes in the opening sentence of his autobiography—and surely it was with no lack of design he chose to begin his story this way. The hilarious doings of "Uncle Phin," who would "go farther, wait longer, work harder and contrive deeper, to carry out a practical joke, than for anything else under heaven," occupy considerable space in his namesake's book; and as he lived to the ripe old age of seventy-seven, he had more than sufficient time to exert his beneficial influence upon his favorite grandchild. Elected on two occasions to represent Danbury in the Connecticut House of Representatives, a local justice of the peace until he was forced to retire at the mandatory age of seventy, he was by turns census taker and deviser of ingenious lottery schemes, as well as one of Bethel's wealthier landowners. The inventory of his personal property, made at the time of his death in 1837 (for he died intestate), shows him to have lived quite comfortably for the period, possessed of such amenities as a gig and carpets, and a good-sized dinner service with silverware.[6] Toward the end of his life he put in for and was granted a government pension on the basis of some four years' service during the Revolutionary War, in which conflict he distinguished himself on several occasions by capturing an enemy cavalryman, uncovering a Tory plot to lead British dragoons to surprise his camp, "capturing" a cache of goods meant for the British, and "recapturing" forty-two hogs they in turn stole from the colonials.[7]

He was decidedly an "original," without question one of the chief formative influences in Barnum's life, and one of the more notorious of his well-blazoned exploits was a carefully incubated joke he played on his own grandson. As Barnum gleefully tells the story in his autobiography, a few days after his birth, in appreciation of his being named after him, he was presented by his grandfather with the deed to a tract of land on the outskirts of Bethel known as "Ivy Island." From the age of four on he was continually reminded of this wonderful present by the members of his family and everyone else in Bethel. "My grandfather," he writes, "never spoke of me in my presence, either to a neighbor or stranger, without saying that I was the richest child in town, because I owned all 'Ivy Island,' the most valuable farm in Connecticut. My mother often reminded me of my immense possessions, and my father occasionally asked me if I would not support the family when I came in possession of my property. . . . Our neighbors, too, reminded me a dozen times a day, that they feared I would refuse to play with their children, because I had inherited such immense wealth, while they had nothing of the sort."

And so it continued until he was around twelve years of age. It was only then he was finally taken to see this fabulous place—but not before his mother had cautioned him not to let his joy make him sick or return home with a swollen head. Barnum then describes how he nearly drowned getting there; landed, while leaping from bog to bog in the swamp surrounding it, on a hornets' nest; and, upon finally arriving at this inaccessible and, as he only then realized, barren piece of land, was nearly scared out of his skin by a monstrous snake that came after him. When he returned that evening to the bosom of his family and his loving grandfather, they and all the neighbors gathered, with the utmost seriousness, to congratulate him on his good fortune and to ask if he had found his domain to be as rich as he expected. And having spent some eight years preparing this joke, the good folk of Bethel then spent the next five laughing over it.[8]

Ivy Island does indeed exist, and is nearly every bit as awful as Barnum makes it out to be. Situated in the midst of East Swamp, the island is somewhat easier to approach than it was in his day, owing to a dirt access road running beneath a power line. Even so, one must be prepared to do some wading, and during the rainy season one is well advised not to go at all. Surprisingly, the surrounding area is quite pretty in its wildness, especially during the summertime, when tall ferns and cattails, purple-plumed swampgrass, black-eyed Susans, Queen Anne's lace and joe-pye weed, and seas of towering purple loosestrife literally overwhelm one on the approach through the swamp. Honey- and bumblebees are everywhere; monarch and yellow swallowtail butterflies undulate across one's path; and if one looks in the direction of the great wooded hill that rises west of the swamp, one may well see a hawk wheeling high up in the air, keeping a sharp eye on the intruder below. The southern half of the island itself, which slopes up from the level of the swamp on the west to a height of some thirty feet on the east, at which point it drops abruptly to a rushing brook, is not unattractive in its own way, with mature trees and shrubs, especially on its elevated part. Mountain laurel blooms there in late spring, and deer are occasional visitors. The northern half of the island—flat and un- interesting, consisting of around five acres of stunted vegetation, bogs, and a few medium-sized trees choked with poison ivy (the only kind of "ivy" to be found on the island)—fully lives up to Barnum's description.[9]

Barnum certainly once owned this valuable piece of property, although his grandfather did not, in fact, make him a gift of it until he was nearly two years old. Nor, it turns out, did he deed him the entire Ivy Island, but only its north- ern, more barren half, naturally enough.[10] A number of writers have claimed or suggested that this "heartless" joke with its crushing dénouement must have had some fatal, malign influence on young Taylor's developing character. But the evidence hardly bears out so compassionate an interpretation. They were all inveterate practical jokers in Barnum's day, and by the age of twelve he had already been witness to, and either the butt of or an eager participant in, hundreds of others. His own mother, as one learns from his narration of the Ivy Island incident, was another proverbial "chip of the old block." Elsewhere in his autobiography he gives sufficient evidence for his father's not being far behind in such matters—in particular, the tale of "Uncle Phile's" passing off a half-dead nag as a famous racehorse and what happened when this valuable animal expired while on loan to a gullible, easily terrified apprentice shoe- maker.[11]

"A joke was never given up in Bethel until the very end of it was unrav- elled," Barnum comments at the end of another telling anecdote.[12] And indeed, to the very end of his life he was himself never able to resist an opportunity to cause someone temporary embarrassment. The jokes were not invariably appreciated and, as Barnum himself acknowledged more than once, sometimes resulted in hurt feelings or the loss of a friend. Occasionally, too, a lifelong enemy would be made. But these were risks he must be prepared to take, for the predilection, he liked to think, was beyond his control. It was something in the blood—congenital. Whether one chooses to accept this explanation or not, it is hardly fair to single out Barnum for particular scrutiny or psycho- logical analysis in the matter. The nineteenth century was the age par excel- lence of the practical joke, and contemporary newspapers and memoirs abound in accounts of those "practiced" by others. Could there be anything more em- barrassing, for example, than the joke Barnum's friend Mark Twain once played on the distinguished author Thomas Bailey Aldrich and his wife while they were visiting at Twain's opulent house in Hartford's Nook Farm community? Early one morning Twain banged on their bedroom door and loudly called for

Aldrich to come out. Their bedroom, Twain informed his alarmed guest, was directly over his and Mrs. Clemens's room, and the latter had a headache and had been disturbed all night by the noises the Aldriches had been making. "Do try to move more quietly," he pleaded, "though Livy would rather suffer than have you give up your game on her account." When the mortified couple finally appeared at breakfast and apologized to their host's wife, Livy, as might be expected, hadn't the faintest idea what they were talking about.[13]

Moreover, as Barnum eventually informs us, it was really he who had the last laugh over Ivy Island. Some twenty years after his one and only visit to his property, when he was down on his luck in New York City and casting about for some way to support his growing family, he learned that the American Museum's collections were up for sale. He felt instinctively that if only he could get his hands on this languishing institution, he could quickly turn it into one of the city's most profitable attractions. The trouble was, he was almost broke at the time and the asking price for the Museum's valuable collections was $15,000. So he boldly wrote to Francis W. Olmsted, a retired merchant who owned the building itself, and asked him to lease him the Museum, buy the collections in his own name, and allow him to pay for them in installments. Olmsted was highly impressed by the cheeky Barnum and by the many glowing testimonials he was able to produce from other showmen, but nonetheless thought he ought to have something other than promises before agreeing to this novel proposal. "Now if you only had a piece of unencumbered real estate that you could offer as additional security," he said, "I think I might venture to negotiate with you." At this point our hero recalled his worthless property in Bethel. He did indeed have some five acres of unencumbered land, he announced, which his wealthy grandfather had presented to him. Olmsted naturally assumed this must be a valuable piece of property and that, in view of its having been a gift from his grandfather, Barnum would not like to risk it as security. But he did "risk" it all the same; bargained the price of the collections down to $12,000; paid off his indebtedness to Olmsted in less than two years; and within a few more years, thanks to this purchase made possible by Ivy Island, had become one of America's richest and most celebrated showmen.[14]

So the long-standing joke played so remorselessly on the credulous boy, and which Barnum is careful to relate in such fine detail, is ultimately revealed to be more than a joke. It becomes a lesson in human resourcefulness—in the laudable Yankee determination to "go ahead." The same inspirational message was to figure repeatedly in his speeches and writings over the following decades, often with the tale of Ivy Island thrown in as a prime example. His audiences never failed to respond to it. But it turns out there was more to the story than Barnum ever chose to reveal in his autobiography or elsewhere. When he originally entered into negotiations with Olmsted, he was no longer the owner of Ivy Island, having sold it for $60 as early as November 1834 to his half-brother Philo F. Barnum. On 30 November 1841 he bought back the property from Philo for the same price, obviously in preparation for his closing with Olmsted. Nor was Francis Olmsted so "green" as the showman makes him out to be. According to the mortgage made between him and Barnum and his wife Charity on 27 December 1841, the date on which Barnum became proprietor of the American Museum, two other parcels of land in Bethel, one with a two-story frame store on it, were pledged as security along with Ivy Island. The combined value of this property was appraised at $2000—not such bad collateral after all when one considers Olmsted also retained title to the Museum's collections until Barnum had repaid the $12,000 advanced on his behalf.[15]

———◆———

ANOTHER MEMORABLE incident in young Taylor's life was the first and only ex-ecution he ever witnessed. The condemned man, a former slave named "Black" Amos Adams, had been sentenced to death for a criminal assault of a "heinous nature" on one Mrs. Thorp. On 13 November 1817, the day of his hanging, Danbury was crowded with people who had walked and ridden in from the surrounding countryside for a distance of up to twenty-five miles, with many arriving the night before so as to be sure not to miss the spectacle. Immense throngs passed through Bethel itself, and when one yokel reined in his horse at the Barnums' house to inquire the way to Danbury, Philo Barnum curtly replied, "Go with the crowd, you fool." As this was only the second execution in the town's history (the first had also been of a Negro), the citizens were determined to see it carried out in proper style. Following a procession of the prisoner and two military companies to the Congregational Church, whose minister preached a full-fledged sermon relevant to the occasion, the parade was continued, to the music of fife and drums, up West Street to the place of execution, where a number of enterprising individuals had erected refreshment booths. The surrounding trees were themselves so crowded with people eager to get a view of the gallows that some of their branches came crashing down. The seven-year-old Barnum and his parents were also present to see the turn-ing off of "Black" Amos, and as he wrote years later to a Danbury friend, "when he dropped & my mother groaned, I was too young to realize that there was any occasion for sorrow." In retrospect the event sickened him, and in later life, while serving in the Connecticut legislature, he was a staunch opponent of capital punishment.[16]

Meanwhile, when not attending on his grandfather's merry pranks or wit-nessing the infrequent diversions Danbury had to offer, he had commenced his formal education. From around the age of six he attended the district common school; and although he later complained that his father often kept him away from his studies to assist him in his work and that he never had any "advan-tages," he seems to have received at least as good an education as did most children of his age and circumstances. Schools did not then indulge their pu-pils with long vacations, but ran throughout the year, and during one summer Taylor did have the advantage of attending, six days a week, the private acad-emy in Danbury. Among his teachers was his uncle Alanson Taylor, who in the 1830s ran a "select school" of his own and appears to have been well educated.

By his own account Barnum was "unusually quick" at mathematics; and that he also received a good grounding in grammar and orthography (although his handwriting itself steadily deteriorated over the years) is attested by his early letters. He soon developed quite a flair for composition, in fact, tossing off essays and doggerel poetry. No doubt he also read widely in the classics of English literature, for he was by no means ignorant of such authors as Shakespeare, Milton, Addison, and Byron, besides being well acquainted with the writings of his fellow countrymen. On the Sabbath he was expected to attend Sunday School, where additional study and writing were required of him.[17]

"Headwork I was excessively fond of," Barnum wrote, but physical labor on his father's farm—where he was expected to plow and rake hay, drive the cows, dig and hoe, and perform all the other duties of a farmer's son—he never liked and shirked whenever he could. His entrepreneurial bent soon manifested itself on days when the local militia assembled to train, on which festive occasions he peddled candy and cookies and rushed among the appreciative soldiers with a wineglass and decanter of cherry-flavored rum. By the age of twelve his profits had enabled him to acquire a calf, some sheep, and other property of his own. His father, eyeing this wealth, "considerately allowed me to purchase my own clothing." Around this time, too, having had sufficient evidence of his son's aversion to manual labor, Philo Barnum put him to work in a country store he and one Hiram Weed had established in Bethel. Since this was a cash-and-barter store, young Taylor soon gained additional knowledge of the great world of business through witnessing and participating in the various swindles merchants and their customers were in the habit of playing on each other. On his own he continued to sell candy and now got up small lotteries, the tickets to which he sold to workers in the local hat and comb factories.

Then came the great disaster of his youth! As Barnum tells the story in his autobiography, Philo Barnum was taken ill with a fever one day in March and died six months later, on 7 September 1825. "I was then fifteen years of age," he writes.

> I stood by his bedside. The world looked dark indeed, when I realized that I was for ever deprived of my paternal protector! I felt that I was a poor inexperienced boy, thrown out on the wide world to shift for myself, and a sense of forlornness completely overcame me. My mother was left with five children. I was the oldest, and the youngest was only seven years of age. We followed the remains of husband and parent to their resting-place, and returned to our desolate home, feeling that we were forsaken by the world, and that but little hope existed for us this side the grave.

Worse still, Philo Barnum had died insolvent, which meant his estate had to be put up at auction to settle his debts; and among the last was a sum owed Taylor, whose claim was ruled out of order, however, since it was decided a minor's property belonged to his father. Even the shoes he wore to his father's funeral, Barnum makes a point of telling us, had not been paid for, so that "I began the world with nothing, and was barefooted at that."[18]

The story of Philo Barnum's dying insolvent and inconsiderately leaving his family, and particularly his eldest child, in such straitened circumstances has its poignant moments, of course, and in later life Barnum was not reluctant to repeat it. As late as 1884, upon the inauguration of the Barnum Museum of Natural History at Tufts College, he was still dwelling on the deprivations of his youth; while the president of that august institution, taking his cue from the school's benefactor, used the same occasion to congratulate him warmly for having conquered the poverty with which he began life, and for having attained, despite his lack of "educational advantages," not only a mind stored with "varied and useful knowledge" but also the mastery of a "vigorous and idiomatic style of English which would put many a college man to shame."[19] No matter that the disadvantaged Taylor was the pet of one of Bethel's wealthiest citizens. No matter that the humane custom of the "widow's dower" reserved to the bankrupt's family a dwelling and sufficient personal property for the duration of Irena Barnum's lifetime. No matter, certainly, that Philo Barnum never departed this life until 7 September 1826, by which date his "inexperienced" son Phineas—then two months beyond his sixteenth birthday—was perfectly capable of shifting for himself.

One of the strangest aspects of Barnum's autobiography is that, in every edition of the work published during his lifetime, its author never got around to reporting correctly the year of his father's death. The confusion is further compounded on Philo's headstone, which may have been ordered at a later date, where the year is recorded as 1828. There is no mention of his death among Danbury's vital statistics; and the parish records of the Bethel Congregational Church are equally silent on the matter, presumably because, although he certainly attended its services and during one year, at least, clubbed together with two other men to rent a pew, he was never actually "received" into the church.[20] But the Danbury Probate Records concerned with the settling of his estate—a process that commenced on 12 September 1826 and continued into October of the following year—amply support the 1826 date, and the genealogists Barnum hired in the 1880s also had no difficulty in arriving at this figure. His mother, who was still living when the first edition of the autobiography appeared, and no doubt any number of other persons must have called his attention to the error as well. If memory really did betray him when he was writing that work, there was certainly no excuse for not correcting the information in the book's 1869 and later editions. But by then the story of the fifteen-year-old thrown out on the wide world to shift for himself had become a part of the established canon. So he chose to ignore reality.[21]

The estate paid its creditors fifty-one cents on the dollar; and its inventory, listing everything down to a cradle, large spinning wheel, elementary reader, and pair of spectacles, is chiefly of interest for those items pertaining to Philo Barnum's occupations as innkeeper, teamster, and livery stable proprietor. A formidable number of sheets, blankets, pillowcases, and towels are individually catalogued, as are beds, chests of drawers, and chamber pots. Numerous decanters, wineglasses, and a lemon press; hogsheads, kegs, and barrels of cider and "poor" wine; and a third interest in a still and stillhouse attest to a copious flow of liquid refreshment at mine host's establishment. Also listed are several wagons, a cart, and a sleigh, with five horses (one blind) to draw them, besides cows, hogs, and fifteen sheep. In all, Philo's personal estate was appraised at $1090, while his real estate—consisting of thirteen pieces of land, a new barn, and the homestead—was valued at an additional $2326.[22] The family home was itself set off as part of Irena's dower and consequently brought at auction only a quarter of its appraised value of $775; but as Barnum relates in his autobiography, his mother, who took over from her husband as landlord of the inn, by dint of industry and economy "succeeded in a few years in redeeming the homestead and becoming its sole possessor."[23] Since he was legally a minor, Taylor was given the opportunity to select his guardian. His choice fell on his uncle Alanson Taylor, some eight years his senior, who was approved and bonded by the court on 16 September 1826.[24] For a short time he continued to clerk in the store Hiram Weed and Philo had established in Bethel, then took similar employment at a country store in Grassy Plain. Since he had now moved the extraordinary distance of one mile from the family homestead, it was necessary that he board there. On weekends he rode back to see how the bereaved widow and younger children were progressing, carrying with him his dirty laundry.

———◆———

WHILE CLERKING at Grassy Plain, he first met a "fair, rosy-cheeked, buxom-looking girl, with beautiful white teeth" named "Chairy" Hallett. She had ridden up from Bethel one Saturday evening to buy a bonnet at a neighboring milliner's, but had become frightened when a storm blew up; and Barnum, who was about to return to his mother's anyway, was asked to escort her back. The sight of this pretty companion sent Taylor into a "state of feeling quite new to me," causing him to regret the distance to Bethel was only one mile instead of twenty, and he shortly ascertained she was a tailoress working for one Zerah Benedict. Haunted by visions of her in his dreams that night, the next day he accompanied his mother to church and there saw her again, and on many subsequent Sundays as well, although their relationship progressed but fitfully until the summer of 1829. "My good mother and some other relatives," Barnum writes, "feared that I was not looking high enough in the world." Over their objections he nevertheless proposed to Charity and was accepted, the two being careful to keep their plans to themselves, however. In October Charity left for New York City on what was ostensibly a visit to her uncle Nathan Beers, and the following month Barnum himself traveled thither on what was supposed to be a business trip. In the presence of Charity's relatives and friends, they were married in Beers's house on 8 November 1829. When the nineteen-year-old bridegroom and his wife returned to Bethel a few days later, taking board in the same house where Charity had previously lived, Irena Barnum showed her displeasure by studiously avoiding any reference to her son's wedding or her new daughter-in-law. "She evidently felt chagrined at the clandestine manner of my marriage," Barnum writes, "but I called on her every day with the same freedom that I had ever done, and within a month she invited me to bring 'my wife' and spend the following Sabbath with her. I did so; and from that day to this, I am sure that neither she nor any other person ever said or believed that I had not been extremely fortunate in the selection of my companion."[25]

Aside from these few paragraphs describing their initial meeting, courtship, and marriage, Barnum had little to say about his wife of forty-four years, either in his autobiography or elsewhere in public. A few tributes to her willingness to stand by him when he was in difficulties ("Without Charity, I am nothing," he was fond of punning around the time of his bankruptcy); a rather perfunctory account, in large part a quotation from a local newspaper, of her death and funeral in 1873, while Barnum himself was in Germany—this and no more he was prepared to offer. Even the twenty-page "memorial" to her published a few months after her death, containing both the funeral address of the Reverend Abel C. Thomas and a tribute to her by her cousin Nathaniel P. Beers, in whose father's house she had celebrated her nuptials, tells us little that is personal about her, other than that she was passionately fond of flowers.[26] Consequently, even to her descendants she presents an enigma; while a number of writers have taken advantage of this elusiveness to theorize most ingeniously about her and her husband's conjugal relations. Others have mistakenly assumed she was herself a native of Bethel, seemingly oblivious to the fact that as late as 1830 the combined population of Danbury-Bethel was only around 4300, and that Barnum and Charity could hardly have grown up in a village of a few hundred inhabitants without being aware of each other's existence.

She was born on 28 October 1808 in Fairfield, Connecticut, the daughter of Benjamin W. and Hannah Hallett. The family does not appear to have been very prosperous, and Benjamin himself seems eventually to have wandered off to seek his fortune elsewhere, possibly on Long Island, where several of his descendants established themselves. At the time of Charity's birth he was around forty-three years old. His wife seems to have managed on her own for much of her life, after giving birth to a numerous family. The 1810 U.S. Census lists four children as then present in the household; and during the summer of 1823 no less than six daughters—ranging in age from three to eighteen, and including Charity—were baptized in Fairfield's Greenfield Hill Congregational Church, in whose membership rolls Hannah's, but not her husband's, name figures.[27] In addition, there was at least one son, John, born in 1809, who was employed by Barnum as an advance agent and manager in the late 1830s and early 1840s. Presumably he was the same Hallett who later began to take on airs at the American Museum and was fired "forever" by his employer in the spring of 1843. "The fact is," Barnum wrote to his friend Moses Kimball at the time, "it has long been a matter of doubt *who* was manager of the American Museum. I have not been *suspected* as such for some time. I guess I *shall* be *slightly* suspected of it hereafter!"[28]

Hannah herself continued to reside in the Greenfield Hill area. In the 1850 U.S. Census she is listed as head of a household—comprising herself, an elderly woman named Betty Bank, and a seventeen-year-old granddaughter named

Sarah Wakeman—and living in Easton, just over the Fairfield town line. Her house there, on Morehouse Highway, is indicated in a map of the area dating from 1867. She lived on to survive most of her family, dying in 1882 at the age of ninety-seven.[29] In her old age she was a frequent guest at the Barnums' homes in Fairfield and Bridgeport, and Barnum continued to keep a kindly eye on her after Charity's death in 1873. She was "full of fun," he remarks in his *Funny Stories*, and liked to think of herself as a great fortune-teller. One also suspects she possessed her share of the native wit. On one occasion, when Barnum was sixty-nine, she consented to read his palm. After studying the various lines, she earnestly looked him in the face and said she dared not tell him what she had seen. When her son-in-law persisted, she finally called his attention to his abbreviated "life line." "You are short-lived," she announced, throwing down his hand as though she expected him to faint.[30]

Her daughter Charity possessed her store of "fun" as well, although one might never suspect it from the colorless portraits of her that have been painted in the past. The well-known Universalist editor the Reverend George H. Emerson, who in the late 1860s became a frequent guest at the Barnums' town house in New York and who thereafter remained a close friend of the family, wrote some revealing recollections of her shortly after her death. Even when she felt compelled to censure her husband for one of his more outrageous pranks, he reports, "I saw that she heartily enjoyed him, as she could not keep the laughter down." Emerson could not recall an instance when Charity had ever started a joke on her own, "but when, as was often the case, a good natured specimen was produced for her special benefit, it rarely failed to be honored with a repartee every whit its equal." Barnum was perfectly delighted on such occasions. "Charity gave me a stinger that time, didn't she?" he would say appreciatively when the two men had reached the sanctuary of the library. The minister adds that Charity herself thoroughly enjoyed such triumphs over her husband.[31] Notwithstanding her lowly profession of tailoress in Bethel, and the initial feeling on the part of Barnum's family that he should look higher (the fact that she was his senior by nearly two years may also have entered into their considerations), she appears to have possessed an adequate education and an independent mind. The few extant letters and other examples of writing by her show she was not deficient in that department. That she eventually attended the Unitarian Church and fervently supported the abolitionist cause testifies to her interest in concerns beyond the home.[32]

Barnum never apologized for or felt ashamed of his wife, even though he did, in a few of the articles he wrote for the *New York Atlas*, poke fun at her provincial pronunciation ("cairds" for cards, "cirkiss" for circus), fearfulness when away from home, and straitlaced morality. On her first trip with him to Europe she was violently seasick during most of the passage over. At other times she so kept the passengers "in a half-suffocation of concealed laughter by her piteous moaning about the dangers of shipwreck" that they and her amused husband could not resist the temptation to add to her misery by solemnly agreeing the ship was doomed to founder at any moment.[33] In another article Barnum rejoiced in reporting to American readers her opinions of the

English ("a wretched nation of drunkards and gamblers"), the French ("they are the *wickedest* and most unprincipled nation I ever heard of . . . they do not know what a Sabbath is"), the opera ("it is nothing but unnatural screechings of men, and immodest screamings of females"), and the ballet ("every one of the half-naked trollops who come out upon the stage to show their legs and expose their nakedness ought to be horsewhipped and kept on bread and water till they are willing to work and gain an honest and a decent livelihood").[34] One gathers Charity herself was not amused by these indiscreet revelations, for her husband did not repeat them in his autobiography.

In the same article in which Barnum jokes about Charity's fear of shipwreck he describes her as being "exceedingly nervous and given to hysterics." Indeed, she seems always to have been of a "nervous," somewhat timorous disposition; and one may be certain that following her initial crossing to Europe, she was not eager to venture upon the high seas again. She was ill—not surprisingly— at the time of Barnum's bankruptcy in 1856. She was ill, George Emerson informs us, to the point of being a semi-invalid during the last eighteen years of her life, although her doctors never could agree on just what her ailment was. "It was, however, somewhat intermittent," he writes.

> It was not an uncommon occurrence that one day she would be under doctor's treatment, and so much a sufferer as not to be able to take her place at the table; while the next day she would be equal to her favorite ride in the Park, for shopping at Stewart's, and for what she never was willing to delegate, the immediate supervision of the household. When the hours of suffering were upon her, the worst effect seemed to be on her nervous system, naturally directing her attention vividly to her infirmity, and perhaps causing her to exaggerate the immediate trouble. At such crises, whatever tended to force her thoughts upon other matters proved a hundred fold more potent than doctor's prescriptions.

During one of these "crises," Emerson continues, she snapped out of her condition when Barnum himself became seriously ill. "She gave him her entire thought and care, and for the time it was difficult to see that she could be the invalid which she nevertheless really was." On another occasion Emerson observed that a funny anecdote told by him at the breakfast table produced the same effect.[35]

The symptoms are curious, to say the least, especially when one considers that Barnum's second wife, Nancy, forty years his junior, became early on in their marriage another "semi-invalid," whose "cures" were best effected by long stays in sanitariums. According to one of Barnum's descendants who knew and visited Nancy at her later home in Paris, she "blossomed" following her husband's death. One need look to no wife-beating or other dark secret to explain these circumstances, for Barnum was most affectionate toward both his wives and his family. Nevertheless, his incessant joking, restless scheming, and inexhaustible energy seem to have produced an overpowering, at times depressing, effect on those nearest him. They could hardly be expected to keep up with him—to remain on the *qui vive*—all of the time, and escape was often necessary. His daughters, reared, like him, in this atmosphere of perpetual "merriment," appear to have found it easier to breathe.

————◆————

BY THE TIME of his marriage in 1829, Barnum had already gained some experience in the great world beyond Bethel. Around the beginning of 1827 he journeyed to Brooklyn, New York, to clerk in a grocery store owned by Oliver Taylor, a relative and former resident of Danbury. Since he was also entrusted with making purchases for the store, he soon became expert at dealing on the wholesale and auction markets. However, he eventually became dissatisfied with working for a fixed salary, because, as he was to remark on more than one occasion, "my disposition is, and ever was, of a speculative character, and I am never content to engage in any business unless it is of such a nature that my profits may be greatly enhanced by an increase of energy, perseverance, attention to business, tact, etc."[36] He therefore left Taylor to open a porterhouse in Brooklyn; sold out at a profit a few months later; then clerked again across the river in New York City at a "similar establishment" that was popular with visiting townspeople from Danbury and Bethel. For amusement he frequently attended the theatre, taking along his Connecticut friends, who were expected to be duly impressed by their seasoned companion's taste and critical acumen in such matters.

But his doting grandfather grew lonesome for him, and to lure him back to Bethel offered him, rent-free, half of his centrally located carriage house, if only he would establish some business in it.[37] Barnum decided to accept this generous offer (which would also, of course, enable him to be near Charity again) and in early May of 1828 opened a fruit and confectionery store, whose stock also included oysters, a variety of "fancy goods" imported from New York, and a generous supply of ale. He prospered, and upon advice from his grandfather again took up the lottery business—this time, however, not on his own, but as an agent for some of the grander schemes around the nation. Working for a generous commission, he soon expanded this operation to branches in other towns and took his uncle Alanson as a partner. "My profits were immense," he writes. "I sold from five hundred to two thousand dollars' worth of tickets per day." Thanks to his lottery business, too, he soon became thoroughly acquainted with the power of the press and advertising.

> I issued handbills, circulars, etc., by tens of thousands, with striking prefixes, affixes, staring capitals, marks of wonder, pictures, etc. The newspapers throughout the region teemed with unique advertisements. Immense gold signs, and placards in inks and papers of all colors, covered my lottery office. As the curious letters of "Joe Strickland" were highly popular at that time, I advertised my office as being under the special favor and protection of "Dr. Peter Strickland," own blood cousin to the renowned Joe Strickland, etc. In my bills and advertisements, I rung all possible changes upon the renowned name. "The ever lucky Dr.

Strickland," "Five more capital prizes sold by Dr. Strickland!" "A fortune for a dollar—apply to Fortune's favorite, Dr. Strickland," "Another mammoth prize!—huzza for Dr. Strickland," etc., etc. Home-made poetry was also frequently brought into requisition to set forth the inducements for patronizing my office.[38]

The office, as one learns from advertisements in the local papers, was itself inspirationally titled the "Temple of Fortune," whose proprietor, readers were assured, "continues to sell and pay more Prizes in every Lottery than any other vender in this county." "Nothing venture, nothing gain," proclaims another advertisement. "Call without delay and load your pockets with the shiners, at the old established *Temple of Fortune.*"[39]

He was bursting with energy and schemes for making money, and as funds continued to pour in, he began dealing in real estate on the true Taylorian scale.[40] In the spring of 1831 he and Charity moved into a new house he had ordered built on three acres of land bought from his grandfather. At the same time he erected and became proprietor of a new country store, whose second and third stories were rented out to tenants, with his uncle Alanson again as his partner. This venture, surprisingly, did not work out—because, as Barnum unconvincingly writes, "like most other persons who engage in a business which they do not understand, we were unsuccessful in the enterprise"—and he bought out Alanson's interest the following October. Another idea that proved abortive was his taking about the countryside books he had purchased in New York and auctioning them off to the local inhabitants. When he set up his block in Litchfield one night, the law students in that town proceeded to steal some of his choicest books. The story was repeated in Newburgh, New York, "and I quit the auction business in disgust."[41]

The store itself, which was alternately known as the "Yellow" and the "Moulton Store," he continued to operate for a time on his own, then in partnership with Horace Fairchild. It was a true country store, run on a cash-or-barter basis and offering just about everything a customer might need, including dry goods and groceries; candles and soap; tea, coffee, and tobacco; Bibles, prayer books, and religious tracts; and, in the related "spirituous" line, an inexhaustible supply of six-year-old cider, currant wines, port, madeira, rum, brandy, gin, and cordials. Barnum's half-brother Philo, who was temporarily following his father in the tailoring trade, had his shop and several workmen in the rear of the building—"wood and all kinds of farmer's produce taken in payment for work."[42] But the store, like the book-auction business, was obviously a disappointment, and as early as March 1832 Barnum was trying to sell out. By then, too, he was advising those who had owed money on their accounts for more than six months that his attorney was in the process of preparing suits, and that they could expect to be served with writs no later than the tenth of the month. "Gentlemen, you will find that I am in earnest," he warned.[43] In his autobiography Barnum quotes several of the entries in the big leather-bound ledger he kept at the time as evidence of how his anonymous debtors managed to cheat him. But the actual ledger, now in the Bridgeport

Public Library, is even more uninhibited in its comments. Besides customers who escaped paying by dying, going bankrupt, or "running away"—and a few whose debts were canceled with the notations "by friendship" or "can't find him"—Squire Knapp, one learns, got out of his debt of fifteen cents "by lying like hell," Luke Newton out of his for $1.18 "by being a damn clever fellow," and Darius Webb his for $1.47 "by swearing to a cursed lie!" Those sterling qualities so admired by his fellow Bethelites when some hilarious joke was in the making, Barnum was beginning to learn, sometimes wore a more sinister aspect when allowed to impinge on the serious world of business. When he finally found a buyer for his share of the store in early 1833, he was more than happy to close out his books.

There was another reason Barnum wanted out of the mercantile line, and for his uncle Alanson's early departure from it as well. They had become bitter enemies over those two subjects guaranteed to produce dissension in any age: politics and religion. The latter will be discussed in the following chapter, although it is difficult to keep the two topics separate, so intertwined were they in early nineteenth-century American thought and action. In Connecticut itself the Congregational Church had been disestablished as recently as 1818 and continued to exert considerable influence in the running of the state, not only in the executive and legislative branches but also among the judiciary. The eminent Congregational minister Lyman Beecher, who from his home base in nearby Litchfield had fought zealously against the forces of disestablishment and democracy, tells in his autobiography how in the early century "the ministers were all politicians." On election days, he writes, there would be a festival to which "all the clergy used to go, walk in procession, smoke pipes, and drink. And, fact is, when they got together, they would talk over who should be governor, and who lieutenant governor, and who in the Upper House, and their counsels would prevail."[44] He was not far from the truth; and on reading the Connecticut newspapers of the first third of the century, one realizes how closely related church and politics were. The Congregationalists were antidemocratic and allied with the Federalist party. Liberal denominations like Universalism—to which Barnum and his grandfather subscribed—were staunch supporters of the Jeffersonian Democrats, who were determined to keep church and state separate. Both parties had their own newspapers, in which politics and religion were the two most pressing issues.

Barnum himself, upon coming of age, was soon in the thick of this controversy. In 1831 the state was swept by a protracted wave of revival meetings—fueled by itinerating evangelists specializing in such histrionics—whose converts, more often than not, were of the Congregational persuasion. There was talk, Barnum writes in his autobiography, of a "Christian party in politics," under whose beneficent reign only professors of the "true" religion would be entitled to the franchise and to public office. And while he goes on to concede that the fear of such a "great religious coalition" taking over the country was no doubt exaggerated, the threat, at the time, seemed real enough. When some letters he wrote on the subject were rejected for publication in a local Danbury newspaper, he indignantly set up and began publishing a paper of his own, the *Herald of Freedom*, whose challenging title, interestingly enough, was later expanded to the *Herald of Freedom and Gospel Witness*. The first issue of this four-page weekly, the first newspaper in the history of Bethel, was published on 19 October 1831.[45]

Copies of Barnum's periodical are today extremely rare, but the few that do survive permit one readily to grasp its tenor. Aside from general news items, anecdotes, humorous poetry (sometimes written by the paper's editor), familiar essays in the Addisonian manner, and a good many advertisements for local products and services, its two main emphases were clearly religion and politics. In the issue of 1 March 1832, for example, one learns of a resolution passed by the bachelors of the nearby towns of Pawling and Dover against the efforts of the local clergy to establish Sunday Schools and thus "corrupt" the minds of children by "sectarian prejudice"; and of another that would forbid the Connecticut legislature from employing chaplains and paying them out of the state treasury. "GO AND DO LIKEWISE," the editor admonishes all men with their country's interest at heart. Another issue contains a long article by "Brutus" on the upcoming elections for the state's General Assembly and on the *"disgraceful aristocratical* party" in Southington—*"purse-proud overbearing lordlings"* who must be taught that their "day of oppression is over" and turned out of office.[46] There were warm endorsements of Andrew Jackson during the 1832 Presidential campaign, and local politicians frequently came in for their share of praise and blame as well.

It was surely no coincidence that Barnum and his uncle Alanson should have parted company around the same time the first issue of the *Herald of Freedom* appeared. The unnamed newspaper that had refused to publish the former's letters was almost certainly the *Danbury Recorder*, which thereafter lost no opportunity to abuse its Bethel rival, of course. Its editor for a time was Alanson Taylor, who in early 1832 bought the paper outright and, after changing its name to the *Connecticut Repository*, "resumed" his editorial charge on 14 March.[47] He did not, in truth, last very long at the job, for on the following 9 January the paper again changed hands and title, with the latter then becoming the *Danbury Gazette*. Meanwhile, poor Alanson suffered mightily at the hands of his erstwhile ward, who in the 21 March 1832 issue of the *Herald of Freedom*, only a week after the first issue of Alanson's retitled paper appeared, accused his uncle of favoring a union of church and state and proceeded to give his reasons for believing so. The attacks grew ever more blistering as the 1832 federal elections approached and were extended to the *Repository*'s "Church and State" contributors as well. At one point Barnum charged his uncle with writing, for publication in his own paper, anonymous "letters to the editor" maligning the *Herald of Freedom*, and with lying in some gossip he had spread about his opponents.[48] Alanson countered with a lawsuit for libel. By the end of the year, however—the politicking over and Jackson safely reelected—the two finally settled their differences. When Barnum later made his mark at the American Museum, Uncle Alanson was another relative who benefited from his largesse.

His uncle was not the only one to sue him for libel during his tenure as editor of the *Herald of Freedom*. On another occasion, after accusing a Danbury butcher named Alfred R. Knapp of being a spy in the caucus of the Democratic party, he was haled into court and ordered to pay $215 and costs.[49] But this was nothing compared to the furor that was created when he was incarcerated for sixty days in the Danbury jail after accusing Bethel's Seth Seelye of being a "canting hypocrite" and "taking usury of an orphan boy." Seelye, born in 1795, was one of the village's more prominent citizens (two of his sons became presidents of Amherst and Smith colleges) and a leading member of the Congregational Church. He was a deacon of this last from 28 September 1832 until his death in 1869 and, according to parish records, not above getting up at church meetings to lecture fellow members on their "unchristian" conduct— citing Scripture to prove his point—in refusing to repay money they owed him.[50] Good Bible-quoting, mercantile Christian that he was, he also ran a store and sold liquor in Bethel. Very likely there was rivalry on this account as well.

The case was heard before the Yale law professor and arch-conservative Federalist judge David Daggett, who, according to a writer for the *New Haven Columbian Register*, directed the jury to return a guilty verdict and delivered a bitter harangue at the time of sentencing.[51] Since Barnum was a Universalist, and the Connecticut Supreme Court of Errors had recently ruled that those who did not believe in accountability to God could not be considered competent, he was denied the opportunity to testify in his own defense. Far from being cast down by these high-handed proceedings, the convicted editor was positively elated by all the attention he was getting. As he wrote from the Danbury jail to his friend Gideon Welles, editor of the *Hartford Times* and a member of the state legislature,

I am by the unhallowed decree of that lump of superstition, David Daggett, sent within these gloomy walls *sixty days* for daring to tell the truth! My trial with Alanson Taylor did not come on this term on account of the absence of witnesses, but my trial with Seth Seelye has come and the best counsel in the county were employed against me. Seelye testified in his own defence, and in his testimony he contradicted four unimpeachable witnesses. Daggett charged the jury in such a manner that many intelligent men who were present remarked that he was the best lawyer that had plead in behalf of the state. The bar and seat of the judge was filled with *priests*, there being no less than eight present. Brother Holly of the *Sentinel* will report the case at length, and I hope you will take the trouble to read the trial and then make such remarks as justice demands. The excitement in this and the neighboring towns is very great, and it will have a grand effect. *Public opinion* is greatly in my favor. After the judge had given his cursed *charge*, I was advised by many to forfeit the bonds, which were but $100, but I chose to go to prison, thinking that such a step would be the means of opening many eyes, as it no doubt will. A number of the Presbyterians in this town have declared it to be oppression and are beginning to raise their voices against it. The same spirit governs my enemies that imprisoned Sellick Osborn and burnt to death Michael Servetus by order of John Calvin. But the *people* are more enlightened than in the days of Calvin, and they will upon reading my trial express their indignation at such oppression and persecution.[52]

The reference to Sellick Osborn, who had been sued and imprisoned for libel while running a Democratic paper in Litchfield, was certainly not malapropos, though one might reasonably question how closely Barnum's persecution paralleled that of Michael Servetus. Nor does Saint Phineas's suffering for daring to tell the truth appear to have been all that intense. From within the "gloomy walls" of his cell—freshly carpeted, papered, and decorated in anticipation of his stay—he continued to edit his offending journal, whose subscription list was now augmented by several hundred names. "I lived well; was even oppressed by the almost constant visits of cordial friends," he writes.

On 5 December, the day of his scheduled deliverance, his friends gathered again to celebrate the occasion. At sunrise the national standard was hoisted on the Danbury green, and at 9 A.M. a "national salute" was fired. A "Committee of Arrangements" waited on Barnum at his cell at 11:30 and politely requested him to accompany them to the courthouse across the green. There, in the very room where he had been sentenced two months earlier—now crowded to suffocation with sympathizers and the merely curious, who overflowed onto the courthouse steps—the "services" commenced with a musical ode, composed expressly for the occasion by Bethel's "Squire" Benjamin Hoyt, a favorite confederate of Phineas Taylor in the plotting of some of his more elaborate jokes. Then followed an eloquent oration on the freedom of the press, delivered with customary fervor by Theophilus Fisk, a Universalist minister and editor of the *New Haven Examiner*, and reputedly one of the finest speakers of his day. When he had finished, a choir sang the anthem "Strike the Cymbal," and the celebrants formed in procession and marched to a neighboring hotel, where a sumptuous banquet had been prepared. This led to more singing, followed by toasts to the guest of honor ("The fearless advocate of truth and liberal principles," "A terror to bigots and tyrants," etc.), and Fisk himself became so moved that he launched into another impassioned speech about the "victim of religious fanaticism" whose emancipation they had gathered to hail, and the dangers of a determined "priesthood" that longed to "tread with a giant's foot upon the necks of a prostrate people." Then came the crowning event of the whole affair. To the blaring of a band and the booming of cannon, the martyred editor was ushered into a six-horse coach (the musicians clambering aboard with him) and conveyed to his home in Bethel. Some forty horsemen and sixty carriages swelled the procession, which was preceded by a marshal bearing the Stars and Stripes, while spectators along the route added their cheers. When the parade had finally covered the three miles to the village, the band struck up "Home, Sweet Home." And all of this, Barnum crows, from that little word "usury," to which the pious Seth Seelye had so foolishly taken exception![53]

The experience was a heady one for the twenty-two-year-old editor and made him even more visible on the political scene. He became a "power" to be reckoned with and was soon taking time off from his paper to travel to Hartford, where he sat in on meetings of the state's Democratic leaders and twisted legislators' arms to get judicial and other appointments for his friends back home (in particular those who had served on the "Committee of Arrangements" and as "Officers of the Day" at his liberation from prison), and incidentally attempted to pay off some old scores. He exerted himself to have removed from the office of probate judge "that cursed Reuben Booth," the same who had presided over the settling of his father's bankrupt estate and disallowed the claim of young "Taylor." When his "much esteemed friend" David Daggett showed up in town, he sought an opportunity to "return him my thanks for his kindness in helping me to 1000 subscribers," then joined with several others in an investigation to ascertain Daggett's true age, with the intention of forcing him from the bench if they could prove he had reached the mandatory retirement age of seventy (he hadn't).[54] There was even talk of some political reward for the fearless editor himself, as friends like Gideon Welles busied themselves in the attempt to secure for him the office of Bethel's postmaster.

Back in Newtown, next door to Bethel, he was again in his element at a grand celebration on the following Fourth of July. Some 2000 loyal Democrats assembled to hear another stirring oration by Fisk, and at the subsequent dinner Barnum was again toasted as "a young man who has been bitterly persecuted by the enemies of civil and religious freedom." In his response he fervently called on his fellow Democrats to remain ever vigilant against the hypocrites and "intriguing knaves" who hated this "birthday of *Freedom*, God's best gift to man," and who were attempting to sneak into and subvert the Jackson Democrats. Meanwhile, at the Federalists' own celebration, in Danbury itself, additional toasts were being drunk in his honor—this time with a distinctly ironic ring. "The Reverend P. T. Barnum," Lewis Starr proposed, "the Don Quixote of the present age; may he not be blown away by his own windmill." Another toast was proposed by William Patch: "The day—we have been permitted to celebrate it, notwithstanding the nullifying proclamations of a self-made priest." The editor delightedly reported these "very sentimental" toasts offered up to him by the "ruffle-shirt gentry," at the same time pretending not to understand why they should refer to him as "Reverend." In appreciation of one such compliment paid him by the editor of the *Danbury Gazette*, he reciprocated by conferring on his rival the title of "E. T. 'Scratch,' Esq., A.S.S." and expressed the hope that he would "hereafter be respected accordingly."[55]

By now he was free from the drudgery and frustrations of the "Yellow Store" and had several able persons assisting him on the *Herald of Freedom*. Among them was the printer John W. Amerman, who had followed him to Bethel from Brooklyn and eventually returned there with Barnum's younger sister Mary, whom he married in 1835. In a display of civic-mindedness, Barnum opened a free reading room where one could make choice among over forty periodicals he received in exchange from fellow editors. His half-brother Philo ran a "refectory" in the same building, where he sold fruit, nuts, lemonade, and ale; and Uncle Alanson, in addition to presiding over his "select school," was now in charge of the Bethel Lyceum. On 27 May 1833 there was further cause for family celebration when Charity gave birth to their first child, a daughter whom they named Caroline Cordelia.

He was in a flourishing estate, but dark clouds were gathering on the horizon. Since the 1820s there had been agitation throughout the country to abolish lotteries on both religious and moral grounds, and by the early 1830s some of these attempts were succeeding. In May of 1834 the Connecticut legislature considered the issue and decided to prohibit them after the following 3 June.[56] The "Temple of Fortune," whose liberal offerings had supplied Barnum with a considerable portion of his income, was thus forced to close, and not all its devotees honored their debts, either. He still owned the paper, of course, but its attractions were beginning to pall. He needed wider scope for his restless imagination than tiny Bethel had to offer, and without having any firm idea of what he would do there, other than that he might reestablish himself in the "mercantile" line, he decided to remove with his family to New York City. On 5 November 1834 the *Herald of Freedom* was issued for the last time under his direct supervision, following which John Amerman briefly continued to publish it for him in Norwalk, Connecticut.[57] And in the winter of 1834–35 Barnum bade goodbye to his boyhood friends and, shaking the dust of Bethel from his feet, was off to the mecca of all ambitious Americans.

———◆———

IN DREAMS and choicest memories one is always young. As the old showman approached his eighth decade, he thought more and more about his early days in Bethel and its euphoniously named districts of Plumtrees, Wildcat, and Wolfpits. The names and peculiarities of the village elders, and of the boys and girls with whom he had played, came crowding in upon his memory, and to those who were still living he sent pressing invitations to visit him at his seaside home in Bridgeport and talk over old times, before it was "too late." He recounted many of their adventures anew in his *Funny Stories* and made several well-publicized pilgrimages back to his native town to see what had become of it in his absence. He even, he claimed on one such occasion, had hopes of revisiting Ivy Island before he died, although it seems reasonably certain he spared himself that ordeal.

And always there were memories of his fun-loving grandfather, in whose fond arms, Barnum once estimated, he had spent the better part of his waking hours during the first six years of his life. It was not his mother, and certainly not his father, who was the first person he could recollect having seen as a child. At the end of his life Barnum was as fascinated as ever by the same legendary figure. One of the last things he did, as late as the summer of 1890, was to request from the federal Bureau of Pensions a copy of his illustrious progenitor's Revolutionary War record. Barnum never escaped the influence of Phineas Taylor.

III

A Religion of Healthy-Mindedness

I have been indebted to Christianity for the most serene happiness of my life, and I would not part with its consolations for all things else in the world.

Autobiography

THE INFLUENCE of Phineas Taylor was also felt in another area. It may seem paradoxical, perhaps even sacrilegious to some, to mention Barnum in the same breath as religion; yet throughout his life he manifested an informed, even scholarly, interest in the subject and was himself a sincere practicing Christian. His earliest religious instruction he received at the local Congregational Church—the only church in Bethel—to which his mother, who assisted him in his Sunday School lessons and catechism, was eventually admitted as a member. Until 1818 Congregationalism remained the official, established religion of Connecticut, and virtually all citizens, unless they were certified as belonging to another approved denomination, were required to contribute to its support.

The doctrines of this church were pleasingly set forth in its *Confession of Faith*, the so-called Saybrook Platform, adopted at Saybrook, Connecticut, in 1708 and published two years later for all to see. Its republication under close church supervision in the year of Barnum's birth amply testifies to its adherents' unshakable faith in their superstitions during the intervening century. For here one could read, to one's heart's content, of the innate depravity of man and the ineffectiveness of all his "good works"; of dead infants not among the "elect" being damned to eternal misery; and of the prohibition against marrying "infidels, papists, or other idolaters," whose master, the Pope, was declared to be Antichrist. In a chapter authoritatively titled "Of God's Eternal Decrees," one could also learn of the "high mystery" of foreordination, by which God, "according to the unsearchable counsel of his own will" and "to the praise of his glorious justice," at the beginning of time irrevocably divided unknowing mankind into two distinct classes: those among the "elect" destined to spend eternity in heaven, and those just as surely doomed to "dishonour and wrath" in the other place.

> By the decree of God, for the manifestation of his glory, some men and angels are predestinated unto everlasting life, and others foreordained to everlasting death. . . . These angels and men, thus predestinated and foreordained, are particularly and unchangeably designed, and their number is so certain and definite, that it cannot be either increased or diminished.[1]

As if these bracing Calvinistic tenets were not enough, New England, at the time of Barnum's growing up, was in the grip of the protracted religious hysteria known as the Second Great Awakening—a revival that endured well into the 1830s and had as one of its objectives the countering of Deism and "infidelity" (to use the quaint term employed at the time), which had been on the increase since the Revolutionary period.[2] A number of dissident ministers could not help observing that these "outpourings of the Holy Spirit" were confined to certain denominations—God was obviously discriminating again—and that they reached their peak around the same time the Congregational Church was disestablished and therefore no longer eligible for support from the local tax rolls. Be that as it may, the effect of such revival meetings on impressionable minds can hardly be overestimated, and Barnum himself later recalled their awful effect on him. "When I was from ten to fourteen years of age," he writes, "I attended prayer meetings where I could almost feel the burning waves and smell the sulphurous fumes. I remember the shrieks and groans of suffering children and parents and even aged grandparents."[3] The text on these occasions was the familiar one of a

> solemn, stern and frowning God, who in the exercise of his Divine sovereignty consigned millions upon millions multiplied by unlimited billions upon billions of human souls and bodies, without regard to their good works, to a hell of literal fire and brimstone, from which there should be no deliverance or mitigation throughout the endless ages of eternity, their prayers for relief being answered, *Never! never! never!*
>
> Many and many a time have I returned home from an evening prayer meeting frightened . . . and almost smelling, feeling and tasting those everlasting waves of boiling sulphur, and hearing the agonizing shrieks and useless prayers of myriads of never ending sufferers, including mothers and their children, or perhaps children whose saved mothers were complacently watching their eternal agonies from the battlements of heaven, and with my eyes streaming with tears, and every fibre of my body trembling with fear, I have dropped upon my bended knees and fervently prayed this cold, stern God to let me die immediately, if thereby it was possible to save my soul and body from His endless wrath. Now these earnest, sincere prayers of mine were caused entirely by abject fear. Certainly I could not truly love such a God. Professing Christians of that

day would say, "I hope I love God. I try to love Him." But they could not love Him.[4]

Had the young "Taylor" continued in thrall to this terrifying God of wrath and misery, it is difficult to imagine what his future direction might have been, even though most of his New England contemporaries did manage to survive and grow up to become sharp Yankees. Others less hardy, ministers among them, were driven to agonizing doubt, mental breakdown, and worse through contemplating these Tartarean vistas of endless punishment.

Fortunately, there was a way out of this morass of fear and despair. During the eighteenth century a number of other churches had made inroads into Connecticut; and while the Congregationalists did not exactly welcome them with open arms, the Baptists, Methodists, and Episcopalians were increasingly tolerated. They were soon in Danbury, if not in Bethel itself, and in the early nineteenth century were joined by members of several other denominations. Among them were the Universalists, who date their beginnings in that town from 1807, when the famous minister Hosea Ballou, journeying through the state, preached a sermon to interested parties in the Danbury courthouse. For some years subsequent, as was common at the time, the followers of this faith were served at intervals by itinerating preachers, although they also must have gathered more regularly in each others' homes for worship and informal discussions. A small society of Universalists was officially organized in the town in 1822; and two years later, around the time Barnum got up off his knees and ceased praying God to take him out of this sinful world, it was sufficiently prosperous to hire its first settled minister.[5]

When Barnum wrote his indignant reply to the review of his autobiography that had appeared in the *Trumpet and Universalist Magazine,* he was quite correct in asserting that he nowhere in that work makes any reference to his being a Universalist. But he does mention that his grandfather was one; and elsewhere that Phineas Taylor, who had contributed generously toward the erection of the "meeting house" in which the Bethel Congregational Church held its services, once became angry and declared the church "might go to the devil" when a clergyman of his own faith was refused permission to preach there.[6] "Uncle Phin" must have attended Universalist meetings in Danbury and nearby Newtown, both of which had active Universalist societies in the early nineteenth century, and no doubt it was he who introduced his grandson to this liberal religion. Unfortunately, the early records of both societies have long been lost; but a later pastor and historian of the Danbury church, who obviously had access to those pertaining to his establishment, writes that for several years young Barnum was clerk to this society.[7]

Universalism takes its name from its central belief that all men and women, not just an "elect" few, are destined for salvation. In contrast to the terrifying pronouncements of the Congregationalists in their Saybrook Platform, the Universalists gently expressed this belief in their own Profession of Faith, adopted at Winchester, New Hampshire, in 1803, as follows:

> We believe that there is one God, whose nature is Love, revealed in one Lord Jesus Christ, by one Holy Spirit of Grace, who will finally restore the whole family of mankind to holiness and happiness.

Like most denominations, Universalism experienced its share of internal dissent and theological controversy, and in the nineteenth century its beliefs underwent a certain degree of evolution. The doctrine of the Trinity was examined and rejected, for example, and in the 1830s the church almost split over the weighty matter of whether there was or was not a period of limited punishment in the afterlife (the so-called Restorationist Controversy). But this belief in the certainty of universal salvation was never challenged from within the church—indeed, could not be challenged without calling into question the very *raison d'être* of the church itself. With its emphasis on God's love and the eventual reconciliation of all mankind with the deity, with its systematic rejection of the doctrines of infinite sin and infinite punishment, Universalism is a prime example of what William James, in his *The Varieties of Religious Experience*, terms a religion of "healthy-mindedness."[8]

As might be expected, the forces of orthodoxy were not about to let this new denomination go unchallenged.[9] Universalists were variously condemned as deists, infidels, and atheists; and the Congregational Church itself lost no time in proclaiming the doctrine of universal salvation a "censurable heresy." For it followed, did it not, that those professing such a belief could hardly be relied on to abide by God's commandments? They were a danger to society and must be persecuted with righteous zeal. The 1828 ruling by the Connecticut Supreme Court of Errors that such persons were incompetent to testify in courts of law was but one result of such enlightened reasoning.[10] That the invigorating doctrine of predestination might start its disciples down the same hedonistic path was simply unthinkable, of course.

The battle lines were clearly drawn and extended into the political arena as well. A religion that denied mankind free will could not be expected to evince much faith in the ability of men to govern themselves; and the Congregationalists, who in an earlier age had been able to limit the franchise in Connecticut to "true" believers in the established religion, were basically antidemocratic in their political sentiments. Even slavery might be defended on orthodox religious grounds: as a punishment sent by God of man's sinfulness and innate depravity. On the opposing side stood the determined band of Universalists and their allies from other liberal religions, whose championing of a "free" electorate (eventually extended to include Negroes and women) was the logical corollary of their egalitarian religious beliefs. The struggle was waged in the press as often as it was from the pulpit, and in the early nineteenth century a surprising number of journals were published by the Universalists. Between 1793 and 1886 at least 182 such periodicals were published around the nation, while during the crucial years 1820 to 1850 no less than 132 were begun.[11] The 14 April 1832 issue of the *Trumpet and Universalist Magazine* lists fourteen Universalist papers as then being available, although the tally is obviously incomplete, since Barnum's own paper is not among them. For the

Herald of Freedom and Gospel Witness was certainly no more political than other denominational journals of its day, and its religious content was always extensive and pungent. The editor and his contributors ridiculed the Congregationalist doctrines of partialism and endless punishment at every opportunity; and the paper frequently published sermons, articles from other Universalist journals, and caustic "letters to the editor" on the same topics. During one period it carried a series entitled "Proofs of Universalism." When the new Presbyterian meetinghouse in one New England town was "converted" to Universalist use, there was understandable jubilation over this event.[12] In other issues the paper chronicled a never-ending string of suicides, murders, and instances of madness, directly inspired (or so the editor asserted) by itinerating evangelists, whose hapless victims were driven to these extremes after becoming convinced they had committed unpardonable sins. A particularly poignant case involved a young girl in New Haven who literally tried to cut out her "bad" heart with a razor. When friends rushed to take the razor away from her, she continued to claw at the incision with her bare hands, actually exposing, one witness claimed, the beating organ. Was this religion? the editor thundered. Or was it the work of *"hireling Priests . . .* relentless savages who would reduce every peaceable dwelling to an insane house, and make every father a *murderer* of his own innocent and helpless offspring, rather than fail in establishing their heart-rending, barbarous and unfeeling creed."[13]

There were also many piquant accounts of the failings of orthodox ministers, like the wayward Presbyterian clergyman who robbed his wife and ran off with one of his parishioners. Others were accused of attempting to ravish their female servants or dying as the result of drunkenness. When the notorious Rhode Island Methodist minister Ephraim K. Avery was acquitted of seducing and then murdering his paramour, the indignant editor, who had been publishing full accounts of the trial, remained convinced of his guilt and wrote a long article on that subject.[14] Even the Reverend Erastus Cole, the local Congregational dominie, was not spared the barbs of the inquiring editor, who openly proclaimed him to be a *"great ladies' man"* and wondered if he still *"carries the ladies a fishing* nowadays."[15] Again, there were threats of lawsuits.

No wonder, then, that his orthodox neighbors soon took to referring to him as a "self-made priest" and the "Reverend P. T. Barnum." There was always in him a strong tendency to "sermonize," although he managed to control it when he came to write his autobiography. As early as his Bethel days he was frequently called upon to speak before Universalist groups, as he twice did at the Weston home of David Thorp on a Sunday in July 1833, choosing for one of his texts the tale of Lazarus and the rich man.[16] In later years, too, a number of people half seriously suggested that he had missed his true calling in life. At a banquet honoring him in 1874, by which time Barnum was well launched on his career in circus management, the Reverend Dr. Hopper remarked that he would have made a good clergyman, mesmerizing and electrifying his congregation. "What a spiritual showman he would have made; how he would have exhibited the menagerie of the heart, in which ferocious beasts, in the form of fiery passions, prey upon the soul."[17] While Barnum later played down his journalistic exploits in Bethel and was even somewhat apologetic about his youthful fanaticism, there can be no doubt about the sincerity of his religious convictions or that he really did feel it necessary to take up the cudgels against orthodoxy. He was to do so time and again on later occasions, whenever the "reverend rascals"—as he sometimes called his opponents—challenged him or his Universalist beliefs. And he always gave at least as good as he got.

Moreover, these same Universalist beliefs informed his later career as a showman and to a large extent explain what many writers have mistakenly interpreted as a lack of compassion, a certain callousness, in his character. "I think I never knew a more heartless man . . . than P. T. Barnum," wrote Major J. B. Pond, who once managed a series of lectures Barnum gave for the Redpath Bureau of Boston. Pond tells of going with the showman to his circus one afternoon, and seeing a female performer run over and killed by a chariot. "That is dreadful, isn't it?" said Pond to Barnum. "Oh," replied the latter, "there is another waiting for a place. It is rather a benefit than a loss."[18] The scene, if accurately reported, seems terrible in its implications and is invariably harped on by Barnum's detractors. But Pond was hardly an intimate friend; and Barnum, who was noted for his bland deportment, did not often parade his feelings in public. That he was sensitive toward others and their needs, often generous in relieving distress, is abundantly evident in his letters and elsewhere. Like the systematic practitioner of the healthy-minded religion described by James, however, he was apt to ignore, even deny, the influence of evil in the affairs of men and to look upon such accidents as part of some divine plan. In an interview toward the end of his life he once stated his conviction that "if one does right, his mind should never be disturbed by anything which he cannot prevent. He should be thoroughly convinced that if he does his duty Providence will take care of the rest, and never send accident, poverty, disease, or any other apparent evil except for an ultimate good purpose."[19]

The truth is, Barnum was not the type given to morbid introspection and self-doubt. He suffered his fair share of personal disasters: the deaths of his first wife and two of his four children; a devastating series of fires that destroyed much of his personal and business property; an even more damaging bankruptcy, when he was in his mid-forties, that would have crushed most other men of his day ten times over. Writing to his friend the Universalist minister Abel C. Thomas shortly after the last, he was pleased to observe, "All praise to Him for permitting me always to look upon the bright side of things"— a sentiment that might easily stand as a motto for his life.[20] On another occasion, in answer to a minister who seems to have wanted to borrow something he had seen at the circus, he closed his letter with the telling statement, "Wishing you success in teaching your people and children the propriety of innocent amusements & recreation—for I believe in a *cheerful* Christianity."[21] This reassuring belief in a "cheerful" Christianity—a belief that encourages one to cast off doubt and the burdens of guilt and go forward secure in the knowledge of God's love and of good in all things—served Barnum as a touchstone throughout his career. And it is this same belief, still incomprehensible to many who call themselves Christians, that continues to interfere with a proper understanding of the showman today. Religion, as those reared in the orthodox Protestant faith know all too well, was never meant to be a joyful affair.

———◆———

AFTER GIVING UP the *Herald of Freedom* and moving with his family to New York City, Barnum continued to take an active interest in Universalism. In the metropolis he attended services of the Fourth Universalist Society, whose building, originally in the vicinity of City Hall, eventually was situated at Fifth Avenue and 45th Street, only a few blocks from his house on Murray Hill.[22] The "Church of the Divine Paternity," as this later building was called, experienced its greatest period under the leadership of the Reverend Edwin H. Chapin, who was pastor to the society from 1848 until his death in 1880. Descended from Puritan stock and raised in the orthodox faith, Chapin, too, had rebelled against the appalling teachings of the latter in the 1830s. Following his ordination in 1838, for a time he was the colleague of Hosea Ballou—the same who had introduced Universalism to Danbury—at the School Street Church in Boston. In New York he quickly attained the reputation of being one of the greatest preachers of his age and a most persuasive advocate of temperance principles.

He was also, like his slightly older parishioner, fond of jokes, conundrums, and especially puns; and although Barnum did not have much to say about him in the first edition of his autobiography, he recorded several horrendous examples of these last by Chapin in later editions and particularly in his *Funny Stories*. The reverend doctor was such an inveterate jokester, Barnum reports, that those familiar with him only in social circles were apt to say, "To see and hear him out of the pulpit, one would think he ought never to go into it," while those who knew him as an eloquent preacher were of the opinion that "he ought never to be out of it." The two men became such fast friends and were so often in each other's company that they were known to their intimates as "Chang and Eng"—after the famous Siamese Twins—with Chapin inscribing copies of books he sent Barnum "From Eng to his friend Chang" and even directing his letters to "Chang."[23] Among other members of Chapin's New York congregation were Charity's cousin Nate Beers and his wife Emma, with the former serving at various times as clerk, treasurer, historian, and deacon of the society; and Julius S. Redfield, the publisher of Barnum's autobiography, who for several years served as a trustee. Barnum himself was never an officer or trustee of the society, although he was for a time on its Sunday School committee. He also gave generously toward the new church on Fifth Avenue, where services were first conducted in 1867; was a life member of the Chapin Home for the Aged and Infirm, which Chapin's wife opened in 1872; and later, following his friend's death, contributed toward the splendid bronze bas-relief of Chapin by Augustus St. Gaudens that may still be seen at the society's present location.

But the Universalist church that above all others benefited from his generosity and attendance was that of Bridgeport's First Universalist Society, in whose affairs Barnum was active from 1848 on. In the fall of that year he moved into his opulent mansion Iranistan, and on 25 September the first reference to him in the society's records occurs, when a resolution was passed thanking "P. T. Barnum Esq. for the manifestation of his good will and liberality by so appropriately (and to the Society highly satisfactorily) painting the interior of their meeting house."[24] Besides his monthly contributions to this society, which were generally in the range of three to six times that of the next biggest contributors, he often gave substantial sums for such purposes as rebuilding the church after it was damaged by fire, installing a furnace and stained glass windows, getting the church steeple repaired, procuring an organ, canceling various debts and mortgages, and constructing Sunday School rooms and a parsonage. From his Bridgeport mansions' luxuriant greenhouses he frequently sent flowers to decorate the church interior; on other occasions he made the society gifts of land. In his will he left it a handsome legacy of $15,000, which came to be known as the "Barnum Fund." Although he never had the desire to serve as an officer, he was decidedly the most popular trustee from 1882 until his death in 1891, and he also served on several committees charged with buildings, music, and missionary work.

For over forty years Barnum was the Bridgeport society's chief and most influential supporter, to the extent that he sometimes felt it necessary to admonish his fellow parishioners that they should not rely so heavily on any one individual. He was, as might be expected, on intimate terms with the several ministers who served the society during this period, "talking Universalism" with them at every opportunity; entertaining them, and occasionally the entire congregation, at the clambakes he loved to throw at the beach on Long Island Sound; running into the parsonage whenever he happened to be passing to speak a few words of greeting and drop off a Thanksgiving turkey or some other gift. Ministerial friends like Chapin, besides many prominent lay individuals, were often invited to Bridgeport to partake of his legendary hospitality and to add variety to the church services. On other occasions he himself occupied the pulpit, following which his remarks were sometimes deemed worthy of publication in such journals as the *Christian Leader*. After a trip out West in 1870, for example, he spoke about his adventures in Salt Lake City and announced to his no doubt startled listeners that he had discovered the Mormons also believed in Universalism.[25] At other times his talks took a more theological bent, as when, on Good Friday Eve of 1877, he spoke long and earnestly on the true nature of the Gospel, in contrast to the fear and terror instilled by orthodox religions. It was a "Red Letter Day" and "the church was filled with an interested audience," noted the society's then official pastor, the Reverend John Lyon, who a few years later went temporarily insane—abandoning wife, parish, and Barnum to run off to New York City. When he was "captured" there a few days later by some members of the society who had gone in search of him, the glad tidings were immediately telegraphed to the anxious showman. After being sent to Atlantic City to recuperate, Lyon continued to serve the parish until his death in 1887.[26]

Strange to relate, it was Lyon who succeeded in convincing Barnum to finally "join" the church, for as the latter was asserting as late as 1872, "I never belonged to the Bridgeport society . . . & I am thankful that I don't *belong* to any ecclesiastical society."[27] He had made the same claim (he "never became a member of any Universalist society") in his 1855 reply to the review of his autobiography in the *Trumpet and Universalist Magazine*, where he also gave his reason for this paradoxical situation: "I knew the prejudice against show-men, and was not willing to saddle my professional responsibilities upon any church."[28] The hostility of which he writes was real enough, a carryover from the days of the English Reformation when "players" and other shiftless cater-ers to public amusement were officially declared to be "rogues, vagabonds, and sturdy beggars" and subject to public whipping as a just chastisement for their shameless way of life. The Puritans had transplanted to America the hatred of such entertainers, whose activities were prohibited by law in several New En-gland states, including Connecticut, until well into the nineteenth century. But even after these laws had been rescinded, there remained many God-fearing citizens who continued to tremble at the thought of entering a theatre or other place of amusement, and who insisted on keeping a charitable eye out for the spiritual well-being of their frail brothers and sisters. Indeed, can one honestly say this innate distrust of persons who make their livings by "playing" rather than by "working"—and who continue to divert our thoughts from the more serious concerns of business and the imperfect state of our souls—is entirely dissipated even in the present age?

Barnum fought this battle all his life without ever conclusively winning it. There were minor, even major, victories along the way, as when he succeeded in getting for publication endorsements from prominent clergymen—Congre-gationalists and Presbyterians among them—testifying to the chaste amuse-ment and instructional value to be found at his circus. When less-enlightened ministers felt it their duty to point out the moral danger of such entertain-ments, he eloquently sprang to their defense. There were lighter, more playful stratagems as well, some of them dating back to the Colonial period, when actors were often billed to present not plays but "moral discourses." If visitors to the American Museum had scruples about setting foot in a theatre, they had no objections whatever to entering a well-equipped "lecture room," where they might be instructed by such "moral" dramas as *Uncle Tom's Cabin* or *The Drunkard*. "Are the services about to commence?" asked one country patron when the gong sounded to announce the play was about to begin. "Yes," re-plied the unruffled manager, "the congregation is now going up."[29]

It was not until 1876, therefore, that Barnum allowed himself to be "elected" a member of the Bridgeport society and actually signed its membership roll. Even then he refrained from taking the final step and did not join the church itself until Easter Sunday of 1879, when, heeding the persuasive appeal of the Reverend John Lyon, he was finally received "by Christian profession and the right hand of fellowship" and remained after services to take Communion.[30] His wives and children went their own ways in religious matters, although they often accompanied him to church services. The latter and their descendants preferred the more fashionable Episcopalian faith, and Charity, as already mentioned, was a Unitarian.[31] As one who was repeatedly condemned for his own religious convictions, Barnum was almost invariably tolerant toward members of other persecuted denominations, not excluding those of the Catholic faith, against whom there was considerable prejudice in nineteenth-century America. He had been favorably impressed by the devoutness and charitable works of Catholics while on his first visit to France, and had generally found the priests he met to be "jolly good fellows."[32] When his fifteen-year-old daughter Caroline, accompanying him on a trip to Montreal in 1848, righteously commented in her diary on the "idolatry" she had witnessed in connection with the worship of a statue of the Virgin Mary, her father, after reading over what she had written, inserted the following correction at the bottom of the page: "*Idolatry* is not the proper word to apply to the Catholics, for they believe in 'God and a Saviour' and appear to be *sincere* in their devotions. It is fortunate that *any* system of religion can be brought to enlist seriously the minds of the 'lower class, including Indians' P.T.B."[33] In a few of his letters Barnum makes unflattering references to the "moneyless Jew brokers" with whom he was involved in an unfortunate real-estate speculation, but nothing of the sort that would surprise or otherwise occasion objection in most well-bred Christians of his day or ours. While serving as mayor of Bridgeport, too, he once got into hot water when he was reported in a local German-language newspaper as using the phrase "miserable Jews" during a heated debate over the city's liquor-licensing laws. His Honor indignantly claimed he had been misquoted and proceeded to collect statements from Jewish friends testifying to his lack of prejudice.[34] There can be no denying, however, that he fervently believed in the superiority of the Christian faith. To this end he was always a generous supporter of its missionary work.

Despite any doctrines he might disagree with, it really made little difference to Barnum in what church he worshiped. When residing in New York, he sometimes journeyed to Brooklyn, the "city of churches," on Sundays to listen to the sermons of Henry Ward Beecher at the Plymouth Congregational Church or those of Theodore Cuyler at the Lafayette Avenue Presbyterian Church. The former, following one of his trials for adultery with the wife of Theodore Tilton, Barnum once offered to send on a lucrative lecture tour, "the lecture to be the *only* entertainment," he emphasized.[35] Cuyler, besides being a brilliant preacher, was an esteemed friend and fellow worker in the temperance movement. During one summer when he was vacationing in the Bridgeport area and was announced as about to preach in the local Methodist church, Barnum wrote to assure him that he would try to be there,

> for I love your fresh, earnest, unctuous, & zealous efforts—though when I see your writings & your efforts so full of *generous love for your fellow men,* I often wonder & regret that you cannot see the final *triumph* of our good Father & Saviour over *all* sin & wickedness, so that all things shall finally be *reconciled* to Him, & He—the Almighty, the *Infinite* in power,

knowledge, & mercy—shall indeed be All, and in all. Thus would all your prayers & the prayers of all good men be answered, and the angels would rejoice forevermore. But never mind. I love and admire you and your works. We cannot all see alike, but *we can all do good.*[36]

Following the death of Chapin in 1880, Barnum regularly attended services at New York's Unitarian Church of the Messiah, whose pastor, the great Robert Collyer, had recently arrived in the city from Chicago. Having begun life as a blacksmith in England, Collyer had also risen from "humble" circumstances, and the two men immediately hit it off and were soon fast friends. When Barnum proudly declared toward the end of his life that "in my long public career at home and abroad, eminent clergymen of every denomination have been among my most cherished and intimate personal friends," he did not exaggerate.[37]

But the majority of these clerical friends, as might be expected, were of the Universalist faith and included nearly every figure of importance within that denomination. Barnum hobnobbed with them at state and national conventions (on at least two occasions he was an official delegate to these last) and at other times invited them to visit him at his home or traveled to theirs. Among his special favorites, aside from Chapin, were Abel C. Thomas, a former Quaker who resided near his Bridgeport friend during the 1860s, although he spent most of his pastoral career in Philadelphia; George H. Emerson, at one time a disciple of Thomas, who particularly distinguished himself as an author and editor of leading Universalist periodicals; and Charles A. Skinner, father and grandfather, respectively, of the actors Otis Skinner and Cornelia Otis Skinner, who was pastor to the Hartford society from 1867 to 1877. In the last decade of his life Barnum was on excellent terms with the Reverend Elmer H. Capen, third president of Tufts College in Medford, Massachusetts, an institution founded by Universalists but run on nonsectarian principles. Barnum had previously served as a trustee of the college from 1851 to 1857. In the 1880s, under Capen's skillful prodding, his interest in the institution spectacularly revived when he pledged $50,000 to build and endow the Barnum Museum of Natural History on its campus.[38] Officially opened during the college's commencement exercises on 18 June 1884, on which occasion the elusive donor's name was finally revealed, the museum became the "pet" project of his later life. Barnum regularly sent it mounted skins and skeletons, often the remains of animals that had died in his circus, including the hide of the great Jumbo himself, who was destined to become the school mascot and whose sterling attributes, along with his donor's, have been extolled in several college songs written by appreciative Tuftonians. The showman also busied himself in acquiring for the museum various duplicates, specimens, and entire collections from the Smithsonian Insitution, Ward's Natural Science Establishment, and other sources. Including the original money for the building and its endowment, supplementary expenditures for acquisitions and other purposes, and a handsome legacy for the addition of two wings, Barnum's contributions to this one project alone amounted to around $100,000.[39] He sometimes gave money to other Universalist schools around the country—St. Lawrence University in Canton, New York, and Lombard College in Galesburg, Illinois, for example—although these contributions, generally in the range of a thousand dollars or so, were on a smaller scale. "Whilst feeding the churches," he had written in the speech that was read for him at the 1884 Tufts commencement, "let us not neglect to foster the colleges, but endeavor to give them such prestige and position as shall enable them to exercise the most salutary influence and do *the very best work.*"[40]

His commitment to education and to "spreading the word" was apparent in other areas as well. When Isaac P. Coddington, the young brother-in-law of Barnum's nephew Charles Benedict, showed interest in a ministerial career, Barnum helped to finance his preparatory schooling and course of studies at St. Lawrence University.[41] During the early years of his connection with the Bridgeport society, the Reverend Moses Ballou—nephew of Hosea—was his pastor. When Moses felt moved to reply to the Reverend Edward Beecher's recently published *The Conflict of Ages; or, The Great Debate on the Moral Relations of God and Man*, Barnum helped place his *The Divine Character Vindicated* with Redfield in New York and subsidized its publication. The book appeared in 1854, and its author paid handsome tribute ("I am more deeply indebted to you for personal favors than to any other living man") to his benefactor in its dedication.[42] In his will Barnum left a total of $7000 to the Universalist Publishing House of Boston, $5000 of which was specifically designated for "the publication of religious and Christian literature," including a sermon and two tracts (one by his friend Abel Thomas) he particularly admired. The income from this "Barnum Tract Fund," as the larger bequest was known, was used to publish many pamphlets, among them tens of thousands of copies of Barnum's own *Why I Am a Universalist*, until well into the present century.[43] Other "Universalist" bequests in the same lengthy document were made to the Connecticut Universalist Convention ($5000, of which half was designated for religious literature and "missionary purposes," the other half for its Ministerial Relief Fund); the Chapin Home for the Aged and Infirm ($1000); the Woman's Centenary Association of the Universalist Church ($500); the settled pastor, whoever he might be at the time of Barnum's death, of the Bridgeport society ($500); and the Reverend Isaac Coddington himself ($1000). And these, one should bear in mind, were but a fraction of the bequests he made to various other organizations and institutions. In his talks before the Bridgeport society Barnum sometimes stressed the crucial role of "charity" in Christian life, and his own life provided an example of this belief that even his most fervent theological opponents could not gainsay. With the exception of the period when he was recovering from bankruptcy, he customarily devoted all his lecture fees to relieving individual cases of distress, or else donated them, after deducting his expenses, to the churches or other organizations sponsoring his talks. The former were by no means restricted to those of the Universalist faith, and in Bridgeport itself he was commonly known to have contributed to every one of its churches at one time or another. Whether in quest of money, a talk, or something for a church bazaar, ministers were rarely refused by the tolerant showman.

—◆—

BESIDES HIS enduring interest in theological matters, Barnum was also actively involved in the progressive social programs advocated by the Universalist Church. Three stand out in particular relief: the abolition of slavery, woman's rights, and temperance. Barnum's relation to the first and to blacks in general will be examined elsewhere in this book. On the subject of suffrage for women, he blew hot and cold and never did really make up his mind. In an 1880 communication to the editor of the *Bridgeport Standard,* enclosing a copy of a letter he had once received from his deceased friend the poetess Phoebe Cary, he extolled its writer as the "wittiest woman in America" and cited her letter as evidence that "we are a little purblind in excluding this class of persons from having a voice in making laws for the observance of *all* the people."[44] Yet, a few weeks before his death in 1891, when asked what he thought about the "woman question" by a female reporter who had traveled to Bridgeport to interview him, he replied that he knew little about it and that "I never believe in woman suffrage only when I'm listening to some woman who does believe in it, and then I wonder whether the ladies would get through talking at one town meeting before it was time for the next. But I do believe that a woman should follow any trade, profession, or occupation that she may select." He went on to add that he was more radical in his thinking on the subject than his second wife, Nancy, who "is an English woman and very modest and conservative."[45] Barnum had seen his widowed mother Irena ably carry on with the management of the Bethel inn, and in the course of his long career as a showman he often had business dealings with female performers. On his first trip abroad he was further enlightened upon observing women in the French countryside plowing, reaping, mowing hay, etc.—work that in America was usually reserved for men. They even rode horses astraddle! he reported with amazement in one of his letters to the *New York Atlas.* When he once stopped to talk with a group of these tough, brawny peasants (many of whom, he noted appreciatively, had beards and mustaches) and questioned them about their "hard" way of life, they laughed at his notions of female delicacy.[46] It was a lesson he did not forget, although he continued to draw the line at strenuous physical labor. Two decades later, upon contributing $50 to the Working Women's Protective Union, he praised that organization for supporting women who wished to gain their own livelihoods and expressed the opinion that more occupations ought to open up for them:

> In France females not only act as accountants, clerks in stores, offices, &c., but they also sell the tickets at public places of amusement and engage in hundreds of other branches of light labor that are here filled by men. I could give permanent employ to several females of good character who are judges of money and competent to sell tickets. In fact, I think they have but to fit themselves for many light and pleasant avocations in order to find plenty of chances for employment at such salaries as will enable them to live comfortably and respectably.[47]

On other occasions he supported such organizations as the Ladies' Cooperative Dress Association, whose secretary was the journalist and popular speaker Kate Field.[48]

If he wavered in his attitude toward suffrage for women, he certainly had no objections to hearing out the arguments of the leading woman's rights advocates, many of whom he personally knew and invited to speak in Bridgeport and stay at his home. When Lucy Stone lectured on the subject in New York's huge Tripler Hall—originally built to accommodate the crush expected at Jenny Lind's concerts—Barnum was there and later reported he "became enchained" to his seat for the one and one-half hours or so she spoke. He afterward published a biographical sketch and engraving of her in his *Illustrated News* and tried to get her to lecture in Bridgeport for the benefit of the local Methodist church. Writing to obtain her address from Dr. Russell T. Trall, a New York physician who had recently established a medical school open to women students, he remarked that "I think the lecture on Woman's Rights would suit them here—at all events, they ought to hear it."[49] Similar invitations were extended to Mary Ashton Livermore, Kate Field, and Isabella Beecher Hooker. The Bridgeport Universalist Church itself was often the site of their talks. During one period in 1874 alone, its pulpit was occupied on three consecutive Sundays by Susan B. Anthony (who spoke on temperance), the Reverend Marianna Thompson of Boston, and Mrs. Livermore.[50]

Even more remarkable is the fact that from 1869 to 1875 his pastor at Bridgeport's First Universalist Society was the Reverend Olympia Brown, a graduate of the Canton Theological School of St. Lawrence University and the first woman in America to be ordained by full denominational authority. Brown had previously served as minister to the Universalist society in Weymouth, Massachusetts, and in 1868, the year before she received her call to Bridgeport, had founded the New England Woman's Suffrage Association. In Bridgeport, where her grocer husband, John H. Willis, was also the society's treasurer, she received frequent encouragement from Barnum himself, who "was very friendly to me," she writes in her autobiography, "and often made some complimentary remark as I came down from my pulpit."[51] Unfortunately, her ever-increasing activities on behalf of the woman's rights movement shortly alienated a vociferous portion of the society's members, who repeatedly attempted to block her reelection at the annual meetings. When the society's constitution was revised during Brown's pastorate, the right to vote in its affairs was restricted to those who had been paying for a seat in church for at least six months, while those ceasing to do so were immediately deprived of their voting rights and membership. Brown's opponents, many of whom suddenly found themselves disenfranchised and, presumably, excluded from the parish, charged that the minister and her allies among the officers and trustees were attempting to rig the elections, and that the new rules were illegal under state laws governing ecclesiastical societies. In addition, a number of dissidents who had been paying for their seats claimed they had been prevented from voting because they had failed to attend their pastor's preaching on a regular basis. Matters were hardly improved when Brown's chief antagonist, James Staples, a prominent banker and real-estate and insurance agent, was accused of mishandling some of the society's money. Staples promptly brought Brown up on charges of "unministerial conduct" at the 1874 state convention. When this attempt to get rid of her also failed, the society's affairs were finally aired in public and a court injunction was sought and obtained barring its officers from rehiring Brown at the expiration of the 1874–75 church year. Olympia Brown was literally forced out of her Bridgeport pulpit by court decree.

As the society's chief supporter, if not its leading "member," Barnum undoubtedly had his say in the initial hiring of Brown. He remained on friendly terms with her throughout this bitter struggle, yet clearly did not wish to take sides in the matter, since he had no desire, as he pointed out to her, to meddle in church politics. When Brown once wrote to him to report some rumors she had heard concerning plans to hire a man in her place, he denied having heard the stories himself or being party to any such plan ("especially if they expect any $4000 man & expensive music") and informed her he was writing to Staples to say "I am not opposed to you, and that if they engage the angel Gabriel I will not pay more than I have done." But the real danger to church unity, as Barnum made clear, was not Brown's sex but her increasingly strident activity on behalf of woman's rights. Rumors had reached him of her going to the polls and associating with some of the more notorious suffragettes, and

> such persons as Claffin [sic] and Woodhull, Tilton & Middlebrook are
> blackening the woman's rights movement so much that I can understand
> that parties in the Universalist society may feel that your position & ac-
> tion on that question may make the Bgt. church a heavier load to carry
> than they can stagger under. . . . if there is serious objections [sic] by
> many of the society to retaining you, then will arise a question of policy
> which the society must decide.[52]

Three years after this exchange, by which time Staples and his allies had begun their court action, he wrote to assure her that while he had "rather favored your side than the other" in the struggle, he was now convinced from conversations he had had with lawyers and Universalists in other cities that the plan to oust her was bound to succeed. Under such circumstances, in order to spare the society further dissension and what he anticipated would be certain destruction, he urged her to resign while she could still honorably do so. He himself, he pointedly added, had decided against any increases in his contributions to the society so long as it remained divided and until "a new state of affairs exists."[53] For a while Brown appears to have given serious consideration to this advice. But she then decided to make a last-ditch stand, in the course of which she wrote for publication a scorching letter in which she complained of "the wickedness which had betrayed a holy cause into the hands of an unjust judge, and subjected our blessed faith to the sneers of irreverent lawyers" and incidentally likened herself to Paul fighting "with the beasts at Ephesus."[54] This outburst, needless to say, did not go down very well with James Staples or the judge who was still trying the case; and when the injunction against rehiring her was soon afterward made permanent, it further enjoined the society's trustees to employ a "gentleman in good standing as clergyman in the Universalist Church."

Even then the squabbles were not over, for at the following annual meeting in March 1876, when the officers and trustees who had favored Brown were again reelected, the old matters of who was qualified to vote and the legality of the society's elections flared up anew, and by then it was obvious the church was hopelessly divided. By then, too, Barnum himself had had enough. At a subsequent meeting on 24 March, to the loud applause of "outside parties" (presumably those who had been deprived of their membership in the parish), he threatened to withdraw his support and go to law to force the resignations of the officers.[55] The meeting was hastily adjourned. The following month, in the midst of a meeting of the harried officers at the moderator's home, word was brought that Staples and his party had broken into the church and seized possession of it. The insurgents proceeded to elect their own officers and demanded that all church property be turned over to them, and for a brief time Bridgeport had two rival Universalist societies. After further skirmishing in the courts, the old officers and trustees finally gave up. On 15 May 1876 they handed in their resignations and "withdrew" from the parish. The breach between the two factions was never healed. With Barnum now officially a "member," the reconstituted society was soon flourishing again, and in November 1876 the Reverend John Lyon, a "gentleman in good standing," was elected its next settled minister. Olympia Brown and her family continued to reside in Bridgeport for some two years after her fall, then left for Racine, Wisconsin, where she had succeeded in obtaining another pastorate. Her faithful enemy James Staples, after serving many years as an esteemed trustee of the new society, was elected its moderator in 1884. Those were days of high drama in the noble attempt to Christianize Bridgeport.

———◆———

OF ALL THE progressive causes in the nineteenth century, temperance was clearly the one Barnum held most closely to heart. By his own account he had barely tasted alcohol before he was twenty-two years of age—despite his having sold copious quantities of it to others—but had then got into the habit of drinking "spirituous" or distilled liquors whenever he was with friends.[56] While abroad with Tom Thumb in the 1840s, he had been introduced to the pleasures of wine-bibbing and become quite a devotee of the grape, enthusiastically reporting in his letters to the *Atlas*, for example, on how he had "revelled and run riot" among vineyards in the French countryside.[57] Back in the States, the wine cellar at Iranistan was plentifully stocked, and the showman took more pride in its contents than he did in any of his other possessions.

All this was to change, however, beginning with a visit to Saratoga in the fall of 1847, when he was so shocked by the drunkenness he witnessed among the fashionable visitors to that place that he began to fear for his own sobriety. He immediately resolved to give up the "hard" stuff, but continued to indulge his taste for fine wines—until, that is, the Reverend Dr. Chapin, at Barnum's express invitation, arrived in Bridgeport to deliver one of his famous temperance lectures. The topics included the "moderate" drinker; and as Chapin eloquently expounded on the dangerous example such persons set for confirmed alcoholics and those who might not otherwise be tempted to drink, the message hit home in at least one of his listeners. After a sleepless night and considerable soul-searching, Barnum emptied the contents of his wine cellar onto Iranistan's grounds, then rushed off to find Chapin and ask him for a copy of the "pledge." The minister, who had assumed Barnum was already a teetotaler when he invited him to speak in Bridgeport, was astonished but happy to comply. Charity herself, upon hearing the glad tidings, wept with relief. The showman now learned that she had spent many a sleepless night of her own, "fearing that my wine-bibbing was leading me to a drunkard's path. I reproached her for not telling me her fears, but she replied that she knew I was self deluded, and that any such hint from her would have been received in anger."[58]

Like many a reformed character before and since, Barnum was soon proselytizing among his friends and acquaintances. The cause of temperance—more accurately, teetotalism—became for him a moral obsession, and he wrote and lectured about it incessantly for the rest of his life. Indeed, his unbounded enthusiasm for this crusade led him to hail it as a "great Christian doctrine." Upon reading an irate letter in the Universalist periodical the *Christian Ambassador* from a person who announced he was canceling his subscription because he was tired of reading so much about temperance in the journal, Barnum was provoked to write a long letter of his own in which he argued for temperance as being "rank out and out Universalism."[59] Whenever he was lecturing and writing for the uninitiated, however, he had the sense not to argue on religious grounds, but instead stressed the practical benefits of abstinence. He used statistics to back his claim that crime and poverty were linked to alcoholism; and he also came down hard on the adulterating of alcoholic drinks with poisonous substances, a practice that was widespread in the nineteenth century and is again coming under scrutiny today. He pointed to the immense financial loss caused by alcoholism to the nation as a whole, and to the suffering it inflicted on innocent women and children. There was no such thing as "moderation" in drinking, he announced, any more than there could be "moderation" in horse-stealing; "A moderate drinker generally commits suicide moderately."[60] His telling arguments on the subject were as much in demand abroad as they were at home, and in 1882 he wrote a letter for publication at the request of one of the leaders in the English temperance crusade. After remarking on the dangers of the "miserable and ruinous habit of 'treating,' being treated, and 'liquoring up,'" he went on to point out that

no man has a right to expect good health, a happy home, or financial prosperity who disorders his system, muddles his brain, and wastes time and money in imbibing intoxicating drinks as a beverage. An acquired taste like drinking or using tobacco not only, like all habits, becomes a "second nature," but these particular habits are stronger than nature, because they continually require *increased* quantities to produce the same effects—which is not true of natural appetites.

Men who abstain from drinking, he continued, "make fewer mistakes, can accomplish more bodily or mental labor, and are therefore more reliable."

> Pure water is the natural drink for man and beast. My lions, tigers, and even the great Jumbo himself drink nothing stronger than water. Their natural strength is enormous, but a constant use of rum, brandy, beer, or "half and half" would disturb their digestive powers, weaken their muscles, poison their blood, and cause suffering, disease, and death—the same as it does in the case of human beings.[61]

Barnum appears to have been deceived—perhaps voluntarily—about Jumbo himself, who according to several witnesses was in the habit of drinking daily a keg of beer. But the arguments remain powerful, reasonable ones all the same. When delivered by the showman in person—in his richly humorous, anecdotal style—they were even more convincing. He could also hold his own with those who came to scoff and heckle during his lectures. On one occasion, when someone in the audience called out to ask whether alcohol affected one "externally or internally," the speaker immediately shot back "e-ternally."[62]

For over forty years he was in the forefront of the temperance and prohibition movements, although he eventually came to doubt that a total ban on alcohol would ever be achieved. Upon being urged by his temperance friends to run for the Presidency during the 1888 campaign on a Prohibition ticket, he replied that such a party hadn't a "ghost of a show" and that he was no longer for prohibition anyway. The answer, he now thought, was to impose stiff licensing fees on all the saloons, thereby driving many of them out of business and making it impossible for their customers to "get around to their old stamping grounds. They might take wet goods home instead, but think of the influence their wives and children would have."[63] He nonetheless continued to require buyers of the homes he sold on easy terms in Bridgeport to sign a pledge not to drink alcohol—a "liquor clause" that aroused hostility particularly in the German community—and also exerted pressure on his dependents and friends to give up the use of tobacco. Again, however, he was careful to justify such requirements on practical grounds: those who did not waste their money on tobacco and alcohol were more likely to pay off their debts.[64] His employees as well, he was fond of proclaiming, were nearly all teetotalers. And when his museums in Philadelphia and New York produced that most famous of all temperance dramas, *The Drunkard*, whose climactic scene arrives when the hero falls down and writhes on the floor in a fearful display of delirium tremens, he was inspired to a pitch of crusading eloquence. "Incorrigible inebriates," he wrote in a circular letter sent to members of the press, "have been brought by their friends a distance of forty miles to witness this drama, and never, to my knowledge, has this been done without resulting in their signing the temperance pledge; and I am personally cognizant of the fact that *thousands* have been induced by this drama to renounce intoxicating drinks *in toto*."[65] Imbibing friends and acquaintances like Jenny Lind, who once gave him a marble statue of Bacchus as a Christmas present, might twit him about these claims and his principles, and Barnum himself was capable of joining in the laughter. But for all the good-natured jokes and repartee, he never flagged in the struggle or lost sight of his goal. The exorcising of the demon rum, as he had written in 1853, was "a work of life and death."[66]

--- ◆ ---

BY THE LATTER half of the nineteenth century Universalism and its denominational rivals had begun to experience some changes in their theological beliefs. On the one hand, most Universalists, Barnum among them, eventually came round to conceding there was a period of limited punishment in the afterlife— a kind of refining process, as it were, although just how long this process would take was a matter for deep speculation. Some thought 50,000 years a reasonable figure. On the other hand, a number of liberally inclined Congregational and Presbyterian ministers, getting away from their denominations' old hell-fire theology, were beginning to emphasize the efficacy of good works; and if they could not yet deny the doctrine of eternal punishment, they at least had the sense to shut up about it. Less than a year before his death Barnum published a statement of his own beliefs in an eloquent essay entitled "Why I Am a Universalist."[67] In it he briefly recounted his youthful terror at the hands of orthodoxy; argued, on the basis of scriptural and other evidence, for his belief in universal salvation; drew a fine distinction between the meanings of "immortal" and "eternal" life (the former, vouchsafed to all, being merely endless existence after bodily death; the latter being an achievable state of spiritual grace, both in this world and the next); and advanced the proposition that death itself does not fix or end character and the soul's moral possibilities, but that they continue to develop in the world to come. "The endless ages of immortal life," he wrote, "are not given to sit on a flower-bed and sing and play harps, but for the endless development of immortal souls." Under such a melioristic plan for the universe, he boldly suggested, even Judas might eventually be found in the company of those spending eternity in heaven.[68]

The appearance of this "confession of faith" in the 8 May 1890 issue of the London journal the *Christian World* was immediately hailed as a major event. It was quickly republished in a number of American Universalist periodicals, read from pulpits by ministers to their enthralled congregations both here and abroad, and issued as a separate pamphlet, some 60,000 copies of which were already in circulation at the time of the author's death. A missionary to Japan, Dr. George L. Perin, was so delighted by it that he promptly translated it for use in that country—the first Universalist tract to be published in Japanese.[69] Predictably, there was an immediate outcry from those clergymen still clinging to orthodox beliefs. The Reverend George A. Hubbell, a local Methodist minister with whom Barnum had tangled several times in the past, made the article the subject of a Sunday sermon and an excuse to attack Universalism in general. A Presbyterian pastor went on record to state that Barnum was "en-

tirely wrong" and that, "while we no longer consider the expressions of punishment and happiness found in the Bible as anything than mere figures of
speech, and do not believe there are actually burning seas or golden streets,
eternal punishment and eternal bliss are believed to be and are taught as cer-
tainties." When their views and those of others were aired in the newspapers,
the old showman joined the fray with characteristic zeal. Things had not changed
that much after all in the intervening half-century.[70]

He finished, then, much the same as he had begun while editing the *Herald
of Freedom and Gospel Witness*: surrounded by controversy, championing an
unpopular religion, never wavering in his "heretical" beliefs. The last his enemies flung in his face throughout his career in the attempt to discredit any
claims he might make to probity and respectability. How much easier it would
have been for him, both personally and professionally, had he only conceded
those billions upon billions of souls to eternal misery! Curiously, too, for all
his support of Universalism and his years of close personal ties with its leading
ministers, there is barely any mention of him in the memoirs of these last.
Even in the case of prominent Universalists who worked for him—and there
were at least two ministers among them—all that one typically finds in their
obituary and biographical notices is that they were for a number of years "engaged in secular life."[71] It seems almost as though they were ashamed to acknowledge him—embarrassed by their connection with the "Prince of Humbugs." "How these Unitarians and Universalists want to be respectable and
orthodox," Walt Whitman wryly remarked toward the end of his life, "just as
much as any of the old line people!"[72]

"Respectable." One wonders what Barnum would make of the word were
he among us today. At this writing a former "player" occupies the White House;
and the nation's women, having long since attained the vote and equality in
education, have begun invading such traditionally male preserves as fire and
police departments, the military, and even the heavy construction industry.
The noble experiment of Prohibition has been tried and found wanting, and
no doubt Barnum would find nothing new in the flourishing state of the liquor
business. Would he recognize the church he once belonged to? At the services
of today's combined Unitarian Universalist societies, which openly boast of
having no creed whatever, one is more likely to hear an erudite lecture on DNA
than any serious mention of a deity. There is nothing in their pastors' sermons
to bring a blush to the cheek of the most devoted atheist, whose attendance
and membership, indeed, are actively courted. Progress or chaos? The former,
one hopes, in a denomination that has traditionally appealed to rebels who
insist on thinking for themselves. Seated somewhere between Jesus and Judas
in the Universalist pantheon, the "Reverend" P. T. Barnum would probably
approve.

IV

Showman Barnum

By this time it was clear to my mind that my proper position in this busy world was not yet reached. I had displayed the faculty of getting money, as well as getting rid of it; but the business for which I was destined, and, I believe, made, had not yet come to me; or rather, I had not found that I was to cater for that insatiate want of human nature—the love of amusement; that I was to make a sensation on two continents; and that fame and fortune awaited me so soon as I should appear before the public in the character of a showman. These things I had not foreseen. I did not seek the position or the character. The business finally came in my way; I fell into the occupation, and far beyond any of my predecessors on this continent, I have succeeded.

Autobiography

"IF BEING MADE for a thing is a divine call to that thing," Barnum's last pastor in Bridgeport, the Reverend Lewis B. Fisher, once wrote of his famous parishioner, "then Mr. Barnum was divinely called to be a showman."[1] But the "call" had not yet come when Barnum moved with his family to New York City, where by his own account he knocked about for several months without finding congenial employment. His hopes of finding something suitable in the "mercantile" line were quickly dissipated, and when his resources began to fail, he took the ignominious position of "drummer" to a cap and stock store, which paid him a small commission on sales made to customers whom he introduced. Meanwhile, he investigated and rejected various business opportunities advertised in the newspapers. One of these, interestingly, took him to the lecture room of Scudder's American Museum, where he was offered by its owner the "great Hydro-oxygen Microscope," whose price of $2000 was beyond his reach. "I had long fancied that I could succeed if I could only get hold of a public exhibition," he writes. On another occasion he applied for the job of bartender at Niblo's Garden, a famous New York pleasure resort, but balked when its proprietor announced he was seeking someone who would agree to remain in the position for a minimum of three years. With money belatedly received from debts owed him in Bethel, in the spring of 1835 he opened a small boardinghouse in Frankfort Street. Around the same time he became partner in a grocery store with John Moody, whose grandson was to found the well-known Moody's Investors Service.[2]

While attending to business at the latter establishment, Barnum learned of the extraordinary opportunity that was to launch him on his career as a showman. And although he somewhat shamefacedly acknowledged in later editions of his autobiography that this was "the least deserving of all my efforts in the show line," he made no such apology in the original edition. Joice Heth is undoubtedly the most enigmatic episode in Barnum's entire career, for one is never certain how much he really knew—or chose not to know—in regard to this imposition. In his writings and public pronouncements he swore he had been taken in like everyone else; and considering this was his first venture in the "show line," and that he made no bones about his involvement in any number of later frauds, we should probably take him at his word. But there is another version of the story, told by a journalist friend who supposedly got it directly from Barnum, which we shall shortly come to.

As Barnum tells the story in his autobiography, toward the end of July 1835 he learned from Coley Bartram, a Connecticut acquaintance, that a Kentuckian named R. W. Lindsay wished to sell his interest in an exhibition known as "Joice Heth." The last was in fact a blind, decrepit, hymn-singing black slave, whom Lindsay had contracted for with her owner, John S. Bowling, also of Kentucky, for a period of twelve months. The original agreement between Lindsay and Bowling, dated 10 June 1835, is extant and reveals both men planned to travel with Heth "in and amongst the cities of the United States," sharing equally in the expenses and profits, although Bowling took the precaution of binding Lindsay to assist him back to Cincinnati in the event his property should expire on the road, "as he is infirm" and obviously could not get around on his own. Apparently John Bowling had second thoughts about this hazardous expedition, for only five days later he sold his half-interest in the exhibition to Coley Bartram, who in turn sold out to Lindsay in Philadelphia on 24 July. As Bartram now assured Barnum, Lindsay was himself anxious to sell the remaining ten months of his contract, since he had not much "tact" as a showman and wished to return home.[3]

These rapid changes in management might in themselves have led a more experienced person to suspect something was amiss; but such was the picture painted by Coley Bartram for his fellow Yankee languishing behind the counter of a grocery store that Barnum became "considerably excited upon the subject" and immediately rushed off to Philadelphia. For the great selling point of Joice Heth was that she had reached the astounding age of 161 years and had once been the "nurse" of George Washington! When Barnum first viewed this wonder lying upon her couch in Philadelphia's Masonic Hall, "she might almost as well have been called a thousand years old as any other age." Her withered legs, drawn up, could not be moved; and her left arm, whose hand possessed nails some four inches long, lay across her breast and was equally rigid. Her blind eyes were so sunken that they seemed to have disappeared altogether; her teeth were entirely gone; and her weight, as reported in bills and other advertising matter, was but forty-six pounds. Yet she could talk, and talk almost incessantly, about her "dear little George" and how she had not only been present at his birth but "raised" him. Besides her store of anecdotes about the "father of our country" and the doings of the "redcoats," Joice was extremely fond of discoursing on religious topics (she had been belatedly baptized in the Potomac in 1719, at the age of forty-five) and singing ancient hymns, many of which, Barnum writes, "were entirely new to me," as indeed they must have been to her other auditors. "She retains her faculties in an unparalleled degree," proclaims a handbill Barnum himself later had printed, "and often laughs heartily at her own remarks."[4] One suspects old Joice would have felt right at home in Connecticut.

The aspiring showman demanded some proof of Joice's extraordinary age, naturally enough, and Lindsay obliged by showing him a crumbling bill of sale, signed by Augustine Washington and dated 5 February 1727, for a Negro woman named Joice Heth, described as then being fifty-four years old. Further inquiry elicited the information that after being sold by Augustine to his neighboring sister-in-law, Joice had assisted at the birth of "little George" and was the first person to clothe him. In time she became the property of the Bowling family and was taken to Kentucky, where she was left to decay unceremoniously in an outbuilding, no one being aware (apparently Joice was not talking much then) of her true age or connection with the illustrious Washington. It was during a visit to Virginia that the son of John Bowling, while looking over some documents in the Virginia Records Office, quite by chance ran across the 1727 bill of sale and became convinced that the Joice Heth named therein was the same as his father's slave. The Virginia officials obligingly let him take the bill of sale home with him, and it was this ancient-looking document, framed under glass, that Lindsay now offered as indisputable proof of his exhibit's remarkable age and history.

Barnum writes that he was satisfied by this story, and that he then received from Lindsay, whose asking price had been $3000, a written promise to sell him the exhibit for $1000 provided he could come up with the money within the next ten days. Returning to New York, he sold out to Moody his interest in their grocery store, borrowed $500 from an unspecified friend, and was back in Philadelphia to clinch the deal on 6 August. The friend, very likely, was William P. Saunders, who initially planned to join Barnum as an equal partner in the exhibiting of Heth. His name appears jointly with Barnum's in the body of the extant agreement between Barnum and Lindsay, but is then crossed out, leaving Barnum as the sole purchaser. Presumably, like John S. Bowling, he too had had second thoughts.

There was no hesitation on the part of Barnum, however, who immediately plunged into the "show line" with a will and from that moment on rarely looked back. He had finally found his true niche in life—had hearkened to the "divine call," his pastor might have said. Returning to William Niblo, to whom he had applied for the position of bartender a few months before, he arranged for the exhibition of Joice in a large room of his house near the Garden, with Niblo agreeing to furnish room, lights, and a ticket seller and to pay the expenses of printing and advertising in return for one-half the gross receipts. On his own

Barnum engaged as his assistant Levi Lyman, a facile conversationalist and onetime lawyer from Penn Yan, New York, whose job was to introduce Joice and answer spectators' questions. Like his employer, Lyman was fond of practical jokes and capable of carrying them off with perfect aplomb. Within a week Barnum had flooded the city with bills and posters and had procured lighted transparencies—a new form of advertising—to announce his attraction. "The result," once Joice arrived from Philadelphia and began exhibiting at Niblo's, "proved an average of about $1500 per week."

The New York newspapers were appropriately impressed, and Barnum was not loath to reprint their glowing notices in his bills and autobiography. When Joice's powers of attraction began to diminish with Manhattan spectators, he took her on a swing through New England. Abolitionist sentiment was already high in that section of the country, and it would hardly have been diplomatic to broadcast the fact that the curiosity he was traveling with was the property of another. He never went so far as to claim Joice was free; but then he never appears to have actually acknowledged to his patrons that she was still a slave, either. By the time they reached Boston, he had devised a strategy to defuse any hostility on this score and was now quoting in his bills a notice he had planted in the *Providence Daily Journal.* "She has been the mother of fifteen children," readers of that newspaper had been informed, "the youngest of whom died two years ago, at 116 years of age. She has five great-grandchildren, now the slaves of Wm. Bowling, Esq., of Paris, Kentucky, to the purchase of whose freedom the proceeds of this exhibition are to be appropriated. She has herself been taken care of many years in Mr. Bowling's family."[5] While exhibiting Joice at Boston's Concert Hall, Barnum made the acquaintance of the German showman Johann Maelzel, who shut down his exhibition of ingenious automatons and famous chess-playing Turk (the "mechanism" of which, exposed by Poe, was a small man or dwarf inside the figure) in the face of such overwhelming competition. Apparently he bore his young rival no grudge, for Barnum writes that they often had long talks together and that Maelzel, impressed by his grasp of the effective use of publicity, even offered to send him on the road with some of his curiosities. In lieu of accepting this interesting offer, when the number of his own patrons began falling off, Barnum took a cue from Maelzel's exhibition and spread the rumor that Joice was an automaton and her manager a ventriloquist. The Hall was quickly crowded again, and many who had previously paid their quarters now returned for a second look at Joice to see if they had indeed been "humbugged."

The exhibition continued through New England and then returned to Niblo's in New York, and later visited several other cities in the East. Eventually Barnum entrusted Joice entirely to Lyman, who in late fall left with her on another tour of New England. Becoming ill, she was taken to the home of Barnum's half-brother Philo in Bethel, where she finally departed this life to join "little George" on 19 February 1836. Philo promptly shipped the remains by sleigh to the house in New York where the Barnums were currently residing.

There now began the most bizarre chapter of all in the history of Joice Heth, who still had one final exhibition to give. For although Barnum assures us he immediately procured a mahogany coffin and nameplate for Joice's body, and that he was determined to see her respectably buried in the Bethel cemetery, he had previously promised Dr. David L. Rogers, an eminent New York surgeon who had examined Joice upon her first arrival in the metropolis, that he would have the opportunity to dissect her should she die while under Barnum's management. After informing Rogers the time had finally arrived, the showman himself "proceeded to arrange for the examination," which took place on the 25th before a large crowd of physicians, medical students, clergymen, and (naturally) editors, each of whom was assessed fifty cents for this extraordinary privilege. Among this eager group of spectators was Richard Adams Locke, editor of the *New York Sun*, who during the previous summer had been behind the famous "Moon" or "Lunar Hoax," a series of sensational articles in his paper describing the pelicans, winged men, and other interesting objects the astronomer John Herschel was supposed to have observed through a powerful telescope trained on the moon. Locke and Rogers were excellent friends. Indeed, the good doctor was widely believed to have been Locke's accomplice, if not the chief instigator, in getting up the "Moon Hoax."

The doctor and his friend were hardly given to hilarity on the present occasion, however. Instead of ruining his precious scalpels on Joice's ossified arteries, from the state of the last Rogers could only conclude there had been some "mistake," for the cadaver before him, he politely informed Barnum, was in all probability that of a person not over eighty years old. When Lyman, who was present, made an offhand remark about the inability of physicians to determine such matters, Rogers went off in a huff on the arm of Locke. Not surprisingly, on the following day the *Sun* carried an article describing the autopsy and what its editor characterized as "one of the most precious humbugs that ever was imposed upon a credulous community." Although Locke charitably allowed that the exhibitors, who took Joice "at a high price, upon the warranty of others," had probably been deceived as much as anyone, he could not help observing they had made at least $10,000 out of the fraud.[6]

The confusion among those who had paid to see Joice and who now read Locke's exposé, Barnum writes, was considerable. They could hardly disbelieve the evidence of their own eyes, which had convinced them she must have been at least a hundred years old, and possibly as old as she was represented to be. At this point, he continues, Lyman decided to play a joke of his own. Calling upon James Gordon Bennett at the *New York Herald*, he assured the editor that Joice was still alive and living in Connecticut, and that the body Rogers had dissected was actually that of a Negress named "Aunt Nelly" who had recently died in Harlem. The selection of Bennett as the conduit for this story was surely no accident, for the previous summer, shortly after establishing the *Herald*, the irascible Scots editor had played a leading role in exposing the "Moon Hoax." The present opportunity to take another swipe at Locke and his rival paper was, of course, irresistible.

Bennett confidently published these startling revelations in his paper of 27 February, together with the information—doubtless also contributed by

Lyman or Barnum—that the present hoax was the work of someone, probably another doctor, who had been taken in by the "Moon Hoax" and who had passed off "Aunt Nelly" as the veritable Joice in order to even the score with Rogers and Locke. When the *Sun*, which claimed Rogers had known in advance, from his earlier examination of her, that Joice could not possibly be over eighty years old, now revealed that her exhibitors had come directly from the *Herald* office to boast of deceiving the "despicable and unprincipled scribbler" who edited that paper, the still unsuspecting Bennett followed by publishing affidavits from two persons who had known "Aunt Nelly" and were positive hers was the body Rogers had dissected.[7]

Barnum lays the responsibility for all this entirely at Lyman's door, and goes on to write that the following September, by which time Bennett realized how badly he had been deceived, the enraged editor blew Lyman "sky high" upon meeting him on the street. Lyman laughingly protested he had meant the tale as a harmless joke and promised to give Bennett the "true" story as a recompense. This the credulous editor also published in a series of four long articles commencing with the paper's 8 September issue. Although Barnum gleefully writes that Lyman, in this latest cock-and-bull invention, revealed how Barnum himself had discovered and coached Joice, there is in fact no reference to him by name in any of the articles. Instead, readers were now duly informed how Joice's anonymous exhibitors had extracted all her teeth after getting her drunk, rehearsed her in the famous "peach tree" and other anecdotes, and had frequently been at pains to keep her from swearing. The fake bill of sale had been aged in tobacco water, but needed redrafting by the time the exhibition reached New York, since by then someone had discovered Virginia was referred to as a "state" in this 1727 document. Once in the metropolis, Joice was additionally coached in religion and hymn-singing, her tutors taking care to oil the rough road of instruction with a plentiful supply of whiskey, of which Joice, when not busy "god damning" everything, was inordinately fond. Despite Bennett's hinting that Joice's New England adventures would make further good reading, at the end of the fourth article the story abruptly broke off. Either Lyman had conveniently drifted into obscurity again, or Bennett—as seems more likely—had finally awakened to the fact that the "complete" story could only conclude with the revelation of how he himself had been so easily duped.[8]

"The question naturally arises," Barnum writes in his autobiography, "if Joice Heth was an imposter, *who* taught her these things? And how happened it that she was so familiar, not only with ancient psalmody, but also with the minute details of the Washington family? To all this, I unhesitatingly answer, *I do not know.* I taught her none of these things. She was perfectly familiar with them all before I ever saw her, and she taught me many facts in relation to the Washington family with which I was not before acquainted." On an earlier occasion he had told another story, however. While visiting England with Tom Thumb in the 1840s, Barnum had gone off on a tour of the Shakespeare country with the journalist Albert Smith. As the two men rattled along in their carriage, the showman regaled his companion with tales of his adventures; and Smith, in a two-part article he later wrote on the subject, assures us he is reporting Barnum's remarks "nearly word for word as the author heard them." When Barnum came to tell the story of Joice Heth, he described how he himself had forged and aged the documents, drilled Joice in her role, and been the prime mover in this extraordinary "do."[9] In essence it was the same tale that had appeared in the *Herald*, only now with Barnum named as the chief instigator. And in fact the showman himself had published this fantastical story a few years before he ever met Smith, in a strange novella he wrote under a pseudonym.[10] But again, there is the later disclaimer in the autobiography, which Barnum also made in a private letter dating from a year or two before the book's publication. By then R. W. Lindsay, who appears to have become an alcoholic, was sick and down on his luck in Boston; and Barnum, in a letter to a Mr. Baker of that city, generously enclosed $100 toward his relief. In reply to some assertions Lindsay had been making that Barnum was under obligations to him, Barnum assured Baker that these were "ridiculously false":

> I never had anything to do with him except to buy from him, in *perfect good faith* & pay him the money for, an old *negress* which he falsely represented as the "nurse of Washington" and which he imposed on me as such by aid of a *forged bill of sale* purporting to have been made by the *father* of George Washington. I honestly *believed* all this & exhibited accordingly, as Lindsay had done for months previous. Finally she died & the imposition became manifest, and *I* have ever since borne the stigma of *originating* that imposture. I never denied it before—but I might have done so truly. This is all the "obligation" I am under to Lindsay, but he is a poor devil, and I hope to see him recover.[11]

The discrepancy between these later accounts and what Barnum reputedly told Smith can best be explained in terms of youthful bravado. When Barnum was whirling through the English countryside in late summer of 1844, fresh from his recent triumphs with Tom Thumb at Buckingham Palace, he was unabashedly reveling in his reputation as a shrewd Yankee "humbug." He was hardly likely to confess that at the very outset of his career he had been "humbugged" himself, and he was more than willing to let the public believe otherwise for years to come. It would have done him little harm, and possibly even some good, had he chosen to continue the lie when he came to write the first edition of his autobiography. Did he then lean a little too far in the opposite direction? Did he never once suspect the truth about Joice Heth during all those months he was exhibiting and, so unreservedly on his own, publicizing her? Certainly James Gordon Bennett, who had been consistently taken in by Lyman, if not by Barnum himself, never accepted this later explanation. For him Barnum was ever afterward a favorite *bête noir*—that "Joyce Heth in breeches," as he sarcastically characterized him.[12]

"I will only add," Barnum piously writes at the end of the chapter detailing his curious involvement with her, "that the remains of Joice were removed to

Bethel, and buried respectably." There is no trace today of Joice Heth in Bethel.

———◆———

LET THERE BE no crocodile tears shed over the fate of Joice Heth. Her managers appear to have treated her decently enough, and for months she had been at the center of public attention, basking in her role of Washington's "nurse." The popular notion of Barnum as a kind of sideshow "talker," vulgarly hawking and parading before a gaping public the freaks and other curiosities he managed, is almost entirely a twentieth-century misconception, based on the tawdry, degraded shows that may still occasionally be found along the midways of American carnivals. Whatever their respective merits may have been, his exhibitions were invariably conducted with decorum, were attractive to all classes of society, and generally followed some carefully thought-out structure. The last achieved perfection during the period when he was managing Tom Thumb; but as early as 1835 one finds evidence of an attempt to make of Joice Heth something more than a raree-show and to impose a measure of order on her exhibition, which usually began with the reciting of her history and the reading of the bill of sale, followed by questions put to her by Barnum and Lyman. Spectators were then given the opportunity to question Joice and her managers, and the former also regaled her auditors with several of her choice hymns. When business was brisk, Barnum writes, this program would be speeded up and abbreviated, and at the end the audience politely shown out while a new crowd of spectators was admitted to the hall by another door.

Here it may also be pointed out, for Joice Heth as well as for his later enterprises, that Barnum's outstanding success as a showman was due above all to his almost intuitive knowledge of human nature and what the public would pay to see; to his willingness to risk all that he had, sometimes even going into debt, to secure such attractions; and to his then skillfully exploiting public opinion through the press so as to build interest in his acquisitions to a perfect furor. This was the scheme he invariably followed, and his genius was evident especially in the realm of publicity. With very few exceptions (Tom Thumb is the one notable example) he was neither the discoverer nor even the original exhibitor of what he offered his patrons. The Fejee Mermaid, the American Museum, Jenny Lind, Commodore Nutt, and the great Jumbo himself had all been before the public when he arrived on the scene. Beneath his sure touch they flourished. When that touch was occasionally withdrawn, as happened following his rupture with Lind, their power to attract plummeted. Yet intrinsically they were no different while under his management from what they were either before or after.

The key to such phenomenal success was his masterful understanding of the nation's press. Many of the notices of Joice Heth were in fact written by the fledgling showman himself, whose earlier career as an editor and publisher had introduced him to how such things were done. Newspaper publishers of the nineteenth century were no less desperate for advertising and ready-made

news than their counterparts of today, and throughout his career Barnum always took care to keep them supplied with a steady stream of both. The promise of the former ("shall advertise liberally with you when I come in the summer") was usually coupled with some specific request—a notice by the paper's
critic, the publication of the latest appendix to the autobiography, the inser-
tion of an enclosure as a "genuine" news item—and most publishers found
such tactics irresistible. Barnum's extant address books are crammed with the
names of journalists and editors he knew, and in one of them there is even a
separate category headed "Newspapers friendly."[13] In New York City itself, the
Atlas, the *Sun* after it came to be owned by members of the Beach family, and
eventually Horace Greeley's *Tribune* were among his favorite allies, although
at times even they were embarrassed by the demands he made upon them. He
made enemies among the press too, of course, chief of them being James
Gordon Bennett, whose powerful *New York Herald*, even after its founder's death
in 1872, continued to lambaste the showman whenever it could.

When the English theatrical manager and would-be poet Alfred Bunn visited America in the early 1850s, he was amazed to learn that in a country of
slightly over 23 million inhabitants there were nearly 3000 newspapers, whose
annual circulation was said to exceed 420 million copies. "A newspaper con-
stitutes the very breath of Jonathan's nostrils," he wrote. "It is the guide of
his opinion, the furtherance of all his views—and its influence therefore over
him is incredible." Experienced puffer that he himself was, Bunn felt compelled to deny the assertion, made by many of her own citizens, that America's
press was "venal to the last degree."[14] His fellow showman at the American
Museum might have convinced him otherwise, for only a short time before his
visit the *Herald* had indignantly charged Barnum with spreading the same
slander.[15] A few years later, however, when Barnum, following another row
with the publisher, was leading a boycott of New York theatrical managers to
withhold all advertising from the *Herald*, Bennett began to change his tune.
The boycott, he sniffed in an editorial, had been caused by his refusing to cater
to the managers, and might even be a *good* thing if it led to greater independence of newspapers and their editors from those taking out advertisements
and who therefore felt entitled to puffs and other favors in return.[16]

If not exactly "venal," most of the editors Barnum dealt with over his lifetime can certainly be described as "accommodating." "Indolent" might better
characterize others among them. The puffs and "genuine" news items he proffered were almost invariably accepted for publication—and why should they
not have been, for they were generally well written and humorous to boot?—
and editors were grateful for such an easy means of filling their columns. The
wonder is that even when he abused their confidence with such out-and-out
frauds as the Fejee Mermaid, the majority of them seem never to have cared
and readily fell into his trap again on later occasions. True, in his early career
he was often anonymous, letting Levi Lyman or some other "professor" front
for him, so that editors did not always realize with whom they were dealing.
But it all came out in the autobiography, following whose publication it was
more advantageous to have his name connected with his exhibitions, and even

then editors remained easy prey to the "Prince of Humbugs." The reams of publicity generated on both sides of the Atlantic by his purchase of Jumbo in 1882, Barnum once boasted to Major Pond, had cost him nothing.[17] The truth is, by then nearly everyone was acquainted with his methods and eagerly looking forward to his next "humbug." The time of moral indignation had long since passed; something outrageous was expected, even required, from him; people were willing to forgive in advance the old showman's buffooneries and harmless impositions. Never behind in such matters, the members of the Fourth Estate had caught on to all this at an earlier date and had obligingly chosen to look the other way. And besides, whether Barnum's enterprises were "genuine" or not, they always made for lively copy.

Barnum played the press for all it was worth, yet was always generous in acknowledging its support. "I am indebted to the press of the United States for almost every dollar which I possess and for every success as an amusement manager which I have ever achieved," he wrote to his partner James A. Bailey a few days before his death in 1891.[18] On earlier occasions he was fond of attributing his success to "printer's ink"—when a friend was expatiating on this topic at a banquet honoring him in 1874, the showman interrupted to remark, "Yes, without printer's ink I should have been no bigger than Tom Thumb"[19]— under which heading he also included advertising. The effective use of the latter, and of publicity in general, was a matter of keen study to him, and especially in his *Humbugs of the World* and *Funny Stories* he recalled those expert practitioners among his contemporaries who had made a lasting impression on him. One of them was Leonard Gosling, the "great French blacking-master," who appeared in New York in 1830 and within three months had made his product a byword in American households. Barnum had himself seen Gosling driving about town behind a team of four magnificent matched horses:

> The carriage was emblazoned with the words "Gosling's Blacking," in large gold letters, and the whole turnout was so elaborately ornamented and bedizened that everybody stopped and gazed with wondering admiration. A bugle-player or a band of music always accompanied the great Gosling, and, of course, helped to attract . . . public attention to his establishment. At the turning of every street corner your eyes rested upon "Gosling's Blacking." From every show-window gilded placards discoursed eloquently of the merits of "Gosling's Blacking." The newspapers teemed with poems written in its praise, and showers of pictorial handbills, illustrated almanacs, and tinseled souvenirs, all lauding the virtues of "Gosling's Blacking," smothered you at every point.

When the famous "Jim Crow" Rice was performing blackface skits at the Bowery Theatre, Gosling paid him to sing a ditty in praise of his product and to hang posters urging spectators to "Use Gosling's Blacking" about the set of a scene that took place in a bootblacking shop. The result, Barnum writes admiringly, was that everybody tried it, and Gosling soon afterward retired with a fortune. Another early practitioner of such uninhibited methods was the patent-pill manufacturer "Doctor" Benjamin Brandreth, who in 1834, his first year of operation, paid the immense sum of $5000 for advertisements in the *New York Sun* alone.[20]

"Advertising," Barnum once told a person who complained that the three notices he had placed in a weekly newspaper had not increased his business, "is like learning—a little is a dangerous thing."[21] From his "Temple of Fortune" days onward he was himself an adept in the art and never spared expense when publicizing his attractions. Yet in the end, he was always careful to point out, no amount of advertising would lead to sustained success if the item being touted were spurious or not worth the money. His own peculiar use of the word "humbug" was closely related to this observation. Although dictionaries variously define the word as a "deceit," "fraud," or "imposture," or else, in the case of an individual, one who practices deception, Barnum himself, in his *Humbugs of the World*, defines it as "putting on glittering appearances—outside show—novel expedients, by which to suddenly arrest public attention and attract the public eye and ear."[22] But again, once having gained the public's attention, it is essential to give it a "full equivalent" for its money. It was with this sense in mind that Barnum, who boasted that he always gave his patrons *at least* their money's worth, audaciously proclaimed himself "Prince of Humbugs." His contemporaries—particularly those who had paid their quarters to look upon the likes of the "Fejee Mermaid"—did not invariably agree with this ingenious definition and often insisted on applying to him the more accepted meaning of the word.

———◆———

MEANWHILE, he had taken under his wing another performer, an Italian juggler and "professor of equilibrium and plate dancing" named "Signor Antonio," whom Barnum first saw while exhibiting Joice in Albany. Antonio's great specialty was his ability to make dinner plates, washbowls, and other species of crockery "jump, fly, and dance quadrilles, minuets, waltzes, and contra dances" in time to music on the ends of sticks and swords, which he either held in his hands or balanced—sometimes with other objects such as forks interposed— on his nose and chin. He could keep as many as ten plates spinning at once; and his other feats included hopping about stage on a single stilt while firing a musket at a target.[23] Barnum was impressed by the novelty of his performance and immediately engaged his services for a year. He then proceeded to change his name to the more foreign-sounding "Signor Vivalla," announced that this wonder had just arrived from Italy, and commenced the usual campaign of puffery in the New York newspapers prior to his protégé's "first" American appearance at the Franklin Theatre. There the manager himself acted as Vivalla's assistant and handed him his props—"*this was my 'first appearance on any stage,'*" Barnum writes delightedly—and afterward, when the artist was called before the curtain, addressed the enthusiastic audience in Vivalla's name, since he did not think it "policy" to reveal that the performer, who had spent several years in Britain, could speak perfectly good English.

From New York they journeyed to several other cities in the East, and in

January 1836 they appeared at Philadelphia's famous Walnut Street Theatre. There Barnum was alarmed to hear Vivalla hissed for the first time, but quickly managed to turn even this to good account. Upon learning that the hisses had come from a party of spectators who were loyal to a local circus juggler named J. B. Roberts, the manager published a challenge in the next day's newspapers, offering to pay $1000 to anyone who could duplicate Vivalla's feats. Roberts swallowed the bait and published his acceptance of the challenge, but soon realized he had been caught in a "Yankee" trap, since, as Barnum coolly pointed out to him, he would have to perform *all* the feats in Vivalla's repertory before he was entitled to the money. This he clearly could not do—no more than Vivalla could duplicate all of Roberts's feats—and the circus performer was about to march off in high dudgeon when the showman smilingly revealed what he really had in mind. If Roberts would agree to meet Vivalla anyway, perform as directed, and keep quiet about the matter, he would receive the handsome sum of $30. Being then "between engagements," the juggler gratefully accepted the offer, and Barnum immediately set the press to working even harder, stoking the fires of this pretended rivalry. The spirit of nationalism was stridently invoked: could not Roberts, an American, beat this foreigner "all hollow"? For his part, Roberts magnanimously announced that a portion of the thousand dollars, which he confidently expected to win, would be distributed among the city's charities. By the time the contest came off before a crowded house on the night of the 30th, Vivalla and Roberts had been thoroughly rehearsed in their parts, thereby ensuring a suspenseful performance that lasted around sixty minutes. By then, too, Barnum was already looking ahead to many more golden harvests and had secretly engaged Roberts for the following month. At the end of the contest the two jugglers, glaring daggers at each other, appeared before the curtain, and Roberts revealed he had been laboring under the handicap of a sprained wrist. He now delivered a fiery challenge of his own: if Vivalla could duplicate all of *his* feats on some future night, he would willingly forfeit $500. The challenge was immediately accepted, of course; and while the audience out front was still in an uproar, the two bitter rivals were laughing and shaking hands on the other side of the curtain, with Vivalla thumbing his nose and making "curious gyrations" in that direction. The same scene was played out at the Franklin Theatre in New York and elsewhere over the following month. In commenting on these and similar "trials of skill" in his autobiography, Barnum expressed his belief that "the entertainment of the time may be an offset to the 'humbug' of the transaction, and it may be doubted whether managers of theatres will be losers by these revelations of mine, for the public appears disposed to be amused even when they are conscious of being deceived." An opinion that would no doubt be enthusiastically endorsed by present-day promoters of wrestling.

When Vivalla's power to draw finally began waning with theatre and lecture-hall audiences, Barnum took him on a six-month tour with the Old Columbian Circus of Aaron Turner. Although circuses were still forbidden to exhibit in Connecticut, Turner operated out of Danbury and therefore was no stranger to Barnum, who signed on as secretary, treasurer, and ticket seller to the show in return for one-fifth of the net profits. The troupe set out from Danbury on 26 April 1836 (in preparation for this departure Barnum had moved Charity and their daughter Caroline into the apartment above the "Yellow Store" in Bethel) and first erected its canvas tent in West Springfield, Massachusetts, two days later. Among the performers, aside from Vivalla, were Turner's two sons, both expert equestrians, and the well-known clown and sometime magician Joe Pentland. Barnum repeatedly refers to the "diary" he began keeping around this time and tells us he can mention only a few of the incidents in it. Would that the precious document were still in existence, for this period of his life is the most difficult to trace. One gathers from some of the anecdotes he relates, however, that Aaron Turner was not devoid of his share of Yankee wit. When the company, after heading south, reached Annapolis on a Saturday evening, and Barnum was strutting about town the next day in a fine black suit he had just purchased, Turner, ensconced in the barroom of the hotel where they had put up, set going the story that the notorious Reverend Ephraim K. Avery—he who had recently been tried for the murder of Miss Cornell in Rhode Island—had arrived in town and wondered aloud how the local populace could tolerate the "black-coated scoundrel." The result was that his unknowing partner was soon beset by a clamorous mob bent on riding him on a rail and giving him a taste of "Lynch law," and it was only after repeated appeals that he was led before Turner, who laughingly acknowledged he had made a "mistake." The fact was, he explained, his colleague's new suit made him look so much like a "priest" that he naturally concluded he must be Avery. The mob relished the joke and joined in the laugh, although Barnum writes that he himself— having had his new coat torn and been "considerably" rolled in the dirt—was "exceedingly vexed." His partner later tried to smooth things over by confiding he had played this joke as a means of gaining "notoriety" for the show, but Barnum found this explanation equally unconvincing. He does not mention that Turner must have been familiar with his earlier career as editor of the *Herald of Freedom and Gospel Witness*, in which he himself had so confidently condemned Avery, as well as with his reputation among their fellow townsmen as a "self-made priest" and the "Reverend P. T. Barnum."

The elder showman may also have been twitting him on another issue, for Barnum writes that while on tour with Turner he often collected the circus company on the Sabbath and read to them printed sermons and passages from the Bible. He made a point of attending local church services, and several times rose to voice his objections when narrow-minded clergy complained about the circus performers who were in their midst. On other occasions during this and the following year he addressed congregations and interested groups entirely on his own; and while he does not say so expressly in the autobiography, one may safely conclude that the comforting Universalist message of salvation for all was an integral part of these "lectures."

At the end of October, by which time the circus had reached North Carolina, his agreement with Turner expired and the two men went their separate ways. Barnum now formed a small troupe of his own—including Vivalla, a blackface singer and dancer named James Sandford, and several musicians—with the intention of spending the winter in the southern states, playing in a small tent they carried with them. When Turner's own company disbanded a few weeks later, Pentland signed on as well. This was not a circus, but rather a traveling variety show, whose awe-inspiring title was "Barnum's Grand Scientific and Musical Theatre." Professional entertainments were still at a premium in that section of the country, and audiences appear to have been easily satisfied. When Sandford unexpectedly ran off from the show in Camden, South Carolina, Barnum valiantly blacked up, sang the Negro songs he had advertised, and was actually encored in two of them. On another occasion he performed less successfully as assistant to Pentland in the latter's magic act (presumably the "scientific" portion of the program), upsetting a table and ruining a trick when a squirrel bit him. As the result of sickness and continuing desertions among the troupe, he became of necessity a magician himself. In later life he retained the reputation of being a fine practitioner of the art and not infrequently performed his feats of "parlor magic" in public—at benefits for the Bridgeport Universalist Church, for example, or in aid of seamen's and other charities during transatlantic crossings.[24] He knew and attended performances of many of the greatest magicians of his day and was delighted whenever he could figure out their secrets. On his first trip abroad he visited Robert-Houdin at his home outside Paris. He was unimpressed when he first saw, on the same trip, the famous "Wizard of the North," John Henry Anderson. The workings of all his tricks were readily apparent to the showman's experienced eye.[25]

The little troupe continued on its way through Georgia, Alabama, Tennessee, and Kentucky and finally disbanded in Nashville the following May. Meanwhile, Barnum had taken on two separate partners, the first of whom, a former clothing salesman he refers to only as "Henry," was fortunately got rid of before he could defraud the company. In Montgomery he was happier in the discovery of a venerable-looking magician named Henry Hawley, whose favorite recreation was to regale the denizens of local barrooms with such tales as would have caused even the Baron Munchausen to blush. No sooner had his auditors, looking dubiously upon his gray hair and grave countenance, decided to swallow one of his stories than he would launch into an even more fantastic tale— until someone would no longer be able to contain himself and would almost involuntarily cry out "That's a lie, by thunder!" "It is just as true as anything I have told you tonight," Hawley would reply, breaking into a hearty laugh. After a few weeks back home, Barnum returned to the West and formed a new company with Hawley, who was shortly succeeded by a person named Z. Graves. At the end of the previous tour Vivalla had gone off on his own, and the present season was off to a poor start, until Pentland was persuaded to rejoin the show in Kentucky. When the company reached Vicksburg, they sold most of their horses and wagons and bought the steamboat *Ceres*, thereafter transporting themselves and their tent by this means. On 19 March 1838 they arrived in New Orleans and later played at various other towns in Louisiana. Barnum writes that at Opelousas the steamer was exchanged for sugar and molasses, which presumably were shipped back East or sold along the way. The manager himself arrived back in New York in early June, fed up with the precarious existence of an itinerant showman and determined to find something in the way of a "respectable" business.

He found it in partnership with a German named Proler, a manufacturer of blacking, cologne, and "bear's grease." The last was made from sheep tallow and guaranteed to grow luxuriant hair on bald heads "as quickly as any other composition yet discovered." This venture lasted until January 1840, when Proler, after Barnum had sunk all his capital into the firm, swindled his partner and ran off to Europe. While struggling to make a success of the business, Barnum had continued to keep an eye out for exceptional attractions in the "show line." For a time he believed he had discovered one in the dancer John Diamond, who had been born in New York City in 1823 and who specialized in "Ethiopian breakdowns." Barnum describes his blackface prodigy as "the prototype of the numerous performers of the sort who have surprised and amused the public these many years"; and his fellow showman Noah Ludlow, who managed several theatres in the West and at one time engaged Diamond, writes that "he could twist his feet and legs, while dancing, into more fantastic forms than I ever witnessed before or since in any human being."[26] Barnum adds that in 1839 he entered into a contract for the youth's services with his father (in a letter dating from early 1841, however, he writes of Diamond's being bound to him by an agreement signed by his guardian, one Joseph W. Harrison of New York) and that he first sent him on the road in the care of an agent. Certainly by the time of his breakup with Proler he was actively engaged in Diamond's management, for in a letter he wrote in January 1840 to Francis Courtney Wemyss, then managing theatres in Philadelphia and Baltimore, he expatiates at some length on Diamond's "*masterly* and *unequalled*" dancing and mentions the outstanding benefit he had received two months earlier at Boston's National Theatre.[27] By the following April he was on the road with Diamond himself, and in another letter to Wemyss, addressed from Boston, writes that he can be reached at Providence, where Diamond is scheduled to dance through the 20th of the month. After that they will be free to perform for Wemyss in either Philadelphia or Baltimore, and if the latter city, Barnum adds significantly, "I expect a *Trial of Skill* can also be got up. I have a good *dancer* ready."[28] Once on to a good thing, Barnum never relinquished it willingly.

In the same letter to Wemyss one detects a note of the desperation he was feeling around this time: "If you say *no* I must try the Holiday St. or else go to Albany &c. & wait for you. Must keep moving somewhere." He was not happy with this nomadic existence and in his autobiography writes that "no one but myself can know how earnestly I struggled against the thought of resuming the life of an itinerant showman." But times were hard, his resources were fast failing him, and only two days after writing to Wemyss, on 18 April, Charity gave birth to their second daughter, Helen. For a few months during the spring and summer he leased the saloon in New York's Vauxhall Garden, hoping to make a go of variety programs there. When this venture also proved disappointing, he finally took the bit firmly between his teeth and started off for the West again, with Master Diamond, two lesser performers, and a single fiddler. By the time he reached New Orleans in early January 1841 only

Diamond and the fiddler remained. Fortune smiled again, however, at the St. Charles Theatre, where his share of the profits sometimes amounted to nearly $500 a night. One of these bumper occasions featured the inevitable "trial of skill," which Noah Ludlow's partner Sol Smith scornfully dismissed in his memoirs as "a humbug dancing-match for a pretended wager of $500 a side."[29] Smith and Ludlow had recently opened their own theatre, the New American, in New Orleans, and competition with the St. Charles was often keen. It seems obvious, too, that Barnum and Smith had not hit it off, for in a truculent letter Barnum addressed to the manager the following March, offering Diamond's services to the New American as an offset to Fanny Elssler who was then dancing at the St. Charles, he goes on to accuse Smith of spreading a "ridiculous story" about his missing a performance at another city along the Mississippi in order to save the paltry sum of two dollars in transportation costs. The real reason he did not sail on the faster, more expensive *Vicksburg*, he writes, "was to prevent a person in your company from tampering with Master D. and attempting to seduce him from my employ."[30]

Barnum had good reason to worry over Master Diamond, for less than a week before writing this letter his charge had temporarily "absconded." The young man had decided to sow some wild oats; and in a circular letter cautioning other managers against hiring him, Barnum complained that he had "overdrawn the money due him to the amount of $95 and has during the last week expended a hundred dollars in brothels and other haunts of dissipation & vice." A full description of his character and conduct, he promised, would shortly appear in the New Orleans papers.[31] The young master soon came to his senses and, according to Ludlow, did indeed dance for a few nights at the New American.[32] By then, however, Barnum was again thoroughly disgusted with the roving life, and they were soon heading up the Mississippi for home. In Pittsburgh he learned that the two other performers who had earlier abandoned his company—a character actor named Jenkins and another "infant phenomenon," Francis Lynch—were holding forth at the city's Museum, with the latter, under Jenkins's direction, billed as the incomparable "Master Diamond." This led to words and the threat of lawsuits, and the two men each had the other briefly jailed. When Barnum finally reached New York in early spring, he resolved—not for the first or last time in his career—to have nothing more to do with the traveling life.

———◆———

BARNUM WAS to visit the antebellum South again, most spectacularly with Jenny Lind, in whose company he gained entrée to some of its most aristocratic homes and plantations. Yet for all his later championing of the northern cause during the Civil War and of civil rights for Negroes in his home state of Connecticut, he barely mentions the institution of slavery or the many blacks he must have seen on these travels in the 1855 edition of his autobiography. In Camden, South Carolina, he writes, a Scottish musician in his company was imprisoned for six months after suggesting to a colored barber that he should run off to

Barnum blowing his own horn at the entrance to the American Museum.

The "Prince of Humbugs" as he appeared in the frontispiece to the notorious first edition of his autobiography.

PHINEAS TAYLOR

Phineas Taylor, Bethel's leading wag, after whom his grandson was named.

Charity Hallett Barnum, the "fair, rosy-cheeked, buxom-looking girl" Barnum married in 1829.

The Reverend Dr. Edwin
H. Chapin, Barnum's pun-
loving "Siamese twin."

The great Unitarian minister Robert Collyer paying a visit to his friend at Waldemere
c. 1885. Barnum's Bridgeport pastor John Lyon, whose wife gazes so rapturously at
the white-haired Collyer, is at the top. The showman himself, with one of his great-
grandchildren on his knee, sits between Mrs. Collyer and Nancy Barnum. The figure
in white tie barely visible through the window is probably Wyatt Roberts, Barnum's
black valet.

The Reverend Olympia Brown, Barnum's embattled Bridgeport pastor, as she appeared around the time of her graduation from St. Lawrence University in 1863.

The Barnum Museum of Natural History at Tufts College as it appeared in 1889 before wings were added to it. The mounted hide of Jumbo is about to be carried inside through the arched entrance, whose granite lintel, with "Barnum Fecit" chiseled on it, may still be seen at the reconstructed building on Medford's College Hill.

Joice Heth, the 161-year-old "nurse" of George Washington. From a rare bill advertising her appearance at "Barnum's Hotel," Bridgeport, in December 1835.

Signor Vivalla, Barnum's "celebrated Professor of Equilibrium and Plate Dancing."

The first American Museum at the corner of Ann Street and Broadway. Although somewhat the worse for wear, this large print, dating from around 1850, is the best representation of the building's exterior. Note in particular the oval portraits of animals between the windows (whose panes also appear to be decorated), the two figures in the display box at the building's corner, the patrons on the balconies, and the shops at street level. Tom Thumb's famous crested carriage, with a crowd gathered around it, is parked directly in front of the entrance to the Museum. The shop of Barnum's hatter friend Genin is next door.

The "Happy Family." A favorite exhibit at the American Museum.

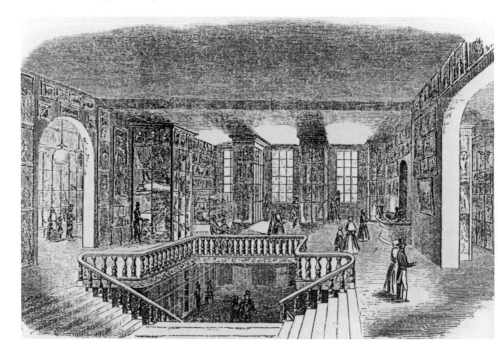

An interior view of the American Museum, showing the staircase leading up from street level to the first "grand hall."

The "What Is It?" One of Barnum's many puzzling exhibits in the "missing-link" category. "Is it a lower order of MAN? Or is it a higher order of MONKEY? None can tell!" Note the costume and imaginative treatment of the feet.

Anna Swan, Barnum's "Nova Scotia Giantess." "She is a whopper!" the showman wrote appreciatively in a letter to a friend.

Rudolphe Lucasie and his wife and son, the troublesome albinos whose behavior, Barnum thought, might be improved with a stay in jail.

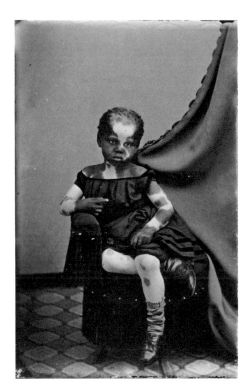

A "leopard child," another example of abnormal pigmentation, in this case vitiligo, whose possessors were favorites with spectators at the American Museum.

Zalumma Agra, the famous "Circassian Girl." The reputedly superior beauty of such attractions was always emphasized, and in this photograph the "Star of the East"—not too happy, it would seem—exhibits more than the usual amount of décolletage.

The first American Museum's "Lecture Room," as fine a theatre as could be found in New York.

Barnum's grandiose proposed museum of 1880. Note the "observatory" at one corner of the building.

The "Fejee Mermaid" as she really appeared.
An accurate representation, supposedly, published by Barnum in the first edition of his autobiography.

The *New York Atlas*'s "foreign correspondent" working at his desk in London.

Tom Thumb's carriage and ponies standing outside London's Egyptian Hall.

the North. In that enlightened town as well he nearly had his brains blown out one night when, still in blackface after singing his Negro songs, he rushed to intercede in a dispute between a native and some of his employees. "You black scoundrel!" cried the enraged spectator, drawing a pistol and cocking it. "Dare you use such language to a white man?" Barnum quickly rolled up one of his sleeves to reveal his true color and announced, "I am as white as *you* are, sir!" His opponent dropped the pistol in fright and instantly apologized.[33]

"I have spent months on the cotton plantations of Mississippi, where I have seen more than one 'Legree,'" he later confided in a letter to the Unitarian minister Thomas Wentworth Higginson, a leader in the abolitionist movement.[34] But in fact he displayed little sympathy for the abolitionists or their cause until almost the eve of the Civil War, and had even argued for the necessity of continuing slavery during his first trip abroad in the 1840s. Passing between Liverpool and Glasgow in November 1844, he had found on board his steamer a party of Scotsmen who were determined to dispute the question with him. Were it not for her toleration of slavery, they began, America would be the greatest nation in the universe. "As it was, however, Americans should almost be ashamed to acknowledge their country." Barnum replied that the British themselves were responsible for introducing slavery to the United States; that it would be "impolitic and unsafe to set free armies of ignorant negroes in such portions of the states that the whites were far inferior in point of numbers"; and that their masters "were induced by interest alone, if they had no higher motive, to use their negroes well—to feed and clothe them well and to administer to their wants when sick—and that the law compelled them to provide for their comfort in decrepitude and old age, and that, on the whole, they were much happier than the *starving workers* of this country, who could scarcely earn a subsistence while in health, and who in sickness and old age frequently died from starvation." When his opponents doggedly insisted on continuing the argument, pointing out that in his "boasted land of freedom of speech" they were prevented from going into its southern states to expose the evils of slavery, he was further moved to state his belief that "if the blacks were unceremoniously set free and there was no army to protect the whites, the blacks would murder them and take possession of their property." One of the Scotsmen said this would serve the slaveholders right and that he could not blame the blacks for at last taking vengeance on their oppressors. "I firmly believe you," Barnum heatedly rejoined, "and if you require 'the freedom of speech' which would permit you to preach that doctrine to the southern slaves, depend on it you will receive all the protection that you deserve!" "I am no apologist for slavery," he added for the benefit of the readers of the *New York Atlas*, in which this debate was reported, "and I abhor its existence as much as any man. But the rabid fanaticism of some abolitionists is more reprehensible than slavery itself and only serves to strengthen instead of weaken the fetters of the enslaved."[35]

More revealing still is his description—also published in the *Atlas*—of a visit one Negro paid to his Tom Thumb exhibition a few months before the above dispute took place:

Very few negroes are seen in London, and when seen at all they are generally walking arm in arm with a white person of the opposite sex. A negro came into the General's exhibition the other night with a well dressed white woman on his arm. The darkey was dressed off in great style, with gold chains, rings, pins, &c. (niggers always like jewels), and his lady love was apparently quite fond of him. I made General Tom Thumb sing all the "nigger songs" that he could think of and dance Lucy Long and several "Wirginny breakdowns." I then asked the General what the negroes called him when he travelled south. "They called me little massa," replied the General, "and they always took their hats off, too." The amalgamating darkey did not like this allusion to his "brack bredren ob de south," nor did he relish the General's songs about Dandy Jim, who was "de finest nigger in de county, O" and who strapped his pantaloons down so fine when "to see Miss Dinah he did go." The General enjoyed the joke and frequently pointed his finger at the negro, much to the discomfiture of "de colored gemman."[36]

Offensive as these articles are to present-day sensibilities, they are as nothing compared to what then came out. Several months after the second of them had been published, when their author was barely halfway through the series of one hundred "letters" he had promised to write for the *Atlas*, a biographical sketch of him appeared in the same paper. Headed by a crude woodcut showing "Our Foreign Correspondent" writing at a desk, the article had been contributed, the editors explained, by "an intimate friend of Barnum's—a very loving one, apparently." From the wealth of personal detail supplied and the comprehensiveness of its subject's history to date, it seems more than likely the showman himself was this "very loving" friend. After chronicling at some length his career in Bethel—where one learns, among other things, that Barnum's mother objected to Charity because "the girl had not got money enough to suit her ideas"—the article goes on to discuss his early tours. While he was traveling with his company through the South during the winter of 1837–38, the roads in Mississippi became almost impassable, and it was on this account that he purchased the steamboat *Ceres* upon arriving at Vicksburg. But he also made another purchase at this time: a Negro to serve as his valet, whom he later suspected of being a thief when he discovered several hundred dollars missing from one of his pockets. Barnum searched the "nigger" and found the money, "gave him fifty lashes, and took him to New Orleans, where he was sold at auction." When the company later terminated its travels in Opelousas and the *Ceres* was sold, Barnum took payment in "cash, sugar, molasses, and *a negro woman and child*. He shipped his sweets to New York, sold his negroes in St. Louis, and arrived in this city in June, after a very successful tour."[37]

Even if Barnum did not write this article himself, much of the information it contains could have come from no other source; and the details in the above account closely coincide with those in the later autobiography—except for mention of the Negroes. Elsewhere, too, he cheerfully acknowledged being familiar with the sketch and never contradicted or protested it.[38] Let us be candid about the matter and have done with it: Barnum's opinion of blacks during the pre–Civil War era was no higher than that of most of his countrymen, whether Southerners or Northerners. They were chattels, things to be bought and sold, like any other commodity. Many people around this time—including eminent scientists like Harvard's Louis Agassiz—were even prepared to argue for their being a separate species, inherently inferior and degenerate. Under such circumstances, why should Barnum not have purchased one of them as a manservant and later taken payment for the *Ceres* in such "coin of the realm"? It was perfectly legal to do so in the South; he was always on the lookout for profitable side speculations; other respectable people he met on his travels, like manager Noah Ludlow, did the same thing.[39] The readers of the *Atlas* no doubt found these revelations amusing enough, and the biographical sketch of the paper's brash "foreign correspondent" was in no sense meant as an exposé or condemnation of his actions. It was, in fact, a generally laudatory account ("Barnum is a man of liberal principles, and a friend of equal rights. . . . He is free, open-hearted, generous and charitable almost to a fault," etc., etc.), of the sort calculated to keep his name favorably before the American public during his long absence abroad.

Aside from the erroneous belief that he had once "owned" Joice Heth, neither his friends nor his enemies during his later life displayed any awareness that he had once traded in human flesh. Mercifully, they were either ignorant of the sketch in the *Atlas* or had long forgotten it. Joice Heth, in whom Barnum himself had initially believed, was hardly "the least deserving of all my efforts in the show line." By the time he came to write those unconvincing words for inclusion in the 1869 edition of his autobiography, however, something else was troubling his conscience.

V

The Wonders of God's Universe

The American Museum was the ladder by which I rose to fortune. . . . The Jenny Lind enterprise was more audacious, more immediately remunerative, and I remember it with a pride which I do not attempt to conceal; but instinctively I often go back and live over again the old days of my struggles and triumphs in the American Museum.

Autobiography

COULD A present-day Manhattanite somehow be transported back to the mid-nineteenth century, he would find little to surprise him in the New York City of that time. Although its teeming boardinghouses and tenements, hotels, pleasure haunts, and thriving businesses were still located mainly in the area from the Battery to just north of City Hall, the inexorable march "uptown" was well under way, with well-to-do citizens erecting their opulent mansions as far north as Union Square at 14th Street, while some visionaries were already predicting the day when every inch of the island would be built upon. Fueled by ambitious natives pouring in from the countryside and by a never-ending stream of immigrants, the city's population, from 60,000 inhabitants at the turn of the century, had been more than doubling every twenty years and by 1850 stood at slightly over half a million (the combined population of Danbury-Bethel was then but 6000). The "Empire City," as some insisted on calling her, already had the reputation of being a cosmopolis—of being, owing to the large number of foreigners in her midst, the least "American" of American cities.

Then as now, extremes were apparent everywhere. The city was exhilarating, and at the same time filthy and barely governable. "What a vast emporium of wholesale commerce, of retail business, of universal bustle!" wrote Alfred Bunn upon first visiting New York in 1853. "Flags flying in every direction—streamers with their owners' trade or calling printed on them, floating out of windows, or waving from one side to the other of every street; flights of omnibus, hack, and car, sailing through broad thoroughfares; lofty stores, rich shops, crowded cellars, choking up every 'block'; huge hotels, restaurants, coffee houses, oyster saloons, here, there, and everywhere; man in every variety of costume, and woman in the loveliest of all costumes—her own native beauty—parading every promenade." Yet the same writer, echoing a familiar lament of many visitors to the city since his time, assured his readers he would never live there, even if "board and lodging were given us gratis." New York was too dirty, too noisy, too "go-aheadish" for his taste. Wherever one looked, buildings were either burning or being pulled down, to be replaced immediately by more ambitious structures; fire bells clanged incessantly and were answered by engines rushing to their calls; sidewalks, often in disrepair, were littered with chests, barrels, cans, etc., to the eternal hindrance of those traveling around town on foot; while the streets themselves, clogged with construction materials and rarely cleaned, were awash in a sea of garbage, ashes, manure, and human spittle whenever it rained, and at other times enveloped in a cloud of dust composed of the same ingredients.[1]

Commerce was the great engine that drove the city. American entrepreneurship had at last come of age, and huge fortunes were being made overnight by former petty tradesmen, farmers, and ship captains. The manners of these parvenus or "shoddyites"—with their ludicrous aping of foreign customs, conspicuous consumption, and putting on of what they considered to be aristocratic airs—were hilariously satirized at New York's Park Theatre in Anna Cora Mowatt's *Fashion* of 1845. But those in more modest circumstances and the industrious poor who jammed into the city were no less engaged in the pell-mell running after riches. And behind the kaleidoscopic whirl of life in Gotham was a darker, less salubrious aspect: in the back slums of Broadway and the city's notorious "Five Points" district, crime, drunkenness, and prostitution openly flourished amidst appalling scenes of misery and squalor.

In the spring of 1841 Barnum was himself an eager participant in this hurried scene, determined once more to succeed at some "respectable" line of business. This time he managed to exhaust his capital as U.S. agent for *Sears' Pictorial Illustrations of the Bible*, a high-toned publication he had first encountered during his recent sojourn in Pittsburgh. "I never could succeed as a merchant," he confessed in his "Rules for Success in Business" published in the first edition of the autobiography; and both here and in his later lecture "The Art of Money-Getting" he stressed the necessity of finding one's natural vocation early in life and sticking to it.[2] Yet throughout his own career he repeatedly violated the same advice, and nearly always with predictable results. "With consistency a great soul has simply nothing to do," Emerson wrote in his famous essay "Self-Reliance," published the same year Barnum returned to New York. His struggling contemporary might have taken some comfort from the observation, even though, paradoxically, there was a certain "consistency" behind his vacillating. The problem was to reconcile somehow his own natural vocation with that withering word "respectable," and as yet he could see no possible way to do so.

When he decided to hazard another summer season of variety performances at New York's Vauxhall Garden, he therefore thought it advisable to keep his name out of the affair; and his brother-in-law John Hallett, who had served as advance agent during the tour with Master Diamond, was nominally in charge.

At the end of three months they had cleared barely $200. Barnum was now reduced to being "about as poor as I should ever wish to be." To eke out a living for himself and his family, who had rejoined him in New York, he took to writing advertisements and puffs for the Bowery Amphitheatre, daily delivering his copy to newspaper offices and making certain it was properly inserted. The pinching salary of $4 per week he received for this work was supplemented by money earned from writing occasional pieces for the Sunday papers.

His hand is frequently evident in the *New York Atlas*, for example, where he published humorous stories under the barely disguised name of "Barnaby Diddleum." Strangest of all these concoctions, commencing in the same paper on 11 April 1841, is a serialized novella he wrote entitled *The Adventures of an Adventurer, Being Some Passages in the Life of Barnaby Diddleum*. The aptly named hero of this tale, after starting out as editor and proprietor of a provincial newspaper known as the *Northern Trust Banner*, decides to get into the "humbug of exhibitions" and is soon traveling around the country with an old Negress and a "very curious monkey." The latter, whose specialty is balancing on its tail, is challenged by another "monkey" in Philadelphia, where "Diddleum" and the rival's manager get up a series of fake competitions. The old Negress, of course, is none other than "Aunt Joice," and here "Diddleum" reveals his true genius. After discovering her in Kentucky, he talks her owner into paying him to take her off his hands (for Joice, like all blacks, has a natural aversion to work), then extracts all her remaining teeth to make her appear more ancient, coaches her in the role of "nurse" to the revered Washington, forges a bill of sale that "proves" her antecedents, and bribes her with whiskey to keep her from swearing before the public. Old Joice, who is described as an "excellent actress" herself, soon becomes expert at taking in people with her supposed piety; and in relating their later adventures in New York City, "Diddleum" ecstatically crows over how they "humbugged" everyone—editors, the public, and even the famous Dr. Rogers. Indeed, the vainglorious boasting of the hero-narrator, who laughs uproariously over his triumphs and proudly styles himself the "king of Humbugs," at times assumes an almost manic air. In another episode containing an ironic thrust at Universalism, he reveals he was once a hypocritical, self-serving minister—the "Reverend Barnaby Diddleum"—who acquired his dignified clothes in a poker game and preached his first sermon on the evils of gambling!

All of these picaresque scenes, readers are informed, are based on a "journal" kept by the author; and nearly all of them reappear in Barnum's autobiography, for which the present work seems almost to have been a rehearsal. But the narrative itself, while obviously founded on the showman's life to date, has been transmuted into fiction, or at least semi-fiction, and the persona of "*Barnaby* Diddle*um*" both is and is not Barnum. For all the humor of the situations he contrives or finds himself in, the cynical, hubristic hero is a telling example of "humbug" carried to excess—a nightmarish projection of what Barnum might have become, perhaps even feared he *was* becoming, now that his craving for "respectability" was again upon him.

Meanwhile, his attention had again been drawn to the American Museum, whose contents, he learned, were up for sale. The nucleus of the Museum's collections had been assembled toward the end of the last century by the Tammany Society and, beginning in 1790, originally exhibited in City Hall. Since 1795, however, they had been owned and managed by a succession of private individuals, the latest of whom, the taxidermist and natural-history enthusiast John Scudder, had died in 1821. For the past twenty years the Museum had been directed for the benefit of his heirs by a group of trustees, who continued to add to the collections and in 1830 moved them into a new five-story building, erected to their specifications, at the corner of Ann Street and Broadway. But unfortunately, squabbling among Scudder's children, declining revenues exacerbated by the great fire of 1835 and financial panic of 1837, and competition with rival establishments such as Rubens Peale's New York Museum had taken their toll; and now that the time had finally arrived to settle the estate, the asking price for the collections, which might have realized $25,000 ten years earlier, was but $15,000.[3]

Barnum writes that he repeatedly visited the Museum around this time as a "thoughtful looker-on" and that he soon became convinced that "only energy, tact and liberality were needed, to give it life and to put it on a profitable footing." Here was an opportunity to ensure for himself and his family a steady source of income, put an end to those frustrating tours with the likes of Master Diamond, and, he might have added, take the first tentative step toward that long-sought goal of "respectability." After boldly writing to and persuading Francis Olmsted, the owner of the building, to buy the collections for him, he still had one more hurdle to overcome. The administrator of the Scudder estate, John Heath, having previously agreed to sell the collections to Barnum for $12,000, unexpectedly announced he had accepted an offer of $15,000, the original asking price, from the directors of the rival New York Museum Company, who had given him a binder of $1000 and promised to pay the balance on 26 December. There had been nothing in writing between Barnum and himself, and he felt duty-bound to realize as much as he could for Scudder's children. Barnum swallowed his disappointment and immediately began making inquiries. Becoming convinced the directors of the New York Museum were out to perpetrate a stock swindle, he was soon busy ridiculing their plans and pointing out in the columns of friendly newspapers the impracticalness of merging the two museums. Once he had sufficiently undermined public confidence in the company and its stock, he returned to Heath and secured from him a secret promise—this time in writing—to sell him the collections for the $12,000 previously agreed on if the company did not pay the balance on the 26th. Meanwhile, the directors of the New York Museum, seeking some way to silence their opponent, had decided to offer him the management of the united museums. Barnum blandly accepted the bribe, named the munificent figure of $3000 as the annual salary he expected to receive, and sat back to await the results. When the directors, confident they were alone in the field and under no pressure to pay Heath on time, failed to keep their appointment with him on the 26th, he again swung into action. On the following day his first act as the new proprietor of the American Museum was to inform the startled directors of the rival company that he had placed their names on the free list of his establishment.[4]

Proprietary museums have largely disappeared from the American scene, and few people today would look upon them as likely business opportunities. But in the mid-nineteenth century, before the great public museums and zoological gardens got under way, nearly every city of any size boasted at least one such establishment, and often these were the principal, most popular cultural institutions of their day. The theatre, still held in disrepute by many respectable citizens, achieved its nadir in 1849 with the bloody Astor Place Riot, the climax in the long rivalry between the brawny American actor Edwin Forrest and the English tragedian William Charles Macready, who supposedly had been behind the cool reception accorded Forrest on his recent visit to England and who now further infuriated the American star's boisterous fans by daring to challenge him on his native soil. Opera and ballet, then barely under way in America, were irrevocably tainted by their theatrical associations, leading so pure-minded an artist as the "divine" Jenny Lind, after achieving her initial success in the former and only slightly less renown as a daughter of Terpsichore, studiously to shun both in later life. Circuses like Aaron Turner's, which sometimes performed in theaters or buildings of their own when not on the road, were fairly common by this time. But here, too, shady practices and loose behavior on the part of employees—not to mention the coarse jests and indelicate references that figured in many clowns' repertoires—frequently outraged the moral element in communities; and traveling establishments, especially, like carnivals in a later day, were often the scenes of bloodshed and violence, frequently brought on by local roughnecks who viewed all such intruding "showfolks" as beyond the pale and thought nothing of killing an innocent performer for their added amusement. "When I consider the kinds of company into which for a number of years I was thrown, the associations with which I was connected, and the strong temptations to wrong-doing and bad habits which lay in my path," Barnum wrote of his early tours with his own and Turner's shows, "I am astonished as well as grateful that I was not utterly ruined."[5]

Menageries were more acceptable, since they were patently "educational" and their denizens were commonly referred to in scriptural terms ("the Great Behemoth of Holy Writ," etc.). Exotic animals, brought to these shores and sold by enterprising ship captains, had been exhibited in America since the Colonial period. Taken about the countryside individually or in small groups, they were a profitable investment for those who bought them; and Barnum himself had been acquainted with one of the more successful of these early entrepreneurs, Hackaliah Bailey, of Somers, New York, who owned the elephant known as "Old Bet" and later built the still-standing Elephant Hotel in Somers with money largely realized from the menagerie business.[6] From these modest beginnings had sprung the great traveling "caravans," which also maintained permanent buildings in cities like New York. When a few hardy keepers belonging to these establishments further gratified spectators by entering the cages of ferocious beasts, biblical parallels were again inevitable. Lion "tamers" in particular, who traditionally made a great show of beating their roaring charges into submission, were advertised to enter "dens"; and when Isaac Van Amburgh, the most celebrated of these early performers, beginning in the 1830s incorporated his act into a number of stage plays, the lion was further made to lie down with the lamb.[7]

Pleasure gardens like William Niblo's, to which Henry James recalled being taken as a boy, were obviously respectable. Here, on a fine summer's evening, a family party or group of friends might take refreshments served in one of the elegantly decorated boxes or "bowers" that surrounded the garden, stroll along its illuminated pathways, and enjoy the light entertainment presented in the adjacent "saloon" or garden itself. Waxworks, also, were deemed innocuous family entertainment, provided they did not dwell too luridly on female anatomy or the horrors of the French Revolution. Music of the nonoperatic variety, performed in numerous "concert halls," was eminently respectable; and so were "Ethiopian" entertainments or minstrel shows, whose greatest period of popularity, however, was to come in the second half of the century.

An appreciation for the fine arts was noticeably on the increase, although here, too, there were as yet no great public institutions to bring together such works. At a time when photography was in its infancy, Americans' curiosity about the Old World and their own nation's remote fastnesses was satisfied by a number of spectacular pictorial entertainments—panoramas, dioramas, etc.—whose huge paintings, often viewed under shifting lighting conditions, with three-dimensional objects in the foreground, special sound effects, and musical accompaniment, were exhibited in specially constructed buildings. A variation, the moving panorama, consisting of a long canvas that slowly unwound from one upright spool and was taken up by another at the opposite side of the stage, was sometimes seen in theatres themselves. When William Dunlap, painter as well as historian and playwright, produced his *A Trip to Niagara* at the Bowery Theatre in 1828, Americans had their first look at this latest wonder: a colossal painting measuring 25,000 square feet in area that depicted scenes one could view while traveling upriver from New York to Albany, and thence to Niagara Falls via the newly opened Erie Canal. One might as well add that lovers of the arts also had at least one "adult" outlet around this time: *tableaux vivants* of the "model artists" variety, whose generous display of undraped female charms pointed the way to another cultural development. But striptease and the raucous "girly-show" phase of burlesque were still some years in the future, as was the cleaner, full-fledged vaudeville show.

Americans were hardly starved for amusement at mid-century, and when one adds to the above the numerous other entertainments then available to them—"legerdemain" or magic shows, puppets, balloon ascensions, annual expositions of arts and industries, country fairs, lectures and other visitations sponsored by local lyceum societies, itinerating freaks, prodigies like Joice Heth and similar interesting objects such as Barnum and his fellow showmen took around the country—one sees to what extent the old Puritans' influence over such godless goings-on had by now declined. But of all these entertainments museums were undoubtedly the most inclusive and least objectionable, combining as they did, rather incongruously, elements of nearly all the above, while at the same time stressing their dedication to "rational" amusement. Such had been the announced policy of America's first great museum, that of the painter, inventor, and naturalist Charles Willson Peale, whose Philadelphia establishment, from the 1780s on, featured wax figures and a notable collection of the founder's own paintings; lectures, scientific demonstrations, and musical evenings; magic-lantern shows and a scenic spectacle with changeable effects, which Peale eventually advertised as "moving pictures"; an adjacent menagerie of living animals; besides the skeletons and mounted skins, collections of insects, minerals, and seashells, anthropological and fossil materials, historical relics, displays of models and curious inventions, and all the other objects associated with a natural-history museum. As at the present-day Smithsonian Institution, almost everything having to do with man and nature was cheerfully accommodated, from a chip of the coronation chair in Westminster Abbey and some "black bugs" that came from the stomach of a distressed Maryland lady, to the tattooed head of a New Zealand chieftain and a living cow with five legs and two tails. The last, after supplying Peale and his large family with milk for several years, eventually found her permanent home in the museum as well, where she was exhibited suckling a two-headed calf.[8]

Peale sometimes expressed impatience with such sports of nature and weird acquisitions, but their inclusion in earlier "cabinets of curiosities" was well-established practice by the time he founded his Philadelphia museum, and neither he nor later museum proprietors dared disappoint their patrons' avid interest in them. The American Museum continued the tradition of faithfully catering to such expectations—not without a frequently humorous note—and under Barnum's direction exhibited such quaint objects as the preserved hand and arm of the pirate Tom Trouble, a great ball of hair found in the belly of a sow, a piece of the door of Columbus's birthplace, a straw from the tick the Russian czar Nicholas slept on while staying at Buckingham Palace, a hat made out of broom splints by a lunatic, and (a traditional Connecticut specialty) a wooden nutmeg. Next to a group of ancient coins, prominently displayed for all to see, were the "handcuffs of a man named George Wilson, who robbed this case many years ago."

But the bulk of the Museum's collections was decidedly of a more legitimate nature and possessed, as Barnum often boasted, considerable scientific and cultural value, even if scholarly visitors did complain about the inadequate labeling and lack of systematic display they sometimes found in their favorite areas. For the American Museum aspired to be—and probably was under Barnum's management—the largest and most comprehensive establishment of its kind in America. Unfortunately, no complete catalogue of its eclectic holdings was ever compiled, almost all of its manuscript records appear to have perished, and the various guidebooks that were published give but a faint indication of the extent of its contents. Under Barnum's direction, too, the Museum pursued an aggressive policy of continual expansion, beginning with the acquisition of the New York Museum of Rubens Peale (with whose directors

Barnum had been in competition for the American Museum) and eventually absorbing even a large part of the elder Peale's celebrated collections, which Barnum bought at sheriff's sale in Philadelphia and divided with Moses Kimball of the Boston Museum. Along the way were numerous purchases, both great and small, made here and abroad; exchanges with Kimball and other museum proprietors; and occasional sales of objects that were no longer wanted. To house all these treasures, the five-story Museum, already of considerable area when Barnum took possession of it, was several times expanded into the upper stories of adjoining buildings, whose ground-floor fronts, as in the Museum building itself, continued to be occupied by shops. At one time the showman even contemplated occupying the entire block between Ann and Fulton streets, but was forced to abandon this ambitious plan when a number of owners refused to go along with it.

While still under the trustees of the Scudder estate, the Museum had published, in 1823, a guide to the "upwards of Fifty Thousand Natural and Foreign Curiosities, Antiquities, and Productions of the Fine Arts" then said to be in its collections, and only three years later the advertised grand total had escalated to no fewer than one hundred fifty thousand.[9] Just how many objects it possessed at any given period is anyone's guess, for museums, from Peale's time on, traditionally preened themselves on such good, round numbers. Some idea of the "million wonders" Barnum was himself trumpeting in 1864, when the Museum was at its most congested, may be gleaned from a guidebook published around that time. There was, to begin with, the usual profusion of skeletons and stuffed animals, particularly birds, which had also been a specialty of the elder Peale. These were scattered throughout the Museum's spacious "saloons," with the majority of specimens secured in glass cases reaching from floor to ceiling. A collection of wax figures—some, like the one of Queen Victoria, notoriously bad—was on display, as were paintings, statues (one of them a "life-size" Venus), daguerreotypes of Barnum and Tom Thumb, the latter's court suit worn on visits to Buckingham Palace, and a painting and bust of Jenny Lind. Elsewhere were Roman, Oriental, and American Indian artifacts; trick mirrors, optical instruments, and a large magnet; various models; facsimiles of famous diamonds; suits of armor; a collection of celebrated individuals' autographs; the mummified body of an Indian found in Mammoth Cave; and four cases of shoes from various nations and periods, another feature of Peale's earlier museum. There were collections of insects and butterflies, minerals and crystals, shells and corals (described in an earlier guidebook as the "ingenious work" of "marine insects"), and horns. A separate room was devoted to one hundred ninety-four "cosmoramas," in effect peepshows, through whose apertures visitors raptly gazed at famous scenes and buildings around the world.[10]

All this was but the beginning, however, for, continuing another tradition established by Peale, the American Museum also had its menagerie of living animals. They were so numerous and at times so large, in fact, that one cannot help wondering how Barnum found space to fit them all in, let alone get them to the Museum's upper stories, where most of them were kept. Besides the usual lions, tigers, bears, ostriches, and primates, at various periods there were the first hippopotamus seen in America, a rhinoceros, the delicate giraffe or "camelopard" as it was still sometimes called, and the entire "California Menagerie" of the legendary "Grizzly" Adams, whose most awesome pupil was the gigantic bear "Old Sampson." During the early years of Barnum's management a gentle orangutan named after the dancer Fanny Elssler was a favorite with Museum visitors; and from the 1840s on a separate feature that never failed to intrigue children and their parents was the "Happy Family," a large collection of natural enemies—cats and rats, owls and mice, eagles and rabbits, hawks and small birds, etc., with one or two monkeys and an armadillo thrown in for good measure—that had been trained to tolerate each other within the confines of the same cage.[11] One wonders if the same patrons were equally delighted by the Museum's anaconda and boa constrictors, whose spectacular alimentary habits, advertised as being on public view, led to Barnum's first run-in with Henry Bergh, president of the newly founded Society for the Prevention of Cruelty to Animals.[12]

Entirely new at Barnum's establishment was the first public aquarium in America. The idea for this project had come to the showman while he was on a trip to England, where he had seen a similar display at London's Regent's Park zoo. Procuring glass tanks and two able assistants from the same institution, in 1857 he inaugurated an elegant exhibit of "Ocean and River Gardens" at the American Museum. By the early sixties a large collection of native and exotic fishes was on display, as were sharks, porpoises, and "sea flowers" or anemones; and so popular did these "crystal ponds" prove with New Yorkers that in 1862 he opened and for several months ran an "Aquarial Gardens" in Boston. To keep them supplied, he regularly fitted out sailing expeditions to the tropics that returned laden with angel, porcupine, and peacock fish, and a variety of other brilliantly colored specimens (the young Albert S. Bickmore, who had studied with Harvard's famed Louis Agassiz and was later to found the American Museum of Natural History, was on board the vessel that visited Bermuda in 1862).[13] Even more remarkable was the expedition he himself made to the mouth of the St. Lawrence River in 1861 to superintend the capture of beluga whales. Transported to New York in a special railway car, the first two of these beautiful creatures were exhibited in a brick and cement tank in the Museum's basement. When they died after a short time, Barnum promptly set about procuring additional specimens, which were now housed on the second floor in a plate-glass tank measuring twenty-four feet on each side. To supply them and his other exhibits with fresh salt water, pipes were laid from the Museum to New York Bay, and a steam engine was set up at dockside to pump the water. The showman also exhibited his white whales in Boston; and when rumors began floating that they were only porpoises, Professor Agassiz himself showed up to vouch for their authenticity.[14] Another famous Museum denizen, also kept for many years in a tank, was the great Pacific sea lion known as "Old Neptune"—described in the Museum's bills as "the most Majestic, Terrific, though yet docile inhabitant of the Great Deep"—who had originally come as part of Adams's menagerie.[15]

Although Barnum sometimes spoke disparagingly about his knowledge of natural history and laughingly informed his friends that he didn't know a clam from a codfish, he had the reputation of being a great zoologist among his contemporaries, many of whom addressed queries to him and sent him specimens to identify. When a Universalist clergyman once sent him an appetizing-looking fish he had caught in a Maine lake, asking him to name the creature and then eat it, he promptly honored the latter part of the request. A number of later writers have gone so far as to assert he had no interest in or love for animals whatever.[16] Yet the truth of the matter—setting aside, for the moment, his evident fondness for the pets he kept on his estates—is that he possessed considerable knowledge of animals and their habits, as is displayed not only in the pages of the autobiography but above all in his extensive correspondence with leading scientists and naturalists, museum curators, animal dealers, and the keepers he employed. Upon learning through the newspapers that the manager of his second American Museum had secured a living gorilla—a huge baboon, he later discovered—he immediately wrote to give expert advice on the care of this long-sought prize. "I have owned many ourang-outangs," he writes in the autobiography, "and all of them die ultimately of pulmonary disease; indeed, it is difficult to keep specimens of the monkey tribe through the winter in our climate, on account of their tendency to consumption. I therefore advised Mr. Ferguson to have a cage so constructed that no draught of air could pass through it, and I further instructed him in methods of guarding against the gorilla's taking cold."[17] When in 1882 the Indian elephant "Queen" gave birth at his circus's Bridgeport winter quarters, and a rival showman tried to top him by claiming he owned a pair of twin elephants just born at sea, Barnum wrote to Alexander Agassiz, son of Louis, to ask for a few lines confirming his belief that "elephants never have *twins*—that a wild elephant was never seen with more than *one* young at its side."[18] A few months later he was writing again to Agassiz at Harvard, as well as to Spencer F. Baird, Secretary of the Smithsonian Institution, Professor Othniel C. Marsh of the Yale College Museum, and Henry A. Ward of Ward's Natural Science Establishment in Rochester, New York, about another elephant he owned—this time an unruly male named "Albert," who was subject, like all of his sex, to those unpredictable periods of frenzy known as "musth." Rather than kill the animal as was usually done on such occasions, the showman was wondering if it might instead be castrated. Apparently the operation had never been attempted on an elephant before, and Charles P. Lyman, chief surgeon at the Harvard School of Veterinary Medicine, after carefully considering the "formidable" problem, decided it would be impracticable. Ward and his colleagues, however, were intrigued by the proposal, and the former even traveled to Bridgeport to examine Albert. But he, too, concluded it could not be done; and Albert, shorn of his tusks and made to dance in an elephant ballet, was allowed to live—a humane but unfortunate decision, as things turned out, since the animal, who understandably resented such treatment, eventually went on the rampage again, ground his keeper into the dust, and had to be shot anyway.[19]

Again, in the midst of the controversy over his famous white elephant (elephants were always particular favorites with Barnum), he took care to read and consult all the available authorities, even informing himself, via government officials at the Siamese court, of the "true characteristics" of these sacred animals.[20] At the Museum itself he delighted in personally showing off the latest arrivals, especially when he could call into play some of the stage presence he had acquired while working at the "legerdemain" business. On 30 June 1864 a delighted visitor wrote to his wife to describe one such spectacle he had seen there that day. Before an audience that included "many literary men" (for which read "reporters and editors"), Barnum had held up a lump of hard, dry clay and informed the skeptical spectators that there was a live fish inside it. When the lump was sawed in two, some sort of creature was indeed found inside that, after exposure to air and then water for a few minutes, swam about like any other respectable member of the finny tribe—the first example of the African lungfish seen in America.[21] And of course there was the oft-repeated performance of the celebrated "cherry-colored" cat, purchased sight unseen by Barnum or his manager (the story of how the animal had been acquired, understandably, was subject to variation) from a smooth-talking farmer for twenty-five dollars. After skillfully working up spectators' curiosity to see this wonderful feline, Barnum would dump from a sack an ordinary black cat. "Well," he would say, repeating the words of the hypothetical farmer, "some cherries, you know, are black."[22]

At his second American Museum farther uptown, where Barnum was in partnership with the Van Amburgh Menagerie Company, even larger animals, including elephants, were accommodated; and when, beginning in the 1870s, he took to the road with his great traveling show, a separate well-stocked menagerie was always a prominent feature of that establishment. Many of his animals, like his genuine white elephant and beluga whales, were of the greatest rarity or the first of their kind to be exhibited in America. Others, like the four giraffes he boasted of in an 1873 letter to Spencer F. Baird, were difficult to transport under the best of circumstances.[23] When these animals died, they were quickly replaced and their hides and skeletons given to scientific institutions, which often entered into fierce competition for them. The Smithsonian Institution's archives contain several incomplete lists of such accessions—during the period 1884–85 alone Barnum presented no less than twenty-four specimens, distributed among carnivores, ungulates, primates, and marsupials—although the National Museum, amidst much bitter feeling, eventually lost out on the greatest prize of all, Jumbo's skeleton, which went to the rival American Museum of Natural History.

For half a century he was actively involved with and made important contributions to the study of natural history; yet today, predictably, he is remembered almost exclusively in this area for such patent frauds as the Woolly Horse and the Fejee Mermaid—those "skyrockets" or "advertisements," as he liked to explain, by which he attracted attention to the bona fide objects he had to offer. At times even he was genuinely puzzled and in danger of being taken advantage of. In the 1880s, in the midst of a spate of sightings of sea serpents and lake monsters (including the perennial "Champ" of Lake Champlain fame), he issued a standing offer of $20,000 to anyone who could capture a specimen and deliver it to him "in a fit state for stuffing and mounting." There seemed to be no reasonable doubt of the creatures' existence, he stated in his announcement, so many "intelligent & respectable" people had reported seeing them. The reward went unclaimed, needless to say, although several such monsters were manufactured around this time. Even before making his offer, Barnum had received a "shameless" letter from a person in Chicago, proposing to make a sea serpent sixty to sixty-five feet long that would defy detection in a glass cage or wagon some four to five feet off. "Some may cry humbug," acknowledged the writer, who had obviously taken a page from the showman's book, but "the one that does only invites 100 to see if it is or not."[24] Strange to relate, there is no evidence Barnum expressed interest in this intriguing proposal—the year was 1881, and by then the period of his more notorious frauds was over—although he does appear to have had some correspondence during the same decade with one J. D. Willman of Vancouver, British Columbia, who had the notion he might succeed in capturing a living mammoth.[25]

And indeed, why should there not have been great woolly mammoths shaking the earth of the Canadian wilderness? Had not Charles Willson Peale, who at the turn of the century excavated the first nearly complete skeleton of a "mammoth"—more accurately, mastodon—for years cherished the belief that this "Great Incognitum" still lived? The idea that species might become extinct, that breaks could occur in the "Great Chain of Being" linking God to the lowliest of his creations, had only recently gained acceptance in the scientific community, and was still vigorously opposed by many outside it. For that matter, were not new species like *Gorilla gorilla*, whose existence had been reported but generally doubted until the explorer Paul du Chaillu showed up in London with his specimens in 1861, being discovered all the time? Perhaps the great sea serpent and its elusive lake brethren also existed—they had been sighted by mariners and others for centuries, after all—and might now finally be taken using such recent inventions as the grenade harpoon. Even more unsettling than the notion of species becoming extinct, to many of Barnum's contemporaries, was the idea that they might not be immutable, but subject to a process of gradual change. It was left to Wallace and Darwin to formulate the theory of natural selection, but even before the publication of the latter's controversial *Origin of Species* in 1859 sufficient evidence had accumulated to convince many scientists that evolution occurred, although its mechanism was then but dimly perceived. The immense geologic record of the earth itself was at last being read, and soon the race would commence for fossil remains far more ancient and unsettling than Peale's mastodon.

To those with an interest in natural history—and this included nearly everyone in the nineteenth century—it was an exciting, yet at the same time confusing, age in which to live. And Barnum, who supplied as best he could legitimate examples of the subject, was not above exploiting his patrons' ignorance and credulousness from time to time, as he certainly did with the Fejee Mermaid and his famous "nondescript," the Little Woolly Horse, not to

mention a tantalizing procession of unicorns, frogs with human hands, phoe-
nixes, and similar curiosities manufactured for him by the ingenious Japanese,
who even then seem to have had a good idea of what would appeal to the
American market.[26] Equally challenging to spectators were some of his exhibits
in the "missing-link" and "descent-of-man" categories. There may have been
some excuse, in the 1840s, for touting "Mlle. Fanny," his celebrated orangutan,
as "the connecting link between man and brute"; but the succession of "What
Is Its?" he exhibited from the same period onward were out-and-out frauds.
The very first of them, the deformed but talented man-monkey Hervey Leach,
who in better days had appeared upon the stage under the name of "Hervio
Nano," provoked such an outcry when Barnum tried to pass him off before the
British public as "The Wild Man of the Prairies" that the showman, genuinely
embarrassed for once, later denied his involvement with him. "Is it an animal?
Is it human? . . . Or is it the long sought for link between man and the
Ourang-Outang, which naturalists have for years decided does exist, but which
has hitherto been undiscovered?" Barnum wrote in the bills and newspaper
advertisements announcing the appearance of this attraction at London's
Egyptian Hall in 1846.

> Its features, hands, and the upper portion of its body are to all appear-
> ances human, the lower part of its body, the hind legs, and haunches are
> decidedly animal. It is entirely covered, except the face and hands, with
> long flowing hair of various shades. It is larger than an ordinary sized
> man, but not quite so tall. . . . its food is chiefly nuts and fruit, though
> it occasionally indulges in a meal of raw meat; it drinks milk, water, and
> tea, and is partial to wine, ale, and porter.[27]

In his autobiography, where he disingenuously claims to have turned down
the opportunity to participate in this speculation, Barnum writes that the "two
Americans" who did exhibit Leach stained his skin and dressed him in a hair
costume, but had to refund the money they had taken less than half an hour
after first opening their doors, when one of the spectators recognized the "What
Is It?" and exposed the "imposition." His uncharacteristic reluctance to acknowledge his own role in this fraud is most likely explained by Leach's untimely death a few months later—brought on, many thought, by the "mal-
treatment" and humiliation he had suffered as the result of his exposure.[28]

At the Museum itself, and in his later circus as well, Barnum nearly always
had some "What Is It?" on display. The most famous of all was the cone-headed
Negro William Henry Johnson, known to generations of Americans as "Zip,"
who continued at his strange vocation until his death in 1926, when he was
variously reported as being anywhere from sixty-three to eighty-four years old.
His sister, in an interview at the time, stated that he had been born as recently
as 1857, but had begun his career at the tender age of four, originally with the
Van Amburgh Circus, and not with Barnum's company until several years later.[29]
Other accounts, however, tell of his being at the old Ann Street museum; and
numerous illustrations of Barnum's "What Is It?" from the early 1860s on—
in bills and guidebooks, lithographs by Currier and Ives in the series "Bar-

num's Gallery of Wonders," etc.—all bear a striking resemblance to "Zip." There one sees him inbecilely grinning and in a characteristic pose, arms crooked and legs splayed outward, supporting himself, in a half-crouching attitude, with a staff. "Is it man? Is it monkey? Or is it both?" queries one bill dating from 1861. In a pamphlet published the previous year, the speech of his "keeper" is even given. He had been captured, according to this account, by a party of adventurers in quest of a gorilla and had only recently been taught to walk upon his feet (hence the awkwardness of his stance). After pointing out a number of interesting physical traits—"the ears are set back about an inch too far for humanity," "the teeth are double nearly all around, and the creature is not able to close its mouth entirely," etc.—the speaker concluded with the announcement that he had been examined "by some of the most scientific men we have, and pronounced by them to be a CONNECTING LINK BETWEEN THE WILD NATIVE AFRICAN AND THE BRUTE CREATION."[30] It was surely no accident that the advent of this particular "What Is It?"—either "Zip" or a predecessor—coincided so closely with the publication of Darwin's Origin of Species, whose original English edition had completely sold out on the first day of issue the previous November. The diarist George Templeton Strong, who was then, like many of his contemporaries, immersed in reading and privately arguing with the work, stopped by the Museum on two consecutive days in early March 1860 to view the "What Is It?" shortly after it was put on exhibit. On his first visit he thought the keeper's story "probably bosh" and the "What Is It?" itself "clearly an idiotic negro dwarf." But its anatomical details, he conceded, were "fearfully simian, and he's a great fact for Darwin."[31]

There were other ethnological exhibits of dubious authenticity, like the "Aztec Children" Maximo and Bartola—diminutive, imbecilic microcephalics or "pinheads" who invariably impressed visitors with their affectionate and confiding natures. They, too, had been "captured," this time somewhere in the wilds of Central America, and were supposed to be descended from the nearly extinct "sacerdotal caste" of their ancient people. "There was nothing monstrous in their appearance," the author and editor Nathaniel P. Willis, who met them privately shortly after their arrival in New York, assured his readers. Their physical and mental degeneration had resulted from the intermarriage imposed on members of their caste in order to keep it "sacred." Even so, he concluded on an elegiac, somewhat mystical note, "with little intelligence, and skulls of such shape that no hope can be entertained of their being ever self-relying or responsible, they still inspire an indefinable feeling of interest, and a deference for the something they vaguely after-shadow."[32] In the 1840s Barnum had the wild boy "Caspar Hauser" under his management (the real Kaspar had died in Germany ten years earlier); and in 1850 he engaged for six years and sent round the country a Chinese Family—a genuine one, presumably, since he was at some pains to find an interpreter who would also "manage them properly so that they behave themselves."[33]

Making employees "behave" was a recurring problem for manager Barnum. With as many as three hundred persons in his employ at any given time during his proprietorship of the American Museum, he needed to be constantly on guard against anything that might offend the more squeamish among his patrons or threaten his authority. Performers who stepped out of line or refused to accede to his wishes were firmly disciplined; employees caught pilfering or guilty of disrespect were promptly discharged.[34] When Dr. Oscar Kohn, the manager of the famous Lucasie family of albinos at the Museum, began experiencing difficulties with his charges, Barnum urged that he be allowed to take over his contract with them. "They are acting very disagreeable with you," he wrote, "but if I have your agreement transferred to me, I will put them in jail if they don't behave."[35] Especially troublesome were the Indians Barnum regularly exhibited at the Museum and elsewhere. If his attitude toward blacks eventually underwent a change, he rarely expressed any sympathy for these indigenous Americans, whom he and most of his contemporaries continued to regard as dirty, treacherous savages. "Damn Indians *anyhow*. They are a lazy, shiftless set of brutes—though they will *draw*," he wrote to Moses Kimball of the Boston Museum, with whom he had arranged to exchange one such group in 1843. "The lazy devils want to be *lying down* nearly all the time, and as it looks so bad for them to be lying about the Museum, I have them stretched out in the workshop all day, some of them occasionally strolling about the Museum."[36] When they were not "lying about" or exhibiting their war dances, tomahawk battles, and other quaint customs on the Lecture Room's stage, Barnum hired them out to compete in boat races—the Indians paddling canoes, of course—as an additional source of income and advertising for the Museum. Two decades later, when a group of chiefs traveled east to visit the "Great White Father" in Washington, Barnum connived with their interpreter to bring them to New York. For several days, under the impression they were "honored guests," they were paraded about the city and led at regular intervals upon the stage of the Museum, where the smiling manager, patting the unsuspecting chief Yellow Bear familiarly on the shoulder, introduced him as "the meanest black-hearted rascal that lives in the West" and as "a lying, thieving, treacherous, murderous monster" who would kill the proprietor in a moment if he understood what was being said about him. In time the chiefs did catch on and angrily made their departure. But not before they had spotted several valuable items, like a suit of antique armor, in the Museum's collections and insisted on having them in exchange for articles of their own clothing.[37]

For all his problems with Indians, however, Barnum was never loath to profit from his patrons' perpetual fascination with them. He sent troupes of redskins to entertain Europeans, and as late as 1888 he was attempting to engage Sitting Bull to travel with his circus.[38] The chief had already appeared before the public with Colonel William F. Cody, who had launched his own peculiar brand of entertainment in 1883. Such was the intuition of Barnum, however, that he had himself foreseen the popularity of the Wild West Show even before the publication of the 1869 edition of his autobiography, in which he prophesies a "sure fortune" for anyone undertaking such an enterprise and writes of having once contemplated getting up such a show of his own. His plan, as he briefly outlines it, was to assemble at least a hundred full-blooded Indians with their squaws and papooses and to send them around the United States and Europe, "the Indians in all the glory of paint and feathers, beads and bright blankets, riding on their ponies, followed by tame buffaloes, elks and antelopes; then an exhibition on a lot large enough to admit of a display of all the Indian games and dances, their method of hunting, their style of cooking, living, etc." When he later fielded his traveling Hippodrome in the mid-1870s, he actually had one such exhibition, which included a fierce battle scene between the Indians and a band of marauding Mexicans.[39] It was left to "Buffalo Bill" and his partners to add the cowboys, troopers, and famous attack on the Deadwood Stage; but may they not have received at least the germ of their idea from Barnum?

Aside from exhibits that can most charitably be termed "ethnographic," there was always a floating population of human abnormalities or freaks to be seen at the American Museum, generally on a platform in one of the saloons, but, in the case of more choice specimens like General Tom Thumb, sometimes on the stage of the Lecture Room, where they might perform in entertainments of their own. The variety and surprising attributes of these oddities can be best appreciated through perusing the newspaper advertisements and bills announcing them: Connecticut's own Jane Campbell, "the largest Mountain of Human Flesh ever seen in the form of a woman," for example, whose juvenile counterpart was "A Mammoth Fat Infant! Only four years old and weighing 220 pounds." There was a formidable assortment of giants and giantesses (their heights nearly always exaggerated, of course), including Barnum's sensational "Nova Scotia Giantess" Anna Swan, who in time married the irascible Captain Martin Bates, another giant, and went off to an Ohio farm in the hope of settling down to a "normal" life. Another giantess, this time from Maine, was Miss Sylvia Hardy, who could easily cradle an infant in the palm of one hand. At the opposite end of the spectrum were Isaac Sprague, the fifty-pound "Living Skeleton," and the "Living Phantom," R. O. Wickware, "whose body is so thin that it is almost transparent, whose limbs, like walking canes, are only about an inch thick, and yet who enjoys a hearty meal, and can wrestle successfully with men of robust constitution and powerful physical development." There was always a pleasing variety of little people—"dwarfs," as Barnum and his contemporaries usually referred to them, but which spectators today, since they were perfectly proportioned, would more likely term "midgets."[40] And what more interesting entertainer could one wish for than the armless wonder S. K. G. Nellis, who played the accordion and the cello with his toes and could also expertly manage a bow and arrow, hitting a quarter held up by any visitor intrepid enough to hazard the experiment?

Equally interesting were those individuals possessing abnormal pigmentation or none at all. The albino family of Rudolph Lucasie—husband, wife, and son, whose marmoreal likenesses are immortalized in a Currier and Ives print— was the best-known example; although at one time Barnum also featured two Negro girls, "Pure White, with White Wool and Pink Eyes," alongside their black mother and baby sister. More startling still were those "leopard-spotted" Negroes whose otherwise dark skins were mottled with areas of perfect whiteness. The result of a harmless depigmentation process known as vitiligo, a more extreme case, in which the skin of a slave had first become spotted, then changed completely to white, had once fascinated Charles Willson Peale, who painted the portrait of James, the "White Negro," and hung it in his Philadelphia museum.[41]

It was a matter of some debate whether the luxuriant hairdos of the several Circassian girls Barnum exhibited were the result of beer. But the pedigree of the most renowned and voluptuous of these beauties—Zalumma Agra, "Star of the East"—was obviously beyond reproach. Supposedly, she had been discovered in Constantinople by John Greenwood Jr., for over twenty years Barnum's assistant manager, confidential agent, and treasurer, who traveled to the Middle East on Museum business in 1864 and 1867 (on the latter trip he was part of the famous *Quaker City* expedition Mark Twain wrote about in *The Innocents Abroad*).[42] From extant correspondence with Greenwood and others, there can be no doubt Barnum was for many years in quest of one or more genuine Circassians, and was prepared to pay as much as four or five thousand dollars in gold for an exceptionally beautiful example—though if bought as slaves, he realized, they would have to be set free or at least given out as being so.[43] Greenwood, who on one occasion donned Turkish costume in order to penetrate the slave market at Constantinople, eventually found the prize in Zalumma Agra, whom he personally exhibited for several years in America and Europe. According to a pamphlet published in 1873, she was the daughter of a prince living along the border of the Black Sea and had fled to Constantinople during a Russian massacre. Presumably she had never been a slave (on this point, as well as her age, the pamphlet is rather vague), although it is hinted she was in imminent danger of becoming one when Greenwood first saw her and somehow got himself appointed her "guardian." Under his tender care and that of the tutors he provided, she had blossomed into a lovely, cultivated woman. Alas, so young was she at the time of the exodus from her native land that her recollections of Circassia were very imperfect, while her knowledge of her mother tongue had been partially, "if not entirely," lost. But she spoke the language of her adopted land, the pamphlet reassuringly continues, with such ease and fluency that it would puzzle the most cunning linguist to discover "she was not a native of America."[44]

Remarkable for her hair as well was Mme Josephine Fortune Clofullia, the celebrated "Swiss Bearded Lady" who appeared at the Museum in the early 1850s. In a repetition of the stratagem that had served so well when he was publicizing Joice Heth in Boston, Barnum orchestrated the charge that she, too, was a "humbug"—a man, in fact, which was indignantly denied by the lady's husband before a large crowd of amused reporters and spectators in a Manhattan courtroom. Any remaining doubts as to her sex were definitively laid to rest a short time later, when she reappeared at the Museum with her "Infant Esau." Less than two years old, he was already "in possession of a Full Beard and Whiskers, while His back, head and limbs are covered with hair in a manner calculated to astonish every beholder." Another artist exhibiting a pleasing hint of sexual ambiguity was Miss Dora Dawron, the "beautiful and accomplished Vocalist." A favorite with Lecture Room audiences in the early sixties, she appeared, flourishing the Stars and Stripes and singing such patriotic songs as "The Flag of Our Union" and "Vive La America," dressed one-half as a man, the other half as a woman. While changing position and shifting between sexes, she then went on to entertain visitors with popular duets, "singing both a deep Tenor and delicate Soprano."

The human phenomena engaged by Barnum were truly legion. First at his museum, later in his circus, often in small independent troupes that he sent on the road, nearly all the famous freaks of his day were at one time or another in his employ. They or their managers wrote to him from all parts of the globe; and he, in turn, seems to have been informed in advance about most of them—sometimes to their chagrin, it may be added, especially when he insisted on verifying some height, weight, or other physical characteristic he had reason to suspect was not exactly as it was represented to be. Aside from the cachet that came from working for him, he had the reputation of being fair in his terms and meticulous in honoring them. When a truly stellar attraction appeared on the horizon, he was prepared to outbid all rival showmen in order to "nail it," but often, so as to keep the price within reasonable bounds, negotiated through a trusted emissary charged with concealing his name until the last possible moment. Another considerable source of income to freaks working for him was a percentage, occasionally all, of the profits arising from the sale of cartes de visite, descriptive pamphlets, tokens, and other souvenirs. The first were supplied in the thousands by Mathew Brady, whose photographic studio was across the street from the Ann Street museum.

Freaks and ethnographic curiosities were by no means the only living hominids to be seen at the American Museum. The halls and saloons were populated by a variety of industrious individuals, for the most part concessionaires, who offered their wares and services at small additional charge. There were Bohemian glassblowers and phrenologists like Professor Livingston, who was advertised to examine his customers and produce correct charts of them in less than ten minutes. A succession of fortune-tellers and clairvoyants with such interchangeable names as "Mlle" or "Mme" DeLang, Dubois, DelMonte, etc. might be consulted in a private office next to the hall of wax figures. In the 1840s this place was occupied by an "eminent petrologist" with the no less intriguing name of Mme Rockwell, "a lady who, by looking into a rock which to common eyes is perfectly opaque, is capable of foretelling events, relating those that are past, describing diseases, revealing mysteries, etc., with the most astonishing accuracy." During the first few years of Barnum's management visitors might purchase multiple silhouettes of themselves made by an individual using an outlining apparatus known as the physiognotrace; in later years daguerreotypists and photographers took over this function. A sewing-machine attachment, invented by a relative and known as "Barnum's Self-Sewer," was demonstrated by two of the showman's nieces. Pet owners who had suffered recent bereavements were encouraged to bring the remains of their dear ones along with them. Upon entering the Museum, they would deposit these with a resident taxidermist, and a few hours later they would retrieve and return home with their pets, freshly mounted and looking as "natural" as ever. In the self-improvement line, Professor Hutchings, the "Lightning Calculator," demonstrated his powers and offered to reveal the secret of his method in a chart he sold for twenty-five cents. Further entertainment might be had in a rifle and pistol gallery in the Museum's basement, while those in need of nourishment could refresh themselves in an oyster saloon. Persons bringing their lunches with them or wishing to partake of the ice cream, doughnuts, or other light fare sold on the premises might regale themselves in what was grandiloquently termed the "aerial garden," consisting of a few small tables and chairs set amid pots of wilted flowers on the Museum's roof.

Finally, there was the Lecture Room—most impressive of all in the eyes of Henry James, who recalled how as a boy he had waited expectantly in the "dusty halls of humbug" for its portals to open so that he might gaze upon his beau ideal, the ranting actress Emily Mestayer, whose "damp-looking short curls," "great play of nostril," and "vast protuberance of bosom" added immeasurably to the entertainment at hand.[45] By Barnum's own admission a "narrow, ill-contrived and uncomfortable" place when he took over the Museum, this feature had been common to all museums since the days of Charles Willson Peale. And originally such rooms had been just that: places in which lectures on natural history and scientific demonstrations were given. As time went on, however, their educational goals were increasingly subverted by less rigorous entertainment—magic-lantern shows, exhibitions of juggling, ventriloquism and legerdemain, dancing and musical numbers, comic skits, etc.— until their programs were barely distinguishable from those of variety halls. From this, once their auditoriums and stage facilities had been suitably improved, it was only a short step to full-scale dramatic entertainments, rivaling or even excelling those of neighboring theatres. But always under the earlier designation of "lecture room" or "hall," thereby ensuring the continuing approbation of spectators who would never dare think of entering a "theatre," but who had no qualms whatever about taking themselves and their families to such entertainments as Barnum and his Boston contemporary, Moses Kimball, presented on their stages.

So much has been made in the past of this subterfuge, of the supposed hypocrisy of Barnum, Kimball, and their fellow museum proprietors, that one tends to overlook the genuine service they rendered to the American stage. In the first half of the nineteenth century theatres were hardly the decorous places to which we are accustomed today. Spectators, particularly those in the upper galleries, were given to demonstrating their disapproval of actors and playwrights in no uncertain terms, often to the detriment of those seated below; drunkenness was rife in the front of the house and, to a somewhat lesser extent, on the other side of the footlights as well; prostitutes openly solicited in corridors and boxes, with a number of the latter commonly set aside for them by calculating managers who, trading on the theatre's reputation as a haunt for dissipation and vice, thereby sought to attract young bloods to their establishments. Unless he were hopelessly addicted to the drama or determined to see some great itinerating "star," a respectable person thought twice about going to the theatre. He thought even harder before exposing his wife or sweetheart to these conditions. Children were almost never taken there.

But all this was gradually to change during the second half of the century, thanks largely to the determined efforts of Barnum and a handful of other managers who felt reform was long overdue. They made theatre into something it had rarely been before: a place of *family* entertainment, where men and women, adults and children, could intermingle safe in the knowledge that no indelicacies would assault their senses either onstage or off, and where all might participate in the same hearty laugh over some innocuous joke by a comic character, weep over the distress of a pretty heroine or become perfectly ecstatic at the final defeat of some blackhearted villain, and perhaps even profit from a cautionary tale. Although Barnum did not himself directly supervise the getting up of these plays—for that department he delegated to a succession of experienced stage managers, including Francis Courtney Wemyss, who had once engaged Barnum and Master Diamond—he was often involved in their selection, writing to solicit plays from well-known authors and arranging for copies and translations of works popular in other countries. In addition to such sterling temperance and abolitionist dramas as *The Drunkard, Ten Nights in a Barroom,* and *Uncle Tom's Cabin* (the last adapted by Henry J. Conway, whose version even Mrs. Stowe had difficulty following), the Lecture Room regularly regaled its audiences with domestic and romantic melodramas, often taken from popular novels and stories of the day, bearing such titles as *The Curate's Daughter; Charlotte Temple; The Old House at Home, or The Trials of a Village Girl; The Sons of the Republic* (set in the days of the French Reign of Terror); *Maremma of Madrid, or The Man, the Spirit and the Mortal; Pale Janet, or The Tragedy at Red Marsh Farm;* and that old standby of innumerable nineteenth-century theatres and circuses, based on Byron's famous poem, *Mazeppa.*

The so-called sensation drama, melodramas that relied on ultrarealistic settings and special effects, was represented by such plays as *The Workmen of New York,* one scene of which was set in an iron foundry with working machinery, and Dion Boucicault's *The Octoroon,* with its burning steamboat at the end of the fourth act. When around 1863 the illusion known as "Pepper's Ghost"— by which spectral figures, often in conjunction with actors who were actually onstage, could be projected onto inclined sheets of invisible glass—was at the height of its popularity, a number of plays were presented that featured this spectacular novelty at climactic moments.[46] Spectacle and fantasy were again frankly in evidence in *The Bower of Beauty, or The Home of the Fairies,* which exhibited forty young "Nymphs of the Air" suspended above the stage in an enchanted forest setting. By the 1860s the proprietor felt sufficiently secure to introduce a *corps de ballet,* whose silk-sheathed limbs were fetchingly revealed in a number of extravaganzas related to the French féerie. There were plays based on biblical subjects—*Moses in Egypt, Joseph and His Brethren,* etc.—and occasional excursions into the "higher" drama. *Macbeth,* performed by the resident company, was hazarded in 1855; and for a time the famous child prodigies the Bateman Sisters, Kate and Ellen, were under Barnum's management and gave their interpretations of Shakespeare at the Museum. Nineteenth-century theatre programs were typically long and varied affairs, and those of the Lecture Room were hardly exceptions. Besides the featured five-act drama or spectacle, there was always some entertainment preceding it or between the acts—a noted violinist, comic singer, or reigning freak, perhaps; at other times Indians performing their dances, "Negro Eccentricities by Master Willie," or Tony Denier in his comic number of the "Great Dancing Giraffe." Equally traditional was the afterpiece, usually a farce or comic burletta, but during one period a Punch and Judy show. On other occasions full-fledged minstrel companies, such as Donaldson's Serenaders or Sanford's Ethiopian Opera Troupe, were engaged.[47]

The actors in these productions were hardly of star caliber, yet many of them gave to the Museum years of yeoman's service. At their head was Corson W. Clarke, for several seasons the company's stage manager or director, who generally played the serious lead roles. Known to his contemporaries as "Drunkard" Clarke, he was acclaimed above all for his portrayal of the dipsomaniacal Edward Middleton, the hero of W. H. Smith's play *The Drunkard*. The English actor Thomas H. Hadaway, who specialized in comic parts, was a favorite with Museum audiences for some fifteen years; and we have Henry James's own word for the prepossessing appearance of Emily Mestayer, who played the part of Madeline Boutard, the "beauty of Brest," in *The Sons of the Republic*, as well as that of Zoe, the distressed heroine who kills herself rather than surrender her honor, in Boucicault's play *The Octoroon*. In his autobiography Barnum points with pride to several other actors who at one time or another appeared briefly on his stage: Mary Gannon, who in the 1840s, before the Lecture Room had expanded into a fully equipped theatre, danced as a child under the sobriquet "la petite Elssler" and who later attained considerable reputation as a comic actress; E. A. Sothern, eventually to become famous as the eccentric Lord Dundreary, a role he himself developed while working at Laura Keene's theatre, in *Our American Cousin;* and the popular Irish comedian Barney Williams. In the scenic and special effects departments the theatre benefited from the talents of artists like George Heilge and Charles Burns, with the latter devising an improvement on "Pepper's Ghost" whereby spectres were not merely projected onto the stage but were seen to move about.

The Lecture Room itself, whose parterre and stage were on a level with the second floor of the Museum, was several times expanded and upgraded from the mid-forties onward, and in 1850, following its most extensive renovation to date, was said to be capable of seating upwards of 3000 people. In an illustrated article published around this time, it was described as "one of the most elegant and recherché halls of its class to be found anywhere . . . fitted up in the most gorgeous style, yet so arranged as not to offend the eye with a multiplicity of ornament."[48] At Barnum's second American Museum farther uptown, the stage measured 50 feet wide by 46 feet deep, and the auditorium seated approximately 2500 spectators.[49] Although admission to the Lecture Room was always included in the price of a ticket to the Museum itself, there were supplementary charges for boxes and the better seats in the parterre and first balcony. Full performances by the dramatic company were given both afternoons and evenings (but never on the Sabbath, naturally); an entertainment following the earlier variety format was presented around 11 A.M. On holidays,

Barnum writes, the performances were continuous—no doubt abbreviated as well, since they were given on an hourly schedule—and the actors, who received extra pay on these occasions, remained in their costumes from eleven in the morning until ten at night.[50]

If he took no active part in the artistic direction of the dramatic company, Barnum nonetheless kept himself informed of the moral state of its members and was ever on the alert for any misconduct or impropriety in the Lecture Room itself. When his first museum burned in 1865, and a supercilious but obviously knowledgeable writer for the *Nation* made this the excuse for some severe reflections on what museums, in contrast to Barnum's chaotic affair, ought to be, the showman was particularly stung by the charge that the Lecture Room had pandered to a degraded class of spectator with "vulgar sensation dramas" and that it had been "many years since a citizen could take his wife or daughter to see a play on that stage." "No vulgar word or gesture, and not a profane expression," he emphasized in his reply, "was *ever* allowed on my stage! Even in Shakespeare's plays, I unflinchingly and invariably cut out vulgarity and profanity." It simply was not true that respectable citizens did not take their wives and daughters to his establishment. "I am sensitive on these points," he added, "because I was always extremely *squeamish* in my determination to allow nothing objectionable on my stage." He went on to point out that no intoxicating liquors were permitted anywhere in the Museum:

> I would not even allow my visitors to "go out to drink" and return again without paying the second time, and this reconciled them to the "ice-water" which was always profuse and free on each floor of the Museum. I could not personally or by proxy examine into the character of every visitor, but I continually had half a score of detectives dressed in plain clothes, who incontinently turned into the street every person of either sex whose actions indicated loose habits. My interest ever depended upon my keeping a good reputation for my Museum, and I did it to a greater degree than one out of ten could attain who had charge of a free museum, or even a free picture gallery.[51]

The showman had no reason to fear for the Museum's reputation, however; nor did he really need to defend it. The charge by the *Nation*'s carping writer that the American Museum had been "largely monopolized" by a "vicious and degraded" class of spectator was patently ridiculous—a libel on the great American public, in fact. From Barnum's acquisition of the Museum at the end of 1841 until its destruction by fire twenty-three and a half years later, nearly 38 million admission tickets were sold; close to 4 million additional tickets were dispensed at his second museum uptown during the two and a half years it was in existence.[52] Many of these were bought by repeat customers, of course; but the record is nevertheless remarkable, especially when one considers that the total population of the United States in 1865 was only around 35 million. As an illustration of the tremendous popularity of Barnum's museums, a comparison may be made with the original Disneyland, which sold its 250 millionth ticket on 24 August 1985, a few months after the park's thirtieth anniversary. If one averages out the Disneyland figures and assumes around 196 million tickets were sold during its first twenty-three and a half years of operation, then a simple calculation—taking into account the fact that the total U.S. population at the beginning of 1979 was approximately 224 million or 6.4 times that in 1865—reveals that the first American Museum, during its years under Barnum's management, actually sold more tickets in proportion to the population than did Disneyland.

Nor did the American Museum ever cater to any particular "class" of spectator. In his reply to the *Nation*, Barnum claimed, rather unconvincingly, that he had "often grieved that the taste of the million was not elevated." With no financial support for his museum other than what he took in at the door, he had been "obliged to popularize it," and while he had indeed offered his visitors a "million" bona fide curiosities, "millions of persons were *only* induced to see them because, at the same time, they could see whales, giants, dwarfs, Albinoes, dog shows, *et cetera.*" It was all an undigested hodgepodge, of course, and in later years the showman was sometimes apologetic about the Museum's lack of system and some of the methods he had employed to lure its patrons. Yet among these same patrons, it must be noted, rubbing elbows with farmers fresh in from the countryside, tradesmen, apprentices and laborers, and "respectable" citizens with their families in tow, were famous scientists like Louis Agassiz and Joseph Henry of the Smithsonian Institution, authors like Walt Whitman and Henry David Thoreau, eminent statesmen, religious leaders, and ambassadors from abroad, and even, in 1860, the visiting Prince of Wales. In an age when public-supported cultural institutions were still the exception rather than the general rule, Barnum's museum filled a definite need in American society and, if it did not always strive to elevate their taste, at least offered its visitors wholesome entertainment. From sunrise until 10 P.M., seven days a week, its untold wonders summoned the democratic multitude. It was one of the greatest, most universally popular institutions of its day. And all this—museum, menagerie, lecture room, and freaks—for the even then bargain price of twenty-five cents![53]

———◆———

BARNUM'S FIRST American Museum burned to the ground on 13 July 1865, while its proprietor was addressing the Connecticut legislature. Unruffled, the showman immediately set to work to assemble a new collection and less than two months later opened his second American Museum farther up Broadway, between Spring and Prince streets, in a building that had once been occupied by the Chinese Museum.[54] For a time, feeling philanthropic—for he had sold the remaining twelve years of his lease on the Ann Street property to James Gordon Bennett for the inflated sum of $200,000—he talked loudly of erecting a *free* museum. He busily solicited endorsements of the project from prominent individuals, including a somewhat reluctant President Andrew Johnson, urging the great benefit he intended to confer on the nation, as well as his demonstrated ability to outshine anything the capital's puny Smithsonian Institution might have to offer. It was to be a perpetual gift to the nation, he solemnly announced, an expression of his gratitude to the "Youth of America" who had helped make him rich, and proof positive that its donor, for all his well-known reputation for humbug, was hardly so bad as he was often made out to be. But some taint of "humbug" in the scheme there certainly was, for next to the free museum, as Barnum confided to his friends, would be his *paying* museum, whose patrons would be entitled to visit the establishment next door during days and hours when those wishing to see only the free museum were excluded from it.[55] After toying with this idea for several months, his enthusiasm for it began to wane; and when his second American Museum burned during the night of 2–3 March 1868, he decided to take his friend Horace Greeley's advice to "go a-fishing" and "retired" from museum management. On 20 May, in a "card" addressed to the public, he announced that he had disposed of his establishment's goodwill to the manager George Wood, who ran a museum of his own— complete with aquarium, a "Happy Family," and a lecture room that was finally acknowledged to be a theatre—at the corner of Broadway and 30th Street. "So far as I shall ever put forth any effort again to obtain curiosities, or shall make suggestions in reference thereto, I shall bestow all upon Wood's Museum," Barnum wrote, adding that he anticipated many happy hours consulting with Wood, whose museum he hoped to "make an agreeable and frequent halting place."[56] In return for his endorsement and expert advice, Wood allowed him 3 percent of the museum's gross receipts.[57]

But he could never keep away long from a more active participation in the business; and besides planning the museum departments that were always a prominent feature of his itinerating shows from 1871 onward, in November 1876 he entered into an equal co-partnership with George B. Bunnell, who ran a large traveling museum and menagerie under canvas and occupied a permanent building in lower Manhattan. Their agreement stipulated that Barnum's name was not to be divulged or used in the enterprise—by then he was well launched on his circus career and his partners in that area were loudly insisting on their right to the exclusive use of his name—although Bunnell did bill his establishment as the "New American Museum" and himself as the "legitimate successor of the great Barnum."[58] When around this same time, unhappily, a writer for the *New York Tribune* complained of recently opened museums in the city that were "only a cloak for 'ways that are dark and tricks that are vain,'" the showman, convinced this was meant as an indirect attack on Bunnell, wrote to the paper's proprietor, Whitelaw Reid, to complain. Reid obligingly published Barnum's defense of the "thoroughly moral & upright" Bunnell and his museum in his 2 December issue, and Barnum reciprocated, as he had privately promised, by seeing that the museum advertised in the *Tribune*.[59]

Then, in what was surely one of his most grandiose schemes ever, he announced his intention to build a new museum in New York on the site of the old Madison Square Garden. In conjunction with William H. Vanderbilt, Henry Cummins, and other prominent businessmen, he had formed a stock corporation entitled "Barnum's Museum Company," whose prospectus, offering 30,000 shares at $100 each, was circulated in early summer of 1880.[60] Scheduled for completion early in the following year, the new "Barnum's Museum" was to be of brick, stone, and iron (and therefore *"thoroughly fire-proof"*), occupy an area measuring 200 by 425 feet, and contain, on its five floors, nearly eleven acres of space. The sunken lower level was to be given over to the "Colosseum," a vast arena suitable for "chariot and hurdle races, walking matches, athletic games, steeple chases, trotting matches, fairs, public balls, large political and religious meetings, military drills, the hippodrome, etc., etc." On the first floor would be "Barnum's Opera House," whose appointments and seating capacity were to exceed those of any other theatre in New York; a smaller theatre or "lecture room," designed for musical, dramatic, and other entertainments such as had been given at his earlier museums; a third, medium-sized auditorium, "Barnum's Museum Hall," devoted to genuine lectures, readings, and select musical entertainments; an aquarium and menagerie; besides shops, offices, and a skating rink. The second and third stories were to contain the museum proper, as well as "what might properly be denominated 'side shows,' or exhibitions of a minor character, such as Punch and Judy, the Marionettes, Chinese Jugglers, Giants, Dwarfs, Fat Women, Glass Blowers, etc., etc." And on the fourth floor, beneath a movable roof, was to be the crowning novelty of the establishment: a great garden with "walks, lawns, bowers, grottoes, arbors, water-falls, palmeries, fountains, parterres, etc., and adorned with the rarest trees, plants, flowers, vines and shrubbery of every zone . . . forming one immense conservatory, dwarfing in its extent and magnificence the most celebrated palatial gardens of the Orient." In this verdant setting grand concerts would be given every afternoon and evening; its elevation above surrounding buildings would make it "the coolest and most delightful summer resort to be found in any large city in the world"; while in winter "its attractions will be heightened and increased by the contrast produced."

The prospectus glowingly goes on to describe the 250-foot-high tower or "observatory," situated at one of the building's corners and encircled by a battery of electric lights sufficiently powerful to be seen for miles, that was to afford visitors an uninterrupted view of the city below. First-class restaurants, elevators, and numerous waiting rooms and lavatories would further minister to the comfort of the museum's patrons, whose numbers, of course, would be simply immense. A permanent annual dividend of 20 to 25 percent was confidently predicted by the company's directors; in a statement of his own published in the prospectus Barnum rapturously estimated the return might run as high as 33 percent. With the experienced showman himself serving as general manager, could there be any reasonable doubt of such phenomenal success?[61]

It was all envisioned as a recapitulation of his earlier career, from the lecture room and fat women to the "aerial garden" above, only now on a permanent, truly colossal scale—"a fitting monument," as the prospectus unabashedly proclaimed, "to his own genius and fame." Even the lights around the "observatory" had been anticipated at his old Ann Street museum, on whose roof he had boldly installed, as an advertising gimmick, powerful Drummond lights; while the great arena projected for the ground-floor level was a repetition of his more recent circus and Roman Hippodrome experiences. In the end, however, this Neronian plan fizzled out, ostensibly because, as Barnum obliquely relates the incident in his *Funny Stories*, he discovered that the person responsible for raising subscriptions for the museum had cheated him out of the price of a $1.50 theatre ticket! Fearing that the agent would be equally dishonest in handling larger sums of money (a conviction that was borne out by the scamp's subsequent history, he writes), he "quickly went to work to break up the whole enterprise" and prevailed on other subscribers, with the "utmost difficulty," to abandon the scheme.[62] More likely, the initial subscription goal of two million dollars had not been achieved. Then, too, in the summer of 1880 Barnum had become acquainted with his young rival in circus management, James A. Bailey, whose retiring manner, yet sure flair for showmanship, immediately captivated him. Within a few weeks they had entered into the first of their several agreements. Thereafter, in whatever major enterprise in the show line Barnum might become involved, the energetic, ruthlessly efficient Bailey was his partner of choice.

They had barely commenced their relationship in earnest when, in the spring of 1882, plans were again announced for a museum in New York City—this time not a stock corporation, however, but a privately owned establishment to be financed by Barnum, Bailey, and their associate James L. Hutchinson. On hearing the glad tidings, Spencer Baird, who had succeeded Joseph Henry as Secretary of the Smithsonian Institution, offered to place the naval vessels under his charge at Barnum's disposal for stocking the museum's aquarium. "I can promise almost anything that is to be found in the North Atlantic," he wrote.[63] In the same year, interestingly, Barnum nearly stole a march on the Smithsonian's National Zoo, again with Baird's active support and encouragement. As early as 1870 Congress had authorized the creation of the Washington Zoological Society, of which Baird was one of the officers and incorporators. With money raised through the sale of its stock, the Society soon afterward purchased fifty-six acres of land in the city's northeast corner, but the project then languished for want of firm direction. Barnum now offered to take it in hand, provided he could get the Congressional charter transferred to himself and would not have to purchase the land already owned by the Society. He was prepared to buy up nearly all the stock, he wrote to Baird, and to ask Congress for a grant of land near the Smithsonian: around thirty acres of that then being reclaimed from the Potomac would be suitable, he thought. If he were to go ahead with these plans, he would see to it that the nation's capital had a zoological garden "that will greatly benefit the city whether it pays me or not—and I don't care much about that point." There would be "very unique & valuable" animals imported from Europe, and even the great Jumbo himself, when not wanted in his circus, would put in an occasional appearance![64]

Yet these plans, also, were never realized; and when Bailey, after becoming his equal partner in 1887, suddenly waxed enthusiastic over the prospect of their establishing a chain of museums in New York and other cities, the old showman urged restraint and uncharacteristically hung back.[65] It was not that he had become timorous or lacked the experience for so extensive a scheme. He had previously experimented, successfully enough, with museums in other cities while running the American Museum. In Baltimore, as early as 1845, he had acquired another museum once belonging to the Peale family and had installed his uncle Alanson as its manager. From 1849 to 1851 he had been proprietor of a museum on Philadelphia's Chestnut Street; a museum and lecture room had also been part of the Aquarial Gardens he ran in Boston during the early 1860s. Only now, as the century drew to its close, he had sense enough to realize that proprietary museums of the type he had owned had nearly run their course. The great public institutions were at last coming into their own, and they were infinitely better organized, more specialized and "scientific," than his old museums had ever been. If these successors were not half so entertaining—if they contained no fat ladies, wooden nutmegs, or Fejee Mermaids—why, such "curiosities" could still be accommodated in the museum or "sideshow" department of a traveling circus.

He therefore increasingly lent his support to the newer institutions, including the burgeoning Smithsonian, whose potential for greatness he had once belittled, and the American Museum of Natural History in New York City. When his own plans to establish a museum in New York fell through in 1882, he almost immediately committed himself to building and stocking the Barnum Museum of Natural History at Tufts College—an act of benevolence that finally made good on his promise of a *free* museum, since its varied displays of mounted hides and skeletons, models, invertebrates and geologic specimens, and all the other wonders he arranged to have sent to it were open to the public. One of the final acts of his life was the creation of the Barnum Institute of Science and History, originally a home for local Bridgeport and Fairfield County medical, scientific, and historical societies—and for museums maintained by these organizations, naturally. For all his reputation today as a "circus man," Barnum was always first and foremost a "museum man." When his great traveling show initially took to the road in 1871, its title, with no lack of deliberation, was "P. T. Barnum's Museum, Menagerie, and Circus."

VI

Of Mermaids and the Man in Miniature

The great secret of success in anything is to get a hearing. Half the object is gained when the audience is assembled.
The Humbugs of the World

"I CONFESS that I liked the Museum mainly for the opportunities it afforded for rapidly making money," Barnum acknowledged in his autobiography; and in truth the American Museum was not only the "ladder" by which he rose to fortune but the springboard to all his successes in the entertainment and business worlds. In the first year alone of his management, its receipts nearly trebled, to $28,000, over what they had been the preceding year. When he was readying the first edition of the autobiography for press, he was able to report they had been slightly over $136,000 in 1853; toward the end of the Museum's career they often amounted to around $300,000 per year.[1] Initially, however, hard work and stringent domestic economy were the order of the day, since, in addition to his indebtedness to Olmsted for the value of the collections, he had agreed to lease the building itself for $3000 per annum and was responsible for its staffing and daily maintenance. After estimating he and his family would need $600 per year for their expenses, he was delighted when Charity, his "treasure of a wife," announced she could make ends meet on as little as $400. Olmsted, too, was ecstatic when, upon paying a call at the Museum a few months after Barnum had taken it over, he discovered the proprietor in his office frugally lunching on cold corned beef. "I have not eaten a warm dinner since I bought the Museum, except on the Sabbath," Barnum proudly informed him, "and I intend never to eat another on a week-day until I am out of debt."[2]

All receipts not going to pay expenses and retire his debt to Olmsted were religiously plowed back into the Museum, especially into advertising its attractions, during his first year of management. Indeed, in this and succeeding years Barnum was constantly busy thinking up new ways to publicize the Museum. "It was the world's way then, as it is now," he wrote, to excite the community with flaming posters, promising almost everything for next to nothing. I confess that I took no pains to set my enterprising fellow-citizens a better example. I fell in with the world's way; and if my "puffing" was more persistent, my advertising more audacious, my posters more glaring, my pictures more exaggerated, my flags more patriotic and my transparencies more brilliant than they would have been under the management of my neighbors, it was not because I had less scruple than they, but more energy, far more ingenuity, and a better foundation for such promises.[3]

Literally overnight the drab, unprepossessing exterior of the Museum underwent a dazzling transformation when the proprietor, who had ordered in advance oval oil paintings of "nearly every important animal known in zoology," had these installed between the windows on the upper stories. This stratagem alone, he reports with some exaggeration, immediately led to an increase in receipts of close to a hundred dollars a day, "and they never fell back again."[4] The flags of various nations—always with Old Glory preeminent, of course— fluttered gaily from the parapet and balconies, adding their color to the spectacle. At night powerful Drummond lights installed on the roof, the first example of limelight used for outdoor advertising in this country, raked the upper and lower reaches of Broadway, further drawing attention to the establishment. There were huge banners and illuminated transparencies, such as he had previously used for Joice Heth, to publicize specific attractions; and besides the perfect deluge of advertisements, puffs, and "genuine" news items in the daily press, the showman took care to furnish his patrons with plenty of free illustrated bills and lithographs, reasoning that these, carried back "to the country," would also help broadcast the fame of the American Museum.

No matter how outlandish or annoying to his neighbors it proved, he was willing to try any scheme that might bring "notoriety" to the Museum and himself. On one occasion he employed an out-of-work laborer to march from corner to corner around the intersection out front, solemnly laying down and exchanging bricks at designated points. He was instructed to pretend to be deaf and to pay no attention to those who might gather to watch him, and to enter the Museum at the end of each hour and walk through its halls. Invariably, a dozen or more curious individuals would purchase tickets to follow him inside, and the bizarre spectacle was continued for several days until the police complained that the crowds it attracted were blocking the sidewalks. Again, for years he had a band of musicians on the lower balcony facing St. Paul's Church directly across Broadway. Its members, however, were always the worst Barnum could find, so that their "Free Music for the Million" might drive passersby *into* the Museum. When their cacophony was finally silenced by the fire in 1865, George Templeton Strong, like many another New Yorker, breathed a great sigh of relief: "The horrible little brass band that was always tooting in its balcony must have produced or aggravated many cases of nervous disease, for it tormented all passengers at the very junction of our two most crowded downtown thoroughfares. May the sins of those six cruel artists be forgiven them. May they henceforth play less hideously false, and may they all find remunerative engagements in some situation where people will not be forced to hear them notwithstanding all they can do."[5] When two vestrymen from St. Paul's objected to Barnum's unauthorized use of a tree in the churchyard to string up a line of flags during the 1842 Independence Day celebration, the showman argued that he always ordered his band to cease playing during church services and that it was only fair they should "return the favor." Failing to persuade the indignant churchmen, he staged a patriotic confrontation in the middle of Broadway, rolling up his sleeves, loudly daring them to take down the American flag on the Fourth of July, and suggesting they must be "Britishers." The crowd that had gathered took up the cry, and the vestrymen beat a strategic retreat. Thereafter, Barnum had free use of the tree on all national holidays.

From time to time, especially in the fifties, the Museum was host to various contests. Certificates and cash awards were presented to the winners of dog, flower, and poultry shows ("Gods! What a crowing!" Barnum wrote to a friend in the midst of one of the last); and in 1855 there was even a "beauty pageant" of sorts, whose anonymous contestants, however, were exhibited only in their photographic likenesses, with each visitor to the Museum given the opportunity to vote for his particular favorites. No portraits were acceptable from "disreputable persons," naturally.[6] Most successful of all were the "baby shows," which Barnum first got up in June of 1855 and later repeated in Boston, Philadelphia, and other cities. Prizes were awarded in such categories as the "Finest Baby," the "Fattest Baby," and for the best sets of certifiable twins, triplets, and quadruplets. Some of the winners, like the "Fattest Child in the World," were then exhibited in the Museum for a few additional days, advertised in the same bills as Barnum's giants, fat ladies, and other freaks. Although these contests were always judged by committees of women, the manager quickly discovered even this could not preserve him from the fury of disappointed parents. After the first "show" ended on a tumultuous note, he took the further precaution of announcing the winners in writing rather than in person. Rumor had it, too, that at the end of this particular contest a number of enraged mothers had flounced out of the Museum taking the wrong children home with them.[7]

A "contest" of another sort—in the proven Signor Vivalla–Master Diamond tradition—was the one Barnum got up with Peale's New York Museum. After trying to compete with Barnum's establishment for several months, its final manager, Henry Bennett, had been forced to close his doors around the beginning of 1843. Barnum secretly purchased the collections of the failed company for $7000, then hired Bennett to reopen and continue running Peale's, the two "rivals" fearfully abusing each other in the press, of course, and generating even more publicity for the American Museum. When the novelty of this ruse finally wore thin, the new acquisitions were transported to Ann Street. Among them was Peale's celebrated "Gallery of American Portraits," most, if not all, of which were probably by members of the Peale family. Together with Indian scenes by Catlin and other paintings Barnum later bought, they all seem to have perished in the 1865 fire.[8]

———◆———

AS BARNUM joyfully recalled his Museum period in his autobiography, it was an unbroken campaign of masterful stratagems, of stunning victories over out-flanked rivals and anyone else who dared oppose him. Over the gullible public too, of course, which soon came to accept him at his own valuation as "Prince of Humbugs." His letters from the same period do not contradict the picture he paints, although they do throw considerable light on his day-to-day concerns and the minor frustrations that often beset him. Chief among his correspondents in the early forties was Moses Kimball, the proprietor of the Boston Museum, who was almost the same age as Barnum and whose chequered career also included stints as a merchant and newspaper publisher. Like Barnum, too, he was to prosper and become "respectable," enter politics and serve as a member of his state's legislature, and engage in various civic and charitable enterprises.[9] Beginning in 1839 he had operated museums in Boston and Lowell, then, in June of 1841, in partnership with his brother David, had opened the Boston Museum, which was almost an exact parallel of Barnum's establishment. This was hardly remarkable, since the two managers often engaged in joint speculations, exchanged performers and exhibits, plays and even scenery, and continually ran errands and did favors for each other. It was a highly profitable relationship, one that had the further advantage of being based on sincere friendship, with the two often sounding out each other on various schemes, comparing notes on receipts and employees, sympathizing with each other when things were not going well, and lustily crowing whenever they did.[10]

Did Kimball, for instance, want a "pretty good sized *bald eagle skin?*" Barnum had just bought two of the birds, shot on Long island. He had finally arranged terms for Kimball with the manager of the juvenile dancer Celeste Williams, who would be in Boston the following Monday. "You can hail her from the National, Opera House, Park, & Mitchell's Olympic, New York, and late of the American Museum, where she has danced to admiring crowds for *three hundred and seventy-one successive nights*! . . .The *puffing* you know she will *bear well.*" He thanked his Boston friend for his perseverance in negotiating for the dog-powered knitting machine, but was not willing to go as high as fifty dollars per month, "especially as there appears to be so much more *poetry* than *reality* about it." After arranging with Kimball for another exchange, he was "grieved, vexed, and disappointed to hear of the sickness and *death* (for I know she will die) of the ourang outang. Damn the luck! I have puffed her high & dry, got a large transparency and a flag 10 by 16 feet painted for her, besides newspaper cut engraved, &c.—and now, curse her, she must up foot and die." Kimball could forget about the small pony he had once wanted to draw Tom Thumb's carriage. Probably it would be no better than the goat he was using, which "*shits* so I can do nothing with him." One of his assistants was about to leave for Baltimore "to get those dirty, lazy, and *lousy* Gipseys. I expect they are too *damned* low for me to do anything with them. However, I *must try*, for if I don't do better than at present, I am sure to bust." "What about the albino lady?"[11]

While putting up with the lazy set of Indians who wanted to be lying about the Museum all day, he nevertheless managed to make additional money out of them by repeating a scheme he had first hit upon in the summer of 1843. Having purchased a herd of scrawny calf buffaloes and hired their former owner "Mr. C. D. French" (whose real name was Fitzhugh) to look after them, he had anonymously advertised a "Grand Buffalo Hunt, Free of Charge," to take place across the river in Hoboken at the end of August. Unfortunately, the promised *"wild sports of the Western Prairies"* proved anything but wild, for when the "daring and experienced hunter" French, who was supposed to pursue and lasso the beasts, appeared on horseback in his Indian costume, the cowering animals refused to move, then, panicked by the laughter and hooting of the crowd, broke through a barrier and ran off into a swamp. The gleeful New Yorkers returned home in high humor, even giving three cheers for the undisclosed author of this humbug. After all, the day's outing had cost them nothing, hadn't it? But of course Barnum had managed to profit all the same, in part through leasing the refreshment privileges, but principally through an arrangement with the ferry company, whereby he was entitled to one-half the day's receipts. The "hunt" was later repeated at Camden, New Jersey, with spectators now being ferried over from Philadelphia. The buffaloes, which had cost $700, were eventually traded or sold.[12]

Barnum soon had his Indians competing in boat races, *"free to all,"* off the same two towns. Before sending them on to Kimball at the end of September, he also made plans for them to race off Chelsea, requesting his friend to sound out the local ferry company on the matter of terms. But he did not, he emphasized, wish to tread on Kimball's toes and was perfectly willing to arrange things so that he, too, might profit from this speculation. "They can increase your receipts a few nights, and on the day of the race they could fill your room *that* night to overflowing, as it *fills* the people with enthusiasm to see the Indians beat their opponents, as they will at the boat race."[13] When the redskins finally departed for Boston, Barnum wrote to advise Kimball to treat their interpreter, the half-breed Cadotte, "like a *man*" and to let him have his own way about giving the troupe whiskey. Kimball apparently did just that. "Damn the Indians," Barnum wrote a few days later. "I fear you give them *too much* whiskey."[14]

Earlier in the same year Kimball had sent Barnum a notorious performer from his own establishment. Miss Mills was a magician who had previously appeared at the American Museum, but whose personal life had taken a fateful turn. After robbing her father and running off with a lover, she had been abandoned by the latter and committed to the Worcester, Massachusetts, insane asylum. Rehabilitated, she had found Kimball willing to take her back, although he does seem to have overcharged her for some apparatus he ordered made for her act. When she arrived in New York and complained to Barnum about this, the showman, forced to concede most of the equipment was really "shabby," relayed the unwelcome news to her benefactor, who thereafter customarily referred to her as "the bitch." His outraged feelings did not prevent him from entering with Barnum into an agreement to engage Mills for a year, however, at the rate of six dollars per week plus her board and traveling expenses. "She thought this was *little enough*," Barnum wrote Kimball, "and it certainly strikes me *that it is*."[15]

The plan in New York was to bill her as "Miss Mary Darling," an English artist who was distantly related, "if at all," to the celebrated heroine Grace Darling, and as just arrived from abroad (where her fame and beauty had "enchanted" the crowned heads of Europe, naturally). To this end Barnum set going the usual press campaign, adding to the mystification by claiming she had once been the pupil of the great "Herr Defrong," while eagerly waiting for her ship to "arrive."[16] Unfortunately, on the very eve of the "Darling's" debut a reporter for the *New York Sunday Times* exposed the scheme, sending Barnum, who suspected a number of his own employees of leaking the tale, into a fury. The paper's owners, in return for a *"large quid pro quo,"* soon appeared on the Museum's doorstep, apologizing and promising to behave better in the future. But the reporter himself, a "brute" named Snelling, attempted to keep up the attack in the *Evening Herald*, another paper whose proprietors expected something in return for suppressing unfavorable news items. "I wrote them that it was of no use, that they could not get a farthing out of me *directly* or *indirectly*," Barnum wrote to Kimball, "and if they published a word disrespectfully of me, my museum, or anyone employed therein, I would sue the whole concern." The threat proved effective, convincing him that in future he should "take that ground and carry it through." He was to act on this resolve a few days later, when Snelling and the owners of the *Sunday Times* tried to blackmail him for another $50. This time he had them all thrown into the Tombs, where the reporter himself languished for lack of bail.[17] All this by the same Barnum who, imperturable in public, at least, was fond of remarking he was "like the man who would rather be kicked than not noticed at all."

But there was money to be made out of "Miss Darling" all the same. With her true history revealed, she became even more attractive in the eyes of those who hoped she was "not quite a saint," although Barnum himself professed to regard her as one—"a vestal, in fact"—and repeatedly defended her against Kimball. She was no "bitch," he assured his colleague: "I have seen nothing like it & *hope* I shall not." Was it not a true act of charity, even if a profitable one, to give her honest employment rather than to see her turned into the streets? If she was really so bad as Kimball, who was still smarting over her complaint about the apparatus, made her out to be, "how comes it that *you* recommended her so strongly to *me* as the very pattern of modesty, repentance, and industry?" When Kimball, chafing under these incessant lectures, suggested Barnum's interest had become more than professional, the showman peremptorily pulled him up. "I have *not* 'taken an *especial* fancy in that quarter' and *only as a matter of business* consider her or wish you to consider her as anything particularly *extra*."[18] Even in his most personal correspondence, he was generally circumspect in his remarks about women. Nor, to his credit, did he patronize them or any of his other employees, including the many freaks who worked for him. An honest worker deserved and received his honest respect, regardless of sex or other considerations.

From Kimball, too, came his most famous "humbug"—the one with which, above all others, the American Museum and Barnum were to be ever afterward identified. The Fejee Mermaid is another example of Barnum's ability to take a mildly interesting object that had been around for some time and to puff it almost overnight into an earthshaking "event." Moreover, the present object was hardly unique, for mermaids are fairly common creatures, of course. They had frequently been exhibited at taverns, coffee houses, and fairs in England from the eighteenth century on; they were often displayed in European museums, particularly Dutch ones, which acquired many of their treasures from the Orient; Peale's New York Museum had one in the 1830s, and the Philadelphia establishment ran one in competition with Barnum's in the 1840s; even today, if one knows where to look, they may be found in many otherwise reputable museums, usually discreetly hidden away. The Fejee lady herself is believed by some to reside currently in Harvard's Peabody Museum of Archaeology and Ethnology, where she shares a locked storage cabinet with a companion mermaid.[19]

To those privileged to gaze upon such sights today—nearly always the head and torso of some little monkey sewn to the body of a fish—they are a source of profound wonder. Wonder over the people who paid to see such things, and even more over the fools who professed to believe in them. But perhaps this opinion is unduly harsh. Perhaps it was the sense of expectation worked up by a master showman of Barnum's caliber, the natural curiosity to view what everyone was talking about, the desire to examine and decide for oneself— despite the feeling that one would almost certainly be cheated—that drew these crowds more than anything else. And having been relieved of their quarters and ushered into the absurd presence, perhaps even then refusing to admit to others what they knew to be true, in the time-honored tradition of sublimating one's own sense of outrage into the innocent delight that comes from seeing one's friends and neighbors humbugged as well. Perhaps.[20]

As Barnum recounts the story in his autobiography, Kimball first showed him the Mermaid in early summer of 1842.[21] It had once belonged to a Boston sea captain, who had been captivated by it on a voyage to Calcutta in 1817 and who had misappropriated $6000 of his ship's money to purchase it, in the certain belief it would be the making of his fortune. In this he was cruelly disappointed, however; and after exhibiting the Mermaid for a time in Europe, he had returned to his old job to pay back the money he had embezzled, leaving no property other than the Mermaid at the time of his death. Kimball had recently purchased it for a low figure from the captain's son, and the question now was, what to do with it? Barnum was immediately intrigued by the possibilities, and the matter was deemed of sufficient promise for the two men to enter into a written agreement, which they signed on 18 June. From this it appears Barnum already had a good idea of the course he would follow, for the name of Levi Lyman—he who had assisted the manager so expertly in the

Joice Heth affair—is specifically mentioned therein. The terms were for Barnum to "hire" the Mermaid, at the rate of $12.50 per week, for a period of four, eight, or twelve weeks at most; to exert himself "to the utmost" to make it into a "highly popular and profitable exhibition"; and to take all proper care to protect it from handling and abuse. At the end of this period Kimball was to have the opportunity to exhibit it for up to twelve weeks in Boston and Lowell, following which, depending on how attractive the Mermaid had proved in the meantime, the managers agreed to share expenses and profits for up to two years while exhibiting it throughout the United States. The person hired to travel with the Mermaid—"Levi Lyman or some other equally capable person" to be determined by Kimball—was to have his salary and expenses paid by both parties and perhaps be entitled to a share of the profits.[22]

Shortly after this agreement had been signed, New York newspapers, including James Gordon Bennett's *Herald*, began receiving interesting communications from obliging correspondents in various parts of the country. Dated and mailed from cities as distant as Montgomery, Alabama, containing local news of crops, commerce, politics, etc., they ran to some length and certainly had the appearance of being genuine. Editors were happy to publish them. Also mentioned in these letters, almost nonchalantly, was a certain "Dr. Griffin," agent for the "Lyceum of Natural History" in London, who was passing through America on his way home to England. As might be expected, he had secured many items of great interest while on his travels; among them was a "veritable mermaid" captured off the Fejee (Fiji) Islands. As the days and weeks went on, and the aptly named "Dr. Griffin" continued his relentless progress toward New York, there was further news of this remarkable curiosity. A correspondent writing from Washington urged New York editors to have a look at it. When "Dr. Griffin" reached Philadelphia, the editors there were given the opportunity to do just that. Feeling highly pleased with his hotel accommodations, the doctor had graciously decided to grant his landlord a peep at the treasure he was carrying. The landlord was so impressed that he begged to be allowed to bring several friends and editors to see it also. Always the perfect gentleman, "Dr. Griffin" could hardly refuse. By the time the good doctor arrived in Gotham—whose reporters, naturally enough, also begged to have a look at the Mermaid—the trap was almost ready to be sprung. "Dr. Griffin" was Levi Lyman, of course.

Meanwhile, Barnum himself, who had *hoped* to be able to exhibit the Mermaid at his museum, was making the rounds of newspaper offices with a tale of woe. In anticipation of what he had expected to be a profitable attraction, he had commissioned an engraving and prepared a written description. But the punctilious "Dr. Griffin" had informed him that, as agent for the "Lyceum of Natural History," he could not possibly comply with Barnum's request to exhibit the Mermaid. The engraving and description were of no use to him, therefore, so he thought he might as well offer them, gratis, to the press. Three editors, James Gordon Bennett among them, fell for the ruse, each thinking he was getting an "exclusive." They learned otherwise on 17 July, when all three published the cuts and description on the same day. There were, in fact, at least four cuts in all (three of them bearing no resemblance whatever to the Fejee Mermaid), and Barnum now rushed the 10,000 copies of the pamphlet he had ordered printed onto the streets, where they were sold at half their actual cost. With excitement to see the Mermaid now at fever pitch, how could "Dr. Griffin" not give in? After repeated solicitations from "scientific gentlemen," he finally consented to exhibit the Mermaid and his other specimens for one week only, beginning 8 August, at Concert Hall.

What paying spectators were at last permitted to see, however, was hardly the seductive bare-breasted creature depicted so winningly on the eight-foot-long transparency outside the hall. Rather, as Barnum himself describes the Mermaid, they saw an "ugly, dried-up, black-looking" specimen "about three feet long," fabricated from a fish and the upper part of a monkey that looked as though it had "died in great agony." A few spectators, he admits, were "slightly surprised." And on one occasion a group of irreverent medical students, while Lyman was out of the room a few minutes, raised the glass bell protecting the Mermaid and stuck a partially consumed cigar into its mouth. Lyman did not notice this sacrilege upon his return and had launched into his usual learned discourse on mermaid lore for the edification of a new group of visitors, when one of them interrupted him and blandly inquired whether her ladyship was "smoking the same cigar when she was captured that she is enjoying at present?" It was probably the only time in his life that Lyman was ever at a complete loss for words, Barnum thought.

When the week at Concert Hall was up, the Mermaid was finally exhibited at the American Museum, whose receipts immediately shot up to three times their previous level. It was afterwards taken around the country, Barnum merely mentions, before being returned to her rightful owner at the Boston Museum. There is evidence in his private correspondence with Kimball, however, that the lady ran into considerably rough seas on this later voyage. After the two showmen had finished with her at their museums, she was taken on tour not by "slow, moping, lazyboned" Lyman, but by Barnum's erudite uncle, Alanson Taylor. Upon the expedition's reaching Charleston, South Carolina, in early 1843, a local naturalist, the Lutheran minister John Bachman, two of whose daughters married the sons of John James Audubon, kicked up such a ruckus that the "bubble" finally burst and poor Uncle Alanson, who had earlier conned the Charleston city fathers into returning to him a licensing fee, was subjected to "*everything* that a mortal could stand." To spare the Mermaid's being made into "mince meat," it was secretly shipped back to New York, where Barnum stowed it away in a box on the top shelf in his office. Some of the "damned skunks" at the Museum noticed it there and tattled about it—and this at the very moment "Miss Darling" was being exposed. "Now how the hell to keep anything from the damned traitors except to do all the work and performing myself, I don't know," Barnum wrote in disgust to Kimball.[23]

It perplexed him to see the Mermaid sitting there, when he knew it should be out somewhere making money. Perhaps they should institute a suit against Bachman? Even if they lost and it cost them as much as $500, the publicity might breathe life into the enterprise again. Kimball was at first cool to the idea. By the time he came round, Barnum was himself having second thoughts, for although "it would be *Almighty Rich* if we *could* sue & *beat* Bachman," he had been informed that the minister had a strong party of friends in Charleston, and besides they would have to prove the Mermaid was a "genuine specimen"—which clearly they could not.[24] While still undecided about going to court, he thought he might bring out the Mermaid at the Museum again on the strength of a *"pretended* law suit," then changed his mind about this (Charity and "all the old maids in town" were of the opinion the business "would *ruin* me"), then changed it back again. He even submitted for Kimball's approval the advertisement he thought they should run:

Engaged for a short time, the animal (regarding which there has been so much dispute in the scientific world) called the
FEJEE MERMAID!
positively asserted by its owner to have been taken alive in the Fejee Islands, and implicitly believed by many scientific persons, while it is pronounced by other scientific persons to be an *artificial* production, and its natural existence claimed by them to be an utter impossibility. The manager can only say that it possesses as much *appearance of reality* as any fish lying on the stalls of our fish markets—but who is to decide when *doctors* disagree? At all events, whether this production is the work of *nature or art*, it is *decidedly* the most stupenduous curiosity ever submitted to the public for inspection. If it is artificial, the senses of sight and touch are useless, for *art* has rendered them totally ineffectual. If it is natural, then all *concur* in declaring it
THE GREATEST CURIOSITY IN THE WORLD

Something in this style might do the trick, and after exhibiting the Mermaid in New York, they could send it on to Havana and elsewhere.[25]

Meanwhile, in what is surely among the most bizarre episodes in this convoluted history, Barnum seems to have persuaded the Universalist minister Edwin H. Chapin to preach a sermon on the subject. At any rate, the showman copied out and sent to Kimball, without comment, an extract that reads as though it could have been inspired by nothing else so timely or appropriate. Beginning with the observation that "it is not only an arrogant but a *shallow* philosophy that says 'the existence of this or that is impossible, it is *contrary to the laws of nature*,'" Chapin astutely pointed out the hopelessness of anyone's ever fully comprehending all the laws and inner secrets of nature and "the *myriad* links of being" that make it up. It was arrogant, the minister continued, for any man to "talk of 'the laws of nature' and what are contrary to them & say there can be no such creature as this or that. Let him set [*sic*] down and study the *wild flower*—the first that comes in spring—and tell how wind and sun and rain could call out such a thing as that from the lap of the dark, unreasoning earth, and he may have more right to sneer at what he arrogantly dares to call something '*contrary* to the laws of nature.'"[26]

But the Fejee Mermaid exhibition was not revived by Barnum, and the "arrogant" Dr. Bachman was soon forgotten amid the whirl of far more exciting developments. Uncle Alanson himself, following the Charleston debacle, traveled in the South for a few months on his own with an exhibition that seems to have included a duckbill platypus and other stuffed animals once part of the Mermaid show.[27] However, the battle with Bachman had taken its toll, and in letters to his nephew written around this time he complained of his evil star's being in the ascendant and fatalistically predicted he would never be able to make a go of things again. He was later hired exclusively by Kimball, who sent him to Philadelphia with a collection of peepshows and employed him in a number of other minor projects, until Barnum, having bought Peale's Baltimore museum in 1845, installed him as manager of that institution. Alanson did not benefit long from his nephew's generosity. He died the following year at the age of forty-four. As to Levi Lyman, he also, after traveling for a time with a painting of *Christ and the Last Supper*, eventually returned to Kimball's employ. Around the beginning of 1845 the latter decided to revive the Mermaid on his own. Who better than the renowned "Dr. Griffin" to assist him in this undertaking? When Barnum, who was then in Europe, learned of these plans, he wished his former partner "joy of *Lyman* & the *baby*." In a footnote to the first edition of the autobiography he informed readers that Lyman later became a "prominent" Mormon and died at Nauvoo, Illinois.[28]

If there was ever one humbug more "shameful" than all the rest of Barnum's manufacture, surely it was the Fejee Mermaid. It might just as well have belonged to him, it became so inextricably woven into the fabric of his career. He joked about it for the rest of his life, as did his friends and nearly everyone else who finally learned, in the first edition of his autobiography, how he had managed things. On the eve of that book's publication, he arranged to "hire" the Mermaid from Kimball again and laughingly invited his readers to return to the Museum for another look, commencing on April Fools' Day, 1855. Again, while lecturing in England a few years later, he carried the Mermaid along with him and brazened it out before British audiences. They, too, professed to find the story highly amusing. After all, this time the joke had not been on them.

THERE WAS good reason for Barnum's waning interest in the Fejee Mermaid toward the end of 1843. He was about to embark on his first trip to Europe, an adventure that was to occupy him for the next three years. The immediate cause of this decision was a sensational discovery he had made late in the previous year while paying a visit to Bridgeport, Connecticut, where his half-brother Philo was now keeping the Franklin House hotel.[29] There he had been introduced to a "remarkably small child"—Barnum was later to refer to him as "my dwarf"—who, at the age of slightly less than five years, measured under two feet in height and weighed less than sixteen pounds. "He was a bright-eyed little fellow," Barnum writes, "with light hair and ruddy cheeks, was perfectly healthy, and as symmetrical as an Apollo." The child's full name was

Charles Sherwood Stratton, and he had been born on 4 January 1838, the son of Sherwood Edward Stratton, a local carpenter in poor circumstances, and his illiterate wife, Cynthia. Young Charley was already something of a local celebrity, but had never been exhibited to this time. Barnum writes that he had heard of him in advance, no doubt from Philo or some of his Connecticut friends. Before returning to New York, he had arranged for the mother and son to follow, at the rate of $3 per week plus their traveling and boarding expenses, for a trial period of four weeks at the American Museum. When they arrived in the city around the beginning of December, Cynthia Stratton was surprised to learn her son was being hailed as "General Tom Thumb, a dwarf of eleven years of age, just arrived from England."[30]

Again there was the irresistible appeal of an "exotic" attraction, which Barnum justified in the first edition of the autobiography on the basis of Americans' "disgraceful preference for foreigners" (a passage he diplomatically deleted from subsequent editions), not to mention the slight exaggeration of Charley's age. In the case of the latter, however, the showman was genuinely concerned that audiences might not be prepared to accept the four-year-old as *"really a dwarf";* and this particular ruse was kept up for so many years that at times, one suspects, little Charley himself must have been confused about his age. No one—not even Queen Victoria—was spared the juggernaut of Barnum's publicity campaigns. Upon receiving the General at Buckingham Palace in 1844, Her Majesty was blandly informed he had been born in 1832, "which makes him 12 years old," she confided to her journal that night.[31]

One thing the showman professed not to worry about was the danger of Charley's experiencing a growth spurt. He had been reliably informed the boy had grown little, if any, since the age of six months; and indeed, Charley added only a few inches to his height during the next several years ("General . . . improves every moment & don't grow a hair," Barnum delightedly wrote to Kimball in the summer of 1844).[32] Perfectly proportioned as he was—an example of what medical authorities refer to as ateliotic dwarfism—his diminutiveness resulted from a deficiency of the growth hormone that is normally produced by the pituitary gland. The condition is believed to be caused by a defective recessive gene, and since Charley's parents were actually first cousins, it seems likely that both inherited the defect, or mutation, from a common ancestor. Under such circumstances the chance of producing a midget is one in four; three other children born to the Strattons were all of normal size.[33]

Announced in advertisements as having been engaged at "extraordinary expense," the General made his debut at the American Museum on 8 December. He was, as Barnum had labored to ensure he would be, favorably received—by no means spectacularly so at this early stage (other attractions, such as the Indians, often drew just as well or better in 1843), but promisingly enough to convince Barnum he had not been mistaken about the boy's potential.[34] Consequently, before the month was out the showman drew up in his own hand another contract, indenturing the tiny Stratton to him until the first day of January 1844. The "extraordinary expense" now amounted to no less than $7 per week, of which $3 was actually for the services of Sherwood Stratton, who agreed to accompany his son and to labor under Barnum's or his agents' direction "at his trade of carpenter or any other respectable employment." Board and traveling expenses for the General and his parents, as well as a bonus of $50 to be paid a month before the year was up, were also specified in the agreement, which Sherwood and his wife (the latter making "her mark") signed on 22 December 1842.[35]

There is no mention of schooling for young Charley in this document, although in later years the General was often said to have received a "very good" education and Barnum did pledge to provide instruction in the basic subjects for other children he employed. Upon departing for Europe with the Strattons in early 1844, the showman made a point of informing readers of his letters to the *New York Atlas*, and later of his autobiography, that Tom Thumb's "tutor" was among their entourage. In the earlier of these sources this individual was further identified as one G. Ciprico—a New York hairdresser, it later came out, who was traveling to Europe to improve himself in his trade.[36] He was shortly succeeded as Tom Thumb's "moral instructor" by H. G. Sherman, a quirky "old stager" with a passion for antiquarianism who had worked for Barnum in the past. Sherman's chief duty now was to take over the day-to-day management of the Tom Thumb Troupe, leaving his employer free to run about Europe.[37]

If Tom Thumb profited at all from such rare educational opportunities during his first few years with Barnum, he most likely did so through another trusted aide, "Parson" Fordyce Hitchcock, who often accompanied the Strattons on their early travels around the United States and was left in charge of the Museum during Barnum's three-year absence abroad. Surprisingly, he really was a minister—not surprisingly, a Universalist. Born around 1813 and, by his own later account, reared in the same neighborhood as Barnum, Hitchcock was ordained at Hartford in 1834. For several years thereafter, while serving as pastor to the Connecticut societies in Newtown, Westport, and Stamford, he seemed headed for a distinguished career in the church. In 1842, for example, while attending the Connecticut Universalist Convention, he introduced a resolution calling for total abstinence from alcoholic drinks (it passed), and he was also a member of that body's committee overseeing the publication of religious tracts. Then, toward the end of the same year, his name vanishes from Connecticut church records—presumably because, as he hinted during the complimentary banquet thrown for Barnum in 1874, he had suffered one of those breakdowns so endemic to nineteenth-century clergymen. His lifelong friend, he claimed on the same occasion, gave him a "helping hand," although the parson did not expand on what that amounted to. In fact, he became Barnum's closest associate and continued so for several years, until he decided to strike out on his own as a businessman—not too successfully, it would seem—in the dry-goods line. By the time Barnum was at work on his autobiography in 1854, Hitchcock had retired to the country where, "shattered in health, he seems resigned to end his days in the honorable and humble position of a tiller of the earth." But the parson was obviously not so resigned after all, for he briefly returned to Barnum's employ in the early sixties, then resumed his ministerial duties in Newark, New Jersey, where he died in 1883. Prior to his death he preached before the Bridgeport Universalist Society several times and shared the hospitality of his old friend on many more occasions.[38]

At the outset, however, it was Barnum himself who took primary responsibility for Charley's "education," coaching him for hours on end in the roles he was shortly to play. The boy was eager to learn and possessed a natural talent for mimicry, so that, in a relatively brief time, he was well settled in his various characters. Most persons today, with perhaps some memory of the degraded "freak shows" that once graced the midways of many carnivals and circuses, have but a vague idea of what Tom Thumb's entertainments were like. They were not "exhibitions" in the usual sense, but carefully crafted performances that eventually evolved into a full evening's (or afternoon's) program. For many years the General appeared in one vehicle, held together by a "Doctor" or straight man, in which he impersonated such characters as a Scottish Highlander, a student at Oxford, an American tar, Frederick the Great bowed down with age, and—most famous of all his impersonations—the Emperor Napoleon. All in appropriate costumes, of course, and with a variety of songs, dances, and wisecracks with the "Doctor" interpolated. Under questioning by the last, who filled in with assorted bits of information whenever the General had to leave the stage to change costumes, Tom Thumb was also given the opportunity to tell audiences something about his personal history. Audience participation was encouraged as well ("plants" were occasionally used for scripted comic business), with children invited to come upon the stage so that their heights might be compared with Tom Thumb's; and there was always a great deal made about the General's notorious partiality for kissing ladies, the prettiest of whom he would sometimes descend into the auditorium to search out—especially those who were prepared to purchase the souvenir pamphlets and photographs he sold. The stage itself would be set with miniature furniture and perhaps even a tiny house. Toward the conclusion of the program the General would don an elastic body stocking to pose in a series of "Grecian Statues," based on famous works of art that most spectators of his day easily recognized. This inspiring finale provided spectators the opportunity to further admire the General's perfect proportions, unencumbered by the sometimes elaborate costumes he wore earlier in the act.

The extant script of the program here described—incomplete, but even so running to fifteen manuscript pages—provides some idea of what the General's audiences found so enjoyable:

. . . .

DOCTOR: You being a general, perhaps you will tell us what army you command?

GENERAL: Cupid's artillery.

DOCTOR: But there are so many generals in the army, perhaps you will tell us whether you are a major general, a brigadier general, or an adjutant general?

GENERAL: I'm a quartermaster general.

DOCTOR: You are? How do you make that out?
GENERAL: Because I look out for the quarters.

.   .   .   .

DOCTOR: What dress is this?
GENERAL: It is my Oxonian dress. [*puts on dress*]
DOCTOR: It is the dress presented to the General by the students at Oxford.
   What do you represent now?
GENERAL: A fellow.
DOCTOR: I understand—a fellow of the university.
GENERAL: No—a little fellow.
DOCTOR: Did you have any degrees conferred upon you?
GENERAL: Yes sir, Master of Hearts.
DOCTOR: You must be aware that you are under great obligations to the
   ladies.
GENERAL: Of course.
DOCTOR: It is reported that you have kissed a good many ladies during
   your travels.
GENERAL: Yes sir, a few.
DOCTOR: How many?
GENERAL: A few.
DOCTOR: Perhaps the ladies would like to know how many you call "a
   few"?
GENERAL: About two millions and a half.

.   .   .   .

DOCTOR: Whom do you represent now, General?
GENERAL: Napoleon Bonaparte.
DOCTOR: Will you have the kindness to represent Napoleon at St. Helena
   in deep meditation? [*business*]
DOCTOR: Napoleon at the Bridge of Lodi? [*business*]
DOCTOR: Napoleon addressing his army? [*business*]
DOCTOR: The statue of Napoleon in France? [*business*]
DOCTOR: Will you give a representation of Napoleon and the manner
   in which he slept on the night previous to the Battle of
   Austerlitz? [*business*]
DOCTOR: Are you asleep, sir?
GENERAL: Yes, sir. [*business*]
DOCTOR: I was not aware that Napoleon slept with one eye open.
GENERAL: I can't close both eyes because I wink at the ladies so much.
DOCTOR: Perhaps you will give us a specimen of the manner in which
   you wink at the ladies. [*business*]

.   .   .   .

DOCTOR: What dress is this, General?
GENERAL: It's my Highland costume.
DOCTOR: . . . What is that in your hand, General?
GENERAL: My claymore.

DOCTOR: To what use do you put it to?

GENERAL: I fight with it.

DOCTOR: Fight! I'd like to know if you've ever been in a battle.

GENERAL: How could I be a general if I have never been in battle?

DOCTOR: Why, sir, I know several generals who have never smelt gunpowder. . . . Will you favor the audience with a Scotch song?

GENERAL: Yes, sir! [*song: "Come Sit Thee Down"*]

DOCTOR: Now, General, will you be kind enough to astonish the audience by dancing the Highland fling? [*dance: Highland fling*]

DOCTOR: I will here state that the General has an interesting book containing an account of his life and travels and also a lithographic portrait which the audience can procure if they desire in the room below at the conclusion of the performance. What do you charge for them, General?

GENERAL: Twenty-five cents.

DOCTOR: A shilling each. And what do you give the ladies when they purchase?

GENERAL: A stamped receipt.

DOCTOR: And what is a "stamped receipt"?

GENERAL: A kiss.

DOCTOR: The General will next appear in his Grecian statuary.[39]

• • • •

The act was subject to modification, of course; and in later years, while traveling with his wife and other midgets, the General was no longer compelled to do so much on his own. Programs then took on more of a variety atmosphere, with each member of the troupe favoring audiences with his or her specialty. These later entertainments, for purposes of contrast, often included at least one normal-sized performer—a magician or ventriloquist, perhaps— while the midgets themselves frequently combined forces in a featured burlesque or dramatic skit. And although the General himself eventually shot up to the astonishing height of forty inches and ballooned to the no less astounding weight of seventy-five pounds (thereby putting an end to the "Grecian Statues" business, obviously), to the time of his death he continued to appear in his most celebrated character, that of Napoleon Bonaparte.[40]

In the early years of his career, however, the burden of these "entertainments" or "levees" fell squarely upon the General's little shoulders. Throughout the months of 1843, when not performing at the American Museum, he was taken around the country by the good Parson Hitchcock, who continued to rehearse him in his various roles and—in return for being "genteel, industrious, and knowing the ways of the boy well"—received $5 more per week than the entire Stratton family. When Kimball, who was champing at the bit to have the General visit his museum, complained about having to pay this exorbitant salary, his friend gave him the option of hiring some other manager during the General's Boston engagement, but cautioned it would have to be "some person who won't *tamper* with the parents" and try to hire them away.[41]

There were morning, afternoon, and evening performances, and between them, as time permitted, supplementary appearances. In October, for example, the popular comic actor John Sefton briefly hired little Charley to bolster his benefit night at another New York theatre. "*I am to take General on the stage & show him off,*" Barnum boasted to Kimball, "*& have somebody in the boxes call out to have him passed round, which I shall decline but express my regret at being obliged to do so, as he must return at once to the American Museum, but that they can see him, shake hands, & converse with him at the Museum any day during the week!* Sefton gives me $50 and will not detain him 30 minutes."[42] At the General's own first "farewell" benefit at the Museum the previous February, receipts, Barnum crowed, had been $280. In Philadelphia, where he next appeared, they had started out at $50 per day, with prospects of increasing to as high as $100. The showman was slightly disappointed by the figures Hitchcock reported when the troupe continued into the South, but they picked up again when the General returned north in early spring. So long as they averaged $50 per day, Barnum would be "satisfied."[43]

There was another aspect of Tom Thumb's early "education" that his wife revealed in her autobiography. In the haste to exploit and turn him into what Barnum was pleased to call "the man in miniature," the boy's natural development was all but forgotten. In later life, his wife reports, he was particularly fond of children and liked to watch them play. "I never had any childhood, any boy-life," he complained to her. "And it somehow seemed pathetic to realize its truth," Lavinia continues. "Mr. Barnum took him when only four years old, and from that time he was trained to speak and act like a man. . . . He was taught to take wine at dinner when only five, to smoke at seven and 'chew' at nine. This was a part of the education which supposably [*sic*] fitted him to fill the role he was expected to play."[44] The charge, certainly a severe one, seems plausible enough, and Lavinia nowhere else in her autobiography has a word to say against her good friend Barnum. The showman has himself left a few telling stories of how Tom Thumb amused himself, and was amused by others, during these formative years. He delighted in setting traps by running twine between chair and table legs, and would "roll upon the floor and shed tears of joy" when Barnum and his parents pretended to trip over them. On one special occasion, knowing the boy's natural inclination to miserliness, his inventive preceptor attempted to cure him of this "meanness." In the midst of entertaining him with the tale of Ali Baba and the Forty Thieves, Barnum broke off just after "Open Sesame!" and pretended to be too tired to continue. The excited General, wriggling on his lap, urged him to go on, but Barnum refused to unless he was first paid a quarter. After thinking long and hard about this, Charley finally dug into his pocket and came up with the amount demanded. "Please don't ever play such a trick as that on me again," he said. "I don't want to pay out money for stories." From that time on, whenever Barnum offered to tell him a story, he would first inquire whether he would have to pay before hearing the end of it. Needless to add, the trick did not cure Charley of his "meanness."[45]

With examples like this to guide him in the Brobdingnagian world he inhabited, is it any wonder spectators paying to gaze upon him sometimes thought they detected a certain mockery in the way he returned their stares? And what can one say about his celebrated ready wit, displayed as early as six years of age when the great Duke of Wellington paid him a visit? Finding the General looking pensive in his Napoleon costume, the Duke asked him what he was thinking about. "I was thinking of the loss of the Battle of Waterloo," was the instant reply. "That brilliant display of wit was chronicled through the country," Barnum writes, "and was of itself worth thousands of pounds to the exhibition."[46] Rehearsed in advance, or a true inspiration? The latter, Barnum would have us believe; and possibly it was. He grew so accustomed to this constant role playing—to being continually on show as the pert "man in miniature," with his repertoire of easily commanded antic expressions, comic gestures, and witty ripostes—that today it is virtually impossible to distinguish the real Charles Stratton from the General Tom Thumb of Barnum's creation. Those who knew him have long been dead, and his wife offers little that is new in her autobiography. Letters and other writings by him are extremely rare, and not all that revealing when they do turn up. Authors who have written about him to date have generally arrived at an impasse once Barnum's own narrative trails off. Which raises the intriguing question of how much, if any, there really was to probe. Was "Tom Thumb" an early example of an almost totally manufactured personality—a personality that, taking hold when he was only four years old, prevented the real Charles Stratton from developing an individuality of his own? An interesting problem for psychologists, perhaps, and possibly for some future biographer.

————◆————

WITH TOM THUMB, his "tutor" and parents, and "Professor" Emile Guillaudeu—the last the Museum's naturalist and taxidermist since 1810—Barnum set off in the packet ship *Yorkshire* in January 1844 with the modest intention of conquering Europe. They were accompanied as far as Sandy Hook by friends and the City Brass Band, and when the time finally came to take leave of the former and the musicians struck up "Home, Sweet Home," the showman was so overcome by emotion that he was reduced to tears. Fortunately, Cynthia Stratton, the only woman making the crossing, soon became seasick, thereby furnishing innocent diversion at her expense; and the "melting mood" was further dispelled through the playing of practical jokes on other passengers, most notably an "Englishman" from Canada who was tricked into standing treat for a dozen bottles of champagne. The ship was becalmed and took nineteen days to reach Liverpool. By then, one imagines, its small party of passengers (they were fourteen in all) must have been surfeited with hilarity.

Before departing from America, Barnum had arranged with the proprietors of the *New York Atlas* to send back accounts of his experiences abroad; and this "European Correspondence," amounting in all to one hundred letters, was published in issues dating from 17 March 1844 through 31 May 1846.[47] Aside from providing readers with his impressions of Europe and its inhabitants, these communications were admirably calculated to keep his name and that of his museum ever before the American public, both of which—along with Tom Thumb, the many attractions he acquired in Europe and sent back to the Museum, hotels whose proprietors were more than ordinarily obliging, etc.— he shamelessly puffed at every opportunity. The patriotic note was sounded as well, with the author frequently comparing American and European forms of government and institutions, although not invariably to the former's advantage. Together with his letters written to Kimball during the same period, the *Atlas* articles provide a revealing, often hilarious, sometimes downright embarrassing portrait of Barnum on his first trip abroad—considerably more comprehensive and less inhibited than the account later published in the autobiography, which was based, to a large extent, on the same correspondence.

After exhibiting Tom Thumb for a few nights in Liverpool and then at London's Princess's Theatre, primarily in order to announce their arrival, Barnum abruptly withdrew his charge from public view and began holding court, as a "private American gentleman," in a furnished mansion he had rented in London's fashionable Grafton Street. The strategy was to inveigle endorsements from editors and the "nobility" by inviting them to the mansion to meet privately with Tom Thumb, while stirring up additional excitement through a few select exhibitions (for which, Barnum writes, he was handsomely rewarded) at the homes of such aristocrats as the Baroness Rothschild. If Americans were given to a "disgraceful preference for foreigners," the English, as he well knew, were equally dazzled by such influential patronage; and with this in mind he had from the very beginning set his sights on the grandest cachet imaginable: a royal "command" from Victoria herself, whose innocent predilection for freaks, lion tamers, and other "curiosities" had often been remarked on in the British press.[48] To this end the showman was soon urging Edward Everett, the U.S. Minister to the Court of St. James, to see what he could do, even though the Royal Family was then officially in mourning for the death of Prince Albert's father.

Meanwhile, uncertain of Everett's success, Barnum had rented one of the rooms in London's Egyptian Hall and commenced exhibiting Tom Thumb in earnest. He had barely done so when a "command" for Tom Thumb to appear at Buckingham Palace on 23 March arrived—an event that, naturally enough, was blazoned forth on the locked doors of the exhibition room that evening. Barnum describes this historic occasion at length in his autobiography: how the General, "looking like a wax-doll gifted with the power of locomotion," advanced with a firm step to the surprised Queen and her circle at the far end of the royal picture gallery, and how they all burst into laughter when he bowed and unceremoniously saluted them with "Good evening, ladies and gentlemen." Before presenting his entertainment, he was led round the gallery by the Queen herself, the General assuring her that her paintings were "first-rate" and inquiring whether he was to meet the two-year-old Prince of Wales (Bertie was in bed by that hour). At the conclusion of the performance there was another comic incident when Barnum and Tom Thumb, following instructions given them by an officious lord-in-waiting, took leave of the royal presence while backing out of the long gallery. Unable to keep up with his manager, the General would back a few steps then turn and run to catch up with him, back a few steps more, and repeat the process. This so excited the Queen's favorite poodle that it began barking and rushed over to Tom Thumb, who brandished the tiny cane he had brought with him and engaged the dog in a "funny fight." The amused Queen immediately sent word that she hoped the General had "sustained no damage." Once outside the picture gallery, the two were served refreshments in another part of the palace; and Barnum, ever with an eye on the main chance, asked to meet with the editor of the *Court Journal*. To his great delight, this gentleman, who was then in the palace, not only agreed to devote more than a "mere line" to Tom Thumb's meeting with the Queen but even invited the showman to write out what he would like to see in the paper. The notice, Barnum was later pleased to discover, was published verbatim.[49]

Victoria's own impressions are contained in the entry she made in her diary that night, although she nowhere refers to Barnum by name:

> After dinner we saw the greatest curiosity I, or indeed anybody, ever saw, viz: a little dwarf, only 25 inches high & 15 lbs in weight. No description can give an idea of this little creature, whose name was Charles Stratton, born they say in 32, which makes him 12 years old. He is American, & gave us his card, with Gen. Tom Thumb written on it. He made the funniest little bow, putting out his hand & saying: "much obliged Mam." One cannot help feeling very sorry for the poor little thing & wishing he could be properly cared for, for the people who show him off tease him a good deal, I should think. He was made to imitate Napoleon & do all sorts of tricks, finally backing the whole way out of the gallery.[50]

Several days later, when Tom Thumb returned to the palace and this time was presented to the Princess Royal and the Prince of Wales, she was still amused:

> Saw the little dwarf in the Yellow Drawingroom, who was very nice, lively & funny, dancing & singing wonderfully. Vicky & Bertie were with us, also Mama, Ldy. Dunmore and her 3 children, & Ldy. Lyttelton. Little "Tom Thumb" does not reach up to Vicky's shoulder.[51]

A third visit to the palace followed on 19 April. This time it was Leopold I, King of the Belgians, and his queen who were "surprised."[52]

Barnum, naturally enough, was in ecstasy. Upon returning from his first visit to the Queen, he immediately wrote to Everett offering him "ten thousand thousand thanks" and assuring him his goodness in arranging the invitation would "never be forgotten."[53] In an excited letter to the *Atlas* written two days after the second of these visits, he could only summarize the recent events that had almost overwhelmed him:

> Since I wrote you last, I have been twice with Tom Thumb before Queen Victoria, at Buckingham Palace—once before the Queen Dowager, at Marlborough House—have exhibited the General to the Queen of the Bel-

gians, Prince Albert, the Duchess of Kent, the Prince of Wales, the young Princess Royal, the Duke of Wellington, and thousands of the nobility—have attended two of the queen's levees at St. James' Palace—visited the first nobility at their residences—passed several hours on three several days in examining all the wonders and magnificence of St. James' Palace—have put my hand on the throne itself, and done many more marvellous things, which I will not mention at present; but I must say that if I was not a remarkably *modest* man, I should probably brag a little, and say that I had done what no American ever before accomplished; but being "remarkably modest," I shall say *nothing*, but wait for an American to appear who has visited the queen at her palace *twice* within eight days, and on each occasion been received with smiles, cordiality, sociability, and royal favor.[54]

There were so many visits to members of the Royal Family that the showman soon felt it necessary to expend nearly one hundred pounds on a court costume for Tom Thumb.[55] The gifts showered upon the latter, like the miniature gold watch made for him at the express order of the Queen Dowager Adelaide, became themselves a part of the exhibition, further testifying to his popularity with the nobility and *beau monde*. Before May was out Barnum had ordered, at a total cost of not less than $2000, an elegant equipage for the General. The body of the coach, painted an ultramarine blue and decorated with a coat of arms and the motto "Go Ahead," measured but twenty inches high by eleven inches wide. Its interior was lined in silk and its windows were of plate glass. Drawn by ponies only twenty-eight inches high and ridden on the outside by children costumed in liveries and wigs, it was bound to provoke a sensation wherever it appeared. It would *"kill the public dead,"* Barnum promised in a letter to his friend Moses Kimball. "It will be the greatest hit in the universe, see if it ain't!"[56] Meanwhile, the showman had made a gift to the Queen: an albino hart, of spotless whiteness, from the Rocky Mountains.[57]

The results of such distinguished patronage were even greater than Barnum had anticipated. During the entire four months Tom Thumb appeared at Egyptian Hall, receipts averaged $500 per day, while total expenses for Barnum and the Strattons—for the rental of the exhibition room and mansion in Grafton Street, printing and advertising, their meals, everything—came to only around one-tenth that amount. And besides the three public performances given each day, the General's presence continued to be requested at more private parties than he could possibly attend, each of which had the potential of realizing an additional forty to fifty dollars. By mid-June the showman was so flush with money that he contemplated sending ten or fifteen thousand dollars to Hitchcock for investment in bonds and mortgages.[58] The Strattons were not doing so badly, either. Although they had bound themselves to the end of 1844 for the weekly sum of $50 plus expenses, by now they were receiving most, if not all, of the profits from Tom Thumb's sale of pamphlets and other souvenirs. Receipts in this area averaged $30 per day, "more than half of which is profit & *their* perquisites."[59] Nor did the interest of the "nobility" show any sign of tapering off. At Egyptian Hall itself, Barnum writes, as many as sixty of their carriages might be seen standing during the "fashionable hour." Indeed, he found it hard to believe that *any* member of the English aristocracy had not seen Tom Thumb at least once that season.[60] On 8 June the Russian Czar Nicholas, then in London with the King of Saxony, was himself introduced to the "man in miniature." The Emperor laughed "immoderately" upon first seeing him, then took little Charley in his arms and invited him to St. Petersburg.[61]

There could be no thought of failure after so spectacular a beginning. By enlisting the Queen of England at the outset of his carefully orchestrated campaign in the Old World, by shrewdly playing upon the innate snobbery of his British hosts, Barnum had managed to snare them all, from prince to lowliest commoner. Setting aside the matter of his age, there was nothing fraudulent about Tom Thumb, for as Victoria herself acknowledged, he certainly was a talented and bona fide "curiosity." What the English found so hard to swallow, what they could not forgive the showman when his autobiography appeared ten years later, was his telling how he had deliberately *used* them and their Queen to attain his goal. As in America itself when that book was first published, he was condemned not so much for "deceiving" the public as for the candor with which he revealed his machinations. And in the running subtext to that bold work, of course—though few cared to admit it openly—for what he revealed about the "deceived" themselves.

VII

The Universal Yankee

Intrepid then, o'er seas and lands he flew;
Europe he saw, and Europe saw him too.
Pope

WITH TOM THUMB well launched before the British public, in June of 1844 Barnum was glad to turn over the day-to-day running of the company to H. G. Sherman—thereby permitting himself more time to write, as he promised readers of the *Atlas*, and incidentally to play the tourist. He was in Paris by the end of the month, ostensibly to attend the quinquennial exposition there with the object of purchasing automatons and other interesting objects for the American Museum. Of course, he could not resist strolling the Champs-Elysées and attending the Cirque D'Eté of the famous Franconi family, or visiting a pleasure garden where he saw the polka and notorious cancan performed. The last, in contrast to the mock horror expressed by Mark Twain when he later saw it in the company of the "innocents abroad," struck him as very funny indeed. He climbed to the top of Notre Dame, visited the Church of the Madeleine and bought an "animated" model of it, and inspected the animals and horticultural exhibits in the Jardin des Plantes. The treasures at Versailles, which he described as an "earthly paradise," set his head spinning; but the Paris morgue, which he also felt compelled to visit, depressed him. In all, he was in France for a little over two weeks and lived so well, he boasted to his readers, that he gained eleven pounds.[1]

Once back in London, he regaled readers of the *Atlas* with a long description of a marvelous group of "Swiss" Bell Ringers he had recently heard and urged some astute American theatre manager to lose no time in snapping them up, since they were bound to prove a sensation and make a pile of money for anyone engaging them. He neglected to mention he had already hired them himself and that they were actually from Lancashire, or that they were about to embark for America under the pretense of going there "on their own hook," so that they might first secure profitable engagements at various theatres and halls around the country before showing up at the American Museum.[2] At the same time he had arranged to bring to London a group of American Indians he intended to exploit in partnership with the artist George Catlin, whose own exhibition of paintings, giant wigwam, Indian costumes, weapons, and other artifacts had been on display at Egyptian Hall for several years. A famous automaton letter-writer, purchased from the great wizard and mechanician Robert-Houdin during his expedition to Paris, was soon on display at London's Adelaide Gallery. For a while the showman toyed with the idea of buying the Gallery and turning over its management to Catlin's nephew, "a regular roarer," as Barnum described him. With similar establishments on both sides of the Atlantic, he could receive novelties sent to him in America by Catlin, "& I could occasionally send him a fat nigger girl or something else." Nothing came of these interesting plans.[3] Meanwhile, he had somehow acquired—by means he refused to specify, although he assured Moses Kimball he had come by it "honestly"—one of the "state robes" worn by Queen Victoria. This he was sending back for exhibit in America, and he begged his friend in Boston to get it through customs duty-free or, failing that, as "second-hand wardrobe."[4]

When the lease on the room at Egyptian Hall expired on 20 July, the Tom Thumb Troupe started on a grand tour of Britain. By then the miniature carriage was ready with its four matched ponies (they had been broken to harness and trained by William Batty, proprietor of Astley's Amphitheatre), and this fairylike equipage, in which the General was driven about in all the towns they visited, became one of the principal means of advertising the show. In mid-August, Barnum reported in genuine terror, Tom Thumb came near to suffering a fatal accident while out for an airing in a full-sized carriage. In the course of a drive through the picturesque countryside around Clifton, the General, along with his "tutor" H. G. Sherman, had mounted the driver's box in order to obtain a better view. On descending a steep hill the horse ran away, crashing into a high stone wall with such force that it broke its neck, and the carriage itself experienced considerable damage. Sherman and Tom Thumb were nowhere to be seen, and Barnum, who was seated inside when the accident occurred, jumped out and began frantically searching for them under the wreckage of horse and carriage. "All right—there's no danger, don't be frightened," called a tiny, high-pitched voice from over the wall. It turned out that Sherman, who had seen the crash coming, had taken the General in his arms and, at the last moment, made a heroic leap over the wall into the soft field beyond. "It was a most remarkable escape, and for which we all feel truly grateful," Barnum wrote. "Every person who examines the wall is astonished that any man could have leaped it at a single bound, and have escaped as Sherman did, free from injury."[5]

It was also during this initial sweep through the provinces that Barnum set out, on 5 September, on a whirlwind tour of the Shakespeare country in the company of the London author and journalist Albert Smith. Smith, who was later to become a showman and popular lecturer himself, most notably in his entertainment based on his bibulous 1851 ascent of Mont Blanc, and who loosely based the character of the showman Rosset on Barnum in his 1845 novel *The Fortunes of the Scattergood Family*, eventually recorded the adventures of their crowded day in a two-part article for *Bentley's Miscellany*.[6] As he describes their travels—which commenced at 5 A.M. in Birmingham and went on to take in all the Stratford sights, Warwick and Kenilworth castles, a fair being held in the vicinity of the former, and Coventry—Barnum attempted to purchase everything that struck his fancy along their route and was indignantly rebuffed when he offered to buy the "wonderful relics" of the legendary giant, Guy of Warwick. In Coventry, however, he did manage to acquire "a wandering exhibition of animals of dissimilar habits all in one cage"—the American Museum's original "Happy Family," obviously. Barnum himself devoted considerable space to this trip in his articles for the *Atlas* and, to a lesser extent, in his autobiography. He makes no mention in either source of trying to purchase Guy of Warwick's "trumpery," but does tell how he complimented the guide who showed them these outsized articles "for having concentrated more *lies* than I ever before heard in so small a compass." The guide laughed at this remark and "evidently felt gratified." At the fair connected with the Warwick Races, the inquisitive showman was knocked flat by a Canadian giantess when he raised her dress to see if some trick was involved (he was right: she was standing on a pedestal). The purchase of the "Happy Family" cost him $2500.[7]

No doubt it was on this first trip to Stratford that he conceived an even more ambitious scheme—namely, the purchase of Shakespeare's birthplace, which he planned to dismantle and transport to New York. Through a friend he obtained a verbal agreement granting him first "refusal" of the house; but when the news leaked out, "British pride was touched, and several English gentlemen interfered and purchased the premises for a Shakespeare Association." Had they delayed a few days longer, Barnum writes in his autobiography, "I should have made a rare speculation, for I was subsequently assured that the British people, rather than suffer that house to be removed to America, would have bought me off with twenty thousand pounds."[8]

In October, without informing his family or friends in advance, he suddenly decided to return to New York. There were business matters that needed settling at the Museum, and for nearly nine months now he had been absent from home. The previous April his third daughter, Frances, had died a few weeks short of her second birthday. When Barnum received news of this in London over four weeks later, he was in the midst of composing one of his letters to the *Atlas* and concluded with a touching, if somewhat philosophical, paragraph on the subject. The toys he had sent his daughter a few days earlier were destined for one who was already

> placed beyond the reach of either pain or pleasure, so far as this world is concerned. I had fondly hoped to meet her on my return, but a good and wise Providence has ordered otherwise; and painful as is the effort to the parental feelings, still the doctrines of Christianity, and a belief and confidence in the goodness of a Creator, whose attributes consist of infinite power, wisdom and *love*, enables me in all humility to say, "not my will but *thine*, oh God, be done." I can write no more today.[9]

Notwithstanding such recent grief, there were the usual practical jokes played on shipboard during the long passage home—and an even bigger one played on his "treasure of a wife" Charity once he had actually arrived. Instead of going home, he proceeded directly to the Museum and had Hitchcock dispatch an urgent message to her, telling her to come immediately to the Museum to hear some news meant for her ears alone from a gentleman who had just arrived from Europe. What thoughts must have crossed Charity's mind while she was rushing to the Museum to hear this news, or what she said to her husband once there, Barnum does not specify. But "I *guess* she was a little astonished," he blithely informed the readers of his next letter to the *Atlas*, "as were also the little ones, and thus ended my sky-larking for that day."[10]

He was in America for less than three weeks, arranging for the first expansion of the Museum's "Lecture Room" and coming to terms with Francis Olmsted, who earlier in the year, eyeing his tenant's phenomenal success with Tom Thumb, had written to say he was thinking of converting the Museum building into office space. He only did so, Barnum felt certain, as a prelude to raising the rent; and he had responded by advising Olmsted to go ahead by all means with his plan, since he had decided that at the expiration of his present lease he would rent some other property in Broadway and build a "larger & more convenient" museum of his own. "I *know* it will scare him," Barnum had confided to Kimball. And of course he was right.[11] On 9 November he set off again for Europe on the steamship *Great Western*, this time taking Charity and their two daughters with him. To occupy himself during the two weeks they were at sea (when not playing jokes on his seasick wife, that is), he reverted to his adventures in France for the benefit of the readers of his *Atlas* articles and reflected, with some asperity, on his recent visit to America. While there he had been quite amused by the warm reception accorded him by the "nabobs" and "codfish aristocracy" of New York who, prior to his success with Tom Thumb,

> would have looked down on me with disdain if I had presumed to have spoken to them. I really forgot, till they forced the truth upon my mind, that since I left them I had accumulated a few more dirty dollars, and that now, therefore, we were upon *equal* ground! Bah! the very thought of money being the standard of merit makes me sick; and the fawning, canting obsequiousness which I witnessed from *many* during my flying visit to America made me despise the sychophants [*sic*] and almost wish I was not worth a shilling in the world! On the other hand, I met some good honest friends in humble circumstances, who almost appeared to approach me with awe—and then again I felt ashamed of human nature. What a miserable, pitiful and disgraceful state of society is it, which elevates a booby or a tyrant to its highest summit, provided he has more gold than others; while a good heart or a wise head is trampled in the dust, if their owner happens to be poor!

He himself, he swore to his readers, could conceive of no other benefit from wealth than the enabling one to provide, "without ostentation," for the comfort of one's family and fellow human beings.

> My sincere prayer is, that I may be reduced to beggary rather than be made a pampered, purse-proud and overbearing aristocrat by the influ-

ence of wealth. This coat, I am sorry to say, is intended for and will fit many of my acquaintances in New York. I beg them, for their own sakes as well as mine, to *wear* it. I wish them and all the world to know that my father was a *tailor*, that I am a *showman* by profession, and all the *gilding* shall make nothing else of me. When a man gets above his business, he is a poor devil, who merits the detestation of all who know him.[12]

The national election for President had also taken place while he was in New York, and he was alarmed to note the great amount of time being devoted to such events. "Should the excitements at our presidential elections continue to increase as they have done during the last eight years, the citizens of America will soon be spending nearly half their time in political meetings, instead of devoting their energies to legitimate and profitable business. These parades are very well for children, but should seldom be resorted to (for political purposes) by grown-up men." There were further reflections on the wasteful practice of replacing minor governmental officials every time a new party attained power ("Uncle Sam is continually taking his apprentices, and as fast as they become useful, the leaders of party turn them adrift and hire a fresh batch to feed at the public crib") and on the need for the states to pay their foreign debts:

No person who has not experienced it can conceive the shame an American is made to feel in a foreign country when attacked regarding the repudiation of debts by the various states. I can stand and defend almost anything else which they can say against America; but this refusing to pay honest debts admits of no defence, and the sooner the stigma is removed by the states paying what they justly owe, the better. When the English attack us upon slavery, we can look them boldly in the face and reply that the institution of slavery in America is of British origin; and after they have proved that the slaves are absolutely worse off than they would be if they were free, or that they are one half so badly provided for as the poorer classes of England and Ireland, then they must contrive some way to abolish slavery without creating a greater evil than at present exists; and until then they must have the credit of its origin and present existence. I would remark, *en passant*, that the abolitionists in America are filling our school books with sentiments against slavery; and thus, in ten years, we shall have a nation of abolitionists who will scarcely know why they are so. This conduct is mean and reprehensible.[13]

No wonder James Gordon Bennett, who sometimes commented sarcastically on Barnum's letters in his *New York Herald*, had taken to referring to him as "Mr. Philosopher Barnum."

In Liverpool he deposited his family at the Waterloo Hotel while he himself continued on to Scotland to catch up with the Tom Thumb Troupe. On the boat to Glasgow he got into a heated argument with several Scotsmen over the subject of slavery in America, which may have influenced his opinion of the Scots in general. They might be strict churchgoers and great sticklers for creeds, he wrote from Edinburgh a few days later, but they were also "the most close-fisted and hardest chaps at driving a bargain and turning a penny that I ever knew. I don't know why it is," he continued,

> but certainly every day's experience proves the fact that where a community or individual is celebrated for *extra* piety, for an unusual stock of sanctity, there is found the hard bargainer, the grinders of the poor—the liberality for heathen in foreign lands, but the cold indifference for suffering humanity at home. I know not how to account for this total disagreement of practice and precept, and am satisfied that it cannot be the fruit of true christianity, whose blessed founder commended charity as the very essence and foundation of pure religion; but it nevertheless *is* the fact that he or they who set themselves up as the very patterns of all that is good, and who pretend far to exceed all others in their devotions, are the most unfriendly, unsociable and unprofitable neighbors in the world. They talk long and loud about the poor unconverted barbarians afar off, but they too often forget the sufferings of the poor widow and orphans who are starving under their very noses.[14]

He had barely delivered himself of this opinion when the Scottish tax commissioners caught up with him and informed him he owed £729 in income tax. The outraged showman, arguing he was a foreigner with no fixed address in the country, refused to give in to their demand and was shortly writing to his friend Everett for advice. The latter diplomatically replied that the tax laws in Britain were interpreted "rigorously" in favor of the treasury and suggested that, unless the sum in question was very large, it might be better to pay it rather than hazard the expense of going to court.[15] Writing to Kimball at the beginning of the new year, Barnum estimated he might have to pay as much as $500 in the end. But as for the original demand of £729 or over $3600, "*they can't come it.*"[16]

Meanwhile, rejoined by Charity, he had been to Ireland, where he had met, and attended a speech by, the great patriot Daniel O'Connell.[17] During one day in Dublin alone, he boasted to Kimball, Tom Thumb had taken in $1300; and on his last day in the city, during the final hour of exhibition, the receipts had amounted to $320, "over five dollars per minute for one straight single hour!"[18] The Strattons were themselves about to participate in this "fairy business." On the first of January 1845 they were advanced to the status of full partners with Barnum, thereafter equally sharing the profits and expenses with him. But the showman, who estimated he could still count on clearing $25,000 per year under the new arrangement, insisted on retaining tight control of managerial operations and resolutely moved to crush any threatened rebellion. "The Strattons are crazy—absolutely deranged with such golden success," he wrote to Kimball toward the end of the month:

> At first they were inclined to take airs, carry high heads, and talk about what *we* were doing; but when Mrs. Stratton began to be too inquisitive about the *business* & to say that *she* thought expences were too high &

that I spent too much for printing &c., I told them both *very decidedly* that *I* was the *manager* & that unless the *whole* was left to my direction I would not stay a single day. Their horns were hauled in very suddenly, you may depend, & they are now down to their *old level*, where you may be sure I shall keep them. I can do business with blockheads & brutes when there is money enough to be made by it, but I can't be tempted by money to associate with them nor allow them to rule.[19]

The "brutes" had in fact been making trouble almost from the very start of their association with him. At one point during the initial tour of the United States, the genteel Parson Hitchcock had thrown up his hands in despair of being able to please them and had begged to be relieved of his onerous duties. It was their "ignorant *pride*," not rum, Barnum assured Kimball at the time, that was at the root of the trouble, for he had recently bribed Stratton to give up drink with the present of a gold watch. If they could not learn to "behave," he warned, he was determined to "blow the concern to hell before I'll allow anybody else to pick up the fruit which I have shaken from the tree."[20]

In Europe his indignation at their feeble attempts to assert themselves soon gave way to amusement over their numerous gaucheries in public and in private. He openly laughed at them in his letters to the *Atlas*, and did so again in his autobiography and *Funny Stories*, where he sometimes disguised their identities, however, by referring to them as the "Simpsons." Stratton himself, who was laying up $500 a week from his share of the profits, functioned as ticket seller to the exhibition. On one occasion, when asked by a somewhat incredulous woman if he really was Tom Thumb's father, he lackadaisically replied, "Wa'al, I have to support him."[21] Another time, Barnum reported in high glee, he expressed surprise upon hearing Flemish, which he confused with Dutch, spoken in the streets of Brussels. He was not aware, he remarked, that the "Dutch" ever traveled so far from home. Upon the showman's slyly asking him where he supposed their "home" was, he answered that "there was a lot of old Dutchmen out in the western part of the state of New York, and he supposed there were no more in the world; but he didn't know that they ever travelled so far off as this."[22] "Wasn't that rich?" Barnum chortled in a letter to Kimball, in which he also described the "daddy & mammy of the General" as "the greatest curiosities living" and acknowledged he could not resist "showing them up a little" in the *Atlas*.[23]

But it was Cynthia Stratton herself, determined to see her husband "be like somebody once in his life," who came in for his most savage ridicule. Henceforth she would look upon New York and Boston as "dirty villages quite beneath her notice," Barnum assured Kimball, adding that "maybe there is not already a display of ringlets, earrings & other jewelry, $50 silk dresses with *low bosoms*, &c. &c.!!!"[24] When he wrote about her as the female half of the "vulgar, ignorant, common people" he dubbed the "Simpsons"—an American couple suddenly become rich whom the showman, supposedly, kept running into on his travels about Europe—he portrayed her as vain and overbearing, loaded down with diamonds and "tawdry jewelry," ostentatiously parading the streets in as many as eight different dresses in a single day. Yet despite her high opinion of herself as the epitome of refinement, she never could break herself of the habit of swearing, as was hilariously demonstrated at a fashionable dinner party in London where she angrily reprimanded her husband for asking for "sass" instead of "sauce" with the added remark—delivered in almost a scream, Barnum writes—that "I'd rather hear you say hell a damned sight!"[25]

There could be no question of parading such louts before the "crowned heads of Europe," and throughout the tour the "Simpsons" were kept in the background as much as possible. One suspects, too, that there must have been some rivalry between the jewel-encrusted "Mrs. Simpson" and Charity Barnum, who remained with her husband for several months in Europe. Certainly the two families were never intimate, although Stratton himself, described elsewhere by Barnum as a good-natured person who was always offering to "stand treat" to his fellow Americans, was for several years afterwards in partnership with the showman. Unfortunately, the "treats" eventually got the better of him. After returning to America and touring with his son for a number of years, he became so hopeless an alcoholic that he had to be committed to an asylum. He died on 29 December 1855 at the age of forty-four. Cynthia herself survived both her husband and her famous son and died in 1884, aged seventy-four.[26]

After visiting several towns in the south and west of England, the troupe finally embarked for the Continent, arriving in Paris on 18 March. Almost immediately the showman and his famous protégé were summoned to the Tuileries palace, where Barnum executed another brilliant publicity coup. Having learned of a forthcoming celebration in the Champs-Elysées and Bois de Boulogne, he boldly asked Louis-Philippe if Tom Thumb and his miniature equipage might drive in the same avenue reserved for the carriages of the court and diplomatic corps. Amused, the King was pleased to grant the request; and when the General and his carriage appeared in the procession, "thousands upon thousands rent the air with cheers for 'Général Tom Pouce.' There never was such an advertisement," Barnum exulted in his autobiography, "and thereafter whenever the General's carriage appeared on the boulevards, as it did daily, the people flocked to the doors of the cafés and shops to see it pass." Three additional visits were paid to the royal family, on the last of which the King expressly asked to see the General in his famous character of Napoleon, an impersonation that, on account of its inflammatory tendency, had been proscribed at public performances in France. It was almost a perfect reprise of their earlier visits to Buckingham Palace, where Victoria had sanctioned a similar indiscretion by encouraging Tom Thumb in his singing of "Yankee Doodle."[27]

Meanwhile, they had again begun giving public exhibitions in a rented hall, which was twice daily crammed to capacity. The receipts were even greater than they had been in London, "compelling" the showman to hire a cab to tote his silver back to the Hotel Bedford each night. In Paris the General became a "furor." Besides the numerous paragraphs about him in the newspapers, "statuettes of 'Tom Pouce' appeared in all the windows, in plaster, Parian, sugar and chocolate; songs were written about him and his lithograph was seen everywhere. A fine café on one of the boulevards took the name of 'Tom Pouce' and displayed over the door a life-size statue of the General." The leading French actors attended his performances, and before leaving the city he was made a member of the Association des Artistes Dramatiques.[28] There were supplementary appearances at private parties, charity fairs, and pleasure gardens patronized by the working classes on the outskirts of Paris; and before long the General was also appearing nightly at the Théâtre du Vaudeville in the first of several longer vehicles featuring him—a play by Clairville and Dumanoir entitled *Le Petit Poucet*, in the course of whose action he was served up in a pie, ran between the legs of ballet dancers, and drove about the stage in his miniature carriage. Adapted by Barnum's friend Albert Smith as *Hop O' My Thumb*, it later proved spectacularly successful in England as well, to which the General returned in the following year while making a long round of "farewell" performances.[29]

Tom Thumb was soon regaling his audiences with a few words of French (his mother, Barnum reports delightedly, never did progress beyond "quacking" in restaurants whenever she wished to order roast duck), and the showman himself, who had conducted some of his business on his first visit to Paris without benefit of an interpreter, eventually boasted of managing the language as well as he did French pastries: "beautifully."[30] When not engaged in business matters, he squired Charity and his daughters around the city and its environs, taking in Versailles, the public buildings and monuments, and other sights that had impressed him on his earlier visit, although his wife obviously did not share his enthusiasm for the Académie Royale, with its *corps de ballet* of "half-naked trollops."[31] From his letters to the *Atlas* it is clear he thoroughly enjoyed his long stay in Paris. He considered the city "paradise" and spent the happiest months of his life there, he raved—reveling in the life of a bon vivant, imbibing copious amounts of champagne and smoking good cigars, savoring the glories of French cuisine, and taking full advantage of the city's cultural offerings. He became friends with the Irish playwright Dion Boucicault, who was then in Paris and who introduced him around; paid several calls on the writer George Sand; and made a point of attending no less than three performances by the great tragedienne Rachel, whose acting was "perfection," he thought, and whose principal charm resided in the fact that "while she throws into every word and gesture a fire and earnestness which bear the stamp of reality, there is no over-acting, no artificial straining; but she acts nature, and she does it with an earnest quietness and fidelity seldom if ever witnessed."[32]

In contrast to his often critical attitude toward the inhabitants of Britain— where he claimed hostility to America and Americans abounded, and where he was sometimes moved to lash out at "bloody tyranny," oppression of the working classes, and "exclusive, over-pious, beggar-hating lordlings" who refused to aid their fellow man—he found himself in sympathy with all levels of French society, from its unpretentious, umbrella-carrying "citizen king" down, and genuinely liked and admired its people. If the bigotry and avariciousness of the followers of John Knox had appalled him during his recent sojourn in

Scotland, here, somewhat to his surprise, he discovered abundant evidence of religious toleration, a great variety of charitable and state-supported institutions dedicated to the relief of the poor and sick, and jolly good fellows among the Catholic priesthood.[33] If he was sometimes shocked by the ignorance and prejudices of the English lower classes, and would no more think of associating with them than he would with those "brutes" the Strattons, he now observed the benefits of a good public education system and felt no hesitation in fraternizing with their French counterparts. On a trip to Rennes around the middle of August, he delighted in riding on the outside of a diligence in the company of a group of rough sailors. Dressed in a slouch hat and an old salt-and-pepper coat, he joined them in singing the choruses of their raucous love songs, puffed contentedly on the stub of a pipe, bought bread and butter for a few sous along the way, and washed them down with a half-pint of cheap wine.[34] In later years, after his own prejudices had mellowed some, he was to look with a more appreciative eye on the "mother country." But on this first trip abroad, while he was still flushed with the exuberance of youth and his first great success, France was the country to which he felt spiritually akin.

In June he saw Charity and his daughters off to America, then left Paris with the company on the 23d of the month. At Rouen he was so moved by the story of Joan of Arc that when he later related it for the benefit of his readers, he became increasingly indignant and concluded with the wish that everyone who had been involved in her death had been "hanged on the spot."[35] Upon preparing to leave the city for Amiens, he decided it would be more convenient, and possibly cheaper, if the troupe had its own transportation. Including servants, a piano player, and a gentlemanly interpreter and guide named Professor Pinte, the party now numbered twelve in all, besides which there were Tom Thumb's carriage and four Shetland ponies, the miniature house and other properties used in his performances, and the company's considerable baggage. To carry all this, Barnum purchased three vehicles and twelve horses—as much for show as for practical purposes, for as he explained to those readers of the *Atlas* who might consider such an act extravagant,

persons catering for the public amusement must dash ahead and damn-dang the expense. Besides . . . it is necessary always to *put on the appearance of business*, in order that the *reality* should follow. When the public sees twelve horses, twelve persons, and three post carriages come into town, they naturally begin to inquire what great personages have arrived; and when told that it is the celebrated General Tom Thumb *and suite*, they will say, "Well, I did not think much of going to see this little chap, but he must be a devil of a fellow to require, or even *afford*, such a 'turn out' as this; really, I must go and see him." And so old daddy goes, and, if daddy goes, of course, mammy goes, and, if they go, "it would be very hard indeed if the dear little children could not go, bless their hearts; a little dear creature like General Tom *Pouce* is just what would please the children." So, somehow or another, the people *all* go, and when they have done going, *we* go—to the next town.

At Amiens, he continues, the inhabitants were half-frightened out of their wits when their "caravan" rolled into town.[36] Upon their crossing into Belgium a few days later, a customs officer, dazzled by all this splendor, seriously inquired if Tom Thumb was a prince in his own country. "Certainly," interjected Sherman, for once stealing a march on his employer, "he is Prince *Charles* the First, of the dukedom of Bridgeport and kingdom of Connecticut."[37]

While they were in Brussels, Barnum decided to visit the site of the Battle of Waterloo, to which he and a friend set out one morning at the early hour of 4 A.M. He could not help being impressed by the brisk traffic he saw there in reputed "relics" of the battle and by the whopping lies told by the guides who swarmed about them. After one of these had pointed out with great authority the place where Wellington had his station, the spot where Sir William Ponsonby fell, etc., Barnum asked if he could show them where Captain Tippitimichet of the Connecticut Fusileers was killed. This the guide promptly did. The precise spots where some twenty other fictitious officers from such exotic locales as Coney Island, Hoboken, and Saratoga Springs had fallen were also obligingly pointed out, following which the showman could not resist asking where "Brigadier General James Gordon Bennett had given up the ghost." This time the guide, who claimed to have been present when Bennett died, excelled himself and recalled the famous general's final words: "Portez moi de l'eau!"[38] "Mr. Philosopher Barnum" was scoring some hits of his own.

When Sherwood Stratton, egged on by his wife, and the other men in the company traveled to Waterloo on the following day, their carriage broke down while they were returning to Brussels. They finally arrived back in the city, drenched by a downpour, riding in a farmer's old dung cart; and Barnum added to their misery by pretending he had not gone ahead with the usual afternoon performance in their absence. Stratton was so depressed by this news and worn out by the day's excursion that he fell asleep in a barber's chair, after giving instructions that he was to be shorn until he gave the word to stop. The barber, not realizing he was asleep, proceeded to carry out the order. When his customer awoke to discover his black, bushy head of hair had almost entirely disappeared and that he would need a wig to look presentable in public, he swore like a trooper and stormed out of the shop. His anger was hardly appeased by the "deafening burst of laughter" that followed his explanation back at the hotel. It was the first time in his life he had gone sight-seeing, he said, and he guessed it would also be his last.[39]

From Brussels they returned to France, where Barnum, traveling days or even weeks ahead of the company, now acted as its advance agent. His duties connected with arranging for exhibition halls and advertising were hardly burdensome, permitting him ample time for writing and sight-seeing. Besides *de rigueur* descriptions (occasionally lifted from guidebooks, as he candidly acknowledged) of all the standard tourist attractions on his route, he continued to supply his readers with reports on his own activities, including a pleasant account of his journey from Orléans to Tours and other cities along the Loire in a small steamboat known as an "inexplosible batteau à vapeur," whose iron-clad hull frequently scraped along the river's gravel bottom. There one finds him, admiring the châteaux and other sights along the way, sometimes ensconced at a small table and glancing out a window almost at water level while writing his letters to the *Atlas* or enjoying a meal. A priest, trying to make off with one of the boat's handsome napkins, momentarily engages his amused attention. At other times he observes women doing their laundry at the river's edge or working in the fields—hard labor that, he chivalrously opines, would best be left to men.[40] In Tours, where he disembarked for a few days, he was appalled by a painting on the subject of the Last Judgment, showing "what strange and horrid conceptions some people have regarding the final destiny of man."

At his Tours hotel he was called on by a quack doctor—"a portly Jew, with keen, piercing eyes, jet black shining hair, and the usual 'Israelitish countenance'"—who insisted on demonstrating his skill at painlessly removing corns. Finding he could not get rid of him otherwise, Barnum finally gave in and accepted his offer to remove the first corn gratis, while keeping a sharp lookout for some trick. After the doctor had performed the operation and extracted, or at least produced, some hard substance around half an inch long that he called the "seed" of the corn, the intrigued showman agreed to pay him ten francs to remove a corn from a second toe. Again the operation was successfully performed. A third toe, this time without the slightest trace of a corn, was now presented for the doctor's ministrations, and again the same hard "kernel" was produced. By now Barnum had figured it out. Pretending to be delighted, he summoned the hotel's proprietor to witness the doctor's wonderful science, and in his presence submitted another healthy toe with the same result. Then, after deliberately taking off his coat and locking the door, he blandly informed the doctor he had "caught a Tartar" this time and could not leave the room until he had been searched. The quack blustered and threatened to take him before the "tribunal," but finally gave in when he saw this was having no effect. Within a few minutes the supply of ready-made "seeds" had been discovered in a secret compartment of his instrument case, and Barnum then took pleasure in kicking the doctor down the hotel's staircase, at the bottom of which, he writes with satisfaction, the proprietor "doubled the dose." The same rascal, he subsequently learned, had amassed a fortune through practicing his deception in Paris and the French provinces. "Be on your guard," he righteously warned readers of the *Atlas*. "Perhaps the same sort of impostors have reached the other side of the Atlantic."[41]

From Tours he continued downriver to Nantes, then on to Angers, Rennes, Brest, and several other towns in Brittany, admiring in particular the Druid remains and finding the native costumes, which reminded him of those he had seen in an illustrated edition of Izaak Walton, "very droll." He returned to Nantes via a different route and continued on his way south to Poitiers, Niort, La Rochelle, and eventually Bordeaux, where he spent several weeks at the height of the vintage season. Provided with letters of introduction to some of the city's leading bankers and wine merchants, he was soon in thick with the latter, frequently visiting their estates in the region of Médoc, rhapsodizing over the beauty of the vineyards, at one point stripping off his stockings and rolling up his trousers to jump into a vat of grapes and enthusiastically tread out the juice in time to a polka played by a fiddler. His temperance friends back home, he had no doubt, would roll up their eyes in horror if they could see him carrying on as he did, but he had "always desired to see these precious specimens of God's bounty at vintage time, when all was life and joy and gladness. This time is the present, and here, day after day, have I revelled and run riot among thousands of acres of ripe luscious grapes, the very sight of which is enough to make anybody but an infernal, cold-hearted rascal drop on his knees and offer up sincere thanks to Heaven for its unbounded munificence!"[42]

He was so often among these gladsome scenes, in fact, that the peasants had nearly all come to know and look upon him as "one of the family"; while in Bordeaux itself, at a dinner attended by the mayor and several prominent citizens, he flattered himself that he and the others had "broached a few bottles of as good wine as was ever tasted since Lot got boozy and played such shameful and ridiculous pranks in his family." From wine the jolly tipplers had progressed to cognac, which was wicked enough in "these days of temperance," he acknowledged. "But any man who can resist the oily, delicious, charming and enchanting temptations of a glass of real Cogniac, twenty-three years of age, can resist the *devil*, and I give him joy—I mean the man, and not the devil."[43] On another day, while touring the city's churches and cultural institutions, he was accosted by an old sailor who insisted on walking with him and telling him something about the city's history. Arriving in front of the sailor's residence, he was invited inside for a glass of wine—an offer Barnum accepted with reluctance, since the house looked poverty-stricken and he suspected his host could hardly afford a glass of *vin ordinaire*. Once inside, however, he found to his surprise that the rooms were handsomely, almost magnificently, furnished, while the wine itself was a fine old bottle of Madeira, the first he had tasted since leaving Paris. There was a valuable moral to be drawn from this: "We should not always judge by appearances."[44]

From Bordeaux, too, he wrote to his friend Moses Kimball, describing the mouth-watering spectacle he had seen in the vineyards and boasting of a trick he had played on some of the local authorities. As was true throughout France, exhibitions like Tom Thumb's were heavily taxed for the benefit of the local hospital and licensed theatre. Elsewhere he had managed to pay hospitals a reduced but guaranteed fee in lieu of the percentage they were entitled to by law, and had come to some mutually satisfactory arrangement with theatre directors. But in Bordeaux the functionaries of the two institutions had stood upon their rights and refused to be satisfied with less than 35 percent of his gross receipts. In vain he had enlisted public support by threatening to cancel Tom Thumb's visit to the city rather than give in to this extortionate demand; in vain had his friend the mayor appealed to the hospital and theatre directors to moderate their expectations. So he gave them instead, as he wrote to Kimball, "a touch of *Yankee*." Upon learning that the village of Vincennes, which had a mayor and municipal government of its own, had over the years been entirely encircled by Bordeaux, he rented a large exhibition hall in that enclave

and arranged to pay its hospital ten francs a day. Since Vincennes had no theatre, he was spared the necessity of paying that tax; and to "revenge" himself
further on the greedy Bordellais, he was raising the admission price from its
usual two to three francs. He would "raise hell here for 10 or 12 days & no
mistake," he promised Kimball, and leave the Bordeaux directors, who would
not realize a sou from his venture, "a lesson they will not soon forget."[45] When
he repeated the story a few days later in a letter to the *Atlas*, he claimed that
the citizens of Bordeaux were themselves delighted by his triumph over the
directors and were flocking to see the General at the rate of 3000 francs per
day. He was proud of having so successfully defended the character of the "universal Yankee nation," and hereafter, he was certain, the theatre director and
his "unprincipled coadjutors will consider a Yankee and the devil as synonymous terms."[46]

In early September, upon receiving an invitation through the Spanish consul at Bordeaux, the company crossed the frontier and journeyed to Pamplona
to appear before the young Queen Isabella and her court. The Queen, Barnum
ungallantly remarks, was a "dumpy little body with no particular beauty to
recommend her," but was obviously impressed by her distinguished guests,
who had several "audiences" with her and were additionally honored by being
invited to join her in the royal box to witness a bullfight. While somewhat
apologetic about being present at such a "cruel practice," Barnum could not
resist giving his readers a long, colorful description of the spectacle. As the
excitement mounted, he quite ceased thinking of the suffering of the animals
and men and "never felt so much like throwing my hat high in the air and
crying *bravo* with all my power of lungs as when I saw the executioner's well
aimed sword enter the fatal spot and lay a sturdy and ponderous bull dead at
his feet."[47] In the end, he reasoned, the *corrida* was hardly any worse than
"other sports in which fish, flesh, and fowl are subject to torture of various
descriptions for the purpose of gratifying the taste of the sportsman." Besides,
it would be futile to deny the irresistible, all-absorbing interest of the bullfight.
Even Spanish women delighted in witnessing it and behaved as "respectably,"
he observed with some irony, "as those of other countries do at executions or
other dreadful scenes, where they crowd with their babies, yearning after strange
excitement."[48] There were visits to the Pamplona theatre as well, where the
showman was amused to see the raven-haired female spectators fluttering their
mantillas and ogling the men from their special gallery, the *cazuela*, and where
he also delighted in witnessing the bolero—"the essence, the cream, the *sauce
piquante* of the night's entertainments"—performed. He could not begin to describe the beauty and fascination of the Spanish women he saw. "Suffice it to
say this is a dangerous country to any except those who, like myself, have lived
long enough to resist all temptations!"[49]

Following this Spanish interlude the company resumed its progress through
southern France, with the showman now recording his impressions of towns
along their route to Marseilles. At Nîmes, where he arrived on 18 October, he
spent five hours surveying the amphitheatre and other Roman antiquities.[50]
By now, however, he was tired of touring and increasingly homesick for Amer-

ica and his family, and Charity had written to say she was expecting again. Shortly after visiting Marseilles he was back in Paris; toward the end of the year the company returned to England, where the General reappeared briefly at Egyptian Hall prior to commencing a "farewell" tour of the British provinces. But his popularity had hardly diminished, and as Barnum wrote to a friend the following April, their business and prospects continued to be so surprisingly good that they had decided to remain in England for another year.[51] By then they had returned once more to Egyptian Hall for a much longer stay (during their final year in England Tom Thumb also appeared at various theatres in Smith's adaptation of *Le Petit Poucet*), which in turn was followed by another obligatory round of "farewell" engagements.

It was during this third stay at Egyptian Hall that the English artist Benjamin Haydon committed suicide following the failure of his own exhibition in the same building. While watching thousands of spectators stream past his door to witness Tom Thumb's performances, he had been bitterly disappointed by the handful of people who were willing to pay to see his own "magnificent" work, two gigantic canvases on the subjects of Aristides being banned by the populace and Nero harping while Rome burned. When he took out a sarcastic newspaper advertisement, headed "Exquisite Feeling of the English People for High Art," in which he complained that Tom Thumb had taken £600 during the previous week while he who had labored forty-two years for the elevation of British taste had received less than a hundredth of that amount, his friends in art circles could only shake their heads. On 21 June, a month after he had been forced to close his exhibition, he slashed his throat and shot himself. Predictably, there were those who, like the poetess Elizabeth Barrett, attributed his death to the "victory" of Tom Thumb. Others, like Dickens, who privately marveled that Haydon's mediocre paintings had attracted as many people as they had, took a more objective view of the matter. Nor did the jingoistic attempts of several journalists and cartoonists to link the artist's suicide to the success of the Yankee showman and his "disgusting dwarf" carry much weight with the British public. At the end of June, in the midst of this uproar, Tom Thumb commenced his final tour of the provinces. Barnum himself, if he was at all affected by Haydon's death, did not mention it in his autobiography.[52]

In the meantime, after deciding to prolong the company's stay in Europe, he had paid a second flying visit to America. Prior to departing on the *Great Western* in mid-April, he had written to his friend John Nimmo in Paris to express his anxiety over Charity's "accouchement." He would not know the result until he arrived home, and meanwhile he could only hope for the best.[53] At sea he composed his final letters to the *Atlas*, fretting over the boredom and monotony of such voyages and extolling the good companionship he found among a group of Catholic priests.[54] Strange to relate, he also struck up a shipboard friendship with a noted Presbyterian clergyman and missionary, Dr. Robert Baird, whose widely read writings, in which he freely attacked liberal denominations like Universalism, had always impressed Barnum as being "very rigid and intolerant." The two men had several friendly tilts on the subject of religion, and Barnum was impressed by the businesslike manner in which the doctor considered various problems. When Sunday rolled round and the ship's martinet captain, a person named Judkins, barked out the Episcopalian service as though he were giving orders, the showman decided it would be a good idea if Baird were to conduct another service. The captain, taking umbrage, refused the request; then, when Barnum persisted in arguing the point, told him to "shut up" and threatened to clap him in irons. High words ensued, during which Barnum dared the captain to lay a finger on him and promised to show him "a touch of Yankee ideas of religious intolerance" when they reached New York, until friends interposed and dragged him off to another part of the ship. On the last night at sea the captain sent a bottle of champagne to his table and asked to be allowed to drink to his health, a proposal to which Barnum grudgingly consented. But in retrospect he was ashamed of making up so easily, and on later crossings, whenever he encountered the irascible Judkins again, he was always reminded of the captain's "coarse and offensive" manner during this 1846 voyage.[55]

Upon arriving home toward the end of April, he learned Charity had been safely delivered on 1 March of another daughter. Pauline, who was destined to become her father's favorite, was their fourth and final child. Since 1842 his family had spent considerable time in Bridgeport, Connecticut, where Barnum's half-brother Philo was permanently settled. He now purchased seventeen acres just over the city line in the town of Fairfield, with the intention of building the first of his mansions thereon. In New York City itself the Museum had continued to flourish under Hitchcock's able direction, and the proprietor, thanks largely to his letters in the *Atlas*, now discovered he had become an even greater object of curiosity than he had been on his previous visit. On 23 May, Walt Whitman, recently hired as editor of the *Brooklyn Daily Eagle*, crossed the East River to interview Barnum, who told him about his tour through Europe and the various kings, queens, and "big bugs" he had met. When the gentle editor inquired if he had seen anything there to make him love Yankeedom less, the showman's gray eyes flashed: "My God! no! not a bit of it! Why, sir, you can't imagine the difference. There everything is frozen—kings and *things*—formal, but absolutely *frozen*. Here it is *life*. Here it is freedom, and here are *men*." Whitman concluded his account of the interview with the prophetic observation that "a whole book might be written on that little speech of Barnum's."[56]

From his office at the Museum Barnum also set about arranging for other curiosities to take back to England with him. Besides the ill-fated Hervey Leach, the first of his "What Is Its?," these included a speaking automaton, dubbed the "Euphonia," invented by a Professor Faber of Philadelphia. Operated by a kind of keyboard, it was a truly ingenious mechanism, popular with audiences in America and Europe for many years afterwards and endorsed in writing by the Duke of Wellington himself, who at first suspected its inventor of being a ventriloquist.[57] At Egyptian Hall, where Barnum exhibited it separately in August at one shilling a head, it was advertised to speak "anything and everything suggested by the audience in all languages, whispers, laughs, and sings all airs, including the air and words of God save the Queen."[58] The initial weekly profits from this one speculation alone, Barnum wrote Kimball, amounted to $300 and would probably be greater once the winter "season" commenced.[59]

To Kimball, too, he confided in the same letter from Brighton that something had gone wrong during his recent stay in America. He had intended to remain in New York until 16 July, "but my troubles only seemed daily to increase, and in a fit of very *desperation* I resolved to leave the 25th June by *G. Western*. So here I am, and although hard at work and not very happy, I have less *troubles* than when I was home." Had he not fled America when he did, he was convinced he would have been confined in an insane asylum before the next steamer left! "I *never* before experienced so much trouble, nay *misery*, in the same space of time as I was forced to endure during my stay in the States, and if I believed I should be obliged to go through the same vexations & annoyances when I returned, I would *never go back, by God!*" Barnum is nowhere specific about the cause of his decampment, but from his reference to "home," which he rarely used in other than a literal sense, one may make a reasonable deduction. In all likelihood Charity, who had given birth to two of their children and seen the death of a third while he was off on his rambles, had been having her say about his decision to remain another year in Europe. Those rollicking letters she and her friends had been reading in the *Atlas*, in which he had publicly made fun of her and boasted of how he had "revelled and run riot" among the heavenly vineyards of France, not to mention his praise of the fascinating señoritas he had seen in Spain, probably played their part in this domestic drama as well.[60]

"Not very happy," then, and at some pains to make things up with Kimball—who was about to open a new museum building in Boston and who had been counting on seeing Barnum there before he left for England—the showman set off on his travels again. From Kidderminster he wrote to his Boston friend in mid-October, chastising him for getting on his "high-heeled shoes" and talking of "'not wishing to continue friendship or advice where it is not wanted,' &c. &c." He was tired of traveling and wished he could learn to be contented and give up the roving life. The General's harvest continued to be good, "but it is not all *cream* as we once had it," he acknowledged, and he was giving some thought to returning to the Continent in the spring.[61] Before he was forced to make that decision, however, things were thrown into turmoil at the American Museum when the good Parson Hitchcock nearly went insane over the death of his wife. As a result, it became necessary to wind up the tour and return to America a few months earlier than anticipated. After spending a few weeks in London, the company sailed on the *Cambria* out of Liverpool on 4 February and arrived back in New York, via Boston, in the middle of the month.

Tom Thumb had been gone from America for over three years, in the course of which he had developed into a seasoned performer. "Cuter than ever . . . in fact a *little brick*," as Barnum described him to Kimball in one of his last letters from Europe, the General continued to astonish all who knew him "more and more every day."[62] He had become famous—"Barnumized," as his awestruck Bridgeport neighbors aptly put it—and had returned from abroad, his discoverer insisted, "an educated, accomplished little man." There could be no question of letting the little wonder rest on his laurels, of course; and after four weeks at the American Museum and a brief "vacation" in Bridgeport (where he was nevertheless pressed into service for the benefit of local charities), Tom Thumb and "suite" returned to the road on a grand tour of Cuba, Canada, and the United States that included a visit to President and Mrs. Polk at the White House.[63]

Barnum himself agreed to continue as manager during the first year of this tour. While arranging with Kimball for the General to appear at his new Boston Museum, he boasted that receipts during the month Tom Thumb performed in New York had amounted to over $16,000. He could have done as well there for two or three weeks longer, for thousands of people were fearful of attending on account of the crowds. At Boston, where the troupe arrived in June after playing in Washington, Richmond, Baltimore, and Philadelphia, the terms— delivered as an "ultimatum" to Kimball by his friend and "Mister Boss Stratton"—were 50 percent of the gross receipts at evening performances; 50 percent of the first $150 taken at morning and afternoon performances and *all* of the money above that figure; with the understanding that the General's sales of pamphlets and other souvenirs were "his own affair." Even under these harsh-sounding terms Barnum estimated Kimball stood to make $6000 or more as his share of the transaction. Moses evidently agreed.[64] When the company performed in rented halls instead of theatres and museums, its share was even greater. Receipts throughout the year's tour averaged close to $500 on days of performing; daily expenses were less than $30.

From New England the company headed into New York State, where at Saratoga the showman served officialdom another "touch of Yankee." The State Agricultural Fair was about to commence, and its trustees, over Barnum's objections, insisted on charging him a $25 licensing fee. Unfortunately for these gentlemen, the wording of the license was so nonspecific—authorizing Barnum to "hold levees and give exhibitions for money"—that he immediately saw a way to recoup his investment. Arriving at the grounds on the first day of the fair, he went around to other exhibitors who had been ordered to pay the same fee, offering to license them under his own general authority. The embarrassed trustees attempted to persuade him to surrender his license and accept a "proper" one, but the triumphant showman refused their kind offer and continued to sell licenses for five and ten dollars apiece.[65] At Saratoga, too, as Barnum writes in his autobiography, he saw so much drunkenness among otherwise respectable people that he began to entertain serious doubts about his own sobriety. Although he did not become a teetotaler all at once, from this visit dates the commencement of his involvement in the temperance movement. Those heavenly days spent treading the grapes and quaffing the delightful wines of France would soon be an embarrassing memory.[66]

———◆———

BARNUM FINALLY gave up actively touring with Tom Thumb in the spring of 1848, but continued in partnership with the General or his parents for many years afterward. On later tours his interests were represented by a succession of qualified managers, of whom Sylvester Bleeker, who accompanied Tom Thumb and his wife on a three-year trip around the world, and George A. Wells were the most notable.[67] But the showman himself, despite all his protests to the contrary, never succeeded in conquering his wanderlust. As early as the summer of 1848 he was off again on a six-week tour of New York State and Canada, ostensibly a "vacation" with Charity and his two older daughters in tow, but in fact a business trip as much as anything else, making frequent contact with the Tom Thumb Troupe. Barnum's fifteen-year-old daughter Caroline kept a diary of the trip, which commenced on 5 July, Barnum's birthday, with a railway journey to Albany, where she and her father immediately went off to the local museum's "lecture room."[68] Two days later they arrived in Rochester in time to catch a performance by the General. After attending another performance on the morning of the 10th, the Barnums and Tom Thumb sailed aboard the same vessel for Kingston, Ontario, and were enthusiastically cheered upon their arrival in that city. At the hotel where they stayed, a mob collected to stare at the General's carriage and ponies outside, while Caroline and Tom Thumb amused themselves by blowing soap bubbles out the windows. There was further fun during a performance the same evening as Barnum raced about catching boys who climbed in through the windows. Then, in the midst of Tom Thumb's Napoleon impersonation, things turned serious when a fully grown man entered the same way and the indignant showman began dragging him from the hall. The intruder suddenly grabbed Barnum by the throat and began throttling him, while the General, jumping up and down on the platform and shaking his fist, made "frightful grimaces" at the man. But "father" had come prepared for just such emergencies and, after hitting the man twice over the head with a loaded cane, turned his dazed attacker over to the police. Upon considering the possible repercussions of this forceful action, he then changed his coat and hat so as not to be recognized and led his family back to the hotel before the performance let out.

A bit later in the month, after they had all arrived in Montreal, the showman took his family and Tom Thumb for a drive around Mont Royal. Observing a fine-looking estate along their route, he ordered the driver to turn into the grounds and, upon being intercepted by a servant, grandiloquently announced that General Tom Thumb had arrived on the premises and would be happy to receive the owner and his family in the garden. They all came running, naturally, and insisted on showing off their distinguished guest to their neighbors as well. On the way back to the city Caroline noted the "priests' farm where they gamble and drink during the night." When Barnum, who was in the habit of reading and correcting his daughter's frequently intolerant opinions in her diary, came to this passage, he marked the word "gamble" and added the comment that it was "rather a *strong term* to apply to persons who play a game of chess or cards for *pastime only*."

Meanwhile, the timorous, easily scandalized Charity had been faring no better than usual on this hurried tour. On a visit to the Kingston penitentiary (such tours were highly popular diversions in the nineteenth century) she was so shocked by what she herself saw that she refused to let her daughters look at the female prisoners. In Quebec, to which they traveled after Montreal, she suddenly became "ill" and confided to her family that she thought she would never be well again. Back in Kingston a few days later, by which time she had recovered, she begged her husband to break their journey and defer his plan to sail across Lake Ontario to Rochester. But her plea went unheeded, a big storm blew up while they were on the lake, and this time, as her less than sympathetic daughter observed, she "was so frightened that she forgot to be sick." On the following day, however, still on the water, all the ladies in the party prepared to be ill and congregated in Charity's stateroom with bowls ready to hand. When the fun-loving Barnum learned about this, he poked his head in through the window and obligingly helped them on their way by telling them some of his "odd stories."

But the highlight of the trip was yet to come, for they had still not gazed upon the mighty cataract of Niagara. They arrived at this majestic scene on the 2d of August and set out for the Canadian side on the following day. The route to the ferry lay down a flight of some two hundred and fifty steps, and Charity required considerable persuading before she agreed to hazard this fearful descent. Halfway down she complained of being dizzy and refused to go on. Barnum and his daughters continued merrily on their way, leaving her to get back to the hotel as best she could. When they returned to the American side later in the day (this time they rode the inclined plane between the river and the top of the cliff), they learned she had fainted on the stairs after they had left and been carried back up by a party of men.

———◆———

BACK IN BRIDGEPORT on the 10th of the month, Barnum might justifiably have taken pride in his progress to date. In a little over six years he had gone, almost literally, from rags to riches and was about to give incontestable evidence of this for all to see. Iranistan, his oriental mansion, was nearing completion and would be inaugurated with a grand housewarming on 14 November. From an obscure, itinerating manager of dubious attractions, he had risen to become America's best-known showman. "Prince of Humbugs" he certainly was. But he was also the discoverer and promoter of the renowned Tom Thumb and proprietor of the no less celebrated American Museum. The latter had continued to prosper during his absence abroad, thanks in large part to the bereaved Parson Hitchcock, who was about to be succeeded by the equally resourceful John Greenwood.[69] Francis Olmsted, the building's owner, had recently died; and while Barnum's present lease still had several years to run, so confident was he of continued success that he had already signed a new lease with Olmsted's heirs that was to commence in 1852 and run for twenty-five years.[70] The future appeared certain and secure enough. But he was not about to retire, as many of his friends contentedly did after making their "piles," and pass the rest of his days among the Bridgeport gentry. New ventures, sirenlike, were already beckoning to him. Some of these would be as ambitious, even more risky, than any he had undertaken to date.

Tom Thumb became famous too, of course, and over his lifetime probably appeared before more spectators than any other performer of the nineteenth century. Fittingly enough, the Strattons themselves became rich beyond their wildest dreams. With part of their profits from the European trip, they built a fine house on the northern outskirts of Bridgeport with a separate apartment scaled to Charley's size. The remainder of their earnings—a large portion of which, Barnum assures us, was settled on the General—was invested in bonds and mortgages. The money continued to pour in during future tours, and in time the General, upon coming of age, developed quite a taste for fleet horses, yachts, and diamonds. Following his marriage to Lavinia Warren and a three-year trip around the world that they, Lavinia's sister Minnie, and Commodore Nutt undertook in 1869–72, he built a splendid house of his own in Lavinia's hometown of Middleboro, Massachusetts.[71] Yet for all the money he earned in a pre-income-tax era, at the time of his death in 1883 his estate was appraised at only slightly over $16,000. Little Charley may have been notoriously tight-fisted or "mean" in his youth, but he was obviously no expert when it came to handling money.

VIII

The Finer Things

"The public" is a very strange animal, and although a good knowledge of human nature will generally lead a caterer of amusements to hit the people right, they are fickle, and oft-times perverse.

Autobiography

FAIRFIELD AT mid-century, as Barnum remarked in one of his letters to the *Atlas*, was a sleepy coastal community with no particular claim to distinction. Yet in its day, before the red-coated troops from the "mother country" burned it on one of their daring punitive expeditions, it had been one of the principal towns in Connecticut, extending as far as Norwalk on the west and Stratford on the east and possessing, in the area known as Black Rock, one of the finest harbors in the state. North of the town center, commanding a spectacular view of Long Island and the intervening Sound, rises Greenfield Hill, up whose steep roads Barnum delighted in driving his phaeton, drawn by his superb black horse Bucephalus, in later years. The handsome colonial church in which Charity and her sisters were baptized still stands at its summit. On the hill's eastern flank, near the old Black Rock Turnpike leading down from Bethel, lies Samp Mortar Rock, a picturesque rockfall once frequented by Indians, in more recent times a favorite picnic spot Barnum and his family sometimes visited. Even the legendary Phineas Taylor is not without some connection to the town's history. His second wife, Sally, widow of David Burr, came from Greenfield; and around 1819 he was one of the projectors of a notorious lottery got up for the ostensible benefit of Fairfield's Episcopal society—an ingenious scheme that proved highly remunerative to its managers, needless to say, and that also caused considerable uproar once its patrons realized how badly they had been swindled.[1]

East of the town, beginning at what was called Division Street (today Park Avenue) and straddling the Pequonnock River, lay the city of Bridgeport. Incorporated first as a town in 1821 and then as a city as early as 1836, it was to continue expanding during the nineteenth century into areas once parts of Fairfield and Stratford, replacing the former as the county seat in 1853 and soon becoming a hub of manufacturing and transportation activity. In the 1840s two railroad lines were constructed linking the city with the interior of the state, Massachusetts, and eventually Albany, where connections might be made with boats traveling the Hudson River and the Erie Canal. In 1849, with the opening of the "shore line" of the New York and New Haven Railroad, rapid commutation to and from the metropolis became a reality, leading to nearly a doubling of the city's population over the next decade—to a little over 13,000 in 1860—and to the decline of the steamship lines that provided similar but slower service.[2]

In the first edition of his autobiography, where he remarks on the pleasant situation of Bridgeport and the "enterprise which . . . seemed to mark it as destined to become the first in the State in size and opulence" (the paeans were to wax more eloquent in later editions, after he had become one of the city's biggest property owners), Barnum merely mentions he had the "concurrence" of his wife in his decision to establish their permanent residence there.[3] Yet his first two mansions, where his family lived for the next two decades, were actually over the city line in neighboring Fairfield, to which the lowly seamstress daughter of Benjamin Hallett now made a triumphant, Cinderella-like return. Iranistan, or "Oriental Villa," as Barnum loosely translated the name, was surely as fabulous a place as showman or any person ever occupied. Set upon the seventeen acres he had purchased a few rods west of Division Street in 1846, it was loosely modeled on the Royal Pavilion at Brighton, England, which Barnum had visited several times during his trip abroad.[4] Measuring 124 feet on its longest axis and 90 feet to the top of its central dome, the house was a medley of Moorish, Byzantine, and Turkish architecture, executed in reddish-brown sandstone. From its front it presented a stepped appearance, with conservatories at each end connecting to two-story wings, and between them the three-story main section of the house, topped by the central dome, some twenty feet in diameter, and four subsidiary domes at each corner. The wings and conservatories had their onion-shaped domes as well and were each in turn set back from the contiguous section. Broad piazzas ran the entire length at all levels of the wings and main section; and these were screened by a rich tracery of carved filigreed arches in the Moorish style, set between graceful columns that terminated above the roof level in slender minarets. From the topmost of these airy perches, which were glazed in during the harsh New England winter, one had a fine view of Bridgeport and Long Island Sound.[5]

One had an even better, if rather bizarre, view from the great dome above, whose circular divan was capable of seating some forty-five persons. Its circumference was pierced by diamond-shaped windows, all of different colors, producing an effect that never failed to fascinate visitors. Writing to his wife, Isabella Beecher Hooker, from Bridgeport on 9 October 1849, the lawyer John Hooker told of being taken on a two-hour tour of Iranistan that morning. "It was the most gorgeous display of earthly splendor that I ever dreamed of," he wrote. "It seemed like being transported into a fairy land." When his host and he finally arrived at the dome and gazed through its windows, "I never saw anything so like enchantment as the effect of those glasses upon the view around. One would give everything an unnatural greenness, the next made it look like mid-winter with everything covered with frost & snow, the next made all look like a world on fire—clouds, the surface of the earth, houses—all lighted up as with a myriad of fires, pouring their baleful light upon them." Upon descending to the yard at the end of this tour, Hooker was startled to meet another guest who was often at Iranistan. Tom Thumb had just driven up in his miniature carriage and was amusing himself by running about the walks. He was "the most curious & comical sight I ever saw. . . . He was dressed in full style as a gentleman, with boots & gaiters, a sack surtout & cap, & walked among us & talked like a man."[6]

Less favored persons were not entirely barred from this earthly paradise, for in keeping with Barnum's policy at several of his Connecticut residences, its grounds were open to the public. The many outbuildings—summer greenhouses, barns, carriage house and stables, a rustic villa, etc.—were also in the oriental style, some like Turkish kiosks, others like Chinese pavilions, including a house for the head gardener that was like a little palace itself. A large fountain threw up its jets at the center of the circular drive in front of the mansion; at the rear was an artificial pond, fed by a running stream, on which swans and eider ducks paddled about. The grounds were planted with hundreds of rare shrubs and fully grown ornamental and fruit trees (Barnum could never wait for his trees to grow); orange and lemon trees, banana and other tropical plants flourished in the long greenhouses; a profusion of flowers bloomed in neatly tended beds, themselves formed in the shape of arabesques and bordered by large seashells, smaller specimens of which were set into the gardens' walkways.[7]

Inside the "palace"—as Hooker and most other visitors insisted on calling it—a central hallway, whose carved walnut staircase spiraled to the great dome above, ran from front to back. Off to one side was the drawing room, decorated with panels representing the Four Seasons and a ceiling of white-and-gold arabesque moldings, with huge pier glasses at either end and mirrored doors that reflected its splendors to infinity. The furniture was of rosewood, the mantels of Italian statuary marble. A royal Wilton carpet covered the floor. Between the drawing room and one of the conservatories was the square dining room, capable of accommodating forty persons, the painted panels of which represented the arts of Music, Painting, and Poetry. Here, too, amidst furniture of black walnut and mahogany, were displayed some of what Hooker termed the "crown jewels" of the establishment: a silver dining service, a china cabinet filled with the richest Sèvres porcelain, and a famous "Harlequin" dessert set with each piece of a different pattern. These, a gold tea set, and various other articles of virtu had been purchased by the showman in Paris when the household effects of a deceased Russian prince came up at auction. Unfortunately, the prince had put his coat of arms and initials on most of the items, thereby decreasing their attractiveness to potential buyers. But as the latter happened to be "P. T.," the resourceful Barnum had snapped them up and hired artists and engravers to add a final "B." The coat of arms, like the one painted on his new carriage with the motto "Love God and Be Merry," he could learn to live with.[8]

On the other side of the downstairs hallway was the "Chinese" library, whose walls were covered with oriental landscapes done in oils. The furniture, with the exception of a superb brass-and-tortoiseshell marquetry cabinet said to date from the Middle Ages, followed an oriental motif as well and included a number of the items today preserved in Bridgeport's Barnum Museum: a settee, armchair, great bookcase, two tables, and several straight-backed chairs, all of light-colored "tiger" maple in late Chinese Chippendale style, upholstered in Indian silk and carved with a surprising variety of dragons, butterflies, birds, snakes, sea monsters, and bells. Beyond this room, in the other wing of the first story, were family apartments consisting of bed- and dressing rooms. The second story was occupied by additional bedrooms, a picture gallery largely devoted to mementos of Napoleon (on his first visit to Madame Tussaud's, Barnum had made a point of climbing into the Emperor's carriage), and what was described as the "bijou" of the entire mansion—the proprietor's private study, whose walls and ceiling were hung with richest orange satin. Adjacent to this was a room containing a bath and shower, supplied with hot-and-cold running water, as were all the bedchambers in the house. On the third floor, opening out onto the porch with its prospect of Long Island Sound, was a large billiard room that at other times served for balls and musical soirées. Illumination throughout the house was by gas manufactured on the premises, and heating was by hot-air furnaces. Not surprisingly, the windows and doors were guarded by Tomlinson's newly patented burglar-alarm system.

To this humble abode, then, whose owner had only a few years earlier proclaimed his goal to be the providing, "without ostentation," for the comfort of his family, some thousand invited guests trooped on the evening of 14 November 1848 for an "old-fashioned" housewarming. He had no desire to ascertain what Iranistan and all its embellishments had cost, Barnum modestly declared in the first edition of his autobiography, although he took care enough to enter the various expenses in the ledgers he kept and boasted to friends they had come to around \$150,000.[9] Besides, had he not given gainful employment to some five hundred of Bridgeport's laborers and artisans? Then, too, he reasoned, would not such a "pile of buildings," easily visible from the Sound and the cars of the soon-to-be-completed New Haven Railroad, serve as a splendid "advertisement" for himself and his enterprises? In the last thought he was quite correct, of course. He even managed to improve on the situation a few years later when, having a spare elephant on his hands, he sent it and its oriental-costumed keeper out to plow, over and over again, a plot of land beside the tracks whenever a train was scheduled to come by. This strange spectacle was also reported in the national press, and Barnum was deluged with letters from agricultural societies seriously inquiring whether elephants could profitably be put to work on other farms.[10]

The Taylorian passion for land was soon upon him. He bought a nearby farm of around a hundred acres, and another piece of land that he fenced in and stocked with elk and reindeer. Somehow this qualified him for the presidency of the Fairfield County Agricultural Society—a position he occupied from 1848 to 1854—at whose annual fairs he addressed his country neighbors on the virtues of manure and "staying on the land"; related hilarious anecdotes that were intended to demonstrate, if anyone had doubts about it, his ignorance of farming; and, whenever attendance showed signs of slacking off, was likely to put in an appearance with his "man in miniature" or place a hand-cuffed pickpocket on display. In his final address he treated his auditors to his thoughts on the "philosophy" of humbug and revealed he had once plotted a hoax even more outrageous than Joice Heth and the Fejee Mermaid. Taking his cue from the surefire biblical passage "There were giants in the earth in those days," he had ordered manufactured, from assorted bones, the skeleton of a man some eighteen feet tall. The idea was to bury it in Ohio for a year or so and then have it dug up "by accident." But his discovery of Tom Thumb had distracted him from these ambitious plans, and he had instructed his manager to sell it. A few years later the owner of a gigantic skeleton discovered somewhere in the South offered to sell it to him for $20,000. Upon investigating the matter, he learned it was his own creation.[11]

Yet behind his self-disparagement and pretended ignorance of farming was a fairly well informed knowledge of the subject—after all, he had learned a few things while toiling for his father in Bethel—particularly as related to fowls and livestock. He was proud of the great variety of birds he possessed (Spanish and African bantams, Egyptian and barnacle geese, mandarin ducks, gold, silver, and English pheasants, etc.); imported at considerable expense Alderney cows, whose milk was "like cream," from the Isle of Jersey; and obtained from Prince Albert's own farm some fine specimens of Suffolk swine— named, appropriately, "Victoria," "Prince Albert," "Empress," "Emperor," and "Lady Suffolk"—whose pedigrees, dates of "pigging," and other vital statistics were meticulously entered in one of the ledgers he kept.[12] And despite the assertion to the contrary by several later writers, there is plenty of evidence for his interest in, even affection for, his domestic animals. His riding and carriage horses were always the fleetest, most magnificent money could buy, and to the end of his life he delighted in showing off their mettle by overtaking his neighbors on the streets of Bridgeport, often arriving back home spattered with mud or snow after these breakneck races. For the amusement of his grandchildren and in time their children, who drove about his estates in carts of their own, he kept a number of goats and donkeys, whose exploits he humorously chronicled in his letters whenever the children were away from "grandpop."[13]

At Iranistan he even had a pet cow named "Bessie," who was given the exclusive use of a plot of grass directly beneath his study window. On one occasion, when Jenny Lind, at the commencement of her American tour, was paying him a visit, a misunderstanding over Bessie's prerogative almost led to the singer's abruptly returning to Europe. Barnum laughingly related the story many years later to an acquaintance he met on a train, but was outraged when he saw it published in the *Hartford Sunday Globe*. As reported in the paper, one of the showman's employees, an individual named Henry, was charged with keeping visitors from trespassing on Bessie's grass; and on the first morning of her stay, out for an early walk, the unsuspecting Jenny was caught by the officious Henry in this sacred precinct. Not recognizing her, he yelled at her to keep off the grass. "Sir," inquired the offended singer, "do you know who I am?" "No," replied Henry, "but I do know you ain't P. T. Barnum's cow." At this propitious moment, while the angelic Jenny stood speechless with rage, Barnum poked his head out the study window. The singer was too near the house for him to see her, but he could see his pet cow rubbing her nose against Henry. "What's the matter, Henry?" he shouted. "Does she want to be milked?" Then Jenny recovered her voice, whose pitch and tone took every curl out of the showman's hair. "No," she screamed up at him, "I don't want to be milked, but I do want to go back to England—and today, too!" A long explanation followed.[14]

His daily routine when in residence at Iranistan, described in an amusing newspaper article dating from 1854, is familiar enough to present-day commuters. Out of bed before sunrise, he jotted down things he meant to do in his "daily remembrancer" while sipping chocolate and munching on rolls. After a turn among the flowers in the conservatories, he tackled more substantial fare in the form of "a bunch of hamburgs," then galloped off to the Bridgeport depot with a groom in attendance. When his train reached Stamford, he bought and read the New York morning papers; once arrived in the city, he hailed a cab and drove to the Museum, where he conferred with Greenwood and his stage manager Corson Clarke, offered advice and hints, looked over the accounts, and spent some time working on the Museum's advertisements and bills. Following this he ran across the street to the Astor House, in one of whose private parlors he wrote and answered letters and met with various persons who had appointments with him. He then walked to Wall Street to take care of banking, insurance, and other business matters, met with his lawyer, lunched, and caught an early train home. Back at Iranistan, he customarily took a brief nap after supper, spent the evening reading in the "Chinese" library if he had no other plans, and retired by eleven.[15]

Elsewhere Barum himself comments on his busy schedule around this time and his habit of writing down everything he meant to do in his "daily remembrancers" or memorandum books. There was danger in relying too much on them, obviously, unless one intended to be thoroughly systematic and inclusive. On one occasion, when he was about to drive into Bridgeport to run some errands he had listed in his book, Charity unexpectedly jumped into the carriage and asked to be dropped at her dressmaker's for a few minutes. Her husband obliged, ran down the list of his chores, crossing them out as he accomplished them, then sprang back into the carriage and returned to Iranistan. A short time later, upon being asked by some guests what had become of his wife, he suddenly remembered he had not "put her in my notebook." The coachman was hastily summoned and ordered to reharness the horses and return to town for Charity, who had been "impatiently" awaiting her husband all the while.[16]

He was not home all that often during his first few years as sultan of Iranistan, having decided, in early 1849, to open a new museum in Philadelphia. Located at the corner of Chestnut and 7th streets, "P. T. Barnum's Museum of Living Wonders," as this establishment was called, regularly exchanged exhibits and performers with the New York museum, presented "moral dramas" in its own lecture room, and featured Barnum's latest hoax got up around this time, the famous "Little Woolly Horse." Sometimes joined by Charity and his daughter Caroline, the showman spent long weeks in the City of Brotherly Love during 1849, overseeing alterations to the building and "identifying" himself with the enterprise. It was afterwards left in the hands of capable assistants, then sold to Clapp Spooner in 1851, at the end of which year it was destroyed by fire. By then, however, as Barnum had promised Moses Kimball in an earlier letter, the "other shop"—meaning what was left of the elder Peale's once celebrated museum—had been "killed" by the competition and the two gloating managers had divided the spoils.[17]

◆

"I MYSELF relished a higher grade of amusement," Barnum writes in his autobiography, after describing the eclectic wonders to be seen in the American Museum's crowded rooms and the melodramatic claptrap produced on its stage, "and I was a frequent attendant at the opera, first-class concerts, lectures, and the like."[18] The claim has been viewed with suspicion by later writers (in a biography of Jenny Lind, one author even goes so far as to assert the showman was tone-deaf), who understandably find it hard to believe anyone pandering so diligently to the many-headed mob could himself possess any appreciation for more refined fare. From his earliest days in New York, however, he had been an avid follower of the legitimate theatre, eventually striking up friendships with Edwin Booth and his English counterpart Henry Irving, who entertained Barnum during his sojourns in London. On his first trip to Europe, as already noted, he attended performances by the actress Rachel and dragged the disapproving Charity along to opera and ballet productions. And it was to opera—more specifically, the concert stage—that he turned for his next managerial venture, the American tour of the great Jenny Lind.

How can one possibly do earthly justice to the "divine," the "angelic" Jenny? Have not her peerless virtues and unparalleled voice already been sufficiently extolled by those who never met or heard her? Did not her meteoric career across the great land of Demos foretell a glorious new era in that country's well-known appreciation for the arts? Has there ever been an instance in the annals of music or any other entertainment when the populace of nearly an entire nation rushed so eagerly to make fools of themselves, and then, once the excitement of the moment had flashed by, just as quickly wondered, shame-facedly, what all the fuss had been about? The legend of the "Swedish Nightingale" has become almost as ingrained in the American consciousness as that of Barnum himself. One must proceed warily when approaching such an idol.

When Barnum first conceived the idea of enticing Lind to visit the United States, he writes in his autobiography, millions of Americans had never heard of her, while millions of others were merely familiar with her name and had no real knowledge of who or what she was.[19] Yet the "Lindomania" he now set about so expertly infecting his compatriots with was hardly unique to America or a new phenomenon, for the English, and to a somewhat lesser extent the

Germans as well, had already lost their heads over Jenny, who for the past several seasons had been singing in London and making royal progresses through the British provinces. Like Tom Thumb, too, she had been petted, only considerably more so, by the "crowned heads" of Europe. Victoria herself, whose favorite singer she was, attended all sixteen of her operatic performances during her first season at London's Her Majesty's Theatre, breaking up other engagements to arrive in her box on time, besides hearing and meeting her at numerous private functions at court and elsewhere.[20] But of course opera, while Jenny's singing in it gave infinite pleasure to the Queen, was nevertheless, owing to its theatrical associations, morally offensive to all right-thinking people; and as Jenny was experiencing a spiritual regeneration around this time—was developing into quite a religious fanatic, in fact—she required little encouragement from the Queen, the Bishop of Norwich, and others among her pious, well-meaning mentors to save her pure soul from this sink of iniquity. It also seems certain the second of her fiancés (there is some doubt whether she had definitively broken with the first by the time of her engagement to Captain Claudius Harris) contributed to this momentous decision by insisting that his future wife not only agree in writing to abandon the "chapel of Satan" but also prepare herself to spend the rest of her life repenting the part she had once played in it. Even angels yearn for respectability.[21]

By the time of her association with Barnum, then, Lind had renounced the scene of her former triumphs (along with the demanding Captain Harris) and was busily at work on the reclamation of her soul. Henceforth she would devote much of her energy to the promoting of "sacred" music—Handel's *Messiah*, Haydn's *Creation*, Mendelssohn's *Elijah*, which the composer wrote with her voice in mind, etc.—although operatic arias like the "Casta diva" from Bellini's *Norma*, in which she had previously made her mark, continued to figure in her concert programs. They were "safe," provided she did not don costume and act them out. Her voice, with a range of nearly three octaves, was then at its peak, excelling at coloratura singing in which she startled her listeners with brilliantly executed cadenzas, chromatic runs, roulades, and an incredibly fast, even trill that, dropping in volume to almost a whisper, reminded many of the warbling of a bird. She was equally celebrated for her breath control, which enabled her to sustain notes, according to some who heard her, for as long as sixty seconds and to project her voice, even in the faintest pianissimo passages, to the farthest reaches of the largest concert halls. Yet, like all truly great artists, she could also move her audiences with the most simple fare: the folk songs of Scandinavia, for example, in one of which, the famous "Herdsman's" or, as it was more popularly known, "Echo Song," she introduced the marvelous effect of echoing her own voice by what one fellow musician described as "a sort of ventriloquism."[22] To be sure, not everyone was swept away by the "Nightingale's" singing. The dissenting opinions of Carlyle, Hawthorne, and Walt Whitman (whose heart Jenny never touched "in the least") have often been noted.[23] But the consensus was that she was the greatest soprano of her day, and there were plenty of qualified judges who concurred in this.

Nor can there be any doubt about Lind's benevolence. She really did give away a substantial portion of the money she earned, endowing hospitals, or-phanages, and scholarship funds for music students, besides contributing to a host of charitable, religious, and humanitarian institutions. She did this with no desire to publicize herself further—wherever she went she was regularly besieged, almost to the point of having no time to herself, by a motley crew of individual and institutional beggars expecting, even demanding, money from her—but through sincere, honest conviction. Her voice, she was convinced, was a God-given gift. Were the fabulous riches earned through this gift in-tended to benefit a single individual? For this reason, too, even when she was almost overwhelmed by the attentions of kings, queens, and church luminaries, she never lost touch with the common people. Like the good, simple girl she pretended to be, she was always deferential to the former, eagerly sought their approval and blessing, and was willing enough to be guided by the gems of wisdom they bestowed upon her (if the Archbishop of Canterbury said it was sinful to sing in a theatre, she once declared in the midst of a heated argument with the Danish choreographer August Bournonville, that was good enough for her). But she was equally pleased to meet, and seems to have felt considerably more at ease with, those from humbler stations in life. In Havana, to which she traveled in early 1851, she was especially delighted when Barnum intro-duced her to his old juggler and plate spinner, the once renowned "Signor Vivalla," who had suffered a stroke and fallen upon hard times. He was then ekeing out a living in the streets with a performing dog, which he had trained to turn a spinning wheel and do other tricks; and Lind, who had heard about him from her manager, ordered $500 set aside from one of her charity concerts so that he might return to Italy and end his days among friends. The juggler was so overwhelmed that he excitedly begged to be allowed to exhibit his dog before his benefactress—a request Barnum promised to transmit to Jenny, al-though he felt certain she would decline the offer, since she disliked receiving thanks for the favors she conferred. In a burst of feeling for the "poor man" and his dog, however, the singer not only agreed to let them perform for her but insisted on personally carrying the spinning wheel upstairs to her sitting room, where she showered Vivalla with questions about his life, went down on her knees to pet his dog, and herself sang and played for her guests. Barnum thought Vivalla had probably never been so happy before. A few months later he was dead.[24]

In preparing for Lind's American tour, Barnum shrewdly chose not to con-centrate on her vocal ability but to emphasize those traits in her character—her piety and benevolence, her "purity" and unaffectedness—that were certain to strike responsive chords in his high-minded, egalitarian countrymen. The outcome of his campaign would depend not on Jenny's reception by a handful of music critics and *cognoscenti* but on how well he managed to endow her with a broad-based, popular appeal. There was need for him to be concerned on this point. He had committed himself to the limit of his resources, and then some, before the singer ever set foot in America; and the success of the venture would hinge on his ability to fill the largest halls with capacity audiences. By the terms of their contract, under which Lind engaged to sing for him at 150 concerts or oratorios over the course of 12 to 18 months, Barnum was obligated to place the entire amount of her remuneration—at the rate of $1000 per concert or $150,000 in all—in the hands of Baring Brothers of London in advance of her departure from Europe; and to do the same in regard to the musical director, Julius Benedict, and baritone singer, Giovanni Belletti, she had selected to accompany her (for an additional $25,000 and $12,500, respectively). After selling several pieces of property and borrowing all he could, the showman still found himself short of the requisite sum. He was rescued from this impasse by his friend the Universalist minister Abel C. Thomas, who loaned him the final $5000.

But the deposit was only the first of many financial obligations he was to incur over the next several months. In addition to the traveling and hotel expenses of Lind's party (everything "first and best class," naturally), he had contracted to pay for a maid, male servant, traveling companion, and personal secretary for the singer during her sojourn in America, and to place at her disposal a carriage and attendants in each city she visited. Another clause in the contract entitled her to a fifth share of the net profits, beyond the guaranteed $1000 per performance, beginning with the seventy-sixth concert, provided Barnum himself had cleared $75,000 by that time. Should the manager be disappointed in his expectations, it was agreed that at the end of fifty concerts their contract would be "reorganized" and thereafter Lind would be content to receive as her sole compensation a mere 50 percent of the gross receipts. The singer retained full liberty to give supplementary concerts for charity along her route, on the condition these were not to be the first or second of her appearances in any city; the number of performances per week, and the number of songs she would sing at each of them, were also left largely to her own discretion. And of course she was "in no case to appear in operas."[25]

Generous as these terms undoubtedly were—it was rumored in Wall Street, Barnum informs us, that they would "ruin" him—the singer was in no rush to close with him. When his agent in Europe, John Hall Wilton, after preliminary correspondence, called on her in Lübeck, he learned his employer was not the only one in the field. Four other impresarios were vying for the honor of taking Jenny on an American tour, and one of them, Chevalier Wikoff—the same who had been managing Fanny Elssler's American tour at the time Barnum was on the road with Master Diamond—had assured her Barnum was a "mere showman" who "would not scruple to put her into a box and exhibit her through the country at twenty-five cents a head."[26] This, Jenny confessed to Wilton, had somewhat alarmed her. Consequently, she had written to several friends in London, among them Joshua Bates of Baring Brothers, to inquire into Barnum's character and "responsibility." Reports from these quarters had convinced her she need have no fears about his integrity and business acumen; and as Barnum, unlike his rivals who were so eager to take her to America, was willing to assume the entire risk of the enterprise without insisting that she should participate in any losses, her preference, obviously, was to sign with him. A sound business decision, one might think, arrived at following patient investigation and deliberation. Once in America, however, Jenny added a charming variation to the story. She would never have consented to see his agent, she confided to Barnum while visiting him in Bridgeport, had it not been for the beautiful engraving of Iranistan on the stationery Wilton had used to write to her. Upon seeing it, she had said to herself, "A gentleman who has been so successful in his business as to be able to build and reside in such a palace cannot be a mere 'adventurer.'"[27] That magnificent "pile of buildings" had paid another dividend.

The contract was signed on 9 January 1850, although Barnum himself, who was still occupied at his Philadelphia museum, received no word of his agent's success until Wilton returned to America nearly six weeks later. Besides scrambling to raise funds to pay the initial deposit (which he finally sent off to London on 17 April), he was soon caught up in a host of other concerns—arranging for steamship and hotel accommodations, the rental of concert halls and theatres, advertising and printing, an orchestra that at times numbered as many as sixty musicians, the hiring of advance agents and ticket sellers, etc.—most of which entailed considerable additional expense. And, as always, there was the press to be "worked." From late February on he bombarded editors with news of Jenny and his preparations to receive her, even enlisting his old enemy James Gordon Bennett in the campaign.[28] From Benedict and others in London he received newspaper cuttings of Jenny's triumphs before European audiences, which he dutifully passed on to American editors. Items published here— regarding the apartments Barnum had taken for Lind and her party in New York's elegant Irving House, for example—were sped across the Atlantic in the opposite direction. In August, immediately prior to her departure for America, Lind gave two farewell concerts in Liverpool. According to Barnum, she did so at his express request, so that a review of the first concert, written by a music critic hired by Wilton and published a few hours later in a Liverpool paper, might be rushed across the ocean the following day. The republication of this flattering account in American newspapers, on the eve of Lind's arrival on these shores, "had the desired effect."[29]

By the time the steamship *Atlantic*, with the "Swedish Nightingale" perched fetchingly on her deck, docked in New York on 1 September, the public's enthusiasm had been worked to fever pitch. Thousands of cheering people jostled for position on the wharves and on ships in adjacent berths; a bower of trees decorated with flags had been erected on the dock; a bit farther off two triumphal arches, surmounted by eagles and bearing legends welcoming Jenny to America, had also mysteriously sprouted overnight. "These decorations were not produced by magic," Barnum later acknowledged in his autobiography, "and I do not know that I can reasonably find fault with those who suspected I had a hand in their erection." Some observers had doubts about the spontaneity of the crowd as well. Scattered among it, or so they thought, were a goodly number of the American Museum's employees.[30] The showman himself had boarded the vessel while it was coming up the Narrows. Upon meeting Jenny for the first time, he candidly confessed he had never heard her sing. When Lind expressed surprise that he would risk so much money under such circumstances, his modest reply was "I risked it on your reputation, which in musical matters I would much rather trust than my own judgment." Now Lind and her party were descending the gangplank to enter his waiting carriage, upon whose high box, next to the driver, the showman took his own seat "as a legitimate advertisement." When they finally reached the Irving House, traveling a route lined with people leaning out of windows and overflowing the sidewalks, another crowd of "not less than twenty thousand persons" gathered within ten minutes of their arrival. At midnight there was a grand torchlight parade to the hotel by red-shirted firemen, escorting two hundred musicians from the Musical Fund Society intent on serenading the singer. The throng in the street was now even greater than it had been during the daytime, Barnum writes, and when he led Jenny out onto a balcony, "the loud cheers from the crowds lasted for several minutes."[31] All this from a populace that, a few months earlier, had possessed but the faintest idea of who Jenny Lind was and whose object of hysterical adoration had yet to sing a note in America.

And so it continued throughout the tour. The singer was mobbed in nearly every public place she appeared; her privacy as well was repeatedly violated by persistent fans and the merely curious determined to get a closer view of her. Newspaper reporters and satirists had a field day, of course, as when a peach pit, carelessly tossed by someone from the balcony outside Jenny's New York rooms, resulted in a nighttime scramble, described as almost a "street fight," among the waiting throng below. A more worrisome aspect of "Lindomania" Barnum never expatiated on became evident when the singer accidentally dropped a shawl in Baltimore. It was seized by the mob and instantly torn into shreds. Elaborate precautions were taken to get her safely into and away from the halls where she sang; in a pathetic attempt at anonymity, when going about on her own she sometimes wore a thick veil. Yet, surprisingly, she was not all that easily recognizable. Early photographic likenesses reveal her to have been quite plain, whereas engravings and lithographic portraits such as those of her on music covers, with which her public would have been more familiar, often appear to be so romanticized that one may be pardoned for wondering if they are of the same person.[32] Her contemporaries often remarked on her mercurial appearance—how, whenever she was singing onstage, her rather coarse, asymmetrical features were transformed into those of an "exceeding beauty." Even the editor and poet Nathaniel P. Willis, who spent many hours in her company, admitted to being puzzled by this. One could not rely on the usual discretion of one's own eyesight, certainly not on the engraved likenesses of her in every shop window, he wrote. While she was singing, there was "an expansion of her irregular features to a noble breadth of harmony, at times, which, had Michael Angelo painted her, would have given to art one of its richest types of female loveliness. Having once seen this, the enchantment of her face has thrown its chain over you, and you watch for its capricious illuminations with an eagerness not excited by perpetual beauty." One Sunday Willis accompanied her on a long walk about New York and was surprised to note that not a single person gave any sign of recognizing her. Yet many of those they passed, he knew, were among Jenny's worshipers and would confidently have offered to describe her features. "So do not be sure that you know

Jenny Lind's looks," he cautioned his readers, "even when you have seen her daguerreotypes and heard her sing."[33]

It was an entirely different matter when she was in Barnum's company, for everyone recognized the showman and naturally assumed she would be with him. On a number of occasions he traded on this confidence to pass off someone else—his daughter Caroline, Lind's companion Josephine Åhmansson, it really made no difference who—as the singer. Upon arriving at New Orleans from Havana, for example, the singer was terrified by the great concourse of people that had collected to greet her. Taking his veiled daughter by the arm, Barnum strode boldly down the gangway to the dock, while Le Grand Smith, his principal agent for the tour, cried out to make way for "Mister Barnum and Miss Lind." The crowd pushed and shoved about them and followed their carriage all the way to the hotel. A few minutes later, the dock now deserted, Jenny and her companion quietly left the ship and drove unnoticed to the same establishment.[34] A more revealing incident occurred earlier in Baltimore, where Caroline, who had been seen in her father's company the day before, was mistaken for the singer while attending church services. She had gone there with a schoolfriend whom she joined in the choir, and as the rumor swept the church that "Jenny Lind" was among its members, the parishioners strained their ears to catch every note. They were transported by the "heavenly sounds" of the "exquisite singer"—and the joke was, Barnum writes, "that we have never discovered that my daughter has any extraordinary claims as a vocalist."[35] So much for Jenny's elevating influence on American musical taste.

Fearful of the "promiscuous crowds" that gathered whenever she was announced to arrive in a city, the singer begged that her travel arrangements be kept secret. But her manager, while seeming to consent to this request, always took care to telegraph the information ahead, knowing "that the interests of the enterprise depended in a great degree upon these excitements."[36] In writing of some of the other "innumerable means and appliances" he set in operation both in advance of and throughout the tour, Barnum boasted that the audience that assembled to hear her inaugural concert "was not gathered by Jenny Lind's musical genius and powers alone. She was effectually introduced to the public before they had seen or heard her. She appeared in the presence of a jury already excited to enthusiasm in her behalf."[37] Among the more public "means" employed to whip up this enthusiasm was a contest for an ode to be set to music by Benedict and sung by Lind. The committee of judges, which included Julius S. Redfield, the publisher of the first edition of Barnum's autobiography, and the Universalist minister Edwin H. Chapin, was hard pressed to come up with a winner; but eventually—*faute de mieux*—awarded the prize of $200 to Bayard Taylor, whose "Greeting" or, as it was often termed in programs, "Welcome to America" was dutifully sung by Lind at the end of her first concert. The judges' agonizing over the hundreds of wretched submissions was humorously commented on in the press, and Barnum himself, who characterized most of the poems as the "merest doggerel trash," appears to have been nearly in despair over the slowness of their deliberations.[38] When a satirical pamphlet entitled *Barnum's Parnassus: Being Confidential Disclosures of the Prize Committee on the Jenny Lind Song* was published shortly afterward, the showman was delighted by the additional publicity, even going so far as to republish some of its verses—ribbing Barnum, Lind, and "Lindomania" in general—in his autobiography. Supposedly, the work had been got up by the prize committee itself (which was said to have kept the contest entries in the same hogshead that once held the Fejee Mermaid) in the futile attempt to vindicate its decision.[39]

The "means" were once more in evidence when Barnum announced that the tickets for Lind's first concert in New York would be sold at auction, a practice he repeated in most other cities they visited. There was nothing so terribly novel in this, for tickets to Fanny Elssler's performances in America had been auctioned off previously. But the showman, with characteristic cunning, turned such sales into huge publicity events by inducing others to bid astronomically for the initial tickets in the hope of achieving "notoriety" for themselves. Prior to the very first of these auctions, he advised his hatter friend John N. Genin, whose shop was in the same block as the American Museum, of the great éclat a successful bid for the first ticket to Lind's inaugural concert would undoubtedly secure to an enterprising businessman. No dumbbell, Genin (who had already presented the singer with a "Jenny Lind" riding hat) immediately took the hint, secured the prize for $225—a seemingly preposterous sum that was broadcast, along with the name and occupation of the fool who had paid it, throughout the land—and thereby almost overnight made a fortune. "Genin" hats became all the rage. Nearly everyone visiting New York was sure to wear one home, striking envy into the hearts of neighbors who were not similarly capped; from distant Iowa came the tale of one such badly battered article being auctioned off on the steps of a post office for fifteen times its actual worth; the London *Times* wryly suggested that a huge hat should be suspended above Genin's seat at the concert so that everyone present might recognize him.[40]

Years later, in an article he wrote for the *Cosmopolitan*, Barnum added an interesting wrinkle to the tale. He had not completely revealed his hand to friend Genin after all. What if, he had thought, there should be no other serious bidders at the auction? If Genin were to carry off the first ticket for a relatively low figure, would not this have a depressing effect on his own business plans? He had therefore gone with the same advice to a second businessman, none other than the great patent-pill manufacturer Benjamin Brandreth, whose own policy of advertising on a grand scale had inspired Barnum at the outset of his career. Strange to relate, his former idol was singularly slow to grasp the significance of the benefit Barnum wished to confer on him. When the "doctor" persisted in seeing only profit for Barnum in the driving up of ticket prices, the showman became increasingly nettled at his "temporary obtuseness." Brandreth finally agreed to bid as high as twenty or thirty dollars, and there the matter rested. When the auction came off at Castle Garden on 7 September, Brandreth's and Genin's agents were indeed the principal bidders. Genin later confided to Barnum that he had instructed his agent to bid as high as $1000, and even beyond that, if necessary, at his own discretion. But the "doctor," with considerably less foresight, had strictly limited his man to $200. He later acknowledged he should have gone as high as $5000 rather than lose "such a splendid chance for notoriety."[41] In other cities along their route the amounts obtained were sometimes even higher. In Boston a local singer named Ossian E. Dodge bid $625 for the first ticket to Lind's initial concert in that city, then used the publicity to advance his musical career, even getting up a song contest of his own for a prize of $50. The highest figure realized anywhere on the tour was $650 at Providence. In this case, in what may well have been the final word on the subject of patronage of the arts in America by businessmen, the purchaser, who owned a local carting company, did not even bother to show up at the concert.

Once the first ticket to an initial concert had been auctioned off, the sums realized by the remainder rapidly declined, and prices were fixed at subsequent performances in most cities. Going to hear the Nightingale, however, was never an inexpensive proposition, although generally one could purchase standing-room or "promenade" tickets for as little as one dollar. During a later round of concerts in New York City, Lind supposedly requested that seats be priced at as little as three dollars and no more than five. This was still at least twelve times the cost of a good day's entertainment at the American Museum, and Barnum, with a grand show of good will, readily complied. In fact, it seems likely he himself suggested the plan as a publicity ploy, giving the benevolent Jenny credit for something he had thought up, for he immediately wrote instructions to a typesetter on Lind's letter to him and his own reply, and both letters were published the next day in the newspapers.[42] By then the bloom was off her New York appearances anyway, and the huge Tripler Hall, seating around 5600 persons and originally built, but not completed in time, for her inaugural concerts, was finally ready to receive her.

As always, the trick was to locate and obtain the largest auditorium in each place they visited—be it concert hall, theatre, or even a church or railway depot—in order to ensure a profit and at the same time keep ticket prices within attainable bounds. Exactly what his average break-even point was Barnum never specified in his autobiography. But since he seems to have been content to profit nearly equally with Lind, and eventually agreed to split with her all receipts above $5500, somewhere around $4500 seems a reasonable estimate—a figure confirmed by Sol Smith, who was privy to Barnum's finances during the tour.[43] This would have included Lind's thousand-dollar fee and the salaries and expenses of everyone else in his employ, besides the rental fee for the hall and all other costs incident to the enterprise, including a sum set aside to cover expenses on days when they were traveling or otherwise between performances. At the end of their nine-month association Barnum tallied the figures and announced that Jenny, after paying a penalty of $32,000 for early termination of the contract, had netted close to $177,000 as her share of their bargain. If, as seems likely, his own net profit was at least the same amount, the payoff had indeed been fabulous. Only six years earlier he had been boasting to Kimball over the prospect of clearing $25,000 per annum with Tom Thumb.[44]

There was another sizable drain on his purse that may have been averaged into the expenses of the regular concerts, although Barnum gallantly never mentioned it in the first edition of the autobiography. He did so in the 1869 edition, however, and neither Lind nor any of those who had so loudly decried his handling of the tour ever contradicted him. In nearly every city where they gave multiple concerts, Jenny exercised her divine right to give one or more performances for charity. By the terms of their contract, Barnum was obligated to pay the living expenses of the singer and her party on these days as well as on all the others during the tour. But he also, on his own volition, assumed the expenses of these supplementary concerts—for the hall, orchestra, printing, etc.—because, as he wrote, "I felt able and willing to contribute my full share towards the worthy objects which prompted these benefits." The singer's sole contribution was that of her voice—at its assessed market value of $1000, naturally—although it was generally believed she paid all the other expenses as well. When Barnum once showed her a humorous poem in which her generosity was contrasted with his acquisitiveness, she laughed, then quickly remarked that it really was not fair, for "you know that you really give more than I do from the proceeds of every one of these charity concerts." But, the showman modestly continued, he had no wish to receive "a larger meed of praise than my qualified generosity merits." In puffing Jenny's benevolence throughout the land, he had anticipated and taken into account the inevitable results. Bread cast upon the waters "would return, perhaps, buttered; for the larger her reputation for liberality, the more liberal the public would surely be to us and our enterprise."[45]

———◆———

FOR ALL THE high-minded talk about "art," "charity," and "divinity," the real object of the Jenny Lind tour was the making of money. And the singer, who could drive a shrewd bargain with the best of them, was as eager as Barnum to make as much as she could. What she really thought of the plebeian masses that rushed pell-mell to her concerts she kept largely to herself, although in a letter written to a musician friend after she had regained the safety of Europe, she complained of the exhaustion she still felt as the result of the tour: "America, the anxiety I experienced there every time I sang to a 'Barnumish' House (you will understand all I mean with that only word) has put me down very considerably and my whole iron constitution was necessary to resist as well as I did."[46] All things considered, she "resisted" remarkably well; if anyone was entitled to break down during the tour, it was surely her manager. From the first concert to the last, over a period of nine long months, he himself "did not know a waking moment that was entirely free from anxiety."[47] There was, to begin with, the matter of the "angel's" disposition. Moody, intolerant, with a well-earned reputation for obstinacy ("mulish" or "pig-headed," as some described her), she prided herself on her lack of affectation and could be sarcastic and crushingly rude. She despised the immoral French, naturally, insulting members of that nationality she met along her route and causing Barnum to fear for her reception in New Orleans.[48] Her own superior religious enlight-enment led her to take a dim view of Catholicism, further threatening to alien-ate the nation's Irish population. In Boston there was a ruckus in the press when a Catholic school for children was excluded from sharing in the largesse following a charity concert in that city. The blame for the omission, fortu-nately, fell upon the committee advising her, one of whose members, Lind's devoted admirer Edward Everett, was particularly anxious to shield the singer.[49] Blacks she found "ugly"; and when a report began circulating that she had contributed to an abolitionist society, Barnum moved swiftly to mollify Southerners. There was not the slightest foundation for the rumor, he assured one Washington editor, and he felt no hesitation in stating that "this lady never gave a farthing for any such purpose, and that her oft expressed admiration for our noble system of government convinces me that she prizes too dearly the glorious institutions of our country to lend the slightest sanction to any attack upon the union of these states."[50] Jews were less of a problem and not all that numerous anyway. Jenny was an expert at converting them.

To those in the know, it was wonderful indeed how Barnum managed to keep Jenny's "angel" side outside. Sol Smith knew and hinted at the truth in the dedication to Barnum prefacing his 1854 book of memoirs; but the man-ager himself remained guarded on the subject until the 1869 edition of his own autobiography. Even then, in acknowledging her fits of temper, "ungovernable" will, and his discovery—contrary to what he had believed "till I knew her"—that she was less than perfect, he refrained from revealing the full extent of his tribulations with Jenny, whose faults he attributed to her having been so extravagantly petted and spoiled in Europe. It would have been strange indeed if she had not "now and then exhibited some phase of human weakness," and he remained convinced—or so he now informed his readers—that "her natural impulses were more simple, childlike, pure and generous than those of almost any other person I ever met."[51] But these were remarks set down in tranquillity, at the distance of almost twenty years when he still had hopes of renewing their profitable association, and his opinion of the singer had not always been so charitable. If, as he now wrote in his expanded account of the tour, "justice to myself and to my management" demanded such a qualified explanation, he had no one but himself to thank for its belatedness. He had so puffed the legend of the Nightingale's "divinity" that any hints of imperfectibility would hardly have been believed at the time of his rupture with her. Then, too, there were those who had predicted all along that Lind was bound to become fed up with his "humbug" and break with him. So he held his peace and put the best light on matters he could. Time was on his side, anyway.

As a result, throughout the tour one senses a curious ambivalence in their relationship. In private, at least during their first few months together, they seem to have genuinely delighted in each other's company: playing for hours at tossing a ball back and forth, dancing uproariously on Christmas Eve in Charleston, impetuously embracing in the wings of a theatre after Jenny had triumphed over an initially hostile audience ("Are you satisfied?" cried the singer; "God bless you, Jenny, you have settled them!"). In public and in their business dealings, however, while the showman continued to set in motion his "innumerable means and appliances," there was always a discreet distance maintained between them, for of course no taint of "humbug" must attach to Jenny herself. It was almost as though the singer's concerts and the blatant publicity surrounding them were two separate things—the one the disinterested warblings of the "Queen of Song," the other the unprincipled scheming of the Fejee Mermaid's onetime exhibitor, into whose snare the Nightingale had so unfortunately fallen. Or so it seemed to many of Lind's worshipers, who were more than willing to absolve her of any complicity in so barefaced a mercantile enterprise.

The showman had anticipated such a reaction, of course, and, like a lone conductor standing guard over a shrine, was prepared to draw all the lightning to himself in order that Jenny's own reputation and popularity might remain unscathed. It was his opinion, as he wrote in a troubled letter to Joshua Bates a little over one month after they were into the tour, that "her mind ought to be as free as air, and she herself as free as a bird." The trouble was, the singer had not fully appreciated the advantage of their symbiotic relationship and had already begun listening to "envious intermeddlers" and "evil advisers" who were "so blind to her interests as to aid in poisoning her mind against me by pouring into her ears the most silly twaddle, all of which amounts to nothing and less than nothing—such as the regret that I was a 'showman,' exhibitor of Tom Thumb, etc. etc."[52] The rumbling had begun around the time of the first concert, in fact, which took place on 11 September in the huge Castle Garden, a converted fort at the foot of Manhattan. According to Barnum, even before the tickets to this event were auctioned off, he had become so convinced of Lind's success in America that he voluntarily offered to share with her all nightly receipts above $5500. But at this point, he adds in the 1869 edition of the autobiography, the chief "intermeddler" in the piece entered upon the scene—the attorney John Jay, who, along with his partner Maunsell B. Field, had been hired by Lind to look after her interests—and insisted on inserting a new condition into the revised contract. This was an article giving the singer the right to terminate her engagement at the end of the sixtieth or one hundredth concert upon returning to Barnum the money she may have received over and above the originally agreed on $1000 per concert.[53] Elsewhere in the autobiography and in his letter to Bates, Barnum complains of suffering much from the "unreasonable interference" of Jay during the tour. At one point, he writes, the lawyer even demanded that he file a daily report of the tour's receipts and swear to its accuracy before a magistrate. The showman shamed him into withdrawing the demand, which Jenny herself, supposedly, had no knowledge of. Indeed, if one cares to rely solely on the testimony of the autobiography, the singer remained amazingly ignorant of all the intrigue swirling about her throughout the tour.

The new contract Barnum refers to was executed on 7 September and now appears lost. It was only the briefest interim agreement, however, for a week later, on 14 September, the two parties entered into a third and final contract governing the tour—a document containing several clauses advantageous to

Barnum, which he neglects to mention in his book. Among them was the release to him of the funds and securities he had previously deposited with Baring Brothers, and the privilege of giving a portion of the concerts in Canada or "any other part of the world" upon mutual agreement with Lind. The latter interesting option was something Barnum had secured and mentioned in a letter to an editor even before Lind's arrival in America (for a while he considered taking her to London in time for the Great Exhibition of 1851).[54] Most likely it had been broached by the singer herself, who, as one learns from another clause in the final contract, was fearful of the effect the American climate might have on her voice. The other terms were essentially the same as in the original contract, except for the sharing of gross receipts above $5500 and the termination clause Barnum found so objectionable. The expenses attendant upon charity concerts were specifically excluded from those for which the manager was responsible.[55]

All told, the new terms were hardly so bad as Barnum made them out to be. Yet he nowhere refers to this third contract in his autobiography, concentrating instead on the interim agreement as though it were the final document, got up before Lind ever sang in America and, he implies, at his own instigation. But again, Sol Smith had another story to tell in the dedication to Barnum in his 1854 book of memoirs—a dedication that Barnum was given the opportunity to read and correct in advance of the book's publication.[56] The lady herself had claimed "various modifications" in her contract after arriving in this country, among them "ONE-HALF OF THE PROFITS of each performance" in addition to her nightly fee of $1000.[57] Here Smith obviously had in mind the one-half the receipts above $5500; and the pianist Richard Hoffman, who was engaged by Barnum to travel with the troupe, was equally positive Lind herself had insisted on altering the original contract, even going so far as to refuse to sing after her first concert until Barnum gave in to her demands.[58] Was the showman, perhaps, protecting his own reputation or that of Lind again when he wrote of voluntarily making over to her half the receipts above $5500, and of John Jay's being the one who insisted on the termination clause? Significantly, the final agreement was executed the day after the second concert, the gross proceeds of which, along with those of the first concert, Barnum had agreed to divide equally with Lind. The singer's share from the two performances came to a little over $16,000, of which $10,000 was devoted to "charity." The expenses of both concerts, which in New York must have amounted to at least the latter figure, were borne entirely by the manager.[59]

Barnum thought that the enthusiasm with which the affectingly white-gowned Jenny was received at her first New York concert "was probably never before equalled in the world." He may have been right, for the audience of 6000—thoroughly prepared by him in advance—was in ecstasy almost from the moment she appeared, cheering and waving their hats and handkerchiefs, hurling bouquets at her feet, drowning the final notes of her first song, the "Casta diva," with a "perfect tempest of acclamation." Other songs by the Nightingale this evening included the trio with two flutes from Meyerbeer's *Ein Feldlager in Schlesien*, an opera especially composed for her; a duet with Belletti from

Rossini's *Il turco in Italia;* and, at the end of the second half of the program, the famous "Herdsman's Song" followed by Bayard Taylor's prize-winning ode "Welcome to America," which Benedict had managed to set to tolerable music. The remainder of the program, rather impatiently endured by the audience, comprised two operatic pieces by Belletti himself; a piano duet by Hoffman and Benedict; and overtures by the select sixty-member orchestra to each half of the concert. At the conclusion of the performance the manager himself was vociferously called for and "reluctantly" appeared upon the stage.[60]

In the midst of this frenzied demonstration one of Lind's admirers, the editor Nathaniel P. Willis, could not help detecting a "countercurrent." Upon traveling into the city to attend the concert, he had been struck by the all-pervasive talk of the impending event. "When before," he asked, "was a foreign singer the only theme among travellers and baggage porters, ladies and loafers, Irishmen and 'coloured folks,' rowdies and the respectable rich?" Even the wheels of his railway carriage seemed to be endlessly repeating the three syllables "Jenny Lind." On making his way with the crowd to Castle Garden, however, he observed several private carriages belonging to fashionable people deliberately traveling in the opposite direction; while at the Garden itself, upon scanning the audience with his opera glass, he was able to count but eleven members of New York's "Five Hundred." "There should, properly, have been no class in New York—at least none that could afford the price of attendance—that was not proportionately represented at that concert," he wrote. Society's distinctions should play no part where the Nightingale was concerned, and he yet hoped to see her as much "the fashion" as she was now "the rage."[61] One of those not attending—though he did finally break down and, not very pleased, go to hear Lind's "foolery" the following May—was George Templeton Strong, who in his diary was appropriately scornful of the "terrible new disorder" known as "Lindomania" and the asses who had fallen victim to it. The singer reminded him of "the good little girl in the fairy story who spat pearls and diamonds out of her mouth whenever she opened it to speak." But in Jenny's case the expectorations were five-dollar bills, "a variation that suits the more prosaic imagery of the nineteenth century."[62]

On 26 September the troupe departed for Boston, sailing part of the way on the *Empire State.* Cheering multitudes and salutes fired from neighboring vessels, of course; and as the ship sailed triumphantly up the East River and into Long Island Sound, the inmates of various charitable institutions along the way were lined up and paraded before their benefactress. At Blackwell's Island even the local prison population turned out—"a proof of very questionable taste either on the part of the Governor or of themselves," opined the music critic Charles Rosenberg, for when Jenny learned from Barnum who these "enthusiastic admirers of music" really were, she rapidly crossed to the other side of the boat.[63] In Boston, where the initial concerts were given at Tremont Temple, there was disagreement with the singer and her "advisers" again following a near riot at the Fitchburg Railroad Depot. Barnum had decided to give the two final concerts there on account of the much larger hall attached to that building. But unfortunately, the hall possessed but two narrow entrances; at the second concert on 12 October those holding "promenade" tickets rushed into the room when the doors were opened, blocking the aisles and preventing others from getting to their seats (the pianist Richard Hoffman writes that he had to be passed over the heads of the crowd in order to reach his place on the stage); the heat became so unbearable that all the windows were smashed during the overture; and there was so much noise and confusion among the audience that Jenny herself could hardly be heard. Meanwhile, hundreds of angry ticket holders had not been able to enter and claim their seats; a rumor started that the hall was unsafe and the floor about to collapse onto the railroad tracks below; and in the ensuing panic the crowd inside surged forward and burst through a door into another part of the building, from which spectators like Rosenberg were glad to make their escape. By this time, too, the manager had prudently left the hall, although he did return before the concert was over to make sure Jenny herself would have no trouble beating a retreat. It was generally believed he had oversold tickets, when in fact fully half the seats were unoccupied. Outside, the most violent threats were uttered against him, fists were shaken under his nose, the police themselves did nothing to protect him or control the crowd. Rosenberg, who witnessed all this, thought it was Barnum's "infinite *sang froid*" that saved the day. Obviously, things might have ended much worse than they did.[64]

They were bad enough, assuredly, since Jenny herself, once she had recovered from her fright, flew into a rage and was not inclined to calm down for several days. Others among the troupe were also indignant. A week after the debacle, on 19 October, Barnum was writing to Edward Everett, asking him to use his influence to placate Benedict and, indirectly, Jenny. The former statesman and Harvard president, who had entertained Lind and her party at his home in Cambridge, wrote to Benedict two days later. It was true he had once expressed to the conductor his "regret" that Jenny should be connected with the showman. But in the present instance he believed allowance should be made for circumstances over which Barnum had no control, and he had no doubt the manager was acting in good faith and would continue to exert himself to the utmost on Lind's behalf. "There is no person in the country," he added, "in whose hands Miss Lind could place the management of her concerts, of equal experience, enterprise, & tact." On the same day, in a sympathetic letter to Barnum, he delivered himself of the opinion that the annoyances besetting him were "pretty sure to be the lot of all persons who meet with distinguished success of any kind." The showman must "lend a ready ear to all reasonable complaints; do the best to accommodate the public; & be patient under injustice."[65] The harried manager had already done his best to accommodate the outraged Boston public by refunding the money of those who had been unable to gain entrance to the hall.[66] But he could not escape so easily the censure of his traveling companions; and a few days after writing Everett he directed a similar request to Joshua Bates, asking him to drop a "line of advice" to Benedict and another to John Jay. If the last continued to spend hours "traducing" him before the singer, there was bound to be unpleasantness. "I am full of perplexity and anxiety," he wrote, "and labor continually for success, and I cannot allow ignorance or envy to rob me of the fruits of my enterprise."[67]

At the time Barnum wrote these letters the troupe was finishing a brief engagement in Philadelphia prior to returning to New York for an extended round of performances at Tripler Hall. Toward the end of November they departed on their "southern" tour, giving a few additional performances in Philadelphia before continuing on to Baltimore and Washington. In the capital the President and his cabinet, along with most of Congress, turned out to hear the Nightingale; and on one evening the singer and her party were entertained by the Fillmores at the White House. Meanwhile, Barnum's seventeen-year-old daughter Caroline had joined her father and was renewing acquaintance with some of her friends and teachers from the private school she had attended in Washington. On 15 December, the day before the first concert there, she had the pleasure of accompanying a group of them to hear Barnum deliver one of his popular temperance lectures ("Father . . . spoke very well"). The showman continued to speak on the topic along their route, and Caroline herself was soon caught up in the "excitement" of pestering everyone she met to sign the "pledge."[68]

Following a single performance in Richmond, where the usual auction of tickets produced close to $12,400, the company traveled by train to Wilmington, North Carolina, then boarded the steamer *Gladiator* for the final leg of the journey to Charleston. Once they were at sea, a fearful storm blew up, extending their passage by nearly twenty hours. By the time they finally arrived in Charleston on the evening of the 23d, the ship and its precious cargo had actually been reported lost in the nation's press, sending, as one of Barnum's New York friends wrote him a few days later, a "thrill of horror" through the whole community.[69] In describing this tempestuous voyage in his autobiography, Barnum remarks that Jenny herself "exhibited more calmness . . . than any other person, the crew excepted." But his daughter Caroline paints another picture, in which the singer appears "very much alarmed" and she herself seasick. The manager, following his usual practice on such occasions, went to bed.[70]

A pleasant interlude occurred on Christmas Eve when the company gathered in Jenny's rooms for the exchanging of gifts and an intimate supper party. The singer had prepared a beautiful tree and bought for each of her guests a number of presents, some of them—like the "jolly" statue of Bacchus Barnum received and the seal with the figure of a singing monkey given to Belletti— obviously not without ironic overtones. The hilarity continued after supper when Jenny insisted her manager dance a cotillion with her. He had never danced in his life before, and this first attempt, his daughter reported, "afforded us a great deal of amusement."[71] There was less cause for joy at the concert two days later, when Caroline was dismayed to notice empty seats for the first time since she had joined the tour. Most of the audience was composed of people from the surrounding countryside: "the Charlestonians are too prejudiced and narrow-minded to come." At the second and final regular concert on the following evening the audience was even thinner.[72] The "countercurrent" Willis had observed was still running strong; and besides, many Charlestonians had still not forgiven Barnum for the Fejee Mermaid. According to an account in the *New York Herald*, when the company belatedly arrived at their hotel on the evening of the 23d, one person in the waiting crowd called for three cheers for Jenny. Someone else had immediately demanded three more for Barnum and the Mermaid.[73]

If Barnum suffered unaccustomedly from anxiety throughout the tour with Jenny, he was also at no other time in his entire career so uncharacteristically vitriolic, so dishonest and downright petty, as he was in his relations with James Gordon Bennett. In the first edition of his autobiography he was pleased to quote one "unbought, unsolicited" (the distinction is an interesting one) editorial from the *Herald* lavishly praising the singer in advance of her debut. But "as usual," he added in the 1869 edition, after Bennett had permitted this "one favorable notice," the *Herald* "very soon 'took it all back' and roundly abused Miss Lind and persistently attacked her manager."[74] From New Orleans, where the troupe arrived in early February, he directed a vicious letter to his friends Moses S. and Alfred Ely Beach, owners of the *New York Sun*, describing the carryings-on of Bennett and his wife in Cuba, a favorite winter resort of wealthy Americans in pre-Florida days. He had seen the "empty champaigne [*sic*] bottles" from one party the *Herald*'s owner had attended the night before; while Mrs. Bennett herself, who openly boasted of editing the *Herald* ("and none doubt it who know much on the subject"), had paid nightly visits to a "drinking shop" frequented mostly by men, where she kept up loud conversations "until an hour arrived at which she declared she must go home, for her husband scolded her strong and had forbid her going to the Dominica." The bibulous couple had later sailed for New Orleans on the same steamer carrying Jenny and Barnum and been snubbed and insulted by everyone from the singer on down to the purser. In Havana, the showman cattily added, a ball given by Mrs. Bennett had been sparsely attended, putting an end to her chances of attaining her "darling object"—namely, admission to fashionable New York society. The Beaches, of course, were free to make use of this information in any way they saw fit. Barnum held himself responsible for all that he wrote, though he wished his name kept "secret" in the matter.[75]

Poor James Gordon Bennett! Repeatedly duped by the showman and his agents, it would have been wondrous indeed had he not now and then retaliated. His *Herald* was among the first of America's truly great newspapers, offering far more news, on a broader range of topics, than most of its puny predecessors had ever done. And whatever one might think of its owner and his opinions—for like all newspapers of the day, the *Herald* certainly had its biases— its articles were generally knowledgeable and engagingly written; its editorials not without humor in their frequent sardonic thrusts; its reviews of books, concerts, and other entertainments more perceptive and fair than Barnum would have us believe. Which was one of the chief sources of friction between its owner-editor and Barnum, of course, since the latter, who could count on having pretty much his way with other metropolitan papers, was never able to "buy" Bennett's good opinion. In private the showman often fretted over Bennett's jibes and lack of appreciation for his enterprises; threatened to "cowhide" him in his letters to Moses Kimball; at one point even wrote to offer the editor a "flag of truce" if he would ease up on him.[76] Publicly, he professed himself "always glad" to be the butt of Bennett's attacks, "for they served as inexpensive advertisements to my Museum, and brought custom to me free of charge"; related a fantastic tale of how he had personally intervened to save the editor from being thrown overboard during the passage to New Orleans (by a demented Henry Bennett, no less, the same who had once managed Peale's New York Museum for Barnum); and finally, following Bennett's death in 1872, belatedly acknowledged the "extraordinary talent and tact of this great journalist" and magnanimously announced his willingness to bury their differences in "forgiving forgetfulness."[77]

In reality, the *Herald*'s coverage of Lind and her tour was as extensive and laudatory as any artist might reasonably desire. From the no less than seven columns that appeared in its 3 September 1850 weekly European edition, describing her last concert in Liverpool and enthusiastic reception in New York (and containing generous praise of Barnum's "managerial skill and enterprise" in bringing her to these shores, incidentally), there was almost daily notice of her movements and concerts, interspersed with many comments on the Lind "fever" in general. Reviews of her concerts were almost unexceptionally favorable, although the paper's critics did occasionally feel compelled to mention certain "small" faults they detected in her performances. What really irked the showman—and in time, inevitably, had a depressing effect on the singer herself—was the *Herald*'s soon focusing on what it considered to be Barnum's own shortcomings and questionable managerial practices: his blatant manipulating of the press; the high price of tickets and his supposed collusion with those speculating in them; his reputed refusal to follow Jenny's example and donate any of his own huge profits to charity; the overcrowding at concerts like the disastrous one in Boston; the frequently expressed regret, in short, that Lind "had the misfortune to be engaged by a showman" when she could obviously do so much better without him. Then, too, there was its continuing mockery of "Lindomania" itself and the fulsome "critics" who buzzed about the singer and spent less time speculating on her voice than they did on her matrimonial prospects.[78] The last was an especially sore point with Jenny, who celebrated her thirtieth birthday early on in the tour and was still casting about for someone to rescue her from spinsterhood.

In Havana, where the company arrived on 4 January 1851, receipts sagged again at the Tacón Opera House as many stayed away in protest against the high price of tickets. Rather than give in to demands that he lower these, the showman decided to teach the ungrateful, penurious Habaneros a lesson, cut short their scheduled twelve performances after the third regular concert (there was a fourth for "charity"), and grandly announced "there was not money enough on the island of Cuba" to induce him to continue. This left them "pleasant opportunity for recreation" during the remainder of their month in Cuba.[79] Another disappointment, presumably, occurred on the 17th when Barnum went to meet the ship that was supposedly bringing Charity to join him. In place of his wife he received a letter, explaining she had not sufficient courage to make the voyage after reading accounts of their perilous passage to Charleston.[80]

On 4 February the troupe set out for New Orleans and the return leg of their journey up the western rivers. For months Barnum had been corresponding and dickering over financial terms with his friend Sol Smith, who, with his partner Noah Ludlow, owned various theatres along the Mississippi. Prior to leaving Charleston, he had sent Smith some publicity materials, requesting him to distribute them discreetly among New Orleans editors. "I need not tell you," he added in the letter accompanying them, "that even *Our Saviour* needed John the Baptist as an *avant courier*. Why then, may not an 'angel' require the heavenly rays of *'Old Sol'* to light her pathway to the Crescent City? The angel Gabriel uses a *'trumpet,'* and *you* know that *we must* do likewise!"[81] While Jenny was again profitably charming audiences at the St. Charles's Theatre, Barnum gave another temperance lecture at the city's Lyceum Hall—an event that was itself reported at length in the daily papers and considerably impressed Charles Rosenberg. Hundreds could not gain entrance to the hall, he writes, while those within would have been content to listen to the lively speaker for another half hour.[82] When the company finally started up the Mississippi in the steamer *Magnolia*, there was a tiny figure at dockside waving them off. Tom Thumb and his parents, on a tour of their own, had just arrived in the Crescent City from Mobile.[83]

Their first few days upon the river passed pleasantly enough. Barnum had arranged with the ship's captain to lay over and wait for them while they gave single performances in Natchez and Memphis. At the latter city, Caroline wrote in her diary, some of the men in the audience looked as though they had never attended a concert before and expressed their appreciation by banging their chairs on the floor.[84] Evenings were occupied with dancing and a private concert on board the *Magnolia* itself, whose captain was so overwhelmed by the Nightingale's singing that he remarked that "if he had a home, if it was only a hollow log, he would go and crawl into it."[85] At Cairo, however, there was dissension again when they were forced to transfer to another boat for the trip to St. Louis. The *Lexington* was crowded and suffocating, the singer decidedly displeased with her new accommodations, and Barnum had to employ all his art of persuasion to induce her to tolerate them for a day or two. On the following morning, a Sunday, there being no clergyman aboard, the passengers asked Barnum to give a temperance lecture. In the evening he followed this up with a display of magic. The singer herself remained shut in her cabin until the boat reached St. Louis.[86]

On the morning after their arrival in the city the "intermeddlers" were busy again when Max Hjortsberg, Lind's cousin and secretary on the tour, announced that the singer wished to exercise her right to terminate her contract following the sixtieth concert. At this point the showman excused himself to consult with his friend Sol Smith, then at his home in the city; calculated the substantial amount Jenny would have to refund under the terms of their contract; and returned to tell Hjortsberg he was ready to settle. The secretary was obviously taken aback, and it then came out that the real object of his mission was to sound out Barnum on the subject of a new arrangement under which he would continue to manage the tour in return for a set fee per concert. The showman belligerently answered he would not do so for less than "a million dollars each" and that it was he who had hired Miss Lind, not the other way around. Hjortsberg quickly retreated and claimed the whole thing was a "joke." Of course, Barnum was convinced Jenny herself was not in on the "joke." Or if she was, she never let on.[87]

From St. Louis they proceeded back down the river and on to Nashville, where Jenny, who wished to visit Mammoth Cave, hired a coach to take her and her party overland to Louisville. In her diary for 31 March, Caroline petulantly remarks that she and her father had decided not to accompany "her Majesty" on this tour, "thinking we might be considered intruders." Instead, the showman and the remainder of the company continued on by boat. Shortly before they reached Louisville, a fight broke out between the musicians and the boat's steward. Pistols were drawn, and Barnum, jumping in to quell the disturbance and siding with the steward, received a terrific slap in the face from one of his employees.[88] After Louisville, the company continued on its fitful course: to Cincinnati, where the receipts from five performances nearly equaled those of the seven they had previously given in Philadelphia; to Wheeling, where a single concert, sold in advance for $5000 to two local entrepreneurs, was given in a church; and to dusky Pittsburgh, where a second planned concert had to be abruptly canceled when the singer, terrified by the drunken factory workers who kept up a row outside the theatre on the night of the first performance, fled from the city the following morning.[89]

By the time they arrived back in New York in early May, they were barely halfway through the 150 concerts. Worn out by his exertions over the past eight months, plunged anew into the stifling atmosphere of intrigue generated by Lind's "advisers" and her lawyer John Jay, the showman no longer cared what course the singer might elect to follow, even devoutly wished for his release at the end of the one hundredth concert. To his joy, Jenny herself informed him she had decided to exercise that option.[90] The final concerts were scheduled for Philadelphia and Boston; but at the former there was another disagreeable scene when one of the "advisers" (Hjortsberg, apparently) stirred up trouble over the theatre Barnum had rented, a house recently used for equestrian entertainments. His patience finally exhausted, the showman offered to relinquish his management at the end of the first Philadelphia concert in return for $1000 for each of the remaining seven nights, in addition to the penalty imposed for terminating their agreement after the one hundredth performance. This time it was the singer's turn to feel relieved.

———◆———

SO THE GREAT Jenny Lind enterprise concluded prematurely on a sour note, although Barnum continued to assure readers of his autobiography that there had never been any disharmony between him and the singer herself. All the same, he took satisfaction in reporting that Jenny's subsequent career in America turned out to be pretty much as he had expected. On her own now, without the experienced showman to keep her "angel" side outside and draw all the thunderbolts to himself, she soon found herself beset by all the petty annoyances of managing her own concerts and by people who, as she later complained to him, swindled her at every turn.[91] Strange to relate, too, for all the carping criticism of Barnum's management she had lent an ear to, there were still outraged complaints about the high cost of tickets and those speculating in them; audiences and mobs outside theatres continued to prove as unpredictable as ever; the press, with little to gain from the "angel" herself, was no longer so lavish or uncritical in its praise. By the time of her final concert on 24 May 1852 in the same Castle Garden where she had commenced her American career—for Jenny was a sentimentalist at heart, and even delayed her departure for Europe in order to sail on the same ship, with the same captain, that had brought her to these shores—a number of critics had perceived the basic incongruity of her "fragmentary and unsatisfactory concert performances" in which the singer, despite her well-known aversion for opera and anything "theatrical," persisted in singing operatic morceaux that "throughout the length and breadth of the country . . . were neither understood nor appreciated, and therefore left no marked impression." Had she been able to conquer her religious scruples in regard to the stage, one writer noted, and performed in full-fledged operas rather than the "elaborate monstrosities" that constituted her programs, "an audience would not have been wanting which would not only have derived rich, rare pleasure from the representation, but a substantial benefit would have been rendered to musical professors and students, which they may now hope for in vain."[92]

But the "divinity" remained adamantly unreceptive to all such mundane reasoning. Her narrow, pietistic mind, her eminently bourgeois craving for "respectability," would never permit her to acknowledge the essential hypocrisy of her position—a position that had been attained through the very institution she so resolutely turned her back on, instead of attempting to elevate it through her own example. In later life, her biographers note, she could not pass the Swedish Royal Theatre where she had celebrated her initial triumphs without an involuntary shudder running down her spine.[93] How fitting, then, that she and her husband, the plodding pianist Otto Goldschmidt—whom she had first converted from Judaism, then married toward the end of her stay in America— should eventually settle upon England as their home. Its climate proved devastating to the health of both. But its "fidelity" impressed Jenny as being far above that of all the other countries she had visited.

And Barnum himself? For the rest of his life he preened himself on having been the manager of the great Jenny Lind and on having introduced thousands of his countrymen to bona fide Art. But the "art," as is obvious even from the less than candid pages of the autobiography, was heavily dependent on "humbug" for its success, while the natural antipathy between the two contributed inexorably to the showman's rupture with his singer. In his spectacular management of the Jenny Lind tour, Barnum was, paradoxically, both within and without his natural element. The methods he used to publicize the singer were essentially the same he employed for all his enterprises, and financially, at least, proved highly gratifying to both parties. Yet the notion that art needed to be hawked like a Fejee Mermaid remained unacceptable to Lind and her friends, many of whom, like Edward Everett—who was certainly sympathetic so long as the showman remained in his proper sphere of influence—felt infinitely relieved when Lind ended her "discreditable" relationship with Barnum.[94] It was a problem nearly insoluble in the nineteenth century, when distinctions between art and commerce were deemed more unbridgeable than they are today. But the showman, with unflagging optimism, refused to be daunted by such prejudices. During his bankruptcy a few years later, when he was desperately searching for ways to raise large sums of money, he conquered his own distasteful memories of their earlier venture and proposed to the singer that they embark on a new tour.[95] As late as the mid-seventies, by which time the Nightingale was long past her prime, he was still wistfully looking back on that golden era and insisting to his jealous circus partners that he had the right to run "Jenny Lind Concerts" if occasion arose.[96] But the singer steadfastly declined to renew her association with her old manager. In public, to be sure, they remained the best of friends.

IX

Bridgeport and Bankruptcy

> The fact is, I am not, nor never was, half so cute nor cunning nor *deep* as many persons suppose. I generally speak right out, just as I think, & have neither time nor inclination to engage in duplicity.
>
> *Barnum to the Reverend Thomas Wentworth Higginson,*
> *c. April 1855*

DURING THE leisurely trip up the western rivers Barnum displayed his usual predilection for practical jokes, among them a flurry of fake telegrams announcing sundry items of good and bad news to nearly all the members of the Jenny Lind troupe on April Fools' Day.[1] Yet the news he had conveyed to his daughter the previous week, he solemnly assured her, was *not* a joke: he had decided to sell or lease Iranistan after the 1st of July and move to the outskirts of Philadelphia, where he had already purchased a furnished country seat. The announcement, Caroline recorded in her diary, reduced her to a "flood of tears"; and she was certain that her mother, who had not yet been informed, would be "perfectly miserable," especially after lavishing so much attention on Iranistan and its grounds. It was "abominable to have to leave them, but we must resign ourselves to our fate." Three days later, her father still adamant, she was writing letters home to tell her mother and friends of the intended move. The mansion, together with its elegant furnishings, Barnum's nearby farm and livestock, were actually advertised to be sold or auctioned off, "without the slightest reserve," on 19 June. Then, just as suddenly, these plans were dropped.[2]

What may have prompted this temporary aberration? Was the troubled manager—the frustrated husband, perhaps—attempting to get back at Charity in some way for refusing to accompany him on the long, arduous tour? Or did he genuinely wish to remove to what he considered to be a more congenial environment? The months he had recently spent in Philadelphia while establishing his new museum there had been pleasant ones. In that city, too, the Reverend Abel C. Thomas—the same who had loaned him the final $5000 to bring Jenny Lind to America, as close a friend as he ever had—was pastor to the First Universalist Church in Lombard Street. But Philadelphia was not to be, and after nursing his wounds for a week at Cape May following the collapse of the Jenny Lind enterprise, Barnum was glad enough to return to Iranistan, where he spent most of the summer of 1851 recuperating.

His attention was soon occupied by other projects, a number of which had been set in motion well in advance of his involvement with Lind. Shortly before breaking with the singer, he had induced her to witness, from a balcony of the Irving House where she was again staying, a grand procession up Broadway inaugurating his "Asiatic Caravan, Museum and Menagerie." To some extent a forerunner of his later circus and its lavish street parades—but actually more an itinerating version of the American Museum—the enterprise had been planned some two years earlier in equal partnership with Sherwood Stratton and the experienced showman Seth B. Howes. Its most impressive feature was a "herd" of ten elephants, by far the largest seen in America until then, to secure which the partners had financed an expedition to Ceylon.[3] Its most diminutive was Tom Thumb himself, who, in addition to performing his usual repertoire of songs, dances, impersonations, and "Grecian Statues," delighted audiences by riding on the back of a baby elephant. The extensive menagerie also included a group of six lions, whose intrepid trainer, Mr. Pierce, entered their cage to give his "classical illustrations" of "Hercules Struggling with the Numidian [sic] Lion" and, predictably, "Daniel in the Lions' Den." Spectators in search of religious enlightenment found equally awesome a great Brahma bull, also from Ceylon, "worshipped there by the pagan natives, and recently taken from their idolatrous temple."

The mammoth museum department included life-size wax figures of all the United States Presidents and the armless wonder S. K. G. Nellis, whose pedal dexterity with bow and arrow, accordian, and cello was advertised as "a wonderful example of what indomitable energy and industry can accomplish, even when laboring under disadvantages apparently the most insurmountable." The exhibiting of these edifying marvels took place inside a great "pavilion" or tent said to be capable of accommodating as many as 15,000 spectators, and the show's arrival in each town it visited was heralded by a street parade in which the elephants drew a monster bandwagon decorated and billed as the "Great Car of Juggernaut"—another fearsome illustration of the idolatrous ways of Hindus.[4] An interesting concomitant to this enterprise was an independent circus troupe that might easily be combined with the menagerie and museum. This was done, Barnum writes in the first edition of his autobiography, out of "self-defence," in order to crush lesser showmen whenever they dared set up their own entertainments in the same neighborhood. For four years the Asiatic Caravan continued to tour, earning its partners respectable profits.[5] At the end of the 1854 season, however, its wagons, cages, horses, and most of its menagerie were put up at auction. The dissolution of the concern was probably hastened by Sherwood Stratton's "return to strong drink" and his subsequent confinement in an asylum.[6]

The spectacular financial success of the Jenny Lind tour had overnight made him a highly desirable manager in the eyes of a host of other performers with pretensions to "legitimacy." Besides managing the famous Bateman children around this time, in 1852 he engaged and sent on a tour of California another opera singer, the well-known Irish soprano Catherine Hayes, who had previously made her mark at La Scala, Covent Garden, and New York's Tripler Hall.[7] One artist he certainly did not engage was the notorious *danseuse* and "female Harry the Eighth" Lola Montez—or, as her recent intimacy with the king of Bavaria had earned her the right to be called, "Countess of Landsfeld"—although James Gordon Bennett insisted Barnum had tried to do so, only to be refused by Lola with the crushing remark that he "should not have her services, for he was too much of a humbug." Rumors of the failed negotiations had originated in some "Paris Correspondence" published in American papers in the fall of 1851, and as Bennett himself was in Paris at the time, there can be little doubt that he was behind or at least abetted them. According to the publisher, it was Le Grand Smith, Barnum's principal agent in the Jenny Lind venture and currently overseeing the British tour of the Bateman children, who had attempted to negotiate with Lola on Barnum's behalf. When Bennett persisted in discrediting Barnum's own statement that "there is not one word of truth in this report," the aroused showman took the extraordinary step of swearing to an affidavit in which he again declared he had never entered into any negotiations with the "notorious Lola"; that while it was "undeniably true" Montez had contacted him, through her own agent, about his managing her forthcoming American tour, he had "instantly and unqualifiedly refused"; and that he verily believed that Bennett himself, while lending credence to the story of Barnum's desiring to associate himself with the dancer, knew it to be "false in every particular." This truculent document was delivered to Bennett by Barnum's New York lawyer, with the demand that both it and a retraction of the *Herald*'s allegations be published "without fail." In the lawyer's letter accompanying the affidavit, the editor was further warned that while he was free to ring as many changes as he liked on Joice Heth and the Fejee Mermaid, he must be careful not to charge or impute to the showman anything "disgraceful or dishonest."[8]

Bennett did indeed publish both the affidavit and Barnum's attorney's letter in the *Herald* of 6 November—and went on to ring a few "changes" not only on Joice Heth and the Fejee Mermaid but also on Tom Thumb, the Woolly Horse, the Happy Family, and Barnum's proselytizing temperance activities. In addition, he supplied some documentary evidence of his own, specifically a letter from the manager of the New York theatre where Montez was scheduled to make her American debut the following month, in confirmation of his earlier statement that Lola had declined an offer made her by Le Grand Smith. What the editor now coyly left in doubt was whether Smith had been negotiating on his own or Barnum's behalf, although much continued to be made of his being the "well-known agent of Mr. Barnum for the Bateman children in London." Perhaps there was truth on both sides of the question, the editor suggested, while adroitly shifting the burden of proof to the dancer. If, upon arriving on these shores, "the notorious Lola—the wonderful Lola—the king-enchanting Lola—should threaten to annihilate the Napoleon of showmen for questioning her veracity, we shall step forward and intercede for his further existence, as an act of charity and mercy."

Somewhat mollified by this halfhearted apology with its flattering epithet, Barnum wrote to Bennett on the same day to "cheerfully" retract his statement about the editor's publishing information he knew to be false. It was nevertheless true, he again emphasized, that he had never for a moment entertained the idea of engaging Montez, and that while Le Grand Smith was indeed his agent in Europe, "it does not follow that every step he takes in Europe is as my agent." The truth, Bennett joyfully proclaimed to his readers, had finally been revealed! "Barnum is a gentleman at last. He begins to be a sensible man, and no humbug." And as "perfect evidence" of the fact that Barnum never had or desired an engagement with Montez, the editor, with a gesture of pretended good will, now published something he had possessed all along: a letter Barnum had written to a third party the previous July, in which he specifically disavowed any interest in managing Lola's American tour. Thus ended the latest skirmish between the showman and his champagne-drinking Scots adversary. This time the latter was clearly the victor.[9]

As usual, he could not resist trying his hand at a number of "respectable" business ventures—and with the usual results. Most laughable of all, in the eyes of his contemporaries, was his agreeing to invest in, and become U.S. general manager and secretary of, a company formed to exploit a newly patented English fire extinguisher, named, rather optimistically, "Phillips' Fire Annihilator." The president of the company was no less a figure than the First Comptroller of the United States Treasury, the Honorable Elisha Whittlesey, who, together with several other Washington politicians, enticed Barnum to join them in this beneficent enterprise. On 22 September 1851 the company opened its office in New York. Sales were off to a brisk start, and Barnum was soon confidently assuring skeptics that the principle of the annihilator was something no one but its inventor, Mr. Phillips, had ever thought of—namely, "an atmosphere in which flame or fire cannot exist, but which can be inhaled with perfect ease and safety." Purchasers of this wonderful discovery, pending a public demonstration of its efficacy, were required to make only a small deposit, which Barnum promised to refund if the test was not successful.[10]

On the day in question, 18 December, Mr. Phillips himself appeared to conduct the demonstration at a specially erected building in Hamilton Square. According to Barnum, he succeeded in putting out the original fire, but was then "knocked down by some rowdies who were opposed to the invention, and the building was ignited and consumed after he had extinguished the previous fire." Apparently the "rowdies" were not the only ones who failed to appreciate what Barnum was trying to do for them, for as the manager wrote, he was so disgusted by the behavior of a "large portion of the public" that he insisted on refunding every cent he had collected till then. While continuing to profess his own faith in the value of Phillips's invention, especially for fires in their incipient state and aboard ships, he subsequently sold his interest in the company to one Horatio Allen. "My experiences in life have convinced me that real merit does not always succeed as well as 'humbug,'" he added in the first edition of the autobiography, "and I consider Phillips's Fire Annihilator a fair exemplification of the fact." But "humbug"—more specifically, his well-earned reputation for it in his usual line of business—was undoubtedly a contributing factor in the public's refusal to take the invention seriously. The irony of his position was not lost on Barnum. Had he been governed by the system of morals prevalent in the "trading community," he bitterly observed, he would have refused to return the deposits he had collected before the demonstration. "Being a mere showman, however, I was actuated by somewhat different principles, and chose voluntarily to make every man whole who had in any manner misapprehended the true merits of the invention."[11]

More in keeping with his past experience as editor and publisher of the *Herald of Freedom*, one would think, was his partnership with Henry D. and Alfred Ely Beach in the founding of the *Illustrated News*. The Beaches were members of the distinguished publishing family that included their brother, Moses Sperry, and father, Moses Yale Beach, all of them at one time or another involved in the conducting of the *New York Sun*, and Alfred himself had already been editor and part-owner of *Scientific American* for several years. Yet this venture, too, after forty-eight weekly issues commencing 1 January 1853, was abruptly terminated and its engravings and "good will" sold to its Boston rival, *Gleason's Pictorial Drawing-Room Companion*—because, as Barnum oddly remarks, the difficulties became almost insurmountable for "novices in the business."[12] Conceivably the "novices" were the paper's chief editors, the first of whom, the brilliant but inflexible Dr. Rufus Griswold, was shortly dismissed after insisting he be given undisputed control of the editorial columns. His successor, Charles Godfrey Leland, did not last long either and reports that he was replaced by an "inexperienced New England clergyman."[13]

Despite these upheavals, the paper was of consistently high quality, with many first-rate engravings by Frank Leslie and others. As announced in its first issue, the *Illustrated News* was to be a journal of "Intelligence, Literature, Art, and Society" appealing to the most fastidious tastes; and with these aims in mind the showman himself frequently solicited stories, articles, and objects that might be illustrated from such friends and acquaintances as Edward Everett, William Makepeace Thackeray (who was then in America), and the celebrated laureate of the Jenny Lind Ode Contest, Bayard Taylor.[14] To be sure, the American Museum and its attractions were not scanted in its pages, and the hazards of gambling and intemperance came in for their fair share of attention. But there were also many illustrations and notices of such figures as President Pierce, Harriet Beecher Stowe, and the woman's rights advocate Lucy Stone; coverage of theatrical, operatic, and a variety of entertainments given by managers other than Barnum; descriptive accounts of Polish salt mines and Commodore Perry's Japan Expedition; besides poetry, fiction, humor, and selected news items. The paper was initially published in editions of 100,000 copies, with a goal of at least 50,000 bona fide subscribers by the end of January. By April Barnum was writing confidently of having "over 100,000 subscribers and possibly 500,000 readers."[15] All told, it was a good American equivalent, as Barnum and his partners intended it to be, of the *Illustrated London News*. The surprising thing is that it lasted so briefly.

Even briefer was his tenure as president of the New York Crystal Palace Company—officially named the Association for the Exhibition of the Industry of All Nations—whose exhibits had often been extolled in the pages of the *Illustrated News*. Directly inspired by London's great Crystal Palace Exhibition of 1851, this organization of private stockholders had opened its own imposing glass-and-iron building in upper Manhattan, adjacent to the site of today's 42d Street library, in July of 1853. Its location so remote from what was then the heart of the city, Barnum writes, "was enough of itself to kill the enterprise." Yet hopes for the Palace, which was to exhibit the arts, manufactures, and latest inventions of "all" nations, originally ran high. Even if those investing in it did not become rich, it was bound to reflect credit on the nation and benefit the city itself, whose businesses would greatly profit from a large influx of visitors. Or so ran the reasoning of at least one group of enthusiastic supporters.

Within a few months, however, the Palace's novelty had begun to pall and fewer and fewer spectators were making the long trip uptown. As debts continued to mount and the value of the Association's stock steadily declined, even the most altruistic of its members began casting about for some way to salvage their investments. Early in 1854 Barnum and his famous hatter-friend Genin were both entreated to stand for election to the board of directors. The showman at first stubbornly refused, but then—following some confusion among the public over whether he was or was not a stockholder in the company (the rumor of the former was sufficient in itself to reverse the stock's decline), repeated pleadings to reconsider his decision, and some particularly nettlesome remarks made about him during a meeting of stockholders—finally decided "to throw no obstacle in the way of my election." He was elected not only a director but almost immediately thereafter the company's president.[16]

For over three months he devoted himself wholeheartedly to the job, working night and day in the hope of breathing new life into a venture that, he shortly discovered, "was a corpse long before I touched it." In an equally futile attempt to allay the fears and prejudices of the stockholders who had opposed him, he even requested James Gordon Bennett to ease up on him, since he was now "engaged in managing a public enterprise which I hope & believe will be made highly conducive to the interests and reputation of this city and the country at large." If the editor would kindly select someone else to be the perennial butt of his sarcasm and, for a change, "begin to speak of me and my efforts with some little degree of respect and encouragement," he would feel obliged.[17] The appeal, needless to say, went unheeded. In May there was a grand "re-inauguration" ceremony at the Palace, and in June it was the scene of several "monster" concerts by the spectacular French conductor Jullien, who assembled some 1500 instrumentalists and singers for the occasion. The diarist George Templeton Strong attended one of them and thought the "conjunction of Barnum and Jullien . . . one of the grandest humbugs on record." Selections from

Handel's *Messiah* and the overtures to *William Tell* and *Tannhäuser* were on the program, but the acoustics of the great domed building were so bad that at times nothing could be heard, while the incessant shuffling about of a crowd estimated to number as many as 40,000 was in itself sufficient to drown the singers' voices. Especially amusing was a "Fireman's Quadrille" composed by Jullien himself, during which military bands, after beginning to play in the distance, marched into the orchestra area; red and blue fireworks were shot off outside the glass dome; and the great chorus, urging on the firemen supposed to be battling this mock conflagration, shouted such compelling phrases as "Go it, 20," "Play away, 49," and "hay-day." "The audacity of the imposition reconciled one to its grossness," wrote Strong, who could not help being impressed by some instrumental passages imitating the "thundering, quivering, shuddering rush and roar of falling walls." But even such monumental claptrap as this, he thought, would not succeed in rescuing the Palace. The building was by then almost empty of exhibits. "Its character has changed. It is now merely an extension of Barnum's Museum."[18]

After one final effort to galvanize the Palace into life with a Fourth of July celebration, the showman resigned his office on 10 July and promptly withdrew to Connecticut. He was "an ass for having anything to do with the Crystal Palace," he wrote to his friend Moses Kimball four days later. "Thank God I have got enough to live comfortably on here in the country & then have enough left to ruin & spoil my children." As a continuing director of the Association, however, Barnum was still not entirely clear of the Palace; and besides, as he complained in his autobiography and elsewhere, he had personally advanced large sums to pay some of its debts—money that might yet be recovered if things were properly managed. To this end he urged Kimball to interest Boston businessmen in buying and moving the Palace to their city, painting a glowing picture of how profitable and civic-minded such an enterprise would be, especially if the Palace were reerected on Boston Common. Philadelphia was also interested in acquiring the building, he wrote, while New York's American Institute, which ran expositions of its own, would like to see some arrangement made to keep it in Manhattan.[19] As late as January of 1858—by which time the Association was bankrupt, the ground-lease had expired, and there was ominous talk of demolition—he was still proposing various ways by which "such a beautiful building" might be preserved.[20] The city had barely taken it over in the same year when, in what would have been a fitting climax to one of Jullien's concerts, the Palace caught fire and was totally destroyed.

Barnum's uncharacteristic lapse in appealing to Bennett to spare him his barbs and the asperity with which he shortly afterwards reflected on some of these failed projects in the first edition of his autobiography (New Yorkers, for example, had "disgraced" themselves by their "coldness" toward the Palace) are indicative of his growing concern over his ambiguous standing in society. It was all well and good to proclaim himself "Prince of Humbugs" when promoting a Fejee Mermaid or Woolly Horse, but since the time of his association with Jenny Lind his reputation in this area had increasingly come home to haunt him. Besides, as he had confessed to Bennett in the same letter, he had a family growing up around him, was no longer so young as he used to be, "and all things considered, I have to request that you will hereafter *not* speak of myself or my actions in a spirit of ridicule or abuse, except I, or they, *really deserve* it." Surely there must be a *few* good streaks in his character, he argued a few months later in his reply to the devastating review of the autobiography that appeared in the *Trumpet and Universalist Magazine*. Had not the same journal, several years earlier while he was promoting that boon to mankind, Phillips's Fire Annihilator, published a testimonial from a person signing himself "One Who Knows" extolling those very accomplishments on which he most prided himself? Not only was he the proprietor or manager of numerous wholesome amusements that gave gainful employment to hundreds of persons, this anonymous writer had justly observed, but he was also an indefatigable supporter of agriculture and temperance.[21] The latter cause, in particular, had occupied him since the time of the Jenny Lind tour. He was frequently on the road at his own expense, lecturing throughout the United States and Canada on the dangers of drink and on behalf of various prohibition movements. In this continuing "work of life and death," as he termed it in his 1854 pamphlet *The Liquor Business*, he was so unsparing of his comfort and health that at one point he was confined to Iranistan for over a week, laid up with "sore throat caused by temperance lecturing."[22]

The writer in the *Trumpet and Universalist Magazine*, in eulogizing the showman's "exemplary" life, also reported that he had given up tea, coffee, and tobacco. There was obviously a considerable amount of backsliding with the last, however, for Barnum himself later told of the difficulty he experienced conquering the nicotine habit and confessed to having been a great smoker of cigars until as late as 1860. Others among his acquaintance were in the same predicament. From Iranistan he wrote to his friend Kimball in early 1852, gaily describing the antics of the fourteen-year-old Tom Thumb, who at the moment was sitting on his knee. "The little General is puffing away at a nasty stinking segar, and my nose is dreadfully offended thereby—nevertheless I can't cure the little rascal from his filthy and disgusting habit. He laughs at this, gives an extra puff and sends his respects."[23] On the same day he wrote to Charity's cousin Nate Beers in New York City, asking him to rush to Bridgeport 500 "segars" via Adams Express. Some he might sell to a local barber; his own modest supply would serve as a "sample."[24] Further jollification occurred at Iranistan on 19 October of the same year, when Caroline Barnum, described in the Fairfield town records as "Lady," married David W. Thompson, a local bookkeeper. The festivities were unexpectedly disrupted when the mansion caught fire only a few hours before the ceremony was scheduled to take place. An anxious Thompson galloped with the news to his future father-in-law, who was then being shaved at a barbershop. "Never mind!" exclaimed the showman philosophically as they rushed back to the house. "We can't help these things; the house will probably be burned; but if no one is killed or injured, you shall be married tonight, if we are obliged to perform the ceremony in the coach-house." But Iranistan, almost miraculously, was spared serious damage, though as Barnum wrote, it "came as near destruction as it well could, and escape."[25]

———◆———

FREED FROM his tribulations as president of the Crystal Palace Company, Barnum concentrated on more congenial projects during the summer of 1854: his autobiography, which he had promised to deliver to Redfield by the end of October, and his continuing promotion of the City of Bridgeport. Together with the American Museum, these were among the most enduring passions of his life; and of the three, none was to command more of his time and energy, or cause him more trouble, than Bridgeport itself. From orphan asylums to hospitals and cemeteries, from banks and water supplies to horse-drawn railways and public parks—whether charitable, civic, or commercial in nature—there was hardly a phase of the city's existence in which he did not take an active interest. All this was to evolve over a period of some forty years, but had almost literally exploded into life in the fall of 1851 when Barnum, in partnership with the lawyer and former schoolteacher William H. Noble (later to serve gallantly as a colonel, then general, during the Civil War), decided to develop the sparsely populated area across the Pequonnock River that soon came to be known as East Bridgeport. The object of their scheme, Barnum modestly declared in his autobiography, was to found a "new city"—complete with factories, residences, churches, schools, and a public park—with its nucleus 50 acres of land that had once belonged to Noble's father. Before revealing the extent of their plans, however, the two men took care to purchase an additional 174 acres, then proceeded to lay out the property in streets and lots, naming several of the former after themselves and their family members. New bridges were built to connect the development with the city across the river; houses, factories, and various commercial establishments were erected and rented out by Barnum and Noble themselves; lots were sold at their original value on condition purchasers promptly erect buildings meeting with the partners' approval. To further encourage rapid growth, financing, sometimes to the full cost of land and buildings, was offered to settlers on easy terms.[26]

Barnum's initial investment in this "new city" was around $20,000, the amount he paid Noble on 31 October 1851 for a half-interest in the original 50 acres. Thereafter he supplied three-quarters of the money for additional land purchases and, as entries in the ledger he had kept since his Bethel days show, was soon pouring thousands more into grading lots, constructing cottages, tenements, single and double houses, bridges and a dock ($6300), a sawmill and hotel ($5200), shops and factories, and various other "improvements."[27] To oversee all these investments he was shortly in need of a full-time agent. Who better qualified than his bookkeeper son-in-law? In the less than three years between his agreement with Noble and the writing of his autobiography, buildings worth nearly a million dollars were erected on the property. All of this was not without some benefit to the partners, of course, who in offering such generous terms to those originally settling in East Bridgeport shrewdly held back every other lot for disposal at a later date. Within two years, Barnum reports, the value of such lots had escalated from $200 to $2000. It was the first example of what he liked to term his "profitable philanthropy."

The wheels of this great enterprise rolled merrily along, while its chief mover continued to work for the glory of his adopted city in other ways. In the spring of 1851 he was elected and served for four years as the first president of the Pequonnock Bank, an institution that existed independently into the present century.[28] Some of its early notes, in what was presumably meant to be an advertisement of the bank's integrity, depicted Barnum and Jenny Lind beaming benignantly at the holder, with a handsome engraving of Iranistan between them. He continued in office as president of the Fairfield County Agricultural Society, whose annual fairs were often held at Bridgeport. And he also found time to drum up support for another pet project to the west of the city, Mountain Grove Cemetery, where, in a setting that remains surprisingly beautiful to this day, Barnum and most of his family, Tom Thumb and his wife, Sherwood and Cynthia Stratton, and many others among the showman's friends and associates were eventually laid to rest. At its founding as a nonprofit corporation in 1849, Barnum himself subscribed for a total of twenty-five shares and later donated some of the lots to which he was thereby entitled for burial of Civil War dead and other charitable purposes. Before seeing her off on her California tour, he induced Catherine Hayes to give a benefit concert for the cemetery, with the proceeds going to build one of its picturesque gateways. At his solicitation, too, the famous actor and playwright Dion Boucicault, who had once introduced Barnum around Paris, traveled to Bridgeport and, for the same worthy cause, delivered his popular lecture "My Literary Life."[29]

———◆———

DESPITE HIS REVERSES with the Annihilator and the Crystal Palace, Barnum and his finances appeared eminently solid at the beginning of 1855. Everyone knew he had made a fortune managing Jenny Lind; his highly popular museum continued to pour money into his pockets; the "new city" growing so reassuringly on the banks of the Pequonnock, like the fabulous "palace" of its energetic projector, was there for all to see. Nor was there so much as a hint that anything might be amiss when, toward the end of 1854, his autobiography appeared—a work that outraged many critics not so much on account of its author's "moral obliquity" as because he had been so successful in making money out of it. At the end of that book Barnum published ten "Rules for Success in Business" he had written two years earlier at the request of a Philadelphia acquaintance who was about to bring out a treatise on the subject. A sensible enough exhortation on such topics as good working habits, the need for sobriety, and the power of advertising, it was remarkable above all, in retrospect, for its admonition to avoid extravagance and to make certain one's income always exceeded expenditures. "Those who live fully up to their means, without any thought of a reverse in life," he sagely counseled, "can never attain to a pecuniary independence." A smaller house with less costly furniture, fewer renewals of one's wardrobe, and such economical entertainments as a "social family chat," an evening's reading, or a fun-filled game of hunt the slipper or blindman's buff—and lo! what infinite pleasure all would derive from watching the family's nest egg grow steadily larger. As a telling example of the folly of those failing to heed such advice, he added the story of the "$30,000 sofa," concerning a friend who, after purchasing an elegant new sofa, felt driven to acquire matching furniture, a new house and carriage, servants, etc., etc. "The truth is," his careworn friend had confided to him, "that sofa would have brought me to inevitable bankruptcy, had not a most unexampled tide of prosperity kept me above it."[30]

Like other gems of wisdom he was fond of dispensing, this "rule" was often more honored in the breach than actual observance by the showman himself. Throughout his life Barnum remained an inveterate borrower—no mortal sin in a driving businessman, certainly—and was continually in debt not only to banks but to partners and friends, relatives and family members, and even to his own employees. They all lent him money willingly enough, for it was always into some promising venture that he turned these funds, and always with the prospect of at least a fair return. Trees, interest-bearing investments, and appreciating real estate, he often remarked, continued to "work" while their owners were sleeping. Of these he was most heavily into real estate—not just in Bridgeport, but in Fairfield, New York City, Brooklyn, and many other parts of the country as well—investing less frequently in bonds and only rarely in stocks. "Land poor," his contemporaries might have said of him, were it not for the spectacular returns from his entertainment ventures.

As late as the spring and summer of 1855, no one could have foreseen the magnitude of the disaster that was about to overtake him. To be sure, there were some minor annoyances around this time. Henry L. Bateman, father of the famous histrionic sisters, was refusing to repay some $4000 he owed the showman, which finally necessitated legal action.[31] Far more troubling, touching as it did on his personal integrity as well as his wallet, was his entanglement in the criminal activities and eventual prosecution of his cousin Edward T. Nichols, son of his aunt Laura Taylor Nichols of Danbury. An exhibitor of a traveling panorama in the 1840s, then one of the hangers-on who speculated in tickets during Jenny Lind's tour, Nichols afterwards gravitated to Cleveland, Ohio, where he set up as a theatre manager, real-estate speculator, and promoter of lotteries. Barnum later stated to the Cleveland prosecuting attorney that he had loaned Nichols money "ever since he was a boy" and that he had himself accepted, in February 1855, loans his cousin insisted on arranging for him. This required the sending of several signed drafts through the mail, and in short order Barnum discovered that over $6000 of the money he was supposed to receive had been squandered by Cousin Edward in a gambling orgy. Confession, a show of contrition, and a promise of restitution promptly followed; and Barnum, after traveling to Cleveland to look over the situation, not only forgave his wayward relative but advanced him several thousand dollars more to tide him over his temporary embarrassment.

But Nichols—whom the showman was shortly calling a "serpent" and "libertine"—was obviously incapable of reform and continued to blow large sums of money on gambling and his actresses. Worse still, in order to cover his mounting debts, he devised an ingenious scheme that involved forging his famous cousin's signature to various bits of paper. When Barnum found out about this toward the end of the year, he nearly exploded. Nichols ran away from Cleveland, was arrested and brought back to stand trial, and spent some time in prison. The trouble was, in his defense he claimed Barnum had *authorized* him to sign his signature; and as the brokers and others who were stuck with the forged paper—the amount was $40,000 in all—naturally preferred to believe him on this point, they eventually succeeded in getting him pardoned. The vexing affair dragged on for over six years and involved Barnum in several trials, lawsuits, and threats of legal action. Cousin Edward, one gathers, was no stranger to the courts. In time, after standing trial for other offences, he drifted off to Colorado.[32]

The discovery of his cousin's treachery came at a particularly awkward moment, for by the end of 1855 Barnum was desperately struggling to keep his own head above water. Early in the new year, in a letter addressed to the agents in Ohio who were handling a mortgage he now held on Nichols's Cleveland property, he urged them to "make it *strong* so that it will stand any investigation," sell it to someone else if they could, and get what was due him into his possession as soon as possible. "The N.Y. papers will very probably announce tomorrow these forgeries," he cautioned, then almost casually added that "in a day or two afterwards I shall be heralded as having failed for half a million! Such is life."[33] And indeed, when Americans awoke to read their newspapers in mid-January 1856, it was just as he had said: the Croesus of Bridgeport had suddenly gone bankrupt, and to the astonishing tune of half a million dollars.

One could easily devote a separate volume to Barnum's bankruptcy, and probably not even then would every detail of that eventful history be brought to light. The showman himself, naturally enough, told his version of the story in later editions of his autobiography. It had all come about, he insisted, through his having "East Bridgeport on the brain" and an ambitious plan to benefit that thriving community. A few years previously he had invested in a small clock factory in Litchfield, Connecticut, which later moved to East Bridgeport and merged with another clock company that had located there. The latter was the former Ansonia Clock Company of Theodore Terry, a major figure in the history of Connecticut clockmaking, who had reestablished his concern in East Bridgeport in 1854 and gone into partnership with Barnum as the Terry and Barnum Manufacturing Company.[34] Sometime in 1855, Barnum writes, he was approached by a "citizen of New Haven" with the suggestion that he negotiate for the removal of still another clock company to East Bridgeport. This was the huge Jerome Manufacturing Company of New Haven and Ansonia, the largest of its kind in the state, whose founder and president, Chauncey Jerome, had made a fortune out of inexpensive one-day movement clocks that were sold throughout the world. Barnum was impressed by Chauncey Jerome. Not only had this venerable gentleman been elected mayor of New Haven the previous year, but he had also financed the construction of a Congregational church in that city and presented a fine clock to one of Bridgeport's own churches. The upshot was that Jerome visited him at Iranistan, and shortly afterwards it was agreed that the company would indeed move to Bridgeport and absorb the Terry and Barnum Company in return for an exchange of stock and Barnum's pledging temporary security to the amount of $110,000. The total assets of the Jerome Company, Barnum was assured, were nearly $600,000; the loan was merely to tide it over a "dull season" and prevent the laying off of some of its workers.

There followed what appears to have been some incredibly inept accounting on the part of Barnum or his bookkeeper son-in-law. The showman had agreed to set his signature to any number of notes and drafts, renewed as often as necessary, with the proviso that the total amount of his indebtedness should not at any time exceed the $110,000. The full amount was outstanding within three months, and he was shortly being called upon to sign new notes as soon as old ones were canceled and returned to him—a process so often repeated, with apparently nothing amiss, that he carelessly began signing notes without checking to see how much might still be out. One day the "frightful fact" dawned upon him. He had been tricked into endorsing notes for half a million dollars, and the agent he had finally sent to look into these matters "came back to me with the refreshing intelligence that I was a ruined man!"

Barnum swore to the end of his life that he had been "swindled" and "deliberately defrauded" in the clock company affair. Old Chauncey Jerome, he claimed, had personally guaranteed that he would not be responsible for a cent in excess of the original $110,000. Yet the company, as he subsequently learned, was already in a precarious state when he became associated with it; and the money he advanced, instead of going for the purpose originally stated, had been swallowed up by debts incurred months and years before. When the Jerome Manufacturing Company itself went into bankruptcy in February 1856, the most it could offer its creditors was twelve to fifteen cents on the dollar. And "to cap the climax," Barnum wrote in exasperation, "it never removed to East Bridgeport at all, notwithstanding this was the only condition which ever prompted me to advance one dollar to the rotten concern!"

Jerome had his version of the story to tell as well, most notably in his own autobiography, which he published in 1860. A disquieting litany of complaints from start to finish, it does little to arouse sympathy for its whining author. Someone was always waiting in the wings to "swindle" poor Chauncey Jerome—to steal an invention or appropriate one of his ideas—though he himself was never guilty of such treachery, of course. Even the hand of the Almighty seemed sometimes to be raised against him, which must have caused Chauncey to wonder, pious Congregationalist that he was, about his status among the "elect." The church he so benevolently got up in New Haven proved unsuccessful and was sold to the Baptists, after costing him four times the amount he had originally subscribed. "Other ministers," he complains, refused to support it, and he was accused by ungrateful journalists of "speculating" in its construction.

Utterly ruined by the debacle of his clock company, at the age of sixty-three he moved to Waterbury and there had another unfortunate experience with a Congregational church, whose steeple came toppling down upon his house in the midst of a hurricane. Even in his poverty he continued to be cheated and betrayed by one associate after another. "Thank God," he remarks with satisfaction at one point in his autobiography, "I have never been the means of such troubles for others." At another, "I love truth, honesty and religion." But he did not mean, he hurriedly added, "the religion that Barnum believes in," for he was of the gratifying conviction that the wicked are punished in another world.[35]

Considering his morose opinion of the rest of mankind, Jerome was remarkably restrained in his comments on Barnum. He repeatedly insisted, however, that he never met the showman until after the failure and that the plan to merge the two companies had been arranged without his knowledge. Then, too, he writes, Barnum had agreed to endorse notes "to any extent" and had grossly understated, by some $50,000, the liabilities of the Terry and Barnum Company, whose debts the Jerome Company was obligated to assume. All told, he concluded, it was this unfortunate connection with Barnum and his failing clock factory that had led to the inevitable collapse of his own company. Nowhere does he hint at any agreement to move the last to East Bridgeport.[36]

To be sure, one wonders how the president and chief stockholder in the Jerome Manufacturing Company, no less than Barnum himself, managed to remain in the dark on so many matters. Earlier in his book—but without directly naming him—Jerome mentions that his son Augustus was secretary and financial manager of the company and "seemed to have a desire to keep things to himself a little too much." Well before Barnum entered the picture, Augustus and some of his pals were making a great many improvements to the New Haven factory that Chauncey thought "quite unnecesary," buying "costly machinery," and laughing at the "old fogy" of a president whenever he objected to what they were doing. "The Secretary thought I was always looking on the dark side and prophesying evil, because I frequently remonstrated with him on the many extravagancies which were constantly being added to the establishment. I frequently told him that if the company should fail, I should have to bear the whole blame, because my name was known all over the world."[37] It was the "Secretary," he elsewhere writes, who did all the negotiating with Barnum. Readers of the upright Chauncey's autobiography were thus offered two attractive alternatives: if they did not choose to believe Barnum was entirely to blame for the company's failure, they might pin at least some of the responsibility on the unheedful Augustus.

Between these two claims of blissful ignorance, one may be pardoned for hesitating to take sides. Conceivably it was a case of two Connecticut Yankees each trying to "come it over" the other, with little thought of what the ultimate consequences might be. Jerome's own tribulations were soon forgotten by the masses; all of the sympathy, he woefully observed, seemed directed toward the Bridgeport showman. And truth to tell, there was a vast outpouring of sympathy when news of Barnum's failure reached the public, with offers of assistance flooding in from friends, associates, and total strangers, and even an unprecedented "sympathy meeting" in Bridgeport's Washington Hall, at which citizens from all walks of life gathered to praise and express their faith in their embarrassed fellow townsman.[38] By then, however, the showman and his family had long been gone from the city, and all his Connecticut assets were in the hands of court-appointed trustees. Other parties, naturally enough, rejoiced in his fall, especially after all the hubris he had exhibited in his recently published autobiography. Here was a terrible illustration of where the practice of humbug must lead, and the righteous and his enemies made the most of it.

As lawyers, trustees, and creditors probed his finances over the following months, it became painfully evident how overextended he was. Nearly every piece of real estate he owned had been mortgaged to the hilt. Iranistan itself, which was appraised in one inventory at $32,000, had been mortgaged three times over within two weeks of his bankruptcy for the astounding total of $102,000.[39] Barnum publicly boasted of having paid many of his personal debts, amounting to over $40,000, immediately before his failure was announced. He was silent or evasive about many of his other actions during this period, like the leasing of Iranistan and its outbuildings to his half-brother Philo and another relative in early January 1856—a maneuver presumably conferring some degree of protection on that property. In the summer of 1855 he had sold the American Museum's collections to John Greenwood Jr. and Henry D. Butler, "previous to my financial troubles," he stressed in later editions of his autobiography. The two partners, possessing little money of their own, had given Barnum notes for "nearly the entire amount," and the mortgage on the collections he held as security was turned over to the New York assignee at the time of his bankruptcy. There were those who suspected this "sale" had taken place much later than the showman claimed, though, to do him justice, Barnum had expressed the hope in the first edition of his autobiography that Greenwood would someday become "at least a partial proprietor" of the establishment.[40] Around the time this sale was supposed to have occurred, there was a related transaction for which one does find documentary evidence. On 17 July 1855, for the "consideration" of one dollar, Barnum transferred his lease on the Museum to Greenwood, who on the following day conveyed it to Barnum's wife Charity for the same "consideration."[41] Property held by Charity in her own name could not, of course, be attached to satisfy her husband's debts, and the same stratagem was employed to secure various pieces of real estate in Bridgeport. When Barnum later turned down offers of assistance from well-meaning friends, some of whom genuinely believed he had been reduced to poverty, he candidly reassured them his wife possessed a fortune in her own right. "Without Charity, I am nothing," he would playfully remark. The lease on the American Museum still had twenty-two years to run, and as Greenwood and Butler were willing to pay $19,000 per year over and above the $10,000 Barnum had agreed to pay Olmsted's heirs, the Barnums, obviously, were not about to find themselves on the street.

The evidence points to Barnum's being uneasy about his financial affairs by no later than the summer of 1855. Even such precautionary measures as he then took, however, could hardly have prepared him and his family for the fall that came several months later, when they were abruptly forced to flee the scenes of their former opulence and take up residence in a rented house (with boarders, again) on New York's West 8th Street. The embarrassment seems to have been hardest felt by Charity, whose psychosomatic ailments commenced in earnest around this time. In an effort to restore her to health, Barnum soon arranged for his family to board with a farmer at Westhampton, Long Island, where she might have the benefit of the ocean air. While out for a walk there one morning, he was intrigued by the body of a small whale that had washed up on the beach. Possibly recalling a similar show he had once seen in England, he shipped it to the American Museum. Greenwood and Butler exhibited the carcass for several days and sent him a share of the profits—sufficient to pay for his entire stay on Long Island, much to the amazement of his hard-working landlord. There was magic still in the showman's touch.[42]

He himself was depressed for a time. The clock business had "wound him up," he complained, and all he could hear was an ominous "ticking" in his head. The move to New York spared him the necessity of appearing in Connecticut courtrooms. He was content to leave his affairs in that state in the hands of trustees, one of whom, James D. Johnson, appointed by the court in Fairfield County, became a close ally and worked behind the scenes for his relief.[43] In New York City itself, however, he was frequently summoned to appear in court and badgered mercilessly by creditors' lawyers, who were determined to sniff out every penny he might have hidden away. It was widely believed he must be shamming—that the "Prince of Humbugs" still had vast resources at his command—with the result that many holders of the notes he had signed were at first unwilling to compromise. And indeed this impression was not without some foundation, considering the property known to be registered in Charity's name.

Had Barnum been another sort, he might have spent the remainder of his days living comfortably enough on Charity's income and died a bankrupt. But at the age of forty-five he was hardly ready to retire, and by April he was tackling his problems with his usual vigor. Certainly he did not hold himself responsible for payment in full of all those notes he had signed on behalf of the failed Jerome Company; many of them, he subsequently learned, had been sold short to speculators at ruinous rates of interest. Other claims, he cautioned the commissioners who were in charge of his New York affairs, were being made by persons who had previously been paid, and there was "a good deal of fraud connected with much of the paper" that was now brought in against him.[44] Yet if ever he was to engage in business on his own again, it was necessary, he realized, to "extinguish" all those clock debts. To effect this he soon hit upon a two-pronged strategy. While friends and trustees negotiated with the holders of notes, he himself acted the part of the broken-down businessman. "I am utterly paralyzed, my ambition is all gone, and can never attempt to rise again, for such an effort were useless with $460,000 debts hanging over my head," he wrote in a letter of 3 April to the *Springfield Republican*, whose editors had recently expressed sympathy for him. If only *all* his creditors would come forward and immediately settle, saving the "world of *costs* which law suits will involve," it would surely be better for everyone concerned. "But I don't know how to bring such a thing about," he pathetically continued. "I never knew anything about commercial business—never having had any experience in that line, and my impulsiveness and confiding disposition in my fellow-men have proved my *ruin*."[45]

While public lamentations like the above were being aimed at his creditors, he was already laying the groundwork for another fortune. His own failure had not much affected East Bridgeport, where real-estate values continued to climb and a thriving sewing machine company soon moved into the factory once occupied by his clock company. When his properties there now came up at auction, his agents were instructed to purchase as much as they could in Charity's name, using money from her own sources of income and (a closely guarded secret, of course) funds supplied him by friends for this purpose. Other money went to take up his notes, whose owners gradually agreed to compromise in the range of 15 to 25 percent. Meanwhile, as in the days when he was starting out at the American Museum, he and his family made a determined effort to economize. Boardinghouses, stays with relatives, and modest rentals sufficed them for the next few years; his own first, ineffectual attempt to stop smoking came about not through health or moral considerations but simply because he wished to save the money his customary ten cigars a day were costing him. The frugality advocated by the author of "Rules for Success in Business," for a time, was rigidly enforced.

It was all a slow, tedious process—too slow for one dying to plunge into business again and regain control of his destiny. In America, where his affairs were subject to constant scrutiny, any money he might earn would be immediately attached; and the more he was known to earn—here was the rub— the less likely his creditors would be willing to compromise. Toward the end of 1856, over the objections of several of the latter, he therefore embarked for London again, taking with him the family of Mr. and Mrs. George C. Howard, famed for their interpretation of *Uncle Tom's Cabin*, in which their daughter Cordelia starred as the heaven-bound Little Eva. By early December Barnum was in residence at number 10 Craven Street, whence he was soon writing theatre managers to offer his actors' services. "I can assure you," he wrote to the actor-manager Charles Kean on the 8th of that month, "that after losing a large portion of an ample fortune, I should not have engaged in any enterprise which I did not *know* contained all the elements of *great* success."[46] They were soon performing at the Royal Marylebone Theatre, the Strand Theatre, and Sadler's Wells, sometimes with Cordelia's scene "The Death of Eva" billed as a separate entertainment.[47] Early in the new year Barnum was joined by Tom Thumb, who occasionally gave his own entertainment at the same theatres where the Howards were playing. The Howards returned to America a few months later, but the General stayed on, repeating his triumphant tour of several years earlier. This time, in addition to London and the British provinces, Barnum took him to Germany, where they found much to wonder over at that country's fashionable gambling spas.[48] His interest in both ventures, Barnum writes, was "not generally known," in order to spare him any "annoyance" from his creditors.

At one point—so strong was the temptation to repeat his earlier successes—he proposed to Jenny Lind that they undertake a new tour. Failing in that, he gave serious thought to sending the entire opera company from London's Her Majesty's Theatre to New York for a season. At various times, too, as in happier days, Charity and his unmarried daughters were with him in London—a welcome respite from their troubles back home. In early summer of 1857, leaving Tom Thumb in other hands, he returned to America, where on 20 October, at her sister Caroline's home in Fairfield, his second eldest daughter, Helen, was married to Samuel H. Hurd. The showman was still in America two months later when his half-brother Philo telegraphed him in New York that Iranistan had just burned to the ground. The house had remained unsold since the time of his bankruptcy; and although Barnum was understandably guarded on the subject, it appears his Fairfield trustee James D. Johnson had been doing his utmost to ensure it would remain so. Very likely, the two had concocted a plan to bid it in at auction, using some of Barnum's London earnings, and repurchase the property in Charity's name. Meanwhile, Johnson had decreed that the Barnums might as well move back into the house and had recently sent painters and carpenters there to set everything in order. One of the workmen may have dropped a lighted pipe onto the circular divan beneath the great central dome. In any event, it all went up in smoke and flame during the night of 17–18 December. "My beautiful Iranistan was gone!" Barnum lamented in his autobiography. "This was not only a serious loss to my estate, for it had probably cost at least $150,000, but it was generally regarded as a public calamity. It was the only building in its peculiar style of architecture, of any pretension, in America, and many persons visited Bridgeport every year expressly to see Iranistan." The insurance on the building, he hastened to add, was only $28,000. Most of the furnishings were saved by firemen, but he could hardly be said to have gained by the disaster.[49]

Back in London the following year, he was encouraged by friends to get up an "entertainment" of his own. "The Art of Money-Getting, or Success in Life" was certainly a provocative subject for a lecture by one who was universally known to have gone bankrupt; and as Barnum sardonically remarked at the time, he might more competently have spoken on "The Art of Money-Losing." But his friends pointed out that he could hardly have lost money if he had not first made it—and with this reassuring thought in mind he set to work. The talk was an expansion of his "Rules for Success in Business," fleshed out with a fund of jokes and personal anecdotes, quotations and literary allusions, words of wisdom from such authorities on the subject as John Jacob Astor and the Rothschild family, and some newly added "rules" with a peculiarly personal ring ("Don't Indorse Without Security").[50] First delivered before an audience of over 2000 at St. James's Hall on the evening of 29 December 1858, it was extensively reviewed in the English press, whose encomiums the showman incorporated into his publicity material. The London *Times* of 30 December favorably compared its systematic organization to that of Cicero's *De Officiis* and praised the speaker for his "fund of dry humour that convulses everybody with laughter, while he himself remains perfectly serious. A sonorous voice, and an admirably clear delivery complete his qualifications as a lecturer." "It was one of the most lively, interesting, and pleasantly delivered lectures of which we have any recollection," reported the reviewer for the *Morning Advertiser* on the same date. "It breathes a wholesome, healthy air, is varied in subject and delivered in such a genial and pleasant style as to constitute an intellectual treat which one does not meet with every day, even in London."[51]

In the following year, besides repeating the lecture on several occasions in London, he delivered it over sixty times in the British provinces, earning considerable sums that went to settling his debts back home, so that the lecture itself, Barnum wryly notes, soon proved an admirable example of the "art of money-getting." His itinerary included Oxford and Cambridge, whose students could not resist interrupting the talk to rag "old Barnum" a little. The delighted showman, long accustomed to hecklers at his temperance lectures, managed to hold his own. The lecture was not the only "entertainment." As early as 28 January a "Bavarian minstrel" named Knope was added to the program. In addition, he carried with him on tour an assistant whose job was to put up and take down some unspecified "paintings" and to "exhibit the Mermaid at the close of the Entertainment." The latter was the notorious Fejee lady herself, whose owner, Moses Kimball, had obligingly loaned her to his friend.[52] "The Art of Money-Getting" proved so successful that Barnum continued to give the lecture for years afterwards in America (the fees he received now going to lower-case "charity"), where his advice was considered so beneficial to youth that he was called upon to repeat it at six-month intervals before the student body of one Poughkeepsie business school. Many of those who came to hear him, he assured one party about to advertise his appearance in a Pennsylvania town in 1868, expected "simply a string of jokes and nonsense conveying no moral, & perhaps quite the reverse. This class of persons are always happily disappointed, and the more refined and intelligent an audience is, the better satisfaction do I give."[53]

The showman spent as much time in America as he did in Europe during these years, frequently crossing the Atlantic (with the inevitable shipboard jokes, naturally), occasionally accompanied by Charity and one or more of his daughters. Throughout this period, too, as on his first trip abroad, he was constantly attentive to the needs of the American Museum, although Greenwood and Butler were now its official proprietors and he himself—or so he gave out in public—was merely their "agent." In private he continued to act as he had always done, engaging performers and freaks, arranging for new plays, buying and selling "curiosities," expostulating with the owners of the *New York Sun* when they threatened to raise their rates for the Museum's advertisements, etc.[54] The pretense was finally laid to rest on 24 March 1860 when Barnum stepped onto the stage of the Museum, which had been gaily decorated as on a holiday, to announce he had repurchased the collections from Greenwood and Butler. Fighting back the tears that rose to his eyes when the audience in the packed Lecture Room gave him a tremendous ovation, he went on to recount his struggles over the past four years, paying generous tribute to Charity, Johnson, and others who had stood by him, and candidly revealed the stratagems that had enabled him to retire his indebtedness. Not all the clock debts, however, had been settled by the time of this announcement of his return to "solvency." Some $20,000 worth of notes, he writes in his autobiography, were still outstanding; and he had given his bond, guaranteed by his friend Johnson, to take them up "within a certain number of months."[55] But in fact, as he revealed in a letter to one noteholder in Massachusetts the following December, more than $67,000 worth of paper was known to be still out, which his "friends" were willing to purchase at the rate of fifteen and twenty-five cents on the dollar. As for himself, he plaintively added, "I tell you candidly & honestly that *I do not possess a dollar's worth of property in the world*, & the prospect of ever doing so grows darker as I grow older. . . . I have lost nearly all of my ambition . . . & if I should die (which I *must* sometime), no note or debt against me will be worth the paper it is written on." Worse still, he was but "ostensibly" the proprietor of the American Museum, having "hired out my name & services to the real owners," Greenwood and Butler, who paid him "a monthly salary, quite inadequate to support my family, except aided by a small income which my wife holds in her own right." Now that the weather had turned cold and business was bad, these "services" might conceivably be dispensed with! This for the benefit of a creditor holding a note for $1500.[56] He had told a slightly different story to "Uncle" Sol Smith the previous April. "I guess you are not sorry I have dug out again," he jubilantly wrote a few days after proclaiming his "solvency" from the stage of the Lecture Room. "I can make $90,000 per annum in this Museum."[57]

The truth lay somewhere between these two postures, for as Barnum acknowledged in his letter to his Massachusetts creditor, notes signed by him for thousands of additional dollars, "of which I have never heard & of which I have no means of knowing," might yet be unexpectedly brought in against him. When Charity executed her last will and testament a year later on 13 September 1861, this possibility was still a source of some anxiety. Provision was carefully made therein to place her entire estate in trust for her husband in the event he should be bankrupt at the time of her death. More curious still is the direction that if such a trust should prove necessary, Barnum might dissolve it himself at any time within the following five years upon simply certifying, as "the sole and exclusive judge" of such matters, to his own solvency. And indeed, in the nearly unfathomable labyrinth he had made of his financial affairs, who better qualified than the showman himself to declare whether he was, or was not, truly "solvent"? The path grew so tortuous, the thread so apt to slip from his fingers, that at times even he lost the way. Upon Charity's death in 1873, neither he nor her court-appointed appraisers were able to trace some fifty-seven pieces of property she owned in East Bridgeport, which consequently were omitted from the inventory of her estate. The oversight was not corrected until as late as 1928, amidst some little wrangling among the showman's descendants and heirs.[58]

———◆———

ARDUOUS AS THE road back from bankruptcy was, Barnum's struggles during these years were not entirely confined to money matters. While loud in his denunciations of the perfidious Jerome Company, in more private moments he came to believe there was some deeper meaning behind his fall. "I have learned to be patient & submissive, & that was a great and most important lesson for me to acquire," he wrote to his friend Abel Thomas from London in 1857. "It was just the lesson which I needed—in fact, my whole troubles have been and are just what I most stood in need of. *Of course* so, for they are sent to me by Divine & Parental wisdom, and I receive them with earnest thankfulness." As a Universalist, he could not allow that evil might be at work in the world: all afflictions, all apparent chaos in one's life, were sent by the "good Father" to convey "lessons of experience & wisdom," if only one were not so blind as to disregard or fail to recognize them. "Last summer, in my poverty & seclusion at the sea-side with my family, I found more peace & contentment than Iranistan ever afforded me—& even on the Atlantic & this side of it, hope & happiness have been and are my handmaidens. All praise to Him for permitting me always to look upon the bright side of things."[59] In an earlier letter read by his partner William H. Noble at the "sympathy" meeting held in Bridgeport, and more briefly in his speech upon regaining possession of the American Museum, he alluded to the same great lesson. "I humbly hope and believe," he wrote in the former,

> that I am being taught humility and reliance upon Providence, which will yet afford a thousand times more peace and true happiness than can be acquired in the din, strife and turmoil, excitements and struggles of this money-worshipping age. The man who coins his brain and blood into gold, who wastes all of his time and thought upon the almighty dollar, who looks no higher than blocks of houses and tracts of land, and whose iron chest is crammed with stocks and mortgages tied up with his own heartstrings, may console himself with the idea of safe investments, but he misses a pleasure which I firmly believe this lesson was intended to secure to me, and which it will secure if I can fully bring my mind to realize its wisdom.[60]

"The man" here described was not dissimilar to Barnum himself—or at least to Barnum as he feared he was fast becoming—whose own ever-quickening pursuit of the "almighty dollar" had so spectacularly brought his world crashing about him.

His tribulations, then, he looked upon as a divine chastening—as a warning to turn back from the reckless, increasingly self-centered course he had pursued for the past several years. Is there any concrete evidence he heeded this warning? That any "change of heart" was sincere and enduring? The money was soon flowing in again, as he resumed his activities as showman and real-estate developer. But he also, in the years that followed, devoted considerably more of his time and resources to philanthropic, educational, and religious causes; to politics and service on the boards of various public institutions; and even, in a complete reversal of his earlier stand on the subject, to championing the rights of the nation's blacks. "He grew more charitable and gentle as he grew older," his friend and lawyer Curtis Thompson later remarked of him.[61] His style of living also underwent a change around this time. No more for him the splendor and ostentation of an Iranistan, nor even a carriage with some controversial motto blazoned on its doors. Henceforth his residences would be unremarkable—solidly constructed and everything of best quality, of course, but hardly of the sort calculated to draw a gaping crowd. The "Prince of Humbugs" commenced his metamorphosis into the "Genial Showman."

Like many people in Barnum's own day, previous biographers, without disputing the evidence above, have tended to view it all as one more instance of the showman's hypocrisy—or at best as proof of his chameleonlike ability to adapt to shifting conditions in the second half of the nineteenth century. To them he appears *semper idem*, incapable of more than superficial change, craftily working his way around or diplomatically coming to terms with new societal values forced on him from without.[62] But these interpretations fail to take into account Barnum's deep religious convictions or, for that matter, his essentially moral nature. His bankruptcy was one of the greatest blows he ever suffered; and although his involvement with the Jerome Company had certainly been the catalyst to that debacle, he was sensible enough—humble enough, even—to profit from the experience and accept it for what his religious faith told him it must be: an admonition from on high that something was seriously amiss in his character. As a Universalist who believed in the perfectibility of his own and others' souls, he was eminently logical in his interpretation of events. Any real changes had to come from within, of his own volition, under the inspiration of divine guidance. There *would* be moral development over the coming years. He could no more think of complacently continuing in the character of the old Barnum than he and his family could return to Iranistan—that gaudy symbol of a closed period in his life that had almost providentially burned down on the eve of their moving back into it.

X

Pro Bono Publico

> For 30 years I have *striven* to *do good*, but (foolishly) stuck my
> worst side outside, until half the Christian community got to
> believe that I wore horns & hoofs.
> *Barnum to Theodore Tilton, 29 May 1865*

AFTER BEING CLOSED a week for renovations, the American Museum—"P. T.
Barnum, Proprietor"—reopened on 31 March 1860. John Greenwood Jr., in his
old position as manager, continued in Barnum's employ for several more years,
making two trips abroad on Museum business in the mid-sixties and for a while
working at the second American Museum farther uptown. Meanwhile, the
showman's two sons-in-law, who eventually made their homes in New York
City, were drafted into Barnum's service during the Civil War years. David W.
Thompson and Samuel H. Hurd were both listed as assistant managers on the
Museum's 1864 letterheads. Thompson soon departed to engage in other occupations (he was an inspector of customs in New York for many years under
Republican administrations and in later life a banker), but Hurd stayed on and
worked for his father-in-law on a number of subsequent ventures. In the seventies he was treasurer and financial agent with Barnum's traveling circus and
hippodrome.

Barnum himself was soon again conspicuous in the Museum's management.
He was especially proud of his aquarium and living whale exhibitions, and in
early 1862 he succeeded in recapturing the nation's imagination with his well-
orchestrated promotion of a sensational new midget. George Washington
Morrison Nutt—or "Commodore" Nutt, as he was better known to the public—was not, as one might believe from reading the autobiography, "discovered" or first exhibited by Barnum.[1] The son of a Manchester, New Hampshire,
farmer named Rodnia Nutt, he was already traveling around the countryside
when Barnum first heard of him, being badly managed by a showman named
Lillie, who sometimes charged as little as five cents to see the boy, took no
care for his education, and "don't understand doing this thing up in the *proper
style.*" Or so Barnum claimed in an 1861 letter to a lawyer-neighbor of the
Nutts named B. P. Cilley, whom he had hired as his confidential agent to lure
the midget to his museum. If Cilley could persuade Rodnia Nutt to sign an
agreement with Barnum for his son's services for a period of three to five years,

the showman promised to "take every pains [sic] to have him *properly educated* and *trained* so that he shall become a genteel, accomplished, and *attractive* little man, the same as I made Genl. Tom Thumb. . . . Mr. Nutt ought to be assured of the *fact* that Lillie is not competent to elevate the thing above a mere tuppenny show—low, common, and unattractive—and that *much valuable reputation* will be gained for the little fellow if he is put in training by the right man." Of course, he was also prepared to pay more than Lillie. But his own name, he stressed, was to be kept out of the affair until Nutt agreed to the terms Cilley thought best to propose. Figures were likely to jump sky-high whenever P. T. Barnum's name was invoked.[2]

Negotiations dragged on through the summer and fall—while the nation was plunged into the gloom of civil war, Lillie struggled to maintain his claim, and Barnum himself suffered a broken arm—and were not concluded until 12 December, when the contract was finally signed in New York. By then Cilley had switched allegiance and was acting as Rodnia Nutt's attorney, and between two such "wide-awake chaps," Barnum jokingly protested, he feared he had made a "pretty bad bargain."[3] The agreement called for the services of both George and his elder brother, Rodnia Jr., twenty-one years old, who often accompanied George on tour and was around forty-nine inches tall. George himself, who had been born on April Fools' Day 1848, stood around twenty-nine inches and weighed close to twenty-five pounds at the time.[4] In addition to binding himself to provide the two boys with room and board, clothing, travel and medical expenses, Barnum promised to "exercise a healthful influence over their morals and teach them both reading and writing and arithmetic." Payment during their first year was to be $12 a week plus 10 percent on all sales of souvenir items, the profits from which were guaranteed to amount to no less than $260 per annum. The weekly salary was to increase to 14, 18, 23, and 30 dollars in each succeeding year, with the guarantee on souvenirs ultimately rising to $440. Upon faithfully completing the final year, the boys were to have all presents, excepting money, made to them during the life of the contract and a carriage and pair of ponies presented by Barnum. A simple calculation shows that salaries and guaranteed returns from souvenirs totaled $6560 over the five-year period, although Barnum was, of course, responsible for the other expenses listed in the agreement.

The ink was hardly dry on this document when an ingenious new publicity campaign was under way. Without revealing he had already secured the Commodore and his brother, Barnum now primed the press with stories of this wonderful prodigy and pretended to be in hot pursuit of the midget himself. A number of rival managers rose to the bait. The circus proprietor Joseph Cushing wrote to Nutt's father on 8 January, offering $5000 per year for his son's services. A few days later the circus of June, Howe, Quick & Co. telegraphed its offer of $16,000 for three years. Somehow these communications soon found their way into the nation's newspapers—together with a "confidential" letter, dated 10 January 1862, from Barnum to his old friend Parson Hitchcock, who had temporarily returned to his former employer and was now, supposedly, operating as his "agent" in the Commodore Nutt affair:

Don't fail to take the first train for Manchester, N.H., and secure if possible the dwarf, Commodore Nutt. . . . Rather than fail in getting him, you may offer him or his father *thirty thousand dollars* for the privilege of exhibiting him three years (this is about $200 per week), besides which I will pay all expenses of board, clothing, costumes and travel of the little commodore; also the expenses of any companion he may select, and will give him the profits of all sales of books, pictures, etc., and present him all cuts, properties and paraphernalia attached to the exhibition at the close of the engagement, including a splendid pair of ponies and carriage. . . . I hear that several showmen are after him. Nail him, and don't let them get ahead of you.[5]

From this it was but a short leap of the imagination to the sobriquet the "$30,000 Nutt," this being the sum Barnum reputedly paid for the Commodore's services. When Cilley wrote to report the amazement of his Manchester neighbors over such wild tales, the showman cited Scripture: " 'He that *believeth not* shall be ———d.' How can your friends disbelieve? Of course 'any *fool*' must know I had to go above the other offers—consequently if I don't give $30,000 I must go over the $16,000. It is generally thought the sum is from $20,000 to $25,000 that I pay. For particulars see all the papers.' "[6]

It was the early history of Tom Thumb all over again. While diligently preparing the great American public for the Commodore's debut, Barnum rushed to have costumes, photographs, and bill cuts made, rehearsed the boy in the roles he was to perform, and ordered a "beautiful little carriage" in which the Commodore was to be driven about town by his liveried brother Rodnia. This unusual vehicle, preserved today at the Barnum Museum in Bridgeport, was fantastically carved in the shape of an English walnut, with the top half of the shell split and hinged at the ends so as to open up, revealing the tiny "nutt" inside. After making his debut at the Museum in early February, the Commodore was taken to Washington, where Barnum was invited to bring him to the White House. They arrived in the midst of a cabinet meeting, were immediately taken before the President anyway, and the inevitable puns and witticisms followed. When Lincoln, taking Nutt by the hand, advised him to "wade ashore" if he should ever find himself in danger while commanding his "fleet," the Commodore coolly surveyed the length of the Presidential legs. "I guess, Mr. President, you could do that better than I could."[7]

The year 1862 was a good one for dwarfs. A few months after the above events, Barnum met and engaged a pretty midget named Mercy Lavinia Warren Bump (the name was quickly shortened to "Lavinia Warren"), who had been born, and for a time taught school, in Middleboro, Massachusetts. Like Nutt, she had already been on exhibition when Barnum first heard of her, traveling the western rivers on a combination showboat-museum, which did not deter the showman from trumpeting her as his latest find. After giving several receptions for the press at New York's St. Nicholas Hotel and briefly appearing before the Boston public, the "Queen of Beauty," as Barnum advertised her, commenced at the Museum at the beginning of 1863. She was then twenty-one years old, weighed twenty-nine pounds, and towered over Nutt at thirty-two inches.[8] Meanwhile, having begun to put on pounds as well as inches, Tom Thumb had continued to tour under Barnum's direction. As the showman tells the story, upon paying a visit to the Museum one day, the General was immediately smitten by the beguiling Lavinia and forthwith announced his determination to make her his wife.[9] Unfortunately, his attentions to Lavinia did not sit very well with the Commodore, who had developed an adolescent crush on the lady and who took out his frustration by beating up the portly General in a dressing room. The courtship was a brief one, the wedding was announced for 10 February, and, as the General had agreed to exhibit himself with Lavinia during the interim, the Museum was daily crowded with spectators eager to gaze upon the prenuptial couple. So much money poured into the Museum's coffers—frequently more than $3000 per day—that Barnum was moved to offer them $15,000 in return for agreeing to postpone their wedding for a month. The offer was instantly refused, and the ceremony, described in the press as the "grand national event of the season," took place as scheduled in New York's Grace Church. Having gotten over his disappointment in love, the Commodore magnanimously agreed to serve as Tom Thumb's best man; and Lavinia's younger sister Minnie, another midget who was even tinier than she, was bridesmaid. The showman was happy to pay all expenses, at the same time valiantly resisting the temptation to make further money out of the affair. "I had promised to give the couple a genteel and graceful wedding," he writes, "and I kept my word."

The "Fairy Wedding," as the event came to be called, was immortalized in numerous photographs and prints by Mathew Brady and others. The church was crowded with a distinguished body of witnesses that included governors, members of Congress, Civil War generals, and the cream of New York society. In the afternoon there was a splendid reception for over 2000 guests at the Metropolitan Hotel, where the gifts to the little couple were also displayed. Among them was a set of Chinese fire screens sent by the Lincolns, who shortly afterwards entertained the Thumbs at the White House while they were on their "bridal tour."[10]

The wedding was too great a coup to let the public ever forget it. After inducing the Bumps to sign Minnie over to his care, Barnum sent the diminutive wedding party on extensive tours of America and Europe, culminating in a grand trip around the world in 1869–72 that took in the American West, Japan and China, Indonesia, Australia and Tasmania, India and Ceylon, Arabia, Egypt, and Europe again. In all, they journeyed nearly 60,000 miles on this one tour alone, giving 1471 entertainments in 587 cities and towns without missing a single performance.[11] In the seventies the Commodore decided to strike out on his own and eventually married a Miss Elston of Redwood City, California, who was only a little below average height. At the time of his death from Bright's disease in 1881, she was seen sobbing over his coffin, calling him her "dear little boy."

All four members of this famous quartet were perfectly proportioned and examples of ateliotic dwarfism, whose sufferers are further classified into "sexual" and "asexual" varieties. The former eventually attain puberty and are capable of reproducing, though not without considerable danger to the females, as may be imagined. Minnie herself married a small person (but not, apparently, a dwarf) named "Major" Edward Newell whose specialty was a song-and-dance number on roller skates. She died in childbirth in 1878 after adamantly refusing the services of an obstetrician Barnum wished to send her. The baby, which weighed six pounds and which nearly everyone thought would also be a "midget," died a few hours later. Tom Thumb and Lavinia also appear to have been sexually mature, but never had any children of their own. This despite the fact that several photographs and a medal depict Lavinia or the couple posing with a baby said to be theirs, and that they were often advertised as taking their "baby" along on their tours. Predictably, the ruse has always been laid at the doorstep of Barnum, who has been accused of originating it in order to sell copies of the photographs. But in an interview published in 1901, Lavinia revealed that she and the General had not been entirely blameless in the matter. The original baby, a boy, she explained, came from a foundling hospital, but by the age of four had already outgrown his "father." Afraid of looking ridiculous alongside of him, they appealed to Barnum to remedy the situation. "He agreed with us. He thought our baby should not grow. Thus we exhibited English babies in England, French babies in France, and German babies in Germany. It was—they were—a great success. Mr. Barnum was a great man."[12] She might have added that on their first tour of Britain, following a tradition begun by Barnum and the General twenty years before, the credulity of the Royal Family was again put to a severe test. In November 1864 the famous wedding party performed before the Prince and Princess of Wales at Marlborough House, and the following June visited Windsor Castle by royal command. On both occasions they carried with them the Thumbs' "infant daughter."[13]

———◆———

NOT EVERYONE, of course, was delighted by Barnum's rebound from bankruptcy. James Gordon Bennett continued to be the proverbial thorn in his side, ridiculing him and his plans at every opportunity. When the *Herald*, at the end of an article on New York's amusement places, characterized the American Museum as dark and dirty, "unselect" in its patrons, and a "moral humbug," the showman angrily demanded the right to reply to these charges that were so patently "calculated to do me serious injury."[14] The same offending article had suggested Barnum ought to tear down the Museum and build another that was "worthy of the city." Ironically, when the American Museum burned to the ground the following year and Barnum decided to open a new establishment farther up Broadway, it was Bennett, searching for some land on which to erect a new *Herald* building, who bought the unexpired lease on the Ann

Tom Thumb as Napoleon. A later depiction of the General in his favorite character, after he had married Lavinia Warren, shown here with him, in 1863.

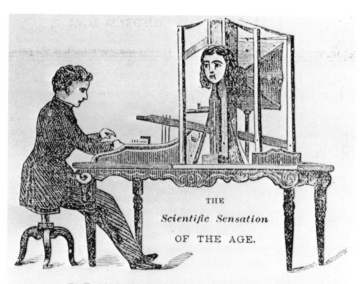

THE
Scientific Sensation
OF THE AGE.

THE MARVELOUS TALKING-MACHINE.

Professor Faber's famous "euphonia" or talking machine, which so puzzled the Duke of Wellington.

anistan, Barnum's first and most opulent mansion, modeled on the Royal Pavilion
Brighton, England. The fountain before the front entrance is not shown in this
int, but note the oriental outbuilding in the distance.

Barnum's daughters Caroline, Pauline, and Helen, as painted by the American artist Frederick Spencer in 1847.

Jenny Lind as she was portrayed on a music cover dating from 1850, the year
in which she commenced her engagement with Barnum. The conductor Julius
Benedict and the baritone Giovanni Belletti, both of whom accompanied the
singer to America, are also represented.

"Barnum's Mammoth Tent," the forerunner of those used in his later circus enterprises, which sheltered his "Asiatic Caravan" in 1851–1854.

A five-dollar note issued by Bridgeport's Pequonnock Bank, of which Barnum was the first president. The showman and Jenny Lind are both depicted, as is Iranistan, whose fountain was in operation by this time.

"The Fairy Wedding." A famous
photograph by Matthew Brady,
commemorating Tom Thumb's
marriage to Lavinia Warren in
1863. Commodore Nutt and Minnie
Warren, Lavinia's sister, complete
the bridal party.

General and Mrs. Tom Thumb
with their "baby." One of several
depictions of this scene of domestic
bliss.

WALDEMERE.

The Home of Hon. P.T. BARNUM. BRIDGEPORT, CONN.

SEA-SIDE PARK

Waldemere, Barnum's second-most famous home, and the one he resided at the longest. As at Iranistan, the grounds were open to the public. The showman's monogrammed flag flies from the cupola.

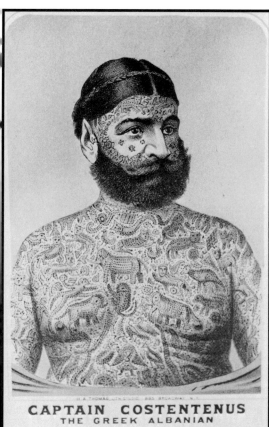

CAPTAIN COSTENTENUS
THE GREEK ALBANIAN

Tattooed from Head to Foot in Chinese Tartary as punishment for enga-
ging in Rebellion against the King, now with P.T. Barnum

Captain Djordji Costentenus, the famous tattooed man, whose authenticity was certified by Oliver Wendell Holmes and other eminent representatives of the medical profession.

Ye Kind-hearted Man.

Ye Kind-hearted Man," lampooning Henry Bergh, Barnum's sometime antagonist. Note whom the president of the SPCA is protecting from the rain.

"The Greatest Show on Earth" in 1873. This rare photograph illustrates well the layout of the various "departments" through whose tents spectators passed on their way to the big top. In the foreground are the canvas banners advertising some of the freaks in the museum department. One of the elaborate tableau wagons used in the street parade is visible at the right.

Charity Barnum, the showman's "poor, nervous wife," as she appeared in later life.

The interior of Barnum's Roman Hippodrome in New York, with a quadriga race in progress on its track.

Nancy Fish Barnum in her boudoir. One in a series of imperial-sized photographs Barnum's "young English wife" had made for sending to her friends and family in England.

The Barnum family
monument in Bridgeport's
Mountain Grove Cemetery.
The sons and grandsons of
Barnum's youngest daughter,
Pauline, who married Nathan
Seeley, are buried in the
same plot.

Thomas Ball's marble bust of
Barnum, before its
destruction in the 1975 fire at
Tufts University.

Thomas Ball posing with his monumental statue of Barnum in Europe. The pencil the showman is holding in his right hand, like the bronze urns about the granite base of the statue in Bridgeport's Seaside Park, has long since disappeared.

"The Perennial P. T.—The Man the Children Love." Barnum as a modern-day Noah. Madison Square Garden, where his circus began each season, is in the background.

Street property from him. The price, supposedly a bargain, was $200,000; but as Bennett wished to own the property outright, he also paid $450,000 for the land, some $100,000 above the figure at which its worth had been appraised. It turned out, however, that the persons doing the appraising had not been aware of the lease held by Barnum; otherwise they would have reduced their figure by the value assigned to it. Upon realizing he had paid nearly double what the land was worth, the publisher did his best to get out of the deal. Too late: he had already paid the showman his $200,000 and had signed a bond for $100,000 toward the purchase of the land.[15]

The showman's refusal to return the money—"I don't make child's bargains," he had informed Bennett's lawyer—inevitably led to more unpleasantness with the *Herald*. This time the paper refused to publish the advertisements for his new museum, a punishment previously inflicted on several other managers who had declined to use the *Herald*'s job printing office for their bills or offended the high-handed publisher in other ways. The showman retaliated by calling a meeting of the Managers' Association, a group to which he and most other New York theatre proprietors belonged, which delegated a committee to wait upon Bennett and ascertain if he was indeed excluding the Museum's advertisements out of personal pique. When the publisher peremptorily refused to accept Barnum's advertisements, the members of the Association unanimously decided to boycott the *Herald*. For a time Bennett tried to dismiss the affair. It had all come about, he loftily informed his readers, through his refusing to kowtow to the managers, led by that "Joyce Heth in breeches of the Museum," who expected puffs and other favors in return for their advertisements.[16] In an unsuccessful effort to divide the Association, he continued to publish gratuitously advertisements for several theatres run by its members, who promptly took to heading their bills and announcements in other papers with the statement that "This Establishment does not advertise in the New York *Herald*." The *Herald* soon fell to abusing the rebellious managers, their productions, and the other newspapers that sided with them. But in reality, Barnum writes, the theatres thrived as they never had before, and thousands of people went to them "merely to show their willingness to support the managers and to spite 'Old Bennett.'" The loss to the *Herald* in advertising revenue was estimated to be as high as $100,000 per year; and since readers no longer looked to its pages for a rundown of the city's amusements, its circulation also "suffered terribly." The triumphant managers, Barnum continues, did not end their boycott until the fall of 1868. By then Bennett had been definitively taught "the lesson of his own insignificance, as he had not learned it since the days when gentlemen used to kick and cowhide him up and down the whole length of Nassau Street."[17]

————◆————

BARNUM'S PRESENCE in the metropolis was even more conspicuous after 1867, the year in which he purchased an elegant town house in the Murray Hill section. Located at the corner of Fifth Avenue and 39th Street, only a stone's throw from the site of the failed Crystal Palace, this was to serve as the showman's "winter" residence—generally from November to June—for the next several years. His youngest daughter, Pauline, had married Nathan Seeley on her birthday, 1 March, the previous year, and as all three of his daughters and their families were now living in New York, he rejoiced in being within easy visiting distance of them. At other times he attended to business, took leisurely drives through Central Park, and entertained friends, some of whom, like Horace Greeley and the Universalist minister and editor George H. Emerson, had their own latchkeys and were free to come and go as they pleased. Emerson, who for several years spent two nights per week at the house while attending to his editorial duties in the metropolis, later set down his recollections of his life with the Barnums. The humor and practical jokes abounded, naturally, and not even the clergyman was spared the latter.[18] Greeley himself was sometimes present for weeks at a time. The famous editor's absentmindedness and habitual inattention to his own comfort, according to another guest, were a continual source of concern to his host, who took care to provide him with slippers and a robe and always insisted he take the easiest chair.[19]

These extended seasons in town also provided Barnum greater opportunity to pursue his cultural interests, for, as has already been noted, he was by no means insensitive to the "finer" things. During the sixties he was even a member of one of America's first "salons," that of the well-known Cary sisters, Alice and Phoebe, a few of whose poems—such as Alice's touching "Pictures of Memory," admired by Poe—were anthologized into the present century. For years the sisters' informal Sunday evening receptions at their home in 20th Street attracted many of the leading writers, editors, clergymen, and celebrities of the day. John Greenleaf Whittier, dressed in his plain Quaker garb, was sometimes present, as were the poets Richard and Elizabeth Stoddard; Bayard Taylor and his wife; the journalist and lecturer Kate Field; the Norwegian violinist Ole Bull; the publisher George W. Carleton, who brought out Barnum's *The Humbugs of the World* in 1865; the ministers Edwin H. Chapin and Charles F. Deems; Robert Bonner, the owner of the *New York Ledger*; Whitelaw Reid, editor of the *Tribune*, who became its proprietor in 1872 and eventually U.S. Minister to France and Ambassador to Great Britain; and the editor of the Congregational journal the *Independent*, Theodore Tilton, who was shortly to figure so prominently in the affairs of another of Barnum's friends, the silver-tongued Henry Ward Beecher of Brooklyn's Plymouth Church. Greeley himself was often there, drinking cups of sweetened milk and water before dashing off to address a temperance meeting or to prepare a leader for the Monday morning edition of his *Tribune*; and Elizabeth Cady Stanton and Susan B. Anthony also put in occasional appearances. They all constituted what one visitor was pleased to term "a Pantheon, a Polytechnic Institute, a room of the Committee on Reconstruction, a gathering place for the ecclesiastical and political 'Happy Family,'" to which the original begetter of that peaceable kingdom at the American Museum, "burly and full of good nature . . . with great brains, which would have made him notable in any department," was always a welcome addition.[20]

Several of these figures—Chapin, Greeley, the Carys themselves (though Phoebe eventually lapsed into Methodism)—were further bound by their Universalist faith, which to some extent explains Barnum's inclusion in their circle. He had led off the very first issue of his 1853 *Illustrated News* with a a poem by Alice, and in later years was so delighted to entertain the sisters at his home in Bridgeport that he named one of the bedrooms after them. Phoebe, in particular, was a great favorite with him and sometimes accompanied him on his drives around New York. Her contemporaries often referred to her as the "wittiest woman in America," and Barnum, who later wrote that she afforded him "hours of rollicking laughter," eventually jotted down a few recollections of her brilliant repartee. Upon accompanying him one day to Wood's Museum, the successor to the American Museum, she asked him to show her the "Infernal Regions," one of the advertised attractions of that establishment. When Barnum learned the exhibit was out of order, he reported to her that "the Infernal Regions are busted, but never mind, Phoebe, you'll see them in time." "No, in *eternity*," was her instant reply. On another, perhaps more revealing occasion, while he was trying to leave one of the Carys' Sunday receptions without attracting attention to himself, Phoebe and her niece followed him into the hallway. "Now why do you follow me out?" he laughingly inquired. "I am not going to carry anything away." "We wish you would," Phoebe quickly replied, invitingly throwing open her arms.[21]

The showman's own legendary "wit" continued unabated, of course, as was evident above all in the horrendous punning in which he and his ministerial friend Edwin Chapin took particular delight. An especially egregious example occurs in a letter Barnum wrote around this time to a Bridgeport resident, Philo H. Skidmore, after the latter had complained about some wagons containing bears—the remnants of "Grizzly" Adams's California Menagerie, including the gigantic bear "Old Sampson"—that had been left parked on Skidmore's street while the wagons were being repainted at Hall's Carriage Shop. Skidmore had threatened some kind of action unless the cages and their occupants were promptly removed; and Barnum, after lamenting the fact that "the artistic display from Hall's Conservatory of Art is more than you are willing to *bear*," promised he would

> not *pause* nor hesitate, especially after reading the finishing *clause* of your eloquent epistle, but shall at once order the bears to "dig out" lest there might be mischief a *brewin'* in your vicinity.
>
> I am rejoiced at the evident tendency to "spiritual things" which is manifest in Elm St. from your desire to cast off the "Old Adam." The proprietors of the "Conservatory" will today *haul* the palaces of "Old Sampson" & his courtiers to "Gaza," in order that more appreciative eyes may *gaze-a* while upon the "wreck of matter" ere it falls (perchance) into the hands of the ruthless "Philistines." I hope that in descending the

hills the horses will be relieved by placing a "skid" upon the wheels, but if they require further relief, I shall be obliged to call on you for one *Skid-more.*

I hardly know where I shall place the "palaces," but if I cannot find a more suitable locality for them, I will *Barnum.*[22]

———◆———

AS IN NEW YORK, he was soon active in Connecticut again. In 1860 he commenced building a new residence for his family, a bit to the west of Iranistan's site on land he owned in Fairfield, next door to a house he had previously built for his daughter Caroline. "Lindencroft" owed nothing to his connection with the Swedish soprano, but was named after a beautiful grove of lindens that stood on the property. A large, substantial mansion with a depth of over a hundred feet, it was set amid the usual profusion of trees, shrubs, and flowers so beloved by Charity and was fronted by an ornate fountain.[23] Here the showman had hoped to spend his "declining years." But Charity's perennial health problems and her increasing inability to look after so large an establishment, he later claimed in his autobiography, led him to sell the house in 1867. After spending the summer of that year and the next at other locations in Bridgeport, in 1869 they moved into a new mansion overlooking Long Island Sound. "Waldemere," or "Woods-by-the-Sea," was a rambling, Victorian-style structure whose rooms and grounds continued to expand over the years. An example of what would be later termed in America a "compound," the spacious estate included summer cottages built to accommodate Barnum's daughters and their families; and the carefully tended grounds—which possessed a fine hickory grove, broad, sweeping lawns with statues and fountains, and flower beds laid out in the English manner—were again open to the public. The house eventually measured 160 feet on its front. Whenever its famous owner was at home, a silken flag with the monogram "P. T. B." streamed from its cupola.[24]

The choice of location for this "summer retreat" was primarily the result of two considerations: Charity's doctor, unable to think of any better medication to prescribe for her ailments, had decreed she should live near the seashore; and Barnum already owned the land on which the house was built. He had acquired the property while pushing another pet project, Seaside Park, originally a rock-strewn shoreline front owned by several farmers, who at first were reluctant to agree that the ceding of their land would in any way benefit Bridgeport or themselves. But the showman, who had envisioned such a pleasure ground as early as 1863, continually harangued his neighbors in the papers and in person, arguing not only that its establishment would attract new residents and increase property values in general but also that it was absurd, almost criminal, "that a beautiful city like Bridgeport, lying on the shore of a broad expanse of salt water, should so cage itself in, that not an inhabitant could approach the beach." Worn down by his persistence and that of a few other public-spirited citizens he had enlisted in the cause, the owners finally agreed to donate a portion of their land to the city and sell the remainder.

Unfortunately, one small farm whose frontage was needed for the park's completion was then tied up in estate proceedings, and neither the heirs nor the administrators felt entitled to give away any portion of it. With characteristic determination, the showman cut through this Gordian knot by purchasing the entire farm for $12,000, then deeded to the city the land required for the park. The rest he kept for himself, and it was there Waldemere arose a few years later.[25]

As one of his own rewards in this civic-minded transaction, Barnum had the honor of naming the park, whose construction got under way in 1865. Its design—though the fact is nowhere mentioned in the autobiography—was at least partially the work of the great creator of New York's Central Park, Frederick Law Olmsted, whom Barnum later consulted about the laying out of roads and grounds around his own residence.[26] The park was expanded westward in later years, often with Barnum himself contributing land and large sums of money for draining and filling projects and the construction of dikes and roadways. In effect, Seaside Park became another striking illustration of his penchant for "profitable philanthropy," providing a gorgeous setting for, almost an extension of, his own estate. There his grandchildren and in time their children drove their donkey carts, rode a merry-go-round, and were taken to concerts at the park's bandstand. For his many guests Barnum often organized clambakes at the water's edge, boating and bathing parties, and drives along the broad boulevards, one of which, appropriately, was named after him. The park soon became the favorite resort of thousands of Bridgeport's and Fairfield's residents, who drove there in their carriages or arrived via a branch of the city's horse-railroad system; and "the main drive," the showman wrote rhapsodically in the 1869 edition of his autobiography, "is already, on a lesser scale, to the citizens of Bridgeport, what the grand avenue in Central Park is to the people of New York; with this priceless advantage, however, in favor of Sea-side Park, of a frontage on the Sound, and a shore on which the waves are ever breaking, and sounding the grand, unending story of the mysteries of the great deep."[27]

THE NEW PARK, fittingly enough, was also chosen as the site of a fine monument commemorating Bridgeport's citizens who had fought in the Civil War. Though not a frontline participant in this struggle, Barnum was profoundly affected by it and contributed more than his fair share to the war effort, sometimes at considerable risk to himself and his business activities. Well before the war had begun, as he wrote the abolitionist minister Thomas Wentworth Higginson in 1855, he had finally come to recognize the "curse" slavery had inflicted on the land, and his own growing abhorrence of the institution was fully matched by that of Charity, who attended the Unitarian church and declared the outspoken abolitionist sentiments of that denomination *"too tame* for her."[28] His liberal-minded friends among the Universalist ministry and laity—many of whom were in the forefront of this movement—undoubtedly influenced his thinking as well; but what definitively led him to reverse his earlier stand on the subject was the "Free-State Struggle" that took place in Kansas, where in the mid-fifties proslavery and antislavery forces massacred each other over the attempt to introduce slavery into that territory. Appalled by these events in "bleeding Kansas" and the Democrats' willingness to temporize over the slavery issue, Barnum also switched his political allegiance around this time and voted for Lincoln in the 1860 Presidential election.[29]

During the war itself Barnum often lashed out at the "Southern slaveholders" and their "Copperhead" sympathizers in the North. He was prepared to be reduced to his last shirt and dollar—"yes, and the *very last* drop of blood," he wrote to his English friend Thomas Brettell—in order to crush the rebellion and preserve the nation.[30] Shortly after the outbreak of hostilities, while compromise was still being urged by many in the North, conservative Democrats in Connecticut staged a series of "peace meetings" around the state that were soon vigorously opposed by local Union and Prudential committees. By far the most dramatic of these confrontations occurred on 24 August 1861, when Ellis B. Schnable, described by Barnum as a "broken-down politician from Pennsylvania," was scheduled to address one such rally at Stepney, a town some ten miles north of Bridgeport. With an eye to determining whether there might be anything treasonable in these activities, Barnum and some of his friends, including the sewing-machine magnate Elias Howe Jr., drove to Stepney on the day in question and, as chance would have it, were joined by two omnibuses crowded with soldiers who were home on furlough. No sooner had they arrived than the meeting was disrupted and the white flag of the Peace party torn from its pole, while some of those who had come to hear Schnable brandished weapons and threatened to fire on the intruders. The soldiers soon had the situation under some degree of control and carried Barnum to the platform to give a speech of his own. According to one account, the featured speaker himself swore to shoot Barnum if he dared address the crowd. When the showman went on anyway, Schnable then fell to heckling and was kicked for it. "The Star-Spangled Banner" was sung and Howe spoke some patriotic words; and having given the Stepney natives some "wholesome advice," the triumphant Union supporters piled back into their coaches and dragged the offending peace flag after them all the way to Bridgeport. There they were greeted by cheering crowds, whose more volatile element, after an impromptu Union meeting in the center of the city that evening, went on to sack the offices of the *Bridgeport Farmer,* a Democratic paper notorious for its pro-Southern sentiments. Four days later, after delivering another inflammatory speech in Litchfield County, Schnable was arrested on direct orders from Secretary of State Seward and spent the duration of the war in jail. The Connecticut legislature promptly passed a law authorizing the seizure of "treasonable flags" and the fining and imprisonment of those owning them; Prudential committees quickly formed throughout the state to squelch any further activities by Secessionists. As Barnum jubilantly wrote President Lincoln only a few days after these stirring scenes, "The late events which have occurred in this vicinity, concluding with the arrest of *Schnabel* [sic], have rendered Secessionists *so scarce,* I cannot find one for exhibition in my museum. Those who one week ago were blatant Secessionists are today publicly announcing themselves as 'in for the country to the end of the war.' The 'strong arm' has a mighty influence here."[31] There were no more "peace meetings" in Connecticut.

Besides paying for several volunteers to serve in the war,[32] Barnum was soon offering advice to his old Hartford friend Gideon Welles, who had become Lincoln's Secretary of the Navy. In September 1861 he asked Welles to use his influence to have the office of local subscription agent for the National Loan taken away from a former Bridgeport mayor, Philo C. Calhoun, whom Barnum characterized as a "rabid political Democrat of the *Bridgeport Farmer* school." Calhoun, he pointed out, was being paid between $30,000 and $50,000 to make harnesses and saddles for the U.S. Government, yet had not contributed a dollar to the war effort. Worse still, Barnum had learned he had invested $100,000 in the same sort of business in Charleston, South Carolina; and his wife and daughters were such undisguised Secessionists that following the Battle of Bull Run "they drove to the *Bridgeport Farmer* office, called out the editors, and gloated & laughed with them in the public streets over our defeat." "For heaven's sake, have an *example* made of this traitorous Calhoun," he pleaded. "It will do *a world of good* to the cause of the Union." On another occasion he wrote to give Welles intelligence he had received concerning Confederate blockade runners that were sailing between Wilmington and Nassau.[33]

His blatant support of the Union and prominence as a member of Bridgeport's Prudential Committee made him a likely target for agents of the Confederacy, and especially after the 1863 draft riots in New York soldiers sometimes stood guard at Lindencroft. The following year, when a group of Southern saboteurs infiltrated New York with orders to fire the metropolis, it was no accident that the American Museum, alone among all the city's amusement places, was one of the buildings in which they planted their incendiary devices.[34] Nothing daunted, the showman continued to champion the Union cause every way he could. In the Lecture Room of the Museum itself, audiences were treated to patriotic dramas and the thrilling narratives of wartime celebrities, including the little drummer boy Robert Hendershot, who had his drum shattered by an enemy shell while crossing the Rappahannock River at Fredericksburg, and the famous Union spy Major Pauline Cushman.[35]

At one point during the conflict, amid rumors that the flag that had flown over Fort Sumter was in rebel hands, Barnum set out to reassure himself and the public on the matter. Upon learning that Major-General Robert Anderson, commander of the Charleston defenses at the time of the fort's surrender, probably had it, he promptly wrote to the general to request the flag's loan. If he were permitted to exhibit it for as little as a week, not only would this gratify the public and "*silence* the claims that the enemy now possess the flag," but he would also be happy to hand the general one hundred dollars "to be used in any way you please." Anderson, who did indeed possess the flag and was to reraise it over Fort Sumter at the end of the war, was unimpressed by this patriotic appeal and refused the request.[36] When the war finally ended and Jefferson Davis, dressed in what were alleged to be his wife's clothes, was captured while attempting to flee Union troops, Barnum dispatched a telegram to Secretary of War Stanton—which was immediately released to the press, of course—offering $500 for "the petticoats in which Jeff Davis was caught."[37] Southerners never forgave him for the role he played during the war, and in later years, after he had embarked on his career as a circus proprietor, his traveling shows usually avoided the South.

Nor did Barnum himself easily forgive what he considered to be the perversity of the South and its Northern sympathizers during this turbulent period. "Was there ever a struggle wherein the hand of a Beneficent and Almighty God was more plainly visible?" he wrote to the New York politician Daniel S. Dickinson two months after Lee's surrender at Appomattox. "Could there ever have been a more pusillanimous termination to the rebellion than Jeff Davis gave it in his petticoats?"[38] A week later he was warning his Danbury friend Frederick Wildman, with whom he had earlier gloated over the "Stepney Raid," that the state's Copperheads were attempting to get the management of all the Fourth of July celebrations into their hands, "just as many of them did in relation to the Lincoln obsequies so as to cover up their infamy & make the people forget the Copperhead rascalities during the last 4 years." In Bridgeport, Barnum and his allies were determined to see they did not succeed, and he hoped Wildman would do the same in Danbury.[39]

He had become so ardent a supporter of the Union, in fact, that even before the war's end he decided to enter politics himself, so that he might, as he wrote, have the honor of voting "for the then proposed amendment to the Constitution of the United States to abolish slavery forever from the land."[40] Since his legal residence was then still in Fairfield, he ran on the Union or Republican ticket to represent that town in the state's General Assembly, was elected by a margin of 187 votes in early April 1865, and won reelection the following year. During these two terms Barnum proved himself an astute, hardworking member of the legislature, chaired the committees on Agriculture and the State House, and regularly did battle with the powerful railroad lobby in the state, at one point hiring detectives to spy on the activities of the directors of the New York and New Haven Railroad and foiling a secret plot to raise commutation fares by the extortionate rate of 20 percent.[41] The directors of the company were so outraged by his "thus securing a righteous law for the protection of its commuters," he wrote in a note appended to later editions of the autobiography, that "as lately as 1871, the venders of books on the trains were prohibited from selling to passengers this book which exposes their cupidity." After becoming convinced that a parallel railroad from New York to New Haven would be a good investment and a means of disrupting the railroad monopoly in Connecticut, for a time he actually busied himself with such a project.[42]

His political shrewdness, not to mention his willingness to risk making powerful enemies, was again demonstrated during the 1866 session, one of whose most pressing issues (for in those days the state legislature, not the people, decided such matters) was the electing of a U.S. Senator. Oddly enough, the American Museum played a role in this little drama, though Barnum chose not to reveal the fact until many years later. During the previous session—while he was in the midst of a key speech attacking the railroad interests—he had been handed a telegram from his son-in-law Samuel Hurd informing him of the destruction of his first museum. Hardly batting an eyelid, he had gone on to finish his exposé of the machinations of the railroad directors, and it was only after a vote had been taken and his bill to protect commuters had been passed that he revealed his loss to his astounded fellow legislators. The Museum was soon back in business at its new location uptown; but for months afterwards, flush with the money he had received from James Gordon Bennett, Barnum also pursued his idea for a great national "free" museum, obtaining endorsements from as many distinguished individuals as he could and even a "memorial," signed by Horace Greeley, Henry Ward Beecher, William Cullen Bryant, and a host of other prominent citizens, addressed to President Andrew Johnson, urging him to lend governmental support to this benevolent enterprise.[43] Johnson, however, who together with Secretary of State Seward expressed concern about "propriety" when Barnum called on them in person, continued to refuse to endorse this document over the next nine months. By early 1866 the showman had nearly given up hope of obtaining Presidential sanction for his project.

Until, that is, the question of who was to be Connecticut's next U.S. Senator arose at the start of the 1866 legislative session. By then Barnum and many other Republicans had become disenchanted with Johnson, and the Republican-controlled General Assembly was determined to send to Washington someone who would staunchly oppose his pro-Southern Reconstruction policies. At first the contest seemed a three-way race between wartime governor William A. Buckingham, Orris S. Ferry, a former state senator and Congressional representative from Norwalk, and incumbent Senator LaFayette S. Foster, who was also president *pro tem* of the U.S. Senate and acting Vice-President—all three of whom, Barnum wrote to a fellow legislator in early April, were admirable choices, though it seemed to him that Foster's position and influence as Vice-President entitled him to the office, and he hoped "we will elect him very early in the session."[44] But before the session got under way, alarming intelligence reached him that Foster's wife had been heard to say that her husband, were he not standing for reelection, would have no hesitation in acknowledging his sympathy for the South; and Barnum, in order to test the truth of this statement, laid for the Vice-President of the United States a most ingenious trap. "Knowing that if this really was true," he writes, "Senator Foster would have a great influence with President Johnson, I wrote to him about my project for a Free National Museum, stating my desire to get the President's influence with our Consuls abroad, and asking him whether he would speak to the President on the subject." Foster cheerfully replied he thought he could sway the President and that he was always glad to do favors for "friends," and two days later, on 27 April 1866, Barnum finally received the long-sought endorsement. When the Connecticut legislature convened the following week, Barnum trotted out both Foster's letter to him and the President's endorsement and "secretly" explained to Republican members from Fairfield County why they should drop their allegiance to the duplicitous Senator. By the time the balloting in the full Republican caucus was over, Foster had been roundly defeated and Ferry, whose champion Barnum had become, elected—all of which went to show, Barnum wrote with considerable satisfaction toward the end of his life, "that Mr. Ferry was elected United States Senator, simply and only because Senator Foster had been detected in his pretence of being a Northern Republican."[45]

The 13th Amendment to the U.S. Constitution had been speedily approved at the start of the 1865 legislative session. What was undoubtedly the finest moment in Barnum's entire political career occurred on 26 May of the same year, when he delivered an eloquent, carefully reasoned speech before both the house and the senate in favor of an amendment to Connecticut's own constitution extending the vote to the state's black population. Unfortunately, the "Land of Steady Habits" was not ready to go so far, and it was not until four years later—by which time the 15th Amendment was about to become the law of the land anyway—that the restrictive word "white" was finally deleted from the state's constitution.[46] But Barnum's own impassioned appeal on this occasion—"the only safe inhabitants of a free country are educated citizens who vote . . . knock off your manacles and let the man go free . . . give him the responsibility of a man and the self-respect of a man, by granting him the right of suffrage"—was widely reported and applauded in the national press. He had made a full turn since the time, twenty years earlier on a boat bound for Glasgow, he had himself heatedly argued against the "unwisdom" of knocking off those manacles. "Where was this poor, down-trodden colored race in this rebellion?" he pointedly asked those who were opposed to the amendment.

> Did they seize the "opportunity," when their masters were engaged with a powerful foe, to break out in insurrection and massacre those tyrants who had so long held them in the most cruel bondage? No, Mr. Speaker, they did not do this. My "democratic" friends would have done it. I would have done it. Irishmen, Chinamen, Portuguese would have done it; any white man would have done it; but the poor black man is like a lamb in his nature compared with the white man. The black man possesses a confiding disposition, thoroughly tinctured with religious enthusiasm, and not characterized by a spirit of revenge. No, the only barbarous massacres we heard of, during the war, were those committed by their white masters on their poor, defenceless white prisoners, and to the eternal disgrace of southern white "democratic" rebels, be it said, these instances of barbarism were numerous all through the war.

To the authors of a minority report who had harped on the differences between the races, he directed the sarcastic inquiry whether they considered the Negro to be a beast.

> If this is the position of the gentlemen, then I confess a beast cannot reason, and this minority committee are right in declaring that "the negro can develop no inventive faculties or genius for the arts." For although the elephant may be taught to plow, or the dog to carry your market-basket by his teeth, you cannot teach them to shave notes, to speculate

in gold, or even to vote; whereas the experience of all political parties shows that men may be taught to vote, even when they do not know what the ticket means.

He did not deny that ignorance, lack of refinement, even barbarism might be found among Negroes. Was this surprising in a people that had been so long kept in servitude in the South and that even in the North "has been tabooed and scarcely permitted to rise above the dignity of whitewashers and boot-blacks"? If those opposed to the amendment were so enamored of white blood, would they be willing to "let a mulatto vote half the time, a quadroon three-fourths, and an octoroon seven-eights of the time? If not, why not?" Given the opportunity to be educated and treated the same as other men, the Negro would

> put to everlasting shame the champions of modern democracy by the overwhelming evidence he will give in his own person of the great Scrip-ture truth, that "God has made of one blood all the nations of men." A human soul, "that God has created and Christ died for," is not to be tri-fled with. It may tenant the body of a Chinaman, a Turk, an Arab or a Hottentot—it is still an immortal spirit; and amid all assumptions of caste, it will in due time vindicate the great fact that, without regard to color or condition, all men are equally children of the common Father.[47]

———◆———

BUOYED BY HIS success as a state legislator, Barnum next sought to enter na-tional politics by running for Connecticut's 4th Congressional District seat in the 1867 elections. His opponent, a distant relation, was the wealthy William H. Barnum of Salisbury, sometimes referred to as the "Iron Barnum" on ac-count of a foundry he owned in Lime Rock, Connecticut. The Democrats were determined to reassert themselves in the state; "the eyes & hopes & fears of all our statesmen are centred & fixed upon Connecticut," Barnum wrote to a friend in late February; and by the end of that month the local Republican committee had set up its headquarters in Bridgeport's Sturdevant Block, whence appeals were issued to state and national figures to visit the city and speak on Barnum's behalf, and Republican editors were politely advised that if they continued to "talk right," extra copies of their papers would be ordered by the hundreds for free distribution among the undecided electorate.[48] The "Iron Barnum" prudently declined an invitation to debate the issues with his Bridgeport namesake. So when a "Republican" in Torrington wrote to warn Barnum that he had learned his "Copperhead" opponent was preparing to spend $50,000 to buy votes and asked whether he intended to "fight fire with fire," the showman eagerly seized upon this opportunity to draw out his rival and forwarded the letter, together with his fervent reply, to his editorial friends at the *New York Tribune*. No money of his would ever be used to purchase votes, he assured readers of that paper. "God grant that I may be a thousand times defeated sooner than permit one grain of gold to be accursed by using it so basely!" He went on at length to express his horror at the thought that New

England voters could be bought "like sheep in the shambles" or that "unprincipled vagabonds," by the lavish expenditure of money, would attempt to bring into disgrace "the noble privilege of the *free elective franchise.*" But if money were indeed being used for such purposes, he trusted it came "from the pockets of those who now (as during the Rebellion) are doing their utmost to aid traitors, and who, still unrepenting, are vindictively striving to secure at the ballot-box what their Southern allies failed to accomplish on the field of battle." In a postscript to this learned disquisition on citizenship he quoted the Connecticut law setting forth the punishment for anyone found guilty of bribing electors. "I shall be the last to consent to its violation," he warned.[49]

What had seemed a perfect excuse for some grandstanding soon showed signs of backfiring, however, when a number of the state's Democratic papers, including the *Bridgeport Farmer*, began claiming the Torrington letter was a forgery or had been written by the showman himself; and the matter became even more complicated when the *New York Herald*, which Barnum characterized during the campaign as "the great Satanic newspaper," entered the fray and reported that a Bridgeport resident, O. J. Hodge, had acknowledged he and "Woolly Horse Barnum" concocted the letter. Hodge denied the story, and Barnum indignantly offered to pay $1000 to the papers if they could prove their allegations.[50] Then, too, rumors were rife that the original letter was some sort of "Democratic *trick*," and Barnum was at pains to verify its author's identity. "The fact is," he wrote to the *Tribune*'s office from Litchfield County, where he was then campaigning, on 13 March, "the Democrats don't care nor is it any matter who wrote the letter. What troubles them is my letter *in reply* in which I denounce fraud & corruption and declare that I will permit no money to be paid to buy voters." He felt sure he could carry his district by 600 to 800 votes, "unless some stupid lie like that about the Torrington letter obtains credence among the Republicans."[51] Greeley's *Tribune* did its best to set the people right, again and again. Besides repeatedly urging Republicans to stand by their candidate and pay no attention to the "babble" against him in the *Herald* and other publications, its editors, taking their cues from information the showman sent them, regularly exposed the villainies of the "Iron Barnum" and his accomplices in their attempts to subvert the Connecticut electoral system.[52]

But the would-be congressman now discovered, again, that he had an even more potent adversary than the Democrats to contend with: his old reputation as "Prince of Humbugs." "For 30 years," he had complained to Theodore Tilton two years earlier at the start of his political career, he had "*striven to do good,* but (foolishly) stuck my worst side outside, until half the Christian community got to believe that I wore horns & hoofs."[53] Now the Democrats—led by a local doctor Barnum had accused of being an abortionist and by ex-Congressman William D. Bishop, president of one of the railroads whose nefarious plots he had checked in the legislature—were warning the same community against him on moral and religious grounds, and a number of Connecticut clergymen had been persuaded to add their names to a circular attacking him.[54] In a curious development, another Barnum—Lewis S., a Danbury saloonkeeper—proclaimed himself the "independent Republican candidate" and, followed by a claque of cane-thumping young men, stumped the district with a speech in which he vilified the showman as a "deceiver," a "noted scoundrel," etc. Republicans soon guessed who was financing this attack and denounced it as another "Democratic trick."[55] The showman himself, at the end of a speech he made at Stamford in early March, hardly helped his campaign when he spontaneously made a clean breast of one episode in his career that was far from admirable. Asked to continue with his remarks until the next speaker, who had been delayed, could arrive, he launched into another attack on the "rebels" in the late war and stressed the need to continue punishing them. "I lived among them myself," he incautiously confessed, "and owned slaves. I did more. I whipped my slaves. I ought to have been whipped a thousand times for this myself. But then I was a Democrat—one of those nondescript Democrats, who are Northern men with Southern principles." But again, with the exception of some predictable fuming over these remarks in Bennett's *Herald*, no one other than the showman seems to have thought or cared much about the matter.[56]

More damaging, in the eyes of his friends, was the fact that the *Nation*, theoretically a Republican weekly, chose this moment to renew its complaints about the vulgarity of his museum and Barnum's own "depraving and demoralizing influence." Surely a state so renowned for education, refinement, and high character as Connecticut could find someone better to represent it in Congress than the proprietor of the Woolly Horse and Bearded Lady![57] The young Mark Twain, then at the beginning of his career, added his voice to this swelling chorus by writing a mildly funny piece for another New York paper, giving his impression of what Barnum's maiden speech in Congress might be. Filled with endless self-congratulation and puffery of the freaks and other curiosities to be seen at the American Museum (the nation was likened to the Happy Family and Congress itself to an "august menagerie"), it was the sort of notice most politicians would be pleased to do without.[58] The old Puritan distrust of those engaged in the frivolous occupation of entertaining others had been stirred into life again, and the thought of sending one of these pariahs to Washington was more than some righteous voters could bear. One local newspaper described the campaign being waged against him as "the most malignant and libelous vituperation ever showered upon the head of a candidate for office in Connecticut."[59]

By the eve of the election (which was held on April Fools' Day that year) Barnum had become considerably less sanguine about his chances for success. Already, he wrote to the *Tribune* on 30 March, "we find at least 300 illegal votes registered for the sham democracy in 4 towns in this district." If it should turn out that he was defeated by anything less than that number, he wished the *Tribune* promptly to inform its readers that he would contest the election results in the "Iron Barnum's" own and neighboring towns, "for I can certainly unseat my opponent for fraud."[60] He lost the election by around 1000 votes— dragging, some said, the Republican state ticket down with him. On the following day Republican governor Joseph Roswell Hawley, who had campaigned with Barnum and been defeated in his bid for reelection, wrote to a Massachusetts friend to give his assessment of the situation. Their platform was the best Connecticut Republicans had ever had, and the party itself cleaner and purer than before, "save for the great blunder (of Talleyrand's kind) in nominating Barnum. But P. T. Barnum," he hastened to add, "horrible as his book is, is a better man than many out of the state suppose. He is one of those fellows who have double characters, one professional & scoundrelly, the other private, church-going, decorous, and utterly abstinent from pocket-picking. We have known such in our profession. He is a teetotaller, generous, hospitable, enterprising as a citizen, &c. &c. But he was a burden, save that by his frightful activity he got out a full vote, at the tail of which he ran."[61]

From what Barnum himself later wrote about this turbulent campaign in his autobiography, one might never suspect he took more than a passing, even reluctant, interest in it. "Politics were always distasteful to me," he writes.

> I possess naturally too much independence of mind, and too strong a determination to do what I believe to be right, regardless of party expediency, to make a lithe and oily politician. To be called on to favor applications from office-seekers, without regard to their merits, and to do the dirty work too often demanded by political parties; to be "all things to all men" though not in the apostolic sense; to shake hands with those whom I despised, and to kiss the dirty babies of those whose votes were courted, were political requirements which I felt I could never acceptably fulfil.

At the insistence of friends, however, he consented to run, and was "neither disappointed nor cast down by my defeat." He was later "surprised" to read in the newspapers that his opponent's election was to be contested on the grounds of bribery and fraud, since he himself "was never, at any time before or afterwards, consulted upon the subject." But, he repeated, "I took no part nor lot in the matter, but concluded that if I had been defeated by fraud, mine was the real success."[62] Far from being dislodged or otherwise embarrassed by these puny protests, the "Iron Barnum" went on to win reelection to the next four Congresses and in 1876 succeeded Barnum's favorite, Orris S. Ferry, in the U.S. Senate.

———◆———

"NEITHER disappointed nor cast down," then, he almost immediately put Lindencroft on the market and bought a town house in New York City. During his term in the 1866 General Assembly he had steered through the legislature an act incorporating the "Barnum and Van Amburgh Museum and Menagerie Company," whose avowed purpose was the "importing, breeding, acclimating, and exhibiting foreign animals, birds, reptiles, insects, and fish, and of establishing, building, furnishing, and conducting a museum or museums, and zoological gardens or collections in connection therewith or otherwise."[63] Under this umbrella his current museum was operating; ideas for his "free" museum and perhaps even a zoo stirred again in his head; and for a time, as toward the end of the Jenny Lind venture, he appears to have given serious thought to abandoning Bridgeport. All these plans went literally up in smoke, however, during the night of 2–3 March 1868 when the second American Museum caught fire and, along with its prized menagerie, was totally destroyed. The showman, who first learned of the catastrophe while breakfasting at his town house with Charity and the wife of Abel Thomas, claimed to have taken the news with characteristic calm; but there could be no denying he had suffered a serious loss.[64] Newspaper reporters, as during the earlier fire in 1865, waxed hilarious over the torments of the poor animals unable to escape from the burning building. Mark Twain, who had visited the establishment while Barnum was running for Congress and called for "some philanthropist [to] burn the Museum again," was probably ecstatic as well.[65]

Nearly sixty years of age, his hopes for a career in national politics dashed and his great amusement establishment lying in ruins, he finally decided to take the advice Horace Greeley had given him at the time of his first museum's destruction and retired to "go a-fishing." He returned to Bridgeport to do just that (fishing was one of his favorite recreations, and in East Bridgeport he even owned a private lake stocked with species recommended by the Smithsonian's curators), to oversee his ever burgeoning real-estate interests, and to plan and commence building his new residence there. With unaccustomed leisure time on his hands, he again turned author—an occupation that had not seriously engaged him since the summer of 1864, when, making good on his promise in the first edition of his autobiography, he began publishing in the *New York Weekly Mercury* the series of articles on frauds and hoaxes in all ages that eventually became *The Humbugs of the World*.[66] Now, with some helpful advice from Whitelaw Reid, he toiled at revising and expanding his notorious *Life*, whose new edition appeared in the fall of 1869.[67] Meanwhile, his mother, Irena, who had been quietly living at the family "homestead" all these years, died of "old age" on 14 March 1868, leaving her son—at the time, typically, $200 in her debt—some nine acres of prime Bethel woodland.[68] And his "poor nervous wife" Charity, who a few years earlier had been so ill that Barnum was convinced she could not live an hour, but had miraculously recovered almost overnight, continued to suffer from her mysterious ailments, restricting him in his plans to entertain friends.[69] Somehow life seemed to be winding down for him, and in the concluding pages of the new autobiography, written on his birthday and entrance upon his sixtieth year, he sounded an almost elegiac note. His public life, he declared, had come to a close with his "formal and final retirement from the managerial profession." Henceforth he would divide his time between the rural felicities of Bridgeport and the cosmopolitan pleasures of New York, while seeking to satisfy his craving for comfort and quiet.

XI

————•—■—•————

A New Beginning

> I have lived so long on excitement, pepper, & mustard that plain
> bread & milk don't agree with me.
> *Barnum to Mrs. Abel C. Thomas, 22 May 1874*

HE COULD NEVER be content to remain entirely out of sight, of course. Even in the midst of what he was pleased to term his "retirement" from public life, Barnum continued to deliver his lectures on temperance and "The Art of Money-Getting," often following a punishing schedule that would have exhausted many a younger man. The latter talk was finally superseded by a new one filled with "old-fashioned truths" and the predictable hilarious anecdotes, "The World and How to Live in It," which he inaugurated during the fall of 1875 under the auspices of the Redpath Lyceum Bureau of Boston.[1] There were the usual recreations of fishing, riding, and long drives to help fill the time; games of backgammon and chess with the Reverend George Emerson in New York; whist during the long summer evenings at Waldemere, where friends and weary relatives, summoned from the cottages on the estate, heroically did their best to overlook his poor play.[2]

He was rescued from these doldrums in the winter of 1869–70 by the arrival of an old friend from abroad. John Fish, the prosperous owner of a cotton mill in Bury, England, was surely as idolatrous a fan as Barnum ever had. They had first met some eleven years earlier while Barnum, on the rebound from bankruptcy, was lecturing in Manchester. On that occasion Fish had sought him out and confided that, but for his reading of the showman's autobiography, he would never have risen from his original position as a lowly mill hand. All of his success he attributed to his study of that book, whole pages of which he could quote by heart; his amused business associates had become so used to his harping on the showman's wisdom that they had actually taken to calling him "Barnum." When he later added two new steam engines to his mill, they were christened, not surprisingly, "Barnum" and "Charity."[3] Now Fish had finally decided to accept Barnum's long-standing invitation to visit him in America, bringing with him his eldest daughter. The showman was suddenly in his element again, playing cicerone to them in their rambles about the country. After doing the sights in and around New York, they traveled to Niagara Falls, viewing the Catskills along the way. Then his guests declared they would like to see Cuba, and for the third time in his life Barnum went there, too. While they were gazing one evening upon a beautiful valley in Matanzas Province, he was pleased to note "tears of joy and gratitude" roll down the cheeks of his friend's daughter. He himself was hugely delighted by the scene, which he had viewed without emotion some twenty years earlier while touring the island with the "divine" Jenny Lind. "And this is a fitting opportunity for saying," he added in the first appendix to his 1869 autobiography, "that in order to enjoy travelling, and indeed almost anything else, it is of the very first importance that it be done without care and with congenial companions."[4]

From Cuba they sailed to New Orleans, then up the Mississippi to visit Memphis and Mammoth Cave (which Barnum had *not* seen while on his travels with Jenny), Louisville, Pittsburgh, Baltimore, and Washington, where they were entertained at the White House by President and Mrs. Grant. After a sidetrip to Richmond and several days in Philadelphia, they returned to New York and immediately commenced planning an even more ambitious tour. Their party now augmented by several other friends of the showman—but without his "poor nervous wife" Charity, who as usual remained at home—they again set out in early spring, traveling to California via the recently completed transcontinental railroad.[5] They broke their journey at Salt Lake City, where Barnum delivered one of his lectures before an audience that included "a dozen or so" of Brigham Young's wives, and where the theatre-loving Apostle himself, upon receiving the travelers at his home, the "Beehive," jokingly asked what Barnum would pay to exhibit him in New York (a guarantee of $200,000 was promptly offered). In California they traveled to The Geysers above San Francisco and spent a week in that city, devoted two weeks to viewing the wonders of Yosemite, and visited Sacramento and Stockton. On their return journey they stopped over in Denver and traveled to a number of sights and settlements in its vicinity. The "truly wonderful town" of Greeley, "guarded by flaming swords of sobriety," impressed the showman in particular. Named after his friend Horace and just begun by the Union Colony, the settlement permitted no intoxicating drinks within its borders.

He was still not finished playing guide to his English friends. After moving his household to Waldemere for the summer and entertaining for a few weeks there, he took them next to Montreal, Quebec, and Saratoga Springs. Then in September, in a change of pace, he set out for Kansas with an all-male party to participate in a buffalo hunt hosted by Colonel George Custer. John Fish was among these intrepid hunters, as were George A. Wells, the sometime manager of Tom Thumb, and David W. Sherwood, who was Barnum's agent and partner in several real-estate schemes. Custer magnanimously supplied the party with horses, guns, ammunition, and an escort of fifty cavalrymen as protection against uncooperative bulls. The chase and slaughter lasted but a few hours, in the course of which Fish became thoroughly saddle-sore and nearly shot one of the troopers and Barnum himself was credited with two and a half kills. At the end of this stirring adventure the majority of the men—somewhat ashamed, one gathers, by the ease of the operation—decided they had "done enough" and voted to return home.

The worshipful John Fish could not get enough of America or his genial host, and in later years he and various members of his family were frequent visitors to these shores. Exactly when Barnum made the acquaintance of his friend's younger daughter Nancy is a matter for some speculation, although the showman later claimed—and there is no real reason to doubt his word—that he first became aware of her through reading the charming letters she wrote to her father while he was on his first trip to America and was thereby moved to correspond with her on his own. Fish's companion on his first trip, he emphasized, was an elder daughter; Nancy and he did not personally meet until 1872, when she accompanied her father on another of his trips to the United States.[6] She was then twenty-two, appears to have spent part of the winter of 1872–73 with Charity's cousin Nate Beers and his wife Emma at their home on Fifth Avenue in New York City, and remained in America until the following summer.[7]

As one result of his trips West around this time, he was soon caught up in a number of new business ventures. In Colorado, especially, he became a heavy investor in real estate, buying lots and erecting a block of buildings in Greeley, for example. In the southern part of the state, outside Pueblo, he purchased a ranch of several thousand acres that took its name from the nearby Huerfano River, then turned its large herd of cattle into a stock company got up by his Fairfield friend Dave Sherwood.[8] By far his most expensive, and ultimately most vexing, investment was in Denver itself, where a group of businessmen had organized a company to develop a large tract of land on the western outskirts of the city. Following an initial payment of $36,000 in 1874, Barnum soon became one of the principal holders in the Denver Villa Park Association and the proud owner of a 765-acre "Barnum" subdivision, including a former hotel, which he and his agents divided into 9000 lots.[9] The trouble was, sales of this desirable property were by no means so brisk as he had been led to expect; his agents and fellow members in the Association proved dilatory and unreliable (which was hardly surprising, considering his blacksheep cousin Edward T. Nichols was for a time entrusted with the superintendence of the property); the railroad that had promised to build a line connecting the development with the city began to balk and demanded Barnum first invest in its stock; there were also problems finding an adequate water supply. By the early eighties the showman had had enough of the "swindle" and was desperately trying to get out of it, simultaneously negotiating with at least three interested parties and not scrupling to play each against the others. At one point, infuriated by the activities of some realtors who were trying to cash in on his difficulties, he railed against the "shysters" and "moneyless Jew brokers" who were "bitching and injuring my property" and ordered that they be cut off and left to "float away and carry their stink with them."[10]

In 1883 he finally agreed to transfer the property, under mutually advantageous terms, to his son-in-law Dr. William H. Buchtel, who for the past several years had been assisting him in its management. Buchtel, who married Barnum's divorced daughter Helen in 1871, had moved to Denver the following year, which was another reason for the showman's interest in Colorado around this time. Several years after Barnum's death, the *New York World* published a slanderous article on him and his "hereditary influence" on a number of his descendants; and these confused tales, contributed by an anonymous "special correspondent" who was in reality one of the most venomous enemies the showman ever had, have been widely and uncritically accepted to the present day. According to this source (who took care not to mention Helen or her husbands by name, however), Helen had been unfaithful to Samuel Hurd while they were living at a mysterious Bridgeport residence named "Lindenhurst," and eventually ran off from her husband and three daughters to live openly in sin with her latest lover, a "doctor," in Chicago. Barnum was embarrassed by the affair and urged Hurd to forgo getting a divorce for the sake of the children; but Helen went ahead and got one herself, married Buchtel, and, at the time of her father's own second marriage, descended upon Bridgeport to make a "terrific scene," presumably over the matter of her inheritance. The old showman adamantly insisted on cutting her off in his will, "her name not even being mentioned in it," but finally, after much "bitter wrangling," agreed to give her some land.[11]

The cause of Helen's breakup with Hurd, her initial meeting with Buchtel, and the progress of their courtship are today only matters for idle speculation.[12] What is certain, however, is that Barnum never repudiated or "cut off" his daughter, frequently visited her and her new family in the West, and continued to be the generous, loving father he had always been. From his vantage point in the East he arranged loans so that she and Buchtel could erect buildings in Colorado, looked after the house he had given her in New York City, and did numerous other favors for her whenever he could. Around the time he definitively made over his Villa Park holdings to the doctor, he also presented her with the deed to his remaining ranch property in Colorado and all the livestock thereon; and it was in consideration of this and other "valuable gifts" received from him in the past that Helen "cheerfully" waived all claims she might eventually have on his estate.[13] By the time of her father's death she had already received various heirlooms, including her mother's gold watch, such as he left to other family members. In his probated will—where she is mentioned several times—her two surviving daughters by Hurd were named residual heirs to a third of his estate, the same as he bequeathed to his other daughters or their children. If the showman, following his second marriage, anticipated any squabbling over this last document, it was Hurd he feared, not his daughter Helen. On 21 April 1882 his secretary Bowser made a partially enciphered entry in the office diary: "Took old Hippodrome Cash Book to Peq. Bk. marked to be delivered to Mrs. Nancy Barnum or H. E. Bowser in regard to [Sam H. Hurd's false footings in said book] the same to be proof of [his dishonesty in case he should] interfere with Mr. Barnum's [will] in favor of [Nancy Barnum]."[14] There may well have been some motive other than love that induced Helen to part from Samuel H. Hurd.

Her new life with the doctor appears to have been a prosperous and happy one. They had at least one child, Leila, who was educated in the East and visited her famous grandfather on several occasions. In the eighties they were joined in Denver by William's younger brother Henry, a former Methodist missionary who became chancellor of the University of Denver and, in 1906, governor of the state. Henry and "Sister Helen," as he affectionately called her, got on particularly well. They met almost weekly at dinner parties, where the often depressed administrator would unburden himself to "Sister Helen" over the coffee cups. Their families were always together at Christmastime, when Helen and the usually sedate Henry would keep everyone in an uproar through their clowning and boisterous merrymaking. During one of these saturnalias, according to Henry's official biographer, who gives no indication of appreciating the irony of the situation, "Helen stopped in her laughter at one of Harry's escapades long enough to shout out at him, 'Henry, I married the wrong man.'"[15] The jovial Helen, who was said to bear a remarkable resemblance to her father in her appearance and disposition, died in December 1915 and was buried beside her husband in Denver's Riverside Cemetery.

———————— ◆ ————————

MEANWHILE, the showman in him—never entirely dormant, to be sure—had been fanned into life again around the time of his friend Fish's first visit. In October 1869 workmen digging a well on a farm outside Cardiff, New York, uncovered a ten-foot petrified man that was soon being exhibited to gawking natives at fifty cents a head. The originator of this hoax, a rather disreputable Binghamton cigar manufacturer named George Hull, seems to have been as eager to embarrass the religious and scientific communities as to profit from the public's credulity. An atheist and sometime alchemist, who was also fascinated by Darwinism, he later claimed he had received the inspiration for his creation while disputing with a Methodist minister on the biblical passage "There were giants in the earth in those days." As the fame of the "Cardiff Giant" spread throughout the land and a group of upstate businessmen rushed to purchase a three-quarter interest in it for $30,000, Barnum, who had once planned such a hoax himself, could not help being impressed.[16] When the Giant arrived in Albany, he went there to see it and offered to buy it from its proprietors. Refused, he then righteously determined to "expose the swindle and punish the perpetrators," hired an artist to visit the exhibition and secretly make a small wax model, and advised his friend George Wood in New York to have a plaster "facsimile" made, based on the model and the rather complete list of dimensions so conveniently available in the Giant's bills. Wood promptly acted on the suggestion, and this "hoax of a hoax" was soon outdrawing the original at his Broadway museum. When the outraged owners of the Giant applied for an injunction to stop this encroachment on what they considered to be their exclusive domain, the judge sagely replied he would be happy to accommodate them if their own giant would first appear before him and swear to his "genuineness."

On Barnum's trip to California he also found much to intrigue him. From Mariposa, where he marveled at a grove of giant sequoias, he sent east a piece of bark thirty-one inches thick. While watching the sea lions frolicking at Seal

Rocks, he was suddenly seized by "show fever" and offered $50,000 to anyone who could deliver ten of the largest specimens to him in New York, where he thought he might "fence in" an area of the East River and exhibit them. His resistance broke down completely during his week in San Francisco when he was introduced to a midget even smaller than Tom Thumb had originally been. The German parents of Leopold Kahn had received offers from other showmen, but had set their hearts on having Barnum manage their son. This time the rank chosen was that of admiral, and "Admiral Dot," as he was thenceforth called, was launched on his career at Woodward's Gardens. It was the "old story" of Tom Thumb over again, Barnum wrote, "with a new liliputian and a new locality." His original "man in miniature," still under his direction, was then on his three-year tour around the world with the wedding party; and about this time he also sent to Europe a group of freaks who had formerly worked for him at his museum, together with the famous Siamese Twins, Chang and Eng.[17]

He was obviously at a disadvantage with no permanent base of his own, even though his arrangement with Wood was still in effect and he could always send curiosities to his museum. Then in the fall of 1870 a new opportunity beckoned, and the showman, as he wrote shortly afterwards to his friend Moses Kimball, decided to "go it once more."[18] The cause of his coming out of "retirement" was a proposition he had received from a young circus manager named William C. Coup, who, together with his partner Dan Castello, wished Barnum to join them in an ambitious enterprise. Coup, born in 1837, had commenced his own career in show business at the age of fourteen by signing on with Barnum's Asiatic Caravan. After working on several other shows, he had teamed up with Castello—a sometime manager, equestrian director, and clown—to found a circus and "Egyptian Caravan" that toured the Great Lakes region during the summer of 1870.[19] The first season of this venture was barely over when the two men decided to approach the veteran showman.

They could hardly have caught him at a more propitious moment. Bored by his relative inactivity, and knowing Coup to be "a capital showman and a man of good judgment, integrity, and excellent executive ability," Barnum eagerly snatched at their offer—over the strong objections of his family and friends, Coup later recalled—and on 8 October agreed to join them. Already he was thinking of what might be included in the expanded show. Admiral Dot would be "well trained" by the spring, he wrote, and several "tip-top museum curiosities" and all of the animals could be had from Wood's establishment. "We can make a stunning museum department," he emphasized. "You can have a Cardiff Giant that won't crack, also a moving figure—Sleeping Beauty or Dying Zouave—a big gymnastic figure like that in Wood's museum, and lots of other good things—only you need time to look them up and prepare wagons &c. &c." The Siamese Twins might also "pay."[20]

Barnum's connection with the American circus has been notoriously misrepresented by past writers on the subject, some of whom have taken a perverse delight in pointing out what he did *not* do in this field, almost as though they were attacking a personal enemy.[21] To some degree attributable to his reputation for "humbug"—to an almost automatic willingness to condemn the showman's version of a story whenever some other interpretation, however specious, presents itself—the origin of this pervasive attitude may be traced to his own era, when a number of calculated tales were set going by his own press agents and business associates. At the time of Barnum's death in 1891, so great was the worry that his demise would adversely affect the receipts of his show that a campaign was immediately launched to belittle his contributions to "The Greatest Show on Earth," while simultaneously puffing those of his surviving partner James A. Bailey. Thenceforth, aside from having furnished his name and money and (naturally) evidenced an avid interest in returns, it was as if he had never set foot inside his own tents.

To be sure, other showmen did covet his name and financial backing, and Barnum made no bones about expecting a premium for the former. It was a name that had been before the public for more than thirty years—a guarantee, in many people's minds, of the biggest and the best, the strangest and most exciting, and possibly something outrageous as well. In his letter to Coup, he suggested calling the museum department *his* museum, in return for the same percentage Wood "allowed" him. Later partners paid him a bonus of upwards of $10,000 per season for the use of his name and bitterly complained when he insisted on his right to attach it to other enterprises. In a field in which circus titles, even those of shows that have been extinct for generations, are still bought and sold, his name to this day is jealously guarded.[22]

Barnum's contract with Coup appears to be lost; but from extant agreements between him and later partners, letters, newspaper articles, and published accounts by the two men themselves, one may arrive at a fair estimate of its terms. The senior partner owned two-thirds of the show, with Coup and Castello dividing the other third. Coup was designated general manager; Castello was in charge of the circus department. One may reasonably assume that Barnum, in addition to visiting the show whenever he could (in later contracts he was sometimes obligated to do so at least twelve times per season), pledged to exert himself in publicizing the enterprise and insisted on being consulted in regard to all major decisions.

The great traveling exhibition that took shape over the winter of 1870–71 was hardly the typical circus of Barnum's or anyone's day. The arenic entertainments were to form but one part of the show, which also embraced an extensive menagerie of exotic animals and—a feature Barnum boasted of having introduced to the circus—a museum containing "an infinite variety of Living and Representative Curiosities from the realms of nature and art," including wax figures, automatons, Indian and Eskimo artifacts, an Egyptian mummy, Hiram Powers's titillating statue *The Greek Slave*, Woods's "facsimile" of the Cardiff Giant, and, predictably, a large contingent of human abnormalities. It was as if the American Museum had been revived and set on wheels, with Castello's "Mammoth Circus" replacing the Lecture Room. For months in advance, to the horror of "Manager Coup," Barnum writes, he spent money "like water" in his determination to get the best of everything.[23] Since this was to be an itinerating show, it was necessary to have tents to house all the attractions and up to an estimated 10,000 spectators. To transport and further advertise the show in the traditional street parade, a fleet of vans, cage wagons, carriages, and ornately carved chariots was also required. Meanwhile, the showman was firing off letters to Kimball inquiring where he could get a mummy or group of living seals.[24] During 1871 and later years he was also actively in pursuit of sea lions, giraffes, hippos, and other rare animals and was constantly in touch with dealers in America and abroad.

Barnum was obviously well qualified to advise in the museum and menagerie departments; nor was he so ignorant of circus matters as is sometimes claimed. He had spent some time traveling with Aaron Turner's circus in the 1830s, and a circus company had been attached to his Asiatic Caravan. He was personally acquainted with, and a shrewd judge of, nearly all the managers in the business (it was a mystery among veteran showmen how he had come to choose the young and relatively unknown Coup as his partner, yet Barnum writes he had been favorably impressed by him for "some years" before) and a frequent spectator at circuses in America and Europe. When necessary, he would "scout" and negotiate for stellar attractions himself, as he did in the case of the sensational human cannonball Zazel.[25] While attending his own show, he would often make notes on how an act or something else might be improved and pass along his suggestions at the end of the performance. And always, of course, he was on the lookout for the slightest indiscretion, the faintest hint of indecency, that might give offense to the "moral community." The lack of riotous conduct and the decorum that prevailed everywhere in his show, he was pleased to report at the end of the 1872 season, were due to a single fact—namely, "that my employees are *teetotalers* and of gentlemanly behavior."[26] Apparently not all his employees fit this glowing description, however, for Coup tells an uproarious story of one whiskey-loving superintendent in the equestrian department whom his fellow workers had ironically taken to calling "Barnum." One day while the real Barnum was walking around the tents and his namesake was sleeping off his latest bout on a pile of hay, someone came rushing up to wake the befuddled superintendent and began bawling "Barnum!" at the top of his voice. The enraged showman, who sized up the situation in an instant, stormed into Coup's office and demanded to know if he had no respect for him and his reason for calling "that drunken, illiterate brute by my name." Coup tried to pacify him with some unconvincing tale about circus employees' fondness for "nicknames." Orders were given that this particular one was not to be used again.[27]

The responsibility for overseeing the day-to-day operation of this colossal enterprise—which involved hundreds of workers, performers, draft and show animals, not to mention the logistics connected with feeding and housing all of them and the problems of transporting, setting up, and taking down the show itself—fell to Coup and his eventual successors. Where Barnum made his greatest contribution was in publicizing the show, to effect which he resorted to a number of time-honored methods and invented a few new ones. He seems to have been the first to think of the circus "courier," for example, in effect a tabloid newspaper containing the show's program, descriptions and illustrations of its acts and novelties, endorsements by prominent individuals, etc., printed in editions of hundreds of thousands and distributed to all the households in a town in advance of the show's arrival. Less than two months after agreeing to join Coup, he was already at work on the first of these annual publications, soliciting "characteristic letters" from well-known persons and begging them not to "mention my paper *at present* in any public way, lest my brother showmen may steal my thunder."[28] His autobiography offered another excellent means of advertising the show, and from early 1872 on, almost as regularly as clockwork, there now appeared the annual "editions" with their appendices and additional chapters that ticked off the triumphal progress of his circus during preceding seasons. Many of the glowing reviews reprinted in these supplements were actually the work of Barnum or his press agents. Newspaper owners and their editors, who stood to benefit considerably from his paid advertisements, were always happy to oblige the great "P. T."[29]

His easy familiarity with the nation's press and his proven ability to "work" it effectively were themselves of inestimable value to the show. And as hundreds of extant letters dating from this and the next decade testify, he was never content to resign this part of the business entirely to his press corps. Nor is it likely there has ever been another showman who could count so many of the world's famous and powerful among his friends and acquaintances. The Reverend Henry Ward Beecher may have argued against the circus as a demoralizing influence in his *Lectures to Young Men*, but he saw no contradiction in adding his name to the list of distinguished clergymen and denominational publications that unqualifiedly endorsed Barnum's "Great Moral and Instructive Exhibition."[30] If there were any doubts about the genuineness of Captain Djordji Costentenus, the "noble Greek" who had been tattooed from head to foot with over seven million blood-producing punctures during his captivity in "Chinese Tartary," one need only read the certificate of authenticity, signed by Oliver Wendell Holmes and other eminent members of the Boston medical fraternity, that appeared in Barnum's courier for 1877.[31] When David Kalakaua, Hawaii's "Merry Monarch," paid a visit to New York and accepted Barnum's invitation to join him at his Hippodrome, he, too, was pressed into service to help publicize the show. Halfway through the performance someone set the audience to shouting for "The King!" and "Barnum!" and at that moment the showman's open carriage drove invitingly into the arena. King Kalakaua, who was considerably more enlightened than the Indians Barnum had similarly tricked at his American Museum, accepted it all with surprisingly good humor. As the two men made their royal progress in front of the cheering spectators, he philosophically remarked to his smiling host, "We are all actors." No one but Barnum, one New York paper observed, would have the temerity to exhibit a living monarch.[32]

He was himself among the show's greatest curiosities, as eagerly looked for as was any star performer. Which was one reason his partners were so anxious to have him among the audience—an obligation he cheerfully accepted, arranging his lecture tours and other business so that he might "hit" the show as many times in a season as he could. Occasionally, when these interests coincided, he would travel with the company for a week or two. The triumphal drive round the arena was often repeated, with the showman, now unaccompanied, stopping the carriage every few moments to address his ecstatic patrons ("You came to see Barnum? Well, I'm Barnum"). And always there was his intuitive grasp of what would capture and hold the public's attention, his almost uncanny ability to exploit situations that, however potentially disastrous at the outset, might further enhance his own and the show's "notoriety": his well-publicized clashes with Henry Bergh, for example, and the latter's Society for the Prevention of Cruelty to Animals.

Barnum's relations with Henry Bergh extended back to the fall of 1866, the year in which the SPCA was chartered by the New York State legislature and the quixotic crusader for the humane treatment of animals was designated its first president. Acting on a complaint from someone who had witnessed the feeding of live rabbits to the boa constrictor at the second American Museum, Bergh had gone there to protest this practice and had later written to Barnum and his managers to threaten them with legal action. The outspoken president—whose proverbial lack of tact on such occasions was exceeded only by his ignorance of natural history—did not hesitate to characterize anyone condoning such an "atrocity" as "semi-barbarian"; and if it was argued that such reptiles would take only living food, he was of the opinion that one should "then let them starve, for it is contrary to the merciful providence of God that wrong should be committed in order to accomplish a supposed right."[33] Barnum personally answered Bergh a few weeks later, enclosing a letter he had received in the meantime from Harvard's famed naturalist, Louis Agassiz, who confirmed that such snakes required living food. The American Museum, Barnum defiantly added, would continue to feed all its animals "in accordance with the laws of nature," and if the president of the SPCA did not write a letter for publication withdrawing his former objections, he would take it upon himself to publish Bergh's original letter in conjunction with that of Professor Agassiz.[34] Meanwhile, the Museum—whose advertisements around this time did indeed promise visitors they would be able to witness such things—had taken the precaution of sending its snakes to New Jersey to be fed, prompting Bergh to begin agitating for the establishment of an SPCA in that state.[35]

Bergh sarcastically replied to Barnum's letter on 7 March, daring the showman to publish their correspondence if he thought any "business capital" could be realized from it and parenthetically throwing in several rather severe remarks on "that delectable volume," the showman's autobiography. But this latest exercise in "humbug," he warned, might turn out otherwise than as planned, causing "parents and other guardians of the morals of the rising generation to discontinue conducting them to a miscalled museum, where the *amusement* chiefly consists in contemplating the prolonged torture of innocent, unresisting, dumb creatures." Stung by this reply, Barnum made good on his threat and published all their correspondence to date, adding to it another letter of his own that he clearly hoped would put an end to his antagonist's career. In it he ridiculed the sentimental account by the witness who had lodged the original complaint; emphasized his own long-standing concern for the humane treatment of animals; then settled down to a long disquisition on the SPCA president himself, whom he accused of ungentlemanly conduct, "low breeding and a surplus of self-conceit," and an insufferable dictatorial air in his futile attempts to overturn the laws of nature. "In attempting to prevent the abuse of *beasts* your influence will not be increased by your abuse of *men.* As you seem to court the pillory by asking for the publication of your last letter, I bow to your request, wondering at your temerity. . . . The public all have an interest in the proper management of a society for the prevention of cruelty to animals, and have a right to know whether its chief officer is fit for his position." While the "public" and presumably the society's board of directors were making up their minds on this matter, there would be no more "tom-foolery" such as sending his snakes out of state to be fed. If Bergh wished to commence his threatened legal action to shut down this part of the Museum's operations, he was free to try.[36]

Bergh valiantly struggled on in his campaign to convince Barnum and other managers to give up feeding their snakes living food, but there was no gain-saying nature or the authority of Professor Agassiz.[37] Eventually a compromise of sorts was reached—with the Museum agreeing to feed its snakes at night after the public had departed—but for years Barnum could not resist taunting Bergh on the subject, especially whenever his tenderhearted opponent sounded off on other matters of which he had little firsthand knowledge. It happened again at the start of the 1880 season, when the highly trained steed "Salamander," imported from Germany's Circus Renz, was billed to gallop through a door panel surrounded by exploding fireworks, then jump through several blazing hoops. Unfortunately, on the evening the act was first pre-sented an attendant let slip one of the hoops, and the animal was seen to run off with its mane and tail apparently on fire. This brought forth Bergh and his officers, who ordered that the number be immediately discontinued. In vain did Barnum and his managers insist that the horse had not even been singed, that it was well sprayed with water before every performance, that the flames themselves, far from being real fire, were "purely scenic" and produced by "harmless chemical liquids."[38] It was "simply abominable," Bergh wrote to Barnum, "that the public cannot be provided with amusement by your show without inflicting torture upon an animal"—a sweeping charge that elicited the usual rejoinder about the SPCA president's rushing to extremes and abus-ing his power like a "despot." On the following Monday, the showman pro-claimed, the act *would* be repeated despite Henry Bergh's order, and he himself would address the audience. Bergh was invited to attend and make any re-sponse he liked.[39]

True to his word, on the day in question the seventy-year-old showman en-tered the arena and delivered a ringing challenge to the president of the SPCA. The circus was packed with spectators and members of the New York press eager to witness the denouement of the well-publicized dispute, and a strong body of police and SPCA officers was stationed menacingly around the ring. "Either Mr. Bergh or I must run this show," Barnum declared, "and I don't think it will be Mr. Bergh." If his opponent dared to order his arrest, he would put a "hoop of fire" around him that would warm him more than he had ever been in the past, and probably more than he would ever be in the future. After discoursing at length on his past history with Bergh—not omitting the oft-told tale of the snakes, and another concerning Bergh's once insisting that a rhinoceros be given a tank of water to swim in—he proceeded to demonstrate the safety of the act. While the horse stood waiting in the ring, the hoops were ignited and the showman, followed by the show's company of clowns, ran his hand through the flames, then stepped, hat in hand, through one of the blazing hoops. The writer for the *New York Evening Post*, who next day ironically described how Barnum and the "other clowns" went through the same act as "Salamander," reported that the showman himself "vaulted about with admired agility." After this, the SPCA superintendent who was present (Bergh had wisely decided to absent himself from these antics) was invited to try the same experiment and, finding nothing of danger, was forced to concede there was no cause for his interference and that his superior had evidently made a mistake.[40]

It was another stunning triumph for Barnum, of course, which brought the show reams of publicity and caused Henry Bergh no little embarrassment. When the exasperated SPCA president protested the story in the *Evening Post* and what its reporter was pleased to describe as Barnum's "rattling victory," the showman, in a letter to the same paper, gave his antagonist a final drubbing. The public's guffaws over Bergh's "late humiliating defeat," he crowed, would never have occurred if Bergh had only taken the trouble to ascertain the truth of the original complaint *before* writing him an insulting letter and libeling him in the press. But instead of doing so, he

> peremptorily ordered me, under pain of immediate arrest and imprisonment, to stop doing what I never had done, and when I persisted in continuing to not do it, and to manage my show in my own way, the irate "President" Bergh dispatched a file of officers of his "Society," backed, as he boasts, "by a large section of the police force, headed by the resolute Captain Gunner," to thrust me into prison. I forgot to be frightened at such a display of tinsel and bombast, so I announced that the show would proceed as usual; and as we were not in Spain or Russia, I hoped the army with banners would dare to arrest an American citizen for lawfully attending to his own business. When it was discovered that my fireproof horse rather liked the fun of going through flames which gave no heat, and that "law and humanity" were my guiding stars, the valiant armies, "headed by the resolute Captain Gunner," ignobly sneaked away, reminding us of Bombastes Furioso, and that great king who marched so many men up the hill and then marched them down again.

Yet despite all their differences, the showman generously concluded, there could be no question that Bergh's intentions were good, even if he did display, from time to time, a lamentable ignorance of both animal and human nature. "We should remember that no man is perfect, and that, with all his faults and shortcomings, Henry Bergh, President of the Society for the Prevention of Cruelty to Animals, is to be honored and respected for his unselfish devotion to such an excellent cause."[41]

As one may gather from the above, there had been some improvement in relations between the two men since the day Barnum had publicly questioned Bergh's fitness for his position. For all their clamorous disputes in the press, they really had the same interests at heart; and Bergh, who belatedly came to recognize this, was soon counting Barnum among his staunchest allies. Only a few weeks before the "Salamander" fracas, in fact, when a former agent of his was organizing a local SPCA in Bridgeport, he had unreservedly recommended that Barnum, as one known to him for his "generous and sympathetic instincts towards the lower animals," be included on its board.[42] The showman, who not only helped found the Bridgeport society but served for many years as one of its vice-presidents, was thereafter fond of referring to himself as the "Bergh of Bridgeport." By 1885 he was also an active member of the New York society and later defended Bergh's nephew and successor, Henry Bergh Jr., when he was forced to resign in the midst of an acrimonious dispute with his board of directors.[43] Most wondrous of all, the respect the two former enemies came to feel for each other eventually ripened into genuine friendship, with the showman inviting Bergh to clambakes at Waldemere and Bergh now eagerly ordering copies of "that delectable volume" for the society's library.[44] On 22 March 1884, signing himself "your friend and admirer," Bergh wrote to Barnum to pay tribute to "the vast amount of pleasure and instruction you have afforded the human family" and to ask that he remember in his will the "poor dumb animals" that had helped him to his fortune. The showman was happy to comply with the request and bequeathed generous sums to both the SPCA and the Connecticut Humane Society. He also left $1000 to the City of Bridgeport toward the erection of a statue honoring his friend Henry Bergh.[45]

———◆———

ON 10 April 1871 "P. T. Barnum's Museum, Menagerie and Circus" opened under canvas in Brooklyn. After exhibiting there for a week, the show began its first seasonal tour, traveling north through New England and into Maine, then across Vermont and New York State as far west as Buffalo before returning to New York City via towns along the Hudson. "Never since Jenny Lind was there such a pronounced success," Barnum boasted in a letter to one editor.[46] Although his tents, covering a total of three acres, could hold as many as 10,000 spectators at each performance, it was common throughout the season for thousands to be turned away. At Waterville, Maine, so many people drove in from the countryside or arrived on excursion trains that Coup, after some perplexity, decided to give continuous performances in the circus department from early morning until 9 o'clock at night.[47] Rather than immediately "winter" the exhibition at the end of the tour, it was decided to continue for a few weeks longer at the Empire Rink in New York City, where operations commenced on 13 November. By this date the show, with the kind of arithmetical legerdemain common to all such entertainments, was being touted as "7 Superior Exhibitions in One!"—consisting of the Museum, Menagerie, Grand International Zoological Garden, Polytechnic Institute, Caravan, Hippodrome, and Dan Castello's Mammoth Circus—and all for the single admission fee of fifty cents.[48]

Throughout the winter of 1871–72 Barnum busied himself with plans to improve the show, adding to it many exotic animals (among them an Italian goat named "Alexis" that had been taught to leap through hoops while riding round the ring on the back of a galloping horse) and what he assured readers of the latest edition of his autobiography was a group of "four wild FIJI CANNIBALS!" As in the case of his Circassian beauties, there were some doubting Thomases who insisted they were of less distant origin; but Barnum swore they had been ransomed by one of his agents from an enemy chieftain who was about to kill, and perhaps eat, them. One of the four, a "half-civilized" woman who had been converted by missionaries, regularly read to the others from a Bible printed in the Fijian language, as the result of which "they earnestly declare their convictions that eating human flesh is wrong, and faithfully promise never again to attempt it." Consequently, there was no cause for young ladies to fear they might be gobbled up while observing these curiosities, whose "characteristic war dances and rude marches, as well as their representations of Cannibal manners and customs, are peculiarly interesting and instructive."[49]

One of the greatest and most far-reaching improvements during the 1872 season resulted from the decision to move the show exclusively by rail. There was nothing startlingly novel in the idea itself, for a number of smaller American circuses had used this mode of transportation in the past and Barnum's own show had taken advantage of railroads along its route while traveling west of the Hudson in 1871.[50] But the decision to put so large an establishment on the rails; on cars that, in time, were entirely owned by the show itself, built to its specifications, and sufficient to make up several trains; and to coordinate all this with a bold, new strategy of marketing was certainly a daring and imaginative experiment, on a scale few managers other than Barnum could have conceived or afforded. Yet in the past any credit for this innovation has generally been denied him, primarily because Coup, in his posthumously published memoirs, claimed to have thought up the whole thing himself and to have forced it through over his "partner's opposition."[51] Which "partner" he does not specify—by the 1872 season there were four of them, Barnum having let in his recently divorced son-in-law Hurd for a share of the show—but the implication is clear enough.

There is another, more plausible version of how the railroad show came about, however, which Barnum himself related in considerable detail in the "Conclusion" to the first appendix of the autobiography—an account that was sent to the printer in March 1872 while Coup and Hurd were both active partners in the firm and that could easily have been deleted or modified had either of them objected to its contents. Instead, it continued to be included in the annual editions of the autobiography over the next several years; but was then dropped, and forgotten, when the book was abridged in 1876.[52] While the show was being readied for the 1872 season, Barnum writes, Coup was constantly "in great agony" over the large sums of money he was spending on new animals and other items. No country could possibly support or make such an expensive show pay, he protested, an opinion that was shared by Barnum's son-in-law Hurd after he joined the partnership and became the show's treasurer. One morning in February, Barnum continues, Coup, Hurd, and a number of their assistants, looking solemn and a little ominous, called at his house and insisted on laying out the figures before him. By their calculations the expenses of the show, with all the additions he had been making to it, would average around $4000 per day for a total of at least $720,000 over the entire 1872 season; yet they had also computed, after looking over the list of towns they planned on visiting, that total receipts could not exceed $350,000. When Barnum questioned these estimates, Coup exclaimed "Figures never lie," pulled a map from his pocket, and earnestly proceeded to demonstrate how the show, dragging its heavy wagonloads an average of twenty miles a day, would be compelled to make no less than seventy-one stands "where there are not people enough within five miles to give us an average of $1000 per day." And this was before making any allowances for storms, accidents, and other risks. The unanimous conclusion of those calling on Barnum, therefore, was that the season would prove ruinous unless he agreed to sell off more than half the curiosities, horses, and wagons the firm had accumulated, or at least to divide them into two, possibly three, separate shows.

After patiently listening to these arguments, Barnum replied that, far from reducing the show by "a single hair or feather," he intended to add five or six hundred dollars to its daily expense. The others rolled their eyes in astonishment, and Hurd, with a look of despair, asked, "Father, are you crazy?" Then the wily showman revealed what he had been thinking all along. During the previous season he had been impressed by the popularity of excursion trains, which had brought spectators from as far away as a hundred miles; and he now proposed to put the show itself on railroad cars, "taking leaps of a hundred miles or more in a single night when necessary, so as to hit good-sized towns every day in the season. If I can do this with sixty or seventy freight cars, six passenger cars and three engines, within such a figure as I think it ought to be done for, I will do it." Five days later, after telegraphing the various railroad companies and receiving their replies, he was able to report to his associates that the plan was indeed feasible, "and we, then and there, resolved to transport the entire Museum, Menagerie and Hippodrome, all of the coming season, by rail, enlisting a power which, if expended on traversing common wagon roads, would be equivalent to *two thousand men and horses.*"

Admittedly, the above was written to help publicize the show and contains some element of exaggeration. But its wealth of detail, Barnum's rather patronizing depiction of Coup and Hurd (repeated elsewhere in the showman's writings), and the fact that it was written not from hindsight but *in advance* of the show's first setting out by rail lend an unmistakable air of authenticity to the whole. At the time of Barnum's death in 1891, Coup himself confirmed his former partner's apparent recklessness, and his own caution, in money matters. "As far as the technical details of the show were concerned," he wrote, "Mr. Barnum was absolutely ignorant, but in its place he possessed an amount of commercial daring and business sagacity which amply atoned for his other shortcomings. He was the most daring manager that ever lived, and would pay almost any price for an attraction. He was easily duped, and had to be almost constantly watched to prevent unnecessary expenditure. Possibly this very fearlessness in money matters was the secret of his success, although without a doubt such lavish and apparently wasteful expenditure, if applied to commercial undertakings, would prove eminently disastrous."[53]

The "fearlessness" paid off during 1872. Despite expenses of around $780,000 plus "wear and tear" on the establishment, at the end of the six-month season Hurd was able to report receipts of over one million dollars, some $600,000 above what the show had grossed the previous year and more than Barnum or any of his partners had anticipated.[54] After opening in New York and making its way into New Jersey, the entire show had first entrained at New Brunswick, originally on some sixty-five cars, most of them leased, including Pullmans and converted sleepers for the performers and laborers. Coup recalled that because his men were new at the job, it took them twelve hours to load the train the first time, and that for the next seven days he was so busy teaching them "the art of loading and unloading, giving attention to the moving of all the wagons, chariots, horses, camels, elephants, etc." that he never once removed the clothes from his back.[55] But the operation, especially after the partners purchased their own flatcars of uniform construction, soon became a model of efficiency, enabling the show to travel up to a hundred miles in a single night, parade through a town early the next day while the tents were being raised, give three complete performances in the morning, afternoon, and evening, then pack up and move on to the next stop in time to begin all over the following day. It was exhausting work for everyone concerned, with the only respites coming on Sundays, when the longest hauls were customarily scheduled and employees had the day largely to themselves. But at least once aboard the trains each night, they were spared the sleepless drives atop jolting vans and chariots, the battles with the elements and country thugs, that were a traditional part of life on wagon shows. Of course, rail travel had its unique dangers, too.

The show, indeed, rolled with the times, taking full advantage of the nation's railroad network that had been aggressively expanding in the aftermath of the Civil War. No longer limited to the distances teams of horses could draw in a night, it now penetrated deep into the Midwest and Plains states, overleaping less profitable stands whose inhabitants were nevertheless given the opportunity to attend. For as Barnum had foreseen and accurately predicted, the success of so vast an enterprise depended not so much on getting the show to the people as it did on getting the people to the show—in some underpopulated regions from distances of up to a hundred miles away—via the same modern mode of transport, which railroad companies were happy to provide at cheap "excursion" rates. The main tent this 1872 season seated 12,000 spectators and was so much larger than any building in the West, he writes, that he offered free use of it, at hours when the show was not playing, for political rallies during the Presidential campaign. The fact that many of those attending such meetings were tempted to remain a few additional hours had obviously not escaped his reckoning.[56]

The exhibition had officially been renamed "P. T. Barnum's Great Traveling Exposition and World's Fair" in preparation for the 1872 season, and for the first time was also being billed by its most enduring title: "The Greatest Show on Earth." Castello's "chaste and refined circus" continued to figure at the bottom of the bills (no need to frighten unnecessarily country parsons and their flocks), yet was certainly dominant in this and later seasons, as is evident from the layout of the show itself. After paying a single admission fee, spectators were directed through a series of five medium-sized tents—housing the museum, menagerie, freaks, etc.—then entered directly into the "big top," where performances commenced an hour after the other departments opened. And although Barnum, oddly enough, does not boast about it in his autobiography, there was something revolutionary to be seen here as well—namely, the addition of a second ring, in which performances were given simultaneously with those in the first.

The continuing development of the American circus, from the time Barnum set out with Aaron Turner's pitifully small wagon show in the 1830s to the period when the great three-ring establishments proudly roamed the rails at the end of the century, is a complex, tortuous story itself, mirroring the nation's own changing mores and beclouded by numerous conflicting claims of "firsts."[57] More than any other nineteenth-century entertainment, the circus paralleled the country's growth, ceaselessly struggling to become more grandiose and inventive, to capture for itself all segments of the expanding population, to outboast and crush lesser rivals with an imperial disdain that was worthy any robber baron or unrestrained monopolist. In terms of the evolving "architecture" of such shows, the small circular tents originally used by Turner and his fellow showmen were greatly enlarged—not so much by increasing the diameter of the round top, however, as by splitting this in half and lacing between what now became the rounded ends of the tent an ever-increasing number of canvas midsections. The circus big top thus took on its characteristic shape, which also permitted the installation of an oval "hippodrome" track, running around the periphery of the arena directly in front of the spectators' seats. On this track spectacular processions, "walkarounds" by the clowns, and races between charioteers, male and female jockeys on individual mounts, ostriches ridden by monkeys (the latter often stuffed, however), elephants and other animals were given—the inference being that there was something "Greek" or "Roman" in all this, and hence constituting a separate "classical" entertainment. In Europe there had been several attempts to revive these ancient "games" earlier in the century, and in 1853 a company of French artists, headed by a member of the distinguished Franconi circus family, had arrived in New York to present such performances in an elegant, specially designed hippodrome building in the vicinity of Madison Square and 23d Street.[58] Barnum had doubtless witnessed some of these entertainments and was about to launch a similar experiment of his own.

But while the hippodrome track added an exciting new dimension to the expanded big top, the circus ring itself was now in danger of being over-whelmed. By tradition its diameter has nearly always been thirteen meters or a little under forty-three feet—an international standard that arose during the age when equestrianism predominated in the circus and horses, schooled to perform in circles of that diameter, traveled widely with their riders and could not be expected to be retrained at each circus engaging them. With little pos-sibility of increasing the ring size, therefore, it was inevitable that spectators should become dissatisfied as they found themselves seated farther and farther away from the action at the center of the tent; and Coup himself indicates that during the 1871 season it was impossible to keep those most distant from standing up or rushing to the front, thereby interfering with the view of others. The new arrangement, however, served to keep audiences in their seats and so hit the "popular fancy," he recalled, that "within a few months smaller show-men all over the country began to give two-ring performances. Indeed, from that time it seemed to me that the old one-ring show was entirely forgotten."[59] He might have added that the two-ring show was itself soon a distant memory, as the American circus, ever augmenting its catalogue of wonders, finally at-tained its most distinctive—and bewildering—format.

The 1872 season concluded in Detroit, after which the show was divided and part of it sent south. It was always a problem what to do over the winter months. Most human employees could loaf or work at other jobs, but the an-imals, in particular, required looking after the year round and were sure to "eat their heads off" whether they were earning money or not. The few weeks spent at the Empire Rink the previous winter had seemed to offer a way out of this dilemma. This year, in what was planned to be a far more ambitious venture, the greater part of the circus, museum, and menagerie moved into the Hippotheatron on New York's 14th Street—a flimsy structure Barnum had purchased from the circus proprietor Lewis B. Lent with the object of turning it into a "permanent" establishment. The renovated building had been open barely five weeks when Barnum, who had gone to New Orleans to visit the southern show, received a telegram from Hurd announcing it had burned down during the early morning of 24 December. The destruction, as at his two Amer-ican Museums, was virtually complete, taking a large part of the neighbor-hood—Grace Chapel included—with it. Nearly all the performers and musi-cians lost their valuable wardrobes and instruments; Admiral Dot's miniature carriage went up in flames as well. Most sickening of all, as usual, were the terrible sufferings of the animals, which the SPCA, in its publication the An-imal Kingdom, bitterly denounced the following month. The heavy cages con-taining the more ferocious beasts were not set on wheels. Consequently, fire-men could not move them to the street and, fearing the results if the animals were released, could only pour water on them until they were forced to retreat. Even less dangerous animals were saved with difficulty. Despite heroic efforts by Barnum's employees to rescue them, four beautiful giraffes were so para-lyzed by fear that they refused to be led from the burning building. When it was all over, only two elephants and a camel had escaped.[60]

Publicly, at least, the showman took the news with his usual imperturbability. By the end of the same day he had cabled his European agents to replace all his losses and was promising a "new and more attractive travelling show than ever early next April." Upon arriving back in New York on the final day of the year, he found Hurd and Coup almost in despair. Hurd, wringing his hands over the $50,000 they might have cleared had they been able to perform through the holiday season, did not see how they could field a new show before July at the earliest. Coup was so overwhelmed by their loss that he thought they should "lie still" the entire season. But all their tents, chariots, wagons, and draft animals had been spared the blaze, the showman gamely argued, and only "energy, pluck, courage, and a liberal outlay of money" were needed to get the show on the road again. Before their meeting was over he received a cable from his London agent, Robert Fillingham Jr., announcing he had already succeeded in purchasing two giraffes and a large number of other animals, and that French and Swiss craftsmen were rushing to completion automatons and other novelties for the burned-out museum department. "Doesn't that electricity beat the world?" Coup exclaimed, his spirits suddenly reviving. "Just put a little of it into your blood," Barnum answered, "and *we* will beat the world."[61] The show opened in early spring, as promised.

———◆———

HIS TRAVELING exhibition having been launched on its 1873 season, Barnum now turned his attention to other enterprises. The Hippotheatron's ashes were barely cold when he declared his intention to "rebuild" in the city and once more set before the public his idea of what a museum should be.[62] In the spring he agreed to advise on and help publicize (for a financial consideration, of course) a scheme by a group of English businessmen, who had purchased several of the gigantic circular paintings from the Colosseum in London and planned to exhibit them in specially designed "cosmorama" buildings in New York and other American cities.[63] Most intriguing of all was his announcement, later in the year, that he intended to finance an expedition to cross the Atlantic in a balloon. The accomplishing of so monumental a voyage had for years been the dream of Professor John Wise, the dean of American aeronauts, who had made several long-distance flights within the continental United States and had long argued for the existence of an "easterly current" in the atmosphere. In the summer of 1873, then in his sixty-fifth year, Wise had finally secured backing for such a flight from the *New York Daily Graphic*, but had later resigned from the project following a dispute with the newspaper's owners. His younger assistant, Washington H. Donaldson, was then placed in charge and, after several delays caused by ripped seams and uncooperative weather, finally lifted off with two of the *Graphic's* reporters on the morning of 6 October—only to crash ignominiously in a Connecticut swamp a few hours later.

While Donaldson was still struggling to get his balloon into the air, the showman, in an interview with a reporter from the *New York Times*, declared he had attempted to secure Wise's services before the professor had signed his contract with the *Daily Graphic's* proprietors, but had failed to reach him in time owing to a misdirected letter. He had long been interested in the subject of aerial navigation himself, had assisted a number of inventors of would-be "flying machines" (one of which, tested from the top of a building in New York, had left its creator with several broken bones), and had discussed the subject, as long as twenty-eight years ago, with the famous English aeronaut Charles Green, who in 1836 had flown the "Great Nassau Balloon" from England to Germany. It was Green, he believed, who had originally advanced the theory of permanent currents in the upper atmosphere—an idea the showman later communicated to Wise, who made an ascent at the New York Crystal Palace while Barnum was its president in 1854. Now that he had decided to take the matter into his own hands, he first planned to travel to Europe to consult with the leading authorities in France and England, then spend any sum deemed necessary in order to ensure that his balloon and equipment were of the best quality. Of course, he candidly added, he fully expected to profit in the end. The money received from exhibiting the balloon after its successful transatlantic voyage would probably repay him at least fourfold. His idea was to have an international crew—an American, an Englishman, and either a French or a German citizen—and to decorate the balloon with his monogram, an American eagle, and "other patriotic devices." "For forty years," he continued, "I have been a showman, and in spite of all talk about humbug, the public have confidence in me, and know that I always carry out what I undertake. I firmly believe that this experiment will be successful. At my time of life I have but a few years left, and in them I intend to do great things. I have reserved the sky-rockets and the grand transformation scenes for the close of the performance."[64]

Despite the obvious opportunism of his announcement, Barnum was genuinely fascinated by the possibilities of manned flight. He subscribed to and studied various journals and books on ballooning, and in the seventies he helped finance the work of one eccentric inventor, "Professor" C. F. Ritchel, who in 1878 successfully piloted a hydrogen-filled airship whose horizontal and vertical motions were controlled by propellers powered by the operator's arms and legs.[65] The showman also corresponded with Joseph Henry, the famous physicist and first Secretary of the Smithsonian Institution, on the subject and received from him a letter of introduction, testifying to Barnum's interest in the "promotion of aerial navigation," prior to making his trip abroad. Henry, who thought some force like guncotton might be of practical use in such flights, later applied to Barnum for the loan of a captive balloon from which he proposed carrying out experiments of his own relating to loud sounds that might be used for fog signals.[66]

Armed with Henry's letter of introduction, then, he set sail for Europe toward the end of September. It was his first trip abroad since the period of his bankruptcy, and the first person to greet him as he stepped off the boat in Liverpool was none other than his faithful friend John Fish. After spending several days with Fish and his family at their home in Southport, he proceeded to London, then on to Cologne, Leipzig, Dresden, and Vienna, arriving in the last city in time for the World's Fair, whose wonders he spent the next ten days studying. From Vienna he traveled to Prague and Berlin, where he received letters from Coup and Hurd informing him they had an option to lease several acres of land in Manhattan "for the purpose of carrying out my long-cherished plan of exhibiting a Roman Hippodrome, Zoological Institute, Aquaria, and Museum of unsurpassable extent and magnificence."[67] He immediately telegraphed them to take the lease, then redoubled his efforts to acquire animals, performers, and novelties to fill this and his other show. He visited all the circuses, zoos, and museums along his route; and in Hamburg he finally made the acquaintance of Carl Hagenbeck, Europe's foremost animal supplier, with whom he had dealt for several years. Hagenbeck, who recalled their meeting in his own published memoirs, was loud in his praises of the "König aller Schausteller." Over the next fortnight, he writes, his guest pumped him on his ideas for the Hippodrome, filling two thick notebooks before they finally parted. Upon Hagenbeck's telling him of the elephant races held in India and suggesting that ostriches also be raced with riders upon them, the showman exclaimed, "Hagenbeck, you are just the man I need. Come to America and I will make you my partner and cut you in for a third of the profits." When the dealer protested he had no money to invest, Barnum replied he had no need of his money: his talent was of greater value to him. But Hagenbeck, after thanking Barnum for the compliment, decided he had better remain in Hamburg after all, enriched by the $15,000 order the showman had just given him.[68]

He was finishing his business in Hamburg when a cable from Hurd arrived, informing him that Charity was dead. The mysterious ailments of the past eighteen years had gradually been superseded by a more diagnosable condition, and for the past two years she had suffered from valvular heart disease. On 18 November she was seized by paralysis and died without pain on the following day.[69] The news was not entirely unexpected, for she had experienced a near fatal attack the previous winter and, Barnum writes, often "prayed for death to come as an angel of mercy to take her 'home.'" But to have lost his companion of forty-four years while he was so distant from America, with no possibility of returning to take final leave of her or to receive comfort from his family and friends, filled him with anguish and almost despair. For the next several days he remained in his room, weeping and praying on the Saturday he knew his friend Abel Thomas was conducting her funeral services and Charity, embalmed and laid to rest in an elegant rosewood casket according to directions he had sent, was taken to the Mountain Grove receiving vault to await his return.[70] Then, having hidden himself and his grief away from it for a while, he sallied forth once more to "beat the world."

XII

---◆■◆---

Crowning Efforts

Look at the conformation of that massive head—how evenly and admirably balanced! Behold the kindness and beneficence of that face; the tenderness of those eyes; the cheerfulness and exuberance of that mild, expressive countenance. Who could dream of shrinking or turning away from such a look—from such a face! That is the head which has planned and carried into successful execution the most gigantic amusement enterprises ever conceived in Europe or America. Those are the quick, piercing eyes which take in at a single *coup d'oeil* the ever-recurring demands of the race for diversion and amusements. Those craniological elevations, so prominently developed, are among the active forces which impel him to blend with those amusements a very large preponderance of wholesome moral instruction. . . . He appears on the theatre of life's busy stage as modifier and purifier of many of the abuses which have crept into public amusements, and, through his persistent efforts to divest them of immoralities, will challenge the admiration of a carping world.

*from a physiognomic description of Barnum in an
1874 booklet describing the animals and other
curiosities in his Great Traveling World's Fair*

BARNUM'S OWN HEALTH was not so robust during the fall and winter of 1873. He had recently begun to complain of dizziness and pain in his head—the symptoms were to recur in later years, and he came to believe they could be alleviated by not thinking too much and by "resting" his brain—and the news of Charity's death dealt his recovery a severe setback.[1] Instead of continuing on to Holland, Belgium, Switzerland, and Italy, as he had originally planned, he therefore returned to London to recuperate among friends. For a while, once his health began to improve, he thought he might go to Italy after all. But upon his doctors' recommending Brighton, he willingly gave up that plan. Besides, as he rather enigmatically wrote his friend George Emerson toward the end of February, "I cannot enjoy sightseeing as I could before Mrs. Barnum died."[2]

There was plenty in England to occupy his time. His Roman Hippodrome was rising apace in New York City, and Coup had dispatched Castello to London to aid him in selecting attractions for that huge establishment. In addition to the elephants, ostriches, camels, elands, blood horses and their riders that were to race on its quarter-mile oval track, and individual artists like Mlle Victoria, "Queen of the Lofty Wire," and the "French Hercule" Joignerey who were to perform at the center of the arena, performances were to commence with a grand spectacle entitled "The Congress of Nations." This was a sumptuous procession, with appropriate music announcing the appearance of each separate division, of gilded cars and chariots, flags and banners, exotic animals and beautifully caparisoned horses, and a human cast dressed in over a thousand historically accurate costumes to represent the "Kings, Queens, Emperors, and other potentates of the civilized world" and their retinues, including those of England, France, ancient Rome, Germany, Turkey, Italy, Egypt, Russia, Ireland, Spain, China, India, and even "Lilliput" and America (the last featuring Washington on a triumphal car and a magnificent gold-and-silver banner fittingly embroidered with "a perfect representation of the greatest showman the world ever saw"). The greater part of this pageant was a recreation of one given several years earlier at London's Agricultural Hall by the English showmen George and John Sanger, with whom Barnum now entered into a contract, for $165,000, to purchase exact duplicates of all the costumes, armor, chariots, and other paraphernalia connected with their spectacle.[3] The Hippodrome building itself, which also encompassed a museum, menagerie, and aquarium, cost Barnum and his partners around $150,000; its dimensions—480 by 240 feet—were sufficient to accommodate between ten and twelve thousand seated spectators at each performance.[4] The venture, Barnum later boasted in a letter to Gordon Ford, business manager of the *New York Tribune*, was to be his "*last* crowning effort," and even if he did not recover all the money he had invested in it, he was satisfied in the belief that he had awakened "a *public taste* which *will not* henceforth be satisfied with namby-pamby nonsense. Managers will be *required* hereafter to give their patrons something *better*—& therein is the public benefitted."[5]

In January, Joseph Henry forwarded to him a resolution by the Smithsonian Institution's Board of Regents thanking him for the donation of dead animals' bodies "which form a very important addition to the collection of specimens necessary to illustrate the science of zoology." In his reply the gratified showman mentioned the large number of Mexican and "other idols" he had recently purchased in Hamburg and invited the Smithsonian to make copies of them.[6] Throughout the winter and early spring he continued to acquire animals, performers, and "curiosities" for his Hippodrome and traveling World's Fair, doing an additional $55,000 worth of business with the Sangers alone. At one point, while Londoners were excitedly preparing for a royal entry by Victoria, the Duke of Edinburgh, and the Duke's new wife, a daughter of the Russian Czar, Barnum jokingly remarked to the journalist George Sala that the Queen and her "grand street show" couldn't "half come up to my big show processions in America." Nevertheless, if he could "have the showing of her 'Edinburgh' & wife a couple of months in America," he would be more than happy to pay the expenses of the recent Ashantee War in Africa.[7]

In the midst of dealing with agents and overseeing the shipment of crates to Hurd in New York, he became embroiled in a minor controversy when the social scientist and author Goldwin Smith, recently returned from a trip to America, delivered an address before the annual Trades' Union Congress in which he warned his listeners against emigrating to the United States, where "the feeling against England is so strong as to bring discomfort, if not injury, to the English immigrant." Upon reading an account of this "astounding assertion" in the London *Times*, Barnum rushed to point out that Smith was "utterly mistaken" and that "a life-long acquaintance with the American people, whose character in every phase of society I have diligently studied for more than 40 years . . . justifies me in declaring that the Americans, as a people, entertain for the English a profound and sincere friendship."[8] He was himself soon the recipient of "scores" of letters from English gentlemen who had resided in America, nearly all of whom attested to the civility they had encountered there; and he then expanded on the topic in a letter addressed to the American journal the *Independent*, which published it in its 9 April issue. While acknowledging, as one correspondent had complained to him, that American schoolbooks unjustifiably "cast slurs upon the English nation on account of the follies of an English king a hundred years ago," he was certain "any intelligent American residing a few years in England will . . . find much to admire in her respect for law and order, good morals, religion, and all those requisites which go to make up a liberal government and a high civilization. I confess that in most respects I admire the English character, and surely all observers acknowledge her claims to literature, science, and humanity."[9]

Barnum's eagerness to defend Anglo-American relations and to proclaim his admiration for the English and their institutions (he had sounded a slightly different note while touring the country thirty years before) was not entirely disinterested, of course. When not at his London address or resting at Brighton, he was often the guest of his Lancashire friend John Fish, whose daughter Nancy had increasingly come to occupy his thoughts. He was in no great hurry to return to America, and before finally setting sail from Liverpool on 18 April, he was again at the home of the Fishes in Southport. By then he had obviously made up his mind. When he arrived back in Bridgeport, he recalled in an interview toward the end of his life, there was "considerable talk" about his marrying a widow around his own age, and every time he took some lady friend out driving, rumors of such an impending union were sure to follow. But he knew where his heart was and kept his own counsel.[10]

He disembarked in New York on 30 April, by which date the Hippodrome had been open for several days. Upon attending a performance that evening, he was called out by the audience and driven around the arena in his open carriage—an enthusiastic reception he was pleased to interpret as "a testimonial of the public appreciation of my greatest effort in my whole managerial career, and a verdict that it was a complete and gratifying success."[11] Besides the great "Congress of Nations" spectacle with which each performance opened, and the various races whose jockeys and drivers were often of the female gender (a piquant "Amazonian" note common to all nineteenth-century hippodromes), there were the recreation of an English stag hunt—with real stags, 150 lady and gentlemen riders in authentic hunting costumes, and 36 staghounds Barnum had purchased in England—and a comic interlude entitled "20 Minutes of Fun, or the Lancashire Races," featuring a steeplechase and a race between donkeys. Later in the season, once the weather turned clement, the proprietor announced the results of his recent inquiries into the feasibility of crossing the Atlantic in a balloon. The experts he had consulted in Europe were of divided opinion on the subject, and even the matter of the most proper equipment was open to debate. So he had decided to become his own experimenter and had engaged Professor Washington H. Donaldson to make twice-weekly ascensions from the Hippodrome, bearing aloft with him the most improved instruments in order to ascertain altitude and temperature and, he hoped, settle once and for all the question of an "easterly current" in the atmosphere. Should its existence be finally established, he was determined to go ahead with his earlier announced plan to build a balloon for the flight to Europe, which would be "as easily and safely accomplished as a journey there in one of our best ocean steamers."[12]

Accordingly, on 9 July Donaldson made a brief, initial ascension over the Hippodrome. A reporter from the *Herald*, who attended the second of these trial flights a day later, was somewhat surprised to see the professor dressed in a thick woolen suit. But he and the other spectators, despite the heat of the day, were willing to give him the benefit of the doubt and to assume he understood the perils of the upper air currents better than they. There were cheers and waving of hats and handkerchiefs as the balloon lifted off and rose above the perimeter of the Hippodrome; and at an altitude of 1500 feet, while floating directly over 40th Street, the professor began throwing overboard "great quantities of business cards, which floated off in the air like a flock of insects."[13] Whatever the outcome of these "experiments," they were superb publicity for the Hippodrome. A few weeks later, when the company, under huge tents Barnum had ordered, took to the road, Donaldson went along. In October he and his balloon were pressed into service for a wedding performed above the clouds—reputedly the first ever—while the Hippodrome was playing at Cincinnati.[14] The following year he was again with the show, though by then Barnum had wisely decided to abandon the attempt to cross the Atlantic and no more was heard about this hazardous scheme. On the afternoon of 15 July the professor and a reporter lifted off from the Chicago showgrounds and were blown out over Lake Michigan when a gale sprang up. The reporter's body washed ashore a month later, but Donaldson and his balloon were never seen again.[15]

The great Traveling World's Fair was again on the road during the 1874 and 1875 seasons, featuring in its Polytechnic department an improved version of Professor Faber's marvelous talking machine—the same invention the Duke of Wellington had found so mystifying thirty years earlier. By the latter season, too, the Hippodrome company (which had spent the intervening winter performing at its newly roofed-over building in New York) had added a stirring scene entitled "Indian Life on the Plains," described by Barnum in a letter to Mark Twain as depicting "scores of Indians of various tribes . . . with their squaws, pappooses, ponies, and wigwams travelling as they do in the Indian territory. They encamp, erect their wigwams, engage in buffalo hunts with real buffaloes, give their Indian war dances, their Indian pony races, snowshoe races, foot races against horses, lasso horses and other animals, and both Indians and squaws give the most amazing specimens of riding at full speed. The Indian camp is surprised by Mexicans, and then ensues such a scene of savage strife and warfare as is never seen except upon our wild western borders."[16]

The extent of these enterprises was so ambitious, in fact, that in July 1874 the showman and his partners thought best to incorporate as "The Barnum Universal Exposition Company," a private stock company with an initial capital of $200,000 and the option to increase this to a maximum of one million dollars.[17] A number of other persons, including Barnum's real-estate partner Dave Sherwood, were now let into the firm; Coup, who was sometimes absent in Europe, could not be expected to oversee everything; and John V. "Pogey" O'Brien, celebrated for his self-serving tolerance of gamblers and pickpockets who formerly attached themselves to many American circuses, was taken into the management and for a time, besides being associated with the World's Fair, ran a third show in which Barnum had an interest. By 1875, as Barnum acknowledged in an interview toward the end of that year, the company had become hopelessly overextended. Receipts were down owing to bad weather and the financial panic of 1873; the profits from the two main shows during the latest season—around $100,000—were barely sufficient to cover wear and tear on the property; the Hippodrome itself, as he and his partners had discovered, did not draw well outside major cities because country patrons were disappointed by the absence of clowns.[18] Other accounts of the firm around this time, while attributing its difficulties primarily to "the subdivision and multiplication of Barnum shows . . . that have been so effectual in the division of both patronage and popularity for the last two years," hinted at troubles with O'Brien and "complications of a peculiarly embarrassing nature."[19]

At the end of the 1875 season, therefore, the Barnum Universal Exposition Company was officially dissolved and nearly all its properties and animals sold at auction.[20] In preparation for the nation's Centennial, the showman now consolidated his resources for a single mighty show and entered into a new association with John J. Nathans, George F. Bailey, Avery Smith, and Lewis June. All four were experienced in the circus and menagerie business, and Bailey, interestingly, was the son-in-law of Aaron Turner, with whose traveling circus Barnum had once toured. Coup himself, who later wrote that his partnership with Barnum "was in every way a pleasant and successful one" and that he was forced to end it owing to poor health, eventually became involved in a New York aquarium and several other shows. From various entries in Barnum's ledgers, it seems obvious the two men continued to have business dealings until at least as late as 1879; and Barnum, in token of their friendship, left his former partner a souvenir at the time of his death.[21] This, too, is at variance with the usual depiction of their relationship, wherein Coup has been described as "infuriated" over Barnum's "leasing" his name to men like O'Brien and only too glad to escape from his overbearing associate.[22]

◆

AFTER SEEING the Hippodrome fairly launched and spending some time with Abel Thomas and his family at their home outside Philadelphia, the showman returned to Waldemere for the summer of 1874 and was the recipient of a signal honor. The mayor of Bridgeport, R. T. Clarke, and over a hundred of the town's most prominent citizens threw a "complimentary banquet" to him on 25 June. The lavish menu, which included clams prepared "Waldemere style" and Indian pudding with "temperance sauce," was notable for the absence of alcoholic beverages—a sacrifice made in deference to Barnum's well-known views on the subject and endured by the good-natured company for nearly six hours while Clarke, William H. Noble, Barnum's former manager "Parson" Fordyce Hitchcock, and numerous others rose to pay tribute to their gratified friend and letters and telegrams were read from those unable to attend. As might be expected, there were many joking allusions to the more notorious episodes in the showman's career—"Mermaid!" Barnum delightedly interjected when Clarke observed they had not assembled "to view some wonderful product of the sea"—though more often the speakers concentrated on his unselfish devotion to Bridgeport and its institutions, and Charity herself was touchingly remembered for inspiring others to adorn their grounds and homes through "her almost idolizing love for all that is beautiful in the world of tree and flower." In his own speech Barnum modestly drew attention to those who had benefited the city no less than he, recalled his reasons for settling in Bridgeport, and emphasized that while it was true he had made some expensive improvements to the city that would never repay him, he was glad to have it understood "that mine is usually a *profitable philanthropy*. I have no desire to be considered much of a philanthropist in any other sense. If by helping those who try to help themselves, I can do it without ultimate loss, the inducement is all the greater to me, and if by improving and beautifying our city and adding to the pleasure and prosperity of my neighbors I can do so at a profit, the incentive to 'good works' will be twice as strong as if it were otherwise." The banquet itself, it turns out, was not without some "profit" to the showman, who took care to ensure there was a goodly number of reporters among the invited guests and devoted considerable space to the festivities in the next appendix to his autobiography.[23]

To friends and relations over the summer he continued to write on black-bordered "mourning" paper. Charity's favorite cousin, Nate Beers, and his wife Emma somehow failed to receive, or else chose to ignore, an invitation to the traditional Fourth of July celebration at Seaside Park. Conceivably they were not eager to meet Barnum's "friends from abroad" mentioned in published accounts of the earlier banquet. Then, in late summer, there was a sudden flurry of activity at Waldemere. The showman was tearing down walls in his house and in a "dreadful muss," he wrote Beers in early September, was *"full of business and overworked,"* was due to spend a few days in New York the following week, taking his horses and carriage with him, but really would be so rushed while in the city that he was not at all certain he would have time to stop by and see him and Emma.[24] The ostensible reason for this progress into the metropolis was the national Universalist Convention, to which Barnum had been elected a delegate. But it soon came out. On 15 September, while the convention was settling down to its first day of business, Nancy Fish and her family arrived in New York aboard the steamship *The City of Montreal*. And on the following day, at one o'clock in the afternoon, she and Barnum were married by the pun-loving Edwin H. Chapin in the Church of the Divine Paternity on Fifth Avenue.[25]

The wedding, Barnum briefly noted in his autobiography, took place before family members and "a large gathering of gratified friends." The latter, he might have added, were surprised as well, for as he wrote apologetically to Nate and Emma Beers later on the same day, only his daughters and sons-in-law, his widowed sister Mary Amerman, who still resided in Brooklyn, and his housekeeper, Miss Ellis, had been let in on the secret. Nate and Emma, it would seem, had received some earlier inkling of the newlyweds' interest in each other and had disapproved. "The river *Lethe* is good to drink from sometimes," Barnum now added in his letter to them. "My wife has done that. The world is large— our hearts should be large. I hope & she hopes that past misunderstandings may be forgotten. I trust we may often meet pleasantly at Waldemere & elsewhere."[26] One gathers Barnum's daughters—the eldest of whom, Caroline, was seventeen years senior to the twenty-four-year-old Nancy—were not exactly overjoyed by this sudden turn of events, either. According to a legend that has been passed down among descendants, when the happy couple arrived back in Bridgeport after honeymooning in the White Mountains and Saratoga, they found the family drawn up to receive them on Waldemere's porch—pointedly dressed in their best mourning clothes.

Despite the inevitable speculation over their "May-December" union, there is no evidence that Barnum or Nancy ever intended it to be "platonic." From several jokes dating from around this time and from provision made for anticipated children in Barnum's 1882 will, one may assume quite the opposite, in fact.[27] The showman was eager for a male heir who would perpetuate his name—so eager that after it became obvious his marriage to Nancy was destined to remain barren, he entered into an arrangement with his grandson Clinton Hallett Seeley who, in return for the consideration of $25,000, agreed to change his middle name to "Barnum" and thereafter to use that name "habitually."[28] By then Nancy, like her predecessor, had developed into a semi-invalid, confined for weeks to her bed or else escaping to sanitariums. Once the initial shock of the wedding was over, relations between her and Barnum's children and grandchildren (to the last she was "Aunt" Nancy) were cordial enough, though there was grumbling again, following the showman's death, over the $40,000 per year the estate was obligated to pay her as a lifetime annuity.[29] In the interim there had been various transactions involving other members of the Fish family. During one extended period Barnum was in debt to his father-in-law for over $66,000, and Fish—who sometimes acted as Barnum's "agent" in England and was in the habit of making his daughter gifts of money on her birthday, ordering Barnum to "charge the same to me"—

was endlessly concerned over the interest due him and the fluctuating rate of exchange. For a time, too, Fish's young son John was employed as a secretary with the traveling show, and Barnum was strictly charged with looking after him.[30] A cousin of Nancy, Benjamin Fish, was first employed by Barnum as treasurer with the circus during the 1877 season, returned to the same post in 1881 and permanently settled in America, and became one of the executors of the showman's estate. Another cousin named Sarah Fish served as housekeeper and traveling companion to both Barnum and Nancy in the mid-1880s.

Nancy herself was a continual source of pride to the aging showman, who reveled almost snobbishly in her youth and "Englishness." Unlike the home-clinging, straitlaced Charity, she possessed considerable enthusiasm for the arts, so that Barnum now had a willing companion on his forays to the opera and theatre during the winter season in New York. There they would customarily put up at one of the city's more luxurious hotels—the Sturtevant House, the Fifth Avenue Hotel, or, especially in later years, the Murray Hill Hotel at Park Avenue and 40th Street—the showman having given up his town house around the time of Charity's death. During the coldest weeks they sometimes sojourned at Point Comfort, Virginia; spring meant the return to Waldemere and the renewal of Barnum's obligation to visit the show whenever he could. A bit later in the year they might venture to England for a few weeks, where in time Nancy was pleased to note, as proof of her "Americanization," that shopkeepers invariably showed her only their most expensive items and quoted prices to her in dollars.[31] At the height of summer, when the heat was most intense, they would escape to fashionable retreats in the Adirondacks and White Mountains (Paul Smith's, whose eponymous proprietor was a friend of Barnum, was a favorite at the former), occasionally Newport or Block Island, to which they might travel aboard friends' yachts. Since Barnum especially enjoyed New England's glorious autumns, that season nearly always found him back at Seaside Park, waiting for the show to finish its annual tour and attending to business and social concerns in Bridgeport. To the extent her health permitted, the showman's "young English bride" accompanied him on his lecture tours and visits to his circus, and even went so far as to submerge her own Episcopalian preferences so she could be with him at Universalist church services.

Besides taking an active interest in her husband's charities and planning entertainments for their numerous guests, Nancy was reputed among those supposedly in the know to be a competent pianist and to possess considerable literary talent. With the onset of middle age, she could no longer resist sharing the latter gift with the public; and the first of her creations in this line to see publication, written for the March 1891 issue of the *Ladies' Home Journal* and coyly entitled "Moths of Modern Marriages," presumed to instruct readers on how to hold onto their husbands. "If you must be absent from him in those leisure hours in which Satan is said to provide 'some mischief still' for idle men to do, it is not incumbent of [sic] you to provide for his solace a companion of the gentler sex, younger and fairer than yourself," she sagely counseled. "Don't stay at home in the autumn while he goes to Europe. It is an

ominous state of things when husband and wife can really enjoy separate pleasures." Charity must have been turning cartwheels in her grave.

Since Nancy also nurtured a passion for American authors, prodding her
husband to obtain autographs and inscribed copies of their works for her, it
was inevitable that Barnum, who in any case sought their endorsements of his
traveling show, should attempt to improve upon his acquaintance in this area.
Rather disappointingly, despite his once having been interviewed by him, there
is no evidence that he was familiar with the works of Walt Whitman, who
sounded his own "barbaric yawp over the roofs of the world" within a few
months of the publication of the showman's autobiography. There were other
parallels in the early careers of the two men: both were newspaper proprietors
and editors at various times, and both had been fervently active on behalf of
the Democratic party. Like Barnum, too, Whitman was an adept in the art of
self-promotion—frequently writing anonymous reviews of his own works, or
preparing defenses and explanations that he published over the signatures of
obliging friends—and spent the remaining years of his life (he died in 1892,
less than a year after Barnum) revising and adding to his own greatest work.
But the author of *Leaves of Grass*, although famous enough in his day, was also
rumored to be "disreputable" and a "loafer," and Barnum obviously did not
think it worthwhile to renew their relationship.

More congenial to his taste were the works of such contemporaries as Whittier
and Holmes, with whom Barnum occasionally corresponded. Writing to Whittier
in 1885, after the Quaker poet had graciously observed, while responding to
the request for his autograph, that they had much in common and that each
of them catered to the public in his own way, a flattered Barnum confided that
"my young English wife has thumbed over and over all of your published writings with great delight & reverence. She takes pleasure in reading them to me,
and I as great pleasure in hearing them—perhaps the greater because I have
read & re-read them *alone* and received higher hopes & aspirations therein
years before I saw my English bride."[32] Although Whittier also expressed his
regret that the two men had never met (apparently their paths had not crossed
at the Carys' salon), Barnum was certainly on more immediate terms with the
author of *The Autocrat of the Breakfast Table*, who attended Barnum's circus
and other exhibitions whenever they played at Boston and even permitted his
name to be used in connection with the famous tattooed man, Captain Djordji
Costentenus. On one occasion, frustrated over having missed Holmes by only
ten minutes when he paid a visit to the show, Barnum rushed to the author's
home and "begged" his way to the inner sanctum of the library. Unfortunately,
the doctor was out, but the showman nevertheless took some consolation from
the thought that he could now make his wife, who was sick at the time and
had remained behind in Bridgeport, "more miserable by telling her what she
has missed."[33]

Both Whittier and Holmes, as Barnum acknowledged toward the end of his
life, were among the authors whose works he most enjoyed. But he also included among this select group Shakespeare, Irving, Franklin, Dickens, Lowell,

Stowe, Twain, and "others of that ilk," together with the *Spectator* papers (the title page of *Funny Stories,* published in 1890, displays a quotation from Addison) and works on travel, history, and biography.[34] His favorite poem around this time, as Nancy informed a correspondent who had written to ask, was Leigh Hunt's "Abou Ben Adhem," whose protagonist, one recalls, wished to be recorded "as one that loves his fellow men."[35] In his early years, one is relieved to discover, he was capable of quoting Byron, Goethe, and even Milton, although Shakespeare, if one excludes scriptural allusions, easily claims precedence in his letters and other writings. He did not, he once confessed in an interview, care much for fiction; yet he appears to have read at least the early works of Melville. He quoted from a moving passage by Hawthorne in his essay "Why I Am a Universalist," was familiar with the works of Emerson, and throughout most of his life was an avid reader of works on theology and the numerous denominational journals to which his many ministerial friends, and sometimes he himself, contributed. And he also dutifully read and praised the works of friends who were minor figures in the literary establishment: the English writers Albert Smith and George Sala, for example, and in this country Bayard Taylor, Joel Benton, and members of the circle that once surrounded Alice and Phoebe Cary.

At times he was apt to wax overly enthusiastic upon discovering some work that struck a responsive chord in his own being. Toward the end of 1870, after giving in to his friend George Emerson's insistence that he read *Vagabond Adventures* by the journalist Ralph Keeler, Barnum wrote to the author's publisher to express his admiration for this "stunning" book and to extend an invitation to Keeler to visit him at his home for a few days so they might "compare notes." The book itself is a rather dull, verbose narrative—hardly the equivalent of the showman's sparkling autobiography, although Emerson assures us Barnum found it to be "so much in the line of his own early experience that it seemed his own story"—which begins by recounting Keeler's adventures as a cabin boy on the Great Lakes and then as a minstrel performer after he had run away from home. Before its author could sink any further into the depths of degradation, however, he entered a Catholic college in the Midwest, eventually graduated from Kenyon College, and left for Europe to travel and continue his studies at the University of Heidelberg, frugally managing to support himself during his two years abroad on the pitifully small sum of money he took with him.[36] The author of "The Art of Money-Getting" was as much impressed by Keeler's economy as he was by his determination to avoid temptation (which included the dangers of intemperance, needless to say). "It is marvellous how he could handle so much pitch without being defiled," he wrote, "but the explanation is that Mr. Keeler's natural taste did not lead him in that direction. . . . And yet how a poor forsaken orphan boy could manage to rise above such degrading surroundings, secure a liberal education, visit the principal cities of the old world, and become a gentleman of culture, and this too all accomplished by the outlay of a sum barely exceeding two hundred dollars, is to me utterly incomprehensible. The story is not only thrillingly interesting, but it is immensely valuable to the rising generation."[37] When Keeler did indeed show up at Barnum's town house to "compare notes" some two weeks later, he was so polished in his speech and neat in his dress that Charity herself was moved to remark, "That man could not be anything but a gentleman, if he tried."[38]

In the early seventies, after both of the Cary sisters had been borne to their final resting place in Brooklyn's Greenwood Cemetery, Barnum became acquainted with another author whose reputation was on the rise. The recent publication of *The Innocents Abroad* had established Mark Twain as one of America's foremost humorists, and in December 1870, at the suggestion of their mutual friend Joel Benton, Barnum first attempted to enlist Twain's aid in publicizing his newly formed show. The invitation must have been extended with some trepidation, for the author had previously satirized both the showman and his museum in none too gentle terms.[39] There were other reasons the two men ought not to have hit it off, although Twain's more sardonic views on human nature—together with his devastating appraisals of relatives, fellow writers, and friends and enemies alike—were in the main withheld from the public during his lifetime. A sometime toper and inveterate smoker, a connoisseur and expert practitioner of the fine art of swearing, a mocker of institutionalized religion who nonetheless believed in predestination and yearned for the approval of "respectable" people, at first sight Twain seems a strange choice of companion for the circumspect Barnum. Yet as a literary and lecture-platform celebrity the young author held considerable appeal for the seasoned showman, who saw in him a potential avant-courrier for himself and his numerous enterprises. Once the ice between the two had been broken, Barnum repeatedly invited Twain to bring his wife and children to spend a few days in Bridgeport; visited, with Nancy, Twain's new home at Hartford's Nook Farm; and expressed his unbounded appreciation upon receipt of autographed copies of the author's latest books, which he once remarked would be used for "family instruction" and by his grown children in "sabbath school."[40]

Although Twain, arguing such things were not in his "line," persistently refused to give in to Barnum's urgings that he write a "funny" article about him and his circus for one of the popular magazines—or something that, in return for the author's usual fee, might be used in the circus's advertising matter—he did mention the showman in at least one of his newspaper pieces. In the summer of 1874 Americans were alternately fascinated and terrified by the approach of the newly discovered comet Coy Coggia, and newspapers were filled with stories of the brilliant celestial visitor, which some observers feared was having an adverse effect on the world's weather. In the midst of this excitement Twain wrote a long-winded "advertisement" for the *New York Herald*, in which he announced he and Barnum had leased the comet, were fitting up a million staterooms in its tail for the accommodation of persons wishing to embark on a grand tour of the heavenly bodies, and would return all passengers to New York on 14 December 1991, "at least forty years quicker than any other comet can do it in." Those desiring further particulars were instructed to apply to Barnum, after whom Twain proposed to rename the comet, since it was necessary, he wrote, "that my mind should not be burdened with small business details."[41] The showman was ecstatic over being unexpectedly drafted into this imaginary partnership, which, as he wrote to Twain a few months later, "added much to my notoriety at home and abroad."[42]

For his part, despite his early opinions of Barnum and his museum, Twain soon became a genuine admirer of the showman's career, particularly after reading about it in the 1869 edition of the autobiography. In later years Barnum faithfully kept his friend abreast of his current activities by sending him the revised editions with their annual supplements—his own "religious work," as he once irreverently described the book in a letter to Twain.[43] Indeed, the latter's change of heart may have begun even earlier, for among the "innocents" who sailed with Twain aboard the *Quaker City* in the latter part of 1867 was Barnum's trusted assistant John Greenwood Jr., charged with collecting "relics from the Holy Land" for the American Museum.[44] The two travelers must have discussed Greenwood's employer from time to time; and Twain's own later wild ideas for such imaginative exhibits as the Virgin Mary's tomb and, during the Columbian Year of 1893, the bones of Christopher Columbus undoubtedly owed much of their inspiration to Barnum's example. The same was probably true of many of his other get-rich-quick schemes, the fatal pursuit of which nearly always turned out disastrously and eventually led to his bankruptcy around the time of Barnum's death. As the result of these ill-fated ventures and his penchant for high living (his extravagant house at Nook Farm, which originally cost over $100,000, became such a drain on his finances that at times he wished it, like the American Museum, would conveniently burn down), Twain was constantly in need of money and frequently in debt. Consequently, he was always on the lookout for literary projects that promised a high rate of return for a minimal investment of his time. One of these had his friend in Bridgeport as an enthusiastic collaborator.

Barnum often complained about the "bushels" of unsolicited letters he received from those asking for handouts and jobs, offering to sell him "curiosities" of dubious authenticity or interest, or attempting to cajole him into investing in harebrained business speculations. The majority were answered by his secretaries and promptly destroyed. A few, on account of their style or content, were deemed worth preserving, like the one from Professor Gardner, the "New-England Soap Man," inviting the showman to invest in his product and "aid in cleaning and purifying at least ten millions of your dirty fellow-citizens," which Barnum published in the first edition of his autobiography.[45] By far the greatest number of what Barnum was pleased to term his "queer letters" were those he or his secretaries classified in their margins as "begging," including one from a practicing physician in Pennsylvania who wanted an unsecured loan of $250 so he could begin manufacturing three "family" remedies: Stomach Elixir, Nervine, and Expectorant Cordial; another from a ne'er-do-well in the backwoods of Indiana, requesting $50 for his "personal use" so he would be able to flee a Benedictine monastery; and a proposition from an obviously eccentric woman in Essex, Connecticut, who wanted Barnum to "aid me by renting my barn & letting me have a donkey or a mare, pony or something to look at. There is space for a large shed or enclosures & deer, eland, any quiet animal. If an elephant or some birds could be trusted with refined keepers—I mean those that do not drink or swear—it would make me so happy." She thoughtfully added that if the animals could be transported by night, her fellow townspeople would not need to know about it.[46]

Did the showman want to buy a three-legged chicken with "two rectums, or two passages by which she passes her dung"? A gentleman in Pennsylvania had one for sale. Would he like a small alligator discovered by a Virginia lady in her milk house? How it got there she had no idea, although she supposed it had been taken up in a storm from some place and deposited there. Another person wrote from Boston to inquire what the showman was willing to pay for quadruplet sisters, twenty-six years old, all less than thirty-six inches tall—or what he would pay for three alone, since the fourth was ill and might not be able to travel. From an American in Moscow came a similar query, this time in reference to Siamese twins and a boy, eight years old, who "has the appearance of only being 3 years old. In the place of legs he has arms & hands, so that in all he has 4 arms & 4 hands." Inanimate objects were also proffered in abundance. From New York came an invitation to view something its discoverer mysteriously termed the "falling" or "meteoric sword," to which Barnum replied he had "not the least desire to see the 'sword'—but any man who believes in it is a marvellous curiosity."

Other correspondents, willing to work, offered their services as "actters," circus performers, and in various other capacities. A would-be playwright, who had discovered "it is the very worst of crimes to be a woman and at the same time presume to any business sense," needed the showman's advice—as well as his financial support, naturally—in regard to a drama she had written ridiculing the Mormons and their marriage ceremony. "If any man upon hearing my statement find no good in it, and if I cannot convince him that there is plenty of money to be made," she pathetically concluded, "I will then be satisfied." Stranger still was a proposal from an archdeacon in Scotland who wanted Barnum to manage his "orchestral Sunday services with oratorios." They had already created a musical revolution in his own land, the writer claimed, and by charging at the church door for "sittings," those who undertook them in America would undoubtedly realize a "very vast financial success."

Sometime around early 1874 Barnum showed a number of these "queer letters" to Twain, who instantly recognized in them the potential for an amusing, profitable piece of work. At Twain's urging, the showman began saving and forwarding them to Nook Farm. Upon receiving one packet of these treasures, the author wrote to express his appreciation for the "admirable lot of letters. Headless mice, four-legged hens, human-handed sacred bulls, 'professional' Gypsies, ditto 'Sacasians,' deformed human beings anxious to trade on their horrors, school-teachers who can't spell—it is a perfect feast of queer literature! Again I beseech you, don't burn a single specimen, but remember that *all* are wanted & possess value in the eyes of your friend."[47] Barnum enthusiastically complied with the request and continued to send Twain batches of letters over the next several years, all the while encouraging him in his publication plans. "I hope I sent you the letter from the man who was going on a lecturing *tower!*" he wrote in early 1875, at the same time regretting he had destroyed so many funny letters in the past. When set before the public, they would constitute, he felt confident, "almost a *new* page in the volume of human nature."[48] "Your big envelope of queer letters keeps swelling," he wrote again a few months later.[49] The following year he forwarded a choice letter from an aspiring actress in Massachusetts with the jocular suggestion that Twain consult Mrs. Clemens in regard to his engaging the writer as a "literary" companion. After describing herself as "American by berth . . . quick in motion & allwase an admirer of Drameticks," the writer suggested that if "Barnoum" could not get her a situation on the stage or in his circus, he might know of "some travling Gentelman that wantes a companon for the winter. I will be verry devoted to eney one that will be kinde to me for I am of an afectunate dispotion & continualy long for something or someone to lavish my afectons on."[50]

When the Reverend Dr. Horatio N. Powers of Bridgeport's Christ Church stopped by Waldemere one day in early 1876 and saw some of these letters lying about, he too was struck by their novelty and wanted to use them in an article. But of course Barnum could not accommodate him, since to do so, as he wrote to Twain, "would convict me of a breach of courtesy & good faith." He went on to add that "I hope to see something in print ere long from your pen on the subject."[51] A few weeks later he again expressed the hope that "you will by & bye slip into the *Atlantic* an article on the subject."[52] As late as 1881, after Barnum's partner Hutchinson had allowed a reporter for the *New York Sun* to copy out and publish a selection of "queer letters" recently received at the circus's Bridgeport office, Barnum was still urging Twain to "utilize" the mass of letters he had previously sent him. But for some unexplained reason, Twain never got around to doing so.[53]

The showman's hopes of inducing the author to write something that would help publicize his circus had evaporated even earlier. At the beginning of 1878, planning the show's advertising campaign for the coming season, he had begged his friend to spare "5 or 10 minutes and as many lines over your fist" to contribute to some "congratulatory utterances &c. &c. upon Mr. Barnum's career as an amusement manager." Twain's refusing even this relatively modest request nettled the showman, who had difficulty understanding why one who had freely bestowed praise on himself and his circus in a private letter three years earlier should object to seeing the same sentiments in print. "All right, Mark," he coolly replied. "It's only a matter of taste anyhow—& I am *content.* Of course, I did not want a quack doctor's certificate. But if 'Mark' could have said as if to a third party something like what you once said in a letter to me, that the greatest wonder about Barnum's show is how it is possible to give so much for so little, or had you said the greatest wonder is to see a man who can manage & control so *big* an affair, or something else—it would have been *nice.* But really I am *quite satisfied* & don't suppose it will make any difference with the *big show.*"[54]

Twain later made up for this breach of friendship to some extent by casting Barnum as a minor character in his tale "The Stolen White Elephant," in which mention is also made of the showman's latest acquisition, Jumbo.[55] There can be little doubt, however, that the writer viewed Barnum's persistent attempts to draft him into the circle of his publicists as a continuing minor nuisance. Albert Bigelow Paine, Twain's official biographer and companion during the writer's final years, and self-appointed guardian of his reputation afterwards, had access to Barnum's letters to Twain, as well as to the author's unpublished reminiscences. In Paine's three-volume biography of Twain published in 1912, Barnum receives scant mention. "Even P. T. Barnum had an ax, the large ax of advertising," he writes, "and he was perpetually trying to grind it on Mark Twain's reputation; in other words, trying to get him to write something that would help to popularize 'The Greatest Show on Earth.'"[56] Was this all that Twain himself—who at the time of his death was absorbed in lacerating both friends and foes in his autobiography meant for posthumous publication—thought worth recollecting about his twenty-year relationship with one who provided him so many hours of amusement and pleasant hospitality? One wonders.

———◆———

MEANWHILE, Barnum's interest in public office had been rekindled when his Republican friends in Bridgeport approached him about running for the mayoralty in the 1875 elections—a nomination he only agreed to accept after being assured by prominent Democrats that his fellow citizens again intended to "compliment" him and he would receive bipartisan support.[57] There was an opposition candidate all the same—Frederick Hurd, whose character and abilities Barnum generously praised on the eve of the election—although the campaign was conducted with remarkable civility and the result, even in a city that by then had become largely Democratic, was a foregone conclusion. This did not prevent Barnum's old enemy the *Bridgeport Farmer* from launching several attacks of its own against him, or from lending its columns to a strange debate over his supposed involvement in "desecrating" the graves of some of the town's leading citizens. The imbroglio had begun two years before when the members of the Bridgeport and Stratfield Burial Association, which owned a cemetery of some twelve acres on the western side of Park Avenue, petitioned the Connecticut legislature for authorization to exchange their land for lots in Mountain Grove Cemetery and to arrange for the removal of remains and monuments to the same place. By the time of the petition the Association's own burial ground, originally established around 1811, was in the midst of an area that was being rapidly developed; at least half the lot owners had already transferred their dead to Mountain Grove; and owing to declining revenues, the Association could no longer afford to maintain its fences and grounds. The cemetery had become what Barnum and others described as a "public nuisance," in fact, with horses, pigs, and cattle roaming it by day, washerwomen spreading their laundry over the headstones to dry, and vagrants and "vile characters" frequenting it by night.

The removal plan, therefore, which was approved in a special law of the

Connecticut legislature on 3 July 1873, seemed to make eminently good sense, and most lot owners were glad to take advantage of it. Under its provisions, remains were to be redeposited in a new section of Mountain Grove recently presented by Barnum's old factotum, David W. Sherwood, who had also agreed to pay all the expenses of removal and to settle with owners whose old lots were determined, by a group of commissioners, to exceed in value the cost of the new. The catch was, Sherwood was to receive all the land belonging to the old cemetery in return. But as the financing of this project (estimated to run between 50 and 75 thousand dollars) proved too much for him alone, Barnum soon purchased from him a half-interest in it "in order to share a part of the burden assumed by his former agent."[58] Within a few months of the legislature's approving this undertaking, over 3000 corpses had been disinterred and carted off to their new home in Mountain Grove Cemetery; and Barnum and his partner Sherwood, having laid out the reclaimed land in lots and streets, were busily erecting elegant cottages and turning the whole into a carefully planned middle-class neighborhood.

The venture was another example of what the former liked to term his "profitable philanthropy." But unfortunately, a few owners of lots in the old cemetery, especially after realizing the profits the partners stood to make, chose to look upon it in another light. Among the most vociferous of these protesters was Daniel H. Sterling, descended from one of the earliest families to settle in the area and therefore, as he and his quondam-historian son were fond of pointing out, entitled to be looked upon as a "Colonial blue-blood." He had also been a three-term mayor of the city in the early 1860s, was a director and eventually president of the Connecticut Bank, and, not surprisingly, figured prominently in the affairs of Bridgeport's First Congregational Society.[59] At the time the remains were being removed from the old cemetery, Sterling, who had already transferred his illustrious ancestors to Mountain Grove, attempted to sell his empty lots for a figure the commissioners judged to be exorbitant. The matter simmered for nearly two years, then boiled up again a few days before the 1875 election, most notably in a letter to the *Bridgeport Farmer* from one signing himself "A Republican all but in the Mayor." There was no doubt in Barnum's mind as to the source of the attack, and charges and countercharges were freely exchanged, culminating in a broadside Barnum issued while the election was actually in progress that ridiculed, in particular, Sterling's boasting of "his *blood*, his caste, his aristocratic ancestors (as if people did not remember *who* they were), and of the prestige of his 'family' name."[60]

This tempest in a teapot might have quickly blown over had not Barnum so indelicately touched Sterling on the sore point of his "noble and ancient lineage." Sterling's son Julian, especially, never forgave him for it. In the course of a fairly long career as a muckraking journalist for the *New York World* and other publications, he took every opportunity to slander and deprecate—often anonymously, almost invariably after the showman was safely dead—Barnum and his accomplishments. From the present quarrel over the price of some empty cemetery lots, thanks largely to his cowardly writings at a later date, arose all the tales of Barnum's desecrating the graves of Bridgeport's most respected citizens ("an outrage on the country . . . which was wept over by countless mourners"); of decaying coffins, disinterred by a former butcher "Barnum" had hired to do the job, being carted twenty at a time through the city in broad daylight and bursting open to scatter bones about the streets; of remains tossed willy-nilly into graves at Mountain Grove; and of headstones and monuments from the old cemetery being set up in the new "wherever it suited the convenience of the workmen." Those that were not used to flag Barnum's driveway or the city's sidewalks, that is.[61] From the implacable Julian Sterling, too, later emanated the sensational allegations of Helen Barnum Hurd's reputed indiscretions at "Lindenhurst" and her running off with Dr. Buchtel ("How could I help it? Am I not P. T. Barnum's daughter?") and an even more titillating tale concerning an illegitimate son Barnum was supposed to have fathered.[62]

In the spring of 1875, however, few Bridgeporters were paying any attention to the Sterlings' complaints; and when the polls closed on the evening of 5 April, Barnum, almost alone among those on the Republican ticket, had been elected to office by a comfortable majority. Around midnight there was a parade of citizens to his home in Seaside Park, where a band struck up "Hail to the Chief" and the delighted showman was introduced to the crowd as "Mayor Barnum." In the course of a brief speech he delivered on the occasion, he gracefully acknowledged the honor he felt was being paid to him, pledged to run the city in a bipartisan manner, and made some joking remarks about his "youthfulness" for the job.[63] During the year of his mayoralty (for that was the term of office in those days) he conscientiously labored for several reforms, among them an improved water supply and the competitive awarding of contracts to light the city's streets with gas. The former was a particularly touchy subject with him, for he was himself a stockholder in the company with which the city had contracted; yet the same company, he acknowledged before the Common Council, owing to the "blind miserly policy" of its president and majority stockholder, had failed to provide either an adequate or a reliable source of water. In a private letter he wrote to the president on 2 August, he urged that the company either sell its works to the city or else put them in order, comply fully with its contract, and "do it regardless of dividends."[64] None of these things had been done by the end of his term as mayor; and a year later, in what amounted to a palace revolution at the annual stockholders' meeting, Barnum maneuvered to have himself elected a director, and two days later president, of the company—an office he faithfully discharged until his resignation in 1886, although he continued as a director up to the time of his death. During this period, largely at his behest, the Bridgeport Hydraulic Company constantly improved its works and vastly expanded its reservoir capacity. The company continues to flourish at the present day, providing Bridgeport and neighboring towns with a never-failing source of pure water.[65]

It was inevitable that his long-held temperance principles should come into play. He harped on the advantages of sobriety in his inaugural message to the Common Council, and he insisted on strict enforcement of the liquor-licensing laws. Citizens were encouraged to report persons seen entering or leaving saloons on Sundays, and the owners of those establishments were immediately arrested, with their patrons subpoenaed to appear as witnesses against them. Understandably, these measures did not go down well with some members of the city's large German population, who had become accustomed, under more relaxed administrations, to drinking their beer in peace. When a member of that community objected that Barnum, before being elected, had promised to "do no more in regard to the Sunday law than Mayor Clarke, or any other mayor," the showman rhetorically asked whether his antagonist meant to imply "that the Germans, after becoming voters and American citizens, sworn to sustain American laws, are determined to perform acts which, though lawful in their native land, are unlawful here? Can my Fiji cannibals slay and eat ladies here because they can in the Fiji Islands? Can circuses perform in Bridgeport Sundays because they can in Paris?"[66] Such logic was unanswerable.

This was nothing, however, compared to the uproar created when he was reported in the local German-language newspaper *Die Zeitung* of having accused Jewish saloonkeepers of violating the Sunday law and, before a meeting of the Board of Police Commissioners, of having used the expression "miserable Jews." His Honor, pointing to his "scores" of Jewish friends around the world, swore he had actually said "miserable whiskey" and threatened to sue the *Zeitung*'s editor for slander unless he promptly printed a retraction. A committee of leading Jewish citizens was formed to hear testimony from Barnum and others who were present at the meeting; and while those appearing before it were fairly evenly divided among those who thought he did or did not use the expression, or *might* have used it in connection with those few Jews who were violating the law, this ad hoc body decided to "fully exonerate" the mayor and published its opinion that "the expressions used at said meeting did not allude particularly to the Jews as a race, but to persons of all creeds who disobey the laws."[67]

Mayor Barnum was equally exercised over the activities of the city's notorious ladies of the evening—who tended to ply their trade, then as now, in the vicinity of the post office—and was particularly indignant when his chief of police, William E. Marsh, philosophically expressed the opinion that nothing much could be done about the problem "while society remains as it is and human passions continue as they have been and are." At one point in this hopeless campaign to reform the morals of his fellow citizens, the mayor threatened to personally descend on the city's bordellos and to "arrest, expose and punish to the extent of the law every person found in such houses."[68] On a lighter note, he continued to rejoice in his role of the city's chief booster, crowing, in particular, over his latest "scientific" discovery: Bridgeport, he had determined after sending chemically treated test paper to forty locales up to a thousand miles distant, possessed "a higher average rate of ozone than has ever before been found on the face of the earth!" The bracing effects of such supercharged oxygen were bound to prove a blessing to invalids, help combat epidemics of yellow fever and other diseases, and "add millions to the material prosperity of our delightful city." To accommodate the scores of persons who would soon be streaming to Bridgeport to avail themselves of this panacea, plans were under consideration to build an Ozone Hotel. If there were any mention of him at all when the nation's 200th birthday rolled round, he modestly proclaimed in a speech he delivered on the Fourth of July, 1876, it would be that he "discovered and proved by the highest scientific authority that *ozone* abounded in Seaside Park."[69]

Obviously, not everything went smoothly during his year in office. The majority of the Common Council were Democrats, and they and the mayor were sometimes at loggerheads. When His Honor, in an effort to reduce expenses, volunteered to take a 15 percent cut in his annual salary of $500 and asked that other municipal salaries be reduced "in the same ratio," the proposal, after languishing ten months in committee, was indefinitely tabled. Accustomed to getting things done and having his own way in his business enterprises, the showman often waxed indignant over such frustrations and endless delays. As early as January 1876, while delivering a temperance lecture at Bridgeport's Opera House, he announced he would not accept the office again "with half the city in the bargain."[70] Still, when he met with the Council for the last time the following March, he concluded his mayoralty on an amicable note. Members found their desks decorated with bouquets furnished by the mayor, who in his farewell address congratulated them on the fact that, now that they were about to "fold their tents" and, like the Arabs, "silently steal away," this was "the only 'stealing' which has been performed by this Honorable Body." The Council itself, on a motion by Barnum's chief antagonist among the Democrats, William H. Stevenson, unanimously adopted, by standing vote, a resolution thanking him for "the very able and impartial manner" in which he had presided over its deliberations.[71]

"My ambition," he wrote to a female admirer who had praised his temperance work in Bridgeport around this time, "is to be a poor politician. The Mayor and Common Council of a city have no right to be influenced by political or personal feelings. Our business is to manage the affairs of the city justly, economically and for the greatest good of the entire community."[72] And before the Common Council itself he expressed the telling observation that "it is an unwise policy to elect men to office whose chief study is how *not* to do their duty."[73] He denied being a strict "party man" and, like at least one famous Republican since his day, was fond of reminding voters he had once been a Democrat, and continued to be a democrat (with a small "d") at heart. When Horace Greeley, fed up with the policies of Grant's first administration, ran for the Presidency on the Democratic ticket in 1872, the showman—to the dismay of many a Republican—not only supported and voted for his friend but, in the midst of the vicious campaign being waged against him, threw a big clambake for the Democratic nominee at Waldemere. By then the exhausted founder of the *Tribune* was within a few weeks of his death, and Barnum, who looked upon him as the "Ben Franklin of our day," could not help expressing the opinion that his election was doubtful. Greeley calmly replied he would be satisfied if, as a result of his liberal platform, all political parties would henceforth feel compelled to adopt higher standards in regard to justice and the rights of individuals. "My chief concern," he added, "is to do nothing in this canvass that I shall look back upon with an unapproving conscience." A sentiment with which his fellow Universalist undoubtedly agreed.[74]

———◆———

BARNUM'S MAYORALTY aptly concluded in the midst of the nation's centennial year, which he literally "rang in" by ordering all of Bridgeport's church bells set going for half an hour at midnight on the last day of 1875.[75] To the great exposition at Philadelphia he sent several exhibits, including two of his reformed Fiji cannibals, for whose contentment and continued good behavior he begged from the Smithsonian an assortment of clubs, bows and arrows, tapa cloth, and other "trinkets."[76] His most spectacular achievement this year, however, was his new traveling show, which he described in a crowded letter to Mark Twain as presenting "a real old-fashioned Yankee-Doodle, Hail-Columbia Fourth-of-July celebration every day." At the start of the morning street parade, he continued,

> we fire a *salute* of 13 guns. In the procession we carry & ring a big *church bell*, and we intend to give such a patriotic demonstration that the authorities will gladly let the *public bells* join in half an hour's jubilee. The procession will abound in American flags, a chariot will be mounted with a group of living characters in the costumes of the Revolution, a large platform car drawn by 8 or 10 horses will carry on it 2 white horses on which will be mounted Genls. Washington and Lafayette, properly costumed, a live eagle will be perched aloft, an old-fashioned drummer & fifer march in procession, &c. During our circus performances we introduce a musical ovation wherein great singers lead a chorus of several hundred voices in singing national songs. While singing "The Star-Spangled Banner," *cannon* will be fired by electricity & the Goddess of Liberty will wave the Stars & Stripes. This ovation to conclude with singing "America," "My Country 'Tis of Thee," at which the whole audience will rise and join. At night we give set pieces of fireworks—representing Washington, the eagle, flags, 1776, 1876—rockets, & send up fire balloons.[77]

He was himself often an irresistible part of the spectacle this year, and for a while toyed with the idea of transporting the entire show to Europe in time for the 1877 season. But in the spring of that year he suffered another painful loss when his youngest daughter, Pauline, who had contracted measles followed by diphtheria, died of congestion of the lungs on 11 April; and letting his business enterprises slide for several weeks, he and Nancy escaped to England on their own.

By then, too, there was friction between him and his new circus partners, one of whom, Avery Smith, had recently died. The showman—who already received half the profits and an annual bonus of upwards of $10,000—was indignant when the remaining three partners opposed his purchasing half of

Smith's share. He was also upset over occasionally being called upon, contrary to their contract, to visit the show when it was more than a twenty-four-hour journey from his home or he was not feeling well. What nettled him more than anything else, however, was his partners' strict insistence on the firm's right to the "exclusive" use of his name—something he would never have agreed to, he complained in a rambling letter to them in early September, had he imagined this clause would have been construed to prevent him from managing a separate troupe of dwarfs, joining the American circus proprietor James Myers in a European venture, or running "Jenny Lind Concerts or anything else that would not clash with our interests." His health permitting, he might still be willing to make longer journeys to visit the show, and he was "glad to volunteer to travel or write, contrive & think for the benefit of our company more than contract requires, when I can do it without injuring health, for I want to see the show prosper. But I do object to your demanding me to risk health & life to go beyond the contract, or to your tying my hands any more than the interest of our Museum, Menagerie & Circus demands. I may not perhaps wish to have any show interests in Europe, but if I can sell the use of my name there to responsible parties, or if I choose to engage in a show speculation in Europe, I insist upon doing so—knowing it could not hurt our show here a hair, but on the contrary it would help add to my notoriety." Their original two-year contract was about to expire, he pointedly added, and if Nathans and the others thought him unreasonable and could not get along with him in a "friendly way," he was fully prepared to wind up the concern. "I have not long to stay on this ball of dirt, and I propose to receive without grumbling something like the worth of my name and powers, and then whoever I am associated with will find me as zealous and ready to further the interests of the show as if I owned the whole of it."[78]

To these complaints George Bailey exasperatedly replied that while he, June, and Nathans did "all the work the year around" and received no salaries, Barnum himself was widely believed to have no real interest in the show aside from "renting" it his name. Such rumors were the result, he implied, of Barnum's unfortunate association with "Pogey" O'Brien; now that the showman had begun to think of making similar arrangements with other parties, this could only work to the further detriment of the show. Barnum could not "for any price" find men willing to work so diligently for the success of the company as he, Nathans, and June were doing. They "liked" him as a partner and were willing to continue with him for another two or three years. But they, too, had legitimate rights that must be insisted upon.[79]

When the four men sat down to iron out their differences a few days later (the show was then in Iowa, and Barnum, who was experiencing stomach trouble at the time, arrived with his personal physician conspicuously in tow), they agreed to continue their association until 1 March 1880. Barnum reluctantly abandoned his efforts to increase his share beyond one-half; the "P. T. Barnum Show Company" was also granted full ownership of all amusement speculations he might get up in America, and half of his share in any European ventures. For his own peace of mind, the showman insisted on adding a clause to the new contract that he not be "compelled to visit the show over 12 times per year unless he likes, and those 12 times shall not exhaust more than one month of his time. He shall not go if he is sick and physically unable to do so."[80]

The renewed association jogged on for three additional seasons, during which Barnum seems to have refrained from making any further demands on his partners. The accounts of the company for several of these years throw interesting light on their business arrangements. At the end of the 1877 season, out of total show receipts amounting to $445,266, Barnum's half-share of the profits came to $56,300. At the end of the 1878 season, out of receipts totaling $461,209, his half-share was $53,269. He received only $36,572 for the 1879 season, whose receipts were $429,765. And at the end of the company's final season in 1880, out of receipts of $573,692, his share of the profits came to $87,850.[81] These figures were arrived at after deducting various expenses and losses, of course, some of them—like the railroad wreck in Iowa that claimed the show's gorgeously decorated advance advertising car and seven of its occupants only a few days before the showman journeyed that way in 1877— totally unexpected, others predictable but unavoidably costly. Expenses connected with wintering the show from December 1876 to March 1877 and purchasing new animals during the same period amounted to over $68,000. Publicizing the show (under which heading were included the costs of the special advertising car, lithographs, billboards, newspaper advertisements, the salaries of agents and billposters, etc.) always claimed a major part of the budget and in 1877 alone amounted to over $100,000. In addition to his half-share of the profits, however, the showman stood to realize considerable money from the "bonus" allowed him—a supplement that customarily came to $10,000 or 5 percent of the first $200,000 of gross receipts, and 6 percent of anything above that figure. For the four above seasons, this amounted to $24,716, $25,673, $23,786, and $32,426, respectively. To set these figures in some kind of perspective, it may here be mentioned that in 1880, while the showman was earning over $120,000 from his half-share and bonus, his private secretary and chief accountant, Henry E. Bowser, was drawing the princely salary of $1404 per annum.

As always, he was at his most inventive when publicizing the show, whether through badgering eminent writers and clergymen he knew to endorse or at least sanction it by attending performances, lauding its wonders in the latest edition of his autobiography, or engaging in controversy with Henry Bergh. In 1876, to add further to his "notoriety" among children, he published the first of his juvenile works, *Lion Jack*, a stirring adventure tale whose adolescent hero participates in an expedition to Africa to capture animals for the circus.[82] Two years later, when the Reverend Samuel Scoville, writing in Henry Ward Beecher's weekly paper the *Christian Union*, learnedly condemned popular amusements in general, and "Barnum's circus" in particular, on account of their "downward" tendency, he was again in his element, championing his own "exalted" brand of entertainment and cautioning against pharisaical critics who would stifle the "natural love of cheerfulness" with their "morose

Christianity." It was a libel on the great public conscience to assert, as Scoville had done, that amusements were "popular" in direct proportion to their "objectionable features." "I have no doubt," he paradoxically argued, "that the practical indifference of the Christian church has done much to lower the standard of public amusements. Had the church in earlier days wisely made use of the means within its power of affording the people innocent, instructive and profitable recreation instead of insisting upon the relinquishment of almost every amusement, popular entertainments would more certainly be exercising their legitimate functions today not only in affording necessary recreation but in being powerful agencies of reform. That indifference should no longer exist in a Christian community."[83] Ministers always found him a formidable opponent.

———◆———

NEITHER HIS partners' objections nor the carping of zealous clergymen could deter him from occasionally engaging in some outrageous side speculation. Only a few days after settling his differences with Nathans and the others in 1877, he was reveling in another mystification, this time a fossilized "Colorado Giant" that was unearthed while he was visiting his daughter Helen in Denver. The object was said to measure seven and one-half feet in length and to resemble in its features a modern-day Ute or Apache Indian. Yet it also possessed a low, apelike forehead, an opposed big toe (described in some newspaper accounts as "prehensile"), and, even more remarkable, a tail some four inches long. Was it, perhaps, the long-sought "missing link"? As news of this amazing discovery reached the East, a number of editors could not help remarking on Barnum's opportune proximity. The showman had promptly appeared to examine the "critter" and offer $25,000 for it, but with the proviso that some scientist like Professor Othniel C. Marsh, the eminent paleontologist from Yale College, should first pronounce it a genuine petrifaction. A learned "professor"—not Marsh, needless to say, who had earlier declared the Cardiff Giant to be a "decided humbug"—soon appeared to do just that.[84]

In early December, prior to being placed on public view at the New York Aquarium, the Giant was indeed examined by a group of reputable scientists and physicians, most of whom could barely suppress their laughter. Among other discrepancies, it was noted that while the simianlike arms of the creature were the same overall length, the left forearm was one and one-quarter inches longer than the right. "The sculptor," one physician who had no doubts about the Giant's origin triumphantly proclaimed, "measured from shoulder to finger tip, but forgot to measure the forearm." But an actual sculptor who was present insisted the figure was "perfect" in its anatomical proportions and that, even if it should turn out to be an ancient statue, it provided conclusive proof of Darwin's theories. When another physician suggested that a section be cut from the figure and examined for bone cells, the Giant's "discoverer"—a Mr. William A. Conant, who gave himself out to be a former member of the New York State legislature and who cited among those who would vouch for his character Barnum's friend the Reverend E. H. Chapin—refused to hear of it. The Aquarium management itself announced it would take no side in the matter, but would advertise the Giant as a petrifaction *or* ancient statue. The possibility that so antique-looking an object might be of recent origin was hardly worth mentioning.

All this, following the well-established formula of "When doctors disagree, who shall decide?" merely served to whet the public's appetite to see the figure. "What would you give to see the Colorado petrified giant?" Barnum laughingly asked another Universalist minister, the Reverend James M. Pullman, a few weeks later.[85] Around the same time a reporter for the *New York Tribune*, which had suspected a second Cardiff Giant from the very beginning, traveled to the hinterlands of northern Pennsylvania and learned the details of the hoax from several persons who had participated in it. The Giant's creator, it turned out, was the same George Hull who had manufactured the earlier giant. In the present instance, however, he had abandoned the easily detected process of sculpting from stone and had spent several years experimenting with and perfecting a composition made out of ground bone and stone, clay, blood, eggs, and other ingredients. After forming the figure from this strange concoction, Hull had baked it in a specially constructed kiln, which he kept going for nearly a year in a laboratory built to look like an icehouse. All this ingenious work had been carried out in strict secrecy and seems to have cost Hull—who had gone bankrupt since his short-lived success with the Cardiff Giant, but who was as determined as ever to create something that would set the scientific and religious communities in an uproar—considerable time and anxiety. When the figure was finally ready in early 1877, he had traveled to Bridgeport to interest Barnum in the hoax. The showman had sent his faithful friend George Wells to investigate and, being satisfied by his report, had set up a shareholding company to exploit the Giant that consisted of himself, Wells, Hull, and Theodore Case, a wealthy hotel owner who had been bankrolling the inventor. Together with a "petrified" snapping turtle and fish that were to be found with it, the Giant was then covertly shipped to Colorado and planted near Barnum's cattle ranch. Its "discoverer," Conant, was in the showman's employ. Hull himself, to prevent his being recognized as the creator of the Cardiff Giant, traveled under the name of George H. Davis and took to wearing an odd disguise that included a hump on his back. When the *Tribune*'s reporter, after piecing together the story from the testimony of several of Hull's neighbors and disaffected business associates, confronted Hull's partner Theodore Case with what he had learned, Case slyly replied, "Well, if it is a humbug, it would be about right, wouldn't it, to have Barnum leading off?"[86]

———◆———

HIS ADMIRING TOWNSMEN again honored Barnum in 1877 and the following year, sending him to represent Bridgeport in the 1878 and 1879 General Assemblies. This time, in place of Agriculture, he chaired the Temperance Committee and led the battle on behalf of another cause dear to Universalists: the abolition of capital punishment.[87] Oddly enough, while serving in the legislature he was again at the center of a cemetery controversy, and another conflict with the ministry. By 1878 Mountain Grove was in need of major improvements, and in order to raise money without taxing lot owners, its directors and a large number of the city's leading citizens decided to get up a grand "Christmas Fair." For over a week leading up to the holiday St. John's Hall was crowded with visitors eager to purchase toys, handcrafted articles, and items contributed by various manufacturers, which were sold at booths tended by Mrs. P. T. Barnum and others. But a good many of these treasures—like the solid silver tea set donated by William D. Bishop, the magnificent card receivers and painted fans Nancy Barnum had obtained from Tiffany's, and the pony with elegant saddle and bridle contributed by Barnum himself—were disposed of through raffles, a scheme that incurred the disapproval of a group of eleven of the city's ministers (John Lyon, Barnum's pastor, among them), who in a "memorial" published in the *Standard* of 25 November stated their objection to raising money by means that were clearly in violation of the state's antilottery law. The punishment for such transgression, they "respectfully" reminded those in charge of the Fair, was a fine of not less than twenty dollars or sixty days in jail.

The result of this righteous protest, aside from offending the several hundred persons who were laboring to make the Fair a success, was an outpouring of letters to the *Standard* beyond all precedent. Nearly everyone in Bridgeport, it seemed, thought the ministers had gone too far; and when Barnum incautiously contributed a letter of his own, in which he advised the ministers "to look after the living, and let business laymen attend to the dead," the battle commenced in earnest. The Episcopalian minister Horatio N. Powers, who admitted to having cast his ballot for the showman "at some personal inconvenience," wanted to know if, as a legislator of the commonwealth, he really advocated breaking the state's laws. The Reverend Mr. Powers fervently hoped to see the Honorable P. T. Barnum, Representative, "relieved" from this embarrassing predicament, and he demanded a simple answer of "yes" or "no."[88]

Clearly stung, the showman replied the following day with an emphatic "NO!" and then went on for nearly a column to belabor the rector of Christ Church for having himself broken the state's laws on several occasions. On one Sunday in particular, he claimed, contrary to the statute against paying, receiving, or promising money on the Sabbath, Powers had engaged and introduced to his congregation a professional fund raiser, who so begged and coaxed, argued and cajoled, that the minister and his agent pocketed several thousand dollars. "You raked in money enough in a few hours on one Sunday to satisfy the Sunday segar sellers and stable keepers of Bridgeport for a year," he charged; and in anticipation of this haul, upon visiting a brother clergyman earlier in the day, the preacher was observed to throw up his hat and kick it "in pious delight"! The showman was sorry the protesting ministers had been led into the "mistake of supposing that they were Popes." If they did not retract their denunciation of "men and motives as good and worthy as you and yours," he was certain they would regret their action to the end of their lives. As for Powers's solicitude over his "relieving" himself, he was of the opinion that the preacher himself was in need of some physicking. "Suppose you apply to the 'Great Physician' for a medicine that will ease you without retching and 'straining' over that very small insect, even when your ravenous appetite and capacious stomach will permit you to swallow, not only a dromedary, but the biggest part of my menagerie?"[89]

The Reverend Mr. Powers, in a letter explaining "the adventures of my hat," made a temperate rejoinder and was content to let the matter rest; but when the pastor to Bridgeport's Methodist community, the Reverend George A. Hubbell, was reported to have denounced Barnum by name from his pulpit the following Sunday, the battle flared anew. This time the antagonists learnedly fell to abusing each other with texts culled from Scripture, with Barnum, citing Matthew and Luke, suggesting that Hubbell, like Judas, go out and hang himself; and the minister, drawing upon Revelation, reminding the showman that "all liars shall have their part in the lake which burneth with fire and brimstone."[90] Meanwhile, any number of other persons were busily writing letters of their own to the *Standard*, causing the paper's harried editors more than once to threaten to cut off all correspondence and to urge restraint and greater understanding of the ministers' position. There was a biblical burlesque on "Phineas the Barnumite"; another local wag succeeded in insulting Bridgeport's black community by contributing an imagined "colored" protest framed in the most approved minstrel-show manner.[91] One group of gentlemen made the serious proposal that Barnum and the ministers debate the issue in the Opera House, with all proceeds going to the cemetery (the showman was willing, but the ministers refused).[92] Finally, on the eve of the Fair, a writer signing himself "Justice" respectfully referred Barnum to Matthew 5:37–39. On the following day, in what proved to be his valedictory on the subject, the showman thanked "Justice" for reminding him of the need for forgiveness and acknowledged he might have exhibited "a slight degree of tartness" when replying to the ministers' attacks on himself. But he "never entertained the slightest ill-feeling towards one of these clergymen or their congregations," he insisted, and would gladly do everything in his power to serve them all. Then the truth— or at least the partial truth—came out at last: "Perhaps I may as well here confess that having made a life-long study of the science of *advertising*, and discovered on this occasion an opportunity of working it to advantage, what I have written for the papers have been chiefly to that end. That it has been *effectual*, none will deny!"[93] The Fair was indeed an immense success; and to benefit the cemetery further, all of the letters and editorials written on the subject were promptly collected and published as a "souvenir" book, with the punning title *Lots About Lots; or, The Great Fair and What Preceded It.*

Early in the following year, still not having learned his lesson from the 1867 debacle, he made another bid for national office. The U.S. Senate seat once occupied by Orris Ferry was about to come up at election; and William H. Barnum, who had been appointed to fill out Ferry's second term following the Senator's untimely death in 1875, was the Democrats' choice to continue in this office. A victory over the "Iron Barnum" would have been especially sweet.

The Republicans were scheduled to select their candidate in mid-January, with the election itself, still by the legislature, to follow on the 21st. And since they were then in control of both houses, the success of their choice was assured. On the 10th of the month Barnum wrote a confidential letter to Whitelaw Reid, who had succeeded Greeley as proprietor of the *New York Tribune*, requesting that if his name should somehow be placed in nomination for the office, the *Tribune* would give him a "fair showing," reprint favorable notices of his candidacy that might appear in "respectable" Connecticut papers, and see to it that "my being a *showman* shall not obscure any good qualities which I may happen to be credited with."[94] Reid was willing to oblige his friend, but Barnum's fellow Republicans had other plans. The nomination and election went to Orville H. Platt, who continued in the U.S. Senate until 1905. Some amends were made to Barnum in the following year, when he received the nomination for the state's 10th senatorial district. Although waged primarily in Bridgeport, the campaign this time was an especially dirty one, with the showman himself at one point angrily accusing the Democrats of resorting to "filth, falsehood, forgery, perjury and rascality beyond all precedent." The *Bridgeport Farmer*, not surprisingly, again led the attack, charging him with amassing a "corruption fund" of $15,000 to buy votes (and this after his "very pious article" on the subject during the 1867 campaign) and with having promised to get one distressed citizen's son released from reform school if he would agree to vote the Republican ticket.[95] When it was all over he had lost to his Democratic opponent—also from Bridgeport—by 500 votes. He was *glad* he had been defeated and would not have to spend the winter months in Hartford away from his family, he wrote to ex-governor Hawley a few days later. All the same, forgetting for the moment his thoughts on capital punishment, William H. Barnum and two-thirds of the Democratic party ought to be hanged![96]

A few days after this outburst, on 16 November, he was in New York City, finally winding up his affairs with his circus partners. While hurrying about in lower Manhattan, he was stricken with excruciating abdominal pain and had to be assisted to his son-in-law Samuel Hurd's house on Lexington Avenue. Doctors were summoned, including his Bridgeport physician Robert Hubbard, who diagnosed the problem as obstruction of the intestines. As his condition became increasingly critical and the pain more unbearable, morphine was finally administered to him. By the 23rd he appeared out of danger, was able to sit up and chat with friends, and gaily announced his intention to eat his Thanksgiving dinner with Hurd. But a relapse followed in early December: he was now racked by vomiting, and his weight dropped precipitously from 215 to 144 pounds. Friends and family members despaired of his life. And on 12 December, at the failing showman's own request, prayers were said for him in all the Bridgeport churches.[97]

XIII

The Children's Friend
and Jumbo

Talk of the songs of a nation! . . . What I say is, "Let me furnish the amusements of a nation and there will be need of very
few laws."

Barnum in an interview in the New York Sun,
5 September 1880

BARNUM'S RECOVERY from his painful illness was frustrated by several setbacks over the next few months. Not until 7 January 1881, looking emaciated and "very much bleached," as his secretary put it, did he feel well enough to return to Bridgeport, where important business matters demanded his attention. In mid-March, still recuperating, he sailed for a vacation in northern Florida, bathing in mineral springs in the neighborhood of Jacksonville. On the 31st he wrote from Green Cove Springs, extolling the salubrious climate and the flow-ers and orange groves he had seen, and predicting a glorious future for the state as a winter resort. His letter, obviously meant for publication, went on to emphasize his continuing active participation in the circus bearing his name and described a new deception he had uncovered. Upon leaving New York he had observed on board his steamer hundreds of crates of cheap Mediterranean oranges bound for Florida, and at Fernandina he had seen the same oranges being repacked and marked as though they had been grown in the state. These were then shipped back to New York to be sold as "Florida" produce, and "this fraud," he cautioned readers, "is constantly practiced." It reminded him of something nearer to home—namely, the shipping of Connecticut River Valley tobacco to Cuba, whence it was returned in the form of first-class "Havana" cigars.[1] At the beginning of April he commenced a leisurely return through the southern states, stopping over in Washington to visit President Garfield. In May he was off to England with Nancy and his grandson Clinton Hallett Seeley. Writing from Southport to his secretary and circus partners the following month, he complained that "I walked & knocked about considerably yesterday, feeling that I was about as well as ever, but I was mistaken for today I am tired & used up almost."[2]

As one result of his near-fatal illness, he now began giving serious thought to setting his house in order. While still at Hurd's and convinced he was dying, he had looked back over his life and "could hardly recall a benefit I had rendered to my fellow-men." He had therefore written in a spirit of reconciliation to his enemies and to others with whom he had had differences, and they had all replied in friendly terms.[3] A few months later, when the Bridgeport Common Council delayed too long in accepting the gift of a large bronze fountain of baroque design, he presented it instead to his "home town" of Bethel, paying additional money for its foundation and installation and journeying to its unveiling on 19 August. The day was transformed into a local festival, with bands, a parade, speeches by Barnum and several other dignitaries, and repeated salutes and acclamations for the town's most celebrated son. The event—reminiscent of his triumph fifty years earlier upon his release from the Danbury jail—let loose a flood of memories in him, and the old showman rejoiced in still being able to recognize and recall the names of many of his childhood friends.[4] His interest in those tender years he had spent in Bethel, as well as his curiosity about his family history, spectacularly revived. He was soon at work on a genealogy, advertising for information in the nation's newspapers.[5] And in a move that recalled another, this time less than glorious episode in his past, he hired a Negro valet, Wyatt B. Roberts, whom he kept by his side, and treated considerately and generously, until the time of his death.[6]

Like more than one American in the present century, Barnum had traveled a long way on the road of tolerance since the period when he had looked upon blacks as chattels to be flogged and sold, or as vindictive savages awaiting an opportunity to murder their masters. Although he was never one to wax sentimental over the matter and remained to the end an unapologetic savorer of racial and ethnic jokes ("Some nigger had the nose-bleed," he solemnly remarked to an amused ministerial companion upon spotting an ink stain on a staircase during a Universalist convention), there can be little doubt that the change in attitude was sincere. "No intelligent observer can fail to be struck by the aptitude of those of African descent for the acquisition of knowledge, and by the readiness with which they assimilate good business ideas," he wrote appreciatively toward the end of his life in his *Funny Stories*, a work that also contains a generous sampling of what Barnum and his contemporaries were pleased to term "nigger jokes."[7]

His final will and testament—which he drafted in his own hand and executed on 30 January 1882, and which he thereafter revised in a series of eight codicils—was an heroic attempt not only to protect and equitably distribute the immense wealth he had accumulated but also to provide for every possible contingency, including challenges to the will itself, in which event those doing so were to suffer immediate disinheritance. As rumors of this document leaked out to the public, even his relatives could not help being amazed. Upon sending New Year's greetings to Charity's cousin Nate Beers at the beginning of 1884, he halfheartedly attributed these "enormously fictitious statements" to his circus partners. "My will & codicil occupy about 20 pages instead of 700," he added in reference to one such tale, "but don't please deny the statements made."[8]

Early in 1880, increasingly encumbered by his real-estate and other business dealings, he had hired away from a Bridgeport lumber company Henry E. Bowser to serve as his chief accountant and private secretary. More than anyone else during the last decade of Barnum's life, Bowser was familiar with the extent and intricacies of these myriad transactions, continuing at his post for several years following the showman's death in order to aid in the settling of the complicated estate. He also was responsible for overseeing the work of several agents in Bridgeport and elsewhere, was party to many of Barnum's private affairs, and, as numerous letters to him testify, enjoyed the unbounded confidence of his employer, who repeatedly stressed that he wished him to be thoroughly posted in all his concerns, since he himself wished to be relieved as much as possible "from the necessity of thinking and of working."[9] Besides the long hours he spent in Barnum's Bridgeport office, Bowser found time to engage in a few speculations of his own (he was a physical fitness buff and for two years managed a gymnasium, complete with smoking room, in a building owned by his employer) and diligently kept an office diary. The last is both a personal and an official document, containing as it does information on Bowser and his wife Jennie, remarks on the writer's own business interests, together with notes on fires, accidents, and murders in Bridgeport and other topics holding peculiar interest for him. The great majority of entries relate to Barnum, however, and constitute an invaluable record of his activities during his final years. Included are copies of letters and memoranda of agreements (some of them initialed by Barnum himself); notes on the circus and its daily fortunes while on the road or in its Bridgeport winter quarters; remarks on rival shows when they played in the city; notices of the comings and goings of Barnum, his family, and friends; as well as many entries relating to the showman's real-estate and business affairs.

Among other agents who served Barnum faithfully during these years were Nancy's cousin Benjamin Fish, who traveled with the circus as the showman's treasurer and personal representative, and Charles R. Brothwell. The latter, a lifelong Bridgeport resident and eventually president of the city's Board of Public Works, was in charge of the development of Barnum's vast real-estate holdings, overseeing the erection of buildings and the maintenance of rental properties, besides helping out in other areas where his expertise in construction proved useful. The activities of these "Busy B's," as they were jokingly referred to, were coordinated by Bowser from a series of ever-expanding offices in Main Street, to which the showman himself paid almost daily visits whenever he was in town. Almost from the beginning of the 1880s, too, his homes in Seaside Park were linked to the office by telephone.

The above were but the principal agents in the management of Barnum's financial empire, which in real estate alone was now of staggering proportions. According to an inventory prepared around the time Bowser came to work for him in early 1880, the showman was then possessed of lots and houses valued at over $400,000 in East Bridgeport itself; some $600,000 worth of property elsewhere in the city; over $300,000 worth in New York City (including Harry Hill's establishment at the corner of Houston and Crosby streets); 20 acres of undeveloped land in Brooklyn valued at $20,000; the 765 acres, worth $60,000, he still owned in Denver's Villa Park; besides property elsewhere in Colorado, lots and farmland in Nebraska, Minnesota, and Wisconsin (in which last state he settled several penurious relatives), and additional Long Island property in Corona and Port Jefferson.[10] Even this lengthy inventory, one suspects, does not detail the full extent of his real-estate holdings, which in Bridgeport continued to change and expand over the following decade. In a year-end report of his own activities in the city during 1883 alone, Brothwell informed his employer he had built 38 single and 28 double houses, sold 88 lots for others to build on, laid sewers, water mains, and over 58,000 feet (square, presumably) of concrete sidewalk, and filled in and graded land for Black Rock Avenue and "Barnum Boulevard" at Seaside Park. In addition, he had superintended the construction of a three-story brick building on Main Street measuring 95 feet on its front and 206 feet in depth. Christened by the showman "Recreation Hall," this pleasure haunt was largely devoted to "healthful amusements" and contained a gymnasium, skating and bicycle rink, bowling alley, shooting gallery, first-class restaurant, dance hall, and a larger hall for public meetings, fairs, and other events.[11] No intoxicating drinks were tolerated within its confines, naturally, though the proprietor did occasionally agree to look the other way when the city's beer-guzzling German population wished to hold some social function there. The "Barnum Gymnasium" briefly managed by Bowser toward the end of the decade was another such establishment designed to benefit Bridgeport's superoxygenated citizens.

By 1883 it was also reported that, taking his combined Bridgeport-Fairfield holdings into consideration, Barnum paid more property taxes than did any other of the region's private citizens. Only the sprawling Wheeler Wilson Company, a manufacturer of sewing machines that had taken over the East Bridgeport site once intended for the failed Jerome Clock Company, paid more than he did.[12] The showman professed to rejoice in this distinction, since it gave him pleasure to know his money was being used to educate the city's children, providing them with the "advantages" he had been denied in his own youth. However, there was no sense in carrying a good thing too far. Because horses and movable items such as railway cars were subject to property taxes if they were within Connecticut's borders on the 1st of October, he took care to instruct his circus partners they should not cross the state line until after that date, even if it meant an annoying delay in getting the show back to winter quarters.[13]

Characteristically, he borrowed left and right to finance these ventures, whose increasing complexity, added to that of his circus and other enterprises, often led him to fear what might happen should Bowser have a sudden "taking off." To guard against confusion in such an event, he soon engaged a second experienced accountant on a part-time basis, with the sole responsibility of looking over Bowser's books each week and keeping himself "in full possession of all the details of my worldly affairs."[14] Yet despite such precautions, he was equally insistent his family and especially his sons-in-law should know as little as possible about these same affairs. For some years past they had been of the opinion that he should rest on his laurels, and the potential value of his estate, one gathers, had not escaped their notice.

His building and endowing the Barnum Museum of Natural History at Tufts College, also dating from 1883, provides a revealing case in point. After initially hesitating when the college's president, Rev. E. H. Capen, approached him on the subject, Barnum almost immediately thought better about it, within a few days signed the agreement obligating him to contribute a total of $50,000, and six months later had already forwarded more than the $30,000 it was estimated the building would cost. At first even Bowser was kept in the dark; and to avoid discovery in Bridgeport, payments were by drafts on which Barnum's name did not appear and were circuitously routed through New York City banks. As late as the college's commencement exercises the following June, at which time it was planned to announce the name of the heretofore anonymous donor, he still had not let his wife or family in on the secret. Capen wanted him to address the graduating class, and the showman had even written his speech and made hotel reservations in Boston. At the last minute, however, racked by sleeplessness and almost sick from anxiety, he felt forced to beg off. *"I cannot & dare not* go next week to Boston," he wrote to the president. Yet as the truth was about to come out anyway, he thought there should be some reporters and a good agent from the Associated Press present, so that his wife and daughters might finally learn what he had done through the newspapers! "Heirs may as well know I do what I like with my own," he added almost defiantly.[15]

But there was no unseemly revolt among his "heirs"; and a few days later, his confidence restored, he was again writing to Capen to express the hope that the museum and its collections would be complete and in order by early September, so that he might bring "Mrs. Barnum" to view them. In the same letter he announced the museum would soon be receiving another handsome present: a marble bust of its donor by the noted sculptor Thomas Ball, in whose Boston studio Barnum had secretly posed for several days during the previous summer.[16] A number of plaster casts were immediately made of this precious object, one of them, at the college president's insistence, destined for Capen's home, another for the Smithsonian Institution in Washington, whose Secretary, Spencer F. Baird, had earlier expressed the desire to have a bust of the showman "to be placed in our series of representations of men who have distinguished themselves for what they have done as promoters of the Natural Sciences."[17] His circus partners at the time, who seem to have had a better notion of his plans than did his family, intimated that they, too, wished to express their esteem and gratitude for his "peculiar genius." To this end they suggested that Ball commence planning a monumental bronze statue of the showman; and when the sculptor returned to Europe to complete work on the bust, he carried with him measurements and photographs to aid him in this grandiose project. Although the list of those contributing to the statue's cost eventually included "wife and family & friends," the showman himself remained remarkably modest about it, insisting that it not be erected during his lifetime. Even then, he wrote to Ball, he had no idea where it might be placed:

"Perhaps my posterity and the public will wisely conclude to *bury* it." By late summer of 1885—the figure of $10,000 and the pose, sitting, having been agreed on—Ball had begun work on the model in his Florence studio. There was no need, Barnum stressed, for him to "hurry" the work, and the statue was not cast until over two years later. After receiving a first-class medal at the International Exhibition in Munich during the summer of 1888, it was shipped to America and stored in a Hoboken warehouse. Early in the following year, accompanied by an entourage that included his circus associates James A. Bailey and James L. Hutchinson, his wife, daughter Caroline, grandchildren, Bowser, and several friends, Barnum journeyed there and viewed, for the first and only time, what he and the others were pleased to declare "the *best executed statue* and the *most perfect likeness* we ever before saw." Then he ordered that it be securely enclosed in its crate again and never brought out until he was "mouldering in the grave."[18]

———◆———

HIS "PET" PROJECT, the Barnum Museum at Tufts, was not the only beneficiary of his generosity during his later years. On 10 January 1882 the Bridgeport Public Library officially opened its doors, and P. T. Barnum, "occupation, showman," was issued its first membership ticket. Over the next few months, and with lesser frequency during later years, he contributed several hundred volumes to the library's initially small stock of books—to the value of $1000, according to a local historian.[19] Many of these donations were undoubtedly purchased to fill specific needs; but other volumes, mirroring his personal interests, were obviously selected by the showman himself and in many instances emanated from his library at Waldemere. Besides bound volumes of *Harper's Magazine*, the *Illustrated London News* (on which his own *Illustrated News* had been patterned), and its French counterpart *L'Illustration*, seven volumes of the papers of the Aeronautical Society of Great Britain and some half-dozen books on ballooning testify to his onetime fascination with that subject. He gave multiple copies of his autobiography, of course, as well as the memoirs of Kossuth and biographies of such figures as Lincoln, Washington Irving, Kit Carson, Thoreau, and the explorers David Livingstone and Sir John Franklin. Several works by the African explorer Paul du Chaillu, whom Barnum knew and invited to lecture in Bridgeport, were also contributed, together with many volumes on anthropology, natural history, and evolution. Other subjects holding particular interest for him are represented by a Universalist hymnbook; a treatise on whist; a book on the kidnapping of the young Charley Ross—a *cause célèbre* in 1874—for whose return Barnum had offered a reward of $10,000; Izaak Walton's *The Compleat Angler;* a collection of temperance dramas and C. Jewett's *Forty Years' Fight with the Drink Demon;* and John Tryon's *Sketches of Show Life* and Thomas Frost's *Circus Life and Circus Celebrities*, together with a classic juvenile on the subject, James Otis's *Toby Tyler, or Ten Weeks with a Circus*. History and travel works, which Barnum professed to enjoy reading, were also contributed in abundance.

Besides continuing to enlarge and improve Seaside Park (by now he was an aggressive member of the Board of Park Commissioners), he subscribed $5000 toward the establishment of Bridgeport Hospital, served as its first president until the time of his death, and bequeathed it an additional $5000 to endow a "Barnum Free Bed." This institution—at whose graduation exercises for nurses the showman passed out diplomas and held forth on the "angelicalness" of their calling—was inaugurated in November 1884 and continues as one of the largest and best-equipped hospitals in Connecticut.[20] In New York City itself he was an incorporator, along with his friend Edwin Booth, of another humanitarian institution that has flourished to the present day: the Actors' Fund of America, on whose board he served as one of the original trustees.[21] As always, too, he remained an inexhaustible supporter of the Universalist Church and its causes.

Of all his charitable and civic activities around this time, however, none gave him more pleasure than those he performed for children. Like his fun-loving Bethel progenitor, he doted on his grandchildren and, eventually, their children, ordering donkeys and Shetland ponies for them to ride on at Waldemere, cramming into a donkey cart with them to take a fast spin around Seaside Park, barking like a dog or performing tricks of magic to amuse them, and slipping out of his coat after tiny hands had grabbed hold of it and pretending such astonishment at finding himself in his shirtsleeves that he set his little playmates wild with delight.[22] He was more subdued when entertaining older children, as might be expected; but his last pastor in Bridgeport, the Reverend Lewis B. Fisher, who later served as president of Lombard College in Illinois, tells one hilarious anecdote about a talk he once gave before the local Boys' Club. His audience, which contained a rough element, was not particularly noted for its manners or attentiveness, and on the present occasion had obviously come expecting more from the world-famous showman than the standard words of wisdom he was giving them. At last, sensing the boys' disappointment and growing restlessness, Barnum announced he would give them a demonstration of his skill as a magician. "Every boy in the room gave a sigh of satisfaction," Fisher writes,

> and prepared himself to watch with every sense alert. Mr. Barnum got a table, put two hats upon it, and produced a common biscuit. He then announced that he would swallow the biscuit and afterwards cause it to come under either one of the hats they chose. All this was done with a great air of mystery and parade, which kept the boys intent on every detail. Their faces made a sight never to be forgotten. At last the cracker is eaten, and Mr. Barnum asks them to name the hat it shall be under. Then he calmly raises the hat designated and puts it on his head, remarking, "Young gentlemen, the cracker is under the hat." There was a second's silence, and then such a yell went up as never assailed my ears before or since.[23]

In his will Barnum remembered both the "young gentlemen" and their sisters in the local Girls' Club, and for a time he also presided over the Bridgeport orphan asylum.[24] During the winter of 1884–85 he established a fund of $1000 whose income was to be used to purchase gold and silver medals for presentation to the Bridgeport High School students who each year wrote and delivered in public the best orations. The contest is held to the present day, though the medals (struck off by Tiffany's) have long since been replaced by paper certificates.[25]

To be sure, his fondness for children, like the "profitable philanthropy" he practiced, was often turned to good advantage in his business dealings. No longer so eager to glory in his "Prince of Humbugs" title, he now thought he might more appropriately be hailed as "The Children's Friend." "It pleases parents & children," as he explained to his circus partners.[26] Nor did his well-publicized concern for the "Youth of America" interfere with his continuing to cast a professional eye on those among its ranks who merited more than ordinary attention. Upon receiving word of an exceedingly small infant born on Fairfield's Greenfield Hill, or a sensationally fat child living in nearby Stratford, he was apt to become as excited as ever. The parents of these prodigies were not always pleased to see the white-haired showman unexpectedly bearing down upon them, flying along in his phaeton behind his magnificent black steed "Bucephalus," while neighbors and their children rushed to the roadside to gawk.

He was on familiar territory again when the Society for the Prevention of Cruelty to Children, in the spring of 1883, prosecuted him for allegedly endangering the health and safety of several children in his circus. At issue was a cycling act by a troupe known as the Elliott Children, whose ages ranged from six to sixteen. A few tenderhearted spectators in New York had written to protest their appearance in the ring; the superintendent of the Society, E. Fellows Jenkins, attended a performance and thought the children looked exhausted; and the Society's gentlemanly president, Elbridge T. Gerry—who was more foresighted than his intemperate colleague at the SPCA and who seems to have resigned himself to what he knew would inevitably follow—therefore had little choice but to forbid the act. The showman rose to the challenge with characteristic spirit, bidding defiance to Gerry in a letter that was simultaneously relased to the newspapers, of course, and striding into the center ring at Madison Square Garden to address a cheering audience. Was he not himself a member and director of the SPCC, he rhetorically asked, and did not his wife serve as a vice-president of the same society in Connecticut? Had not the late President Garfield once referred to him as the "Kris Kringle of America"? There was nothing in the Elliott Children's brilliant performance that was not "healthful, invigorating, and within the bounds of law and propriety," or which he would not permit his own children and grandchildren to do.

To prove his assertions, he scheduled a private exhibition by the children before leading members of the city's medical and legal fraternities. Meanwhile, since he had no intention of disappointing the "millions" who came to the circus expecting to see these wonderful artists, he and his partners suffered arrest, with the old showman himself gaily remarking to the judge as he was led before the bench that this was not the first time he had been in a police court or been faced with the prospect of a term in jail. As things turned out, the three justices who heard the case were all among those who witnessed the private performance (and were taken on a free tour of the menagerie afterwards). And since the physicians who were present unanimously declared the children's exercises to be "very beautiful and beneficial to their health," the court quickly arrived at a verdict of "not guilty." The enthusiastic applause greeting this decision was still dying down when the showman coolly walked up to Jenkins, who had brought the charge, and offered him $200 a week if he would consent to be exhibited as "the man who wanted to take the bread out of those children's mouths." "Go away, sir, go away," his embarrassed antagonist mumbled. It was remarkable, an editor of the *New York Times* wrote somewhat wistfully the following day, how much gratuitous advertising Barnum had managed to receive during his long and "conspicuous" career through playing upon people who had no interest whatever in helping him to notoriety.[27]

———◆———

BARNUM'S LONG ILLNESS toward the end of 1880 came at a crucial juncture in his business affairs. He had already announced his decision to break with his circus partners of the past five seasons—was stricken while visiting New York to settle with them, in fact—and the chief incentive for this was the appearance of a powerful new rival with whom he had wisely concluded to ally himself.[28] James Anthony Bailey, considered by many to be the greatest circus manager America ever produced, was in many respects the exact opposite of Barnum. A small, wiry, retiring individual who shunned personal publicity and was given to chewing on rubber bands to allay his habitual nervousness, secretive almost to the point of paranoia about his origins (he had been born "McGinnis" in 1847, took his adopted name from a circus agent who befriended him, and later sacked at least one star performer who knew and was indiscreet enough to broadcast his true name), he had worked as an advance agent, billposter, and at several other jobs before becoming a partner in James E. Cooper's International Circus in 1873. Described by one artist as "likeable but hard-headed," he was a strict disciplinarian and an almost unerring judge of performers and their acts, a driven figure who was typically at his post from dawn until the last wagons were loaded late at night, worrying over the weather and the moral welfare of his employees and busying himself with every detail of the show, down to the purchase of a pot of paint. The strain of such a lifestyle was bound to tell. On at least one occasion he suffered mental collapse.[29]

After taking their circus to the West Coast, Cooper and Bailey embarked for Australia in the fall of 1876, stopping at Honolulu and the Fiji Islands along the way, and successfully toured the continent, Tasmania, the Dutch East Indies, and New Zealand. The toll on animals was high, however, and on the way home most of the profits were dissipated during a disastrous tour of South America. Back in New York toward the end of 1878, the partners refurbished their sagging enterprise by purchasing The Great London Circus (formerly owned by Barnum's onetime partner Seth B. Howes), whose resounding titles also included "Sanger's Royal British Menagerie." The revitalized circus was soon providing "The Greatest Show on Earth" with stiff competition, often performing in the same towns and on the same dates as it did ("day-and-dating," as this cutthroat practice is known in the profession), particularly during the 1880 season when The Great London held an undeniable trump. On 10 March of that year, at the circus's Philadelphia winter quarters, the Indian elephant Hebe gave birth to the first baby elephant conceived and born in America. The event was immediately trumpeted to the press, naturally, and the public became so wild to view this infant wonder that the experienced exhibitor of the Woolly Horse was himself stampeded into making a major tactical error. He offered to purchase little "Columbia" for a huge sum of money, reputedly $100,000. Its delighted owners promptly refused, then gleefully set about incorporating his offer into their bills and advertisements, so that people might see what the great Barnum thought of their baby elephant. The showman, as he acknowledged in his autobiography, found he had finally met foemen "worthy of my steel" and was soon engaged in negotiating an alliance with them.[30]

Their preliminary agreements were soon afterwards destroyed; but the final one—dated as early as 26 August 1880—essentially set forth the terms that governed the show during the next five years. Cooper himself now retired as Bailey's partner and was replaced by James L. Hutchinson, a former member of the press corps and agent for Barnum's autobiography with "The Greatest Show on Earth," but who most recently had been "director of privileges" (for which read "concessions") on the Cooper and Bailey show. Within the triumvirate of the newly formed organization, he was to have primary responsibility for finances, although he also substituted for Bailey as general manager whenever the latter was sick or away from the show. The capital, expenses, profits, and losses were all to be supplied and distributed on the following basis: Barnum paying and receiving one-half, and Bailey and Hutchinson each one-quarter. None of them was to receive any salary or other compensation for his services, and Bailey and Hutchinson were to devote themselves entirely to the "successful prosecution" of the business and to the managing of its "details." All "important points" were to be submitted to the senior partner, who was also entitled to place one or two personal representatives on the show's payroll, and acted upon only after mutual agreement.

For his part, Barnum, who no longer insisted on being paid a premium for its value, granted the company the exclusive use of his name "in all civilized countries for Circus, Menagerie, and animal exhibitions and all shows incidental thereto," reserving to himself, however, its use for any museum he might wish to establish in New York or several other cities. As in previous contracts, too, he promised to "use his influence and abilities in behalf of said show or shows, and shall when able devote his talents, knowledge and experience to writing for them, and shall identify himself therewith as one of the owners thereof. He will also, when he feels able and willing only, appear before the patrons of the same and address them." The use of the term "show or shows" here and elsewhere in the agreement was deliberate. The original idea was to keep the two shows separate and send them alternately to Europe on five-year

tours; in his autobiography Barnum stressed that the merging of the two circuses during the 1881 season was only an "experiment." Yet the agreement
itself was to remain in force until the first Monday in November 1899. Should
the huge show envisioned for the initial season prove unprofitable or too cum-
bersome, doubtless the partners would have to rethink their plans.[31]

So the great combination was finally launched. In the introverted yet supremely competent Bailey, Barnum had found the partner and foil of his dreams.
Their relationship, as in his earlier association with Jenny Lind, proved to be
almost a symbiotic one. If Bailey preferred to remain a shadowy, self-effacing
figure, silently working all the strings from behind the scenes, his hearty partner, overflowing with good humor, jokes, and outrageous puns, liked nothing
better than to hold center stage. If the aging showman himself professedly wished
to be spared as much as possible "the necessity of thinking and of working"—
notwithstanding his obvious relish for a knockdown bout with Elbridge Gerry
or some other escapade that was certain to redound to the circus's glory—the
young, nervously energetic Bailey was more than willing to look after the "details." "*You suit me exactly* as a partner and as a friend," Barnum wrote admiringly to his junior colleague a few years into their association.[32] His advice,
although frequent, was rarely insistent, coming rather in the form of queries
and gentle persuasion. Like a spectator at a game of checkers, as he wrote in
another letter, he thought he might sometimes claim to see a shrewd move
undiscerned by the players themselves, "so I give you a friendly hint if I think
it is worth anything—& perhaps it is not."[33] Unfortunately, Bailey's own letters to Barnum appear to be lost, but is it reasonable to believe they were any
less appreciative? The generally accepted portrait of the senior showman as a
bumbling, barely tolerated nuisance is as unfair to Bailey as it is to Barnum.

At the outset, however, owing largely to Barnum's recent illness and con-
sequent infrequent visits to the show, there was certainly anxiety among the
subsidiary players. It took Barnum's secretary Bowser, who sometimes thought
his employer was being lied to and cheated by his partners, several years to
accustom himself to the new regime, and even then there was never any doubt
where his loyalties lay. Hutchinson—"Lord Hutchinson," as Barnum's agents
soon took to calling him—seems to have been especially abrasive at times. On
the final day of 1880, while Barnum was still lying ill at Hurd's home in New
York, he paid a visit to the Bridgeport office and began going on about how
the showman had been "stung" by his former partners at the final settling of
their affairs. "I told him that was bad but P.T.B. was not generally beaten,"
Bowser primly replied.[34] The new show had been on the road less than a month
when Charles P. Cary, Barnum's original representative and bookkeeper with
it, was writing to Bowser to complain about his and others' treatment. Charlie
Benedict, a rather troublesome relative of Barnum who was married to the
equestrienne Mattie Jackson and who had functioned as doorkeeper to the reserved seat section in the showman's circus for the past three years, had been
summarily discharged from his sinecure. Cary was sorry for him, and sorrier
still "to see Mr. Barnum so much in the control of these men." Letters to him,
he cautioned, were apt to be opened and read by "Lord Hutchinson," and he

was not given much opportunity to talk with Barnum whenever he visited the show.[35] A few weeks later, "overworked" and in poor health, complaining that no respect was shown to his position and that Barnum's partners, who were denying he owned more than a third of the show, "seem fairly to hate the sight of a Barnum man," he telegraphed his resignation.[36] Upon Barnum's proposing Nancy's cousin Benjamin Fish as his replacement, Bailey and Hutchinson objected because they did not believe in having relatives on the show.[37] But Fish, summoned from England, took up the position anyway and, a greater diplomat than Cary, managed to outlast both Hutchinson and his employer. From a confidential letter he wrote to Barnum several years later (by which time Bailey's brother-in-law Joseph T. McCaddon had done a stint as the show's assistant treasurer), one gathers Bailey's accounts did not bear very close inspection. However, it was best to forgo claiming these "few dollars" and prevent Bowser from making a fuss about them, he sagely advised, rather than to annoy Bailey, who was "worth nursing" for the sake of the "hundreds of thousands" the partners stood to make otherwise.[38] When Fish himself later began complaining about being overworked and hinting at a raise, Barnum left it to Bailey to decide whether he should be paid more or let go. Fish was honest, experienced, and "correct" in his accounts, he wrote at the time, but "nobody must think we cannot do without them."[39] In the exhilarating world of business, Barnum could be as tough-minded as the next person. "Business is business" is a recurring phrase in his letters dating from the 1880s.

Despite the petty jealousies and intrigue that swirled around them, the three partners pulled together for a mighty effort. They began with a decision that was to have a peculiar effect on Barnum's beloved city of Bridgeport. The Great London Show had previously wintered in Philadelphia; and Barnum himself, although he scattered some animals and paraphernalia about Bridgeport from the very start of his circus career, had generally sought to keep at least part of his show exhibiting during the winter months, often loaning his animals to zoos like Central Park's or sending them on tours that took them to southern climes (where they sometimes perished all the same). Now, in time for the end of the 1880 season, a permanent winter quarters was erected for the combined shows upon some five acres of the showman's Bridgeport land where he had formerly set his elephant plowing. Throughout the late summer and early fall of that year, Bailey was frequently in town as the huge buildings went up under Brothwell's supervision. The car barn alone, originally 350 and in later years nearly 500 feet in length, covered eight lines of track connecting with the adjacent New York, New Haven & Hartford Railroad. Passengers on the road's main line were given an eyeful as they whirled by the site, whose buildings were decorated with flags, gaily colored paintings and expansive signs proclaiming the owners' names and the show's multitudinous titles, and, atop one gigantic shed, a row of cut-out, painted animals marching up the two sides of a gable. Here the carved and gorgeously decorated parade wagons were stored, repaired, and regilt during the winter months; the expansive tents were mended; the miles of harnesses were made. There were separate buildings and areas within them, each heated by steam to appropriate temperatures, for the monkeys and big cats, the hippopotami and sea lions, the camels, giraffes, and elephants (up to forty of the last), and a great stable capable of accommodating several hundred horses. Even then some of the animals, especially the draft horses, continued to be sent to outlying farms and towns like Danbury, returning each spring before the show entrained for New York in time to be hitched up and sent clattering through the city's streets on "practice" runs. In another building the human performers had a regulation-size ring in which to perfect their acts; additional areas were set aside for training the animals, in particular the elephants, who also did all the work of moving the heavy chariots and railway cars on the grounds, their ears and tails snugly covered to protect them from the cold. When the weather was warm enough, to the delight and sometimes anxiety of people along the way, they would all be led the few blocks south to bathe and frolic in Seaside Park. Even the great Jumbo himself might sometimes be seen splashing in the waters of Long Island Sound.[40]

In effect, Bridgeport became, and for the next half-century remained, America's foremost "circus town." The artists, laborers, and other employees often made their homes there, and a large segment of the community not directly connected with the show derived much of its income from supplying the circus's needs. The old showman himself never tired of playing cicerone to friends visiting the city, sometimes holding out the winter quarters' wonders as an added inducement. If Mary Ashton Livermore would be so kind as to deliver one of her lectures before the Bridgeport Universalist Society, not only would he guarantee her expenses and a fee of $50, but "I will show Jumbo & 40 other elephants."[41] The winter before, while Barnum was boasting of possessing no less than twelve giraffes and the same number of ostriches, the same promise had been made his amused friend Oliver Wendell Holmes. If the writer would only pay him a visit at Waldemere, he would "*see sights*" and the great menagerie in its "shirt sleeves."[42] On another occasion, after taking some friends to watch a group of elephants being taught by "Professor" Arstingstall to play on musical instruments, he blithely invited the ladies in the party to fondle a two-week-old panther cub. The mother, the reporter who accompanied them laconically remarked, "took it all good naturedly."[43] Bowser, too, often found some excuse to escape from his ledgers to the exciting world a few blocks away. Like everyone else, he was particularly intrigued by the elephants, one of whom, Albert, the same who later killed his keeper and was shot in New Hampshire, he attempted to ride—a lark that ended ignominiously in a mud puddle. Following the birth of a second baby, appropriately christened "Bridgeport," in early 1882, a systematic program was inaugurated to breed the elephants, and the fascinated secretary frequently rushed over whenever they were scheduled to copulate. All this regimented dalliance, or "sub-agitation," as Bowser coyly termed it in his diary, ended in nothing; but at one point—so confident were the trainers of success—plans were laid to mate the mighty Jumbo with the Indian elephant Hebe, then take the happy pair to England to await the accouchement.[44]

When "P. T. Barnum's Greatest Show on Earth, Sanger's Royal British Menagerie, The Great London Circus & Grand International Allied Shows" (to give all the titles proudly set forth in the circus's bills and letterheads) first set out in 1881, the American public had even more things to wonder over. Beginning a tradition that endured for many years, the show led off with an evening torchlight parade through the streets of New York before settling in for several weeks at Madison Square Garden. There spectators and reporters were overwhelmed by another innovation that has since become a distinctive hallmark of the American circus: the three-ring format, often with one or two platforms in between for cycle and other acts requiring a firm surface, augmented by the great hippodrome track surrounding the whole and the rigging for trapeze, high-wire, and other aerial numbers taking place above. Curiously, as was also true for his two-ring circus, Barnum made no claim to being the first to introduce this confusion, possibly because he knew better (the English showman George Sanger insisted he experimented with three rings as early as 1860), possibly because he did not wish to become embroiled in controversy over the sometimes loose interpretation of the word "ring."[45] Some managers with aspirations beyond their means were prepared to argue that the oval hippodrome track itself constituted a separate "ring," by which logic Barnum and his partners might have claimed that theirs was in fact a "four-ring" circus. And indeed, for a single week during the 1886 season, when the show performed jointly with the circus of Adam Forepaugh in Philadelphia, four rings and two platforms were used in addition to the hippodrome track.[46]

Continuing an improvement introduced by Cooper and Bailey, the circus was illumined by arc lights, powered by a steam generator, this season; while the museum or sideshow department featured several of Barnum's old friends, among them the original Fejee Mermaid and General and Mrs. Tom Thumb. Once the weather turned warmer and the tenting season commenced, the show journeyed as far east as Bangor and as far west and south as Omaha and Galveston. To anyone harboring notions about the predictability and smoothness of this colossal operation, Bowser's office diary and the circus's annual route books make for instructive reading. On at least four occasions during the 1881 season alone the show was hindered by train collisions and instances of cars running off the tracks. When Bailey's own private car became one of these casualties, Tom Thumb, already nervous, swore they would "never get home safe."[47] From St. Louis, where he had gone in September to meet the show, Barnum fretted over a falling-off in receipts and wrote to Bowser that he expected the show to make no more money the rest of the season.[48] As always, too, there were fierce competitors in the field. For a while Bailey and Hutchinson were convinced that an opposition circus run by Barnum's former partner Coup would "surely hurt" their business. Should they buy him out? they anxiously telegraphed their colleague. But Coup's show, as Barnum suspected and soon confirmed, was on its last legs, so he eventually wrote to veto this plan.[49]

Of far greater concern was the circus of Philadelphia's Adam Forepaugh, a powerful, unrelenting rival who had once been a butcher and later the partner of "Pogey" O'Brien. Forepaugh and his son Adam Junior—the latter an animal trainer of exceptional ability who once taught the horse "Blondin" to walk a fifty-foot tightrope—ran a large, highly popular railroad circus of their own, and "Old Adam" was particularly fond of puncturing in his bills what he considered to be the exaggerated claims of Barnum. At the start of the 1881 season, for example, in preparation for a battle over patronage in Washington and Baltimore, he issued one such "rat sheet" calling attention to the "discrepancy" between the number of elephants, animal cages, mounted riders, etc. advertised to be in Barnum's recent New York City street parade and what their numbers had actually been. The "Old Reliable Great Forepaugh Show," which was not above making some wildly exaggerated claims of its own, was releasing these figures in order to protect the public against "Fraud! Falsehood! and Downright Deceit!"[50] Obviously, something had to be done about "4 Paws," as Barnum characterized him, and in their own bills and advertising matter Barnum and his agents gave as good as they got. A humorous colored poster dating from this period portrays the two showmen as characters out of one of Aesop's fables. To the right, barely deigning to look at his dwarfish rival, stands the "gigantic Barnum ox," bearing the well-known visage of the showman. Beneath him, about to explode in the vain attempt to puff himself up to the same size, the confidently smiling, muttonchopped head of Forepaugh has been grafted to the body of a "four-clawed" frog.

Forepaugh soon expressed his willingness to end their "show warfare," and in time for the 1882 and 1883 seasons a secret agreement, "not [to] be published or in any manner made known to the public," was signed by him and his three rivals, setting forth the respective routes of the two circuses during those years and placing strict limitations on where and when they could advertise.[51] Once this agreement had expired, however, relations between the two shows were as bad as before. For the remainder of the decade Barnum continued to view Forepaugh's circus as an "annoyance and injury to us—and also a *menace*," and on several occasions laid plans to buy him out. That done, he thought Bailey and he might "sweep the board for all time" and establish "a complete *monopoly* which nobody would ever *dare* to assail" on circus entertainments in America.[52] The scheme was finally realized upon Adam Senior's death in 1890, when James E. Cooper, negotiating covertly on behalf of Barnum and Bailey, purchased the show for $160,000. Cooper, who held a one-third interest in this arrangement, continued to manage the circus under its "Forepaugh" title. By then, of course, the Ringlings were beginning to make a stir.[53]

Aside from engaging in such strategic planning and visiting the circus whenever he could, Barnum continued to secure endorsements from distinguished individuals who attended the show, including President Garfield and members of his cabinet; the Civil War general William Tecumseh Sherman; Robert "Todd" Lincoln, son of the martyred President; and numerous politicians, foreign ambassadors, and, naturally, religious leaders.[54] Some idea of how he viewed his own status in society around this time may be gleaned from his contribution to an 1881 testimonial honoring Mrs. Rutherford B. Hayes, who was sometimes referred to by her contemporaries as "Lemonade Lucy." At the end of a letter praising the temperance-minded wife of the former President for her courage in excluding alcohol from the White House, he proudly identified himself as "Director of Moral & Refined Exhibitions for the Amusement & Instruction of the Public."[55] Among other influential friends—despite his having once voted against him—he counted Ulysses S. Grant, who journeyed to Connecticut and dined with him while Barnum was waging his unsuccessful 1880 campaign for the state senate. When the general later fell on hard times, Barnum offered him $100,000 and a share of the profits in return for permission to exhibit his "trophies." But Grant, who graciously informed him that on his recent trip around the world he had discovered the showman's name was "familiar to multitudes who never heard of me," replied that he had already made them over to William H. Vanderbilt. "I shall always believe, regardless of any profit (or loss) which might have accrued to me," Barnum writes somewhat defensively in his autobiography, "that my plan was one creditable to all concerned."[56]

He continued adding to the autobiography, of course, and to write—or at least publish over his signature—books and stories for younger readers that were also calculated to keep his name before the public. The authorship of these juvenile works has been a matter of some contention in the past, although no one has ever argued they were written by Barnum. Generally, they are believed to have been produced by circus press agents, while at least one person has suggested that the prolific children's author Edward S. Ellis wrote most of them.[57] Certainly their style differs from that found in Barnum's other works, and in one of the last of them, *The Wild Beasts, Birds and Reptiles of the World: The Story of Their Capture*, the showman does acknowledge his indebtedness to "my friend Edward S. Ellis, A.M., for his help in the preparation of these pages" and for "many valuable suggestions as to arrangement, style and method of treatment."[58] It is nonetheless worth pointing out that Barnum could, as is evident from extant letters to his great-grandchildren, readily adapt his writing to younger persons; that royalties on these works were paid to him (and their copyrights sometimes renewed by his widow into the present century); and that there exists an undated letter in his hand to an unidentified publisher—very likely dating from 1887, the year before the above-mentioned book appeared—offering to prepare several chapters of a story "concerning wild animals and the novel adventures of those who capture and train them" during a forthcoming vacation in the Adirondacks. The showman adds that "for some months past" he has been devoting his spare time to the writing of such stories and that "all remunerations which I receive for these articles are devoted to certain special objects of charity which I personally know need it."[59] If Barnum did not write these stories himself, one wonders why he thought it necessary to keep up the pretense in his private correspondence with publishers, most of whom, if they did not know him personally, were quite capable of putting two and two together. Interestingly, too, the very first of these works dates from shortly after his marriage to his second wife, whose writing abilities, even before she began publishing over her own name, were occasionally remarked on by interviewers. "I worked with & for Mr. Barnum in all literary work about which he cared particularly," Nancy Barnum wrote to a friend a few months after the showman's death.[60] It would come as no surprise to the present writer to learn that Nancy was herself the author, or at least joint-author, of some of these stories, working from ideas and perhaps outlines supplied by her husband.

Lion Jack: A Story of Perilous Adventures Among Wild Men and the Capturing of Wild Beasts, Showing How Menageries Are Made, dedicated to the "Many Boys of America," was the first and most popular of these works. According to a notice in the 4 May 1876 issue of the *Bridgeport Standard,* the showman, with nothing else to do (his term as mayor had recently concluded), was then at work on the first chapter of the book, which his friend Frank Leslie had talked him into writing. After being serialized in Leslie's *Boys' and Girls' Magazine,* it was revised and issued in book form the same year by another old friend, the New York publisher George W. Carleton, and in later years by Carleton's successor, Dillingham. Meanwhile, in anticipation of what Barnum hoped would be a visit by his show to Britain in the spring of 1877, the book was published by Sampson Low, using electrotypes of Carleton's illustrations. "I want the boys of Great Britain to know of me before my great traveling show arrives," Barnum wrote in November to the London publisher, adding that he also looked forward to a *"large sale."*[61]

The plot of this entertaining yarn centers upon the sixteen-year-old "Lion Jack," who joins an expedition to Africa in search of animals for the circus. Along the way Jack and the other good characters manage to quell a shipboard mutiny; and on the Dark Continent itself, in addition to exciting episodes involving the capture of animals, the hero and his companions are further menaced by hordes of savage Zulus. The book ends inconclusively with Jack still in Africa—which is hardly surprising, since by the time of its publication Leslie was already serializing its sequel. *Jack in the Jungle,* in which the hero's travels are expanded to include "asiatic deserts," finally returns the characters to New York, where Jack himself—now an experienced young man with a fortune in jewels—renounces further adventures to settle down with a girl he once rescued from the East River.[62] There were many similar tales serialized in magazines and published as books over Barnum's name in later years—*My Plucky Boy Tom, or Searching for Curiosities in India for My Show; Dick Broadhead, a Tale of Perilous Adventures,* told by "Mr. Barnum" himself; *The Wild Beasts, Birds, and Reptiles of the World,* which also takes the form of an adventure narrative; etc.—but again, none of them displays the showman's characteristic style. Several of the episodes in these stories do bear some resemblance to passages in Carl Hagenbeck's later memoirs, however, leading one to suspect that those "two thick notebooks" Barnum filled during his meetings with the animal dealer in the fall of 1873 were being put to good use. In the late 1880s, too, a number of charmingly illustrated books for younger children were published on such topics as Barnum's circus, menagerie, and museum. His collaborator on these volumes was Sarah J. Burke, who shared equal billing with the showman on their title pages.

———◆———

ANOTHER MEANS by which Barnum sought to ensure continuing "notoriety" for his show was by attempting to get at least one new, sensational attraction each year. Friends and even strangers sometimes aided him with advice, as did Schuyler Colfax, Vice-President under Grant and a great circus buff, who once urged him to engage the female human cannonball Zazel.[63] As early as 1881 a railroad executive named George P. Harlow wrote to suggest that the Indian chief Sitting Bull would make a great attraction. The showman eventually did seek permission from the government to exhibit the chief and his "family," although by then the "killer of Custer" had already spent some time with Buffalo Bill's Wild West Show.[64] For years he was in pursuit of a living gorilla—a fruitless quest that also figures in the plot of *The Wild Beasts, Birds and Reptiles of the World*—not to mention sea serpents, giant horses, and anything else that might capture the public's imagination. He did so spectacularly in early 1882 with the acquisition of the great African elephant that, besides adding a new adjective to the language, more than anything else came to epitomize Barnum's association with the circus.

The story of Jumbo, like those of Tom Thumb and Jenny Lind, has been told many times, and not always with scrupulous regard for the facts or Barnum's true role in it.[65] At the time the circus purchased him for $10,000 from the London Zoological Society, he had long been an "institution" with English children and their parents, thousands of whom had ridden on his back and fed him buns at the Regent's Park zoo. The showman writes that he himself had often "wistfully" gazed upon the huge elephant while on his visits to London, never imagining that the Society would ever agree to sell him. When one of the circus's agents dared propose such a sale to the park's superintendent, however, the answer soon came back in the affirmative. Upon receiving a telegram to this effect, Barnum continues, he immediately dispatched another agent, J. R. Davis, to England with a draft for the amount stipulated.[66] The park's superintendent, A. D. Bartlett, who for many years had been among the showman's friends, recalled these events somewhat differently in his own memoirs. It was Barnum, he writes, who originally broached the subject in a letter to him. After receiving permission from the Zoological Society's council to sell the animal, he "wrote immediately to Mr. Barnum telling him that he could have 'Jumbo' for £2000 'as he stands,' my object being to save the Society the expense of packing and forwarding this huge animal to America. Mr. Barnum replied by telegram—'I accept your offer; my agents will be with you in a few days.' "[67] In either case it seems obvious the showman was a principal in these negotiations from their very beginning—a point worth remembering when one comes to the strange aftermath of Jumbo's history.

Jumbo had come to the London zoo in an 1865 exchange with the Jardin des Plantes—dirty, ill, and then around four feet in height. Bartlett had handed him over to the keeper Matthew Scott, who soon nursed him back to health, gave him a good thrashing whenever he became too "frolicsome" (those were the days when it was still an article of faith that keepers must demonstrate physical mastery over their charges), and soon formed a bond with the elephant that permitted him, and him alone, to exercise effective control over him. As one of the interesting perquisites of this job, "Scotty" was allowed to pocket the twopence collected from each person clambering aboard the "howdah" strapped to Jumbo's back, a supplement to his income that easily amounted to several hundred pounds a year. At the time of his sale Jumbo was around twenty-one years old, weighed approximately six tons, and, according to Bartlett, stood eleven feet tall. He continued to grow until the time of his death—Bartlett writes that he had gained another seven inches by March 1883— when his height to the top of the back between his shoulders (the highest point on an elephant) was reported to be twelve feet and his weight was said to be around seven tons.[68] As might be expected, Barnum persistently refused to allow accurate measurements to be taken by outsiders and exaggerated the elephant's size outrageously in his posters and advertisements. There can be no doubt, however, that Jumbo, aside from his impressive big-eared "African" appearance, was the largest elephant of his type in captivity at the time.

There was also good reason for Bartlett's haste in deciding to sell Jumbo. The animal had already gone through at least two seasons of "musth," had driven his tusks through iron plates and nearly demolished the reinforced house set aside for him, and had become so violent during these periods that Bartlett, who was convinced Scott himself might be "murdered" at any moment, had taken the precaution of applying to the Society's council for permission to buy an elephant gun. The strange thing was—and neither Bartlett nor Scott could account for this—the elephant invariably became calm again when allowed to roam freely about the zoo's gardens. But the thought of the huge beast suddenly running amok among children or breaking uncontrollably out of his house filled the superintendent with genuine terror. It was therefore with a sense of relief that he accepted Barnum's offer to buy Jumbo, though one might reasonably ask (and there were some who did) why, if the elephant really was so dangerous, he should be sold to anyone at all.[69]

Once the significance of the Society's action finally dawned upon the British public, there was a tremendous outcry against the sale of this old favorite to the Yankee "humbug." Journalists avidly seized on the story, embellishing it with many fanciful details of their own; the question was raised in the House of Commons; the Queen and the Prince of Wales expressed their concern and were later reported to have telegraphed and summoned Bartlett to Marlborough House for particulars. The RSPCA, worried that cruelty might be employed during the elephant's removal, also became involved; and several outraged fellows of the Zoological Society itself, to the consternation of Bartlett and the Society's much maligned council, initiated a court action to set aside the sale—a useless proceeding, as things turned out, for the sale was ruled to be perfectly legal, although the trial also led to considerable coverage in the press. Barnum, naturally, was ecstatic over all this free publicity and used it to excellent advantage on both sides of the Atlantic. When Davis and Arstingstall's assistant, "Elephant Bill" Newman, arrived at the zoo to take charge of Jumbo, they were repeatedly frustrated in their attempts to get the elephant to enter a large wagon-crate they had brought with them. They finally hit upon the plan to walk him through the streets to the ship that was waiting to carry him to America; but again Jumbo showed his reluctance to leave his English "friends" and "wife" Alice—another African elephant the press and public insisted on sentimentally pairing with Jumbo, but toward whom he showed no love at all and often menaced with "angry and violent conduct"—by lying down in the street outside the zoo and refusing to get up. Upon receiving a cable from his baffled agents requesting instructions, the delighted showman immediately ordered them to "let him lie there a week if he wants to. It is the best advertisement in the world."[70]

Meanwhile, America as well as England had been seized with "Jumbomania." Enterprising merchants hawked hundreds of hastily thought-up "Jumbo" souvenirs, including "jumbo" fans, "jumbo" neckties, "jumbo" hats, "jumbo" bracelets, and even "jumbo" earrings. Prints and trade cards of the elephant refusing to leave his London home, being transported to America, joining the other elephants at Barnum's circus, and in more fanciful situations ("Jumbo at the Opera," "Jumbo at the Bar," and, inspired by Gilbert and Sullivan's *Patience*, "Jumbo Aesthetic") were run off in editions of tens of thousands and used by manufacturers, sometimes most ingeniously, to advertise their products. Songs and poems were written on the subject; hundreds of affectionate letters, to Bartlett's increasing dismay, were addressed to Jumbo at the zoo; a bride sent him part of her wedding cake; a "Jumbo Retention Fund" was begun to which one admirer hastily contributed her new sewing machine. An American living in London at the time wrote to a friend that Jumbo was "the great topic which has recently been on everyone's tongue" and that the late attempt to assassinate the Queen "has not made one half the excitement."[71] The showman himself received scores of appeals from British schoolchildren, editors, and other parties asking him to name the price for which he would give up his title to Jumbo and let the old fellow peacefully end his days in England. When one of these was addressed to Barnum by the editor of the *Daily Telegraph*, inviting him to cable his reply "prepaid, unlimited," he promptly obliged with a polite refusal, then went on at considerable length to catalogue all his show's other wonders.[72]

Nearly everyone involved managed to profit from this furor over the elephant's removal, not excepting the Zoological Society, whose gate receipts climbed astronomically as visitors flocked to see Jumbo during his last days in England. But there was also a darker, potentially dangerous side to the affair, which Barnum acknowledged in a letter to a friend a few months later: some English citizens, incapable of seeing or appreciating the humor of the situation, had threatened his agents with violence and poison. "It was as big a job as I ever undertook to get Jumbo away from London when I had bought him fair and square, paid their price in British gold for him," and such a job, he added, as "I do not want to undertake again."[73] Bartlett, of course, despite the increased revenues at the zoo, had reasons of his own for wishing to expedite Jumbo's removal. When it finally became evident to him that Scott, about to be deprived of a sizable portion of his income, was exercising some subtle control to keep Jumbo from entering the crate, he decided to adopt a carrot-and-stick approach. He therefore threatened to remove the keeper from the job of "assisting" Newman, at the same time mentioning that "Mr. Barnum had made him a most liberal offer if he would accompany the animal to America, and that his place would be kept open for him here should he return in a specified time." Scott quickly got the point, begged for one more day in which to accomplish the task, and on the following morning Jumbo did indeed calmly enter the crate.[74]

So the great wagon-crate, with Jumbo securely chained inside and ten horses struggling to move it, was finally drawn to the London docks, there to be taken aboard a barge and ferried downriver to the waiting *Assyrian Monarch*. Despite the raw March weather and a departure time from the zoo of 2 A.M., the procession was accompanied by a numerous crowd, some of its members "groaning" for Barnum and others roundly abusing "Elephant Bill." On the steamship itself, after Jumbo and his crate had been safely housed in a forward hold, a sumptuous dinner was given to a large party of invited guests, during which many principals in the drama made speeches and proposed toasts, and Newman himself was presented with a gold medal subscribed to by several (but not all) fellows of the Zoological Society. The comedy was not yet ended by any means. The Baroness Burdett-Coutts, a great patron of Jumbo, had been invited to the dinner, but instead waited until the ship made its last stop at Gravesend before coming down from London with an aristocratic party of her own in order to feed her old friend his last English buns. As the ship passed down the Thames, boys aboard the training ships scurried aloft to give Jumbo a royal salute, lining up precariously on the yardarms. The *Assyrian Monarch*, although an English vessel, gallantly broke out the Stars and Stripes. Arrangements were made to deposit bulletins on Jumbo's health and well-being in rubber bags that, thrown overboard, might providentially wash up on British shores.[75]

Back in America, impatiently awaiting Jumbo's arrival, Barnum had more than enough to occupy his time. On 2 February the Indian elephant "Queen" had given birth at the circus's winter quarters, and as the showman wrote punningly to a correspondent a few weeks later, "All my thoughts & cares at present are locked up in two *trunks*—one of which belongs to *Jumbo* & the other to little 'Bridgeport.' If both trunks arrive in New York and our citizens possess the keys, a world of treasure will be exposed to public view."[76] His partners Bailey and Hutchinson had meanwhile been laying some plans of their own, one of which was a publicity campaign in which Jumbo was to be favorably compared to, or even identified with, the extinct mastodon. When the showman got wind of this, he promptly telegraphed them that the story "could not be allowed."[77]

On 8 April, after thirteen days at sea, the *Assyrian Monarch* was sighted off Sandy Hook. Early the next morning Barnum, his partners, and a large contingent of reporters boarded the vessel off Castle Garden, the showman being in an especially jovial mood and likening the event to Jenny Lind's arrival in America. Once aboard, they headed straight for the elephant's quarters, where he again held forth on "Jumbomania" and the trouble he had experienced in wresting Jumbo from the English. The U.S. Treasury Department had been considerably more obliging: its Secretary had agreed to pass Jumbo duty-free since the showman claimed he was importing him for "breeding purposes." Another showman who was present had the bad grace to suggest Jumbo was not always of a peaceful disposition; Barnum insisted he was "perfectly lamb-like." Then Newman began mentioning the many gifts passengers had made Jumbo on the voyage over. One solicitous lady had sent him twelve fine oysters, which "Elephant Bill" and Scott had promptly devoured. Other passengers, he incautiously reported, had been equally lavish with beer and champagne—at which Barnum looked pointedly at Scott and said, "That animal's growth has been stunted by the use of beer." While everyone was laughing over this, a ship's officer butted in and added that Jumbo was as fond of whiskey as he was of beer and, to prove his point, poured a full bottle into the animal's trunk. "I protest, I protest!" the showman shouted in mock horror. But by then Jumbo had raised his trunk to his mouth and, apparently in raptures, swallowed it all.[78]

After several unexpected delays, and a bottle of port to further steady his nerves, Jumbo and his crate were transferred to a lighter and finally offloaded at a Battery pier. By then it was dark and raining, Barnum himself had long since departed, and the crowd that had been impatiently waiting through most of the day began shouting for Jumbo to be let out of his box and walked up Broadway to Madison Square Garden, where the circus had been playing for the past four weeks. Hutchinson thought they might try the experiment, but Bailey, fearful that Jumbo would attack the crowd, insisted he be moved in his wheeled crate. When sixteen horses and a rope pulled by four to five hundred men failed to budge it, the order went up to the Garden to "send some elephants." Before they arrived, however, the crate started to move; and it was this ponderous, slow-moving parade, with the summoned elephants pushing whenever necessary, that finally reached Madison Square Garden at 1 o'clock in the morning. Davis, who had sailed from Europe aboard another ship, showed up later on the same day and expatiated further on the London adventure and Jumbo's drinking habits.[79]

To be sure, American journalists were not behind their English colleagues in stoking the fires of "Jumbomania." Nor were they inhibited by any fear of committing *lèse majesté*. Taking his cue from the "wild and eloquent song of victory" Barnum was singing in his newspaper advertisements, an editor of the *New York Times* was inspired to add a few details of his own. In English court circles, this writer claimed, the intimacy that had long existed between Jumbo and Queen Victoria was a well-known fact. For years Her Majesty was in the habit of keeping the elephant in Windsor Castle Park, "where she would often romp with him by the hour, making him fetch and carry like a dog and rolling with him in innocent delight upon the turf. Later in life, when the danger that her Majesty might by accident roll upon *Jumbo* and seriously injure him became too obvious to be disregarded, the Queen ceased to romp with him, though she still kept up the custom of having him sit by her side at the tea-table and 'beg' for lumps of sugar like a trained poodle." After Lord Beaconsfield obtained for her the title "Empress of India," it then became the

Queen's pleasure to ride in a howdah atop Jumbo in the "back yard" of Buckingham Palace, with her devoted minister mounted astride Jumbo's neck and acting as mahout. All of this was kept secret from the Liberals, of course, until the unfortunate day when Jumbo got tangled in a palace clothesline, knocked over the laundress and a chicken coop, and became so excited that he threw the Queen and her minister, thereby necessitating the intervention of the police. After exposing several other interesting details of Jumbo's heretofore private life, the writer concluded by wondering how Barnum, once reputed to be genial and law-abiding, could now so heartlessly gloat over his triumph in wresting Jumbo from the English—a loss that was not only being mourned by millions of British children but was also wringing the Queen's bosom with "vain regret." The showman immediately composed a reply to this pasquinade, in which he generously offered to "assuage the royal grief and stop the flow of royal tears" by returning to England with Jumbo the following October. "Meanwhile, from the most disinterested motives, and purely for the public good, I will whisper that Jumbo, 'the largest and noblest animal on the face of the earth,' is being exhibited at this Garden to 20,000 delighted citizens daily—'for 10 days longer.' "[80]

Within two weeks of Jumbo's arrival, Barnum writes in his autobiography, the animal had more than repaid the $30,000 his purchase and removal had cost the circus. Drawn by the sensational publicity surrounding his acquisition, spectators flocked to see the "great, noble" beast, who was daily exhibited in the menagerie and circus parades. Bartlett had sent along the elephant's old howdah, and although Jumbo never performed as did the other elephants in the show—for it was then widely believed African elephants could not be trained—he continued to be ridden by thousands of visitors.

After spending some time with the circus at the start of the 1882 tenting season, Barnum sailed for England with Nancy, J. R. Davis, and the Baileys toward the end of May. Understandably, he was by no means certain what his reception might be like in Britain; but he was nonetheless determined, as he had hinted in his letter to the *New York Times*, to make arrangements for his circus to visit London the following autumn. Upon learning that the two buildings large enough to hold the show would not then be available, he and Bailey leased some ground on the Thames Embankment and began making plans to erect an iron building of their own. But when the management of a local hotel and neighborhood residents voiced strong objections to having "Barnum's show" in their midst, threatening to obtain a court injunction, this scheme was held up and eventually abandoned.

Wherever he went in England, Barnum reported in an interview upon his return, he was beset by bootblacks, newsboys, and children in general who crowded around him and shouted about Jumbo: "I almost came near being the victim of one or two juvenile mobs on account of having carried off the great pet of the English people." At other times, as in Southport, where he lectured on Jumbo for the benefit of charity, he was more amiably received; and on 25 June he was invited to a memorable dinner given by the great actor Henry Irving on the stage of his Lyceum Theatre. Barnum's friends George

Augustus Sala, Dion Boucicault, and Julius Benedict, Jenny Lind's old conductor, were among the seventy or so distinguished guests, and when the Lord Mayor of London playfully asked him what nationality he was, the showman roguishly shot back, "A Yankee." A. D. Bartlett, who acknowledged receipt of a "very handsome present" (probably a deluxe edition of the autobiography), wrote to him around this time to express his appreciation for the showman's years of "kind and generous friendship" and his own satisfaction in having been able to render "all the assistance in my power, to carry out the very difficult undertaking in which your great spirit and unbounded liberality had embarked."[81] On another occasion, while he was attending a grand military entertainment at Agricultural Hall, the showman observed the Prince of Wales and the Duke of Cambridge giving him a good "looking-over." A few moments later a military attaché came to his box with the message that the Prince had noticed him taking a particular interest in a musical ride performed by the Life Guards and hoped he would "not conclude to take them off to America with him."[82]

For nearly four seasons Jumbo was the undisputed star of "The Greatest Show on Earth," while Barnum continued to dream up schemes to further publicize him. In the spring of 1883, when the long-awaited Brooklyn Bridge was finally completed, he offered the directors of the bridge company a "toll" of $5000 if they would allow Jumbo to walk "quietly and secretly" over the bridge before the official opening. Jumbo was far too valuable an animal, he argued in a meeting with the directors, to risk transporting to Brooklyn, where the circus also played, by ferryboat, and the previous year the elephant had been nearly "lost" during one such crossing. The potential publicity value to the circus of this "secret" crossing did not escape the directors, who refused the request with some show of indignation.[83] Jumbo never did, as Bartlett feared he might, run amok among spectators or cause serious injuries to his handlers, although he continued to test his immense strength by playfully breaking down walls at winter quarters.[84] Nor is there any hard evidence, as some writers have claimed, that he was in declining health; the occasional illnesses he experienced were nearly always cured by a change of diet. Wherever the elephant went, his keeper notes rather comically in his "biography" of Jumbo, people would wave their handkerchiefs and call affectionately to him, thousands of spectators came to the circus to look at nothing else, "the shouting at Jerusalem for the 'Son of Man,' when he rode triumphantly on an ass, could not have exceeded the shout that has gone up from the children of the United States, as they have watched and waited long hours to get a sight of Jumbo."[85]

All the more painful, therefore, was the news flashed round the world during the night of 15–16 September 1885 that the great elephant had been killed in an accident. The circus was just finishing a performance at St. Thomas, Ontario, and Jumbo and the other elephants were being led down the railroad's main line when an unscheduled freight train came rushing down a grade toward them. The circus train itself was on an adjacent track; on the other side of the main line was a steep embankment, down which the handlers frantically urged the elephants. Most got out of the way in time, though at least one of them was scraped by the onrushing engine and the dwarf elephant "Tom Thumb" was knocked under one of the circus's flatcars and suffered a broken leg. There was no escape for the ponderous Jumbo, however, who refused to descend the embankment and, trumpeting loudly and tossing his head, went rushing down the track, lifting "Scotty," who was holding on by a strap and desperately trying to guide him to an opening between the cars, into the air with each step he took. They had almost reached safety when the engine struck him from behind, knocking him down and wedging him half over, half under one of the flatcars. Jumbo's skull was badly fractured in several places, and he sustained serious internal injuries as well, causing blood to pour from his trunk and mouth. A few minutes later he breathed his last, while "Scotty," sobbing his heart out, stood helplessly by. The locomotive and several cars of the freight train were derailed and demolished by the impact.[86]

The financial loss to the circus was feared to be considerable—according to one preliminary estimate the show's value had decreased by as much as one-half—and for the next few days its affairs were in a state of turmoil. Bailey was not with the show when the accident occurred. Suffering from a nervous breakdown, he had been absent for most of the season and was about to sell out his share and retire from management. Barnum was at his home in Bridgeport. This left Hutchinson to deal with the immediate job of sorting things out and getting the show on the move again. Among the first outsiders to arrive on the scene were the taxidermists from Ward's Natural Science Establishment in Rochester, New York, with whose founder Barnum had arranged in advance to salvage Jumbo's hide and skeleton in case of just such an accident.[87]

As he had done on similar occasions in the past, the old showman quickly moved to minimize his losses by turning the disaster into another public relations event. Less than three days later he was proposing to Harper Brothers that they publish, in time for the holidays, an illustrated children's book on the subject, to be entitled *The Life, History, and Death of Jumbo;* and he was soon circulating among journalists a highly fictionalized account of Jumbo's last moments, which had the elephant heroically pushing his keeper and "Tom Thumb" to safety, then, unable to save himself, defiantly charging the locomotive head-on.[88] That he was not altogether confident about the circus's prospects at the time, however—that he may even have anticipated bankruptcy proceedings—is attested by a secret document executed just two days after the accident, by which he conveyed his entire interest in the show's animals and various properties to his granddaughter Helen B. Rennell in return for the nominal sum of one dollar. Under the terms of this heretofore unrevealed agreement, the showman retained the right to continue to "use" such properties; and his granddaughter, in her accompanying acceptance, promised "to reconvey the same to you on demand"—which she obviously did at a later date, since none of Barnum's descendants was ever acknowledged to own an interest in the circus during his lifetime and there is no mention of any such agreement in his will or codicils.[89]

Fortunately, the show's treasurer, Merritt F. Young, was soon able to report Jumbo's death did not seem to be having any appreciable effect on receipts, which did not prevent Hutchinson from trying to pressure the sick Bailey into accepting $40,000 for his share of the show instead of the $50,000 previously agreed on.[90] Barnum personally intervened in this dispute a few weeks later and saw to it that Bailey was paid the full amount, generously praising his retiring partner for his "manliness & integrity," his "marvellous perceptions of how to hit public taste," and expressing the hope that something they had recently discussed might indeed occur—presumably a renewal of their business relationship at some future date.[91] Meanwhile, both the Smithsonian Institution and the American Museum of Natural History had begun clamoring for Jumbo's skeleton, it having been agreed over a year before that the mounted hide would in time go to Barnum's "pet" museum at Tufts College. The showman had already as good as promised that the Washington institution, which so often had benefited from deaths in his menageries, would eventually receive the skeleton.[92] Here again, however, Hutchinson (who continued to hope Jumbo might be found to bear some "peculiar resemblances to the mastodon") had firm ideas on the subject, possibly inspired by a brainstorm one of the show's advertising agents had had only a few hours after the accident. This was to exhibit both the skeleton and the mounted hide in two enormous cages, a scheme that, Hutchinson was convinced, would "prove a bigger card where he has been seen alive so often & would make him draw more than ever."[93] Barnum quickly assented to this ingenious plan, and Ward—over the objections of the Smithsonian's taxidermists, who thought it would take at least "a year or two" to prepare the skeleton properly—was ordered to rush the "double Jumbo" to completion in time for the start of the 1886 season. When Spencer F. Baird, the Smithsonian's Secretary, also dropped the hint that the hide itself could be "made considerably larger than in nature" during the mounting process, the showman was almost beside himself with delight. "By all means let that *show* as *large as possible*," he immediately wrote to Ward. "It will be a *grand* thing to take all advantage possible in *this* direction! Let him show like a mountain!"[94]

So Jumbo—the "greatest, gentlest and most famous and heroic beast that ever lived," as Henry Ward celebrated him in an amusing pamphlet of his own—trooped forth again in time for the 1886 season, traveling, as he had in life, in a special "palace" railway car.[95] The idea of exhibiting him behind bars had been abandoned by then, but the morbid spectacle was enlivened by a humorous note anyway: Alice, the "wife" Jumbo had been so reluctant to leave at the London zoo, had finally arrived in America to join her "husband." British cartoonists had recently depicted her wearing a widow's cap that was an exact replica of the Queen's, and now, tethered beside the remains of the once mighty beast, she was lugubriously billed as Jumbo's "widow."[96] After circus patrons had gazed their fill on the "double Jumbo," the hide was sent to Tufts College and the skeleton loaned to the American Museum of Natural History, to be reunited one final time during the winter of 1889–90 when Barnum realized his great ambition of taking his circus to England. By then he was thoroughly irritated by what he considered to be the Smithsonian Institution's niggardliness in meeting its promise to supply his Tufts museum with casts, models, and duplicates of its specimens; and he had already confided to Morris K. Jesup, president of the American Museum of Natural History, that he and his partners had decided that Jesup's institution should have "first chance" to secure the skeleton permanently.[97] When the Smithsonian's chief taxidermist, William T. Hornaday, who had labored mightily to mollify the showman in the past, finally became convinced that his institution would "never get Jumbo's skeleton," he nearly exploded. Barnum's museum at Tufts, he wrote in exasperation to George B. Goode, director of the Smithsonian's National Museum, was "utterly insatiable" and they might just as well close their books with the showman and "*call* it square, and quit!" Goode obviously agreed, for he annotated Hornaday's memorandum with the order "File all *Barnum*" and, at the top of his colleague's fiery communication, added the valedictory "R.I.P."[98] The skeleton reposes to this day at the museum in New York City, but the mounted hide of Jumbo suffered a crueler fate. After majestically presiding as the Tufts mascot for nearly a century, it was totally destroyed, together with Ball's marble bust of Barnum, during the burning of the museum in 1975. Jumbo's memory is recalled in several of the school's songs, however; a small exhibit has been consecrated to him in the rebuilt biological sciences building; and the Tufts athletic teams are still cheered on with the rousing cry of "Jumbos!"

IN DEATH as in life Jumbo was the subject of many strange tales, beginning with a story that appeared in the *Hartford Sunday Globe* less than two weeks after the accident. According to its anonymous author, Barnum and his partners, knowing Jumbo was ill with tuberculosis and could not live much longer anyway, had actually planned his death as a means of generating publicity for the circus. Upon reading this fantastic tale, the showman was stirred to unaccustomed fury, immediately slapped the publisher with a $50,000 libel suit, and obtained an order for the Hartford sheriff to attach the newspaper's offices. The identity of the "Bridgeport special correspondent" who had sent in the story was no secret to him. The writer was none other than the eccentric, ne'er-do-well inventor C. F. Ritchel, whom he had once staked in his attempts to perfect a "flying machine," but who lately had fallen under the influence of Barnum's old nemesis, Julian Sterling. Sterling had encouraged the impecunious Ritchel to try his hand at journalism, supplying him with hints as to where he might attack or ridicule Barnum; had helped him place articles with the *New York World* and other papers; and had even employed him as a ghostwriter for his own articles in the *New Haven Register*. Several months prior to the appearance of the Jumbo story the two men had collaborated on what was supposed to be an exposé of Barnum's involvement with the Jerome Clock Company and the ruses he had employed to avoid his creditors. The *World*, which had earlier instructed Sterling to "go for Barnum strong," had a temporary change of heart and decided against publishing the article, but the manuscript itself was carried to Barnum by another person, who suggested Barnum might at least pay Ritchel something for his wasted time! The showman's outburst of indignation was so "tremendous" that it unnerved the intermediary, who fled back to Ritchel to report his conviction that the story, dreamed up by Sterling, *must* be a lie. Barnum promptly branded Ritchel a "blackmailer" in public, and now did so again upon the publication of the Jumbo article.[99]

As a result of this fracas the *Globe*'s proprietor hastened to Bridgeport, interviewed Barnum and Matthew Scott and examined various documents testifying to Jumbo's excellent health and Ritchel's perfidy, printed a full retraction in the paper's next issue, and summarily discharged the "Bridgeport special correspondent." Ritchel himself made an abject apology to the showman and promised never again to "masquerade in the garb of a journalist."[100] And there the matter ought surely to have ended. Instead, rumors have persisted to the present day of Jumbo's being afflicted with some chronic, perhaps fatal, illness and of Barnum's complicity in his death. One writer, attributing the elephant's downfall to Barnum's winking at his well-known penchant for alcohol, describes Jumbo stumbling down the railroad track at St. Thomas in a "drunken stupor" and concludes it was only fitting he should go to a "drunkard's grave."[101] Another, in a generally respectable telling of the elephant's history, argues that the precautionary arrangements made with Henry Ward and his taxidermists are evidence Barnum and his partners secretly knew Jumbo was suffering from a "chronic debility"; a theory that fails to take into account, however, what was common knowledge at the time—namely, that Jumbo's final disposition was of keen interest to the Smithsonian and other museums almost from the day of his arrival in the United States, and that the showman, who had long resigned himself to heavy losses in his menageries each season, habitually made similar arrangements for his other animals.[102]

Considerably more inflammatory, not to say ridiculous, was a "conspiracy theory" advanced in the 1960s by a person who claimed actually to have interviewed Jumbo's "assassin." If one may trust this account, Jumbo was indeed afflicted with a long-standing complaint: a mammoth case of flatulence! The huge animal so stank up the circus and was forever making such a mess in other ways that Barnum and his partners, out of sheer embarrassment, decided they had no choice but to do away with him. Accordingly, the showman personally traveled to St. Thomas to meet the circus, armed the assassin (one "Larry Quigle of the London Zoo") with a pistol, and ordered him to shoot Jumbo through the eye while the circus cars were being coupled. Mortally wounded, the elephant first fell on top of the smaller elephant, then between the moving engine and one of the flatcars, while "P. T. ranted and raved about the stupidity of the engine crew whom he charged with crushing the skull of his fabulous elephant." One would like to believe the whole thing was meant as a joke, but apparently it wasn't. And again, one can still encounter, around Bridgeport, at least, the odd individual who is prepared to swear to this cock-and-bull story.[103]

What was undoubtedly the unkindest cut of all, however, came not from enemies and crackpots like the above, but from Barnum's own associates of many years' standing. At the time of his death in 1891, in a situation that paralleled the accident to Jumbo some six years earlier, there was considerable uncertainty over what his own loss might mean to the show. A frantic publicity campaign was soon under way to convince the public that nothing had changed and to puff the colorless, normally retiring Bailey, who by then had returned to the management, up to the size of the "mighty Barnum ox." For the past dozen years, the world was now informed, Bailey had been the "master spirit" of the circus and responsible for its "every achievement," while the aging Barnum, who "never during his life made a pretence of knowing anything about the circus business," left everything to his younger partner but was allowed all the credit. "That," the authors of this rhodomontade modestly proclaimed, "is Bailey's way." When it came to Jumbo's history, the story waxed even more poetic. It was Bailey who first heard of and decided to go after the elephant, and Bailey who bought him, and Bailey again who had the inspiration to walk the great animal across Brooklyn Bridge. What role did his veteran partner play in all this? "Barnum never heard that Jumbo was in the possession of the show until he saw the big beast here."[104] The propaganda was so persuasive and so unrelenting that Barnum's contemporaries soon came to minimize or entirely forgot his contributions to the circus, and a good many people, historians among them, have continued to place their faith in these press agents' fabrications to the present day.

But "business is business," as the showman might have said.

XIV

—◆■◆—

The Sun of the
Amusement World

I awaken each morning with surprise & gratitude to find myself
so vigorous and free from aches & pains at my time of life. But
the closing scene is near, and it is *all right*. Our last hours will
be all the more pleasant if, with all our faults, we can feel assured that the world is better & happier for our having lived
in it.

Barnum to John J. Nathans, 20 July 1888

BARNUM WAS preoccupied with elephants in early 1882. Well before Jumbo and
baby Bridgeport made their debuts, he had become intrigued by the possibility
of unlocking to his patrons an even rarer "trunk"—a genuine example of the
"sacred" white elephant, which had never before been exhibited in the West.
To this end he had already written to the king of Siam and sent him a copy
of his autobiography and a photograph of himself; and in early 1882 he further
discussed his plans with the Civil War general John A. Halderman, who in 1880
had been appointed consul at Bangkok and was now about to return there as
the first U.S. minister to Siam. In a cryptic, confidential letter to the general
written after their meeting, Barnum expressed his confidence in the success of
the scheme, adding that "ten thousand dollars is certain for you if you accomplish the work." From England he again wrote to Halderman a few weeks later.
Bailey, who was temporarily with him in Europe, had been briefed on the "whole
affair" and was empowered to make "arrangements," and his junior partner
would like to meet with the general sometime in July.[1]

As Barnum and especially journalists eventually related these events, the
quest for the white elephant was a classic tale of derring-do: of intrigue and
corruption in the highest places, of fabulous sums expended to attain the rare
prize, of poisonings and threats of violence to the circus's faithful agents, who
were sometimes forced to flee from outraged Buddhist mobs and who did indeed suffer one brief period of arrest in Burma. Not surprisingly, too, Halderman
later denied any desire to profit from his position at the Siamese court; while
Barnum himself, one twentieth-century writer has claimed, so mismanaged
things in publicizing the elephant that his partners "put a hypothetical gag on
him" and decreed that in future "all news pertaining to the circus must em-

anate from the press department"—an edict to which the chagrined showman, we are assured, obediently "bowed."[2] What appears to have really happened is that Barnum, after obtaining Halderman's promise to exert his influence in Siam, first entrusted the mission to a person named DeWitt Clinton Wheeler, who leaked the story to the press and further irritated the showman by failing to get the animal. As a result, Barnum renewed his financial offer to the minister himself, promising him an additional $5000 for each year the elephant was exhibited. Since there was some doubt whether so recherché an animal could ever be purchased outright, he also guaranteed to furnish security for its safe return and "ample evidence" (including an endorsement by Spencer Baird of the Smithsonian Institution) of his and his partners' "responsibility." "It would be a grand idea," he thoughtfully added in a letter to Halderman, "to have some Buddhist priests come with the animal and preach Buddhism, circulate their tracts (printed here), and thus spread their doctrine." All this to reassure the Siamese and their king, whose nation was bound to benefit from his taking one of their "sacred" elephants around the United States in his circus.[3]

By early 1883 another of Barnum's agents, J. B. Gaylord, was in Bangkok. Halderman, who sent Barnum a gift through this envoy and professed his eagerness to serve "you or him as your representative, whenever or wherever I could," repeated to him what he had previously written to Barnum—namely, that "a white elephant could not be obtained here for love or money."[4] Nothing daunted, the persistent Gaylord boldly marched into the Siamese court with his employer's interesting proposition, and for his "blasphemous presumption" was obliged to take himself off to India. Word of the huge sum of money being offered soon spread through the East—according to American newspapers, the showman and his partners were prepared to pay $100,000 and up—tempting a Siamese noble to part with a white elephant he owned. The animal was secretly brought by night marches to the port of Moulmein in Burma, whence Gaylord, who had rounded up some Buddhist priests in the meantime, jubilantly announced he was preparing to sail on 13 May.[5] A few days later in Singapore, however, the white elephant suddenly died, presumably poisoned by fanatical Buddhists who may have been sent there by the outraged Siamese king. "Bring skin, tusks, and bones enough to stuff," Barnum promptly cabled his discouraged agent.[6]

Early in the following autumn Gaylord expressed confidence he could secure another specimen—this time from Burma, whose King Theebau and court officials were not opposed to making money—and on 24 November cabled he had finally succeeded. Again, Americans were soon agog over the astronomical sum the animal was supposed to have cost. Two hundred thousand dollars in gold was generally bruited in the newspapers, although Barnum's chief accountant, Bowser, entered a more realistic figure in the office diary that day. Together with its "royal documents," Toung Taloung—for that was this famous elephant's name—had cost the circus all of $6000. The show was then in winter quarters, so the elephant, protected in a warm building erected on a steamship's deck, was first sent to London's Regent's Park zoo, there to occupy Jumbo's old quarters.

White elephants are examples of albinism, of course, though they are hardly so "white" or consistent in color as Barnum and the public had been led to expect. Consequently, the reception of Toung Taloung at the zoo was an ominous disappointment; and the situation showed signs of deteriorating further when the Siamese minister in London perversely declared that the existence of "sacred" elephants, white or black, was unknown in his country. To this the showman indignantly replied, citing the obvious annoyance of the Siamese court at his finally obtaining a specimen in neighboring Burma, and offering to pay $100,000 for any two elephants his agent might select from those belonging to the Siamese king—an offer that should prove irresistible if, as was claimed, there were no such things as "sacred" elephants in Siam.

> I expect my sacred white elephant will be pronounced jet black, and profane, before he reaches New York, and perhaps it will be proved that I have not got and never had an elephant of any kind in the London Zoological Gardens; that the whole thing is a myth—a dream (and it almost seems like a dream to me); but if no accident occurs before May next it will prove as it did with Jumbo—that my elephant is even more extraordinary than represented, and as to the tact and cunning which my agent used in quieting the conscience (!) and replenishing the treasury of its royal owner, "thereby hangs a tale"—as well as a trunk.[7]

Despite the showman's attempts to drum up enthusiasm, the elephant's reception in America proved disappointing also. As scientists and those familiar with the East repeatedly acknowledged, Toung Taloung was indeed a genuine example of the sacred white elephant, and a number of these individuals declared it to be the best example they had ever seen. Its light-colored hide, eyes and nails, its pinkish trunk and patches of similar coloration elsewhere on its body, all proclaimed it to be what it was represented to be. But this was hardly enough for "the masses"—or "them asses," as Barnum deliberately reconstructed the words in a letter he wrote to Halderman—who would be satisfied with "nothing short of a *snow-white* elephant *all over*, and therefore don't think much of mine." In his continuing determination to prove how good his specimen was, he had earlier asked the minister for details of those belonging to the Siamese king; and in the summer of 1884 Halderman had forwarded to him a report by one Captain Richelieu, who held a commission in the Siamese navy. Richelieu, who was familiar with the white elephants belonging to the king and appears to have been an expert on the subject, described in some detail the "signs" (among them the "organ of generation") by which such animals were known, and further pointed out how they were graded into three "classes." Upon receiving this information, Barnum jubilantly announced his elephant filled the bill "in every particular" and stood the test "with all intelligent people."[8]

To further stir up interest among the public, the showman—taking a leaf from his tour with Jenny Lind—offered a prize of $500 for the best poem commemorating Toung Taloung. Barnum's minister friend Robert Collyer had the unenviable task of presiding over the jury that was to select the winner. After narrowing the over one thousand submissions down to three (one of them by the "western" poet Joaquin Miller), the jurors conveyed to Barnum their opinion that none of them was worth $500 and left the final decision to him.[9] The showman divided the money among the finalists; offered to purchase at least one other "funny" poem he wished to set "afloat" in newspapers and elsewhere; and seems to have wished to commit the circus to some further expense in keeping up the "excitement," since a few weeks later Bailey and Hutchinson telegraphed him from Boston that they had had enough of the "poem business" and "therefore decline positively to pay another dollar in any manner."[10] As in the case of the earlier "prize ode" contest, too, there were any number of parodies. Some of the best appeared in the *New York Times*, which pretended to set before its readers the submissions by Swinburne, Tennyson, Whittier, and Whitman. That by "Swinburne" went as follows:

> From the purple and passion of rivers
>> Filled full with bright panthers and priests;
> From jungles where juniper quivers
>> With longings for fish and for feasts;
> With the sound and the shudder of tresses,
>> With the silence and shimmer of song;
> Thou art come to our clasp and caresses,
>> Our Toung Talong.

"Tennyson's" entry opened with the poignant lamentation

> I could not trumpet; thick my voice with sighs,
>> As in a dream. Dimly I then descried
> The sad Shakesperean clowns with weary eyes,
>> Waiting to see me dyed.

"Whitman's" poem, beginning with an almost endless enumeration of land measurements around Madison Square Garden, was said to have inspired an "eminent real estate lawyer" to telegraph the poet, "I greet you at the beginning of a grand career."[11]

It was all great fun for the showman, of course, who by the summer of 1884 was as resigned to his elephant's lack of "whiteness" as were most of his disappointed patrons. What he did not find amusing around this time, however, was a trick his arch-rival Adam Forepaugh, now that their two-year truce was ended, decided to play on him. Like everyone else, "4 Paws" had been eagerly following Barnum's attempts to secure a white elephant. The news that he had finally succeeded was barely out when the Philadelphia showman announced that his circus would also feature a sacred white elephant during the 1884 season. Toward the end of March, only a few days before Toung Taloung arrived in New York, Forepaugh's "Light of Asia" landed from Liverpool. Unlike Barnum's animal, this elephant really was "white"—almost to the complexion of driven snow! Barnum and his partners, understandably vexed by this blatant attempt to steal their thunder, wasted no time in exposing the hoax: the "Light of Asia" had been whitewashed in Liverpool, and they soon had affi-

arnum and his partner James A. Bailey.

...rnum in his phaeton, drawn by "Bucephalus." A portion of Waldemere is in
...e background.

The Bridgeport winter quarters of "The Greatest Show on Earth." Note the cutouts of animals on the building to the left and the elephants at work in the yard.

INTERIOR VIEW OF THE Elephant CONTAINING THE 22 ELEPHANTS AT OUR Winter Quarters in Bridgeport BUILDING IN WHICH THE BABY ELEPHANT WAS BORN FEB. 2ND 1882. WEIGHT 145 POUNDS. HEIGHT 30 AND LENGTH 36 INCHES. THE FATHER. MOTHER AND BABY A HAPPY ELEPHANT FAMILY. HALF HOUR AFTER THE BIRTH WHEN BABY TOOK ITS FIRST MEAL

A blessed event at winter quarters. "Queen" nursing baby "Bridgeport" in the presence of the proud father.

"The Frog and the Ox." An 1880s poster linking Barnum and his fierce rival Adam Forepaugh with the tale by Aesop.

Scenes from the life of Jumbo. At the center the keeper Matthew Scott strikes a nonchalant pose on the elephant's trunk. The special "palace" railway car in which Jumbo traveled is at lower left.

"Mutual Admiration," a cartoon by Thomas Nast. "You are a *humbug* after my own heart," Barnum says to Jumbo in the caption. "You have even beat me in advertising."

JUMBO AT THE BAR.

JUMBO ÆSTHETIC.

"Jumbo at the Bar" and "Jumbo Aesthetic." Two examples of the many trade cards—in this case advertising a thread company's products—inspired by Jumbo. The first is a comment on the elephant's reputed drinking habits. The second is in reference to Gilbert and Sullivan's *Patience*, which had its premiere the year before Jumbo was purchased by Barnum.

Jumbo with his keeper Matthew Scott. This photograph, taken at the show's Bridgeport winter quarters, gives a good idea of the animal's impressive size. The sticker of the little elephant in the lower left corner, placed there by a prudish librarian, conceals something that may easily be conjectured from the position of Jumbo's tail.

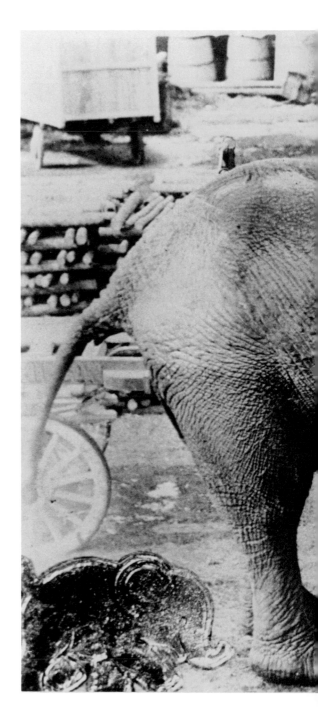

Jumbo dead. The elephant lies on the railroad embankment at St. Thomas, Ontario. Matthew Scott stands near Jumbo's head; the figure at the center appears to be James L. Hutchinson.

The "double Jumbo" on display in the circus's menagerie tent. A rare photograph dating from 1888, the last season this mournful exhibit toured the United States.

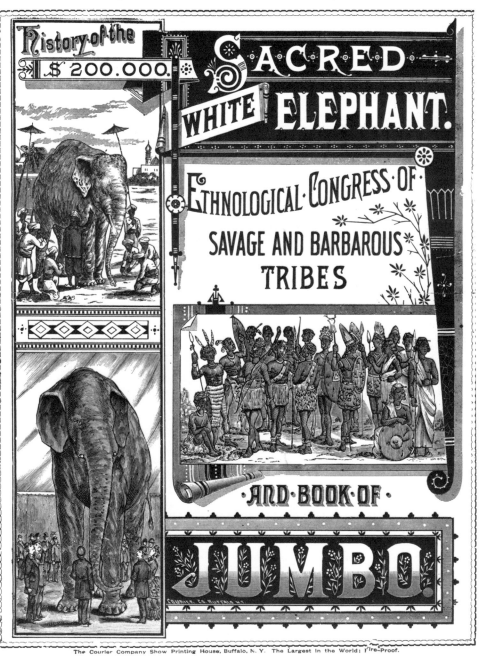

BOSTON, ON COLOSSEUM GROUNDS, FOR A BRIEF SEASON, COMMENCING MONDAY, **JUNE 16**

History of the $200,000. SACRED WHITE ELEPHANT.

ETHNOLOGICAL·CONGRESS·OF· SAVAGE AND BARBAROUS TRIBES

·AND·BOOK·OF· JUMBO.

The Courier Company Show Printing House, Buffalo, N. Y. The Largest in the World; Fire-Proof.

Cover of the 1884 advance "courier" advertising Barnum's circus. The showman's disappointing white elephant and Jumbo are both portrayed, as are some of the "savage" peoples in the grand Ethnological Congress of that season.

Marina, the showman's final Bridgeport home, while it was still under construction. A remnant of Waldemere, not yet entirely demolished, is at the left.

The showman dressed in the height of fashion, as he appeared around the time of his final visit to England.

Barnum and the heir apparent to his show titles, Clinton Hallett ("Barnum") Seeley. Compare the showman's pose in this photograph with that of his statue by Thomas Ball.

Nero, **Imre Kiralfy's great pantomimic spectacle presented as part of the circus's program in 1889 and 1890.**

Barnum in a sunburst. A letterhead, printed in gold, used by the showman and his company in the mid-1880s.

The baronne Nancy Barnum d'Alexandry with her dog "Folette." A photograph of the showman's second wife after she had settled in France.

Barnum on his last visit to London. A colored lithograph after "Spy" (Sir Leslie Ward), published in *Vanity Fair.*

Barnum and the ballet dancer Ernestine de Faiber. The stage box is a photographer's prop, in this case Matthew Brady's.

davits from animal keepers and reporters (one of whom had gotten close enough to test the animal with a wet finger) to prove it.[12] Even in the face of such conclusive evidence, however, "them asses" perversely continued to flock to see Forepaugh's counterfeit animal, driven by much the same kind of curiosity, no doubt, as had once enabled an English menagerie proprietor to triumph over a detested rival. When the single elephant belonging to his establishment unexpectedly died, leaving the field apparently clear for his competitor at a fair, he brazenly advertised he would exhibit the only *dead* elephant.[13]

Forepaugh brazened it out, too, and the warfare between the two circuses lasted the entire 1884 season. When Barnum's show arrived in Philadelphia toward the end of April, another elephant, Tip, ironically renamed the "Light of America," was "bleached out as white as snow" and marched in a street parade headed by the showman himself. "The White Fraud," a banner belligerently proclaimed, "an exact copy of the other whitewashed elephant now being imposed upon the public as a genuine one. A better job by better artists."[14] As late as October, Barnum was still fuming over Forepaugh's treachery. "I hope you will *examine* the coming 'White Elephant' & have your reporters do the same," he wrote to a newspaper friend in Danbury shortly before his rival's circus visited that town. "*Feel* of him, for as true as God reigns, it is exactly as those two Englishmen *who helped paint* him in Liverpool made solemn oath to. He is a common $1500 small India elephant *painted*, & the paint renewed every week or two." If Old Adam and his agents would dare to swear otherwise in a court of justice, where false evidence would subject them to penalties for perjury, he would willingly donate $10,000 to his "native town" of Danbury.[15] At the end of the season Forepaugh announced his white elephant had suddenly "died." But "it was dyed already," Barnum wrote in another letter, "and its only death consisted in rubbing off the white paint and restoring it to its original color!"[16]

———◆———

NOTWITHSTANDING the lack of enthusiasm for the "sacred" white elephant and the increasing severity of Bailey's nervous ailments, which compelled his absence for nearly two months during the season, the show continued to do good business during 1884. For the old showman had finally realized another project he had been maturing for many years, a spectacular procession and series of exhibits illustrating a grand "Congress of Nations"—this time not of proud monarchs and their retinues but rather a kind of "human menagerie," made up of the world's "savage" peoples. In keeping with his plan to feature at least one outstanding novelty each season, he had hoped to have such an exhibition ready in time for 1883. Throughout the preceding summer and fall, Barnum's granddaughter Carrie Hurd and his secretary Bowser laboriously prepared and sent to consular officials and influential persons abroad hundreds of handwritten copies of a circular letter, soliciting their aid in making "a collection, in pairs or otherwise, of all the uncivilized races in existence," together with any interesting examples of freaks or individuals with singular talents they might know about.[17] At the same time Barnum asked his friend Spencer Baird to provide him with an endorsement of his and his partners' "honor" and fiscal responsibility, since some governments, he knew from past experience, were reluctant to permit their natives to be taken abroad unless assurances were given that they would eventually be returned. Baird was somewhat nonplussed by the request—there were "regulations" at the Smithsonian that prevented him from writing such recommendations, he explained—but nonetheless furnished him with an "official" letter testifying to his reputation as a "kind and considerate employer" and praising the proposed exhibition as holding "the highest interest in an anthropological point of view."[18]

Meanwhile, he had dispatched to various parts of the globe J. B. Gaylord, Joel E. Warner, a former mayor of Lansing, Michigan, James R. Davis of Jumbo fame, his brother Thomas H. Davis, and several others with authority to act and negotiate as the show's agents.[19] Their efforts, as in the case of the white elephant, did not always meet with immediate success; but by the following year a good collection of Nubians, "hairy people," Nautch dancing girls, sacred cattle, and a "sacred" white monkey (the last to accompany the white elephant) had been assembled, with Gaylord and the others reporting regularly on their progress. The showman himself occasionally entered into negotiations with persons responding to his circular. He would indeed be interested in engaging some Laplanders, he replied to one correspondent, but did not want any of their reindeer, since experience had proved they "cannot live after their moss is all eaten."[20] By the start of the 1884 season the "Ethnological Congress of Savage Tribes" had finally been completed and was being sensationally described in the circus's courier of that year as consisting of

> Bestial Australian Cannibals; Mysterious Aztecs; Embruited Big-Lipped Botocudoes; Wild Moslem Nubians; Ferocious Zulus; Buddhist Monks; Invincible Afghans; Pagan Burmese Priests; Ishmaelitish Todars; Dusky Idolatrous Hindus; Sinuous Nautch Girls; Annamite Dwarfs; Haughty Syrians; Oriental Giants; Herculean Japanese; Kaffres; Arabs; Persians; Kurds; Ethiopians; Circassians; Polynesians; Tasmanians; Tartars; Patans; Etc.

All this in addition to Jumbo, baby Bridgeport, and the celebrated white elephant, which was similarly hailed as "the Deified Brute of the Benighted Orient."[21] A comparison of this lurid catalogue with the show's 1884 route book leads one to suspect not all these attractions were exactly as represented. But the majority of them undoubtedly were authentic, and they made an overwhelming impression on audiences as, dressed in their native costumes, they were introduced in the course of a grand "Allegoric March" around the hippodrome track. To nineteenth-century American spectators, most of whom had never laid eyes on, if they had even heard of, such "savage" peoples, it was an illustrated lesson in human diversity. The members of the New York Ethnological Society eagerly attended the show while it was in that city, and Baird and others among the nation's scientists were similarly impressed.

Bailey fell ill again early in the 1885 season and was forced to leave the show on 20 May. He was not to fret over or even *think* about the circus for the next six months, Barnum solicitously wrote to his wife a few weeks later, since Hutchinson, Fish, and the various heads of departments were keeping everything "straight" and business was not suffering in his absence. "I have worked hard during my life and sometimes I have overworked my *brain*," he added in an oblique reference to his junior partner's illness. "I found the only sure cure was a season of *brain-rest* and *not thinking*."[22] Privately, he and Hutchinson were themselves worrying over what they would do if Bailey did not recover. When Barnum ran into his old associate Seth B. Howes one day and the latter suggested the wealthy Chicago circus proprietor William W. Cole would make a good replacement, the two partners began giving the matter serious consideration.[23] At the end of the season Bailey voluntarily retired and was succeeded by both Cole and Bailey's old partner, James E. Cooper. The new contract drawn up at this time was essentially the same as the one five years before, except that Barnum's share of the show was now reduced to three-eighths, while Cole owned one-quarter and Hutchinson and Cooper each three-sixteenths.[24] As the showman soon realized, he had made a serious mistake, since his new partners were now in a position to "outvote" him. Hutchinson and he were long familiar with each other's quirks; and Cole, who was known in the profession as "Chilly Billy," proved agreeable enough. But Cooper, who assumed control of the menagerie department, soon began insisting that the circus's dead animals be sold to the highest bidders, which put a serious crimp in Barnum's arrangements for his "pet" museum at Tufts. He was "more *illiberal* than my other two partners," Barnum wrote irritably to the college's president a few months later, and "takes pride in cutting me off from obtaining our dead animals free."[25]

Barnum and his competitors continually boasted of the "millions" of dollars of capital invested in their shows and of the "hundreds of thousands" expended on white elephants and similar exotic attractions. Yet as the total valuation of the circus's "business and property" in this 1885 agreement was set at $200,000, and as the by no means inconsiderable circus of Adam Forepaugh was purchased several years later for a mere $160,000, one may reasonably inquire what their true worth was and how much they actually returned to their owners. Barnum's former partner Coup, in his book *Sawdust & Spangles*, provides some hard figures to puncture such exaggerated claims, illustrating how the average "million-dollar" circus might be got up for as little as $86,000. Of all the circuses on the road in the latter part of the century, he states (and Barnum & Bailey must have been one of them), no more than three had cost more than this figure. Elsewhere he estimates the capital value of the hundreds of tented exhibitions then touring America as ranging from $5000 to $250,000.[26]

Which is not to say that shows like Barnum's were not "million-dollar" affairs in other respects, since the expenses of operating them and their receipts were sometimes enormous, and part of a show's value might be attributable to its proprietor's name and to other intangibles. Barnum himself occasionally trotted out his bookkeepers' figures for reporters to gape over, or blazoned them forth in various editions of his autobiography, though again, as was true for his tour with Jenny Lind, he never revealed his exact share of the profits. During one interview with a reporter for the *New York Sun*, he demonstrated how the show's expenses during 1883 amounted to $1,034,000, or slightly more than $6000 for each of the 170 days it exhibited that season, then proceeded to call the reporter's attention to the receipts on selected days: $14,376 for a single day in Pittsburgh, a total of $80,130 for six days in Philadelphia, $119,172 for ten days in Chicago, etc.[27] Bowser's own incomplete accounts in the office diary would seem to confirm some of these figures. The show's expenses for 1884, he noted at the start of the following year, had totaled $948,253, of which $203,000 had gone for salaries, $49,000 for transportation, $44,000 for the cook tent, and nearly all the rest for printing and engraving, newspaper advertisements, lithographed posters, and the expenses of the agents and others responsible for publicizing the circus.[28] Neither of these accounts mentions the expense of wintering the show or of purchasing animals, costumes, wagons, and other paraphernalia—all of which "putting in order," Barnum seems to indicate in a statement released to the press toward the end of 1882, came to around $225,000 before the commencement of that year's season.[29] The complete accounts of the show now appear lost, but fortunately one invaluable document has survived: a small "private" book made for Bailey by his brother-in-law, Joseph T. McCaddon, who copied into it a table summarizing the show's total receipts, expenses, and "dividends" during each season from 1881 through 1897, together with a daily record of receipts, expenses, and the names of cities the show visited from 1881 until early on in the 1893 season.[30] McCaddon's table summarizing these seasons is reproduced below, with figures rounded off to the nearest dollar or pound.

For 1883, as these figures illustrate, over a relatively brief season of 30 weeks, the show took in $1,419,498 and incurred expenses of $850,159, while the total "dividend" paid to the partners amounted to $560,000. The expenses, it will be noted, do not tally with those given by Barnum in his interview with the *Sun*, but the difference of $183,841 may well represent the costs of wintering the show and other incidental items, including Gaylord's expedition in quest of a white elephant. Presumably, these additional expenses were paid by the partners "on demand"—that is, they were not deducted from the "dividend" or profits from each touring season—though at the end of some years a comparatively small amount of cash was kept in reserve. For the years 1888 through 1894, McCaddon records what appear to have been the actual winter expenses ("Cash in Winter"), which ranged from a low of $55,403 (in 1894) to a high of $180,000 (in 1891). As will be noted in this table, too, the year of Jumbo's arrival in the United States (1882, a season of 31 weeks) produced the largest dividend ever for Barnum and his partners, although total receipts were somewhat greater in the following season. Receipts for 1884 were barely less than they had been in 1882, but the cost of producing the spectacular "Congress of Savage Tribes" considerably reduced the show's profits this season (33 weeks). Expenses again ate away at profits during the 1888 season; the generally reduced sums in 1889 were occasioned to some extent by preparations to take the show to England, where during a brief winter season of 14 weeks income exceeded costs by some $125,000. From 1892 on the figures speak for themselves. Barnum had died early in the previous season, and Bailey, by then back in circus management, was entirely on his own.

The circus made considerable money during all the years Barnum was associated with it. If one accepts his figure (exaggerated, if anything) of $225,000 for expenses before the 1882 season commenced, and deducts this from the dividend paid that year, his own half-share of profits still came to $188,500; while even during the unspectacular season of 1889, his share, after winter expenses, amounted to a respectable $49,000. To again set these figures in some kind of perspective: in 1884 the annual salary of Barnum's chief accountant, Bowser, was $2500; a good middle-class home in Bridgeport could be purchased for a little over $4000; while farmland in neighboring Easton was selling for $100 an acre. Nearly all of Barnum's partners retired and died wealthy men.

From his opulent mansion on New York's upper west side, Bailey must have wistfully followed the show's progress during the 1886 and 1887 seasons, while Barnum continued to chafe under the "illiberality" and rule of his junior partners. Little Bridgeport died at winter quarters on 12 April 1886, was stuffed by Ward, and was temporarily deposited in the Tufts museum.[31] Later that month the show played a combined engagement with Forepaugh's circus in Philadelphia—an experiment that was repeated the following year during the

McCaddon's Tabulation of the Show's Finances for the
1881 through 1897 Seasons

Season	Cash in Winter	Total Receipts	Expenses	Dividend
1881		$1,166,391	$740,758	$410,000
1882		1,333,788	730,854	602,000
1883		1,419,498	850,159	560,000
1884		1,226,081	948,253	277,000
1885		960,382	648,530	311,562
1886		932,904	639,788	293,116
1887		999,746	720,810	272,750
1888	$ 90,000	1,034,219	800,392	200,000
1889	92,000	891,653	658,231	190,000
London		£ 134,932	£110,010	
1890	130,000	1,257,351	790,603	425,000
1891	180,000	1,216,433	851,843	364,590
1892	120,000	1,188,089	932,917	250,000
1893	85,000	924,436	801,378	126,558
1894	55,403	884,618	690,866	192,782
1895		975,269	803,447	125,307
1896				112,479
1897		791,000	728,105	62,894

show's prestigious opening stand at Madison Square Garden, which could not have been entirely to Barnum's liking. There were unaccustomed labor troubles as well. In August 1886 some kind of mutiny broke out in Oshkosh, Wisconsin, and was only quelled when Hutchinson waded in and summarily fired several employees. During the 1887 season the circus confined its travels to the East and for a time, at least, seems to have been reduced to exhibiting in two rings.[32]

It was with an unmitigated feeling of relief, therefore, that Barnum viewed the departure of his three partners at the end of the 1887 season and the return of the efficient, dependable James A. Bailey. From their renewed association dates the true beginning of the great concern known as "Barnum & Bailey," an equal co-partnership that, their agreement optimistically declared, was to continue for the next fifty years. The terms contained in this document are similar to those Barnum executed in earlier contracts—only now, for the first time, he unreservedly granted the show company the sole and exclusive use of his name in "all" public exhibitions. Bailey, who was to share profits and expenses equally with Barnum, paid for his interest in the show $150,000, "which sum is the estimated value of one half of the property and rights contributed by the said Barnum."[33]

Oddly enough, just as the untimely death of Jumbo had threatened to interfere with his retirement in 1885, Bailey had barely returned when another disaster struck the show. On the evening of 20 November a fierce fire broke out in the main building at winter quarters, and before it was over, with the exception of most of the elephants and a single lion (later shot after it escaped into a neighbor's barn, however), nearly all the animals were said to have been "burned to a crisp." The white elephant, Barnum complacently noted in his autobiography, refused to leave the building and "determinedly committed suicide," while a large portrait of himself, painted on the building's exterior, picturesquely glowed for several minutes in "an unbroken frame of flame" before it, too, was finally consumed. Jumbo's "widow," Alice, and a large elephant belonging to Cole also perished in the blaze, and a fourth elephant named Gracie very sensibly ran off to Long Island Sound, but died from exposure the following day. The big cats in particular were so badly burned that even their bones "crumbled at the touch," reported Professor John Marshall of Tufts, who hurried down to Bridgeport in the futile hope of getting a few more specimens for the college museum. Yale's Professor Othniel C. Marsh and his students were also soon on the scene, valiantly attempting to salvage the skeleton of a hippopotamus by hacking their way through fried muscle and fat. Valuable chariots and other equipment stored in the building were totally destroyed. The cause of the fire was never determined—there had been attempts at arson in previous years—and as usual, insurance covered only a fraction of the loss.[34]

The showman was in New York at the time. Upon his wife's waking him to tell him the news, he took it with his usual composure, rolled over in bed, and was soon fast asleep again. A few days later he found Bailey studying a pile of telegrams and letters from animal dealers. When he inquired what he was doing, his partner coolly replied he was "ordering a menagerie." And within six hours he had done just that, assembling a finer one than the show had lost. The winter quarters, under Brothwell's supervision, were themselves speedily rebuilt, expanded, and greatly improved. Bailey soon had everything running smoothly again; and from this time forward the old showman, who was now approaching his seventy-eighth birthday, was content to give his young partner greater leeway to operate on his own, although he continued to exercise his judgment on major matters and, like that spectator at a game of checkers, to offer frequent words of friendly "advice."

———◆———

THE UNIVERSALIST minister Abel C. Thomas, one of the closest, dearest friends Barnum ever had, died at his home outside Philadelphia in September 1880, and was followed a few months later by the showman's pun-loving "Siamese Twin," the Reverend Dr. Edwin H. Chapin. Tom Thumb, grown stout and nervous, dropped dead in his Middleboro home in July 1883; and four years later, on the same day Bailey first returned to Bridgeport as Barnum's sole partner, word was flashed to the city that the Swedish Nightingale had gone to meet her stern, untheatrical-minded maker. Friends and old acquaintances began falling like autumn leaves, yet the showman's own health—despite occasional "stomach" complaints and his increasing inability to tolerate Bridgeport's summer heat—remained amazingly robust. The same could hardly be said of his "young English bride" Nancy, who by now had determinedly entered upon her career as an "interesting" semi-invalid. "She has her ups & downs, the latter being twice as numerous as the former," Barnum wrote somewhat disconcertingly to a friend in 1886, though he hastened to add "she really suffers much."[35] Nancy's seasonal progresses between Waldemere and the metropolis, between winter and summer resorts, interrupted by frequent ocean crossings to visit her family and friends in England, now included increasingly long stopovers in fashionable New York sanitariums, which left her doting husband feeling bored and lonely.

There could be no question of Nancy's looking after a complicated household or accompanying her husband on all his own expeditions, and in the mid-eighties she persuaded a young unmarried cousin, Sarah J. Fish, to assume these functions. "Miss Fish," who was paid a salary as Waldemere's housekeeper, often figures as Barnum's companion around this time, as in June 1886 when, out of concern for his wife's health, he was again about to decline an invitation to attend commencement exercises at his beloved Tufts College. But "Mrs. Barnum, although weak & sick herself," as he wrote to John Marshall, curator of the museum there, "says if I excuse myself on account of 'old age,' I shall never be younger, & that she thinks I ought to go." Besides, he added wistfully, "I *want* to be present on commencement day, as I never attended a 'commencement' of any college."[36] Accordingly, on 15 June he and Nancy's cousin settled in at Boston's Hotel Vendome, and the next few days were spent in joyous reunions with friends, attending a celebration at Bunker Hill, and traveling about to view the city's sights. The highlight of the trip occurred on the 16th, when the showman not only finally made it to commencement but also spoke glowingly about Tufts at the college dinner, after receiving a tumultuous welcome from the students. As the latter cheered and set up a thunderous ovation upon his entering the hall, their benefactor hid his face behind his hands in "pretended shyness." The college's glee club further honored him by singing "The Barnum Song," whose verses humorously tell how the school's president, in order to build a fine "mews-yum," relieved the showman of some of his "tin." On the same day Tufts conferred on Barnum's once demented Bridgeport pastor, the Reverend John Lyon, who was himself to die a little over a year later, the degree of A.M. Needless to say, the showman was immensely gratified by all these proceedings and took care to see they were properly reported.[37]

His solicitude for his young wife extended to what she would do when he, too, was gone; and in early 1888, to the astonishment of nearly everyone, he announced he was putting most of his estate of Waldemere on the market. So many people wished to live next to Seaside Park, he explained, that it seemed "unreasonably selfish" to continue to hold on to his more than twenty acres. Besides, his rambling mansion was much too large for him and his wife, and he had decided to build a smaller, more modern home—an "ideal" house in which Nancy could comfortably continue to live after he was gone, incorporating everything she might like to see in such an establishment. By April, Bowser and Brothwell were busy staking out streets through Waldemere's grounds, while "Marina," as the new house of brick and stone was called, took shape only a few feet east of the old mansion. The showman and his wife remained in Bridgeport during the early part of the following winter, and on 10 January 1889 held a leavetaking for nine hundred guests at Waldemere. Almost predictably, the new house caught fire while it was still under construction. Fortunately, the blaze was quickly brought under control, and Barnum immediately ordered his secretary to insure "Mrs. Nancy Barnum's new house" for $15,000. On 4 February workers arrived to begin pulling down Waldemere. By then the rest of the estate had been laid out in "villas," although Marina itself was hardly devoid of attractive grounds. Between the house and Seaside Park was a large grassy oval, which Barnum deeded to the public on the condition nothing be planted on it that would obstruct his wife's view. When the mansion was completed and everything to Nancy's liking, he gallantly presented her with the deed.[38]

By the mid-1880s, too, although Nancy was still in her thirties, he had given up hope of having any children by her. His grandchildren, for whom he generously provided, were already starting families of their own, and he consoled himself by playing with their offspring. Helen Hurd, who married Frank W. Rennell in June 1883, produced several fine "baby double-grands" over the next few years, the first of whom, Henry—or "P. T. Rennell," as Barnum sometimes playfully addressed him—was a particular favorite with the showman.[39] But the matter of a suitable male successor demanded a more immediate solution; and here, almost perforce, the choice fell on his deceased daughter Pauline's older son, who had been born Clinton Hallett Seeley in 1867. "Clinte," as his grandfather called him and usually spelled the name, appears to have been an affable but rather unambitious young man, who nonetheless held a seat on the New York stock exchange and dabbled in Bridgeport real estate. His chief interest around this time was yachting, however, often in company with his good friend Wilson Marshall, who later married Clinton's sister Jessie. Bowser, who noted in the office diary as early as February 1887 that Clinte seemed destined "to go with the show," seems to have felt some sympathy for the callow youth; but Bailey obviously looked upon him as a potential nuisance and a threat to his authority. In early 1889, after Clinte had been persuaded to change his middle name to "Barnum," his grandfather attempted to reassure both men. It was to everyone's advantage that he have a successor named "Barnum" who would also look after his estate's interest in the show, and Clinte, he pointed out rather ambiguously, was the "best" representative he could find. "He thinks everything of you and your management," he wrote to Bailey, adding that while he himself lived, his grandson would have *nothing to say.*"[40] To Bowser he confided that Clinte had "felt modest & half frightened about taking my name, lest some of my progeny should be jealous. But they need not be, though I think him more capable than any & all of them of doing business properly, and I hope he will by & bye quit the brokers' board & attend to his own building & get posted as much as he can about the show business & my real estate."[41]

For a single season Clinte did indeed travel with the circus and "work"—rather desultorily, it later came out—at selling tickets, occasionally glancing over the payroll, and other odd jobs. He later claimed to have also served a few months as his grandfather's "sort of confidential secretary." But C. Barnum Seeley's career as a showman was mercifully brief. In a heated argument with his senior partner, Bailey refused absolutely to have him continue on the show; and Barnum, according to his treasurer and executor, Benjamin Fish, was himself eventually moved to declare that Clinte was "not a businessman and never will be." These revelations came to light some months following the showman's death, when Seeley, who had been left 3 percent of the show's annual profits on condition he travel with and render it appropriate services, brought suit against his aunt Caroline Thompson and the estate's executors because they had refused such services, thereby denying him the special legacy to which he felt entitled. In their defense the executors replied they would "never have dreamed of considering him a competent or proper person for the position." And besides, Bailey, who had a perfect right to dispense with any representative not to his liking, had several times voiced his adamant opposition to Seeley and had even declared he would break up the concern rather than have him forced upon him.[42]

C. Barnum Seeley was to cause his relatives further distress when he later instituted other actions bearing on his grandfather's estate.[43] And in 1896 he was at the center of an affair that scandalized quite a few people when his scapegrace younger brother, Herbert Barnum Seeley, threw a bachelor party for him at Sherry's restaurant in New York. The principal entertainment at this soirée was the celebrated dancer "Little Egypt," who reputedly performed her peculiar gyrations, while nearly nude, on a tabletop. The "notorious" or "awful Seeley dinner," as the event came to be blazoned in the press, would cause barely a ripple in today's jaded society, while the archaic costume exposing the dancer's "nudity" would probably elicit nothing more than a hearty guffaw. In their day, however, they were thought "awful" enough, providing preachers and other watchdogs of public morality a splendid opportunity to thunder against the degeneracy of the upper class, and an excuse for at least one muckraking journalist—Julian Sterling, again—to speculate on the "hereditary influence" that was obviously at work. If C. Barnum Seeley was the "best" representative the showman could find among his descendants to carry on his name, what must the "worst," or even middling ones, be like![44]

But all this was still some years in the future, and for the moment the showman was as active as ever. He was determined to "wear out" rather than "rust out," he repeatedly informed friends in the eighties, despite persistent rumors that he had already done both. "My impression is that I am not dead," he dryly replied to an Iowa correspondent who had politely written to him about one such rumor.[45] Bailey himself, while traveling abroad during the summer of 1884, became alarmed upon reading a similar tale in the Paris newspapers and cabled Hutchinson to ask if Barnum really was dead.[46] Two years later, when another of these stories began making the rounds, the showman gave his personal assurance that there was "not a word of truth in it."[47] His interest in and enthusiasm for his favorite city remained undiminished. He faithfully attended meetings of the Bridgeport Hydraulic Company, Pequonnock Bank, Parks Commission, and local horse-railway company—on all of whose boards he served as a director—and in November 1883 was elected the first president of the Bridgeport and Port Jefferson Steamboat Company, whose ferries still ply the waters between Bridgeport and Long Island. In Port Jefferson itself, where an avenue is named after him, he bought and partially developed some twenty-two acres of land, but later anxiously ordered his secretary to sell out after becoming convinced he was being "swindled" by contractors.[48] Local legend has it that in the late 1870s he contemplated establishing his circus's winter quarters in the same town; more likely, this rumor dates from the period following the burning of the Bridgeport winter quarters, when some kind of "proposal," possibly at Bailey's instigation, was indeed made to rebuild elsewhere. On 23 November 1887 a petition signed by over one hundred prominent Bridgeport citizens and businessmen was addressed to Barnum and his partner, urging that they not entertain such a move in view of the "great injury" to the city that would inevitably result.[49] It seems inconceivable Barnum himself would have seriously considered such a plan. Instead, the following year he proudly trotted out a dozen of the circus's elephants to "test" a new bridge spanning the Pequonnock River (he had earlier sold to the city the bridges he and Noble constructed while they were developing East Bridgeport), posing bareheaded for photographers in the chill December weather so as to be easily distinguishable in the crowd of pachyderms and politicians.[50] His charitable works around the city also continued unabated. At Mountain Grove Cemetery, where he now ordered Brothwell to install a secure vault to receive Charity's and his remains, he donated a large number of additional plots for use by the city's poor, insisting that they be democratically scattered among the grave sites of more affluent citizens, since he did not believe in "potter's fields."[51]

Surprisingly, in his seventy-eighth year he was again tempted into thinking of running for national office—this time for nothing less than the Presidency. Four years earlier he had intemperately spoken out against the Democratic candidate, Grover Cleveland, who was widely believed to harbor pro-Southern sentiments and was known to oppose the country's protective tariff policies. To the horror of his circus associates, in a blistering letter identifying its author as proprietor of "The Greatest Show on Earth," he had written to the *New York Tribune* on the eve of the election to "pledge" he would sell all his Bridgeport property for one-quarter less than its appraised value if the Democrats succeeded in electing their nominee. "Every taxpayer and every workingman and woman will see business permanently palsied if the South gets into the saddle," he wrote. "It will establish free trade, get pay for its slaves, and obtain pensions for all rebel soldiers."[52] But Cleveland won all the same, and Barnum, in place of selling his Bridgeport real estate, invited the President and his family to the circus.[53]

He was no less belligerent during the 1888 campaign, again railing against the dangers of free trade and incidentally offering a lame excuse for not having kept his earlier "pledge" (for a time after his election, Cleveland's "fair promises" had maintained public confidence, and consequently real-estate values had not been depressed).[54] A few months before their own candidate was selected, a number of Republicans had given serious thought to running Barnum as their nominee. And in truth he might easily have been a third-party candidate in the 1888 election, since his many friends in the temperance movement actually offered to run him on a Prohibition ticket. He had promptly declined the honor, however, arguing, as he had during previous elections, that the formation of such a party would be a "suicidal act." Most good temperance men, he pointed out, were already Republicans; and if these were to cast their votes for a Prohibition ticket, the result would be to split the party of Lincoln and play directly into the hands of the liquor-loving Democrats. Still, as he coyly remarked in an interview published in the *New York Times*, if his *Republican* friends wished to nominate him, that would be a "different consideration." He had even given some thought to who his Vice-Presidential running mate might be—someone from Illinois or Indiana, he hinted.[55] But the invitation never came, and Benjamin Harrison, whom the showman congratulated and at the same time "sympathized" with, went on to defeat the beer-drinking Cleveland.[56] It was the old showman's final bid for public office, denied him, as always, whenever he attempted to reach beyond his Bridgeport friends and neighbors.

———◆———

IN MARCH 1889, as was customary by now, the show opened at Madison Square Garden following an evening torchlight parade. Among the "museum" or sideshow attractions this year were Barnum's old protégé Admiral Dot and Dr. Frank Hoffman's puzzling "Black Tent," which featured a number of fetching young ladies in such illusions as a disembodied head and a smiling, breathing mermaid of "prepossessing appearance," whose torso and tail protruded teasingly from a vase. Barnum and Nancy remained at the Murray Hill Hotel until well after the show had ended its stands in New York and Brooklyn, then, in mid-May, moved into Marina, which was finally ready to receive them. The following month the showman rejoined the circus in Boston and Providence, taking the opportunity to revisit Tufts College and look up old friends along the route. Thomas Ball, whose statue of the showman had been examined by Barnum and his family earlier in the year, paid a visit to Bridgeport on the same day the circus played there and was taken on a whirlwind behind-the-scenes tour. Upon entering the big top he was startled when his host gripped him firmly by the arm and, instead of conducting him to a seat, dragged him around the hippodrome track, while the audience lustily cheered and applauded their celebrated townsman. Midway through the performance a thunderstorm blew up and the tent began to leak. The spectators stoically raised a forest of unbrellas over their heads—which did not prevent Ball and the showman, who occupied front seats, from being liberally spattered with mud each time the horses and chariots in the races rushed by.[57]

Late summer found the Barnums once more enjoying the coolness and "pinery" at Paul Smith's in the Adirondacks, where the showman nonetheless fretted over a recent accident that had cost the circus several railway cars and close to forty animals. What if they "should somehow kill 50 persons instead of 30 horses," he anxiously wrote to Bailey, and find themselves personally liable for a quarter-million dollars in damages? In his opinion they ought to make the show into a private stock company, the value of whose assets would be the maximum they would have to pay in any such mishap.[58] Toward the end of September the Reverend Robert Collyer paid a visit to Marina and preached in Bridgeport's Universalist Church. Earlier in the summer, accompanied by his daughter Caroline, the showman made another nostalgic, highly publicized tour of Bethel and its environs. Nearly the entire population turned out to greet him again; and in October appreciative Bridgeporters followed suit by throwing a reception for him at the city's exclusive Seaside Club.

If there was a certain valedictory air in much of this, it was not because he felt himself to be in failing health. Rather, he was about to embark on a new adventure he had been dreaming of since the mid-seventies—namely, taking his "Greatest Show on Earth" to perform before English audiences—and at times worried he or the show might not safely make it back. The arrangements for transporting the colossal enterprise across the Atlantic occupied much of his and especially Bailey's time during the summer of 1889. On 12 October, four days after the reception given him in Bridgeport, Barnum, Nancy, and Clinton Barnum Seeley sailed for England aboard the *Etruria*. The show's artists, employees, horses, menagerie, and paraphernalia all followed a few days later and arrived without incident at London's great exhibition hall, Olympia, where they performed for three months beginning 11 November. Although the showman boasted in advance that he would not be particularly disturbed if he lost half a million dollars in his determination "to show our Mother Country what her daughter America could do in the way of novel and instructive amusement," and although many of the hall's 12,000 seats were priced as low as one and two shillings (25 and 50 cents), business remained profitable and so brisk during the entire period that would-be patrons were often turned away.

The entertainment, even by American standards, was indeed overwhelming. If reporters for the English press had ever seen or heard of their compatriot George Sanger's reputed three-ring circus, they gave no indication of it in their reviews, nearly all of which remarked on the "indigestion" one was likely to suffer while attempting to keep up with the simultaneous action in Barnum's three rings—a concept so bewildering to English audiences that it almost *compelled* them to return again and again. Still, as the critic for the "Thunderer" itself was forced to concede, there could be no denying the impressiveness such multiplication of effects lent to the spectacle as a whole: "The surpassing greatness of the show is no vain boast." Twice daily, too, patrons were given the opportunity to view what was undoubtedly the greatest curiosity of all, when at the conclusion of the opening parade the action throughout the great hall suddenly ceased, an open carriage with liveried footman and coachman entered the arena, and the white-haired showman, dressed in his "best Prince Albert," made his own stately progress before the spectators. The men in the audience, Barnum later crowed to an American reporter, respectfully removed their hats as though he were royalty, while the ladies gaily waved their hand-kerchiefs at him. The Princess of Wales, who was present during one of these exhibitions, afterwards said to him, "I'm so glad I came in time to see you drive around." If any irony was intended by the remark, the delighted show-man preferred not to notice.[59]

Aside from the kaleidoscopic circus performance, the traditional races round the hippodrome track, the menagerie and "museum" with its own collection of freaks and interesting oddities—not to mention the slightly mournful pres-ence of the "double Jumbo" himself, whom Barnum, true to his earlier prom-ise, had finally brought back to England—there was an entirely new addition to the program with which even American audiences were not yet acquainted. This was a magnificent concluding "ballet" or pantomime by the noted pro-ducer and director Imre Kiralfy, whose reputation for breathtaking, histori-cally based spectacles easily equaled that of Cecil B. De Mille in a later day and medium. *Nero; or, The Destruction of Rome*, with scenery and costumes built in Europe and music by the Milanese composer Angelo Venanzi, was per-formed on a huge stage at one side of the hall and involved over a thousand actors, dancers, and supernumeraries in addition to a fair number of the show's animals. The mimed action, accompanied by an orchestra and a great choir that sang several hymns and odes, illustrated the usual clash between pagans and Christians; and the depraved emperor himself, who was depicted lusting after a fair representative of the latter, came off no better than he has since the day Suetonius and Tacitus composed their fables. All such slender plotting was subservient to the real objective of the production, however: the spectacular staging of a gorgeous triumphal procession of Nero into Rome; gladiatorial combats and races between horse-drawn chariots, camels, and elephants, respectively, in the "circus"; and an orgiastic feast and "grand festal dance" in the palace of the emperor, who exulted while his innocent victims were being tortured and Rome burned in the background. At the conclusion, while Nero lay dying and the victorious Galba marched into the city, there was a "Glorious Apotheosis" and "Celestial Vision of the Dawn of Christianity." The great spectacle absolutely beggared anything ever seen on London stages, and as one reviewer rapturously described it to his readers,

> Imagine a line of stage about half a mile long, backed by a vista of lordly palaces and temples, and of blue sea and sky; people it with five hundred ballet girls, massed in a triple line, and as many men in splendid classic garb. Get this thousand of gorgeously clad figures in motion under the rays of limelight; break this sea of brilliant colour into waves of blue and gold, and scarlet and white, and every harmonious tint you can conceive; let their motion be as regular and brisk as the rhythm of a lively dance tune, and the ripple of movement agitate the vast crowd as a slow summer wind stirs the ears of corn in a wheatfield. Then yon ballet on the Titanic scale of Barnum's show. . . . A gladiatorial combat is shown—we have not a dozen or a score of brawny combatants, but a hundred—and the stage is presently strewn with enough corpses to keep all the coroners in England busy for a month. A procession is desirable—straightway files on a column longer than a Lord Mayor's Show, and many times more splendid, legionaries in golden armour, vestal virgins in draperies of snowy white, bearded senators in voluminous togas, fair-haired barbarians from the north and swarthy Nubians from the south, priests, dancing girls, allegorical tableaux, elephants in gorgeous trappings, camels freighted with cargoes of youth and beauty, all manner of men, and beasts, and gods, and devils of the period. There is about the spectacle a healthy local flavour of barbarism. Our stage managers in England descend to calculation of ways and means, and of the capacity of their stages and audiences. Barnum does not. He has one idea—the show, the whole show, and nothing but the show. The audience does not matter, nor the stage, nor the expense. He piles on crowds on crowds, throws in a dozen of elephants here, a hundred ballet girls there, with a splendid audacity worthy of Nero himself.[60]

The applause and ringing cheers that rewarded this massive spectacle, another critic remarked, were proof that "The Greatest Show on Earth" had not crossed the Atlantic in vain.

Like Nero, too, the old showman was himself fêted and treated almost like visiting royalty during his several months' stay in England. The Prince and Princess of Wales, the great minister Gladstone and his wife, the king of Greece, and a large portion of the British aristocracy patronized the show, made a point of shaking his hand, invited him into their boxes, and amiably chatted with him. The Queen herself, who was then on the Isle of Wight, indicated she wished to attend sometime early in the following year, but the circus could not wait upon her return. If she did not hurry up to London, Barnum informed Lady Churchill, "I shall be sorry for her, as she'll never see such another show." Even before the opening at Olympia, a welcoming banquet, presided over by the Earl of Kilmorey, had been given him at the Hotel Victoria. The distinguished committee charged with organizing the evening included the Earls of Rosebery, Ilchester, and Aberdeen, Lord Randolph Churchill, Alfred and Leopold de Rothschild, Richard D'Oyly Carte of Gilbert and Sullivan fame, Jenny Lind's husband Otto Goldschmidt, Henry Irving, and Oscar Wilde. Among the many speeches made on this occasion, that by Barnum's old friend George Augustus Sala, who proposed the toast to the showman himself, was particularly felicitous for comparing its subject to Caesar, Alexander the Great, and Napoleon—with the distinction, however, that while their careers were associated with human misery and bloodshed, Barnum had been content to amuse and instruct his subjects. In his response to this salutation, the showman so tickled the celebrants with several of his anecdotes that it was some time before they let him resume his seat.[61] Irving invited him to another of his celebrated midnight suppers; he was a guest at the Lord Mayor of London's annual civic feast; several of the city's more distinguished clubs conferred honorary membership on him.

He was the subject of so many articles, interviews, illustrations, and caricatures in the English press that he ordered his secretaries to purchase multiple copies and paste them into scrapbooks, which he later distributed among his descendants and to institutions like Tufts.[62] Madame Tussaud's modeled him in wax, and he insisted on donating to the museum a complete outfit, down to shoes and stockings, from his personal wardrobe—"everything of Barnum but Barnum," he joked—so that his effigy might be properly clothed. Sometime during this visit, too—possibly as early as Irving's supper party on the night of 9 December, but more likely somewhat later—he registered on a wax cylinder the only known recording of his voice, in which he expressed his "parting thanks to the British public" and the prophetic hope "that my voice, like my great show, will reach future generations and be heard centuries after I have joined the great and, as I believe, happy majority."[63]

Like Jenny Lind some forty years before, he found himself deluged with requests for money from begging individuals and charities, offers to sell him curious articles, and invitations to social functions both in and outside London. He was unable to accept even a tenth of these last, he explained to those he was forced to disappoint, but did find time to lecture occasionally for the benefit of charities, as on behalf of an Irish fund at Lord Aberdeen's Grosvenor Square mansion on 30 January, when he regaled an audience, at half a guinea a head, with his rich store of anecdotes. His aristocratic listeners, whom he familiarly addressed as "boys and girls," roared with laughter as he told anew the story of the "dog with two tails," which some of them must have already known from his autobiography. They roared again—and he laughed with them—as he described his adventures with Tom Thumb and their meetings with the Queen.[64] It was a far cry from the day his autobiography had first appeared and he had been pilloried in Britain as the great Yankee "humbug," a shameless hypocrite whose "moral obliquity" was apparent to everyone but himself. Now he was likened to the legendary King Cole, "a jolly old soul," termed a "gentleman" and an "American grand old man," and hailed as the "beneficent" or "genial showman." The hospitality everywhere extended to himself, his wife, and grandson, he wrote to a friend, exceeded all his expectations, "especially from the class of dignitaries who do it." He added that he "never allowed any person to patronize me—neither did my wife ever permit it to her, she says—but it has not been attempted here in a single instance. We all meet as friends & on *equal* ground, & much pleasure is thereby mutually enjoyed."[65]

The anecdotal talks he gave in London and elsewhere around this time had their own ulterior purpose, of course. He was refining and "rehearsing" a new book for press, in which he resurrected several of the original tales omitted from later editions of his autobiography, added many new ones, and carried his history down to the end of his present London visit. Published simultaneously in England and America in 1890, *Funny Stories Told by Phineas T. Barnum*, unlike many other works purportedly by him during this period, was entirely Barnum's own, as is evidenced not only by its characteristic style throughout but also by an extant "memorandum" book filled with his notes and rough drafts for the stories it contains.[66] While still in London, too, he was persuaded by friends to allow publication of his essay "Why I Am a Universalist" in a forthcoming issue of the *Christian World*, thereby firing the opening salvo in what was to be his final battle against the forces of religious "orthodoxy."[67] The *North American Review*, which had requested his ideas on the forthcoming Columbian Exposition, also published a communication from him in early 1890, although in this case it would appear he turned over the actual writing to someone else. But the views advanced in it have the true Barnum ring: the coming world's fair should be held in no place other than New York City; and among its novel features might be the recently discovered mummy of Ramses II, the pharoah of Moses and the book of Exodus, so that visitors might gaze on the perfectly preserved features of the despot who so influenced the world's history, and who lived nearly three thousand years before America was even discovered.[68]

Nancy was ill again—first with the flu, then with assorted other ailments—forcing him to postpone his return to the States until several weeks after the show had departed. At the final performance on 15 February, however, she managed to leave her bed long enough to sit with Lord Chief Justice Coleridge and a host of other distinguished guests in her husband's box at Olympia. Four days later, after the animals had been safely loaded, the showman, who arrived dressed in a magnificent fur coat, threw a luncheon party for the press aboard the ship that was carrying them to America. Bailey himself, in an interview published the next day, revealed the show had lost between twenty and thirty horses at Olympia—mainly through having their legs broken by chariots in the hippodrome races—and that one keeper had been killed by two unruly elephants.[69] Before he and the circus had even reached New York, his lingering partner was bombarding him with letters, inquiring whether the purchase of Forepaugh's show had been successfully negotiated, recommending they get a horse-riding lion such as he had recently seen in London, worrying that if the show opened too early under canvas (Madison Square Garden was being re-built, and their first stand this year was to be at the uptown Polo Grounds) there would be problems with mud and bad weather. It had been "almost a case of life and death" with Nancy, he confided, but her physician had recently assured her she was "making blood & good blood," and he himself was deter-mined to return in time for the show's opening, "even if I have to leave my wife behind."[70] He did just that a few weeks later, leaving Nancy to languish in England for an additional three months.

Nero continued as the featured attraction this year, during which the show made one of its rare forays into the nation's Deep South. Imre Kiralfy was often present during the early weeks, but eventually left to oversee another colossal pantomime for the company, *The Fall of Babylon*, which was entirely independent of the circus. This time the cast of one thousand actors and dan-cers, the hundred-member choir, the camels, horses, elephants, etc. were em-ployed in depicting the mournful history of the great King Belshazzar, who was first shown heroically repulsing the Persians before the walls of Babylon. Like Nero, alas, he soon fell to drunken revelry in his palace, desecrating the sacred vessels of the Jews while four hundred maidens, "richly and diaphan-ously costumed," danced amidst scenes of unprecedented riot. The mysterious writing appeared on the wall, and Daniel was summoned to interpret it. In between there were victory and wedding processions, the inevitable "sports" and "games" in the arena, and the sung lamentations of the Jews at the riv-erbank. The action concluded with the night attack by the Persians, featuring great scenes of carnage and the burning of the city. Twice daily, beginning 30 June and extending over the next three months, the spectacle was presented at Boston's Oakland Garden, which had been extensively rebuilt to accom-modate a grandstand for 10,000 spectators and a stage opposite that was five hundred feet long. The old showman himself, to the audience's immense de-light, made his customary tour of the arena on opening night, an occasion that was marked by its fair share of theatrical contretemps. By the time Daniel made his way across the huge stage to the wall, one amused reviewer reported, the writing on it had long disappeared.[71]

Around this time, too, the showman was said to be one of the authors of a "composite" novel, serialized in the *Boston Globe* beginning 5 July, whose eleven other creators included such improbable figures as the actress Mary Eastlake and the prizefighter John L. Sullivan. In style, *His Fleeting Ideal; or, A Romance of Baffled Hypnotism* certainly varies from chapter to chapter, and several of these last are hilarious enough. But "Lena Makes a Discovery," the chapter advertised as being by Barnum, was obviously not his doing and reads so much like the genteel, humorless, long-winded fiction of its day that one suspects here, if anywhere, his wife's talented hand was at work. No doubt his objective in permitting his name to be attached to this piece was the further publicizing of his new Kiralfy spectacle.[72]

Temporarily restored to health, Nancy had arrived back at Marina around the middle of June, in celebration of which her overjoyed husband had forthwith increased her "pin money" to $4000 per year. On 5 July, his eightieth birthday—"hale, hearty, and smiling," as his secretary described him—he entertained nearly two hundred guests at a clambake in Seaside Park. He went yachting with his Fairfield neighbor Dr. I. DeVer Warner, of corset fame, to New London and Newport; and in late July he and Nancy were again off to the Adirondacks, where he could not resist playing a final practical joke on his friend Paul Smith. After first preparing his host with a speech about the widespread adulterating of food and drink, Barnum solemnly went on to assure Smith that the ground pepper on his tables was at least one-half "peas." The unsuspecting Smith fired off an indignant letter to his grocer, in which he threatened to withdraw his custom unless pure pepper, without any "peas" mixed in, was immediately sent him. When the grocer humbly confessed to having been found out by that "merry old wag of a showman," P. T. Barnum, but went on to point out that even the purest pepper on the market consisted of one half "p's," all the guests had a good laugh on Smith, who somewhat sourly replied he would be glad to stand them a basket or two of champagne, were it not for the fact Barnum was such a well-known temperance man.[73] In September, after returning to Bridgeport, Barnum purchased an interest in a schooner to be named after him, welcomed to Marina his daughter Helen and her daughter Leila, and spoke about his religious convictions, to a "full house," at Bridgeport's Universalist Church. He was in excellent spirits throughout the summer, even if the same could not always be said of his nervous partner Bailey: at least twice during the season the show experienced serious railway accidents, and on both occasions human lives were lost.[74]

Autumn, his favorite time of year, found Barnum and Nancy on their way to Colorado, stopping over in Chicago and Kansas City to be interviewed by the press and to visit the show. The mellow October days were pleasantly spent with his daughter Helen and her family in Denver. As Nancy rather effusively recalled the trip in her memoir of their last days together, it was a month of "flawless happiness," during which Barnum insisted on entering "with boyish eagerness into every excursion, regardless of all entreaties to be careful, regardless of all cautions as to the possible ill effects of such an altitude."[75] He was feeling so vigorous that for a while he thought of extending their vacation in order to take in Mexico and the Southwest, visit the Grand Canyon, southern California and Los Angeles, and return for another look at San Francisco. Reports in the Denver papers even had it he would embark for Japan—a rumor he promptly scotched in an affectionate letter to his granddaughter Helen Rennell, longingly adding how much he missed her and her children and how such separations, "& others harder to bear, *must* frequently occur in this life."[76] Some hint, some intimation of mortality had been given him, and time, he realized, was finally running out. He did not go to Mexico and California after all, but hastened back to Bridgeport at the end of the month.

He was uptown tending to business on the morning of 6 November, and was planning to go to a meeting of the water company the next day. Instead, as

Bowser noted in the office diary, he came down with a "bad cold" and was confined to his home. Like most other people at the time, his secretary seems to have been initially ignorant of, perhaps deliberately kept in the dark about, the true nature of his illness. Even when he did find out, he never mentioned it in the diary. Nancy herself later revealed how on the afternoon of the 6th Barnum became unaccustomedly "drowsy" and listless following a nap, and how a few days later he was felled by a full-blown stroke. He was out of danger within three weeks, but by then the progressive weakening of his heart, which he and his physicians had known about for some years, was well advanced. There was no immediate cause for alarm, the doctors gently informed her, but he had entered upon his "last sickness." They also decreed, she continues, that the truth about his condition be rigorously withheld from the patient, who might otherwise become depressed, "and depression would quickly cause death."[77]

But the failing showman, as he had tacitly acknowledged in his letters to his granddaughter and to others around the same time, knew perfectly well the end was approaching and cheerfully played his own role in this little charade. Spiritually, he assured close friends like his lawyer Curtis Thompson, whom he had known since his early days in the Connecticut legislature, he was ready to go; but there still remained much he wished to accomplish in the temporal world. Over the next few months, beginning as early as 25 November, he added no less than five codicils to his already lengthy will, taking particular care, in view of his late "mental disturbances," to execute these in the presence of witnesses who were qualified to testify to his sanity. Since early 1887 both the president of Tufts College and Professor John Marshall had been urging the desirability of adding two wings to the museum building, and he now increased his legacy for this purpose to a total of $40,000.[78] At Thanksgiving time he deeded a house and lot worth $10,000 to the Bridgeport Universalist Society for use as a parsonage—thereby setting off an outburst of gratitude from his pastor, the Reverend Lewis B. Fisher—besides leaving thousands more to the Universalist Publishing House in Boston, local charities, and the Bridgeport Scientific and Fairfield County Historical societies. The last two organizations, with no permanent homes of their own, had previously been given a piece of land in downtown Bridgeport and left $50,000 with which to build a "Barnum Institute of Science and History," which was also to house the local medical society. On his deathbed Barnum now approved the plans and signed the contracts for this building's construction, at the same time ordering his executors, in a final codicil to his will dated 30 March 1891, to pay whatever its cost might be. Today known simply as the "Barnum Museum," the handsome Romanesque structure is presently devoted entirely to exhibits illustrating the history of Bridgeport and the circus, and to the showman's own eclectic career, appropriately enough.[79]

Meanwhile, the *P. T. Barnum*—the three-masted schooner he had invested in and the first ship of any size to be built in Bridgeport for many years—was nearing completion, and he eagerly looked forward to seeing her sail out of Bridgeport Harbor and past Seaside Park. On 10 December, gaily decorated with flags on her spars, sporting the showman's name in beautifully wrought letters and a large medallion of him on her stern, she was finally launched, got stuck in the mud, and had to remain there overnight. The invalid was up and in good spirits as the ship was towed past Marina the following day, prior to sailing to Philadelphia on her maiden voyage.[80]

There was no question of his ever leaving Marina again, although he was usually allowed up for several hours each day and would longingly gaze out the windows at his beloved Seaside Park. He was attended round the clock by private nurses and his personal physicians; Bowser and others sometimes sat up with him overnight; Dr. A. L. Loomis, an eminent New York heart specialist, occasionally traveled up to examine him. Friends, family members, and business associates constantly came and went, and to all he appeared cheerful, "smart," sometimes downright "jolly." He laughed uproariously over jokes he or they told; merrily remarked on the "scaly pair of callers" when Benjamin Fish and the Reverend Mr. Fisher happened to visit him at the same time; and now inscribed and presented to a few cherished friends the last of his copies of the 1855 autobiography.[81] Reporters, like the sea gulls he ordered daily fed in Seaside Park, flocked to him as well. The *New York Evening Sun*, upon learning he had expressed curiosity over what the newspapers would say about him after he was gone, obligingly published an account of his life in its 24 March issue—only two days before the circus was scheduled to open at Madison Square Garden, it may be worth pointing out. In gratifying the showman's wish to read this premature "obituary," however, the editors decently (if somewhat disingenuously) explained that they did so in the belief he was now on the road to recovery.

What appears to have been the last interview he ever gave—published posthumously in the *Newtown* (Connecticut) *Bee* of 10 April 1891—took place only a day or two after the show's opening in New York. The reporter found the showman rested and professing to be without an ache or a pain, yet eager to volunteer information about the arrangements for his funeral. The staging of this event, he had decreed, would be strictly according to "English custom," with the viewing of his remains restricted to close relatives. Not for him the "old heathenish way" of letting every Tom, Dick, and Harry rush in to gape at the corpse and to stand about remarking on "a black streak on the side of his nose, a discolored spot near the ear, or the expression of his face." If only there were one in the neighborhood, he would much prefer that his body be taken to a crematory—on which solemn note he launched into a favorite tale ("Now a joke or story, else it would not be Barnum") about the widower who had his wife cremated and lovingly preserved her ashes in a glass jar, but who, upon remarrying, used them to sprinkle the steps in front of his house when he feared his new bride might slip on some ice. Here the dying showman broke into a hearty laugh, and the *Bee*'s reporter could not resist joining in.

His physicians had also ordered that he be spared business worries and letter-writing, which did not entirely prevent Bowser, Bailey, and others from consulting him. The contracts to produce another Kiralfy-style spectacle, *Moses in Egypt*, were canceled a few days following his stroke; Bowser and Curtis

Thompson now took over the task of answering most of his voluminous correspondence; his 1891 engagement book, stamped with his name in gold and delivered to him at the beginning of the year, remained entirely blank. His condition steadily deteriorated in the new year, while his two daughters and grandchildren hovered about Marina and visited him with increasing frequency. On the evening of 6 April, when it became evident he had but a few hours to live, telegrams were sent to summon absent family members; and his doctors, who had been ordered to refrain from doing so until death was imminent, began administering morphine to alleviate any pain. He spoke with his lawyer and Ben Fish about a few last-minute business matters, calmly remarked that his old friend Robert Collyer would soon be preaching his funeral sermon from one of his favorite texts, "Not my will, but Thine, be done," and at 2 A.M., before sinking into a heavy sleep, was heard to remark to his wife, who was led away in tears, "Nancy, I want you to know that my last thoughts were of you."

The morning of the 7th dawned cool and clear, and from time to time he roused himself from his lethargy to ask a question or speak a few words of farewell to his sorrowing friends and family. His pastor spoke comfortingly to him and remained by his bedside afterwards, and his sister Mary Amerman, daughters Caroline and Helen, and several of their children were also present to the end. A particularly "pathetic" scene occurred, according to a local paper, when C. Barnum Seeley belatedly arrived and his grandfather, gazing vacantly at him, gave no sign of recognizing his "successor" or his name. As the day progressed, his pulse and respiration continued to weaken, while his periods of consciousness became shorter and less frequent. He was gently, peacefully drifting off to his final rest, "asleep by the gates of light," as his friend Alice Cary had written in one of her poems. And a little after half past six in the evening, he was there.[82]

EPILOGUE

THE FUNERAL took place on 10 April. In accordance with the showman's instructions, his body, unembalmed and cooled by ice, had lain in a darkened room at Marina the preceding two days. Then, following private services at the house in early afternoon, it was conveyed to the South Congregational Church, the city's largest, where Barnum's pastor, Lewis B. Fisher, and Robert Collyer conducted a public ceremony. The church was packed with mourners and clergy of all denominations, while outside and along the entire route from Marina, and thence to the cemetery, crowds thronged the sidewalks to pay final tribute to their fellow citizen. A Sunday-like quiet hung over the city. Businesses shut down, buildings and homes were everywhere decorated with crape and portraits of the showman, even ships in the harbor flew their flags at half-mast. The circus itself canceled performances at Madison Square Garden, and Bailey and many of its employees journeyed to Bridgeport to attend the services.

Inside the church, hymns by Whittier and Holmes, chosen by Barnum from a Universalist hymnal, were sung; and Collyer delivered both the address and the closing prayer. In the former the white-haired minister expatiated on Barnum's frequent championing the cause of the oppressed, his generosity toward his fellow man and adopted city, which he had improved and beautified in so many ways, and his sincere religious faith. During the prayer his voice, strong and distinct till then, became husky and finally broke down, and tears streamed down his cheeks as he gazed from the elevated pulpit on the flower-strewn casket of his friend. This set many others in the church to weeping, which continued through the final hymn set to the tune of "Auld Lang Syne."[1]

In his sermon Collyer had assured his listeners that the showman, crowned with glory, was already with his Father in heaven. A resurrection of another sort nearly occurred the following month. On the morning of 29 May, Bridgeporters were shocked to learn an attempt to steal the corpse had been made the night before. The nation's newspapers, picking up on the story, were not certain what to make of it—the *Hartford Courant* proclaimed the whole thing to be an "advertising dodge"—but city residents and Barnum's secretary, Bowser, who had recently taken to carrying a pistol, were in no doubt about its veracity. The ghouls were at work when they were discovered and chased off by watchmen hired to foil just such an attempt. Presumably, their plan was to hold the body for ransom.

The following month Ball's statue of the showman was shipped to Bridgeport and stored at winter quarters, there to remain an additional two years until the handsome granite base and pedestal, largely paid for by Bridgeport's citizens, were ready to receive it. Bailey, who had contributed to the statue's cost, thought it might appropriately be dedicated on Washington's birthday, 1893, but the ceremonies were delayed until the following Fourth of July, when Collyer again traveled to Bridgeport to give an address and the statue was unveiled by one of Barnum's great-granddaughters. Earlier in the same year, on 18 February, the Barnum Institute of Science and History had opened with a full program of speeches and musical selections.

The value of the estate was declared to be close to $4.3 million—a tremendous sum in those days, of course—and as soon as possible its executors unloaded the show properties, which neither C. Barnum Seeley nor any other family member was capable of managing. Barnum's share in the Forepaugh show was sold at the end of the 1891 season; but since his agreement with Bailey compelled his estate to continue his interest in "The Greatest Show on Earth" for three years following his death, it was not until 1894 that Bailey became the circus's sole owner. After Bailey's death in 1906 the show became the property of the Ringling brothers, who continued to run it separately until the end of the 1918 season, when it was finally merged with their own circus. The combined show continued to winter in Bridgeport until 1927, then moved to Florida, dealing a severe blow to the city's economy. The winter quarters buildings were torn down and the land became an athletic field. Wagons and other equipment unprized by the Ringling organization rotted about the city for years afterwards, a forlorn reminder of the days when Bridgeport had been America's premier "circus town."

The later life of Barnum's wife Nancy is not without interest. Within a few weeks of the showman's death she developed into quite a traveler, dragging Dr. Godfrey, one of the family physicians, off to remote health spas with her, venturing to Europe, Scandinavia, Egypt, etc. At the age of forty-one—wealthy, cultivated, with a reputation for wit—she still possessed attractions; and in the summer of 1895, after shutting up Marina and announcing she was about to return to Egypt to recuperate from some "throat trouble," she astonished everyone by instead marrying a Greek named Dimitri Callias Bey, whom she had met in Cairo some time before (according to one romantic tale, their introduction occurred when Callias, who was some distance below, caught Nancy while she was toppling off the Great Pyramid). The bey, two years her elder, was reputedly a millionaire and the owner of olive groves on one of the Greek islands, though there were rumors that Nancy, upon visiting these fabled properties with her husband, was somewhat disturbed by what she found. By all accounts, however, the fine-looking Callias was the great love of her life. All the more tragic, therefore, was his death from liver disease in Constantinople barely a year after their marriage, while Nancy was paying a brief visit to America.

Following this latest bereavement, Nancy took up permanent residence in the place Malesherbes in Paris, where she maintained an elegant apartment furnished with silk carpets and an ever-expanding collection of paintings by fashionable "salon" artists, whose names are unknown today to all but art historians. In France, too, she found a third husband in the person of a widowed baron, Lucien d'Alexandry d'Orengiani, from whom she soon separated on amicable terms. According to one Barnum descendant who visited her early in the present century, the marriage was purely a business arrangement, whereby Nancy agreed to settle the baron's debts in return for the opportunity to "play the lady." As the "baronne Nancy Barnum d'Alexandry," she now had entrée to the best French society; purchased a coronet that she wore on special occasions; took daily drives in the Bois with a female companion and a dog named "Folette"; and soon managed to ingratiate herself with the widow of Napoléon III. Nancy's fixation on Eugénie, whom she visited both in France and at her English estate "Farnborough," became so great, in fact, that she nearly filled her apartment with paintings, porcelains, and all sorts of bric-a-brac relating to the empress, Napoléon III, and their son "Pom-Pom," who was killed in the Zulu War, later donating these items to the French government, which placed them on exhibit at Malmaison. Among these treasures was the famous Winterhalter painting of Eugénie surrounded by her ladies-in-waiting in the garden at Compiègne, a favorite with the empress who once owned it herself, but which was about to be sold at auction when Nancy purchased it as a gift to the French nation.

Following Eugénie's death in 1920, the "baronne" seems to have returned at least partially to her senses. According to those who visited her during her final years, she now spoke more frequently about her showman-husband, whose charm and intelligence she praised above those of all the interesting men she had met. After suffering a series of strokes, she died at Cannes on 23 June 1927, was cremated wearing her favorite jewelry, and was buried beside her beloved Dimitri Callias. Somewhat relieved, the showman's heirs were then free to divide the sizable real-estate trust Barnum had established to ensure her annuity of $40,000 per year. By the terms of his will, the estate had been obligated to pay this figure regardless of the fluctuating value of the trust and its income; and although C. Barnum Seeley and the others never actually had to dig into their own pockets, a question frequently on their minds was "How soon are we going to have to pay for 'Aunt' Nancy?" Barnum's descendants have continued to flourish to the present day in such diverse professions as the law, the ministry, education, and manufacturing—though few of them seem to have inherited their ancestor's flair for showmanship. Nancy herself never had children by any of her husbands.[2]

———◆———

AS ONE TRAVELS today down Iranistan Avenue and into Bridgeport's Seaside Park, a green object near the water's edge looms larger and larger. Thomas Ball's monumental statue sits high atop its granite pedestal, both only slightly the worse for wear, unlike Barnum's favorite city itself, which has suffered more than its fair share of ills in the twentieth century. The seated, curly-haired showman, looking comfortable but alert, gazes outward over the gently rolling waters of Long Island Sound. In his left hand he holds a partially open memorandum book. What visionary plan has he just recorded or reviewed in that ever-present companion? What accounts for the look of anticipation on his face? If not "Jenny Lind Concerts" or some novel scheme to publicize his circus, does he dream of Jumbo, his "man in miniature," his American Museum? Do mermaids and the great leviathans of the deep sing to him as they pass by in the night?

Through an ideal combination of heredity, ambition, and to some extent luck, in a little over a decade Barnum rose to become America's foremost caterer to the public's love of amusement, which he himself expanded and in large part defined at a time when the Puritans' grip on the nation's conscience was finally relaxing. He was, as his pastor Lewis B. Fisher once remarked, a genius in his way who seemed almost divinely called to become a showman; and among his greatest shows, for over fifty years' running, was Barnum himself. "Prince of Humbugs," "The Children's Friend," "The World's Greatest Showman"—the epithets he or others attached to him roll on and on. In the 1880s, in posters advertising his circus, he was sometimes proclaimed "The Sun of the Amusement World." For one who let sunlight into so many lives, that title will serve as well as any.

APPENDIX: BARNUM APOCRYPHA

SO MANY preposterous tales, rumors, and misconceptions about Barnum are current that one could easily assemble a sizable volume cataloguing and examining them alone. Rather than impede my narrative by repeatedly calling attention to them, I have usually chosen to limit my comments to those that significantly influenced the way in which the showman's contemporaries viewed him, touching on a few others in the notes or, especially in the case of those that are patently absurd, simply ignoring them or letting the counterevidence speak for itself. Much of this misinformation, although originating during Barnum's lifetime, was broadcast in the first and very imperfect biography by M. R. Werner, which was thought wonderful enough in its day. Unfortunately, subsequent authors—particularly those attempting to analyze the showman's character in the twenties and early thirties, when there was a minor boom in such exercises—often employed this as their chief or sole guide to Barnum's life, thereby perpetuating its errors and seriously undermining the value of their own studies.

Without feeling any compulsion to address or comment further on such topics as Barnum's reputed lack of interest in animals, his parsimoniousness toward his family, his "last words" inquiring anxiously about the show's receipts, his boorishly slapping the Duke of Argyll on the back and bawling out, "Well, how are you, Duke?" his offering $10,000 to exhibit the actress Sarah Bernhardt's leg (amputated in 1914, no less), etc., etc., I have nonetheless reserved for this section a few widely accepted tales that, it seemed to me, merited more critical examination. The first of them, to which Werner also contributes (p. 328), concerns

Barnum's Physical Appearance & Voice

NOT SURPRISINGLY, even Barnum's physical characteristics have been subject to considerable confusion in the present century. Nearly everyone has the impression he was a "tall" man (he is vaguely mentioned as being so in one interview published toward the end of his life), and I myself have heard him described as a "six-footer" by several of his descendants, one of whom even assured me the showman stood as tall as six feet four inches. His voice, on the other hand, is generally believed to have been high-pitched, and was even recalled as "squeaky" by the animal trainer George Conklin, who worked for the Barnum & Bailey show from the late 1880s on (*The Ways of the Circus*, pp. 253, 291).

More accurately, Major J. B. Pond, in his *Eccentricities of Genius* (pp. 350–51), describes him as a "handsome, medium-sized man . . . with a wealth of curly black hair" at the time he first saw him in 1853; while a reporter for *Frank Leslie's Illustrated Newspaper*, in an article published in the 23 July 1864 issue of that periodical, gives his height as around five feet ten inches and his weight as then around one hundred seventy pounds. The same reporter also mentions Barnum's gray eyes and fair complexion, and the former were remarked on by Walt Whitman in an interview some twenty years earlier (see above, p. 150).

I am satisfied that the reporter's estimate of Barnum's height was essentially correct, for being the same height myself, and having access to various items of clothing the showman wore, I have made the experiment of trying these on. But I have hardly been so successful in competing with his other dimensions, for he seems always to have been on the fleshy side; although during his illness over the winter of 1880–81 his weight, as his secretary recorded in the office diary on 7 January 1881, plummeted from its then usual 215 to 144 pounds. Three years earlier the fledgling actor Otis Skinner had visited Barnum at his Bridgeport home and found him "big, corpulent and smiling, with an air of having lunched heartily." As he gazed appreciatively at his host's red nose, loose lips, bald head, and "immense bulk," he thought, "What a make-up for Falstaff" (*Footlights and Spotlights*, p. 4). The often reproduced portrait by "Spy" in *Vanity Fair*, depicting Barnum at breakfast while in London with his circus during the winter of 1889–90, confirms this impression. At the time of his death, the showman was said to weigh a little over 200 pounds.

During his last visit to London a cylinder recording of his voice was made, and as this has been re-recorded and released on at least two occasions in the present century (see "I Thus Address the World" in the Bibliography), there need be little debate on this subject. Neither "squeaky" nor high-pitched by American standards, his voice possessed a faint New England twang and accent ("world" is pronounced "warld," e.g.); while his speech was slightly clipped rather than drawled, precise in its enunciation, and easily understood. Barnum was in great demand as a speaker during most of his life and lectured before the public on hundreds, if not thousands, of occasions both in America and in Britain. Reviewers frequently commented on his elegance of diction and distinct articulation, his "sonorous" voice (by which was meant his ability to project his words into every part of a hall), and his thoroughly polished delivery. I have never encountered in any of these reviews any mention of "squeakiness."

There's a Sucker Born Every Minute (But None of Them Ever Die)

OF ALL THE pithy, eminently quotable statements by Barnum that might have become part of the English language's store of bons mots, it is remarkable that the one nearly everybody associates with his name—"There's a sucker born every minute"—was never spoken or written by him. In fairness to the *Oxford Dictionary of Quotations* and *Bartlett's Familiar Quotations*, both of which include the saying as their single entry under Barnum's name, it should be acknowledged that the editors of these works possessed sufficient caution to list it as "attributed" to him. Those among the showman's contemporaries who addressed the subject were unanimous in insisting he never said it; previous biographers have generally accepted their assertions; the recent CBS movie *Barnum*, which featured Burt Lancaster in the title role, had the hero-narrator of that "true story," for all its other factual errors, indignantly declaring at several points that he was never guilty of making such a statement.

None of these sources, however, has shed any additional light on the topic or, needless to say, made much impression on the host of journalists, songwriters, and others who continue to delight in laying the statement at Barnum's doorstep. At least one of his contemporaries—Joseph McCaddon, Bailey's brother-in-law, who certainly bore no love for the showman and was eager enough to attack him on other occasions—even went so far as to claim the "slang" meaning of the word was not in use during Barnum's lifetime. No matter how often Barnum deceived the public with such humbugs as Joice Heth and the Woolly Horse, McCaddon continues in the manuscript history of Bailey and the circus he wrote (p. 317, in the Bridgeport Public Library, Historical Collections), he was too "shrewd an advertiser and well educated a man to directly accuse his public of ignorance, and of being suckers."

In letters from the 1840s to his intimate friend Moses Kimball of the Boston Museum, Barnum sometimes vulgarly used the word "suck" in both its noun and verb forms to signify a swindle or being deceived ("it was a suck," "got sucked," etc.); and as twentieth-century parents of schoolchildren have sometimes learned to their horror, the word still possesses the related meaning of something worthless in such expressions as "it sucks." In the nineteenth century "sucker" was often used to designate an inhabitant of the Upper Midwest, whose settlers at one time purified their drinking water by "sucking" it through straws; but Stuart Berg Flexner, in his *Listening to America* (p. 320), traces its present-day meaning of "one as innocent as a suckling" as far back as 1831. Certainly Barnum was aware of both meanings, as is evidenced by his once playing with the word at an 1875 political rally when, upon introducing a former governor of Illinois, he referred to the speaker as "a good, genuine Sucker, a citizen of Illinois," but also, amidst much appreciative laughter, as a "sucker" for having married a young woman (*Bridgeport Standard*, 24 March 1875).

Ten years later, when the orthodox minister F. E. Hopkins of East Bridgeport, in a temporary fit of pique, wished to attack Barnum as a hypocrite, the worst he could accuse him of was that he had once reputedly remarked that "the people like to be humbugged"—a statement that surely has a more authentic ring, although Barnum himself immediately replied that he had been "misquoted" and went on to explain that "I said that the people like to be humbugged when, as in my case, there is no humbuggery except that which consists in throwing up sky-rockets and issuing flaming bills and advertisements to attract public attention to shows which all acknowledge are always clean, moral, instructive, elevating, and give back to their patrons in every case several times their money's worth" (*Bridgeport Standard*, 1 and 2 October 1885). He did not really deny making the statement, it will be noted, but simply wished to qualify it with reference to the rather imaginative interpretation he had given the word "humbug" in his 1865 book on the subject; and his first use of the expression may date from around that time or, perhaps, from the period ten years earlier when, in conjunction with the first edition of his autobiography, he was traveling around the country delivering his lecture on the "philosophy" of humbug.

"The people like to be humbugged," then, is one statement that may unequivocally be assigned to Barnum; and a number of his friends and associates, while not always certain of its exact wording (see, e.g., Coup's *Sawdust & Spangles*, p. 35), were in agreement on this point. But this still does not dispose of the "suckers" statement, of course, for obviously someone must have been responsible for it, and it remains a mighty good statement. While researching his book *Only in Bridgeport: An Illustrated History of the Park City*, Mr. Lennie Grimaldi chanced upon a tantalizing clue, which he communicated to me, buried in the files of the *Bridgeport Post*. In a typewritten story bearing a 1948 date, the claim is made that Barnum's great rival, Adam Forepaugh, made the statement in the course of a late 1880s newspaper interview. Upon being asked by the reporter if he might be quoted on this, Forepaugh nonchalantly replied, "Just say it's one of Barnum's slogans which I am borrowing for the occasion. It sounds more like him than it does me, anyway." The story's anonymous writer goes on to report that "Barnum is said to have personally thanked his competitor for the publicity—a gesture which made Forepaugh furious for having mentioned Barnum in the interview at all." Unfortunately, the source of the original interview is not given in this account, and neither Mr. Grimaldi nor I have succeeded in running it down. My own hunch, however, is that this story also is apocryphal, considering the showman's haste to "explain" the comparatively innocuous statement with which he was charged in the 1880s by the Reverend Mr. Hopkins. As McCaddon justly observed, Barnum was too "shrewd" a businessman ever to lay claim to any such saying—a saying that most certainly would have given offense to a large portion of his circus patrons.

But there is another, more plausible tale concerning the origin of the statement, also stemming from McCaddon (pp. 317–18), which I am inclined to accept. He in turn received it from a friend, one Alex Williams, who was an inspector in the New York City Police Department. Captain Alexander Williams, incidentally, was certainly familiar with Barnum in the 1880s, since his precinct included Madison Square Garden where the circus played each spring and he was also one of the witnesses who testified at the 1883 trial over the Elliott Children. According to Williams, the expression was first used in the early 1880s by a notorious confidence man known to the police as "Paper Collar Joe" (real name, Joseph Bessimer). And the complete statement, as McCaddon reports it, was "There is a sucker born every minute, but none of them ever die."

An improvement over what has been accepted and broadcast till now, and in future, one would like to think, better attributed to "Paper Collar Joe" than to P. T. Barnum.

Barnum's Illegitimate Son (and Daughter)

CERTAINLY THE most titillating of all the tales surrounding Barnum concern his alleged sexual indiscretions, in particular his supposed fathering of an illegitimate son. In a footnote to his 1923 biography, Werner (pp. 314–15) drew attention to these "persistent rumors of Barnum's moral irregularity"; dutifully reported some gossip he had heard about the showman's being "an old devil" (though he obviously was uncertain how the expression was meant to be taken); lamented the fact, à la Constance Rourke, that verification of such tales was "closed completely by the comprehensible secrecy of family pride"; but nevertheless felt compelled to hint darkly at the "principle of the co-existence of smoke and fire." He was particularly intrigued by an article that had appeared in the *New York World* of 17 January 1897, wherein the claim was made that Barnum had fathered a son off a "French actress" at the American Museum. The article to which Werner refers goes on to point out that Barnum "never denied" the paternity of this son, but looked after and educated him as a physician. Shortly after the showman's second marriage, this individual made a "sudden and by no means welcome descent upon Bridgeport" and demanded that his father settle some property on him. The showman did so in a "cast-iron contract," granting him $60,000 on the condition that he never annoy the legitimate heirs or make any claim on the estate after Barnum was gone. The son, the article's anonymous "special Bridgeport correspondent" goes on to concede, had "kept the contract faithfully" and was then "holding an honored place among the medical practitioners of an important city of the Union."

Irving Wallace briefly took up the same tale in his biography of Barnum (pp. 201–2), further confusing the issue with some gossip attributed to a Bridgeport resident named Mrs. Candee, who used to speak of "a dashing young man named Phineas Taylor, who was said to be P. T. Barnum's illegitimate son" and whose mother was thought by some to have been a dancer and actress named Ernestine de Faiber. Wallace also alludes to a later exposé on the topic by Julian H. Sterling, whom he mistakenly identifies as a "Barnum relative." This last piece of misinformation he probably received from an eccentric Bridgeport resident who liked to claim (though I have heard it indignantly denied by Barnum's descendants) that she herself was in some way related to the showman.

As the reader has probably inferred by now, we are again dealing with Barnum's unforgiving enemy Julian H. Sterling, who has already been identified as the anonymous author of the article in the *New York World*—a malicious piece that, besides lying outrageously about Barnum's daughter Helen, was directly inspired by the "awful Seeley dinner" and made much of the "hereditary influence" supposedly at work on the two sons of Barnum's daughter

Pauline (see above, pp. 229 and 315–16). Somehow, it would appear, even the showman's alleged son was to be drawn into this maelstrom of scientific determinism, for as Sterling thoughtfully adds at one point in his narrative, "This gentleman, of course, is Mr. Seeley's uncle."

Julian H. Sterling, it may here be pointed out, was born in 1845 and died in 1924. A graduate of Yale's class of 1868, he later studied at that university's School of Fine Arts, taught mechanical drawing for some ten years in the Bridgeport school system, designed the city's official seal, and was a portrait artist of some repute. His real forte, however, was journalism—of the sensational, muckraking kind favored by Joseph Pulitzer—and besides contributing regularly to the *New York World*, he sometimes wrote for the *New York Times*, *Boston Globe*, *St. Louis Dispatch*, and any number of Connecticut papers. Although Barnum befriended him on several occasions—letting him occupy his private box at the circus on nights he was not using it, employing him to design posters for the show, etc.—I find no evidence Sterling ever reciprocated these favors. On the contrary, acting on the *World*'s instructions to "go for Barnum strong," he was only too happy to attack the showman at every opportunity, although he was usually circumspect enough to stop short of libel during Barnum's lifetime. At other times he either hid behind his "special correspondent's" label or put would-be authors like the inventor C. F. Ritchel up to writing the more scandalous items (see above, pp. 300–301). Sterling never got over the affront to the "family honor" at the time of the 1875 mayoral campaign (see above, pp. 262–63); and that the original insult was still rankling in him as late as 1904 is evident from a book he published that year, *Space*, originally issued as a series of newspaper articles in connection with Bridgeport's "Old Home Week" celebration in 1903 and purporting to be a collection of interviews with dead Bridgeport residents. The showman appears several times in this bizarre narration and at one point (p. 122) expresses dismay upon learning a blazing likeness of him set off during a fireworks display was mistaken for another prominent citizen. "What's that?" he says. "Mistook somebody else for me. That's dreadful." "Oh, no," Sterling himself replies, "don't you care. They mistook you for a blue blood and the most important citizen of Bridgeport." The later account of the illegitimate son referred to by Wallace also appears in this gossipy work—only now we are informed the mother was a "circus woman," the birth occurred in Bridgeport, and the boy "turned out well and now lives in Richmond" (p. 11).

If the journalist was ever inclined to let up on the showman for once having ridiculed the Sterlings' pretensions to "Colonial blue-bloodedness," he must surely have thought better of it upon receiving a letter from Barnum written on the last day of 1889. At the time Barnum was with his show in London, musing over a letter, "couched in friendly terms," he had received from Sterling some weeks before. Very likely this was a request for some information Sterling wished to use in one of his articles; but in any case Barnum had hesitated to answer him until now, in view of some "wrongs" the journalist had recently done him in the columns of the *World*. In particular, he had been disturbed by Sterling's reporting on two separate occasions that he had "retired" from show business—a deliberate lie that, had it not been promptly contradicted, would have "injured my business hundreds of thousands of dollars." On this the final day of the year, however, he wished to forget past injuries and was ready to meet Sterling halfway to make up their differences, provided the journalist was willing to reform and turn his "future behaviour, as a correspondent of the *World*, into better paths." Unfortunately, to this reasonable proposal the showman added several animadversions on Sterling's standing in Bridgeport society, whose members had too often "smarted under your ungenerous attacks and insinuations. . . . The *Seaside Club* of Bridgeport," he reminded his antagonist, "of which I am a member, although I never attended it except by invitation a few days before sailing for England, as a body, you know, refused to receive you and would have blackballed you had your name been submitted for election. Many families in society in Bridgeport, who otherwise would be glad to receive you kindly, dislike you on account of your attacks upon them and their friends, but, unlike myself, *they* fear a repetition of them in the papers if they do not receive you. Thus your admission into society is permitted through fear rather than good feeling."

Predictably, this brought forth a stinging reply, in which Sterling sarcastically inquired what Barnum could possibly know about true "society." "You are now eighty years old and your life, both public and private, is well known to me as indeed to all residents of Bridgeport. Your integrity! truthfulness! chastity! and social standing! are the themes of constant admiration of all familiar with your course from the time you left old Bethel until today. No dishonest transaction has ever been imputed to you! No lie has ever been traced to your door! No bastard of your begetting has ever been supported by you! You have never so far forgotten yourself as to jump out of a hotel window into a cistern. Neither have you been compelled to flee to a faith that insured final salvation to all men no matter how wicked, and never have doors of decent people been slammed in your face." After similar reflections on Barnum's involvement with the failed Jerome Clock Company and the removal of the corpses from the old Division Street Cemetery, the journalist pointedly added in a postscript that he was "undecided whether this correspondence should be published or not."

It wasn't, and the provenance of both these letters remains somewhat clouded. The original of Barnum's letter, in the hand of a secretary except for its concluding paragraph and signature, is now in the Bridgeport Public Library and is certainly genuine. Presumably it was donated by Sterling's widow, Elida, who must also have given a copy of her husband's reply at the same time. The latter document has been lost or misplaced; but before that occurred, fortunately, photocopies of both letters were acquired by the New-York Historical Society. At the top of the rather poorly typed copy of Sterling's letter, which is dated 18 January 1890, his widow has written "This is a copy of my late husband's letter to Mr. Barnum." The question naturally arises whether Sterling's letter was ever sent, since I have discovered no indication, in manuscript sources or elsewhere, that Barnum was aware of or replied to it, as he was certainly likely to have done in view of his past experiences with Sterling and his sidekick Ritchel and the implied threat of blackmail contained in the postscript. From the letter's contents and its angry, almost furious tone throughout, however, I have no doubt it was indeed written upon receipt of the showman's letter. And again, this time as early as 1890, one finds Sterling eager to dredge up the story of Barnum's "bastard."

Later attempts to identify the showman's supposed paramour have focused on such unlikely candidates as the Austrian dancer Fanny Elssler (another inspiration by one of Bridgeport's famed corps of researchers) or, somewhat less implausibly, the ballet dancer known as Ernestine de Faiber (the "French" connection, obviously). But the only evidence for believing there may have been a liaison between Barnum and the latter is a photograph, taken in Mathew Brady's studio, in which the costumed dancer strikes a pose while Barnum appears to be leering at her from a stage box. The photograph seems so suggestive, one might even say "compromising," that when I first saw it I suspected it might be one of Brady's composites. But my subsequent investigations have revealed this was not the case.

Ernestine de Faiber, or "Mlle. Ernestine," as she was usually billed while in Barnum's employ, did indeed appear as a solo dancer at the American Museum during the spring and summer of 1864; and a good many photographs, meant to be made into cartes de visite and sold as souvenirs, were taken of her around that time. Their glass negatives are now in the National Portrait Gallery's Meserve Collection, and I imagine the dancer, in order to add to her own notoriety and profit, induced the showman to stroll across the street to Brady's studio and pose with her for the one in question. Barnum himself seems to have been embarrassed by the photograph in later years. When a correspondent named F. J. Walton—apparently a publisher or editor—sent him a copy of the carte de visite in 1885 with the suggestion it be used as an illustration in a forthcoming edition of the showman's autobiography, he claimed he could not remember who the dancer was, "only that she was not much of a dancer," and that he believed the photograph might have been taken as an "*advertising* dodge" to excite public curiosity while he was managing variety seasons at New York's Vauxhall Garden. "At all events," he continued, "although the photo reminds me that I saw such a thing 40 or 45 years ago, I have no distinct recollection about it, & therefore it would not be a proper picture to use in illustrating my autobiography." In its place he returned to his correspondent a photograph of himself alone, taken on his seventy-fifth birthday (14 July 1885, Columbia University Rare Book and Manuscript Library).

Odell, in his *Annals of the New York Stage*, notes appearances by de Faiber at various New York theatres during the years 1857 through 1865. In 1864, the same year she was at the American Museum, she was also a principal dancer at the New York Academy of Music and with Max Maretzek's Italian opera company, so one assumes she possessed more talent than Barnum later gave her credit for. In his *History of the American Stage* (p. 94), T. Allston Brown reports de Faiber was born in the American West in 1843, adding that she was of German parentage (elsewhere her name is sometimes spelled "Fieber"). She would therefore have been around twenty-one years old when she danced at the American Museum, and Brady's photographs of her would seem to confirm this. Barnum himself, of course, had he studied his own person in the photograph sent him, would have realized it could not possibly have been taken as long ago as the 1840s, when he was managing entertainments at Vauxhall Garden. Was he being disingenuous with his correspondent? Did he, perhaps, leer at Ernestine de Faiber after all? In any event, as we shall shortly see, the dancer was far too young to have been the mother of Barnum's "bastard."

Before continuing with this saga, however, I feel compelled to make a personal observation. Despite the "comprehensible secrecy of family pride" that presumably prevented Werner and others from getting to the bottom of such tales, I can truly report that in the over ten years I have been studying Barnum's career, never once have I been denied information or access to materials I wished to see by any of his descendants or residual heirs. Indeed, I have generally found his descendants to be as eager as anyone to settle these rumors and was rather surprised when, at the commencement of my research, while I was still hesitant to bring up such matters, a number of them broached the subject of the illegitimate son, asked what I knew about it, and suggested various avenues of approach. They have no family legends or materials bearing on any such son—no "cast-iron contract" or other incriminating evidence—and are nearly as ignorant on this topic as was Werner himself after writing his biography.

In the end, the tale of the "irregular" son always comes back to Barnum's implacable enemy Julian Sterling, who was too young to have had firsthand knowledge of the indiscretion at the time it allegedly occurred, but who acknowledged in his book *Space* that he was frequently indebted to his aged mother for stories concerning Bridgeport's former residents. By the time he wrote that book, too, the reader will have observed, the "French actress" at the American Museum who appears in his *World* article had been transformed into a "circus woman" who gave birth in Bridgeport, so that one gathers either Sterling or his venerable mother had been improving on the tale in the meantime. The story in the *World* about the son's sudden and unwelcome descent upon Bridgeport at the time of Barnum's second marriage recalls all too well the scene Barnum's daughter Helen was supposed to have made following the same event. It, too, never happened. Nor is it at all surprising that Barnum "never denied" the paternity of this "son." Considering Sterling never dared publish his allegations while the showman was alive, there was no cause for him to do so.

He might well have done so had he been in the habit of answering slander alone or—assuming he ever received it—such malicious gossip as was contained in Sterling's 1890 letter to him. "My dear Uncle," begins a letter to Barnum dated 12 December 1887. "Will you loan me $50 until spring? I have lost so much time last season, all through vile people with your show, and some of those nasty women saying you were my father, which was as false as God was just, and also through sickness, that I have not one cent." The writer was the featured equestrienne Mattie Jackson, who had married, and by this date perhaps been abandoned by, Barnum's grand-nephew Charles Benedict, and who in the past, following accidents and other tribulations, had made similar desperate appeals to her "uncle." Barnum simply instructed his secretary to send her the money, without commenting on the tale being spread by the "nasty women" (Fred D. Pfening III Collection). His concern for the equestrienne's welfare had obviously been misinterpreted by some, possibly contributing to those rumors, spread by Conklin and others, about his being an "old devil."

And indeed, if I read the evidence aright, misinterpretation and confusion, sometimes deliberate, on the part of outsiders—coupled with the generally held belief that the showman was incapable of a generous, disinterested action—are at the root of nearly all these tales concerning Barnum's "moral irregularity." Mrs. Candee was correct in her recollection of the "dashing young man" who used to visit Bridgeport—but wrong about his name and relationship to Barnum. Even the calculating Julian Sterling, who obviously knew but never dared publish the real name of this person, took care, for the sake of Bridgeporters, at least, to invest his tale with a specious aura of authenticity by reporting Barnum educated the boy as a physician and that he later practiced in Richmond. For the true identity of this individual—the mysterious "bastard" for whom we have been searching all along—was Philip (or, as he himself often preferred to spell it, "Phillip") Taylor, who was educated by Barnum at a private school in Great Barrington, Massachusetts; graduated from Columbia University's College of Physicians and Surgeons in 1876; and eventually took up practice in Richmond, Virginia, where he married into the distinguished Lovell family and died in 1922. Before moving to Richmond in the early eighties, Philip Taylor completed a residency at the Royal Eye and Ear Hospital in Manchester, England, and for a brief period practiced medicine in Denver, where he also became involved in Barnum's real-estate speculations. Dr. Taylor's obituary in the *Richmond Times Dispatch* of 2 August 1922 and the biographical sketch of him in *Virginia: Rebirth of the Old Dominion* (IV, 390–91) both record his birth as taking place in New York City on 9 April 1850, and the latter work adds that he was the only child of Philip and Louise Taylor. Neither source, predictably, makes any reference to his connection with the "Prince of Humbugs"; nor have I been able to confirm the information on his birth, since the New York City Municipal Archives department, also predictably, has lost all the vital statistics for the period in question. There is no record of Philip Taylor's birth among Bridgeport's and Fairfield's own vital statistics, incidentally, or in the extensive archives housed in the state library at Hartford. Nor have I succeeded in tracing him or his parents in the various Taylor genealogies and New York City street directories I have consulted.

Barnum himself enters the picture—officially, at least—on 8 August 1866, when he was appointed guardian to Philip Taylor before the probate court of Fairfield (Fairfield Town Hall Probate Records, Vol. 38, pp. 518–19). Philip was then said to be fatherless, sixteen years of age, but was obviously not without resources, since the showman was bound by this agreement for the sum of $14,000, and his friend the Universalist minister Abel C. Thomas, who also signed the document, was surety for it. Over the next two decades there were a good many transactions involving Barnum, Taylor, and money held in trust for the latter; and it was not until as late as May 1887 that Barnum's trusteeship of these funds was finally settled. Meanwhile, the money—which seems ultimately to have totaled around $24,000—had been invested in Bridgeport real estate and Kansas farmland, or simply loaned to Barnum, who faithfully paid or reinvested the interest. All of this can be traced in numerous extant documents and letters, as well as through entries in Bowser's office diary and the "Salmagundi" ledger in the Bridgeport Public Library, and everything was done in proper "business" fashion. On one occasion, after Dr. Taylor had been overpaid some interest, Barnum promptly ordered Bowser to recover the difference. When Taylor, who around 1880 was trying to establish a practice in Denver, had the mistaken notion he might take over and dispose of, at a tidy profit, Barnum's Villa Park holdings, the showman, anxious to disburden himself of this "swindle," conditionally agreed to let him have them at a favorable price, but secretly continued to entertain schemes and offers by other parties. Aside from documents pertaining to the final settling of the trusteeship, which Barnum partially paid in stocks, there was no "cast-iron contract" and certainly no exchange of $60,000 between them.

Neither was there any sudden, unwelcome descent upon Bridgeport at the time of Barnum's marriage to Nancy. Philip Taylor came and went freely during the lifetimes of both of Barnum's wives and even, as Bowser noted in the office diary on 12 October 1892, returned to Bridgeport following his guardian's death in order to introduce his new wife, Sally Williams Lovell, daughter of Judge John T. Lovell, of Front Royal, Virginia, around the town. Barnum refers to his "ward," later "Dr. Taylor," in several of his extant letters dating from the late 1860s on. There was never any attempt by him to hide Philip Taylor from his wives, his friends, or the public in general. And apparently the showman never felt any pressing need to explain their relationship, any more than he did when the Reverend Ike Coddington, whom he supported through preparatory and divinity school, paid him visits. Philip may well have been related to Barnum through Irena Taylor's side of the family tree, or perhaps was the son of a deceased friend or employee, like the Mr. Taylor who looked after the "Happy Family" at the American Museum. The showman himself, one recalls, had become the ward of another Taylor when he, too, was sixteen.

It is always difficult—some would say impossible—to prove a negative, and in a case such as this the only thing that could satisfy everyone would be a declaration by Barnum acknowledging he *was* Taylor's father. Even if the showman had been called upon to deny publicly his paternity of Philip Taylor, we might still not believe him. Similarly, the absence of his name in Philip Taylor's birth record, if ever found, would "prove" nothing. Would the showman have been able to keep such a secret from both of his wives, his family, and friends like Abel C. Thomas? If he did have such a secret to conceal, would he have chanced bringing his "bastard" so conspicuously into his life?

Alternatively, if Barnum really was Taylor's father and privately made a clean breast of it, we may be certain the news would have had a devastating effect on his moralistic wife Charity. Others among his family and inner circle would have been shocked as well, and undoubtedly some echo of this sensational revelation would still reverberate among his descendants. In time, the secret would inevitably have leaked abroad. Ministerial friends like Theodore Cuyler, however sympathetic they might be, would have necessarily thought twice before eulogizing the showman for the "chasteness" of his life (Benton, *Life*, p. 615). Dr. Taylor himself, assuming he could have passed inspection with the Virginia Lovells, would hardly have paraded his new bride before knowing Bridgeporters. Bastards were hardly so esteemed in his day as they are in our own.

Having presented the evidence as comprehensively as I can, I leave the final decision to the reader. For my part, while I cannot say with absolute certainty Barnum was *not* Philip Taylor's father, I would be very surprised to learn that he was.

An amusing medal issued by the Paris Mint in 1986. The obverse depicts a balloon taking off from a hippodrome and carries the ironic inscription "Quelle entreprise! Un spectacle qui etonnera L'UNIVERS. L'honnêteté est la meilleure POLITIQUE."

NOTES

The following abbreviations are used throughout the documentation:

- *AB*: various editions of Barnum's autobiography (followed by date of edition, occasionally "Bryan" to designate the edition by George S. Bryan, in parentheses)
- BA: Boston Athenaeum Library
- BM: Barnum Museum, Bridgeport, Connecticut
- BPL: Bridgeport Public Library, Historical Collections
- FDP: Fred D. Pfening III Collection, Columbus, Ohio
- HCC: Hertzberg Circus Collection, San Antonio Public Library, Texas
- HL: Huntington Library, San Marino, California
- HU: Harvard University, Houghton Library
- ISU: Illinois State University at Normal, Milner Library Circus Collection
- JAB: James A. Bailey
- LC: Library of Congress, Manuscript Division (followed by name of particular collection in parentheses)
- MAHS: Massachusetts Historical Society
- MDU: Collection of Mary D. Upton
- MOHS: Missouri Historical Society, Sol Smith Collection
- MTP: Mark Twain Project, Bancroft Library, University of California at Berkeley
- NYHS: New-York Historical Society
- NYPL: New York Public Library, Rare Books and Manuscripts Division (P. T. Barnum Papers)
- PTB: P. T. Barnum
- PUTC: Princeton University Library, Theatre Collection
- SIA: Smithsonian Institution Archives
- *SL*: *Selected Letters of P. T. Barnum*
- TU: Tufts University, Archives and Special Collections (Barnum Collection)
- UR: University of Rochester Library, Department of Rare Books and Special Collections (Henry Augustus Ward Papers)
- UTX: University of Texas at Austin, Humanities Research Center, Hoblitzelle Theatre Arts Library
- YU: Yale University Sterling Library (Miscellaneous Manuscripts Collection: Barnum)

Prologue

1. George Speaight, *A History of the Circus*, p. 143.

2. *Mémoires historiques et littéraires*, p. 101.

3. *The Mighty Barnum*, Twentieth Century Pictures, 1934. Screenplay by Bess Meredyth and Gene Fowler.

4. The musical *Barnum!* with book by Mark Bramble, lyrics by Michael Stewart, and music by Cy Coleman, opened at New York's St. James Theatre on 30 April 1980. There have been any number of fictional and dramatic treatments of Barnum, but the other work here referred to, whose tryouts were held in Bridgeport during the summer of 1983,

was a one-man play entitled *First Time Anywhere!* with the actor Ted van Griethuysen in the role of Barnum. To the somewhat dubious credit of the play's author, Leo Meyer, the feelings entertained by the showman for his singer were not presented as actually having been requited, although there was much wishful thinking on the subject. Roderick Thorp's novel *Jenny and Barnum*, related to the musical and modestly advertised as "the greatest love story on earth," was published by Doubleday in 1981.

5. PTB to Theodore Tilton, 29 May 1865, *SL*, p. 134.

6. Among the attempts to psychoanalyze Barnum, perhaps the best known, not to say most flagrant, example is that in Harvey O'Higgins and Edward H. Reede's *The American Mind in Action*, pp. 140–54. Based to a large extent on M. R. Werner's biography, this study is fatally flawed by its authors' ignorance or deliberate distortion of some of the basic facts of Barnum's life—most notably, his religious convictions—and by their determination to prove he remained a "Puritan" at heart whose contempt for himself subconsciously led him to feel contempt for the race as a whole.

7. Rourke, *Trumpets of Jubilee*, pp. 370–71.

8. *Humbug*, pp. 4–5.

9. "P. T. Barnum, Esq.," *Trumpet and Universalist Magazine*, 11 October 1851.

10. On the provenance of this statement, see the Appendix.

11. *Auto-Biography of Barnum*, p. 3.

12. PTB to H. E. Bowser, 20 June 1881, *SL*, p. 220.

13. Lest the reader think this interpretation somewhat strained, I will here cite the observation of an anonymous contemporary, presumably a Bridgeport clergyman, which I encountered after forming my own opinion on the subject. Writing in the May 1891 issue of the denominational journal the *Independent*, this individual remarks that the "autobiography of the Great Showman, as entertaining as it is, coming from the source it did, only partially tells the story of his life and fails to do justice in all parts to his memory. It is the business side of his life and the side which he presented to the world at large in the furtherance of his business interests. But he had another side, by which Bridgeport knew him, his home side. The side he presented to friends and neighbors."

Chapter I: A Life in Progress

1. The title page of this first edition of Barnum's autobiography bears the date 1855, but the dedication on the overleaf is dated 30 November 1854 and the book was copyrighted in Barnum's name in the same year. In a letter of 30 November 1854 that accompanied an unbound review copy of the book, Barnum wrote to his friend Moses S. Beach of the *New York Sun* that publication was scheduled for the 14th of the following month and asked that he not let his review appear before the 11th (*SL*, p. 84).

2. On Barnum's physical appearance, see the Appendix.

3. PTB to Various Editors, 6 October 1854, *SL*, p. 83.

4. See, e.g., the *Worcester* (Massachusetts) *National Aegis*, 1 November 1854, which reports on the bidding. In a letter of 6 September 1854 to his friend Moses Kimball, Barnum states that "Redfield publishes my book with illustrations—retail $1.25. He *starts* with an edition of 50,000. Will have all the *MSS* in his hands 15th Oct." (*SL*, p. 81).

5. The contract is in the NYHS.

6. These and many later editions of the autobiography are listed and commented on in the separate section devoted to Barnum in the first volume of R. Toole-Stott's *Circus and Allied Arts*, pp. 147 ff. But as Toole-Stott acknowledged to the present author on several occasions, the task of running down all the editions seems a never-ending one. There was also, e.g., at least one German translation published in the United States. This was issued by Warren, Johnson of Buffalo in 1875 and was aimed at the German-American population.

7. References to the various editions of Barnum's autobiography will be given as "*AB* (1855)" for the first edition, "*AB* (1869)" for the second, and so on. As discussed in the

Bibliography, the best and most complete twentieth-century edition is that by George S. Bryan, published in two volumes but with consecutive pagination. Occasional references to that work will be designated "*AB* (Bryan)." The present citation would thus be *AB* (1855), p. 105. This particular passage is omitted in the Bryan edition.

8. *AB* (1855), p. 350. The *New York Herald*, presided over by Barnum's inveterate enemy James Gordon Bennett, later reprinted this and other lengthy extracts from the autobiography in an attempt to discredit the showman while he was running for Congress in 1867. In the present instance, the editor insisted in a "correction" to Barnum's tale, the showman *was* compelled to discontinue exhibiting his Woolly Horse in Washington on pain of being sent to jail. See the *Herald* of 8 March 1867, pp. 4 and 7.

9. *AB* (1855), pp. 399–401.

10. See below, pp. 15–17.

11. *Knickerbocker Magazine*, January 1855.

12. *Forty Years of American Life, 1821–1861* (New York: Stackpole Sons, 1937), p. 55.

13. See, e.g., Harris, *Humbug*, pp. 227–29; Irving Wallace, *The Fabulous Showman*, pp. 213–14.

14. *Memoirs*, I, 294.

15. *Ibid.*, I, 275, 284. On Barnum and his partners' problems with Griswold, see the showman's two letters to Edward Everett, 7 and 19 February 1853, *SL*, pp. 63–64.

16. *Memoirs*, I, 292–93.

17. *SL*, p. 69. Smith's own work, entitled *The Theatrical Journey-Work and Anecdotal Recollections of Sol Smith . . . Comprising a Sketch of the Second Seven Years of His Professional Life*, was published by the Philadelphia firm of T. B. Peterson in the following year. No doubt in recognition of Barnum's heroic efforts on its author's behalf, the book contained a long, flattering dedication to him, which he had previously been given the opportunity to read and correct.

18. PTB to Sol Smith, 5 January 1854 (MOHS).

19. PTB to Bayard Taylor, 24 August 1854, *SL*, pp. 79–80.

20. PTB to Moses S. Beach, 5 September 1854 (TU).

21. See, e.g., Barnum's letters to Kimball of 4, 6 and 28 September 1854, *SL*, pp. 80–82.

22. PTB to George H. Emerson (TU).

23. PTB to Whitelaw Reid, 20 May 1869 (LC, Reid Family Papers).

24. See, e.g., Barnum's letter of 24 September 1869 to the editor of the *Agriculturist* (HL).

25. See, e.g., Bryan's introduction to his edition of the autobiography, p. xix; Wallace, *The Fabulous Showman*, pp. 214–15.

26. *AB* (1869), pp. 585–607.

27. Bryan, p. lv. And cf. Harris, *Humbug*, p. 21 ("became Joice Heth's sole owner"); Wallace, *The Fabulous Showman*, p. 10 ("overnight became showman and slaveholder"); etc. But why go on? The present writer was himself guilty of the same misconception in his edition of Barnum's letters (pp. xxvi, 7).

28. The agreement between Lindsay and Bowling is now in the private collection of Fred D. Pfening III.

29. See PTB to the Librarian of Congress, Ainsworth R. Spofford, 11 March 1871 (LC, Ainsworth R. Spofford Papers).

30. A copy of this particular appendix is in the NYHS.

31. In the preface to this nineteen-page pamphlet, privately published in 1893 and most conveniently available in the Bryan edition of the autobiography, Nancy relates that it was Barnum's custom each spring to write a résumé of his life during the preceding year to add to his autobiography, and that he last did so in the spring of 1890. But in fact his final addition to the autobiography was composed in September of the preceding year. Most likely Nancy was thinking of Barnum's description of his experiences while with his circus at London's Olympia during the winter of 1889–90, an account that was indeed published, but in his *Funny Stories* of 1890. The showman fol-

lowed no invariable schedule in the composing of these additions, though obviously it was advantageous to have a "new" edition available in time for the start of each circus season.

32. PTB to JAB, 17 July 1888 (PUTC).

33. The book was published by Edgewood of Philadelphia in 1891. Benton's own "Some Reminiscences of P. T. Barnum," occupying but thirteen pages, appears toward the end of the volume and was later reworked into an equally undistinguished article, "P. T. Barnum, Showman and Humorist," for the August 1902 issue of the *Century Magazine*. So desperate have twentieth-century writers been for anything touching on Barnum's personal life that a number of them have hailed these "reminiscences" as a rich mine of information. Considering Benton's claim that he and Barnum had been friends for more than twenty years, it is remarkable how little of true substance they contain.

34. *Expression in America*, pp. 103–4.

Chapter II: Bethel

1. The standard work on the town's early history is James Montgomery Bailey's *History of Danbury, Conn., 1684–1896*, which also contains a separate chapter on Bethel. A useful history of Bethel itself, published by the Bethel Historical Society on the occasion of the nation's bicentennial, is *A History of Bethel, 1759–1976* (Hamden, Conn.: Columbia Printing Co., [1976]).

2. In the early 1880s Barnum became fascinated by the subject of his genealogy and advertised extensively in the nation's papers for information. The BPL possesses correspondence relating to this research, as well as the abortive manuscript history he himself began. He soon recognized the need to employ competent researchers, however, and the first attempt at a complete genealogy was compiled, also in 1882, by Frank Farnsworth Starr, a member of the Worcester Society of Antiquity. The manuscript of this history, with corrections and additions in Barnum's hand, is also in the BPL. A somewhat later genealogy, typewritten copies of which are in the possession of Barnum's descendants, may have been prepared by the local Bridgeport historian, the Reverend Samuel Orcutt, who in 1887 had the loan of the data previously assembled by Barnum. Finally, in 1912 there was published a *Genealogical Record of the Barnum Family, Presenting a Conspectus of the Male Descendants of Thomas Barnum, 1625–1695* (Gardner, Mass.: Meals Printing Co.), compiled by Eben Lewis Barnum and the Reverend Francis Barnum, tracing eight generations of male descendants. All of these studies were hampered by the incompleteness of early Danbury records, largely destroyed when the British fired the town in 1777, and by their compilers' inability to locate certain later records as well. I have occasionally been able to supplement the information in these sources through discoveries made in parish records, cemeteries, early newspapers, correspondence, etc. As an example of how serendipity often plays a part in such work, I will mention that on a recent vacation in California, where I paid a visit to Glendale's Forest Lawn Cemetery, I happened to drop something while gazing at one of the "artistic" absurdities that abound in that fabled place. On stooping down to retrieve the object, I discovered I was standing on the memorial plaque of one Starr H. Barnum, deceased as recently as 1976. "Starr" as well as "Barnum" figures prominently among the names of Danbury's early inhabitants, and one of Phineas's uncles was a Col. Starr Barnum.

3. This information is based on various land, tax assessment, and probate records preserved in the Danbury Town Hall, where some 150 land transactions are recorded for Phineas Taylor alone.

4. The complete text of Barnum's speech is given in Bailey, *History of Danbury*, pp. 540–48, and in *AB* (1889), pp. 328–29. An abbreviated version may be found in *AB* (Bryan), pp. 749–53.

5. I am indebted to Mr. and Mrs. George C. Reimers for kindly allowing me to inspect the house while they were the owners of it. It was built sometime in the eighteenth century and originally belonged to the Hickok family, who sold it to Capt. Ephraim Barnum

and regained possession of it after Irena Barnum's death in 1868. Owing to extensive renovations made over the years, including repairs following a fire, it is difficult to judge the appearance of the house and the arrangement of rooms as they must have been in Barnum's day. An illustration in the first edition of the autobiography, showing the elm tree in front and an extension at the rear of the house that still exists, would seem to be a fairly accurate representation.

6. Danbury Probate Records 18:463–66.

7. His war record is contained in his application for a pension, made in 1832, a copy of which, now in the BPL, was obtained by his grandson in the summer of 1890. This news will no doubt come as a surprise to the citizens of Bethel, where Phineas Taylor's name is absent from the bronze plaque commemorating local citizens who fought in the War of Independence, and where his grave is undistinguished by the emblem and other special features accorded to veterans of that struggle.

8. *AB* (1855), pp. 30–35.

9. I am indebted to Mr. Thaddeus E. Carzasty, Bethel Tax Assessor, for aid in locating Ivy Island, and to Mr. and Mrs. Michael Walters, the owners of the southern half of the island, who gave me permission to visit their property. I might add that on my first trip to the island I nearly drowned getting there myself and found one of those big snakes awaiting me.

10. The deed, dated 25 June 1812, is among the Danbury Land Records, 15:563, in the Danbury Town Hall.

11. *AB* (1855), pp. 69–73.

12. *AB* (1855), p. 120.

13. See Justin Kaplan, *Mr. Clemens and Mark Twain: A Biography* (New York: Simon and Schuster, 1966), pp. 173–74.

14. *AB* (1855), pp. 215–23.

15. The mortgage between Olmsted and the Barnums, and the later quit claim to the secured properties—dated 20 November 1843 and signed by both Olmsted and John Heath, who represented the estate that owned the Museum's collections—are among the Danbury Land Records (32:18–20 and 33:491), as are the documents pertaining to the exchange of Ivy Island between Barnum and his half-brother Philo (27:547 and 31:442). The later history of this "white elephant" is rather obscure, and I have been unable to locate either in Danbury or in Bethel any record of Barnum's final disposition of the property, although he does seem to have definitively unloaded it before his bankruptcy in 1856, since Ivy Island is not listed in the inventory of real estate he then possessed. Nor is there any mention of it in the inventories prepared when his wife Charity's and his own wills were probated. The record recommences toward the end of the century, when one Llewellyn Barnum of New York City (the same who was later buried in Fairfield's East Cemetery, I suspect) sold the northern half of the island to William H. Wildman on 11 July 1892. After changing hands on several additional occasions, the property was finally sold in 1937 to the Danbury and Bethel Gas and Electric Light Co., and today belongs to its successor, the Connecticut Light and Power Co. The southern half of the island remains in private hands.

16. PTB to Frederick S. Wildman, 16 July 1886 (MDU). Barnum also comments on the event in a letter to the editor of the *Bridgeport Evening Farmer*, published in its 17 July 1886 issue, where he adds that it was "the only execution I ever saw or desire to." Bailey, *History of Danbury*, pp. 117–18, describes the hanging of Adams, but gives no indication of his race.

17. Barnum makes scattered references to his education among the early chapters of his autobiography, although he does not specify when this formal schooling ended. A reasonable estimate would seem to be around the age of fourteen. An advertisement for Alanson Taylor's school in Bethel, which was to open its doors, perhaps appropriately, on the following 1 April, appears in the *Danbury Gazette* of 13 March 1833. Its master also hoped to attract boarders and "foreign" students to his establishment, and gave assurance that "care will be taken that no vicious or immoral habits be contracted."

18. *AB* (1855), pp. 91–92.

19. Barnum's speech written for this occasion (he did not deliver it in person) and that of Tufts' president E. H. Capen are both given in *AB* (1889), pp. 341–42. The former may also be found in *SL*, pp. 252–54.

20. An explanation that is not entirely satisfactory, however, owing to the incompleteness and inconsistency that is often evident in these records. Phineas Taylor's death is recorded, e.g., and although he also rented pew space in the church, we know he was a Universalist. I am indebted to the Reverend Michael S. Strah, pastor of the Bethel First Congregational Church, for permitting me to examine these records.

21. Prior to the publication of the first edition of the autobiography, Barnum sometimes claimed to have suffered his great bereavement at an even tenderer age. In the biographical sketch of him that appeared in the 20 April 1845 issue of the *New York Atlas*, e.g., his age at the time is said to have been fourteen. As explained below, Barnum himself was most likely the author of this article.

22. Danbury Probate Records 15:333–37, 516–19.

23. *AB* (1855), p. 92. Following Irena's death, the property was sold by Barnum and her other heirs for $3675 to Horace E. Hickok on 14 May 1868 (Bethel Land Records 4:291). The inn and livery stable themselves were evidently never owned by Philo Barnum, but merely kept by him and his wife. From statements made elsewhere by Barnum, it appears he and the younger children sometimes slept at the inn with their parents. It also seems likely that whenever the inn was full, the overflow of travelers was accommodated in the family home.

24. Danbury Probate Records 15:296–97.

25. *AB* (1855), pp. 98, 130–31.

26. *Funeral of Mrs. Charity Barnum, Wife of P. T. Barnum.*

27. The early archives of this church may be consulted at the Connecticut State Library in Hartford. Such wholesale baptisms were not uncommon in America and England during the nineteenth century. Expense was sometimes a factor; repentance and fear of damnation generated by revival meetings another; and still another, one often suspects, was the opportune absence from home of a disapproving husband.

28. PTB to Moses Kimball, 15 May 1843 (BA). The breach was soon healed, however, and for a while in the late 1840s John traveled as Barnum's representative with the Tom Thumb troupe and managed another museum the showman had established in Philadelphia. He died in February 1855 and was buried in Bridgeport's Mountain Grove Cemetery, a respectable distance behind his famous brother-in-law's more grandiose monument.

29. Her grave is in the Easton cemetery, next to those of Daniel and Mary Wakeman (1805–85). The latter was one of her daughters.

30. *Funny Stories*, pp. 274–75.

31. "The Barnums," p. 216.

32. See, e.g., PTB to Rev. Thomas Wentworth Higginson, c. April 1855, *SL*, p. 86.

33. *New York Atlas*, 2 February 1845.

34. *Ibid.*, 24 August 1845.

35. "The Barnums," pp. 219–20.

36. *AB* (1855), p. 107.

37. In fact, as there had to be some "consideration" to make the transaction legally binding, Barnum paid Phineas Taylor $5 for a seven-year lease on the property. The lease, dated 12 June 1828, mentions Barnum as already using the property as a "confectionery store" (Danbury Land Records 24:727). On 13 March 1829 Barnum bought the building outright from his grandfather for $50, with the privilege of leaving it on its site for the next seven years and then removing it (Danbury Land Records 24:613).

38. *AB* (1855), pp. 128–29.

39. Clipped advertisement, bearing printed date 15 April 1831, in the BM from an unidentified newspaper; *Danbury Recorder*, 13 April 1831.

40. The Danbury Land Records alone contain some forty transactions in which he is listed as "grantor."

41. *AB* (1855), pp. 135–36.

42. This and much of the information below has been gleaned from numerous advertisements in contemporary newspapers, as well as from the store ledger Barnum kept at the time.

43. Advertisement in *Herald of Freedom*, 1 March 1832.

44. *Autobiography, Correspondence, Etc., of Lyman Beecher, D.D.*, ed. Charles Beecher (New York: Harper and Bros., 1865), I, 259.

45. *AB* (1855), pp. 136–38.

46. *Herald of Freedom*, 21 March 1832.

47. See the announcement in the *Danbury Recorder* for 7 March 1832. I am uncertain whether Alanson was actually the editor of the paper when Barnum's letters were rejected, although, as the announcement makes clear, he had obviously been so at some time in the past and must have had influence there. According to Bailey (*History of Danbury*, p. 196), the paper, founded in 1826, originally adopted a "neutral" political stance.

48. *Herald of Freedom*, 6 June 1832.

49. The incomplete records of this case, which was precipitated by an article in the 28 March 1832 issue of the *Herald of Freedom*, are among the Superior Court Papers in the Connecticut State Library. Barnum appealed the verdict and was apparently granted a new trial. In the first edition of the autobiography, where he was careful to conceal the names of those who had brought suits against him, he reports that "on the first trial the jury could not agree; on the second I was fined several hundred dollars" (p. 138).

50. The date of his being made a deacon is deliberately stressed, since it is often stated Seelye was already so when he brought suit against Barnum. It is nevertheless interesting that Seelye should have attained this high dignity around the time of the trial. Were the orthodox citizens of Bethel expressing their approval of his action against the editor?

51. The article, signed "Ariel" and published in the 24 November issue of the *Columbian Register*, was reprinted in Barnum's own paper on 5 December 1832, the day of his release from prison. Unfortunately, there appear to be no records of the trial among the court papers preserved in the Connecticut State Library. It was Daggett, incidentally, who in 1833 presided with similar effect over the infamous trial of Prudence Crandall, who was convicted for daring to teach "nonresident" Negroes at her school for girls in Canterbury, Connecticut.

52. PTB to Gideon Welles, 7 October 1832, *SL*, p. 2.

53. The event was described at length in the 12 December 1832 issue of the *Herald of Freedom* and in abbreviated form in *AB* (1855), pp. 139–40. The longer description also appears in the printed version of Theophilus Fisk's *The Nation's Bulwark*.

54. PTB to John W. Amerman and Zalmon Wildman, 17 May 1833 (MDU). Two other letters to Wildman on these topics, dated 14 and 15 May 1833, may be found in *SL*, pp. 3–7.

55. *Herald of Freedom*, 10 and 17 July 1833.

56. See John Samuel Ezell, *Fortune's Merry Wheel*, pp. 196–97, 218. As in the case of liquor and other alcoholic beverages, Barnum himself eventually became "converted" on this subject and exposed the schemes of lottery operators in his autobiography and elsewhere. In fact, either through moral doubts or other causes, for a period in 1833 he actually gave up, or perhaps lost, his Bethel agency—but then resumed its operations, as he jokingly remarked in the *Herald of Freedom* of 20 November 1833, in order to relieve his neighbors' and his own "poverty." Lotteries and other forms of gambling—now run by the state ostensibly for the benefit of its overburdened taxpayers—have been reintroduced into Connecticut in recent years.

57. *AB* (1855), p. 141. No copies of the paper from this later period appear to be extant, and Barnum does not specify who its subsequent editors may have been. Con-

ceivably, he continued to edit it himself for a few more issues, since Norwalk was within easy reach of New York by boat, although he also writes that the paper was sold to one George Taylor "in the course of the year ensuing." In a later syndicated article recounting his experiences with the press ("Barnum and the Editors," *Bridgeport Standard*, 27 June 1887), he tells of selling it to his brother-in-law. Amerman very likely was its owner during this interim period.

Chapter III: A Religion of Healthy-Mindedness

1. *A Confession of Faith, Owned and Consented to, by the Elders and Messengers of the Churches in the Colony of Connecticut, in New-England, Assembled by Delegation at Saybrook, September 9th, 1708* (New London, Conn.: n.p., 1710; rpt. Bridgeport, Conn.: Lockwood and Backus, 1810), *passim*. This last "decree of God" actually appeared on the state's lawbooks until 1784. It was not until 1939 that the "Land of Steady Habits" finally got around to ratifying the Bill of Rights, with its provision that "Congress shall make no law respecting an establishment of religion."

2. The early history of this movement has been told, from a basically Congregational viewpoint, by Charles Roy Keller in his *The Second Great Awakening in Connecticut* (New Haven, Conn.: Yale Univ. Press, 1942).

3. *Why I Am a Universalist*, p. 1. Note that a considerably abbreviated version of this tract continued to be published until well into the present century.

4. From the welcoming address by Barnum, delivered on 13 September 1886, at the annual Connecticut Universalist Convention, which was held that year in Bridgeport. The speech was published in the *Christian Leader* of 23 September 1886.

5. The early history of this society is briefly recounted by the Reverend James Vincent, then pastor of the Danbury church, in Bailey's *History of Danbury*, pp. 322–26. Some additional information may be found in a four-page manuscript history, originally deposited in the cornerstone of the third church building in 1892 and now in the Scott-Fanton Museum of Danbury. There is no comprehensive history of Universalism in Connecticut, and the early records of many pioneering societies now appear lost. In his *The Larger Hope: The First Century of the Universalist Church in America, 1770–1870*, Russell E. Miller devotes a few pages (674–79) to the Connecticut societies; and Donald Watt, in his *From Heresy Toward Truth: The Story of Universalism in Greater Hartford and Connecticut, 1821–1971* (West Hartford, Conn.: Universalist Church of West Hartford, 1971), occasionally touches on events outside the Hartford area. More recently, Stephen A. Marini, in his *Radical Sects of Revolutionary New England* (Cambridge, Mass.: Harvard Univ. Press, 1982), has focused on the background and origins of Universalism in rural New England.

6. *AB* (1855), pp. 49, 87. As mentioned in the previous chapter, Phineas Taylor, notwithstanding his religious preferences, paid for a pew in the Bethel Congregational Church and attended its services, although he was never, according to parish records, actually a member. Among his friends he numbered several Congregational ministers, with whom he was fond of engaging in disputations on religion.

7. Rev. James Vincent, in Bailey, *History of Danbury*, p. 323. In the *Herald of Freedom*, too, Barnum often signals activities at these and other Universalist societies around the state.

8. See Lectures IV and V, in particular.

9. In early nineteenth-century New England the word "orthodoxy" was generally synonymous with Congregationalism. The latter term actually refers to a form of church organization; doctrinally, the denomination was virtually identical with Presbyterianism, with which a union was contemplated, but ultimately never realized, during the first half of the century. During this period the ministers of the two denominations— often referred to as the "United Ministers"—might be called to serve in either church, as was true in the case of the eminent Lyman Beecher, who served alternately in Congregational and Presbyterian churches and institutions, "tried both ways," and didn't "give a snap between them" (*Autobiography, Correspondence, Etc., of Lyman Beecher, D.D.*,

ed. Charles Beecher [New York: Harper and Bros., 1865], II, 500). Thus Barnum, who attended the Bethel Congregational Church, writes of having been brought up in the "Presbyterian" faith. His later attacks on "Presbyterian priests" were also directed mainly against the Congregational clergy.

10. It was Barnum's friend Gideon Welles, while serving as a member of the state legislature, who led the successful struggle to change this requirement of belief in heaven and hell to the more reasonable one of belief in God.

11. See Alan Seaburg, "Remembering Publishing History: Universalist Periodicals."

12. *Herald of Freedom*, 21 March 1832.

13. *Ibid.*, 6 June 1832.

14. *Ibid.*, 17 July 1833.

15. *Ibid.*, 6 June 1832.

16. *Ibid.*, 10 July 1833.

17. *Complimentary Banquet*, p. 21.

18. Pond, *Eccentricities of Genius*, pp. 353–54.

19. From an interview originally published in the *New York Sun* and reprinted, with commentary by the Reverend Dr. T. J. Sawyer, in the 17 May 1888 issue of the *Christian Leader*.

20. PTB to Rev. Abel C. Thomas, 9 March 1857, *SL*, pp. 96–97.

21. PTB to Rev. Alex McMillan, 4 September 1886, *SL*, p. 281.

22. The church is today located at Central Park West and 76th Street. I am indebted to the Reverend Joel Schofield and to Mr. David Dunlop, business manager of the church, for permitting me to study the society's records. To avoid confusion in the minds of the uninitiated, it should be pointed out that in 1961 the Universalist Church of America and the American Unitarian Association merged, and that the former churches of these two denominations are today often, but not invariably, referred to as "Unitarian Universalist."

23. See *Funny Stories*, pp. 114–22.

24. The complete records of the society are extant and preserved at the Unitarian Universalist Church of Greater Bridgeport, which today is located in neighboring Stratford. I am especially grateful to the Reverend Albert F. Ciarcia, pastor of the society, for permitting me to examine these records and for aiding me in my research on numerous occasions. Unless otherwise indicated, it may be assumed that information on the society's affairs is drawn from these sources, which comprise, for Barnum's period, some dozen manuscript volumes containing minutes of meetings, treasurer's accounts, missionary guild records, membership rolls, the society's several constitutions, a few records kept by individual pastors, together with records and lists of baptisms, deaths, conferences, pulpit exchanges, etc.

25. See the *Bridgeport Standard*, 11 July 1870.

26. Lyon had been born in Glasgow in 1844 and was a former teacher and Episcopalian minister. His wife, Carrie, was the daughter of Henry Barnum, who lived in Detroit but was originally from Bridgeport. Interestingly, his madness in early 1884 came shortly after he had entered into a much-publicized debate on the subject of endless punishment with the Reverend R. G. S. McNeille of Bridgeport's South Congregational Church. Nineteenth-century ministers were especially susceptible to mental and physical breakdown, or at the very least to long bouts of depression, and Barnum's friend Chapin and even the stern Lyman Beecher were not proof against these occupational hazards. Afflicted clergymen from more affluent churches were often sent abroad for a year or two by their solicitous congregations.

27. PTB to Rev. Olympia Brown, 6 April 1872, *SL*, p. 168.

28. *Trumpet and Universalist Magazine*, 24 March 1855.

29. *AB* (1869), pp. 154–55.

30. According to the Bridgeport society's archives, Barnum officially became a member on 9 June 1876. I find no record of his ever joining Chapin's or any other church. Lack of membership in Universalist societies did not necessarily prevent one from par-

ticipating in and even voting in the conduct of their affairs. Depending on the qualifications specified by the societies' individual constitutions, the right to vote might be accorded to anyone occupying and paying for pew space over a certain period of time, as was the case in the Bridgeport society.

31. On the differences between Universalists and Unitarians—which were thought to be genuine enough during much of the nineteenth century, however—Barnum was fond of quoting a contemporary bon mot that "the former believe that God is too good to damn anyone, and the latter believe that man is too good to be damned."

32. See especially his letters to the *New York Atlas*, 7 September and 21 December 1845.

33. Entry for 18 July 1848 in "Diary, July 5–Aug. 11, 1848: Trip Across New York State, to Montreal and Quebec, and Return to Bridgeport" (BPL). After reflecting on what her father had written, Caroline changed the offending word to "mockery."

34. See below, p. 264.

35. PTB to Rev. Henry Ward Beecher, 10 August 1874, *SL*, p. 183.

36. PTB to Rev. Theodore L. Cuyler, 3 August 1864, *SL*, p. 129.

37. *Funny Stories*, p. 44.

38. The agreement for this building, dated 3 May 1883, and much of Barnum's correspondence with Capen and others regarding it may be found in *SL*, pp. 234 ff.

39. The museum was largely destroyed, together with Jumbo and other Barnum memorabilia, during a fire in 1975. It has since been rebuilt on a less imposing scale and remains a center for study in the biological sciences. The lower story of the new buiding preserves the gray stone exterior of the original structure, and above the front entrance may still be seen "Barnum Fecit A.D. MDCCCLXXXIII."

40. *SL*, p. 254.

41. The Reverend Mr. Coddington, who eventually was entitled to inscribe "D.D." after his name, ably served a number of Universalist parishes up to the time of his death in 1912.

42. See *AB* (1869), p. 383. Watt, in his *From Heresy Toward Truth*, p. 88, reveals that Barnum subsidized the book.

43. *Will & Codicils*, pp. 26, 43–44. The records of the Universalist Publishing House, containing entries on the status of the money left by Barnum and how it was expended, are now in the Andover-Harvard Theological Library at the Harvard Divinity School. During his lifetime, too, Barnum sometimes ordered and distributed copies of sermons that especially impressed him. In October 1890, e.g., he placed one such order with the Standard Company of Bridgeport for 500 copies of a sermon on Universalist beliefs recently delivered by his last Bridgeport pastor, the Reverend L. B. Fisher.

44. *Bridgeport Standard*, 24 February 1880.

45. Edith Sessions Tupper, "P. T. Barnum at Home."

46. *New York Atlas*, 12 October 1845, 1 March 1846.

47. PTB to Moses S. Beach, 22 March 1864, *SL*, pp. 123–24. Beach was treasurer of the Union.

48. An order in Barnum's hand, dated 3 March 1880, for two shares in this organization is in the Boston Public Library.

49. PTB to Dr. Russell T. Trall (?), 11 February 1854, *SL*, pp. 70–71. See also Barnum's letters to Trall of 27 April [1853], *SL*, pp. 68–69; and to Rev. Thomas Wentworth Higginson, c. April 1855, *SL*, p. 87.

50. Their appearances are announced in the 6, 13, and 20 June 1874 issues of the *Bridgeport Standard*.

51. *Olympia Brown: An Autobiography*, edited and completed by Gwendolen B. Willis, *Annual Journal of the Universalist Historical Society*, 4 (1963), 39. Brown has little to say about her Bridgeport pastorate in her autobiography and even reports incorrectly the year of her beginning there (1870, she writes). I have explored in detail this neglected period of her life and have written about it in "Olympia Brown in Bridgeport: 'Acts of Injustice' or a Failed Ministry?" from which much of the following information is drawn.

52. PTB to Rev. Olympia Brown, 6 April 1872, *SL*, pp. 167–68.

53. PTB to Mrs. Willis, 20 April 1875 (TU).

54. The letter was published in the *Bridgeport Standard* of 25 May 1875.

55. According to the society's clerk (an interested party, however) who kept the minutes of this meeting, the showman also demanded that he be given the right to select a new slate of officers.

56. For Barnum's remarks on his drinking habits and conversion, see *AB* (1855), pp. 109, 359–66.

57. See below, pp. 146–47.

58. *AB* (1855), p. 361. In an interview in the *New York Sun* of 13 January 1884, reprinted in the "Appendix" to the 1884 "Author's Edition" of *AB* (Courier Co., pp. 341–44), Barnum later told a slightly different story—namely, that when his mother-in-law reproached him at the dinner table for drinking too much wine, which left him feeling groggy during the afternoon, he threatened to go back to drinking hard liquor.

59. *Christian Ambassador*, 27 August 1853. More puzzling yet is the claim he sometimes made that there were no true Universalists in prisons.

60. These and other arguments are contained in a twelve-page pamphlet Barnum wrote in 1853 entitled *The Liquor Business: Its Effects Upon the Minds, Morals, and Pockets of Our People*, No. 4 in the Whole World's Temperance Tracts.

61. PTB to Rev. Dixon Spain, 18 November 1882, *SL*, pp. 230–32.

62. *AB* (1855), pp. 363–65.

63. See the *New York Times*, 20 February 1888.

64. Barnum himself, by his own admission, was a mighty smoker of cigars until 1860, when he finally stopped after becoming alarmed over some heart palpitations—see the 13 January 1884 interview in the *New York Sun*, also available, but abridged, in *AB* (1889), pp. 336–37, and (Bryan), pp. 766–70. For a more extensive account of his horrendous experiences with tobacco, see the remarks in his lecture "The Art of Money-Getting," *AB* (1869), pp. 466–67, also in (Bryan), pp. 841–43.

65. Printed Circular Letter, c. June 1850, *SL*, p. 43.

66. *The Liquor Business*, p. 2.

67. In a note to the early editions of this article, Barnum writes that its publication was occasioned "in part" by the recent appearance of an English secularist's tract entitled *The Christian Doctrine of Hell*. From evidence in his letters and elsewhere, it would seem he originally wrote it, under the interrogatory title "Why Am I a Universalist?" during the summer of 1888 with a view toward publication in the *North American Review*. The editors of that journal apparently thought it too controversial, however, and it was only at the urging of English friends that he finally consented to its publication in the *Christian World*.

68. A few years earlier, in the interview published in the *New York Sun* of 13 January 1884, he had given his views on the insufficiency of repentance and the value of punishment in this world and the next: "I believe there is a great Creator, infinite in his attributes of wisdom, power and mercy: that His name is Love. I believe He is a God of all justice, and that He will chasten every person whom He ever created sufficiently to reform him, in this world or some other. In other words, I believe that no man ever committed a sin that he did not have to pay for it. Even repentance will not save him. When a man who has committed a murder swings off the gallows, proclaiming, 'I'm going to swing into an eternity of bliss among the redeemed,' I don't believe him. . . . No law of nature or of God can be transgressed and the transgressor evade the penalty, even by repentance. Suppose a poor man goes out on a Saturday night, gets drunk and spends his week's wages. The next morning he may sincerely repent for what he has done, but that will not stop his headache or bring back the money he has squandered. If his repentance is sincere, perhaps he will not do it again, but whatever he does he has to pay for, in this world or the next. In many instances, I have no doubt, the payment is made in the next world, which I think will be found much the same as this, only that there we will not be surrounded by so many temptations. I do not believe in an eternal

contest between evil and good, in an infinite devil and an infinite God, but believe that God will do that which he demands of man, 'overcome evil with good,' so that eventually, after everyone has received proper punishment and chastening—disciplinary and not vindictive—all will become good, and holy, and happy."

69. A glowing letter from Perin to Barnum, reprinted from the *Christian Leader*, was published in the 16 August 1890 issue of the *Bridgeport Standard*.

70. The controversy was written up in a number of Bridgeport and New York newspapers and is summarized in an undated, unidentified clipping in the Andover-Harvard Theological Library.

71. One such minister, according to Bailey in his *History of Danbury*, p. 197, was the Reverend Lewis F. W. Andrews, who briefly assisted Barnum on the *Herald of Freedom* before he was called to the Second Universalist Church of Philadelphia. See also PTB to Gideon Welles, 7 October 1832 (*SL*, p. 3), for a reference to "Andrews" at the start of his employment with Barnum.

72. Cited in Justin Kaplan, *Walt Whitman: A Life* (New York: Simon and Schuster, 1980), p. 231.

Chapter IV: Showman Barnum

1. "Recollections of P. T. Barnum," *Christian Leader*, 16 November 1929. This article was first published in 1894 in the *Laurentian* of St. Lawrence University, one of the Universalist schools Barnum helped support.

2. *AB* (1855), pp. 142–46.

3. Barnum tells the story of his involvement with Heth and the Italian juggler "Signor Vivalla" in Chapter 7 of the first edition of *AB*, pp. 148–76. As noted above, the originals of the agreements between Lindsay and Bowling and between Lindsay and Barnum for the exhibiting of Heth are now in the Fred D. Pfening III Collection and the Boston Public Library.

4. Undated handbill for Boston's Concert Hall (Chicago Historical Society).

5. *Ibid.*

6. *New York Sun*, 26 February 1836. The figure was revised upwards to between ten and twelve thousand dollars, including admission fees taken at the autopsy, in the issue of 1 March. Bennett, in the *Herald* of 29 February, asserted $700 had been realized by the autopsy. Here it may be pointed out that in the nineteenth century surgeons themselves customarily charged medical students and others to view them at work and realized a considerable portion of their incomes from these fees. In the present instance those who complained about the admission fee were not objecting to the practice itself but rather to the fact they had not gotten their money's worth.

7. See the *Herald* of 27 and 29 February and 2 March 1836, and the *Sun* of 1 March 1836. While referring to neither Barnum nor Lyman by name, it is interesting that Locke, in telling how he was let in on the deception of Bennett, always writes of Joice's "exhibitors" in the plural.

8. The four articles appear in the 8, 13, 17, and 24 September 1836 issues of the *Herald*.

9. "A Go-A-Head Day with Barnum," p. 627. Smith's assurances about the veracity of his tale occur at the head of the first part of the article, p. 522.

10. See below, p. 88.

11. PTB to Mr. Baker, c. March 1853, *SL*, p. 8. In his autobiography, too, Barnum writes that the next contact he had with Lindsay was in Pittsburgh in 1841, when Lindsay, at the instigation of a rival manager, pretended Barnum still owed him a pipe of brandy for the Joice Heth transaction and had him thrown into jail. "Twelve years afterwards," he continues (p. 213), "he called upon me in Boston, with an apology. He was miserably poor, and I was highly prosperous. I hope I may be allowed to add that he did not afterwards lack a friend."

12. See, e.g., the *Herald* of 3 October 1865.

13. This particular address book, which appears to have been used by Barnum around the period 1888–89, is in the BM.

14. Bunn, *Old England and New England*, pp. 62–63.

15. This occurred during Barnum's tour with Jenny Lind, when the showman—or so the *Herald* claimed—accused a number of editors and reporters of trying to "blackmail" him through offering to suppress unfavorable news items and publish only good ones. The showman had answered they were free to publish anything they liked, but had then made public their letters to him and his replies. Bennett, typically, insisted on putting the worst construction on the affair, even going so far as to suggest Barnum had manufactured all the correspondence himself. See, in particular, the *Herald* of 15, 17, and 26 October and 9 November 1850.

16. *New York Herald*, 3 October 1865.

17. Pond, *Eccentricities of Genius*, p. 354.

18. PTB to JAB, 2 April 1891, *SL*, p. 332.

19. *Complimentary Banquet*, p. 15.

20. *The Humbugs of the World*, pp. 24–25; *Funny Stories*, pp. 265–67, 269–70.

21. *AB* (1869), p. 493.

22. *The Humbugs of the World*, p. 20. In a speech Barnum delivered several years earlier at an agricultural fair held at Stamford, Connecticut, he gave a somewhat different definition: "A humbug is an imposter; but, in my opinion, the true meaning of humbug is management—tact—to take an old truth and put it in an attractive form." The speech is reported in an undated, unidentified newspaper clipping in Vol. 7 of the "Barnum's Enterprises" scrapbooks in the NYHS and was no doubt his unpublished lecture on the "philosophy" or "science of humbug," which he consulted Bayard Taylor about during the summer of 1854 (see PTB to Bayard Taylor, 4 and 24 August 1854, *SL*, pp. 79–80). In the first edition of the autobiography Barnum informs us that he originally delivered the lecture at the Fairfield County Agricultural Fair in 1854 (p. 374). Toward the end of the same edition he mentions his researches into the "history of humbug" and that he is "preparing, and hope in good time to publish, a work that I trust will do full justice to that universal science" (p. 381).

23. Bill for Vivalla at Hinman's Hotel, Bridgeport, 1 and 2 April [1836] (Somers Historical Society, New York); *AB* (1855), pp. 160–61.

24. A printed program for one such entertainment, featuring "Sleight-of-Hand & Mesmerism by the Hon. P. T. Barnum," given aboard the Cunard steamer *Etruria* on 17 October 1889, is in the FDP. In a note to the first edition of the autobiography (p. 333), Barnum comments on the causes of his becoming a magician.

25. *New York Atlas*, 26 May 1844.

26. *AB* (1855), p. 210; Noah M. Ludlow, *Dramatic Life as I Found It*, p. 533.

27. PTB to Francis Courtney Wemyss, 21 January 1840, *SL*, pp. 9–10. This letter is addressed from number 101½ Bowery, the site of Barnum and Proler's business establishment.

28. PTB to Francis Courtney Wemyss, 16 April 1840 (Columbia University Rare Book and Manuscript Library).

29. *Theatrical Management in the West and South for Thirty Years*, p. 155.

30. PTB to Sol Smith, 3 March [1841], *SL*, p. 12.

31. PTB to Various Fellow Showmen, 27 February 1841, *SL*, pp. 10–11.

32. Ludlow, *Dramatic Life as I Found It*, p. 533.

33. *AB* (1855), pp. 189–90.

34. PTB to Rev. Thomas Wentworth Higginson, c. April 1855, *SL*, p. 86.

35. *New York Atlas*, 16 February 1845.

36. *Ibid.*, 21 July 1844.

37. *Ibid.*, 20 April 1845.

38. See, e.g., *AB* (1855), p. 356.

39. The Missouri Historical Society possesses an interesting letter by Ludlow dating from the period when he and his partner Sol Smith were negotiating with Barnum for

the use of their St. Louis theatre during his Jenny Lind tour. Writing to his daughter from New Orleans on 2 February 1851, Ludlow tells of the difficulty he is having in hiring out their slave "Betsy," who evidently was in the habit of misbehaving. Unless she mends her ways, he writes, he will sell her. On the subject of racism among American scientists around this time, see Robert V. Bruce, *The Launching of Modern American Science, 1846–1876* (New York: Alfred A. Knopf, 1987), pp. 124–25.

Chapter V: The Wonders of God's Universe

1. Bunn, *Old England and New England*, pp. 48–49, 57, 64.
2. *AB* (1855), p. 394; (1869), pp. 468–69.
3. On the early history of the American Museum, see Robert M. and Gale S. McClung, "Tammany's Remarkable Gardiner Baker: New York's First Museum Proprietor," *New-York Historical Society Quarterly*, 42 (1958), 142–69; and Loyd Haberly, "The American Museum from Baker to Barnum," *ibid.*, 43 (1959), 272–87. Scattered references to the early Museum also appear in Charles Coleman Sellers's *Mr. Peale's Museum: Charles Willson Peale and the First Popular Museum of Natural Science and Art*. The later history of the Museum while under Barnum's management has been entertainingly summarized in William W. Appleton's "The Marvellous Museum of P. T. Barnum," in *Le Merveilleux et les Arts du Spectacle*, Actes du IIIe Congrès International d'Histoire du Théâtre, pp. 57–62. I have myself written about the establishment in "P. T. Barnum's American Museum," published in *Seaport*, the history magazine of New York's South Street Seaport Museum, 20, No. 3 (Winter 1986–87), 27–33.
4. *AB* (1855), pp. 215–22. And for Barnum's dealings with Olmsted himself, see above, pp. 31–32.
5. *AB* (1855), p. 190.
6. *AB* (1855), pp. 111–15; *Funny Stories*, pp. 46–48. Both Bailey's Christian name and surname are variously spelled in contemporary documents and on his tombstone in the town cemetery at Somers, and Barnum himself spells the former as "Hackariah." The spellings I give appear to be those eventually settled on.
7. Not always peaceably, it should be added. On the stage career of Van Amburgh, see A. H. Saxon, *The Life and Art of Andrew Ducrow & The Romantic Age of the English Circus*, pp. 321–40.
8. Sellers, *Mr. Peale's Museum*, p. 42 and *passim*.
9. See Haberly, "The American Museum from Baker to Barnum," pp. 282–83.
10. *Catalogue or Guide Book of Barnum's American Museum, New York, Containing Descriptions and Illustrations of the Various Wonders and Curiosities of This Immense Establishment . . .* (New York: printed for the proprietor by Wynkoop, Hallenbeck & Thomas, n.d.). An amusing earlier guidebook, in which occurs the description of corals, masquerades as a children's narrative wherein "Uncle Timothy Find-Out" conducts his nephews on a tour of the Museum: *Sights and Wonders in New York; Including a Description of the Mysteries, Miracles, Marvels, Phenomena, Curiosities, and Nondescripts Contained in that Great Congress of Wonders, Barnum's Museum; also, a Memoir of Barnum Himself, with a Description and Engraving of His Oriental Villa . . .* (New York: J. S. Redfield, 1849).
11. Barnum had first seen and purchased the exhibition—whose inhabitants obviously had to be renewed from time to time—during his initial trip to England. Such "peaceable kingdoms" had been exhibited for ages in Europe.
12. See below, pp. 235–36. The poet and playwright Percy MacKaye, in his biography of his famous father, tells of Steele MacKaye's once buying an anaconda from Barnum and keeping it as a pet. Elsewhere in this work Percy tells of once being taken by his father to meet the great showman, whom he describes as "that imperishable Yankee of the twilight zone of veracity . . . now become the immortal Oberon of a saw-dust Fairyland." See *Epoch: The Life of Steele MacKaye* (New York: Boni & Liveright, 1927), I, 236–37; II, 117.
13. The 1862 catch and Aquarial Gardens themselves are described in a printed cir-

cular letter dated 27 August 1862, a copy of which is among the Oliver Wendell Holmes Papers in the Library of Congress Manuscript Division. On 29 July 1862 Barnum wrote directly to Holmes, who was a friend of the showman, enclosing a free season ticket to the Boston establishment (HU).

14. *AB* (1869), pp. 561–66.

15. Bill for the American Museum, 27 February 1861 (ISU).

16. See, e.g., Werner, *Barnum*, p. 332; Irving, *The Fabulous Showman*, pp. 193–94. The late John Rickards Betts, who at one time contemplated a separate work on Barnum's most famous animal, Jumbo, was one of the first to appreciate Barnum's contributions to natural history. His "P. T. Barnum and the Popularization of Natural History" is an expert summing up of the topic. Readers interested in the broader aspects of the subject will profit from Lynn Barber's admirable work, *The Heyday of Natural History, 1820–1870*.

17. *AB* (1869), p. 694. The "gorilla" in this case, as Barnum makes clear, was a patent fraud, which he invited his friend the African explorer Paul du Chaillu, then lecturing in this country, to expose and make the most of. Du Chaillu, an American and himself a controversial figure in his day, had startled the London scientific community by showing up there in 1861 with a large collection of stuffed gorillas he had shot and collected, thereby adding further fuel to the "descent-of-man" controversy. The bills for the second American Museum around the period Barnum writes of (1867) do indeed advertise this acquisition, touted as "the most remarkable curiosity ever presented" and the "first and only living gorilla" ever captured alive. All such advertising notwithstanding, it seems certain his museums and circuses never possessed a living gorilla during his lifetime, although Barnum repeatedly expressed his desire to obtain one. The closest he came was in 1882, when he had the offer of two preserved adult skins, which he consulted the Smithsonian about—PTB to Spencer F. Baird, 18 September 1882, and Baird to Barnum, 28 September 1882 (SIA).

18. PTB to Alexander Agassiz, 13 February 1882 (Museum of Comparative Zoology, Harvard University).

19. PTB to Henry A. Ward, 30 October 1883 (UR); PTB to Spencer F. Baird, 31 October 1883 (SIA); Alexander Agassiz to PTB, 1 November 1883 (BPL); O. C. Marsh to PTB, 2 November 1883 (BPL); Charles P. Lyman to John Collins Warren, 6 November 1883 (TU). "What shall I say to P. T. Barnum? who is in the habit of castrating wild elephants," Agassiz wrote on 1 November to Warren, who was Professor of Surgery at the Harvard Medical School and who referred the matter to his veterinarian colleague Lyman (MAHS, J. C. Warren Papers). The flippant question has often been construed by later writers as one more condemnation of Barnum's "insensitivity"; yet in his letter of the same date to the showman, the zoologist concluded there "seems to be little choice" in attempting the "dangerous experiment," considering the alternative was to destroy the animal. Yale's Professor Marsh was of the same opinion. Ward's visit to Bridgeport and Albert's later career and death are chronicled in entries in the office diary of Barnum's secretary Bowser—for 20 October, 10 and 11 November 1883, and 20 July 1885.

20. Some of Barnum's correspondence on the subject with John A. Halderman, then U.S. Minister to the court of Siam, is in the Smithsonian Institution's National Museum of American History. And see below, p. 305.

21. John Emory Bryant to his wife, 28 June–2 July 1864 (William R. Perkins Library Manuscript Department, Duke University).

22. See, e.g., *AB* (1869), pp. 560–61. According to Yale University's legendary English professor William ("Billy") Lyons Phelps, who prefaced an early recording of Barnum's "I Thus Address the World" with some remarks of his own, Barnum continued to exhibit the cherry-colored cat when later traveling with his circus. Phelps claimed to have seen one such performance himself while the circus was playing in New Haven, and he "knew" the cat, which had been borrowed by Barnum from one of Phelps's neighbors. See, e.g., Phelps's *Autobiography with Letters* (New York: Oxford Univ. Press, 1939), pp. 183–84. Billy Phelps was a great tale-spinner.

23. PTB to Baird, 22 July 1873 (SIA).

24. "Letters That Barnum Gets," *New York Sun*, 23 January 1881. And see, on this subject, *SL*, pp. 279–81, 290–91; and A. H. Saxon, "P. T. Barnum and the Great Sea Serpent," in *Bandwagon*, journal of the Circus Historical Society.

25. Barnum Museum address book, under "M" for "Mammoths."

26. Correspondence relating to the ordering of these later curiosities, as well as for an additional mermaid, triple-headed snake, and other items, occurs on pp. 31 and 106, with insertions, in the BPL "Salmagundi" ledger (see Bibliography, "Manuscripts" section). They were supplied through a Yokohama firm in 1880 for exhibition in the museum department of Barnum's traveling circus. After outliving their usefulness on the show, several of them, including the fabulous phoenix itself, were donated to the Smithsonian Institution, whose Secretary, predictably, was happy to accept these "very interesting objects"—PTB to Spencer F. Baird, 18 September 1882, and Baird to Barnum, 29 September 1882 (SIA). Further mention of these donations is made in an interview Barnum gave a reporter for an unidentified Boston newspaper in 1883. A clipping of this was enclosed with another letter he wrote Baird on 20 June 1883 (SIA).

27. Advertisement in the London *Times*, 29 August 1846. An illustrated bill with the same wording is in the Playbills Collection at the British Library, No. 41 in Vol. 366.

28. *AB* (1855), p. 346. Barnum's connection with Leach is established in the letters he wrote to Moses Kimball around this time: "The *animal* that I spoke to you & Hale about comes out at Egyptian Hall, London, next Monday, and I half fear that it will not only be exposed, but that *I* shall be *found out* in the matter"—PTB to Kimball, 18 August 1846, *SL*, p. 35. In his next letter to his friend, remarking on the failure of the exhibition, he acknowledged that "it was *rayther* too big a pill for John Bull to swallow! Still, he has a most capacious throat and stomach!"—PTB to Kimball, 18 October 1846 (NYPL).

29. The interview with "Zip's" sister appears in the *Bound Brook* (New Jersey) *Chronicle* of 30 April 1926. The *New York Times*, *New York World*, and many other newspapers published articles on him around the time of his final illness and death, which occurred on 24 April 1926. Professor Bernth Lindfors of the University of Texas has done extensive research on "Zip" and has kindly made available to me the fruits of his labor. He has himself briefly traced "Zip's" career in his article "P. T. Barnum and Africa," *Studies in Popular Culture*, 7 (1984), 18–25. On this topic, too, see pp. 134–42 of Robert Bogdan's *Freak Show: Presenting Human Oddities for Amusement and Profit*, an unsentimental study by a sociologist with an interest in physical and mental disability who also remarks on several other freaks in Barnum's employ.

30. The speech and a cut of the "What Is It?" appear on pp. 46–47 of Barnum's pamphlet *Illustrated Memoir of an Eventful Expedition into Central America Resulting in the Discovery of the Idolatrous City of Iximaya, in an Unexplored Region; and the Possession of Two Remarkable Aztec Children, Maximo (the Boy), and Bartola (the Girl), Descendants and Specimens of the Sacerdotal Caste (now nearly Extinct), of the Ancient Aztec Founders of the Ruined Temples of That Country* (New York: Wynkoop, Hallenbeck & Thomas, 1860).

31. Strong, *Diary*, III, 12 (entry for 2 March 1860).

32. N. P. Willis, *Famous Persons and Famous Places*, pp. 234–35. The cock-and-bull history of these children, as published at various times by Barnum and their managers, may be found in the pamphlet referred to in note 30 above.

33. PTB to Moses Kimball, 26 August 1850 (BA).

34. See, e.g., PTB to Henri Drayton, 4 March 1861, *SL*, pp. 111–12; *Funny Stories*, pp. 323–24.

35. PTB to Oscar Kohn, 8 March 1861, *SL*, pp. 112–13. Kohn was himself for many years in Barnum's employ, looking after the animals exhibited at the Museum and in Barnum's early circus and acting as his agent in securing other attractions. When Barnum, during his term as mayor of Bridgeport, was accused of maligning the city's Jewish community, Kohn was one of his Jewish friends who testified to his lack of prejudice—see above, p. 56.

36. PTB to Kimball, 26 September 1843, *SL*, p. 22.

37. *AB* (1869), pp. 573–78.

38. See below, p. 291.

39. *AB* (1869), p. 543. And see below, pp. 250–51.

40. In a few letters written toward the end of his life, Barnum does occasionally employ the word "midget"; and in deference to the tender sensibilities of readers and editors, the same term is usually employed in the course of this work. However, it must be noted that all diminutive individuals—including those suffering from hypopituitarism—are more properly referred to as "dwarfs," and that, despite the often forbidding connotations of the word, the national organization known as the Little People of America encourages its members to use and accept the medically correct term. "Midget," as a director of this organization once complained to the author, is usually employed in "a most derogatory manner by the general public." Interestingly, within recent years many members of the LPA have also voiced objections to "little people" itself as being too "cute" and condescending; and they most emphatically reject descriptions of them by well-intentioned but sentimental authors as "very special people." This last term, of course, has even more peculiar connotations for those familiar with the euphemisms currently employed by the educational establishment. While on this subject, it may be worth mentioning that the author feels no need to apologize for his use of the word "freak." There have been many determined efforts to find and force into general usage a gentler sounding term. None has succeeded to date.

41. Sellers, *Mr. Peale's Museum*, p. 53.

42. English by birth, the son of a Presbyterian minister who was pastor to Bethel's Congregational community at the time Barnum became proprietor of the American Museum, Greenwood ended his days as American consul in Brunswick, Germany, where he died of a carbuncle in 1876. His body was shipped home for burial in Bethel, where he rests with his two wives in the municipal cemetery. The *New York Times* published his obituary in its issue of 4 March 1876; additional references to him and his father occur in the parish records of Bethel's Congregational Church. And see above, p. 28, and below, p. 258.

43. See, e.g., PTB to Unidentified Correspondent, 2 February 1856, *SL*, pp. 91–92; and PTB to Greenwood, 14 May 1864, *SL*, pp. 125–27. The earlier of these letters, as I discovered after my edition of Barnum's letters had gone to press, was in fact addressed to the Massachusetts legislator and dentist Dr. David K. Hitchcock, who at one time numbered a Turk among his students.

44. *Biographical Sketch of the Circassian Girl, Zalumma Agra; or "Star of the East"* (Philadelphia: James B. Rodgers, 1873), p. 11.

45. James describes his formative experiences at the Museum and his ambiguous memories of it in Chapter 12 of his *A Small Boy and Others*, pp. 154–65.

46. The illusion may be viewed today in some of the effects in Walt Disney's "Haunted Mansions." Even more spectacular is its employment in a terrifying illusion that is exhibited on carnival midways and sometimes as an independent attraction—that in which a woman, after being placed in a trance and bound to a stake inside a cage, is gradually, before spectators' eyes, transformed into a gorilla. The climax arrives when the animal wakes and opens its eyes, breaks its bonds and charges to the front of the cage, and begins shaking and demolishing the bars. The act is customarily presented inside a tent whose sidewalls, in order to minimize accidents should a panic ensue, are deliberately left hanging loose and unstaked to the ground.

47. Here, as in the above section dealing with freaks, my information is drawn primarily from bills and advertisements for the Museum during the years of Barnum's management. For the history of Barnum's Lecture Room, I must also acknowledge my indebtedness to the work of Miss Camille Calman, who, as a student in the Barnum seminar I once taught at Yale, researched the topic and presented her findings in an excellent term paper.

48. *Gleason's Pictorial Drawing-Room Companion*, 29 January 1853.

49. *Frank Leslie's Illustrated Newspaper*, 30 September 1865.

50. *AB* (1869), pp. 120, 135.

51. The original article, entitled "A Word about Museums," was published in the *Nation* of 27 July 1865. Barnum's reply, dated 29 July, was published in the 10 August issue. From letters he wrote to friends around this time, it appears he did not intend his reply for publication, but merely hoped to convince the anonymous critic to "do him justice." He was, in fact, impressed by the writer's ideas for improvement and his knowledge of European museums, and hoped to benefit from his advice in the setting up of his new museum.

52. The figures for ticket sales at the two museums are reported by Barnum in Chapter 49 of later editions of the autobiography—(1889), p. 314, e.g.

53. Children half price, it should perhaps be added. Toward the end of the Ann Street museum's career, and at Barnum's second establishment uptown, the admission fee was thirty cents, fifteen cents for children. This was the only increase during the nearly thirty years of his management.

54. *AB* (1869), pp. 638–48. The Chinese Museum was another institution with Philadelphia antecedents whose collections Barnum had absorbed at an earlier date. The new American Museum opened its doors on 6 September, although Barnum gives the date as 13 November in his autobiography. Considering his usual reliability in dating, the slip seems curious, perhaps deliberate. By the time he came to write of the burning of his two museums in the 1869 edition of the autobiography, he had already suffered from three devastating fires, including the destruction of his oriental mansion Iranistan. The possibility of arson occurred to several of his contemporaries, and the showman seems to have been sensitive on this point. Certainly the opening of his second museum within the brief period of four months, let alone two, struck many readers of the autobiography as little short of miraculous. Yet in the same work Barnum assures us that the destruction of his first museum was complete—"not a thousand dollars' worth of the entire property was saved"—and that the total amount of insurance was "but forty thousand dollars."

55. *AB* (1869), pp. 698–700; and see, in particular, PTB to Bayard Taylor, 16, 22, and 28 July 1865, *SL*, pp. 136–45. In addition to consulting Taylor about these ambitious plans, Barnum hoped he would travel to Europe as his agent and acquire objects for him.

56. The "card," signed by Barnum, continued to figure as an advertisement for the museum on Wood's engraved stationery, which Barnum now felt entitled to use for his personal correspondence.

57. See PTB to W. C. Coup, 8 October 1870, *SL*, p. 163.

58. The contract between Barnum and Bunnell, dated 2 November 1876, is in the BPL. Each man agreed to furnish half the capital, and curiosities were to be purchased from Wood's Museum.

59. Barnum's private letter to Reid, dated 29 November 1876, is among the Reid Family Papers in the LC's Manuscript Division. The accompanying letter meant for publication is dated at Bridgeport on 28 November.

60. *Prospectus of Barnum's Museum Company*. The prospectus, a copy of which may be found in the Theatre Collection of the Museum of the City of New York, was sent to various newspapers and journals around the time of its publication. *Harper's Weekly* for 17 July 1880, e.g., published a long summary of its contents and reproduced the accompanying illustration of the proposed building.

61. From letters he wrote to friends and business associates, it is obvious Barnum was involved in this ambitious project by the summer of 1879. A year later, on 3 July 1880, although not yet sure all the stock would be taken ("*I think it will*, but will never move towards starting the colossal enterprise unless it is *all* taken"), he was writing to Professor Ward of Ward's Natural Science Establishment, assuring him he would receive a contract to supply the museum with exhibits provided "you are the man who can best & cheapest fill the department you name" (UR). According to the prospectus, William H. Vanderbilt had already subscribed $250,000 to the project, but monies were not to

be called in, nor work on the building begun, until the amount subscribed had reached two million dollars.

62. *Funny Stories*, pp. 320–23.

63. Baird to Barnum, 9 May 1882 (SIA).

64. PTB to Spencer F. Baird, 10 June 1882 (SIA). The two men had been corresponding about the zoo since at least early May—see Baird to Barnum, 9 May 1882 (SIA). In 1886 there was further talk of Barnum's participating in the establishment of a zoo at Washington, but again he pulled out, this time, as he wrote to William Temple Hornaday, the chief taxidermist and curator of living animals at the Smithsonian's National Museum, because his circus partners "cannot raise courage at present"—PTB to Hornaday, 4 September 1886 (SIA). It was Hornaday, more than anyone else, who lobbied for and was responsible for the eventual creation of the National Zoological Park, established by a new Congressional Act on 2 March 1889. He served briefly but unofficially as the park's first superintendent—soliciting and receiving advice from Barnum while in this position—but was forced to resign from the Smithsonian in June 1890 owing to differences with the new Secretary, Samuel P. Langley. In 1896 he became the first director of the New York Zoological Park, more familiarly known as the Bronx Zoo, a position he occupied with the greatest distinction until his retirement in 1926.

Here it may be added that the association between zoos and circuses was quite common in the nineteenth century, particularly before the latter established their winter quarters. Circuses often deposited their animals in zoos during the months they were not traveling—an arrangement that was mutually beneficial, since the zoos were thereby enabled to exhibit exotic specimens they might not themselves possess or be able to afford, while the circuses were relieved of the expense of feeding and caring for their animals during the off-season. Before establishing his own winter quarters, Barnum often sent his animals to New York's Central Park Zoo. When later they instead showed up in Bridgeport each winter, he complained about their "eating their heads off." Zoos and circuses also frequently exchanged animals (a practice that, to a lesser degree, continues to the present day), and keepers moved freely back and forth between the two types of establishment.

65. The Articles of Agreement between the two partners, entered into on 26 October 1887, state that one of the objectives of this association will be "the conduct of a permanent museum or other exhibition in such cities of the United States as may be mutually agreed upon."

Chapter VI: Of Mermaids and the Man in Miniature

1. *AB* (1855), p. 242. The 1853 receipts are confirmed in the big ledger Barnum had kept since his Bethel days, on page 250 of which occurs the statement for the Museum in 1853. The receipts for that year were $135,249; expenses were $80,598.40; and profits were $55,650.60 (BPL). The figure of $300,000 per year is the one Barnum gives in the 1880 Prospectus for Barnum's Museum Company, p. 8.

2. *AB* (1855), pp. 218, 222–23.

3. *AB* (1869), pp. 125–26.

4. *AB* (1869), pp. 141–42.

5. Strong, *Diary*, IV, 18 (entry for 13 July 1865).

6. This particular contest, which commenced in late 1855, was ingeniously planned to extend over the greater part of a year, although it appears to have petered out following Barnum's bankruptcy in early 1856. After visitors had been given a month in which to view and vote by paper ballot on all the photographs and daguerreotypes submitted, the field was narrowed to one hundred "female beauties," whose protraits were to be painted in oils and displayed for several additional months. The "people" were then to be given again the opportunity to decide the issue, and premiums, ranging from a first prize of $1000 to $20 apiece for the last ninety contestants, were to be awarded to all these finalists.

7. *AB* (1869), pp. 146–48.

8. *AB* (1869), pp. 158–59. *Gleason's Pictorial Drawing-Room Companion* for 29 January 1853 comments in particular on the Museum's "valuable collection of portraits of distinguished Americans, which the elder Peale spent his entire lifetime in collecting. . . . it is invaluable to the American public, and can never be replaced should accident befall it, which Heaven avert!"

9. On Kimball, whose dates are 1809–95, and the early years of his Boston Museum, see Claire McGlinchee, *The First Decade of the Boston Museum;* the *National Cyclopaedia of American Biography*, 20:70; the obituary notice and reminiscences of him in the *Boston Transcript* for 21 February 1895; and, most informative of all, the biographical sketch by Charles A. Cummings in the *New-England Historical and Genealogical Register*, 56 (1902), 334–40. The English writer Alfred Bunn briefly describes a meeting with Kimball in his *Old England and New England*, pp. 214–16.

10. Kimball's letters to Barnum appear to be no longer extant, while most of those extant by Barnum date from 1843, with lesser numbers in later years. The majority of these are today in the Boston Athenaeum, many of them scorched and damaged by a fire, which may also account for the loss of Barnum's earlier letters. A smaller cache of undamaged letters is in the New York Public Library.

11. PTB to Kimball, 8 March 1843, *SL*, p. 17; 31 March 1843; 15 July 1843; 1 September 1843, *SL*, p. 21; 26 October 1843; 8 November 1843, *SL*, p. 24; 15 November 1843 (all in BA).

12. *AB* (1855), pp. 352–56. Twenty-four thousand persons traveled to Hoboken, Barnum writes in the autobiography, and the total receipts were $3500. In a letter to Kimball of 30 August 1843, the day before the hunt, he writes of expecting 16,000 persons and $1000 as his half-share of the ferry receipts (BA). On 1 September the figures still were not tallied, but "probably about 12,000" had attended, "giving me some $600—possibly more" (BA).

13. PTB to Kimball, 21 September 1843 (BA); see also his letter to Kimball of the previous 18 September (BA).

14. PTB to Kimball, 30 September and 6 October 1843 (BA).

15. PTB to Kimball, 3 March 1843; 8 March 1843, *SL*, pp. 16–17; 16 March 1843 (all in BA).

16. See, e.g., the puffs and advertisements in the *Herald* of 22 and 25 March.

17. PTB to Kimball, 20 March 1843, *SL*, pp. 17–18; 22 March 1843, *SL*, pp. 18–19; 29 March 1843; 4 April 1843; 8 April 1843 (all in BA). The original exposé evidently occurred in the 19 March issue of the *New York Sunday Times*, copies of which no longer appear to be extant, and was then repeated in other papers whose editors were not under Barnum's thumb. See, e.g., the Philadelphia *Spirit of the Times* for 29 March 1843.

18. PTB to Kimball, 21 March 1843; 22 March 1843, *SL*, pp. 18–19; 27 March 1843, *SL*, pp. 20–21 (all in BA).

19. The Lysons Collection in the British Library contains several interesting items relating to the exhibiting of mermaids in England, including an account of an attempt to kidnap one of them; and the circus collection once belonging to Frederick Martin, then to Baron Sidney Bernstein (but which was recently auctioned off at Sotheby's), possessed many prints and articles on the subject dating from the mid-eighteenth century on. Thomas Frost, in his *The Old Showmen and the Old London Fairs* (London: Chatto & Windus, 1881), p. 162, mentions one mermaid that was exhibited at a Charing Cross tavern around the middle of the same century. Mermaids in Dutch collections, some of which Barnum visited during a later trip abroad, are touched on in Marja Keyser's *Komt dat Zien! De Amsterdamse Kermis in de negentiende eeuw* (Amsterdam and Rotterdam: B. M. Israel and Ad. Donker, 1976), pp. 202–3. The author once told me she had seen many such specimens in Dutch museums. On mermaids at the Peale museums, see Haberly, "The American Museum from Baker to Barnum," p. 286; and Sellers, *Mr. Peale's Museum*, pp. 299 and 318. The mermaid exhibited at the Philadelphia Peale's was probably among the objects Barnum and Kimball later bought and divided. In any event, Barnum

writes in the 1855 edition of his autobiography (p. 236) that "smaller specimens . . . less elaborately gotten up" than the Fejee Mermaid were exhibited in other museums of his day, and that he purchased one of these from the Peale collection in Philadelphia and exhibited it at his own museum in that city. When that establishment was destroyed by fire in 1851, the mermaid perished along with it. As mentioned in a preceding note, at least one additional mermaid was ordered by Barnum from Japan in 1880. Kimball and other American museum proprietors may well have done likewise.

On page 301 of Sellers's book the author reproduces a photograph of the two mermaids at Harvard, which eventually came to possess many of the objects once in the Boston Museum. They are identified in the legend as the "Rival Mermaids"—i.e., the Fejee Mermaid and her Philadelphia competitor, with the former described as being at the bottom of the photograph and the latter at the top. Yet, as an indication of how uncertain these matters are, when I visited the museum to examine and photograph these creatures myself, I was assured they had been misidentified in Sellers's legend and that the one at the *top* of his illustration was the real Fejee Mermaid. Although their provenance seems sound enough, I remain unconvinced that either of them is the Fejee Mermaid (for that matter, considering what Barnum writes in the autobiography, it seems unlikely either of them is the Philadelphia "rival"). Neither possesses a good or even adequate resemblance to the "Correct Likeness of the Fejee Mermaid" published in the first edition of Barnum's autobiography—an engraving that, in point of hideousness and unromantic verisimilitude, was probably just that. Nor do the tiny creatures at Harvard correspond with Barnum's written account, wherein he describes the Mermaid as being "about three feet long" and makes a point of distinguishing it from the "smaller specimens" in other museums. The explanation sometimes advanced that the Harvard specimens have shrunken (to around half that length) does not hold up, since the Mermaid was at least twenty years old when it came into Barnum's hands, who also writes that it was already "dried-up." To the above I shall only add that as recently as 1950 another mermaid, also identified as the "Fejee" one and looking every bit as authentic as her sisters at Harvard, surfaced during the auction of the Stanford White Collection in New York City. It came into the possession of a Franciscan friar.

20. Then again, perhaps one should not be too quick to condemn the credulity of our forefathers, considering what passes for "fact" in the present day. A few weeks before the above lines were written, one of America's sensational weekly tabloids, whose readers number in the millions, was proclaiming on its front page the discovery of an entire family of mermaids in some eastern ocean. Within the past few years, too, "scientific" expeditions have been sent out and "societies" and "projects" have been established to chase after the nebulous monsters of Loch Ness and Lake Champlain; a blurred film of some hairy creature running through woods—looking for all the world like Hervey Leach out for an airing in his "What Is It?" costume—has been shown in movie houses and on late-night television, with a narrator assuring us, in suitably pompous tones, that we are witnessing the antics of the legendary "Sasquatch"; an expedition has been announced as about to depart for darkest Africa, with the object of capturing an evil-tempered swamp-dwelling dinosaur given to frightening Pygmies and other easily terrified individuals (the inspiration for this last hoax, incidentally, may be found in Carl Hagenbeck's 1909 book *Von Tieren und Menschen*). When one considers the body of scientific knowledge that has accumulated since Barnum's day, then weighs it against stories like the above and all the other superstitions that continue to beset the human race, one could easily despair of ever seeing man evolve into a rational being. More to the point, Barnum would have felt right at home and flourished in such a "modern" environment.

21. For Barnum's own account of the Mermaid, see *AB* (1855), pp. 230–42; and his later remarks on its history in the 1869 edition, pp. 129–30.

22. The agreement is now in the FDP.

23. PTB to Moses Kimball, 5, 10, 13, and 21 February; 20 March 1843, *SL*, p. 18 (all in BA). On the furor over the Mermaid in Charleston, see Harris, *Humbug*, pp. 65–67, who studied and pieced together local newspaper articles bearing on the controversy.

24. PTB to Kimball, 21 February 1843 (BA); 27 March 1843, *SL*, p. 20.

25. PTB to Kimball, 4 September 1843 (BA).

26. The undated extract was included in an undated letter, apparently written in early May 1843, and was sent to Kimball with a brief note appended (BA). Chapin was actually pastor to the Charlestown, Massachusetts, Universalist society at the time and did not commence his ministry in New York City until 1848. Like many of his colleagues, however, he was often invited to preach elsewhere and no doubt visited the New York society from time to time.

27. The newspapers barely mention the other curiosities that were in the Mermaid show, and neither Barnum nor anyone else seems to have attached much value to them, although several of these preserved objects genuinely merited naturalists' attention. The rare duckbill platypus, for example, was a creature that struck so many nineteenth-century scientists and laymen as preposterous that, not having yet had the opportunity to view living specimens, they were prepared to swear *it* was a fabrication and therefore dismissed it out-of-hand.

28. PTB to Kimball, 30 January 1845 (BA); *AB* (1855), p. 241. The Temple Records of the Church of Jesus Christ of Latter-Day Saints do indeed contain some information on Lyman, whose date of death, however, is not given. He was born "about 1803." For this and other information on Lyman, I am indebted to Mr. Monte Burr McLaw of the church's Genealogical Library in Salt Lake City.

29. After working for his father as a teamster and then as a tailor and constable in his native Bethel, Philo Fairchild Barnum had gravitated to Bridgeport around 1838. He was later, at various times, a deputy U.S. marshal; deputy, then high sheriff of Fairfield County; the Bridgeport postmaster; and, for many years, the city sheriff. Occasionally, too, he functioned as agent for his half-brother in the latter's Bridgeport real-estate transactions. Philo died in February 1878, aged seventy-one, and was buried in Mountain Grove Cemetery.

30. Barnum tells the story of Tom Thumb and his adventures while traveling with him on pp. 243–95 of the first edition of the autobiography; and again, with expansion and modification, on pp. 163–261 of the 1869 edition. The Bryan edition of the autobiography, pp. 240–309, essentially follows the later account. For reasons alluded to elsewhere in this chapter, there probably never will be a "definitive" biography of Tom Thumb. Still useful to anyone coming to the topic for the first time, however, although fictionalized and written for "younger readers," is *Barnum Presents General Tom Thumb* by Alice Curtis Desmond, who had the advantage of growing up in Bridgeport and knew or was related to many persons once associated with Barnum and Tom Thumb. Mertie E. Romaine's *General Tom Thumb and His Lady*, written by one who personally knew Mrs. Tom Thumb during the last two decades of her life, is primarily of interest for its depiction of the famous couple during their later years and of Lavinia herself and the other midgets with whom she continued to work following Tom Thumb's death in 1883. I have myself edited *The Autobiography of Mrs. Tom Thumb* and written about Tom Thumb and his wife in the introduction to that work. Finally, although limiting itself largely to Barnum's first visit to England, Raymund Fitzsimons's *Barnum in London* is a well-researched, remarkably balanced account of British reaction to Barnum and his famous prodigy, their connection with the suicide of the distraught painter Benjamin Haydon, and of nineteenth-century British attitudes toward America and Americans in general.

31. Royal Archives, "Queen Victoria's Journal," entry for 23 March 1844 (by gracious permission of Her Majesty Queen Elizabeth II).

32. PTB to Kimball, 29 July 1844, *SL*, p. 27.

33. On the genetic mechanism of ateliotic dwarfism and the pedigrees of the Stratton and Bump families (Tom Thumb's wife, Lavinia, came from the latter), see Victor A. McKusick and David L. Rimoin, "General Tom Thumb and Other Midgets," *Scientific American*, July 1967, pp. 103–10.

34. The date of Charley's debut, which coincided with Thanksgiving Day that year, is confirmed in brief puff-notices in the *Herald* of 8 and 9 December. At the time he

received barely more mention than did other performers in the Museum's advertisements, and the few notices of him that were published in the papers were probably supplied by Barnum himself. To settle a matter that a number of writers have questioned, Barnum advertised him as "General Tom Thumb" from the very beginning. He was then sometimes also billed as "General Tom Thumb Junior," however, which was probably done to distinguish him from another popular midget, "Major" Stevens, who had been appearing at theatres in a vehicle entitled *Tom Thumb*, but whose own career—owing to his renewed growth in later life—had seriously declined by the time of the General's debut. On Stevens, Hervio Nano, Tom Thumb, and other freaks who performed in nineteenth-century plays, see Alvin Goldfarb, "Gigantic and Miniscule Actors on the Nineteenth-Century American Stage."

35. Agreement in the FDP. The figures in the manuscript agreement are precisely the same as those Barnum reports in the autobiography, where he adds that before the year was out he voluntarily increased the weekly amount to $25.

36. *New York Atlas*, 17 March, 9 June, and 7 July 1844.

37. *Ibid.*, 14 July 1844 and 31 August 1845.

38. My information on Hitchcock is derived primarily from Universalist archives at the Andover-Harvard Theological Library and the Greater Bridgeport Unitarian Universalist Church; his obituary in the *Universalist Register* for 1884 (where his long association with Barnum is discreetly summed up in the statement that he "for a number of years was engaged in secular life"); *Complimentary Banquet*, p. 20; and *AB* (1855), p. 393.

39. This particular text, whose manuscript is in the New-York Historical Society, appears to have been in use from around 1856 to 1858, as well as during a British tour. Elsewhere in the text, the General is mentioned as now being thirty-one inches tall, twenty-five pounds in weight, and as having been exhibited for "thirteen/fourteen years" (there are minor revisions in the script to keep it up-to-date). By this time, too, it was no longer deemed necessary to lie about the General's age, for the "Doctor" gives this information as "nineteen."

40. The General's final height and weight are reported in his obituary notice that appeared in the *New York Times* of 16 July 1883. It is not uncommon for ateliotic dwarfs to resume growing in later life, and most of the other midgets associated with Tom Thumb also suffered from this phenomenon.

41. PTB to Kimball, 30 January 1843, *SL*, pp. 13–14.

42. PTB to Kimball, 12 October 1843, *SL*, p. 23.

43. PTB to Kimball, 5 February 1843, *SL*, p. 14; 10 February, 25 March, 15 April, and 25 May 1843 (all in BA).

44. *Autobiography of Mrs. Tom Thumb*, pp. 115–16. The *Norwich* (Connecticut) *Weekly Courier* for 21 January 1857 contains an interesting account of Tom Thumb by a fellow passenger on a steamship bound for Europe around that time. After describing the General promenading the deck with a cigar nearly as big as himself in his mouth and making a fine show at the card table, the writer concludes with the observation that Tom Thumb is "a fair specimen of Young America, who has afforded the passengers a vast fund of amusement. It is a pity that the mind could not have better cultivation, for it is not without considerable capacity." The last statement touches on a common prejudice that Tom Thumb and other dwarfs of his day were forced to endure—namely, the belief that their mental powers were in direct proportion to their brain size. In her autobiography, Mrs. Tom Thumb remarks at several places on this misconception.

45. *Funny Stories*, pp. 241–43.

46. *AB* (1855), p. 263.

47. The numbering of these letters in the *Atlas* is sometimes erratic or altogether lacking, and, depending on the schedules and sailing conditions encountered by the ships carrying them, they were not always published in the order Barnum wrote them. In addition, the same issue of the paper might contain two or three letters; one letter is divided into two parts; another is designated "supplementary"; and so on. Their pub-

lication generally followed by one to two months (occasionally more) the dates on which they were written. Thus Barnum's first two letters (the earlier unnumbered, the later designated "number 2"), in which he describes the ocean crossing, are dated from Liverpool on 6 and 9 February and were published in the *Atlas* on 17 March and 7 April 1844. On 31 March, however, the paper published the first of his letters (also unnumbered) from London, dated there on 4 March; while the same issue that carried the Liverpool letter of 9 February printed two other letters (designated "3" and "4") written at Liverpool on 13 and 17 February. In documenting these letters I shall entirely dispense with their numbering and generally confine myself to their dates of publication in the *Atlas*.

48. She was an ardent fan of the American lion trainer Isaac Van Amburgh, for example, who had appeared at Astley's Amphitheatre and on the stage of Drury Lane by this date, and commissioned Edwin Landseer to do a painting of him and his big cats for the Royal Collection. On Victoria's visits to Drury Lane while Van Amburgh was performing there (on one occasion she remained behind after the other spectators had left in order to watch the animals being fed) and the outrage this occasioned among some members of the British press and acting profession, see Saxon, *The Life and Art of Andrew Ducrow*, pp. 321–27.

49. *AB* (1855), pp. 256–60. In his letters to the *Atlas*, Barnum belatedly describes this first visit to the Queen, along with his two subsequent visits, in his communication dated 29 April and published in the issue of 9 June 1844. The description given there is almost exactly the same as that in the autobiography, although the latter was purged of some observations on Victoria herself, whom Barnum considered "not of the most beautiful form or countenance."

50. Royal Archives, "Queen Victoria's Journal," entry for 23 March 1844.

51. *Ibid.*, entry for 1 April 1844. And cf. *AB* (1855), pp. 260–61.

52. *Ibid.*, entry for 19 April 1844.

53. PTB to Edward Everett, 23 March 1844, *SL*, pp. 24–25. Barnum was soon commending Everett in his *Atlas* columns; and when James Gordon Bennett shortly began attacking the minister (and incidentally Barnum) in his *New York Herald*, the showman rushed to take up the cudgels in his friend's defense. Bennett's allusions to Mr. Everett, he wrote in the *Atlas* for 16 June 1844, "have about a millionth part as much weight and influence with that gentleman as the buzzing of a musquito would have upon the granite statue of Nelson in Trafalgar Square."

54. *Atlas*, 5 May 1844.

55. *Ibid.*, 12 May 1844. There are at least two tiny court costumes supposedly worn by Tom Thumb currently on display in American collections. Barnum immediately had one replica made and sent back to America for exhibit, and boasted to his friend Albert Smith that even the tailor could not tell the original from the copy—Smith, "A Go-A-Head Day with Barnum," pp. 625–26.

56. PTB to Kimball, 18 August 1844, *SL*, p. 30.

57. *Atlas*, 23 June 1844.

58. PTB to Kimball, 17 June 1844 (BA).

59. PTB to Kimball, 18 August 1844, *SL*, p. 30.

60. *AB* (1855), pp. 261, 264.

61. *Atlas*, 14 July 1844.

Chapter VII: The Universal Yankee

1. *New York Atlas*, 28 July, 18 August, 8, 15, and 29 September 1844; 12, 19, and 26 January 1845. Descriptions of his first trip to Paris continue through several of Barnum's letters written after he had returned to England and even after his first return trip to America. He never felt compelled to keep to a strict geographical sequence in these writings and often reverted to places he had earlier visited when he had nothing particular to say about his present activities.

2. *Atlas*, 25 August 1844; PTB to Moses Kimball, 29 July 1844, *SL*, pp. 25–26; *AB* (1855), p. 345.

3. PTB to Kimball, 18 August 1844, *SL*, p. 28. "I now have got the Indians under full blast," Barnum wrote in the same letter; while in an addendum, dated 1 August, to his letter of 29 July, he expressed the belief that he and Catlin would make a large amount of money out of them. In the autobiography (1855, pp. 345–46), Barnum writes that he dispatched an unnamed agent to America to bring back from Iowa a party of Indians, which Catlin exhibited on "our joint account." Rather curiously, in his own published memoirs of his extended stay in Europe, which commenced in 1839, Catlin makes no reference to Barnum or Tom Thumb, although he does mention a group of "Ioways" he exhibited in London and Paris, brought to Europe, he writes, by one G. H. C. Melody. At least some of the "Ojibbeways" he exhibited in London during another period must have been the same as Barnum shared with Kimball in 1843, for among them was the handsome half-breed interpreter Cadotte, who fell in love with and married a white girl over Catlin's objections. The "Ojibbeways" were brought to England and managed by one Arthur Rankin, Catlin adds, who left Cadotte and his bride behind when their engagement with Catlin terminated. See *Catlin's Notes of Eight Years' Travels and Residence in Europe, with His North American Indian Collection*, 3d ed. (London: by the author, 1848), I, 110, 183 ff., 293–95; II, 1; and above, p. 117.

4. PTB to Kimball, 29 July 1844, *SL*, pp. 26–27.

5. *Atlas*, 29 September 1844.

6. Smith, "A Go-A-Head Day with Barnum." "If there was anything making a noise in the world, I got it," Rosset boasts at one point in the novel. "If I couldn't do that, I made one like it. Look at the mermaid, and the club that killed Captain Cook, with the very native who used it." He continues by describing how he once engaged "a fellow from Lambeth, Signor Genoa Verona, to spin the basin, you know, on the fishing-rod, at my circus."

7. *Atlas*, 13 and 20 October (two letters each issue) and 27 October 1844; *AB* (1855), pp. 275–81.

8. *AB* (1855), p. 344. Smith, who did not believe Shakespeare had been born in the house and consequently cared nothing about it, remarks on the indignation aroused by the threatened purchase in his "A Go-A-Head Day with Barnum," p. 525. There were many similar tales—some apocryphal, but by no means contradicted by the showman—about Barnum's outrageous attempts to purchase other national treasures and monuments: a tree on which Lord Byron had carved his initials, e.g., and, at one time, even Niagara Falls.

9. *Atlas*, 16 June 1844.

10. *Ibid.*, 29 December 1844.

11. PTB to Kimball, 29 July 1844, *SL*, p. 27; *AB* (1869), p. 225.

12. *Atlas*, 5 January 1845. In the first edition of the autobiography (p. 274) Barnum reprinted some of this article, but omitted several of his harsher criticisms and an illustration he provided of society's being "cursed," through the power of money, "with a Dogberry of a judge, or an ass of a legislator, who would disgrace a legislative body composed of boys of ordinary intelligence ten years of age." He had known a good New England "mechanic," he writes, who, through the accidental accumulation of wealth, was sent to represent his state in Congress. "Knowing that if he could be induced to write a letter his ignorance and the folly of his constituents would be exposed, I wrote him a letter and got an answer, in which he spelt corporal, 'korpril,' pleasure, 'pleashure,' and so on to the end of the chapter. This is an absolute truth, and I still have his letter. For his family's sake it may perhaps never again see the light, but I name this case merely to show the folly of setting up money as the standard of respectability."

13. *Atlas*, 5 January 1845. These reflections and many more, including the entirety of Barnum's thoughts on slavery and the abolitionists, were omitted from the autobiography.

14. *Ibid.*, 16 February 1845. In a note to this letter Barnum was careful to point out that his remarks were not occasioned by any lack of success with Tom Thumb in Scotland, for in his case the Scots' curiosity exceeded their avarice. "I have found many Scotch who are exceptions to the character I have given them," he adds, "but they are ONLY exceptions."

15. PTB to Edward Everett, 25 December 1844; Edward Everett to PTB, 29 December 1844 (both in MAHS, Edward Everett Papers).

16. PTB to Kimball, 1 January 1845 (BA).

17. *Atlas*, 9 March 1845.

18. PTB to Kimball, 1 January 1845 (BA).

19. PTB to Kimball, 30 January 1845, *SL*, pp. 30–31.

20. PTB to Kimball, 3 and 4 April and 15 May 1843 (all in BA).

21. *AB* (1869), p. 229.

22. *Atlas*, 14 September 1845.

23. PTB to Kimball, 26 August 1845, *SL*, p. 33.

24. PTB to Kimball, 30 April 1845, *SL*, p. 32.

25. *AB* (1869), pp. 247–49. For other anecdotes relating to the Strattons and "Simpsons" abroad, see, in the same edition, pp. 213–22, 250–53; and *Funny Stories*, pp. 298–304.

26. On Sherwood Stratton's return to strong drink and his resultant commitment to an "insane retreat," see PTB to Thomas Brettell, 8 May 1855, *SL*, p. 90. Desmond, in her biography of Tom Thumb (pp. 174–75), omits all reference to these events and merely mentions that Sherwood died of a "heart ailment."

27. *AB* (1869), pp. 181, 190–95.

28. *Atlas*, 18 May, 8 June, and 7 September 1845. In France a small umbrella or parasol carried by women is still referred to as a "Tom Pouce."

29. *AB* (1869), pp. 194, 224; and see Fitzsimons, *Barnum in London*, pp. 122–24.

30. PTB to Kimball, 26 August 1845, *SL*, p. 33.

31. See above, pp. 37–38.

32. *Atlas*, 10 and 24 August 1845.

33. See, e.g., the *Atlas* for 23 March, 11 May, 19 October, and 21 December 1845.

34. *Atlas*, 23 November 1845. And cf. the issue of 26 October 1845.

35. *Ibid.*, 31 August 1845.

36. *Ibid.*, 7 September 1845.

37. *Ibid.*, 14 September 1845.

38. *Ibid.*, 28 September 1845.

39. *Ibid.*

40. *Ibid.*, 12 and 26 October and 2 November 1845.

41. *Ibid.*, 19 October 1845. Barnum later repeated the story, with some variations, in his autobiography (see pp. 728–30 in the 1869 edition, e.g.), but deleted all references to the "doctor's" race.

42. *Atlas*, 18 January 1846.

43. *Ibid.*, 25 January 1846.

44. *Ibid.*

45. PTB to Kimball, 26 August 1845, *SL*, pp. 33–34.

46. *Atlas*, 1 February 1846.

47. *Ibid.*, 8 February 1846.

48. *Ibid.*, 15 February 1846.

49. *Ibid.*, 22 February 1846.

50. *Ibid.*, 22 March 1846.

51. PTB to John Nimmo, 3 April 1846 (Columbia University Rare Book and Manuscript Library).

52. On Haydon's career and his connection with Tom Thumb, see Fitzsimons, *Barnum in London*, pp. 108–50. Barnum was in America when Haydon killed himself, and the company had left Egyptian Hall and London by the time of his return. The *Atlas* does mention the artist's suicide in its issue of 26 July 1846.

53. PTB to Nimmo, 3 April 1846. Nimmo was connected with the English-language newspaper *Galignani's Messenger* in Paris. He subsequently performed many errands for the showman in that city, obtaining texts of plays Barnum was interested in, etc.

54. *Atlas*, 10, 17, and 31 May 1846.

55. *AB* (1869), pp. 240–47.

56. *Brooklyn Daily Eagle*, 25 May 1846.

57. *Funny Stories*, pp. 234–37.

58. London *Times*, 24 August 1846.

59. PTB to Kimball, 18 August 1846, *SL*, p. 35.

60. In the last of his articles for the *Atlas*, dated at sea on 23 April and published in the issue of 31 May 1846, Barnum promises to renew the history of his adventures in France in future letters. But there were no more "letters," although the showman does appear to have contributed at least one anonymous article to subsequent issues of the paper.

61. PTB to Kimball, c. 18 October 1846 (NYPL).

62. PTB to Kimball, 4 January 1847 (BA).

63. For Barnum's brief account of this tour, see *AB* (1855), pp. 293–95.

64. Barnum's arrangements with Kimball are specified in three letters written by the showman on 30 March (*SL*, pp. 37–38), 9 April, and 10 May 1847 (all in NYPL). Originally, the demand was to share only the first $120 from daytime performances. Over Stratton's objections, Barnum acceded to Kimball's request that this be increased to $150.

65. *Westchester and Putnam Republican*, 5 October 1847.

66. See above, pp. 62–65.

67. On Bleeker, the tour, and Tom Thumb and his wife in general, see the introduction to *The Autobiography of Mrs. Tom Thumb*. Wells himself, who was employed by Barnum on a variety of projects, is buried in Mountain Grove Cemetery nearly midway between Barnum's and Tom Thumb's monuments.

68. "Diary, July 5–Aug. 11, 1848: Trip across New York State, to Montreal and Quebec, and Return to Bridgeport," unpaginated notebook, with corrections in the hand of PTB, in the Bridgeport Public Library.

69. See PTB to Kimball, *SL*, pp. 39–40. The date of this letter, which is in the NYPL, is recorded at the library and in my edition of Barnum's letters as "2 February [1848]." The correct year, I am now convinced, is 1849.

70. New York City Conveyances, Liber 493, p. 611. The new lease, which was to commence on 1 May 1852 at an annual rent of $10,000 with no increases during the entire twenty-five-year period, was signed by Olmsted's daughter Caroline and her husband, Henry W. Sargent, on 4 October 1847. The BPL possesses another interesting document pertaining to Barnum's relations with Olmsted's heirs. On 7 February 1851 the Sargents and Olmsted's widow, Helen, pledged the Museum property as security for a loan of $30,000 Barnum made to Henry.

71. As has been the fate of so many of Bridgeport's historical buildings, the Strattons' home on Main Street was demolished a few years ago to make way for a bank's parking lot. The house in Middleboro is still standing and has been fairly well maintained by a succession of private owners.

Chapter VIII: The Finer Things

1. *AB* (1855), pp. 75–77.

2. On the history of Bridgeport for the period under discussion, the most complete and useful work remains the Reverend Samuel Orcutt's two-volume *A History of the Old Town of Stratford and the City of Bridgeport, Connecticut*. A survey of the city's history to the present day, with hundreds of well-chosen photographs and illustrations, is David W. Palmquist's *Bridgeport: A Pictorial History*. Of particular value for its surprisingly— some might say devastatingly—candid description of the city's more recent past and its

continuing problems is Lennie Grimaldi's *Only in Bridgeport*, which also contains many fine illustrations.

3. *AB* (1855), p. 401; and cf. (1869), p. 769.

4. In the autobiography Barnum writes that he employed an unnamed London architect to furnish him with a set of drawings in the style of the Pavilion and that he brought these to a "competent architect and builder" in this country. A contemporary description of Iranistan in the weekly edition of the *New Haven Columbian Register* of 13 November 1847 [*sic*] credits Thomas P. Dixon of Stamford, Connecticut, as "the architect under whose superintendence the villa and its appendages have been erected." According to the *Macmillan Encyclopedia of Architects* (II, 15), however, the house was the work of the eminent architect Leopold Eidlitz, who later designed, with H. H. Richardson and Frederick Law Olmsted, the New York State Capitol. The source of this statement appears to be the architectural historian Montgomery Schuyler, who knew Eidlitz well and in 1908, the year of Eidlitz's death, published a three-part article on his friend's career in the *Architectural Record*. As Schuyler tells the story, the "drawings were ordered through an agent, in which the architect undertook the architectural expression of Humbug, mainly in lath and plaster, and succeeded, as he found on visiting the executed work long after, beyond his wildest dreams. In the same spirit of mischief which had inspired the design, he rang the doorbell, which was answered by the showman in person. The visitor, professing admiration for the edifice, inquired the name of the architect, and was informed that the architecture was the result of a cosmopolitan competition, had cost the showman $10,000. 'No it didn't,' retorted the actual designer, whereto the showman, with a presence of mind which at once explained and justified his success in humbug, softly queried, 'Is your name Eidlitz?'" See *Architectural Record*, 24 (September 1908), 169–70. The tale may be apocryphal, of course, although one gathers from Schuyler that Eidlitz himself enjoyed repeating it. Conceivably, Dixon, functioning primarily as a builder or contractor, farmed out the design work to Eidlitz. The latter, who was born in 1823 and educated in Vienna, had emigrated to America in 1843 and was then at the start of his distinguished career.

5. The account given here is based primarily on the long descriptive article published in the *New Haven Columbian Register* (essentially the same as that later published in the 1849 guidebook to the American Museum and memoir of Barnum, *Sights and Wonders in New York*, by "Uncle Timothy Find-Out"); a description of a visit to Iranistan by Charles Spear, editor of the *Prisoners' Friend*, in the March 1849 issue of that journal; an 1850 map of Bridgeport, with daguerreotyped views by C. S. Middlebrook, published by Collins and Clark of Philadelphia; and several contemporary engravings, lithographs, and original works of art.

6. Stowe-Day Foundation, Hartford, Connecticut.

7. The beauties of the grounds are described in a letter dating from 9 August 1852 that Harriet P. Miner wrote to her sister, Sabra C. Sturgiss (Sturgiss Collection, West Virginia University Library). On entering the grounds as a "public visitor," Harriet writes, she felt as though she were entering the gate of Paradise and could not help exclaiming "Visions of Glory, spare my aching eyes!" This particular letter, in which the writer makes a point of underlining the third syllable in "Iran*ist*an," is also of interest for indicating how the name was accented in Barnum's day. The late Mrs. Mildred Breul, the last of Barnum's great-grandchildren, emphasized to the author on several occasions that the stress should be placed on the third syllable and the name pronounced ī-rən-'ist-ən. Most people today accent the second syllable or, in the case of longtime residents of Bridgeport (where the name is perpetuated in an avenue), mumble something that sounds like 'ī(-ə)rn-ist-ən.

8. See *AB* (1869), pp. 199–200. A number of these items are still in the possession of Barnum's descendants.

9. See, e.g., the articles in the *New Haven Columbian Register* and the *Prisoners' Friend*. In later editions of the autobiography Barnum was more open on the subject—e.g., the 1869 edition, p. 453.

10. *AB* (1869), pp. 357–62.

11. Undated, unidentified clipping in Vol. 7 of the "Barnum's Enterprises" scrapbooks (NYHS). On Barnum's agricultural activities and presidency of the Fairfield County society, see *AB* (1855), pp. 366–78.

12. *AB* (1855), p. 377. Information on Barnum's swine and fowls is entered on p. 270 and several unpaginated leaves toward the rear of the big ledger he had kept since his Bethel days (BPL). Additional information on his swine and cows is contained in a letter he wrote on 18 May 1856 to Edwin B. Williams (Holley-Williams Collection of the Salisbury Association, Salisbury, Connecticut).

13. See, e.g., Barnum's letters to his great-grandson Henry Rennell, 12 September 1887 and 10 and 15 August 1888, *SL*, pp. 292, 300, and 301. In another letter to "Harry" (27 July 1887, *SL*, p. 288), Barnum writes he must ride with him to "see the pigs and other nice things when I get home."

14. A clipping from the *Globe* relating this anecdote, presumably published in the issue of 6 September 1885, is among the Barnum–C. F. Ritchel correspondence in the FDP. Ritchel himself, an inventor and sometime journalist with whom Barnum had other unfortunate dealings, appears to have been the author. For additional comment on his often erratic career, see below, pp. 245, 300–301.

15. Undated, unidentified article entitled "The Crystal Palace and Mr. Barnum" in Vol. 7 of the "Barnum's Enterprises" scrapbooks (NYHS). The article was written shortly after Barnum's election to the presidency of the Crystal Palace and therefore dates from around March 1854.

16. *Funny Stories*, pp. 276–77.

17. *AB* (1869), pp. 264–65. Two ledgers pertaining to the Philadelphia museum are in the LC and the ISU. The Philadelphia Library Company possesses at least one bill for the museum, dating from 23 December 1850, while it was under Barnum's ownership, together with a watercolor showing the exterior of the building. Another bill, for 3 November 1849, is in the Theatre Collection of the Free Library of Philadelphia. Two letters from Barnum to Kimball on the subject of the museum, dated 3 and 10 April 1849, are among the Barnum Papers at the NYPL; a third letter, dating from 4 April of the same year, is at the Shelburne Museum in Vermont.

18. *AB* (1869), p. 135.

19. Barnum's management of Lind's American tour is covered in Chapter 11, pp. 296–343, of the first edition of the autobiography. His more candid account, published in Chapters 17 to 22 of the 1869 edition, pp. 270–354, may conveniently be followed in Bryan, pp. 317–90. Of biographies of Lind, the "official," sometimes termed "definitive" *Memoir of Madame Jenny Lind-Goldschmidt* by Henry Scott Holland and W. S. Rockstro, prepared under the supervision of Lind's husband, Otto Goldschmidt, following her death, is as adulatory, almost impossible to read a work as one could desire. In two volumes of unprecedented prolixity and circumlocution, its authors barely manage to cover the first thirty years of their subject's life—with the more embarrassing events, if they or Goldschmidt were aware of them, entirely omitted, of course. The beatification of the singer has continued in any number of later works, and *P. T. Barnum Presents Jenny Lind* by W. Porter Ware and Thaddeus C. Lockard Jr. is essentially another uncritical, wearying chronicle of Jenny's "goodness," although occasionally of interest for the reviews and other contemporary descriptions it contains. The last, it should be noted, are sometimes rather imaginatively interpreted by the moonstruck authors, whose documentation as well is not invariably to be trusted. For readers in search of comprehensive, more objective studies, *Jenny Lind: A Biography* by Joan Bulman—an author who, in addition to going to Swedish sources, displays considerable knowledge of music, singing, and opera—can be recommended as among the very best. While slightly fictionalized, Gladys Denny Shultz's very readable *Jenny Lind: The Swedish Nightingale* is also quite respectable. Among contemporary accounts of Lind's American tour, *Jenny Lind in America* by C. G. Rosenberg, an English visitor who traveled with the company, is undoubtedly the most complete and valuable, although the author, unfortunately, concludes his narrative

shortly before the rupture between the singer and her manager. Rosenberg does not attempt to conceal his admiration for Lind, but he is also eminently fair in his appraisal of Barnum. On an obviously less objective level, the impresario Max Maretzek, who struggled valiantly to present a season of Italian opera in New York City while Lind was touring with Barnum, writes entertainingly about the singer and her manager in the third "Letter" of his *Crotchets and Quavers*, a work that abounds in satiric thrusts at the showman and his recently published autobiography.

20. See George Rowell, *Queen Victoria Goes to the Theatre* (London: Paul Elek, 1978), pp. 35–36.

21. Lind's romantic entanglements are covered in Bulman and Shultz, although, owing to the destruction of certain letters, it appears the full story will never be known. In Sweden she had earlier been an object of scandal occasioned by her moving in with two married friends—at one point the self-sacrificing Sophie Lindblad offered to surrender her husband to Jenny—a curious, apparently unconsummated ménage-à-trois that Lind blithely renewed upon returning from her studies in Paris. Her treatment of Hans Christian Andersen, who fell in love with her and wrote several of his stories under her inspiration, has provided another telling anecdote of Lind's characteristic tact: upon being pressed by the writer to give her reason for rejecting him, she is reputed to have handed him a mirror.

22. For descriptions of Lind's singing, see especially Richard Hoffman, *Some Musical Recollections*, pp. 112–14, 116; and Bulman, *Jenny Lind*, pp. 52–53, 84, 113.

23. On Whitman's impressions of Lind and the influence of opera on his work, see Justin Kaplan, *Walt Whitman: A Life* (New York: Simon and Schuster, 1980), pp. 176–78.

24. *AB* (1855), pp. 328–31.

25. Barnum faithfully reproduced his initial contract with Lind and the letter authorizing his agent John Hall Wilton to negotiate for him in the first and later editions of the autobiography—see, e.g., (1855), pp. 299–302. The original of the first of these documents, signed by Lind, Benedict, and Belletti, together with a certified copy of Barnum's letter to Wilton at the bottom of its second leaf, is in the NYHS.

26. *AB* (1869), p. 274. In the first edition of the autobiography, pp. 298–99, Barnum does not refer to Wyckoff by name.

27. *AB* (1869), p. 307.

28. Three letters from Barnum to Bennett, dated 27 March, 16 April, and 15 May 1850, which accompanied items Barnum wished to see in the *Herald*, are in the ISU.

29. *AB* (1855), p. 306.

30. *AB* (1869), p. 288. The *New York Tribune* of 2 September 1850, in its account of Lind's reception, names the "attachés" of the Museum responsible for getting up the arches and other decorations and adds that "a large number of the Museum's people were on the ground, most of them carrying bouquets."

31. *AB* (1869), pp. 287–89.

32. The same may be said of other representations of her. For many years Bridgeport's Museum of Art, Science and Industry possessed a large pastel portrait confidently said to be of Lind. The author viewed its strikingly beautiful subject many times without ever being able to make up his mind about the sitter's identity.

33. Willis, *Famous Persons and Famous Places*, p. 221.

34. *AB* (1869), p. 329.

35. *AB* (1869), p. 309. Caroline, who accompanied her father on Lind's southern tour, kept a diary of this trip as well. The incident occurred on 8 December and commenced, she writes, even before she entered the church, when a crowd of boys surrounded her carriage shouting "Jenny Lind, Jenny Lind." Inside the church, she continues, she had the pleasure of "being gazed at all the more"; and the scene was twice repeated later in the day when she visited two other churches: "The people were determined to have it that I was Jenny Lind and there was no use trying to convince them to the contrary."

Under her entry for 7 February 1851 she tells of her father's scheme to get Lind safely to the hotel in New Orleans and complains that she herself was almost "crushed to death"— "Diary of Caroline Barnum During the Jenny Lind Tour, 4 December 1850–7 April 1851" (BPL).

36. *AB* (1869), pp. 307–8.

37. *AB* (1869), pp. 301–2.

38. See PTB to J. S. Redfield, [2 September 1850], *SL*, p. 46.

39. The anonymous author of this 52-page pamphlet, whose full title is *Barnum's Parnassus: Being Confidential Disclosures of the Prize Committee on the Jenny Lind Song, with Specimens of the Leading American Poets in the Happiest Effulgence of Their Genius, Respectfully Dedicated to the American Eagle*, was William Allen Butler.

40. *AB* (1869), p. 294; *The Humbugs of the World*, pp. 22–23. Genin himself, who published *An Illustrated History of the Hat* in 1845, is credited with being one of America's first retail merchants to make extensive use of publicity. His wife was later one of the judges at Barnum's baby shows.

41. See "The First Jenny Lind Ticket."

42. See PTB to Lind, 24 October 1850, *SL*, pp. 51–52; and cf. the *New York Herald* for 25 October. This and Lind's letter to Barnum are both in the NYHS, contrary to what Ware and Lockard report in their book. The "request" was not so disinterested as it may have seemed, for it had been Barnum's intention all along, from Lind's first concert on, to fix the price of tickets at $3, provided he was able to secure auditoriums large enough to ensure a fair return. The auctions of tickets to initial concerts actually gave successful bidders the right to select the locations of their seats. See, e.g., the *New York Tribune* for 4 September 1850.

43. Smith, *The Theatrical Journey-Work and Anecdotal Recollections of Sol Smith . . . Comprising a Sketch of the Second Seven Years of His Professional Life*, p. 9. On a few occasions in the West, Barnum agreed to let local entrepreneurs take over the management of concerts in return for a flat fee of $5000. But he was not then responsible for the expense of hall rental, advertising, and ticket selling.

44. Barnum's cash book for the Jenny Lind concerts, which was donated to the Fairfield County Historical Society, has long since disappeared. In all editions of the autobiography, however, he reported the amount of money realized at each concert, together with figures for Lind's net profit from the tour and his gross receipts. The last, he writes, were a little over $712,000 for 95 concerts. Allowing $4500 for each concert's average expense, his own net profit would have been around $285,000. Of course, had Lind not forfeited the $32,000, her profit from the 95 concerts would have increased to nearly $209,000 and Barnum's would have correspondingly diminished to around $253,000.

45. *AB* (1869), pp. 342–43. And cf. Smith in his 1854 *Theatrical Journey-Work*, p. 8: "You *know*, Mr. Barnum, if you would only tell . . . who actually gave the larger portion of those sums which you heralded to the world as the sole gifts of the 'divine Jenny.'" Since Smith also reports (p. 9) that Barnum's profit from the tour was slightly less than $200,000, it may be that the showman's overall expenses were even greater than in the above estimate. Assuming, for example, that the expenses of the charity concerts were not averaged into those of the regular ones, these would have cost him around $3500 each, after deducting Lind's usual fee, which she did not receive for such performances. In her biography of the singer, Shultz writes (p. 282) that there were twenty such concerts in all, so that this item alone would have cost the showman some $70,000. In addition, as was customary in those days, there were "benefit" performances toward the end of the tour for the orchestra, Le Grand Smith, and "other persons and objects," as Barnum writes. He does not specify whether these were "clear" benefits—i.e., with all house expenses assumed by the management. If they were, this item also would have substantially diminished his profits.

46. Jenny Lind Goldschmidt to Joseph Burke, 17 February 1853, quoted in Hoffman, *Some Musical Recollections*, p. 121.

47. *AB* (1869), p. 303.

48. See PTB to Sol Smith and Noah Ludlow, 26 December 1850, *SL*, p. 53. On this point Lind's feelings were so strong that she never sang in Paris.

49. Edward Everett to B. Seaver, 20 October 1850 (MAHS, Edward Everett Papers). Lind's prejudice against Catholics is well documented by her biographers—see, e.g., Bulman, *Jenny Lind*, p. 298.

50. PTB to Thomas Ritchie, 14 December 1850, *SL*, p. 52.

51. *AB* (1869), p. 341.

52. PTB to Joshua Bates, 23 October 1850, *SL*, pp. 50–51. Barnum published this letter in the 1869 and later editions of the autobiography.

53. *AB* (1869), pp. 295–96.

54. See PTB to O. C. Gardiner, 16 August [1850], *SL*, p. 44. The date of the interim agreement is specified in the final contract. But apparently there had been discussion of its terms at least two days before, since the *New York Tribune* of 6 September tells of its being "ratified" the previous night.

55. This contract is also in the NYHS.

56. "You will see I took some liberties with the Preface. You must fix it, however, to suit youself"—PTB to Sol Smith, 24 January 1854 (MOHS).

57. Smith, *Theatrical Journey-Work*, pp. 7–8.

58. Hoffman, *Some Musical Recollections*, pp. 107–8.

59. According to Barnum, the total bid at auction and otherwise paid for tickets to the first concert amounted to over $20,000 (various contemporary newspaper accounts, which predicted a final figure between 30 and 40 thousand dollars, were considerably more sanguine), and on this basis he informed Lind that her share would come to $10,000. But some bidders did not call for their expensive tickets, and the sum finally realized was a little less than $18,000. At this point, he continues, he "proposed" that they equally divide the receipts from the first two concerts—not counting them as part of their written agreement—in order that Lind's contribution to the city's charities would not fall short of its already announced $10,000. A simple calculation shows that Lind's profit from the first concert, before Barnum made his "proposal," would have been around $7250 ($1000 plus one-half the receipts above $5500, or $6250). Rumor had it, however, that when the singer learned her share from the first concert was only around $7000, she informed her manager in no uncertain terms that the $10,000 pledge to charity had been made on the faith of his earlier declaration to her, and that consequently he would have to make up the difference out of his own pocket. Very likely this initial misunderstanding was the basis for Hoffman's statement that Lind refused to sing for Barnum after her *first* concert.

60. *AB* (1869), pp. 298–99.

61. Willis, *Famous Persons and Famous Places*, p. 209.

62. Strong, *Diary*, II, 20–21, 47 (entries for 17 September and 5 October 1850 and 16 May 1851). And see the entries for 2 and 9 September 1850.

63. Rosenberg, *Jenny Lind in America*, p. 37. Cf. the saccharine reconstruction of this scene found in Ware and Lockard (*P. T. Barnum Presents Jenny Lind*, p. 30): "As the ship passed Blackwell's Island, prisoners let out cheers, and Jenny, sympathetic as usual toward all luckless human beings, could feel only pity for these unfortunates."

64. On this incident, which Barnum does not mention in the autobiography, see especially Rosenberg, *Jenny Lind in America*, pp. 57–64. Hoffman, *Some Musical Recollections*, pp. 117–19, comments on it as well.

65. Both these letters, dated 21 October 1850, are among the Edward Everett Papers in the MAHS.

66. See Rosenberg, *Jenny Lind in America*, pp. 62–64. The receipts for *both* concerts at the Fitchburg Depot, interestingly, were less than those for any of the previous regular concerts at the smaller Tremont Temple. The first concert at the Depot, which passed without incident, realized only $5240, almost precisely half the amount taken at the last

concert at the Temple. Here the showman appears to have miscalculated on another front, for the Depot, Rosenberg writes (p. 58), was in an "unfashionable" part of the city, and many persons stayed away on that account. No doubt this fact and the reduced receipts also contributed to Jenny's ire.

67. PTB to Joshua Bates, 23 October 1850, *SL*, pp. 50–51.

68. "Diary of Caroline Barnum During the Jenny Lind Tour," entries for 15 and 17 December 1850.

69. George P. Morris to PTB, 7 January 1851 (HCC).

70. *AB* (1869), p. 314; "Diary," 23 December 1850.

71. "Diary," 24 December 1850. Barnum himself, in his autobiography, confuses his display of awkwardness with a second party given by Lind on New Year's Eve.

72. "Diary," 26 and 27 December 1850. The receipts at this second concert—only $3654—were the lowest taken anywhere to date. The first concert produced $6775.

73. *New York Herald*, 28 December 1850.

74. *AB* (1855), pp. 316–17; (1869), pp. 302–3.

75. PTB to Moses S. and Alfred Ely Beach, 10 February 1851, *SL*, pp. 56–57.

76. See below, p. 189. One threat to "cowhide" Bennett occurs in a letter Barnum wrote to Moses Kimball as early as 29 July 1844 (*SL*, p. 27). The showman was then abroad and indignant over some remarks in the *Herald* concerning one of the American Museum's attractions.

77. *AB* (1869), pp. 327–28; (1889), p. 256.

78. See, e.g., the issues of 7, 15, 19, 23, and 26 October, 9 November, and 12 December 1850.

79. *AB* (1869), pp. 319–21. In her diary for 14 January 1851, Caroline Barnum writes that Lind herself decided to cut short the Havana season after giving a fourth and final concert for charity. The receipts at the second and third regular performances—$2838 and $2932, respectively—were the lowest anywhere on the tour. Those for the first concert were only $4666.

80. "Diary of Caroline Barnum," 17 January 1851.

81. PTB to Sol Smith, 31 December 1850, *SL*, p. 55.

82. Rosenberg, *Jenny Lind in America*, pp. 156–58.

83. "Diary of Caroline Barnum," 10 March 1851.

84. *Ibid.*, 14 March 1851.

85. *Ibid.*, 13 March 1851.

86. *Ibid.*, 15 and 16 March 1851. And cf. Ware and Lockard (*P.T. Barnum Presents Jenny Lind*, p. 73): "Jenny seems to have endured the discomforts of this passage with her habitual graciousness."

87. *AB* (1869), pp. 334–37.

88. "Diary of Caroline Barnum," 5 April 1851.

89. See Rosenberg, *Jenny Lind in America*, pp. 216–19.

90. As indeed she seems to have been intent on doing since at least early March. On the 1st of that month she wrote to a friend in Sweden that she hoped to be "finished" with Barnum by the middle of June—see Bulman, *Jenny Lind*, p. 272.

91. *AB* (1869), p. 351.

92. *American Whig Review*, August 1852. And cf. the remarks of Lind's admirer Nathaniel P. Willis, who had the benefit of hearing Lind in Europe before she had forsaken the stage and observed that at the conclusion of a performance of *La sonnambula* she seemed to wish to convey "in her manner of acknowledging the applause . . . that her profession was distasteful to her." He goes on to note that while there was plenty of "soul" in her singing, it contained no "flesh and blood"—that her "angelic" nature prevented her from comparing favorably, in both dramatic and musical terms, with singers like Giulia Grisi who were better able to throw themselves into the characters and feelings of "the impassioned sinners of the opera" (*Famous Persons and Famous Places*, pp. 210–11).

93. See, e.g., Bulman, *Jenny Lind*, p. 313.

94. Edward Everett to Henry Holland, 24 November 1851 (MAHS, Edward Everett Papers).

95. Bulman, *Jenny Lind*, p. 297; Shultz, *Jenny Lind*, p. 321.

96. See below, p. 267. Lind last sang in public in 1883. She died on 2 November 1887.

Chapter IX: Bridgeport and Bankruptcy

1. *AB* (1855), pp. 336–37. And see pp. 333–35 in the same edition for the tricks he played on the mulatto barber who traveled aboard the *Magnolia*.

2. "Diary of Caroline Barnum During the Jenny Lind Tour, 4 December 1850–7 April 1851," 23 and 26 March 1851; advertisement in the *Bridgeport Standard*, 21 April 1851.

3. *AB* (1855), pp. 348–49; (1869), pp. 355–57. In the hyperbolical language of the circus, a "herd" is any number above a single elephant. For an example of Barnum's "preparing the way" for this attraction, see his letter of 31 May 1851 to the editor of the *Sunday Courier*, in *SL*, p. 58. The parade up Broadway took place on the morning of 2 June. Lind gave her last three New York concerts under Barnum's management during the same week.

4. Advertisements in the *Hartford Weekly Times*, 24 May 1851 (reproduced in *AB* [Bryan], f. p. 390); *Norwich* (Connecticut) *Weekly Courier*, 11 June 1851.

5. In the first edition of the autobiography (p. 349) Barnum writes that the receipts for these four years totaled nearly one million dollars; in the 1869 (p. 357) and later editions, that the profits were "immense." But apparently both declined rather sharply as the show's novelty wore off, for in the big ledger Barnum had kept since his Bethel days, a statement for the 1853 season (p. 241) lists receipts as only $115,054 and profits as $48,547 (BPL). By that season, too, Howes had been replaced in the concern by Lewis B. Lent, another veteran showman.

6. See above, p. 142. The forthcoming auctions (there were two) of the animals and all the Caravan's "paraphernalia" were advertised in the American Museum's bills—that for 25 October 1854, e.g. One of the elephants, retained by Barnum, was the same he set to plowing in the field near Iranistan.

7. *AB* (1869), p. 367. For a brief summary of Hayes's career (but omitting any mention of her connection with Barnum), see Brown's *History of the American Stage*, p. 167. Barnum did not himself accompany her to California, but sent as his agents W. A. Bushnell and George A. Wells. Bushnell, after being divorced by his wife, married Hayes in 1857. Wells, a longtime Bridgeport resident and personal friend of Barnum, was also involved in the Jenny Lind tour besides serving, at various times, as Barnum's representative and manager of Tom Thumb.

8. See the *New York Herald*, 1 and 6 November 1851.

9. *New York Herald*, 8 November 1851. The letter itself, whose recipient Bennett did not identify, was probably addressed to Barnum's friend George P. Morris, editor and publisher of the *New York Home Journal*, with the request that he forward it to Edward P. Willis, who at the time was Montez's secretary in Paris. Willis was brother to the writer Nathaniel P. Willis, who was also associated with the *Home Journal*, which explains how Morris came to be a go-between in the affair. In a letter to Barnum dated 8 November 1851, Morris wrote that Willis must have shown or given the letter to Bennett in Paris, thereby accounting for its publication in the *Herald* on the same date (University of Virginia Library Manuscripts Department, Barrett-Morris Collection). Most likely it was Edward Willis who contacted Barnum about the possibility of his managing Montez's American tour; and Barnum's roundabout manner of communicating with him is additional evidence for his wishing to keep his distance from the "notorious Lola," whose amorous escapades were well known to all and whose peculiar style of dancing was likened by Max Maretzek to the "Memoirs of Casanova." In view of the showman's circumspection on this occasion and his outraged reaction to Bennett's charges, it seems hardly necessary to remark that there is no truth whatever to the absurd claim made

by some writers that he had a hand in establishing the girly-show phase of burlesque in America; or that, as Peter Leslie writes in his *A Hard Act to Follow: A Music Hall Review* (New York: Paddington [1978], p. 28), Barnum "compounded salaciousness with exotica by signing up Lydia Thompson and her Imported English Blondes."

10. PTB to Mr. M'Makin, editor of the *Courier*, 1 November 1851, *SL*, p. 59. And see the letter from Barnum, containing his personal guarantee, in the *New York Tribune* of 31 October.

11. *AB* (1855), pp. 379–81. And see the detailed account of the experiment and its failure in the *New York Tribune* of 19 December, which describes a near riot among a crowd of 3000 persons, who also "annihilated" a number of the extinguishers. For another tale of the "public's" interference at the trial of the annihilator, see *Everybody a Ventriloquist: A History of Ventriloquism, with Instructions and Anecdotes Combined, Being a Highly Diverting Combination of Eccentric and Amusing Anecdotes, Illustrating the Astonishing Effects Produced by the Remarkable Faculty of Ventriloquism, as Practised by Signor Blitz* (Philadelphia: Crown's Steam Power Book, 1856), pp. 15–16. According to this source, Blitz, hiding in the crowd, threw his voice into the building when it was about to be set afire, crying "Don't! Don't! Let me out! Don't burn me up!" etc. The building was searched, preparations were again made to set it afire, and again the voice was heard crying out. On the third attempt the ventriloquist began imitating pigs and other animals, at which point Barnum, who had invited Blitz to witness the demonstration, finally realized what was happening. The writer of this pamphlet suggests that the confusion created by Blitz may have contributed to the failure of the experiment, and reports that another result of the fiasco was a long-standing feud between Barnum and Blitz. Whether apocryphal or not, the story does provide a fair indication of the almost universal hilarity produced by Barnum's involvement with the "failed" annihilator. He did not, incidentally, dispose of his interest in the invention as quickly as one might be led to believe through a reading of the relevant passages in the autobiography. The showman's own *Illustrated News* of 3 September 1853 contains a notice that he had sold out to Allen only a few weeks previously, and that the annihilator had recently been used to put out a fire in a factory.

12. *AB* (1855), pp. 385–86.

13. See above, p. 17; and Leland, *Memoirs*, I, 289. The clergyman was in all probability one of Barnum's Universalist friends.

14. See, e.g., PTB to Edward Everett, 7 and 19 February 1853; to William Makepeace Thackeray, 29 November 1852; to Bayard Taylor, 16 December 1852—all in *SL*, pp. 61–65. That Everett, recently elected to the U.S. Senate, himself prized the journal is attested in a letter he wrote Barnum on 27 June 1853. He was then about to have the first volume's issues bound, but lacked two numbers that he hoped his friend could supply. He was sorry to trouble the showman with such trifling matters, he wrote, but had the notion "that your mind, as has been said of the trunk of the elephant, is able alike to pick up a needle & rend an oak" (Bridgeport Museum of Art, Science and Industry).

15. See PTB to Dr. Russell T. Trall, 27 April [1853], *SL*, p. 68.

16. PTB to Horace Greeley, 8 March 1854, *SL*, pp. 71–74. In this long letter to his editor-friend and fellow director, written shortly before he became the Association's president, Barnum relates in considerable detail the events preceding his election to its board. The account in the first edition of the autobiography is somewhat less complete, although the overall story of his connection with the Palace is more fully told there (pp. 386–89) than in later editions.

17. PTB to James Gordon Bennett, 28 April 1854, *SL*, pp. 75–76.

18. Strong, *Diary*, II, 176–77 (18 June 1854).

19. PTB to Moses Kimball, 14 July 1854, *SL*, pp. 76–78. In a letter to Kimball dating from 22 July, an alternative site suggested was the Public Garden (Shelburne Museum). The idea of transporting the Palace to Boston was hardly so harebrained as it might first appear. London's Crystal Palace had already been moved to Sydenham, where it remained until destroyed by fire in 1936. Despite their vast sizes, such buildings were

relatively lightweight affairs that were easily erected and taken down. That they were also combustible is obvious; a good deal of wood was employed in their construction.

20. See, e.g., PTB to Moses S. Beach, 1 January 1858 (TU); 11 January 1858, *SL*, pp. 98–99.

21. *Trumpet and Universalist Magazine*, 11 October 1851. And see above, p. 16.

22. PTB to Edward Everett, 19 February 1853, *SL*, p. 64.

23. PTB to Moses Kimball, 6 February 1852 (BPL). And see above, p. 64 and note.

24. PTB to Nathaniel P. Beers, 6 February 1852, *SL*, p. 60.

25. *AB* (1869), pp. 367–69.

26. Barnum relates the story of his early involvement with East Bridgeport on pp. 383–85 of the 1855 edition of his autobiography; and, together with the story of his bankruptcy, on pp. 386 ff. of the 1869 edition. Noble himself wrote a manuscript history of East Bridgeport that Orcutt cites on pp. 853–54 of his *History of the Old Town of Stratford and the City of Bridgeport;* some additional information is supplied on p. 20 of the *Reports of the Fairfield County Historical Society for 1893–5*. The same publication contains a long obituary notice of Noble on pp. lix–lxiii.

27. Ledger (BPL), pp. 235–52 *passim*.

28. *AB* (1855), pp. 381–83. In 1913 the Pequonnock merged with the First National Bank, which later became the still operating Connecticut National Bank.

29. On Barnum's involvement with Mountain Grove Cemetery, see *AB* (1869), pp. 369–70; and below, pp. 271–72. The cemetery's articles of incorporation, with a list of the original shareholders, are in the Fairfield Town Records, Vol. 48, pp. 740–43. Hayes, who attended Caroline's wedding, gave her concert around that time; a letter from Boucicault to Barnum, dated 15 February 1854 and confirming the date of his lecture as the 24th of the same month, is in the Manuscripts Department of the Lilly Library at Indiana University.

30. *AB* (1855), pp. 394–99.

31. See PTB to Sol Smith, 2 November 1855, *SL*, pp. 90–91; and PTB to John A. Kasson, 31 January 1856 (MOHS).

32. The BPL, in addition to an 1861 statement addressed to the Cleveland prosecuting attorney detailing Barnum's past association with Nichols, possesses an extensive amount of correspondence by Barnum and others on the subject. Additional letters and documents are in the HL, MDU, NYHS, and Ringling Museum of the Circus in Sarasota, Florida.

33. PTB to Messrs. Curtis and Scribner, 11 January 1856 (BPL). The mortgage, which Barnum later complained had proved worthless, was unloaded onto the recently widowed Cynthia Stratton, who years later was still trying to collect on it—see PTB to Messrs. Curtis and Scribner, 19 January 1856, and PTB to H. B. Curtis, 28 June 1862 (both in Ringling Museum of the Circus). How close he was skating to the brink of financial disaster by late 1855 is attested in a letter Barnum wrote to John Greenwood Jr. on 10 October of that year, shortly after he had first learned of Nichols's forgeries. H. D. Beach, one of Barnum's partners on the *Illustrated News*, had tempted him into backing a new business venture, and a note he had signed for nearly $13,000 was about to fall due. He could not raise "a dollar" to pay it himself, and unless Beach, as he had promised, came through with the money, the note would surely be protested. "He knows the importance of it & that not only my salvation, but his own integrity & honor depend on it" (MDU).

34. Mr. Chris H. Bailey, former managing director of the American Clock & Watch Museum in Bristol, Connecticut, has intensively researched the history of Connecticut clockmaking and elucidates Barnum's connection with the subject in his *From Rags to Riches to Rags*. The Terry and Barnum Company, Mr. Bailey writes, was incorporated on 14 September 1854; and the Litchfield Manufacturing Company, in which Barnum was the largest stockholder, merged with it in March of 1855 (pp. 100–101). Additional information on Barnum's association with Terry may be found in Mr. Bailey's pamphlet

Theodore Terry's Ansonia Clock Company and Its Successors (Bristol, Conn.: American Clock & Watch Museum, 1978).

35. Jerome, *History of the American Clock Business*, pp. 111, 118.

36. Jerome tells the story of Barnum's connection with his company in Chapter 10 of his *History of the American Clock Business*, pp. 106–16. His son Samuel, one of the company's directors, made essentially the same claims in a long letter published in the *New York Tribune* of 21 April 1856. "Mr. Barnum's name did not add to the credit of the Jerome Company," he dourly volunteered. On the following day Barnum briefly replied to these "glaring misstatements and inconsistencies" in the same paper.

37. Jerome, *History of the American Clock Business*, pp. 94–96.

38. The meeting, which was held on 24 April, was widely reported in the nation's press—see, e.g., the *New York Tribune* of 25 April and *Frank Leslie's Illustrated Newspaper* of 10 May 1856. For a "characteristic" letter Barnum sent to be read on the occasion, together with examples of the many offers of assistance he received around this time, see *AB* (1869), pp. 397–404; *SL*, pp. 92–95.

39. Inventory of 14 April 1856, Probate Records in the Archives Department of the Connecticut State Library.

40. *AB* (1855), pp. 393–94.

41. New York City Conveyances, Liber 691, pp. 235–36.

42. *AB* (1869), pp. 413–14; and see Barnum's letter to the *New York Atlas*, 6 October 1844, on the dead whale he viewed in Bristol.

43. Johnson and Henry Sanford were appointed trustees of Barnum's estate on behalf of the Farmers Bank of Bridgeport on 31 January 1856. In New Haven itself, Frederick Croswell was appointed a trustee by the probate court of that county on behalf of the New Haven County Bank. Documents pertaining to these appointments are in the Probate Records of the Connecticut State Library and the Fairfield Town Records, Vol. 52, p. 705.

44. PTB to Dwight Morris [4 May 1856]. The Shelburne Museum in Vermont possesses this and several other letters on the same topic written by Barnum to Morris in April and May of 1856. At the same time he was protesting these fraudulent claims, he urged that full allowance be made for legitimate ones, including a loan he had received from his friend Abel C. Thomas and another for nearly $19,000 from the Nassau Bank in New York.

45. *Springfield* (Massachusetts) *Republican*, 5 April 1856. And see the editorial on Barnum in the 22 March issue of the same paper.

46. PTB to Charles Kean, 8 December 1856 (HCC). Another letter on the same subject addressed to the manager Benjamin Webster on 20 December is in the NYHS. In his autobiography Barnum mistakenly writes that he did not set sail for England until early 1857.

47. They opened in *Uncle Tom's Cabin* at the Royal Marylebone on 26 January 1857. At the Strand Theatre, to which they transferred on 23 February, Cordelia also appeared as Tom Tit, the slave boy. For these and other engagements, see the advertisements and reviews in the London *Times*.

48. Barnum relates his latest adventures with Tom Thumb on pp. 429–46 and 455 in the 1869 edition of the autobiography. Again, however, he is often careless with chronology during this period, leading the reader to believe, e.g., that their tour of the Continent was restricted to 1857. They were certainly in Germany together in 1858, for the Barnum Museum in Bridgeport possesses an unusual letter written by both the showman and the General, dated 4 September of that year, endorsing a hall in Frankfurt where they had just finished exhibiting.

49. *AB* (1869), p. 453.

50. Barnum eventually published the lecture in the 1869 edition of the autobiography, pp. 457–500, although by then it had been adapted to American audiences and considerably revised. His remarks on the "poisonous, filthy weed" tobacco, e.g., were

obviously added at a later date. Meanwhile, he writes, he had refused an offer of $6000 for the copyright from an English publisher.

51. These and many other reviews were appended to various editions of the printed "synopsis" of the lecture that Barnum circulated over the next several years. Eventually, reviews from American newspapers were also included, that from the *Troy Daily Times* of 6 December 1862, e.g., remarking on the showman's "scholarship and elegance of diction," while the *Albany Knickerbocker* of the same month reported Barnum had drawn four hundred more auditors to his lecture in that city than had Henry Ward Beecher the week before. "The audience was kept in a roar of laughter from beginning to end, and left in the best possible humor."

52. "I have returned bringing the Mermaid in good order, & for which I give you many thanks & owe you heaps of gratitude. Greenwood will send the 'crittur' by express," Barnum wrote Kimball from Bridgeport on 25 June 1859. While in London, he added, he had done some research among newspapers and found evidence of the Mermaid's having been exhibited in that city in the fall of 1822 (Shelburne Museum; given in part in *SL*, p. 102). Further mention of Herr Knope and the Mermaid is in PTB's letter of 5 April 1859 to the Dublin manager W. Guernsey. The showman demanded £25 per night plus travel expenses for himself and his two men, but only because Guernsey wanted him to lecture on twelve consecutive weeknights. When he gave single lectures elsewhere, he writes, his fee was three times as much (UTX; given in part in *SL*, pp. 100–101).

53. PTB to J. A. Woodward, 22 February 1868, *SL*, p. 158.

54. See, e.g., PTB to Alfred Ely Beach (?), 9 July 1857, *SL*, p. 98.

55. *AB* (1869), p. 517.

56. PTB to J. B. Tohey, 4 December 1860, *SL*, pp. 108–10.

57. PTB to Sol Smith, 4 April 1860, *SL*, p. 104.

58. Charity's will and the inventory of her estate, dated 22 May 1874, are among the Probate Records in the Connecticut State Library. Also here is the petition for the supplemental inventory, granted in 1928, filed by her grandson Clinton Barnum Seeley, who had discovered Barnum's "oversight." For a joke Barnum liked to tell on himself, concerning his offer to buy some property he already owned, see *AB* (1875), pp. 856–57 (App. IV); (Bryan), p. 702.

59. PTB to Rev. Abel C. Thomas, 9 March 1857, *SL*, pp. 96–97.

60. *AB* (1869), p. 403; *SL*, p. 94. On the final page (780) of the 1869 edition of the autobiography, too, Barnum reverted to the subject of the lesson "intended for my ultimate benefit." Had he been convinced his troubles were the result of blind chance, he was certain he would "have been tempted, as others have been, to suicide."

61. *Reports of the Fairfield County Historical Society for 1893–5*, p. 21.

62. See, e.g., Harris's *Humbug*, in which this view figures as a major thesis.

Chapter X: Pro Bono Publico

1. For Barnum's account of his first meeting and engagement with the Commodore, see *AB* (1869), pp. 567–71.

2. PTB to B. P. Cilley, 26 March 1861 (BM). Possibly Lillie was not the only early exhibitor of Nutt. Another showman named William C. Walker, who operated a small circus out of Manchester, claimed to have discovered and first exhibited him and his brother Rodnia as early as 1854. For a transcription of a handwritten statement by Walker on his connection with the Nutts and further remarks by a grandnephew whose family donated several mementos of the Commodore to the Manchester Historical Society, see the letter from Frank A. Walker in the February 1954 issue of *New Hampshire Profiles*.

3. PTB to Cilley, 14 December 1861 (BM). Several more of Barnum's letters to Cilley, dated 22 July and 20 November 1861, and 7 and 16 January 1862, together with the contract itself, were recently donated to the Barnum Museum.

4. For obvious reasons, Barnum was often reluctant to give accurate dimensions of his dwarfs, giants, elephants, and other phenomena whenever size was a principal consideration. He nowhere in his autobiography specifies the Commodore's height, and the figure here given is an estimate based on several contemporary sources. The year of the Commodore's birth is also cause for some confusion. In a souvenir pamphlet and various newspaper accounts published around the time of his debut, he was said to have been born on 2 April 1844; while at his death on 25 May 1881, the *New York Times* and other newspapers reported he had been born on 1 April 1844, a date that has been repeated in many publications to the present day. In his *Manchester of Yesterday* (Manchester, N.H.: Granite State Press, 1939), however, L. Ashton Thorpe, who researched the history and genealogy of the Nutt family, reports that a daughter, Mary Ann, was born to Rodnia Nutt and his wife, Maria Dodge, on 22 September 1844; whereas Rodnia Jr. was born on 11 October 1840 and George on 1 April 1848 (p. 160). This information was gleaned from a family Bible that, at the time of Thorpe's writing, was owned by a half-sister of George.

5. See, e.g., the *New York Times, Tribune,* and *World* for 16 January 1862. Conceivably it was Hitchcock, the original tutor of Tom Thumb, who was engaged as teacher to the two Nutt boys. Among the treasures in Bridgeport's Barnum Museum is a barely legible letter from the Commodore to Cilley, dated from New York on 5 February 1862, informing the family friend that he and his brother Rodnia are well and asking him to say as much to their father. Was this, perhaps, one of the firstfruits of the parson's tutelage in writing?

6. PTB to Cilley, 16 January 1862 (BM).

7. *AB* (1869), pp. 572–73.

8. For the story of Lavinia's life, see the author's edition of *The Autobiography of Mrs. Tom Thumb.* Barnum writes of Lavinia and her marriage to Tom Thumb in Chapter 37 of his autobiography (1869 ed., pp. 582–608).

9. *AB* (1869), p. 586. Barnum confusedly writes that this occurred in the autumn of 1862, when in reality Lavinia did not begin at the Museum until 2 January 1863. In her own autobiography (p. 49), Lavinia emphasizes that she did not make the acquaintance of Tom Thumb at the Museum, but had been introduced to him a few weeks prior to her first meeting with Barnum the previous year.

10. *Autobiography of Mrs. Tom Thumb,* pp. 61–62.

11. An interesting account of the world tour was almost immediately written by Sylvester Bleeker, the manager Barnum had assigned to the troupe, and was then sold as a souvenir wherever they appeared: *Gen. Tom Thumb's Three Years' Tour Around the World, Accompanied by His Wife—Lavinia Warren Stratton, Commodore Nutt, Miss Minnie Warren, and Party.* Lavinia herself covers the tour in her autobiography, but shamelessly cribs most of this part of her narrative from Bleeker.

12. "Tom Thumb's Widow Reveals Secrets of the Show," *New York World* Sunday Magazine section, 21 April 1901; rpt. in *Billboard,* 4 May 1901.

13. Both these events, which occurred on 23 November 1864 and 24 June 1865, respectively, were made much of in the party's illustrated bills dating from around this period. One such item, for a performance at Ashby-de-la-Zouch on 20 November 1866, in the private collection of M. José Dugardein of Belgium, features a cut of the quartet standing around a chair on which this infant "Wonder of the Age" is seated.

14. The article appeared in the 25 January 1864 issue of the *Herald.* Barnum wrote the paper's editors on the same date (ISU), enclosing his reply, which was published in the 27 January issue.

15. Barnum ecstatically reported these figures to his friend Bayard Taylor in a letter dated 22 July 1865: "I have sold my 12-year lease of the old museum. The price which I get for it in cash is fabulous, incredible—indeed, for the present I dare not speak it loud, for it must not go into the papers until the millionaire purchaser consents. So I tell you *in confidence* . . . the sum I get in cash is Two Hundred Thousand Dollars! $200,000!" (*SL,* p. 140). In the same letter he writes that Bennett had paid $450,000 for

the land itself—not $500,000, as he writes in the autobiography—though he did not name the purchaser to Taylor until a few days later.

16. See the *Herald* of 3 October 1865.

17. *AB* (1869), p. 675.

18. "The Barnums," pp. 215–20.

19. Joel Benton, "Some Reminiscences of P. T. Barnum," in *Life of Hon. Phineas T. Barnum*, p. 612.

20. Charles F. Deems, "Alice and Phoebe Cary: Their Home and Friends," pp. 49–52. On the Carys and their receptions, see also Mary Clemmer Ames, *A Memorial of Alice and Phoebe Cary, with Some of Their Later Poems*, pp. 60–69; and a comprehensive article by Janice Goldsmith Pulsifer, "Alice and Phoebe Cary, Whittier's Sweet Singers of the West."

21. PTB to Mary Clemmer Ames, 24 July 1871, *SL*, p. 171; and see *Funny Stories*, pp. 342–44. Ames, in her published *Memorial* of the Carys (pp. 186–87), used several anecdotes furnished her by Barnum, but prudently omitted the second of these stories. Nine years after Phoebe's death, in a letter to the *Bridgeport Standard* of 24 February 1880, Barnum again recalled his friend's reputation for wit and enclosed as evidence a punning letter she had written him in 1869.

22. PTB to Philo H. Skidmore, 17 May 1862, *SL*, pp. 118–19.

23. Barnum always took particular care with the naming of his homes, and in the present instance even consulted Bayard Taylor on the subject. In a long letter to Taylor dated 13 April 1861, he relates how he and his daughter Caroline eventually hit upon the name. "Beachcroft," "Ivycroft," and "Clovercroft" were among other names they considered, and for a time, harking back to Iranistan or "Oriental Villa" as that name was sometimes translated, they thought of calling the new house "Villanova" (Cornell University Library). The house is described by Barnum on pp. 549–50 and 772–73 in the 1869 edition of the autobiography. Around 1888 it came into the possession of Edmund C. Bassick, who had made a fortune out of a Colorado gold mine, and in the present century was finally torn down to be replaced by Bridgeport's Bassick High School. A grandson of Bassick, Mr. Charles H. Parks of Southport, Connecticut, was often there as a boy and describes the house and its grounds in a privately published biography of his grandfather (*Unbeatable Bassick*, 1981, pp. 83–86, 102). The author is indebted to Mr. Parks for the loan of a copy of this work and for additional recollections that he supplied of the house.

24. The showman again consulted Bayard Taylor on the name of his new house, though by then he had already settled on the title and was primarily concerned over how he should best spell it—see PTB to Bayard Taylor, 28 May 1869, *SL*, p. 160. The house and its grounds are described on pp. 774–76 of the 1869 edition of the autobiography; and in the second appendix to that edition (pp. 873–74) Barnum humorously tells how in 1871, after spending $10,000 to add a wing that contained his octagonal library, he then felt compelled to expend an additional $30,000 to make the rest of the house "correspond" and, since the grounds of the estate now looked a little "narrow," $50,000 for seven acres of land to add to them. "It was the old story of the man's new sofa over again," he writes, alluding to the cautionary tale he had told in his "Rules for Success in Business."

25. Barnum devoted a separate chapter to the establishment of Seaside Park in the 1869 edition of the autobiography (pp. 758–67). For his donations of land and money to expand the park in later years, see the 1889 edition, pp. 319–20 and 355.

26. PTB to Frederick Law Olmsted, 15 September 1873 (LC, Frederick Law Olmsted Papers). Olmsted's connection with Seaside Park is established elsewhere among his papers at the Library of Congress: specifically in a list of his "more notable public works" that he drew up on 15 June 1893 for the architectural critic Mariana G. Van Renssalaer, who was then writing an article on him for the *Century* magazine; and indirectly in a long letter he wrote to Elizabeth B. Whitney on 16 December 1890 ("We made a plan for a park, perhaps twenty years ago, in Bridgeport"). In fact, it seems likely Olmsted

and his partners were active at some subsequent stage in the park's development—possibly around the time of Barnum's 1873 letter to him—since Olmsted was in California during most of 1865 and Barnum originally requested a General Adams to run up to Bridgeport from New York City and "look over a piece of land 35 acres & give us your ideas as to how we can best lay it out in a *public park*" (PTB to Genl. Adams, 17 August 1865, Theatre Collection, Museum of the City of New York). Olmsted was later involved in the design of Bridgeport's Beardsley Park to the north of the city; and as general superintendent of Central Park, he sometimes had dealings with Barnum in connection with the zoo there. On 8 March 1873, e.g., the showman wrote him to request the loan of a young camel for his circus that season, and promised to "place a Sea Lion there with pleasure and reciprocate in any other way I can" (LC, FLO Papers).

27. *AB* (1869), p: 767.

28. PTB to Higginson, c. April 1855, *SL*, p. 86.

29. See *AB* (1869), pp. 609–10; and the report of a political speech by Barnum in the 24 March 1875 issue of the *Bridgeport Standard*. In an 1865 speech before the Connecticut legislature, Barnum claimed to have voted for every Democratic Presidential candidate from Jackson to Pierce, "for I really thought Pierce was a Democrat until he proved the contrary, as I conceived, in the Kansas question"—*AB* (1869), p. 622. He does not mention whom he voted for in the 1856 election, and most likely did not vote at all in that year, since he then had no permanent place of residence and was preparing for his campaign in Europe with the Howards and Tom Thumb. In any event, one gathers from his remarks in the autobiography and elsewhere that he would have voted for neither the Democratic nor the Republican candidate, despite the latter's association with the famous "Little Woolly Horse." Fillmore, the nominee of the American or "Know Nothing" party, who as President in 1850 had signed the hateful Fugitive Slave Law and vowed to enforce it, would hardly have been an attractive alternative.

30. PTB to Thomas Brettell, 10 October 1862, *SL*, p. 120.

31. PTB to Abraham Lincoln, 30 August 1861, *SL*, p. 113. For accounts of the "Stepney Raid" and sacking of the *Farmer*, see *AB* (1869), pp. 611–14; and John Niven, *Connecticut for the Union*, pp. 300–303. Although Barnum writes that he did his best to dissuade his fellow Bridgeporters from sacking the *Farmer*'s offices and later offered to assist the editors in starting up the paper again, he did not conceal his opinion of the paper in letters he wrote around this time. For contemporary descriptions of these events (some of them by Barnum himself), see the *New York Times* for 25 and 28 August. The *Bridgeport Standard* of 26 August carries a long description of the affair and also reports on Barnum's speech at Stepney.

32. Four, he writes in *AB* (1869), p. 611. A letter to Barnum from an agent named R. Tomlinson, dated 9 January 1864, acknowledges receipt of his check to pay for three such volunteers at that time (FDP).

33. PTB to Gideon Welles, 14 September 1861 and 4 February 1864, *SL*, pp. 114–15, 122–23.

34. See Strong, *Diary*, III, 521–22 (26 November 1864). The other buildings included several hotels.

35. Hendershot, who was at the Museum in early 1863, was only twelve years old when he joined the 8th Michigan Infantry in 1861. He later traveled around the country giving exhibitions of his drumming and was a member of the party Mark Twain commemorated in his *The Innocents Abroad*. For a letter in which Barnum writes about the "little hero," see PTB to Sydney Howard Gay, 16 April 1863, *SL*, p. 122. Major Cushman, who appeared onstage in her uniform and whose story included details of her spying activities, capture, death sentence, and rescue, made her debut at the Museum on 6 June 1864.

36. PTB to Robert Anderson, 16 September 1863 (LC, Robert Anderson Papers). The general's refusal is noted at the top of the same letter.

37. PTB to Edwin M. Stanton, 15 May [1865], *SL*, p. 132.

38. PTB to Daniel Stevens Dickinson, 7 June 1865, *SL*, p. 135.

39. PTB to Frederick S. Wildman, 13 June 1865 (MDU).

40. *AB* (1869), p. 617. Years before, "in 1852 or 1853," Barnum vaguely writes in the autobiography, he had "peremptorily refused" the pleadings of some prominent members of the Democratic party that he run for the office of governor. The Democrats were "then in the ascendancy," he continues, "and a nomination would have been equivalent to an election" (p. 609). In fact, the plan, which was hatched around the fall of 1851, was to run him as the nominee of both the Democratic and Temperance parties in the 1852 election, as a replacement for the current Democratic governor, Thomas H. Seymour, who had evinced little enthusiasm for the "Maine Law" or prohibition in general (see, e.g., the *New York Tribune* of 22 October 1851); and Barnum, then at the crest of his fame following the Jenny Lind tour, does not appear to have been all that reluctant. Various newspapers around the nation referred to his "candidacy" for the office, and Bennett and the *Herald*, as might be expected, were not silent on the matter (see, e.g., the issue of 6 November 1851, with the publisher's ironic avowal that, while broadcasting Barnum's supposed involvement with Lola Montez, he had no desire to "lessen the interest which may still be felt by Tom Thumb for his successful political career in Connecticut"). In March 1852 the showman published "Barnum's Appeal to Democratic Electors of Connecticut," a two-page leaflet attacking Seymour and urging voters to support candidates favoring temperance principles. Seymour, however, was again the party's choice and won reelection to the governorship. As a representative in the General Assembly, he later became one of the state's most outspoken "peace" Democrats at the start of the Civil War—for which he was again roundly abused by Barnum, of course.

41. Barnum's adventures during these two legislative terms are recounted on pp. 617–37 and 649–57 of the 1869 edition of the autobiography. Harvey Root, in discussing "Barnum as Legislator" in his book *The Unknown Barnum*, somewhat expands the record of Barnum's political triumphs and points out that another reason he gave for originally running for office was to "save the reputation of the family" from his son-in-law David Thompson, who was a candidate for the state senate in the same election and was likely, Barnum feared, to vote against the 13th Amendment. Thompson lost the election by a little over 300 votes (out of a total of some 4900 ballots cast), gave up his political aspirations in Connecticut, and moved to New York City in the fall of 1866.

42. Especially after 1872, the year in which the New York and New Haven merged with the Hartford and New Haven and began aggressively acquiring nearly all the other rail lines in the state, there were a number of such rival railroads—none ever completed—proposed by Barnum and others. At one time the showman pledged to contribute $100,000 toward the construction of a "parallel" line between New York and New Haven; and ex-governor William T. Minor of Stamford, one of the organizers of this project, even attempted to persuade Barnum to accept the presidency of the railroad— see, e.g., the *Bridgeport Standard* of 3 April 1875 and William T. Minor to D. N. Stanton, 15 May 1874 (YU). On the history of railroading in Connecticut, see Gregg M. Turner and Melancthon W. Jacobus, *Connecticut Railroads*; and on projected "parallel" railroads in the state, pp. 211 and 304 in the same work.

43. See *AB* (1869), pp. 698–99; and above, pp. 108–9.

44. PTB to William G. Coe, 7 April 1866 (FDP).

45. Barnum only hints at these events in the 1869 edition of the autobiography (p. 656), but tells the tale with considerable relish in his *Funny Stories* (pp. 315–20). "Of course," he writes in the latter, "in these circumstances I should never use President Johnson's circular for my business purposes." But he did use it all the same, not only in the autobiography from the 1869 edition on (p. 699), but in a printed circular he almost immediately prepared for sending to American citizens and officials abroad (see, e.g., PTB to Charles Hale, Consul-General to Egypt, 23 August 1866, *SL*, pp. 151–52) and in his later pamphlets and advertising material for his traveling circus. Ferry himself continued to serve in the U.S. Senate until his death in 1875.

46. It had first been placed there, ironically, in 1818, the year in which the state received a new constitution and the Congregational Church was disestablished.

47. The complete text of the speech is given on pp. 621–37 of the 1869 edition of the autobiography. For comments on the speech and its reception in letters Barnum wrote around this time, see PTB to Theodore Tilton, 29 May [1865], and PTB to Daniel Stevens Dickinson, 7 June 1865, both in *SL*, pp. 133–35. Interestingly enough, Barnum's progressive views as a legislator and especially his stand on Negro rights were recalled and praised at the height of the 1944 national elections in the Socialist newspaper the *New York Worker*. See the article "P. T. Barnum Fought the Clare Boothe Luces of 1865" by David Platt in the 5 November issue.

48. PTB to Mr. Morris, 20 February 1867 (ISU); PTB to William G. Coe, 25 February 1867 (FDP). And see *AB* (1869), pp. 657–64.

49. *New York Tribune*, 27 February 1867. The original letter and Barnum's reply were also published in *AB* (1869), pp. 660–63; and the reply itself is quoted in part in *SL*, pp. 153–55.

50. The "Torrington Letter" affair received extensive coverage in the *Bridgeport Standard* from 9 March on (the same paper had reprinted the original letter and Barnum's reply in its 28 February issue), together with frequent mention of the effect this "thunderbolt" had upon Democratic aspirations in the state. See also the *New York Herald* of 13 March, which carried the "dispatch" from an anonymous Bridgeport correspondent who claimed Hodge had announced he and Barnum fabricated the letter; and the *New York Tribune* of 18 March, which denounced the lie, pointed out Hodge was actually a resident of Winsted, and speculated that the "dispatch" had been written in the *Herald*'s own office.

51. PTB to Unidentified Correspondent (probably Eugene V. Smalley), 13 March [1867] (LC, John Russell Young Papers).

52. See, e.g., the issues of 14, 27, and 29 March; and, in connection with the editorial in the second of these issues, PTB's letter of 26 March to Eugene V. Smalley, giving essentially the same information that was published in the *Tribune* (in *SL*, pp. 155–56).

53. PTB to Theodore Tilton, 19 May [1865], *SL*, p. 134.

54. PTB to Eugene V. Smalley, 26 March 1867, *SL*, pp. 155–56. Some three years prior to these events, Dr. Jacques had abruptly departed Bridgeport when the body of one of his patients was discovered anchored in the Housatonic River. Upon his return to the city two years later, Barnum had urged that he be arrested and prosecuted for murder. Bishop, who ran the railroad that served the Naugatuck Valley, had at one time enjoyed Barnum's support when he expressed interest in constructing a parallel railroad that would compete with the New York and New Haven. When the showman later became convinced he had no intention of doing so, but was actually out to hinder others who might wish to build such a railroad, he led the fight in the legislature to deny Bishop permission to extend the Naugatuck line. As might be expected, Barnum was not slow in countering the local clergy who attacked him. He solicited endorsements from the "eminent divines" he knew, and Theodore Cuyler, for one, wrote a letter testifying to his upright character that was published in the *Bridgeport Standard* of 27 February.

55. See, e.g., the *Stamford Advocate* of 22 March 1867, which reports on the reception of Lewis Barnum and his harangue in that town.

56. Barnum's speech at Stamford, delivered on 8 March, was objectively reported by a special correspondent and published without editorial comment in the next day's *Herald*. The 10 March issue of the paper, however, carried a scathing editorial entitled "Barnum and His Niggers."

57. "The Two Hundred Thousand and First Curiosity in Congress," *The Nation*, 7 March 1867. This editorial, too, was faithfully answered by the *Tribune*, which in its issue of 25 March attacked the "third-rate" weekly for insulting those who had nominated Barnum. By harping against the showman on moral and religious grounds, the editor continued, this reputedly Republican paper had played directly into the hands of the Democrats, who were distributing large numbers of the offending issue in Connecticut.

58. "Barnum's First Speech in Congress," *New York Evening Express*, 5 March 1867.

59. *Bridgeport Standard*, 2 April 1867. Among other desperate attempts to smear his

reputation was the accusation that, thirty-six years earlier, he had had an immoral relationship with a woman in Newtown!

60. PTB to Eugene V. Smalley (?), 30 March 1867, *SL*, p. 157.

61. Joseph Roswell Hawley to Richard Henry Dana Jr., 2 April 1867 (MAHS, Dana Papers). The Republicans did win at the local level in Bridgeport and Fairfield, where the same "frightful activity" was credited with helping to ensure these victories.

62. *AB* (1869), pp. 657–64. Cf. the *Tribune* of 2 April, which, following Barnum's earlier instructions to the editor of that paper, announces Barnum will contest the election "on the ground of gross frauds."

63. *Special Laws of the State of Connecticut* (Hartford, 1872), VI, 11–13. The act was approved on 30 May 1866.

64. See *AB* (1869), pp. 700–702.

65. See *Mark Twain's Travels with Mr. Brown*, pp. 116–19 (Letter XI, dated 2 March 1867).

66. The book was a revision of the earlier articles in the *Mercury* and was first published by Carleton in 1865, although most copies seen by this author bear an 1866 imprint. In its own day Barnum's exposé of the spiritualists, in particular, aroused the hostility of several of those individuals, who threatened him and the *Mercury*'s publisher.

67. See above, pp. 19–20.

68. Bethel Probate Records, 1:430–32 and 435–36. Irena's estate, the total worth of which was appraised at $4874, was divided among Barnum, his sister Mary Amerman, and Barnum's nephew Charles Benedict, the son of his deceased sister Cordelia.

69. PTB to W. C. Curry, 21 March 1862 (MDU). Barnum alludes to his wife's continuing poor health around this time at several places in the autobiography.

Chapter XI: A New Beginning

1. The lecture was first tried out, as was customary under the Redpath system, in the Boston suburbs, then officially introduced during the "Star Course" of lectures at Boston's Music Hall. Barnum's debut there on 12 October was highly praised in the Boston press, with the *Globe* of the following day remarking that "it is safe to say that as a humorist he could soon make a reputation as a lecturer second only to Mark Twain."

2. Whist was a special passion with him and he even studied books on the subject, despite which one friend later recalled Barnum as the worst player he had ever met— see the interview with Col. T. B. Warren in the *Bridgeport Post*, 24 June 1934.

3. Barnum devotes an entire chapter (No. 32) to Fish in the 1869 edition of the autobiography, but originally concealed his identity under the name "Mr. Wilson."

4. The showman recounts his travels with the Fishes on pp. 846–56 of this first addition to the autobiography (1872 edition) and later supplied several more anecdotes in his *Funny Stories*, pp. 347–49.

5. On Barnum's plans for this trip and his hope that Charity would be well enough to "spare" him, see PTB to Mr. Thomas, 19 March 1870, *SL*, pp. 161–62. Around this time, too, he consulted with his friend Moses Beach, who had visited California, about their proposed itinerary—PTB to Moses Beach, 14 and 24 March 1870 (TU).

6. See, e.g., *AB* (1872), p. 846 (App. I); the *Bridgeport Standard* of 6 February 1875; and the biographical sketch by Alice Graham Lanigan, "Mrs. Phineas T. Barnum," in the *Ladies' Home Journal* of February 1891 (the last source based on information supplied by Nancy). Toward the end of his life Barnum became forgetful of, or careless with, some of the details. Fish himself, he sometimes claimed, did not visit America until after Charity's death.

7. PTB to Emma [Beers], 22 January 1873 (BPL); PTB to Nate [Beers], 2 July 1873 (BPL).

8. Various statements concerning the ranch and Barnum's involvement in the Colorado Cattle Company may be found in the BPL's "Salmagundi" ledger, pp. 1 ff.; and see PTB to Schuyler Colfax, 15 August 1878, *SL*, pp. 209–10. References to his holdings in Greeley

occur on pp. 26 ff. of the "Salmagundi" volume; and his secretary, Bowser, in his office diary entry for 28 June 1883, mentions a plan to renovate Barnum's buildings in that city. See also *AB* (1889), p. 285.

9. A copy of the Association's published Articles of Incorporation, notarized on 5 September 1871, is in the ISU, which also possesses a substantial number of letters, manuscript agreements, printed descriptions, and other materials pertaining to Barnum's involvement in this speculation. Another large cache of materials on the complicated topic is at the BPL, particularly in the "Salmagundi" ledger; additional manuscripts and related items pertaining to Barnum's investments in Colorado real estate are in the Western History Department of the Denver Public Library. The streets in Barnum's portion of the Denver development were named after friends and places associated with the showman's career (there were "Barnum," "Genin," "Greeley," "Jumbo," and "Waldemere" avenues, e.g., besides those named after his ministerial friends "Emerson," "Chapin," and "Collyer"). Few traces of them remain today.

10. PTB to A. A. Mason, 20 February 1882; and cf. his letter to Dr. William H. Buchtel, 21 February 1882 (transcripts in "Salmagundi" ledger, pp. 144–47).

11. *New York World*, 17 January 1897. And cf. Wallace, *The Fabulous Showman*, pp. 204–7, who elaborates considerably on these sensational stories. The identity and motives of the "special correspondent" will be discussed below.

12. Mrs. Mildred Breul, one of Helen's granddaughters, once informed the author that family members rarely discussed her on account of the "scandal" attaching to anyone getting a divorce in those days; a lawyer-son of Mrs. Breul added, somewhat indignantly, that he had been kept in the dark about the divorce until he was twenty-one, and then only learned about it through a friend. Needless to say, there are no family legends concerning Helen's supposed infidelities to Hurd, who was himself recalled by some descendants as an "old fuddy-duddy." On the subject of how Helen may have come to know Buchtel, it is intriguing to note that while the doctor, who had been born in Ohio in 1845 and later practiced medicine in South Bend, Indiana, was a Methodist, a wealthy cousin, John R. Buchtel, was a Universalist and the principal benefactor of Buchtel College, a denominational school chartered in 1870 that continues today as the University of Akron. Barnum was acquainted with John Buchtel, visited and lectured at the college on at least one occasion, and contributed to its support. Here, as with so many other unexpected events and relationships in his life, the possibility exists that Universalism may have been the common denominator.

13. A transcript of Helen's agreement to this effect, signed and dated by her on 2 May 1884, is in the "Salmagundi" ledger, pp. 161–62, together with an agreement signed by Buchtel on the 30th of the same month, releasing Barnum, in return for similar "valuable considerations," from any responsibility for future claims arising from the doctor's Villa Park real-estate transactions. Page 161 of the same ledger also contains the transcript of a letter written by Helen to her father on the following 13 June, thanking him for the deeds to the ranch and other property, which had just been delivered. The doctor was then very ill, she continues, "and I now make deeds myself . . . With love, affectionately your daughter, Helen." Transcripts of letters Barnum wrote to Helen on 26 October 1880 and 25 May 1882, pertaining, respectively, to a loan he had secured for her and his suggestion that she sell, rather than rent, her house in New York, are in "Salmagundi," p. 60, and on the page for 24 May 1882 of the office diary. The latter source, which begins in 1880, contains many entries recording visits Helen and her daughter Leila paid to Bridgeport and New York during the eighties; in the seventies, as various letters by Barnum attest, Helen also traveled East to visit her father and relatives.

14. Office Diary (FDP). Hurd died in 1898 and was buried in Mountain Grove Cemetery alongside his unmarried daughter Caroline, who had died in 1883 at the age of twenty-one. Helen's other two children by Hurd were Helen and Julia, both of whom had married by the time of Barnum's death.

15. Thomas Russell Garth, *The Life of Henry Augustus Buchtel*, p. 159.

16. See above, p. 160. The showman, at least, had sense enough to plan a gigantic

skeleton. The fact that all of the Cardiff Giant's flesh seemed to have been preserved was an immediate tip-off to scientists. At one time Hull had even intended to give his creation "petrified" hair and a beard. On the history of the Giant, which is exhibited today at the Farmers' Museum in Cooperstown, New York, see the pamphlet by Barbara Franco, *The Cardiff Giant*; and Barnum, *Funny Stories*, pp. 332–35.

17. *AB* (1872), pp. 851–54 (App. I).

18. PTB to Kimball, 18 February 1871, *SL*, p. 165.

19. Information on Coup's life may be found in Richard E. Conover's "William Cameron Coup of Delavan," a chapter in the same author's *The Circus*, pp. 20–24; and in Coup's own *Sawdust & Spangles*. The latter work, one of the more fascinating accounts of the American circus, is disjointed and often short on dates and names, presumably because it was dictated by Coup at odd moments snatched from work and the manager never found time to revise and set these "notes" in proper order. Following Coup's death in 1895, this task was undertaken by one Forrest Crissey, who in the book's Foreword claimed to have done his best to preserve the narrative's "original quality." Castello's name, incidentally, is frequently spelled "Costello" in various histories of the circus and by Barnum himself, and it would appear his real name was John Costello. In contemporary bills and circus letterheads, however, the spelling here given is consistently followed.

20. PTB to W. C. Coup, 8 October 1870, *SL*, pp. 162–63. On Barnum's previous acquaintance with Coup, see *AB* (1872), p. 856 (App. I).

21. The statement cited on p. 1 above, which appears in a work that professes to be an objective history of the circus, may be taken as a typical example.

22. And not only his name, it may here be added. In the 1960s the Barnum Festival Society of Bridgeport was threatened with a lawsuit by Ringling Bros. and Barnum & Bailey Shows, the legal owner of the Barnum show titles, when that organization discovered the Festival had been using "Greatest Show on Earth" in its publicity materials. This indiscretion cost the Society $10,000 in an out-of-court settlement. A major circus in East Germany today goes by the curious name of "Barum."

23. For Barnum's account of the formation of the show and its first season on the road, see *AB* (1872), pp. 856–64 (App. I).

24. PTB to Kimball, 22 November 1870 and 18 February 1871, *SL*, pp. 163 and 165.

25. See below, p. 291 and note.

26. *AB* (1872), p. 872 (App. II).

27. *Sawdust & Spangles*, pp. 225–26.

28. See, e.g., PTB to Mark Twain, 17 December 1870, *SL*, p. 164. The circulation of his courier during the 1872 season, he later wrote to Whitelaw Reid, was "considerably over 500,000 copies," and he anticipated the same number for the 1873 season—PTB to Whitelaw Reid, 18 January 1873 (NYPL).

29. To cite but one example of this continuing practice (and see above, pp. 74–75), the very first extract in the first appendix to the autobiography (1872 ed., pp. 858–59), "from a two-column article in the Boston *Journal*," seems almost certainly to have originated in this manner. In a letter dated 21 April 1871 to an editor named Smith, Barnum expressed the wish that one of his writers would "tell what immense success I get & deserve—but *not yet*, for my agt. will see the *Journal* next week & probably have all said that is needful for the present" (Pennsylvania Historical Society, Gratz Collection).

30. See, e.g., *AB* (1889), pp. 350–51.

31. For a joking letter from Barnum, dated 19 June 1876, thanking Holmes for endorsing the Captain's "genuineness" earlier on the same date, see *SL*, p. 200; and p. 201 for a reproduction of the pertinent page from the following year's courier, misdated in the legend as being from 1879. "The certificate is all right," Holmes wrote to someone who had questioned its authenticity after seeing it in Barnum's courier. He had written it "after a personal examination of Captain Costentenus, whom I was asked to look at by Mr. Barnum"—O. W. Holmes to "Dear Sir," 24 July 1877 (BPL).

32. *AB* (1889), pp. 305–6.

33. Bergh to the managers of the American Museum, 11 December 1866. The entire Bergh-Barnum correspondence on this subject, together with the letter from Agassiz, may be read in the *New York World* of 19 March 1867. Transcripts of all this correspondence are also in the Archives of the ASPCA; the original of Bergh's first letter on the topic is in the NYHS, while that of 7 March 1867 is at Tufts. Here it should perhaps be pointed out that although Barnum often omitted it in his letters and elsewhere, the "American" was part of the ASPCA's official title from its incorporation by the New York legislature in April 1866.

34. PTB to Bergh, 4 March 1867; Agassiz to PTB, 28 February 1867.

35. Bergh to Archibald Russell, 7 January 1867 (transcript in ASPCA Archives).

36. PTB to Bergh, 11 March 1867.

37. On 20 March 1867, e.g., Bergh wrote privately to Manton Marble, the editor of the *World*, objecting to that paper's apparent siding with Barnum and its publication of their correspondence. He was concerned about Barnum's pronouncing him unfit for his job and appealed for "the moral support of gentlemen so able, intelligent, and influential as yourself." In his reply to Bergh four days later, Marble candidly told him he considered his position on the feeding of snakes "untenable" and suggested that in future he direct his energies to "those inhumanities to animals which everybody recognizes to be inhumanities without excuse of any sort." The SPCA president had earlier become involved in an equally ludicrous dispute over the most humane way of transporting turtles destined for the table (transcripts of these letters in the ASPCA Archives).

38. See, e.g., the *New York Herald*, 15 April 1880.

39. Bergh to PTB, 13 April 1880; PTB to Bergh, 16 April 1880 (transcripts in ASPCA Archives).

40. *New York Evening Post*, 20 April 1880; *AB* (1889), pp. 322–23.

41. *New York Evening Post*, 24 April 1880. Bergh's letter that triggered this reaction had been published in the same paper on the preceding day.

42. Bergh to Edgar S. Nichols, 1 March 1880 (Collection of Bob Mathiesen). And see, on the society's founding, the *Bridgeport Standard* of 3 March 1880.

43. See, e.g., the *New York Tribune* for 13 and 14 March 1889. The junior Bergh, who seems to have possessed much the same sort of disposition as his uncle, had offended several board members by campaigning against the docking of horses' tails and August Belmont's rabbit-baiting at the Hempstead Coursing Club.

44. PTB to Bergh, 15 August 1885; Bergh to PTB, 17 August 1885 (transcripts in ASPCA Archives).

45. Bergh to PTB (BPL). The statue of Bergh was never erected, but a "Bergh Memorial Fountain," with basins of various heights and surmounted by the statue of a horse (the animal whose preservation launched Bergh on his lifelong career), stands at the Main Street entrance to Seaside Park.

46. PTB to Mr. Smith, 21 April 1871 (Pennsylvania Historical Society, Gratz Collection).

47. *AB* (1872), pp. 857, 860 (App. I).

48. Bill for 13 November 1871 (BPL; ISU).

49. "Conclusion" to App. I (1872 ed.), pp. 866–67. The cannibals continued with Barnum for several years and, from correspondence between the showman and Joseph Henry, Secretary of the Smithsonian, appear to have been genuine.

50. *AB* (1872), p. 860 (App. I). For a comprehensive study of early railroad circuses, including Barnum's, see the four-part article by Fred Dahlinger Jr., "The Development of the Railroad Circus."

51. *Sawdust & Spangles*, pp. 61–69.

52. See "Conclusion" to App. I (1872 ed.), pp. 868–70. And cf. what little remains of the account in the 1889 edition, pp. 283–84.

53. "How Barnum Circus Was Started," *New York Clipper*, 16 May 1891.

54. *AB* (1872), p. 872 (App. II).

55. *Sawdust & Spangles*, pp. 62–65.

56. *AB* (1872), p. 873 (App. II).

57. Of the many works available on the history of the American circus, the continuing "annals" of Stuart Thayer, privately published in limited editions, may be cited as particularly valuable to scholars and others in search of reliable information. To date these include *Annals of the American Circus, 1793–1829* and *Annals of the American Circus, 1830–1847*. A third volume by the same author, continuing the story to around 1870, is in preparation. Still of considerable value to those researching the early years of the subject is R. W. G. Vail's *Random Notes on the History of the Early American Circus*, which contains chapters not only on the circus and the performers who appeared in it but also on animals and early menageries, freaks, and Indians. The present author has himself summarized the topic in a chapter entitled "Le Cirque Américain" in *Le Grand Livre du cirque*, ed. Monica J. Renevey, I, 347–85. For what are primarily pictorial treatments, see John and Alice Durant, *Pictorial History of the American Circus*, and Charles Philip Fox and Tom Parkinson, *The Circus in America*.

58. See, e.g., A. H. Saxon, "A Franconi in America: The New York Hippodrome of 1853."

59. *Sawdust & Spangles*, p. 63.

60. See, e.g, the *New York Weekly Tribune*, 1 January 1873; Strong, *Diary*, IV, 464 (entry for 24 December 1872); *AB* (1872), pp. 876–77 (App. II).

61. *AB* (1872), pp. 878–80 (App. II).

62. PTB to Whitelaw Reid, 15 January 1873 (LC, Reid Family Papers); and see the *Tribune* of the following day.

63. See, e.g., the *New York Tribune* of 22 May 1873; *AB* (1873), p. 841 (App. III).

64. *New York Times*, 18 September 1873. The interview took place at Waldemere on 16 September.

65. A description of this machine and one of its early tests (at which Barnum was present) inside Ritchel's East Bridgeport workshop appears in the *Bridgeport Standard* of 16 February 1878. It was flown over Hartford in June of the same year. On Barnum's other relations with Ritchel, see above, pp. 160–61 and note; and below, pp. 300–301.

66. PTB to Joseph Henry, 19 September 1873, *SL*, pp. 177–78; and Joseph Henry to PTB, 22 September 1873 and 2 June 1875 (SIA).

67. *AB* (1873), p. 843 (App. III).

68. Carl Hagenbeck, *Von Tieren und Menschen*, pp. 90, 429–32. The English translation of this work, published in the same year, is severely abridged in this and other passages. Hagenbeck's memory was off by a year on the date of Barnum's arrival in Hamburg: he writes that they first met there in November 1872.

69. Death certificate, New York City Municipal Archives.

70. *Bridgeport Standard*, 22 November 1873. And see *AB* (1873), pp. 844–45 (App. III).

Chapter XII: Crowning Efforts

1. PTB to [John] G[reenwood], 6 November [1873] (HCC); PTB to G[reenwood], 19 December 1873, *SL*, p. 178.

2. PTB to Rev. George H. Emerson, 21 February 1874, *SL*, p. 179.

3. See, e.g., *AB* (1873), pp. 846–47 (App. III), where Barnum also reprints his contract with the Sangers; (1875), pp. 849–50 (App. IV), which describes performances at the Hippodrome during the initial season; also (1889), pp. 290–92 and 305–6. A program for the first season in New York is in the Theatre Collection of the Museum of the City of New York.

4. PTB to Gordon Ford, 17 January 1874 (NYPL); PTB to Edward Ledger, 16 April 1874 (MDU).

5. PTB to Gordon Ford, 30 May 1874, *SL*, p. 181.

6. Joseph Henry to PTB, 27 January 1874; and PTB to Henry, 25 February 1874 (both in SIA).

7. PTB to George Sala, 10 March 1874 (PUTC); and cf. the articles on the subjects of "Edinburgh" and the Ashantee War in the London *Times* of 10 and 13 March.

8. See the London *Times* of 16 and 17 January 1874. The original of Barnum's letter that appears in the second of these issues, dated 16 January, is at the UTX.

9. The second page of the MS of this letter is in the Lilly Library at Indiana University, and the private letter to the editor that accompanied it is in the HCC. In the latter Barnum writes, "The English & Americans are now pretty good friends, & *they ought to be much more so.* England, America & Germany ought, I think, to stand united (& will) against unwarrantable Papal aggressions." Both these documents are dated 26 February 1874 and, curiously, from "Rome, Italy." He certainly did not visit that country, but obviously wished some persons to believe he was there.

10. Tupper, "P. T. Barnum at Home." This is the same interview in which Barnum mistakenly recalled that Fish first visited America after the death of Charity. He goes on to say that as the result of reading the letters Nancy wrote to her father while he was on that visit, "I fell in love with my second wife before I had ever seen her. Those charming letters did the work."

11. *AB* (1875), p. 849 (App. IV).

12. *New York Times*, 5 July 1874. The same announcement was published in any number of other newspapers.

13. *New York Herald*, 11 July 1874. For an interesting account of Donaldson's life and his career with Barnum, see "The Circus in the Skies," Chapter 4 in John C. Kunzog's *Tanbark and Tinsel*, pp. 46–74. Elsewhere in this work the author displays the usual circus fan's animus toward Barnum.

14. Kunzog, *Tanbark and Tinsel*, pp. 60–70.

15. *AB* (1889), p. 310; Kunzog, *Tanbark and Tinsel*, pp. 71–74.

16. PTB to Mark Twain, 19 January 1875, *SL*, pp. 190–91.

17. *Special Laws of the State of Connecticut* (Hartford, 1880), VII, 823–25 (this volume for the years 1871–75). The company was approved by the Connecticut General Assembly on 24 July 1874.

18. *New York Sun*, 16 November 1875. In a letter of 24 April 1875 to the Buffalo publisher of his autobiography, J. M. Johnson, whose wife had complained because Barnum had refused to let her husband take stock in the firm, the showman wrote that he "*never* had a harder load to carry according to my strength than during the last two years & especially *this* one" (Shelburne Museum).

19. See, e.g., the *Cleveland Herald* of 22 December 1875. The "complications," if not occasioned by O'Brien's usual practices, may have included several lawsuits, one of which dragged on for years and was brought by the proprietors of a rival hippodrome and "Congress of Nations" who claimed Barnum and Coup had forced them out of business.

20. A copy of the catalogue of the auction, which took place at the Hippodrome building and in Bridgeport, respectively, on 26 and 29 November, is in the Missouri Historical Society.

21. "How Barnum Circus Was Started," *New York Clipper*, 16 May 1891. The BPL "Salmagundi" ledger, pp. 69–71, contains lists of accounts between Barnum and Coup for the years 1876–79, together with references to a "Show No. 3" (conceivably the one O'Brien ran) in which the two men had an interest.

22. See, e.g., Fox and Parkinson, *The Circus in America*, p. 80. Cf. Conover, "William Cameron Coup of Delavan," p. 24, who nevertheless concedes Coup must have been a "full partner" in at least one such deal; and Speaight, *A History of the Circus*, p. 143, who offers as his explanation for the breakup the trenchant observation that "Barnum was a difficult man to work with."

23. See, e.g., PTB to Gordon Ford, 18 June 1874, enclosing an invitation to Whitelaw Reid. Or if Reid cannot attend, Barnum continues, he hopes he will nevertheless "send a reporter & I shall be glad to pay his expenses" (NYPL). A full account of the affair was separately published in *Complimentary Banquet to P. T. Barnum, from Citizens of Bridgeport, Conn.*, and, somewhat abbreviated, in Appendix IV (pp. 850–63) and subsequent editions of the autobiography. The original of Barnum's letter accepting the invitation to the banquet, dated 6 June 1874, is in the BM; a copy of the printed menu is in the BPL.

24. PTB to Nate Beers, 9 and 11 September 1874 (BPL).

25. *Bridgeport Standard,* 16 September 1874; and see the brief mention Barnum makes of the wedding in *AB* (1875), p. 867 (App. V).

26. PTB to Nathaniel P. and Emma Beers, 16 September 1874, *SL,* p. 185.

27. See, e.g., the anecdote of the "silver cradle"—to which English mayors were entitled upon additions to their families during their terms of office—in *Funny Stories,* pp. 349–50. Another slightly risqué joke that went the rounds during Barnum's mayoralty concerned his ordering his coachman to whip up the horses when he and some guests were on their way to a clambake. "Please have some consideration for the horses," Nancy pleaded with him. "They have a heavy load, and they will be covered with sweat." "Isn't it lucky you are not my horse," Barnum said to her. "It is lucky you are my *mayor*" was the punning reply (*Bridgeport Standard,* 27 August 1875). The provision for their children occurs on p. 1 of his published will.

28. *Will & Codicils,* p. 21 (in Codicil No. 1, dated 24 May 1889). Clinton Hallett Seeley was born on 10 August 1867. His younger brother was actually christened Herbert Barnum Seeley, but by the late 1880s Barnum had decided "Clinte" was the most promising representative of the family to succeed him. The original heir apparent, presumably, had been Caroline's only son, P. T. Barnum Thompson, who died in 1868 shortly before his third birthday. Barnum's other surviving grandchildren were all female.

29. The original annuity, agreed upon in the marriage settlement, had been $2500, but Barnum kept increasing this in his will and subsequent codicils. In addition, Nancy received a cash legacy of $100,000 and various items of personal property. Barnum's fourth mansion, Marina, had been deeded to her previously. See *Will & Codicils,* pp. 1 and 46.

30. Letters and records concerning Barnum's often tedious financial dealings with Fish occur throughout the BPL "Salmagundi" ledger—on pp. 33, 48, 51, 55, 105, etc. Fish's son John seems to have been employed, or perhaps apprenticed, as a secretary to Barnum's show as early as the 1872 season.

31. Biographical information on Nancy may be found in an interview by Alice Graham Lanigan, "Mrs. Phineas T. Barnum," in the series Unknown Wives of Well-Known Men, published in the *Ladies' Home Journal* of February 1891; and in an article by Anne Whelan, "Looking Back at Romantic Career of Second Mrs. Barnum," based on interviews with Nancy's relatives and Barnum's descendants, published in the *Bridgeport Post* of 26 July 1936. Additional information is supplied by Barnum in several interviews published toward the end of his life. In the manuscript genealogy of the Barnum family prepared by F. F. Starr, Barnum has himself added the information that Nancy was born on 22 April 1850 (BPL).

32. PTB to John Greenleaf Whittier, 11 March 1885, *SL,* pp. 260–61. Whittier's letter of 16 January 1885 to Barnum is in the Swarthmore College Library.

33. PTB to Oliver Wendell Holmes, 20 June 1889, *SL,* p. 313. And see, on p. 312 of the same edition, Barnum's letter of 5 June 1889 to Holmes, announcing his impending visit to Boston with "my 40-year-old English wife," whose "highest aspiration is to see the author of the 'Autocrat.'"

34. PTB to Frank Parsons, 20 May 1890, *SL,* p. 325.

35. Nancy Barnum to Joseph P. Smith, 15 December 1890 (TU).

36. Ralph Keeler, *Vagabond Adventures* (Boston: Osgood & Co., 1870).

37. PTB to Messrs. Fields, Osgood & Co., 22 November 1870 (NYHS).

38. George H. Emerson, "The Barnums," pp. 218–19.

39. PTB to Mark Twain, 17 December 1870, *SL,* p. 164. And see above, pp. 223, 225.

40. PTB to Mark Twain, 13 August 1874 and 24 March 1875, *SL,* pp. 184 and 192.

41. *New York Herald,* 6 July 1874; and see the issue of 15 July for a reprint of a humorous comment on the piece originally published in the *New York Sun.*

42. PTB to Twain, 19 January 1875, *SL,* p. 189. And see Barnum's earlier reaction to the story in his letter to Twain dating from 16 July 1874, *SL,* p. 182.

43. PTB to Twain, 24 March 1875, *SL,* p. 192.

44. *AB* (1869), p. 697.

45. *AB* (1855), pp. 391–92. For additional anecdotes of Gardner and his impudence, see *Funny Stories*, pp. 147–51.

46. Unless otherwise noted, the letters cited here and below are preserved in the BPL.

47. Mark Twain to PTB, 19 February [1875?] (private collection).

48. PTB to Twain, 19 January and 23 March 1875, *SL*, pp. 188, 191–92.

49. PTB to Twain, 21 October 1875 (MTP).

50. PTB to Twain, 29 November 1876. Barnum's letter to Twain, as well as the letter from Barnum's correspondent, is preserved in the Samuel C. Webster Collection at the Vassar College Library.

51. PTB to Twain, 22 March 1876 (MTP).

52. PTB to Twain, 12 April 1876 (MTP).

53. PTB to Twain, 24 January 1881, enclosing the article from the *Sun* of the day before (MTP). Twain never returned the letters, either—an omission that, according to one of Barnum's descendants, led to some unpleasantness between the two families after Barnum's death. By then, perhaps, Twain no longer had them, since nearly all of the letters sent to him appear to have disappeared. The family's desire to reclaim the letters may have had something to do with the literary projects of Barnum's crony Joel Benton, who seems to have been encouraged to write an article on the "queer letters" himself after Barnum had given up hope of Twain's ever doing so. On 27 May 1889, e.g., Benton wrote to Barnum to say he would do the best he could in regard to the "Letters" and asked the showman how he would like to receive his half of the fee if he succeeded in marketing them (FDP).

54. PTB to Twain, 14 January 1878, *SL*, p. 205. And see PTB to Twain, 10 January 1878, *SL*, p. 204, for the original request. The letter Barnum refers to, dated 3 February [1875], contains an earlier refusal by Twain to write an article about the show (in this case the Hippodrome), but goes on to state that "of all the amazing shows that ever were conceived of, I think this of yours must surely take the lead! I hardly know which to wonder at most—its stupendousness, or the pluck of the man who has dared to venture upon so vast an enterprise. I mean to come to see the show—but to me you are the biggest marvel connected with it after all" (Humanities Research Center, University of Texas at Austin).

55. One might also plausibly argue, of course, that the King's delectable performance of "The Royal Nonesuch" in Chapter 23 of *Huckleberry Finn* owes something to Barnum's own outrageous hoaxes in the "nondescript" and "What-Is-It?" line. In a brief article entitled "Barnum, Bridgeport, and *The Connecticut Yankee*," published in the *American Quarterly*, 16 (1964), 615–16, Hamlin Hill argues—not altogether convincingly, in my opinion—that the character of Hank Morgan in Twain's *A Connecticut Yankee in King Arthur's Court* is based on Barnum.

56. Paine, *Mark Twain: A Biography* (New York: Harper & Bros., 1912), II, 564. The metaphor of the ax seems to have been directly inspired by a letter Barnum wrote to Twain on 19 January 1875 (*SL*, p. 188). Although Barnum and Twain occasionally corresponded during the 1880s, their relationship appears to have been at a decidedly less fervent level following Twain's 1878 refusal to help publicize the show. Barnum's renewed appeal to Twain to do something with the "queer letters" in his letter dating from early 1881, e.g., was actually in response to a message from Twain, who had written after learning the showman was seriously ill.

57. On Barnum's career as mayor of Bridgeport, see *AB* (1889), pp. 307–10, 313–14; and the chapter entitled "When Barnum Was Mayor" in Harvey Root's *The Unknown Barnum*, pp. 153–77. This period is best traced in the published *Proceedings of the Common Council of 1875–76*, a copy of which is in the BPL, and in the city's daily newspapers.

58. An explanation supplied in an anonymous letter—most likely written by Barnum himself—that appeared in the 1 April 1875 issue of the *Bridgeport Standard*. On the following day the same paper carried another letter from a writer signing himself "H" who

also defended the removal scheme and attributed it to Barnum alone ("I think one of the best things Mr. Barnum ever did was to have the bodies removed to Mountain Grove Cemetery"). The original petition and the act authorizing the exchange of land, which make no mention of Barnum or Sherwood, are contained in *Special Laws of the State of Connecticut*, VII (1871–75) (Hartford: Case, Lockwood & Brainard, 1880), 560–62.

59. His history and that of his ancestors are more than amply described in his son Julian H. Sterling's two-part article "Bridgeport—A Story of Progress," published in the *Connecticut Magazine*, 8 (1903–4), 785–802; 9 (1905), 349–83.

60. A copy of this publication, which was distributed with the *Bridgeport Standard* of 5 April, is in the BPL. Sterling replied to it, rather lamely, in the 6 April issue of the same paper. For the original attack and subsequent exchanges, see the *Bridgeport Farmer* of 30 March, the two letters cited in n. 58 above, the 3 April issue of the *Farmer*, and another letter from Barnum in the 5 April issue of the *Standard*. Sterling's lots in the old cemetery, incidentally, were not entirely empty when Sherwood and Barnum commenced their work. Upon removing his ancestors' bones to Mountain Grove Cemetery, he had left behind those of his brother-in-law, reputedly remarking that he "didn't care what was done with them." In statements of his own made during this fracas, Sherwood stressed that he had removed the remains anyway—and redeposited them in a *separate* lot.

61. Sterling tells the story briefly in the first part of his "Bridgeport—A Story of Progress," p. 800, a work one of whose chief aims was to belittle everything Barnum had done for the city; and more sensationally in an unsigned article for the *New York Sunday World*, inspired by the discovery of three forgotten skeletons beneath the street running through the center of Barnum's development (a clipping of this article, hand-dated 1897, is in a BPL scrapbook). On the persistence of this legend among Bridgeport residents, see above, p. 5, to which the author will only add that he was once informed by an official charged with the redevelopment of this section of the city (many of the original cottages still remain, and the area is being restored as a "historic" district) that he "shudders" whenever he hears excavations are to be made in it. Certainly a number of remains and coffins were overlooked at the time, and Barnum himself was sometimes distressed by such unexpected discoveries. On 10 June 1880, e.g., he ordered two skulls and some arm bones dug out of a cellar on Cottage Street be given proper burial in Mountain Grove Cemetery; three weeks earlier two coffins had been unearthed during excavations for a sewer in the same street. "Covered them right up," is the comment in the office diary kept by Barnum's private secretary.

62. See above, p. 229, and the Appendix.

63. *Bridgeport Standard*, 6 April 1875. As reported in the *Standard* of the same date, Barnum's margin of victory, out of a little over 4000 ballots cast, was 141 votes. As an interesting comparison, the 1981 mayoral contest in Bridgeport, which by then was the most populous city in Connecticut, was decided by as little as 64 votes. The victor in that case was also a Republican.

64. PTB to Joseph Richardson, 2 August 1875 (transcription in the "Records A" volume, containing minutes of stockholders' and directors' meetings, of the Bridgeport Hydraulic Company). Barnum's complaints about the company and the improvements he hoped to see it make are contained in his final address before the Common Council on 29 March 1876 (*Proceedings*, p. 136). The author is indebted to the officers of the BHC for permitting him access to their archives.

65. The minutes of all the meetings Barnum presided over or attended as a director are also in the "Records A" volume of the company's archives. Those for the meetings of 11 and 14 June 1877 contain several cryptic references to the struggle that was then under way to replace Richardson, whose system of accounting, one gathers from the minutes of another meeting on the following 24 December, left something to be desired. There was a rival "Citizens' Water Company" projected for Bridgeport in the mid-1880s, chartered by the Connecticut General Assembly in January 1886. Barnum was a stockholder in this company as well, and his fellow Universalist James Staples was its treas-

urer. But the company was never a success and less than two years after its incorporation made over its land and equipment to Barnum, who carried on with the construction of a dam and reservoir and sold them to the Bridgeport Hydraulic Company (the records of this later company are in the BM).

66. *Bridgeport Standard*, 7 June 1875.

67. See the *Standard* for 31 May, 7 June, and 10 and 15 July 1875.

68. *Bridgeport Standard*, 26 February 1876.

69. On Barnum's experiments with and boasts about ozone around this time, see his remarks reported in the 1874 *Complimentary Banquet* (pp. 10–11), his inaugural address to the Common Council (*Proceedings*, p. 2), the *Bridgeport Standard* of 6 December 1875 and 24 February 1876, and, in the 5 July 1876 issue of the same paper, the text of the speech he delivered at Seaside Park on the Fourth of July. He regularly pestered friends around the country to test their atmospheres for him, sending them chemically treated papers to hang up outdoors and read against a color scale—see, e.g., PTB to Mrs. Abel C. Thomas, 22 May [1874], *SL*, p. 180—and no doubt would have been delighted to learn that the concentration of ozone in Bridgeport's atmosphere is still among the highest anywhere.

70. *Bridgeport Standard*, 3 January 1876. On another occasion he indiscreetly remarked that before there could be any improvements in Bridgeport, there would have to be some "first-class funerals."

71. *Proceedings*, pp. 133, 137.

72. *Bridgeport Standard*, 29 March 1876.

73. *Proceedings*, p. 134.

74. *AB* (1872), p. 874 (App. II). The influence of Greeley, who stayed for weeks at a time at Barnum's New York town house and was the recipient of numerous acts of kindness from his host (at Waldemere itself another bedroom was named after him), was far greater on the showman than has generally been recognized. Aside from his interest in the Colorado colony named after and supported by the publisher, as early as the mid-1840s Barnum contributed money to the Fourierites at the same time Greeley was promoting their schemes for Utopian communities (see, e.g., the biographical sketch of Barnum in the *New York Atlas* of 20 April 1845). Yet for all his independence and well-known disregard of public opinion, in his own book of memoirs, *Recollections of a Busy Life* (New York: J. B. Ford, 1868), Greeley, like so many of Barnum's friends, omitted all reference to the "Prince of Humbugs."

75. PTB to City of Bridgeport Auditor, 30 December 1875, *SL*, p. 196. And see *AB* (1889), p. 310.

76. PTB to Joseph Henry, 15 June 1876 (*SL*, p. 199), and to Spencer F. Baird, 23 June (SIA) and 3 July 1876 (HL); Baird to PTB, 17, 21, and 26 June [1876] (SIA).

77. PTB to Mark Twain, 20 March 1876, *SL*, p. 197.

78. PTB to Nathans, Bailey & Co., 2 September 1877 (private collection of Fred and John Avery Nathans).

79. George F. Bailey to PTB, undated (Nathans Collection).

80. Draft MS of agreement, dated 7 September 1877, in PTB's hand (Nathans Collection).

81. The accounts cited here and below are found in the BPL "Salmagundi" ledger, pp. 10–13, 37–38, 72–74, and 108–9. In all these records only Nathans is named, and then as though he were Barnum's equal partner. From other sources, however, it seems obvious Bailey, June, and Avery were in for a part of his share.

82. On this and other juvenile works supposedly written by Barnum, see below, pp. 289–90.

83. Scoville's two-part article, entitled "The Christian View of Popular Amusements," was published in the 6 and 13 November 1878 issues of the *Christian Union*. Barnum's reply, "Popular Amusements," was published in the 4 December issue of the same paper and subsequently in other journals.

84. The "professor" was one J. K. Taylor, a Bridgeport chemist. Marsh's involvement

with the Cardiff Giant is commented on in Franco (*The Cardiff Giant*, pp. 438–39) and is documented in a half-box of materials on the subject among his papers at Yale.

85. PTB to "My dear hatless friend," 25 January 1878 (Andover-Harvard Theological Library).

86. *New York Tribune*, 24 January 1878. For previous notices of the Colorado Giant in the *Tribune*, see especially the issues of 4 and 5 October and 8 December 1877 (the 5 October issue contains a letter from Barnum on the subject). The *New York Herald*, in its issue of 8 December 1877, also describes the private viewing that was held for scientists and provides further information on Conant and the earlier examination of the figure by "Professor" Taylor. The *New York Times* of 9 December 1877, in an article entitled "Is It the Missing Link?" reports the opinion of the sculptor Wilson McDonald, who acknowledged being a follower of Darwin and was so excited by this "proof" of his theories that he planned to send a full description of the figure to the English scientist.

87. By this time state elections in Connecticut took place in November, rather than April, with sessions of the General Assembly commencing the following January; and meetings of the legislature, which previously had alternated between Hartford and New Haven, were held exclusively in the former city. For Barnum's own brief remarks on his career during these two terms, see *AB* (1889), pp. 318, 321. For his views on capital punishment, which was not abolished, see above, p. 32 and note.

88. *Bridgeport Standard*, 27 and 29 November 1878.

89. See the *Standard* of 30 November; and 2 December for Powers's reply.

90. *Bridgeport Standard*, 11, 12, and 13 December 1878.

91. *Ibid.*, 30 November, 4 and 5 December 1878.

92. *Ibid.*, 3 December 1878.

93. *Ibid.*, 14 December 1878.

94. PTB to Whitelaw Reid, 10 January [1879] (LC, Reid Family Papers). Barnum mistakenly dates this letter "1878." And see, in the same collection, Barnum's letter to Reid dated 13 January 1879.

95. See, e.g., the *Farmer* of 1 and 2 November and the *Standard* of 2 and 3 November 1880.

96. PTB to Joseph Roswell Hawley, 9 November [1880], *SL*, pp. 214–15.

97. See the *New York Tribune* of 24 November and the *New York Times* of 25 November and 14 December 1880. Additional information on Barnum's fluctuating condition is contained in the office diary kept by his secretary Bowser.

Chapter XIII: The Children's Friend and Jumbo

1. Extracts from this letter, which was addressed to Barnum's secretary, H. E. Bowser, were published in the *Bridgeport Standard* of 5 April 1881.

2. Extracts from this letter, dated 4 June, are in Bowser's office diary under 15 June 1881.

3. *New York Tribune*, 14 Janury 1881.

4. Barnum writes of the celebration in his autobiography (see, e.g., the 1889 edition, pp. 327–29, which includes an illustration of the fountain); the office diary kept by his secretary contains several references to the fountain's first being offered to Bridgeport, then to Bethel, its installation, etc. (e.g., the entries for 9, 19, and 22 June and 19 August 1881); and see above, p. 27. In a letter addressed to his friend the Reverend George Emerson on 25 July 1881, Barnum writes of the forthcoming celebration and mentions the fountain's costing $7000 (Ringling Museum of the Circus). The town was supposed to assume responsibility for its maintenance, but in the present century it was allowed to freeze and crack, and in time it was carted away as scrap metal. A World War I "doughboy" statue occupies the site today.

5. See below, p. 348 n. 2.

6. Roberts, who had earlier worked as a "hall boy" in a hotel, began service with Barnum on 1 March 1881. His initial salary, $40 per month, was second only to that of

the highest paid member of Barnum's household staff, Hugh Brady, for many years the Barnums' coachman, who generally earned $5 more.

7. *Funny Stories*, p. 294. The companion at the time of Barnum's bon mot about the "ink spot" was the Reverend Charles A. Skinner, and the story, according to his famous actor-son, was told over and over again in the family circle—see Otis Skinner, *Footlights and Spotlights*, p. 3.

8. PTB to Nathaniel P. Beers, 1 January 1884, *SL*, p. 248. The MS of the original 1882 document, which today is in the Connecticut State Library, runs to seventeen pages.

9. PTB to H. E. Bowser, 4 May 1880 (FDP). Bowser had been born in New Brunswick, Canada, in 1838 and died in New York City in 1911. The office diary he kept for the years 1880–95, a notebook and "day-book" containing more personal information, numerous letters to him from Barnum, and a considerable amount of other Barnum memorabilia once in his possession are now in the Fred D. Pfening III Collection. Here it may be apropos to mention that following Barnum's death and for many years afterwards, very little value was attached to such documents, even by his descendants. They were pitched out wholesale, in fact, including what appears to have been over seventy volumes of business correspondence, although occasionally some curious Bridgeporter would salvage an item or two from a pile of "waste paper" that was about to be carted off from some building or business once associated with the showman. Bowser, at least, had enough presence of mind to recognize the historical significance of such documents and in 1893 deposited a large cache of them in a "long box." Many of these items are today in the BPL. Others, which he appears to have carried away with him, are now in the Pfening Collection. A few additional materials preserved by him, also in private hands, are currently inaccessible to the public.

10. BPL "Salmagundi" ledger, pp. 90–100.

11. *AB* (1884), pp. 340–41 (Appendix).

12. *Bridgeport Standard*, 10 January 1883.

13. See, e.g., PTB to James A. Bailey, 26 August 1889, *SL*, p. 314.

14. PTB to H. E. Bowser, 2 and 4 May 1881 (FDP). The other accountant, who had recommended Bowser to Barnum, was a local bank cashier named Prindle. For a time in the early 1880s, too, Julius J. Gorham, Bowser's predecessor, remained at his post, primarily looking after Barnum's interests in New York City. There were numerous other full- and part-time agents in Barnum's employ, some, like Fish, attached to his circus and his various traveling exhibits, others stationed abroad or roaming the world in search of attractions.

15. See PTB to Rev. E. H. Capen, 28 May and 10, 12, and 15 June 1884, *SL*, pp. 250–52, 255. Barnum's earlier correspondence with Capen on the subject of the museum, the agreement signed by them, and the showman's speech that Capen read for him at the college's commencement exercises on 18 June 1884 may be found on pp. 234 ff. of the same edition. And see above, pp. 57, 112.

16. PTB to Rev. E. H. Capen, 20 June 1884, *SL*, p. 256. And cf. PTB to Capen, 4 and 16 May 1883, *SL*, pp. 236 and 238.

17. Spencer F. Baird to PTB, 1 May 1882 (SIA). The Smithsonian had actually commissioned the artist Clark Mills to make such a bust, but he died before completing the work. Before modeling his subject at his Boston studio, Ball visited the Smithsonian to study Mills's incomplete work and took measurements of Barnum in Bridgeport. The sculptor writes of these sittings in his *My Threescore Years and Ten*, pp. 310–11. The plaster copy presented to the Smithsonian was later used to make the bronze cast of Barnum that is today in the National Portrait Gallery. There are several plaster casts extant in Bridgeport: in the Barnum Museum, the Bridgeport Public Library, and the offices of the Barnum Festival Society.

18. Four of Ball's 1885 letters to Barnum—dated 28 March, 30 May, 5 July, and 6 September and written while they were still discussing size, price, pose, etc.—are in the FDP, and at least two of these, from notations in Barnum's hand, appear to have been passed on to Hutchinson. Also in the same collection is Barnum's note to Bowser, dated

14 September 1885, authorizing him to begin making payments to the sculptor. In his own autobiography (*My Threescore Years and Ten*, pp. 310–11, 317–19) Ball writes of his work on the statue and reprints two letters from Barnum, dated 8 and c. 14 February 1889, telling of the statue's arrival in America and the showman and his party's delight upon viewing it.

19. Orcutt, *A History of the Old Town of Stratford and the City of Bridgeport*, I, 690. Specific donations by Barnum are recorded in the library's accessions books.

20. Office Diary, 4 August 1882, 11 November 1884; *Will & Codicils*, pp. 25–26.

21. See Louis M. Simon, *A History of the Actors' Fund of America* (New York: Theatre Arts Books, 1972), pp. 2, 225. The early archives of the Fund, which began in 1882, were destroyed, but there is no doubt of Barnum's role in its founding. At the end of the first year, however, he declined serving another term as trustee, since he did not believe he could devote sufficient time to meetings—PTB to Daniel Frohman, 28 June 1883 (Folger Shakespeare Library).

22. These intimate details of Barnum's playing the fool, reported by an English visitor in a March 1877 issue of the *London World*, were reprinted in the following year's edition of the autobiography (p. 318), but were deleted from later editions.

23. Fisher, "Recollections of P. T. Barnum." The date of this event, from an entry in Bowser's office diary, would appear to have been 22 December 1888, on which occasion Barnum also presented each boy with a copy of his *Life*.

24. He left the Boys' and Girls' clubs each $1000. The local rumor that he refused to leave a bequest to the Bridgeport YMCA because it refused to "accept" him, and left money instead to build the "competing" Barnum Institute of Science and History (see, e.g., Harris, *Humbug*, p. 204), is clearly an exaggeration. The two institutions were hardly in "competition" with each other; the Bridgeport YMCA did not move into its own building until nearly a year after Barnum's death; and there is no evidence that he ever sought membership in or bore a grudge against this organization, several of whose Bridgeport supporters were among his closest friends. Indeed, although the YMCA did exclude Universalists—together with Unitarians, Jews, and Catholics—from membership in the nineteenth century, Barnum writes in his autobiography that he sometimes lectured on temperance before such groups, the only condition being that his talks should be free and open to all.

25. Orcutt, *A History of the Old Town of Stratford and the City of Bridgeport*, I, 685; PTB to Messrs. Tiffany & Co., 2 July 1885 (YU).

26. See, e.g., PTB to JAB, 24 August 1890, *SL*, p. 328.

27. The history of this farce may be traced in the *New York Times* of 30 and 31 March and 3 and 5 April 1883 (with both an article and an editorial in the final issue).

28. Again, while rumors of bad feelings between Barnum and his partners George F. Bailey, John J. Nathans, and Lewis June have persisted to the present day—and Bowser himself reports, in the office diary for 9 March 1881, "All showman [*sic*] down on P.T.B. because threw up all old managers & foreman & took in new ones. Will be dead as a showman in two years!!!"—their winding up the business and their subsequent relations seem to have been amicable enough. On 9 September 1880, e.g., Barnum wrote to Nathans to invite him, his brother Addison, and June to join him in another show he was thinking of forming; and the following 8 November, by which time they had definitively decided to terminate their association, Barnum again wrote to Nathans, assuring him he was prepared to pay the partners all money due them as soon as the circus returned to winter quarters, or to keep the money on hand until they needed it, paying them 6 percent interest in the meantime. "I hope you & June & Bailey will all come up and see how things are fixed here for the accommodation of show stuff," he added, "and I think it is a great pity if we do not all remain good friends always. I am certain I feel perfectly friendly to you all—and I feel grateful that we have got along together so pleasantly & profitably for five years" (both letters in Nathans Collection).

29. There is no satisfactory biography of Bailey, and what little has been published on him is generally, and unnecessarily, prejudicial to Barnum. Aside from the confused

entry in the *National Cyclopaedia of American Biography* and several belated attempts to glorify him following his senior partner's death (see, e.g., the article entitled "A Caesar Among Showmen," which contains its own fair share of exaggeration and inaccuracies, in the *New York Times* of 19 April 1891), George Conklin, in his *The Ways of the Circus*, pp. 295–302, has left some revealing recollections of his onetime employer, as has the English clown George Sanger Coleman, who also worked for Bailey, in John Lukens's *The Sanger Story* (London: Hodder and Stoughton, 1956), pp. 193–203. In 1957 the American circus historian Richard E. Conover privately published a seventeen-page pamphlet, *The Affairs of James A. Bailey: New Revelations on the Career of the World's Most Successful Showman*, a work whose overall tenor is sufficiently indicated by its title. While certainly adding to our knowledge of Bailey's later career, its author could not help regretting that the biography Bailey's brother-in-law, Joseph T. McCaddon, was reputedly laboring on at the time of his death in 1938 was not available ("He should have finished it, as it would have been much better than this one"). McCaddon's long-lost manuscript history of the circus and biography of Bailey unexpectedly surfaced in 1986 and was promptly purchased by the BPL. Although it throws more light on the subject than anything published to date, this work, too, must be used with considerable caution, since McCaddon, who worked for his brother-in-law on several of his shows, also chose to interpret the relationship between Bailey and Barnum more as a rivalry than as a complementary partnership. Bailey's date of birth, incidentally, is almost everywhere given as 4 July 1847, though one or two historians have argued for 1845. The spelling of his original name is also a matter of some confusion (it is sometimes spelled "McGuinness")—which is hardly surprising, since he actually married his wife under another assumed surname ("Gordon") and for many years was known to her and members of her family only by that name.

30. See, e.g., *AB* (1889), p. 324. Both Barnum and the 1880 Cooper & Bailey route book give the mother elephant's name as "Hebe," and the latter source lists the father's name as "Mandrin" [*sic*]. Conklin (*The Ways of the Circus*, pp. 135–36) later recalled the parents' names as "Babe" and "Mandarin," adding that the baby itself, which he claims was killed in 1907 after becoming unmanageable, was called "Columbia." The last is confirmed in the Great London's posters and other advertising matter dating from the 1880 season, although Barnum himself, in his correspondence around this time, refers to the baby as "America." His confusion may have been occasioned, at least in part, by the fact that the baby was not immediately christened. Suggestions for naming it poured in by the thousands; several fanatics, including at least one man oblivious to the fact it was a female, offered money and other gifts in return for having the baby named after them. It is not uncommon for circus elephants, incidentally, to experience one or more changes of name during their lifetimes, especially after being sold to another show or causing some trainer or spectator grievous injury.

31. A copy of the agreement, certified by Bowser as "correct," is in the BPL "Salmagundi" ledger, pp. 116–19; another copy, also made by Bowser, is in the FDP. And see PTB to JAB, 16 October 1880, *SL*, pp. 213–14, for a reference to an inadvertently omitted clause (or perhaps to an entirely separate agreement) that seems to have made provision for the two shows' no longer competing with each other should they again go their separate ways. Barnum discussed his and his partners' plans for the two shows in an interview published in the 5 September 1880 issue of the *New York Sun*, wherein a description of the new winter quarters, then being erected in Bridgeport, is also given.

32. PTB to JAB, 14 April 1889, *SL*, p. 312.

33. PTB to JAB, 5 July 1888, *SL*, p. 298.

34. Office Diary, 31 December 1880.

35. Cary to Bowser, 25 April 1881 (FDP). There were, in fact, two Charles Benedicts who recur throughout Barnum's history, and keeping them separate is not an easy task. One of them, the son of Barnum's sister Cordelia, married the sister of Isaac Coddington—the Universalist minister Barnum helped put through divinity school—appears to have become incompetent, and was left $3000 in trust in Barnum's will (pp. 4, 37). The other,

Charles Washington Benedict, son of the elder Charles's brother Henry Benedict, must have been the one married to Mattie Jackson; and probably it was he, too, who at various times worked at Woodward's Gardens in San Francisco (a job Barnum obtained for him) and as a railroad conductor in the Southwest, and in early 1891 caused his relatives further grief when he was accused of absconding with money belonging to the owner of a Mississippi River store-boat. Bowser himself seems to have thought little of him and noted in the office diary on 7 April 1882 that "Chas. Benedict has no work, and they say will do nothing as long as his wife will earn $25 per week." For further information on Mattie Jackson, who may have divorced, or been abandoned by, her husband, see the Appendix, pp. 341–42.

36. Cary to Bowser, 5 July 1881 (FDP); Office Diary, 6 and 7 July 1881.

37. Office Diary, 14 July 1881. What about Bailey's wife and Merritt Young? Bowser acidly noted in the same entry. The former often accompanied her husband in his private railway car, and the latter was another Bailey relative.

38. This advice is in a two-page letter fragment, identified by Bowser as written by Fish in early 1888 (FDP).

39. PTB to JAB, 24 August 1890, *SL*, p. 329.

40. Barnum briefly describes the new winter quarters in *AB* (1889), pp. 324–25; and they were also written up in many contemporary periodicals. A particularly fine article, with illustrations by James Beard showing the interiors of the buildings and training methods, appears in *Harper's Weekly* for 18 February 1882; and the *Hartford Courant*, around the time the Ringlings moved the quarters to Sarasota, Florida, published a long article on their history in its issue of 29 December 1929. Several persons who worked at or visited the winter quarters have also volunteered their recollections to the author, and a few of these have been incorporated into the narrative. The animal trainer George Conklin, who did not join the show until less than three years before Barnum's death, also remarks on the winter quarters and tells an absurd story about Barnum's once wandering through them, pausing before cages to examine the nameplates identifying the animals within, and "squeaking" out, "That ain't spelled right." In spite of which, Conklin continues, "the spellings were never altered, as the managers of the show preferred to have the names agree with Webster rather than Barnum" (Conklin, *The Ways of the Circus*, p. 291). It would be instructive to see those nameplates today. In the approximately 4000 manuscripts by Barnum that I have perused, including hundreds of letters relating to animals and natural history, I doubt if I have encountered a dozen misspelled words.

41. PTB to Mary A. Livermore, 12 January 1884, *SL*, p. 249.

42. PTB to Oliver Wendell Holmes, 22 December 1882 (HU).

43. *Bridgeport Standard*, 25 November 1882. George Arstingstall, the original elephant superintendent with the combined show, had earlier worked for Cooper and Bailey. Upon his retirement a few years later, he was succeeded by his second-in-command, "Elephant Bill" Newman.

44. Office Diary, 10 and 22 February and 14 March 1883; 10 and 26 February 1884.

45. See Sanger, who also complained neither Barnum nor Bailey paid him for the use of his name in their titles, *Seventy Years a Showman*, p. 190; and cf. George Sanger Coleman in Lukens's *The Sanger Story*, p. 98, who mentions that his grandfather later employed three rings at London's Agricultural Hall. "England has nothing to learn from America," the great "Lord" George proclaimed in his memoirs. "There is nothing that American showmen have ever done that Englishmen have not done first and done better."

46. Barnum writes about the show's first season, which commenced on 28 March, and its reception in *AB* (1889), pp. 325–27, 329. The information on the show's temporarily merging with Forepaugh's circus is from the 1886 route book (BPL). Here it may be added that The Great London Show, like Barnum's earlier circus, was a two-ring affair as recently as its 1880 season.

47. Office Diary, 31 October 1881.

48. *Ibid.*, 21 September 1881.

49. *Ibid.*, 21 August and 2 December 1881.

50. Bill for Forepaugh's circus in Washington on 4 and 5 April and in Baltimore on 6–9 April 1881 (BPL).

51. Draft of agreement dated [   ] March 1882, in BPL "Salmagundi" ledger, pp. 148–50. In the office diary Bowser notes as early as 9 April 1881 that Forepaugh was signaling his desire to end the "warfare," and, somewhat mysteriously on 4 November of the same year, that "I learn BB&H have bought into Adam." To my knowledge there was no financial involvement with Forepaugh during this period. Bowser may simply be indicating that the showmen had finally agreed to compromise.

52. See PTB to JAB, 7 and 10 June and especially 27 August 1888, SL, pp. 293–95, 302–4.

53. Memorandum of Agreement dated 6 March 1890, BPL "Salmagundi" ledger, pp. 183–87. And cf. PTB to JAB, 22 and 26 February 1890, and PTB to Cooper, 9 April 1890, in SL, pp. 319–22.

54. For an invitation to Garfield to visit the circus, see PTB to James A. Garfield, 12 March 1881, SL, pp. 217–18. And cf. AB (1889), p. 327, where the showman writes of stopping over in Washington on his way home from Florida and of Garfield's then referring to him as the "Kris Kringle of America."

55. PTB to Secretary of the Testimonial Association for Mrs. Rutherford B. Hayes, 27 January 1881, SL, pp. 215–16.

56. AB (1889), pp. 342–43. References to Barnum's meeting and dining with Grant during the 1880 campaign and to his later attending the general's funeral procession in New York City are in the office diary for 21 October 1880 and 7 August 1885. Under 6 November 1882, also, Bowser noted what he assumed to be another meeting between the two men in New York City.

57. For a listing of "juveniles" attributed to Barnum and remarks on their possible authorship, see Toole-Stott, Circus and Allied Arts, I, 160–62, and especially entries 1425 and 1435. As is true for the autobiography itself, it should be pointed out that Toole-Stott did not succeed in running down, in this section or in subsequent volumes of his bibliography, all editions of such works bearing Barnum's name. Again, the task appears to be almost endless.

58. The Wild Beasts, Birds and Reptiles of the World: The Story of Their Capture, by P. T. Barnum (Chicago: R. S. Peale, 1892), pp. 486–88. This work, which contains a two-page preface in facsimile of Barnum's handwriting, dated at Waldemere in April 1888, was first published by Peale in the same year, at the end of which Barnum received royalties of $785 for copies "sold to date" (Office Diary, 18 January 1889). The original of the preface, with several corrections in Barnum's hand, is at the University of Texas. In later years, beginning in 1896, the book was often republished under the title Forest and Jungle, but without two later chapters entitled "A Brief Résumé of My Life" and "How to Get Rich, and How to Live Long and Happy." Toole-Stott (no. 1430) is willing to concede these two chapters were written by Barnum, but in fact their style is the same as that found throughout the book. Among other evidence pointing to Barnum's having had at least a "finger" in the work is a reference to "my old friend Du Chaillu" (pp. 484–85), whom Barnum had known since his days at the American Museum. The one-page introduction also refers to Barnum as having "produced" the book and certainly leads one to believe he wrote it. Again, on 17 August 1888, while he was vacationing once more at Paul Smith's in the Adirondacks, Barnum responded to another publisher who had solicited something by him: "I have as much to write for the next 2 weeks as I care to do. After 1st to 16 Sept. I hope to be able to give you a proper story of real occurrences connected with capture of some of my wild animals—of 3000 words or less. If I can do it earlier I shall gladly do so" (PTB to Messrs. Perry, Mason & Co., FDP). The essay he was then at work on was his "Why I Am a Universalist" (originally titled "Why Am I a Universalist?"), which the editors of the North American Review had requested but decided not to publish.

59. HCC. Barnum did spend part of the summer of 1887 at Paul Smith's in the Adirondacks.

60. Nancy Barnum to Henry Hale, 19 November 1891 (YU). On Nancy's writing career, see above, pp. 254–55.

61. PTB to Messrs. S. Low, Marston & Co., 13 November 1876 (Collection of Ricky Jay). And cf. *AB* (1889), p. 315.

62. *Jack in the Jungle: A Tale of Land and Sea, Being Perilous Adventures Among Wild Men and the Capturing of Wild Beasts, Showing How Menageries Are Made* (New York: G. W. Carleton, 1880). Neither Toole-Stott, the Library of Congress, nor the National Union Catalog (as of 1988) lists any edition earlier than this one, which seems rather late for a sequel to a novel published in 1876. I have not seen an earlier edition myself.

63. PTB to Schuyler Colfax, 15 August 1878, *SL*, p. 209. And see Barnum's letter of 3 August 1878 to Colfax, *SL*, p. 208, wherein reference is made to several other suggestions by the Vice-President. A letter to Barnum from the owner of the cannonball act, "Professor" G. A. Farini (whose real name was Hunt), dated at London on 2 February 1879, is in the FDP. After several delays, Zazel made her debut in Barnum's circus during the 1880 season.

64. Bowser, in the office diary for 20 June 1881, reports on Harlow's suggestion. And see PTB to William F. Vilas, Secretary of the Interior, 25 September 1888, *SL*, pp. 306–7.

65. It would be a hopeless task to attempt to list all the books and articles on the "King of Elephants," but the following, in addition to the sources cited elsewhere, are of more than usual interest: Barnum, *AB* (1889), pp. 330–33, 344–45; W. P. Jolly, *Jumbo*; *Autobiography of Matthew Scott, Jumbo's Keeper . . . also Jumbo's Biography,* "by the same author," presumably Thomas E. Lowe, a book written for children and therefore containing many delightful lies; Bella C. Landauer, "Jumbo's Influence on Advertising or Some *Jumbo* Trade-Cards," *New-York Historical Society Quarterly Bulletin,* October 1934; Russell L. Carpenter, "P. T. Barnum's Jumbo," *The Tuftonian* (published by Tufts University), January 1941; John R. Russell, "Jumbo," *University of Rochester Library Bulletin,* Autumn 1947; George G. Goodwin, "What Ever Became of Jumbo," *Natural History,* January 1952; and the author's own "Jumbo: Vita, morte e resurrezione," published on the occasion of the hundredth anniversary of Jumbo's death in the September and October 1985 issues of the Italian journal *Circo.* Additional sources may be found in Toole-Stott, *Circus and Allied Arts,* and at the end of an article by Sandra Lash Shoshani, Jeheskel Shoshani, and Fred Dahlinger Jr., "Jumbo: Origin of the Word and History of the Elephant," *Elephant* (published by the Elephant Interest Group at Wayne State University, Detroit), Fall 1986.

66. *AB* (1889), pp. 330–31.

67. A. D. Bartlett, *Wild Animals in Captivity,* p. 49.

68. *Ibid.,* pp. 45–46, 61; *Ward's Natural Science Bulletin,* 1 May 1886. The naturalist William T. Hornaday, who bore Barnum a grudge over Jumbo, later claimed that the elephant's height in early 1883 was "precisely" 10 feet 9 inches, this figure having been surreptitiously and indirectly arrived at by one of the circus's artists during the stand at Madison Square Garden. See Hornaday, *The American Natural History,* Fireside Edition (New York: Charles Scribner's Sons, 1914), II, 135–36. Jumbo's height and age at the time of his acquisition by the London Zoological Society in June 1865 are variously reported. Bartlett, whom I follow in this instance, writes he was then "about 4 ft. high," and that he was "about twenty-one years old" at the time of his sale to Barnum. The *Animal World* reports Jumbo was "not more than six years old and five feet high" in June 1865; Jolly (*Jumbo,* p. 16) writes he was then "just over five feet high and was judged to be about four years old."

69. On the subject of Jumbo's periods of "musth" and his occasional violence, see Bartlett, *Wild Animals in Captivity,* pp. 46–47; and an informative article on "'Jumbo' and His Last Days in England," which includes interviews with Scott and Bartlett, published in the RSPCA's *Animal World* (London), 1 April 1882. A number of ingenious theories have been proposed to explain Jumbo's violence at the zoo, one of them being that the elephant was suffering from "teething" problems around this time (see Jolly, *Jumbo,* pp. 41–43). There was no doubt in Bartlett's and Scott's minds about its origin, however.

They were on the scene, thoroughly familiar with Jumbo, and the former, at least, had had sufficient experience with these things in the past.

70. *AB* (1889), p. 332. On Jumbo's true feelings toward his "wife" Alice, see the 1 April 1882 article in the *Animal World*.

71. M. O. Hunter to Mrs. Rackliffe, 28 March 1882 (TU).

72. PTB to Mr. Lesarge, 23 February 1882, in *AB* (1889), p. 331.

73. PTB to Edward A. Webster, 2 June 1882, published in the *Jackson* (Michigan) *Daily Citizen*, 15 June 1882. Webster owned the company that built the wagon-crate used to transport Jumbo.

74. Bartlett, *Wild Animals in Captivity*, pp. 50–51.

75. M. O. Hunter to Mrs. Rackliffe, 28 March 1882; and see Jolly, *Jumbo*, pp. 88–106.

76. PTB to Unidentified Correspondent, 7 March 1882, *SL*, p. 223.

77. Office Diary, 25 January 1882.

78. *New York Times*, 10 April 1882.

79. *Ibid.*, 10 and 11 April 1882.

80. *Ibid.*, 11 and 12 April 1882.

81. A. D. Bartlett to PTB, 7 June 1882 (BPL).

82. On Barnum's 1882 visit to England, see the interview with him in the *New York Tribune* of 30 July 1882; and cf. *AB* (1889), p. 333.

83. Office Diary, 21 April 1883; *Bridgeport Standard*, 21 April 1883. Scott, *Autobiography*, pp. 86–95, gives a highly imaginative description of a later crossing over the bridge with Jumbo. The elephant set up a "great vibration," he claims.

84. Scott, *Autobiography*, pp. 81–84, notes several "accidents" he experienced while looking after Jumbo. The *Bridgeport Standard* of 13 November 1882 and the July 1883 issue of the SPCA journal *Our Animal Friends* both describe the elephant's once bashing through a wall and escaping at winter quarters.

85. Scott, *Autobiography*, pp. 77–79.

86. Description based primarily on two manuscript eyewitness accounts—one by Merritt F. Young, treasurer with the show, the other by Joseph T. McCaddon, Bailey's brother-in-law and the show's assistant treasurer—which were written and sent, respectively, to Bailey and to Mrs. Bailey and her sister Mary on the following day (BPL).

87. Barnum's correspondence with Ward, Spencer F. Baird (who offered advice) of the Smithsonian Institution, and other individuals on the mounting of Jumbo is quite extensive and is partially represented in *SL*, pp. 241, 244, 265, 268–69, and 274–78. Other letters by and to Barnum on the subject are among the Ward Papers at the University of Rochester and in the Smithsonian Institution's Archives.

88. PTB to Messrs. Harper Bros. & Co., 18 September 1885, and PTB to William A. Croffut, 20 October 1885, *SL*, pp. 266 and 273.

89. These two documents, both dated 17 September 1885, were among the Barnum papers preserved by Bowser and are presently in the FDP.

90. Merritt F. Young to JAB, 17 September 1885 (BPL); James L. Hutchinson to JAB, 25 and 26 September 1885 (BPL).

91. Office Diary, 10 October 1885; PTB to JAB, 12 October 1885, *SL*, p. 271. The UTX possesses a copy of a letter Barnum wrote to Hutchinson following a meeting he had with Bailey on 10 October. In it the showman announces his intention to waive any claim against Bailey on account of Jumbo's death and urges Hutchinson to do the same. The manuscript appears to be in Bailey's hand; and at its bottom Joseph T. McCaddon, who was always eager to disparage his brother-in-law's partner, claims Bailey himself drafted it "when on the verge of a nervous breakdown," then gave it to Barnum to copy and send to Hutchinson.

92. See, e.g., PTB to Rev. E. H. Capen [16 June 1883], *SL*, p. 239; and PTB to Spencer F. Baird, 21 June 1884, *SL*, pp. 256–57.

93. James L. Hutchinson to JAB, 16 September 1885 (BPL). Hutchinson's hope that Ward might discover antediluvian characteristics in Jumbo is expressed in a letter he wrote the naturalist on 11 January 1886 (UR).

94. Spencer F. Baird to PTB, 26 September 1885 (SIA); PTB to Henry A. Ward, 26 September 1885, *SL*, pp. 268–69. Hutchinson, who insisted that the skeleton be ready in time for the 1886 season, tried to convince Barnum to give up this plan. "It is vastly more important that he should look natural than that his size should be increased," he wrote the showman on 6 October (UR). Two days later Barnum forwarded his partner's instructions about the skeleton to Ward, but neglected to make any mention of Hutchinson's reservations about the mounted hide (Ward's Natural Science Establishment, Rochester, New York).

95. The full title of Ward's fifteen-page pamphlet is *The Life and Death of Jumbo: An Illustrated History of the Greatest, Gentlest and Most Famous and Heroic Beast That Ever Lived*.

96. As Barnum hinted in a letter published in the 29 March 1882 issue of the *New York Tribune* ("While Jumbo is awaiting the arrival of his so-called 'wife' Alice . . ."), he was even then hoping to purchase and bring Alice to America. Negotiations continued over the next few years and were finally consummated on 8 January 1886, when the showman cabled Bartlett he would take Alice and had sent her purchase price (London Zoological Society Archives).

97. See PTB to Morris K. Jesup, 28 April 1887, *SL*, pp. 284–86.

98. Hornaday's memorandum, dated 17 April 1890, was attached to a letter Barnum had written and addressed to him on the preceding day (see *SL*, pp. 322–24). Here it may be added that Matthew Scott himself, shortly after Jumbo's death, was reported to have "started on a life of dissipation." He continued to look after small animals at the circus's winter quarters until early in this century, but was finally let go and took up residence in the Bridgeport almshouse, where he died in 1914 at the reputed age of seventy-four (his "autobiography" gives 1834 as his year of birth).

99. Barnum's relations with Ritchel and Sterling were extremely complex and are referred to at several other points in this narrative. The Pfening Collection contains a considerable number of letters and documents addressed by the inventor to Barnum in late 1884 and 1885, "explaining" his role in these and other schemes, condemning Sterling as the real instigator of various libels, harping on his and his family's destitution, and repeatedly begging Barnum for money or a "situation." Oddly enough, Barnum soon forgave him for his article about Jumbo, which appeared in the *Hartford Sunday Globe* of 27 September.

100. *Hartford Sunday Globe*, 4 October 1885; and see PTB to JAB, 4 October 1885, *SL*, p. 270. The affair is further reported on in the *Bridgeport Standard* of 28 and 29 September and 3, 5, 8, and 10 October 1885.

101. Roy Floyd Dibble, *Strenuous Americans* (New York: Boni and Liveright, 1923), p. 328.

102. Jolly, *Jumbo*, pp. 139–40. And see, e.g., PTB to Henry A. Ward, 22 July 1883, *SL*, p. 241 ("I want hereafter during this season or longer to have my managers forward to you all specimens which die in our menagerie, and wish you to preserve the skins for me, ready for mounting, including everything from a monkey to an elephant"). By the time of Jumbo's death the showman was also anxious to supply specimens to his "pet" museum at Tufts, which was given first choice, with other dead animals going to the Smithsonian and occasionally the American Museum of Natural History. The financial arrangements, at least at the outset, were such that the college paid Ward the cost of mounting and shipping the specimens it desired, but was allowed credit for those it declined and that Ward disposed of elsewhere. On numerous occasions the showman himself chipped in when the school did not possess sufficient funds or "credit" to purchase some specimen it particularly desired, and he continued to support the museum in various other ways. There were several adjustments in these arrangements over the next few years; and in 1889 the American Museum of Natural History—in return for past favors and the anticipated gift of Jumbo's skeleton—agreed to prepare and supply specimens to the college without charge.

103. This ingenious piece of research was the inspiration of one C. Manly Lang and

was commented on, with extracts from the work, in the *Connecticut Sunday Herald* of 2 June 1968. The newspaper article further identifies Mr. Lang as the author of "Here Comes Jumbo," but whether this was an article or a book, or indeed ever published, escapes me. The Library of Congress catalogue lists no such work, and I have not felt any great need to pursue the matter further. Except, that is, in a "Barnum" letter I once wrote myself and privately published in a pamphlet entitled *Letters I Wish P. T. Barnum Had Written*.

104. See, e.g., the *New York Times* for 19 April 1891; and "The World's Opinion as Expressed Through the Columns of the Daily Press: The Past and Present," an advertising flyer published and distributed by the circus soon after Barnum's death (a copy of the latter is in Bridgeport's Museum of Art, Science and Industry). The McCaddon Collection at Princeton University possesses similar materials; and McCaddon himself, in his adulatory manuscript biography of his brother-in-law, dwells on these same themes at numerous points. To be sure, the press agents' wizardry must have irritated some of Barnum's former colleagues, like W. C. Coup, who were still living. Among other absurd claims now put forward was the one that Bailey was responsible for the multiple-ring circus and, around 1880, "started the two-ring circus" while he was competing with Barnum. Coup and Barnum, as noted above, had hit upon this innovation as early as 1872.

Chapter XIV: The Sun of the Amusement World

1. PTB to John A. Halderman, 27 May 1882. This letter was written on the day of Barnum's sailing for Europe with Bailey. His later communication is contained in an undated postscript to a letter that has not been located. In another letter to Halderman, written the following 24 October, Barnum mentions the items he once sent to the Siamese king through Halderman's predecessor, Colonel Daniel B. Sickles. All three of these manuscripts are now in the Smithsonian Institution's National Museum of American History.

2. Barnum briefly relates the story of the white elephant on pp. 338–40 of *AB* (1889); the appendix to the 1884 edition, pp. 339–40, contains a few additional details. The *New York Tribune* of 19 January 1896, in an article on Halderman and some of his correspondence recently donated to the Smithsonian Institution, inaccurately reports on the general's relations with Barnum; and John Kunzog, while interestingly describing the warfare that raged between Barnum and Forepaugh over their respective "white" elephants, cannot resist gratuitously flailing at the showman again (*Tanbark and Tinsel*, pp. 23–45).

3. PTB to John A. Halderman, 24 October 1882.

4. John A. Halderman to PTB, 8 February 1883 (BPL).

5. Office Diary, 8 May 1883.

6. *Ibid.*, 22 May 1883.

7. PTB to the Editor of the *New York Tribune*, [3] February 1884, published in the *Tribune* on 4 February. On this controversy and Toung Taloung's reception in London, see also the *Tribune* of 2 and 3 February 1884; and Jolly, *Jumbo*, pp. 140–145.

8. PTB to John A. Halderman, 22 December 1884 (Alexander P. Clark Collection). Richelieu's report to the minister, dated 5 August 1884 and apparently copied and forwarded to Barnum a few days later, is among Halderman's papers at the National Museum of American History.

9. "Thumbs Down All Around," *New York Times*, 4 June 1884.

10. Office Diary, 24 June 1884. Barnum's offer to purchase, for $25, a poem by another contestant is contained in a 4 June 1884 letter he wrote to a Mrs. Cornell (NYHS).

11. "The Prize Odes," *New York Times*, 1 June 1884.

12. The famous circus press agent Dexter W. Fellows writes amusingly about this rivalry in his *This Way to the Big Show* (New York: Halcyon House, 1936), pp. 272–279; and Kunzog, in his account of the white elephant war in *Tanbark and Tinsel*, reprints

several informative paragraphs from contemporary newspapers. The latter writer argues, incidentally, that Forepaugh's elephant was bleached rather than whitewashed, and he even employed a chemist to evaluate the bleaching compound's supposed formula.

13. The resourceful proprietor was the celebrated George Wombwell, and the incident occurred at Bartholomew Fair early in the nineteenth century. See, e.g., Ruth Manning-Sanders, *The English Circus* (London: Werner Laurie, 1952), pp. 128–29.

14. *Bridgeport Standard*, 19 April 1884; Kunzog, *Tanbark and Tinsel*, p. 37. The Philadelphia Free Library possesses an interesting courier circulated in advance of this engagement, exposing in detail Forepaugh's fraudulent elephant and accusing the showman of also advertising dead artists.

15. PTB to James Montgomery Bailey, 1 October 1884 (Scott-Fanton Museum, Danbury).

16. PTB to John A. Halderman, 22 December 1884.

17. An example of this circular letter, dated 9 August 1882, is included in *SL*, pp. 226–27. Bowser notes in the office diary that additional letters, as many as seventy-four at a time, were copied and sent out on 24 September, 8 October, and 8 November 1882. Among the Barnum Papers in the NYPL is an undated letter to an unidentified recipient, on engraved stationery depicting the first American Museum, setting forth essentially the same scheme for a "Congress of Nations" or "Human Menagerie" that the showman hoped to exhibit "in my Museum and elsewhere." From this it seems evident the idea for such an exhibition occurred to him years before he began his circus career.

18. PTB to Spencer F. Baird, 25 October 1882, *SL*, pp. 228–29; Baird to PTB, 31 October 1882, personal letter and accompanying endorsement (SIA).

19. No less than four letters authorizing J. R. Davis to act as the show's representative, signed by Barnum and in one case witnessed by Bridgeport's mayor, Carlos Curtis, are in the HCC.

20. PTB to Hon. G. Gade, 27 December 1882 (TU).

21. BPL. The wording of these announcements was likely the work of the press agent R. F. "Tody" Hamilton, famed in circus annals for his adjectival, often alliterative constructions.

22. PTB to Mrs. James A. Bailey, 5 July 1885, *SL*, pp. 264–65.

23. PTB to James L. Hutchinson, 29 June 1885, *SL*, pp. 262–64.

24. Agreement dated 30 October 1885, BPL "Salmagundi" ledger, pp. 154–59.

25. PTB to Rev. E. H. Capen, 27 January 1887, *SL*, pp. 282–83.

26. *Sawdust & Spangles*, pp. 129–38.

27. *New York Sun*, 13 January 1884; reprinted in the appendix to the 1884 edition of *AB*, p. 344.

28. Office Diary, 4 January 1885.

29. Statement dated 16 October 1882 and published in the *New York Clipper* and various other newspapers around the country.

30. This document is now in the BPL. A similar, but less complete, record is in the FDP.

31. Barnum made a gift of the stuffed hide to the Fairfield County Historical Society, which did not then have a building of its own. Today this historic elephant, somewhat the worse for wear, may be seen at the Barnum Museum in Bridgeport.

32. Information derived primarily from the 1886 and 1887 route books; also Office Diary, 14 March 1887.

33. Agreement dated 26 October 1887, BPL "Salmagundi" ledger, pp. 164–73.

34. *AB* (1889), pp. 352–54, 358; John P. Marshall to Henry A. Ward, 22 November 1887 (UR). Additional interesting descriptions of the fire were published in *Harper's Weekly* of 3 December 1887 and the *Hartford Courant* of 29 December 1929, with the latter source containing the recollections of a fireman who fought the blaze.

35. PTB to Mrs. Lucy A. Thomas, 10 July 1886, *SL*, p. 279.

36. PTB to John P. Marshall, 31 May 1886, *SL*, p. 278.

37. PTB to Rev. E. H. Capen, 20 June 1886 (TU); Harry Adams Hersey, *A History of*

Music in Tufts College, p. 332. The composer of "The Barnum Song," Leo Rich Lewis, was a member of the class of '87 and must have received some acknowledgment of Barnum's pleasure, since his name and address were entered in the showman's address book (BM). The awarding to Lyon of a master's degree, judging from correspondence dating from around this time, seems to have been largely at Barnum's instigation. The show- · man himself never received any honorary degrees, nor did he ever seek them.

38. *New York Times*, 4 January 1888; *AB* (1889), p. 359; Office Diary, 1, 2, and 4 February 1889; 1889 Memorandum Book, 16 August (BPL). Not all of Waldemere was demolished. The original plan called for moving it to another site and converting it into a summer hotel. Instead, at least two parts of the mansion were salvaged and moved elsewhere to serve as private homes. One of these was floated across the water to nearby Stratford and is presently the property of a well-known actress. Most of Barnum's former estate is today owned by the University of Bridgeport, which demolished Marina in 1961 to make room for an undistinguished brick dining hall.

39. For several letters Barnum wrote to his favorite great-grandson, see *SL*, pp. 283–85, 288–90, 292, 300–301, and 304–6.

40. PTB to JAB, [14 April 1889], *SL*, pp. 311–12.

41. PTB to H. E. Bowser, 12 April 1889, *SL*, pp. 310–11.

42. The office diary contains several clippings from 1892 and 1893 Bridgeport newspapers that bear on the progress of this suit.

43. See above, pp. 203–4 and note.

44. See, e.g., Lucius Beebe, *The Big Spenders*, pp. 110–15. On what Sterling made of the affair, see above, p. 229, and below, pp. 337–38. C. Barnum Seeley, who rendered several services to Bridgeport during his lifetime (like his grandfather, he was for many years a member of the Parks Commission) but who was viewed by other descendants as being somewhat "acquisitive," died in 1958. His brother, Herbert Barnum Seeley, about whom several other outrageous stories are treasured by family members, died in 1914.

45. PTB to J. A. McGonagle, 21 July 1880, *SL*, p. 213.

46. Office Diary, 23 July 1884.

47. *Ibid.*, 24 June 1886.

48. *Ibid.*, 17 June and 31 August 1887; 1889 Memorandum Book, 3 January and 5 August (BPL); PTB to H. E. Bowser, 17 April 1889 (FDP).

49. See Gordon Welles and William Proios, *Port Jefferson*, p. 29; and cf. *AB* (1889), p. 353, where Barnum reprints the petition and claims it was signed by "more than one thousand" persons. The original of the petition is in the BM.

50. Office Diary, 8 December 1888.

51. *Ibid.*, 30 September 1882; and see the *New York Sun* interview reprinted in *AB* (1889), p. 337.

52. *New York Tribune*, 3 November 1884, *SL*, p. 257. Bailey's brother-in-law, Joseph McCaddon, in the manuscript history of the circus he wrote (pp. 233–34), comments on the chilling effect this announcement had on Southern audiences.

53. See, e.g., PTB to Col. Lamont, 27 April 1888 (LC Presidential Papers: Cleveland).

54. See the summary of a speech he delivered at Bridgeport's Second Ward Republican Club in the 19 and 20 September 1888 issues of the *Bridgeport Standard*.

55. *New York Times*, 20 February 1888. For Barnum's thoughts about a Prohibition ticket during the 1872 Connecticut elections, see the letter from "A Good Templar" (the name comes from one of the temperance organizations to which he belonged) in the 24 January 1872 issue of the *New York Tribune*. The authorship of this letter is established in a letter Barnum wrote to Whitelaw Reid on 22 January of the same year (LC, Reid Family Papers).

56. PTB to Benjamin Harrison, telegram of 12 November 1888 (LC Presidential Papers: Harrison). Earlier in the campaign, on 22 September, Barnum had invited Harrison to be his guest at Waldemere. If the Republican candidate would come to Connecticut, he would "do a *world of good*" (Presidential Papers).

57. Ball, *My Threescore Years and Ten*, pp. 334–38.

58. PTB to JAB, 26 August 1889, *SL*, p. 315. On Barnum's earlier ideas for such a scheme, see his letters to Bailey of c. July 1888 and 27 August 1888, *SL*, pp. 298 and 302–4.

59. See, e.g., the London *Times* of 12 November 1889. Barnum himself never got around to writing up this trip for publication in his autobiography (the last addition to that work was written shortly before the show embarked for London), but did report on it fairly extensively in his *Funny Stories*, pp. 357–71, and in an interview published in the 7 May 1890 issue of *Kate Field's Washington*. Nancy Barnum briefly refers to the trip in her *The Last Chapter*, and George Conklin also tells about it in his *The Ways of the Circus*, pp. 251–55. In addition, an interesting route-book-like account of the show during this particular season—giving the show's program and a roster of its personnel, a description of Olympia itself, a listing of daily occurrences, etc.—was compiled by a "Professor" Wendell H. Ordway and entitled *Olympia Gleanings: A Review of the Winter Season of 1889–90 in London, England, with P. T. Barnum's Greatest Show on Earth*. Among unpublished sources containing information on this sojourn in London, Barnum's 1889 memorandum book is particularly valuable.

60. *London Evening News and Post*, 12 November 1889. In America the program and synopsis of this spectacle were published by the Courier Co. of Buffalo in 1890.

61. The banquet, which occurred on 8 November, was extensively written up in the London *Times* of 9 and 11 November. A copy of the printed "program" for the affair—with the American and British flags on its covers and including the menu, seating plan for 150 guests, and lists of songs and orchestral pieces that were performed while the dinner was in progress—is in the BPL.

62. Several of these scrapbooks are still in the possession of Barnum's descendants; others may be seen at the BPL (two copies), Smithsonian Institution, and Princeton and Tufts universities. And see the illustrated article based on one such copy (that presented by the showman to his daughter Caroline) by Eric Larrabee, "The Old Showman's Last Triumph." There appear to have been at least fifteen copies made.

63. A complete transcription of the recording may be found in *SL*, p. 335.

64. *Pall Mall Gazette*, 31 January 1890.

65. PTB to Isaac T. Rogers [?], 10 January 1890, *SL*, p. 316.

66. This small engagement book, supposedly for October 1888 but in reality having nothing to do with Barnum's activities during that month, is in the BPL. *Funny Stories* itself was published by George Routledge of London and New York, with the same plates used for both the English and American editions. As was true for the 1869 edition of his autobiography, the showman no doubt benefited from occasional advice by friends while he was preparing this work. While still in England, e.g., he wrote to his good friend George Sala to ask if he could think of a better title than *Funny Stories*. Sala obviously could not—PTB to George Sala, 9 March 1890 (YU).

67. See above, pp. 65–66.

68. "What the Fair Should Be," *North American Review*, March 1890, pp. 400–401.

69. *Pall Mall Budget*, 20 February 1890.

70. PTB to JAB, 22 and 26 February 1890, *SL*, pp. 319–21; and 1 March 1890 (BPL).

71. *Boston Globe*, 1 July 1890. The BPL possesses several copies of the program for this spectacle and an eight-page courier for its season in Boston.

72. "Barnum's" chapter appears in the 17 July issue of the *Globe*. The novel was published in book form in the same year by J. S. Ogilvie of New York.

73. *AB* (1889), pp. 359–60.

74. Office Diary, 22 August and 27 October 1890.

75. *The Last Chapter*, p. 9.

76. PTB to Helen Hurd Rennell, 10 October 1890, *SL*, p. 330. Barnum's plans to extend his trip are contained in jottings he made in the memorandum book he filled this month (BPL).

77. *The Last Chapter*, pp. 9–10.

78. See, e.g., PTB to Rev. E. H. Capen, 5 February 1887 and 22 May 1890, *SL*, pp.

283, 326; PTB to John P. Marshall, 22 May 1890, *SL*, p. 327; *Will & Codicils*, pp. 25, 43. On 24 November 1890, the day before Barnum signed the codicil pertaining to this gift, his lawyer Curtis Thompson wrote to Capen to say he could go ahead with the wings as soon as he liked. The following month, on 22 December, he wrote again to convey Barnum's wish that previous correspondence on the subject be preserved, in order to prove he intended to make the gift before he suffered his stroke, and to assure the president the codicil had been executed in the presence of "at least five good witnesses to his sanity," although only three of them actually signed the document (TU).

79. *Will & Codicils*, pp. 27–29, 43, 52. And see the description of the building and the account of the "opening exercises" in the *Reports of the Fairfield County Historical Society for 1893–5*. The final cost, building and land, came to around $85,000. Unfortunately, the building was never endowed; and in the early twentieth century, after the City of Bridgeport took it over for nonpayment of taxes, it was for many years occupied by municipal offices, then nearly demolished to make way for an exit ramp during construction of the New England Thruway. But an aroused citizenry, which had witnessed so much of Bridgeport's history destroyed in the past, sprang to its defense; and in the years since then, under more enlightened administrations and through generous infusions of money from the city, state, and local business community, both the building and its collections have been substantially restored.

80. Office Diary, 10 and 11 December 1890, 10 February 1891.

81. The copy he presented to one of his physicians, Dr. Charles C. Godfrey, on 11 January 1891 is now in the BPL. Earlier he had given another copy to his "beloved pastor—the Fisher of Men (and Women)," which some years ago was in the library of a Massachusetts congregation.

82. Both Nancy in her *The Last Chapter* and Curtis Thompson in his address at the opening of the Barnum Institute recalled Barnum's last days and hours in some detail. The *Bridgeport Standard* of 8 April 1891 also carried a detailed description of his final moments and death. The showman's death certificate, signed by Dr. Charles C. Godfrey, is in Bridgeport's Office of Vital Statistics. The cause of death was officially listed as heart failure brought on by "fatty degeneration of the heart"—more precisely, by atherosclerosis of the coronary arteries, which interfered with the heart's blood supply.

Epilogue

1. The *Bridgeport Standard* of 10 April and *New York Tribune* of 11 April 1891 describe the funeral and services at some length, as do Nancy Barnum in *The Last Chapter*, pp. 17–18, and Joel Benton in his purported *Life of Hon. Phineas T. Barnum*, pp. 616–19. Bowser also comments on the crowds that packed the sidewalks all the way from Marina to the cemetery (Office Diary, 10 April 1891). Copies of the program of services are in the BPL.

2. In addition to frequent mention of Nancy's activities in the office diary, Bowser pasted into one of his scrapbooks several newspaper clippings relating to her and her second husband (FDP). The *New Yorker* of 11 April 1936 contains an informative article entitled "P. T. Barnum's Second Wife" by Clara de Morinni, who seems to have known Nancy during her later years in Paris; and the *Bridgeport Post* of 26 July 1936 carried a long, illustrated article on her based primarily on information supplied by Barnum descendants, in particular Mrs. Mildred Breul, who later permitted the present writer to record her candid recollections. Nearly all the correspondence and documents pertaining to the settling of Nancy's estate, together with a collection of her personal photographs, clothing, and other effects, are in the author's possession.

SELECT BIBLIOGRAPHY

So much has been written by and about Barnum that the following is perforce a very select list, representing primarily those works I consider essential to any collection of "Barnumiana" or that have been of particular use in the writing of this biography. Sources of letters, contracts, and other manuscript materials; contemporary newspaper and magazine articles; bills, advertisements, prints, scrapbooks, and similar ephemera are given in the text or notes and generally not repeated here.

Anyone possessing even a casual interest in Barnum should, of course, read his autobiography, the various editions and states of which are discussed in Chapter I. Of these, the 1855 original edition is the most desirable from the bibliophile's viewpoint, followed by the second edition of 1869. Researchers and serious students should keep in mind, however, that the plates of the latter were used in several of the "editions," to which appendices were added, published in the early 1870s, so that these later, less commercially valuable volumes may prove even more useful for their purposes. The many abridgments of the autobiography published in the seventies and eighties are primarily of value for the information (again, sometimes in appendices) they contain on Barnum's latest activities, although it is nevertheless of interest to note what was deleted from the main text and how the appendices themselves were abridged and rewritten prior to their eventual incorporation into the same.

Of the several editions of the autobiography published in the present century, that by George S. Bryan is undoubtedly the best. Based on the 1855, 1869, and 1889 editions, and omitting little that is contained in them, this work also includes Nancy Barnum's separately published *The Last Chapter* and therefore has the advantage of tracing the full history of its subject. The editor, moreover, has supplied a superb introduction, together with notes, bibliography, and a generous selection of illustrations; and the only deficiency in this otherwise exemplary work—one that is common to all editions of the autobiography, however—is its lack of an index. Again, for the sake of those researching the life of Barnum, it should be pointed out that the few passages deleted by Bryan may be found to contain information of particular interest to them, and that this work does not really take into account the initial state of the appendices before they were revised and incorporated into the main text. To appreciate fully what went on in that area, there is no substitute for locating and examining the various editions themselves.

In the same year (1927) that Bryan's work appeared, a severely abridged, unannotated, altogether inferior edition of the autobiography by Waldo R. Browne, entitled *Barnum's Own Story*, was published by Viking. It was later reissued by Dover in paperback, at which time some forty-eight pages of illustrations, whose legends are not always to be trusted, were added. The same edition, taken over in 1972 by Peter Smith and again bound in hard covers, is still available. More recently, in 1981 Penguin Books published the autobiography in paperback, edited and abridged by Carl Bode. Based on the 1869 *Struggles and Triumphs* with additions only to 1871, this edition, headed by a pedestrian introduction, is so unskillfully blue-penciled at points that the reader has difficulty following Barnum's narrative. To those unfamiliar with the ways of publishers, it must seem strange that no one within the past half-century has seen fit to do the job properly, or even to reprint the admirable (but lengthy) edition by Bryan.

After the autobiography, one should at least glance at Barnum's *Funny Stories*, the author's memoranda for which are in the Bridgeport Public Library. A compilation of anecdotes, the book was primarily intended, as Barnum acknowledges in the preface, to retrieve material that had been deleted from the autobiography; and for this reason it has largely been ignored by biographers to date. But in fact many of these stories are new or throw new and interesting light on old subject matter (on the late Tom Thumb's character, for example) and, coming as they do within a few months of the author's death, represent the final written expression of his thoughts on these topics, as well as his own description of the 1889–90 visit of his show to England. Barnum's much earlier work, *The Humbugs of the World*—the "true History of Humbug" he promised readers of the first edition of his autobiography—was originally published, beginning in 1864, as a series of articles in the *New York Weekly Mercury* and is another assemblage of anecdotes, in this case largely taken or retold from other works. Particularly in the early chapters, however, he discusses individuals and schemes with which he was personally familiar, and in Chapter 2 he gives and defends as best he can his own peculiar definition of "humbug." The several juveniles and the book on natural history sometimes attributed to Barnum are discussed above in Chapter XIII.

The present author has edited a selection of over three hundred of the showman's letters and has ready for press a second volume of his letters and papers. The one hundred lengthy "letters" Barnum wrote for the *New York Atlas* during his first trip abroad were never collected and were employed in small part only when he came to write the autobiography. Strange to relate, although the showman makes no attempt to conceal the origin of this material and previous biographers have certainly been aware of the articles' existence, no one in the past seems to have been sufficiently curious to go directly to them and thereby profit from the often revealing information they contain. They would constitute an interesting volume in themselves—representing the showman-author when he was at his youthful, democratic best, proudly comparing the institutions and customs of the country he loved to those he observed in monarchical Europe, looking at everything with a fresh, unjaundiced eye. And so, too, I have little doubt, would the impassioned editorials and lighter fare he composed for his own *Herald of Freedom*, were it not for the fact that extant copies of this periodical are extremely rare, while those deposited in public institutions have been reduced to an ever-diminishing handful.

If I have only infrequently cited the studies of other writers who have preceded me into the field—and then mainly to quarrel with them—it is not because I have failed to enjoy or profit from them. In many instances they challenged and set me to thinking, besides suggesting new territory ripe for exploration. As a matter of principle, however, even when entering *terra cognita*, I have preferred to travel my own way, basing my narrative and interpretations on primary or at least contemporary sources. Over the course of nearly two decades I have probably examined more such materials, particularly manuscripts, than anyone, and my hard-won victory over the peculiarities of Barnum's handwriting has enabled me to avoid pitfalls others writing about him have not always escaped. Added to this, my location and roster of acquaintances could not have been more fortunate, with the former permitting me to visit all of the major places associated with the showman as often as I wished, and the latter embracing, besides a good many of his descendants, several private individuals possessing interesting memorabilia and knowledge of Barnum.

From a listing of truly significant works written about the showman, I naturally exclude those productions, often of European manufacture, that are little more than retellings and simpleminded "analyses" of the autobiography itself; although, to tell truth, what is probably the most egregious example of this sort of hackwork was perpetrated by the American writer Joel Benton, whose *Life of Hon. Phineas T. Barnum* is mentioned in Chapter I. The first bona fide biography was M. R. Werner's *Barnum*, published in 1923, which quickly went through several printings and was also distributed as a book-club selection. A highly touted work in a day when Freudian analysis of historical figures was just getting under way, it was the inspiration for a number of attempts to probe

Barnum's character, including the ludicrous foray into this area by Harvey O'Higgins and Edward H. Reede, whose *The American Mind in Action* was published in the following year. Unfortunately for these and later authors who relied on Werner for their facts, his book contains a fair number of errors.

Lesser known but of greater value to the serious student is Harvey W. Root's *The Unknown Barnum* (1927). Although it, too, is undocumented, it is nevertheless based in large part on the author's patient investigation of primary sources and is of particular interest for its chapters on Barnum's career in Connecticut politics and his life among his Bridgeport neighbors. More recently, Irving Wallace—no mean researcher when he is not busy writing novels—has recounted Barnum's career in his *The Fabulous Showman: The Life and Times of P. T. Barnum* (1959). Besides being highly readable, this work is especially engrossing for its examination of Barnum's family relationships. Finally, in a book that is primarily a critical rather than a biographical study, Neil Harris has explored the showman's public career and "operational esthetic" in his *Humbug: The Art of P. T. Barnum* (1973). My opinion of this scholarly, thoroughly original work may be read in the March 1975 issue of *Nineteenth Century Theatre Research*.

There have been many books on the showman and his attractions addressed to younger readers (Harvey Root, e.g., also did a *Boys' Life of Barnum*); and a number of authors have written or fantasied about Barnum in chapter-length studies. Those in the books by Gamaliel Bradford and Constance M. Rourke are certainly among the most stimulating, whatever one may think of their authors' interpretations. Of all the scholarly articles written about Barnum, John Rickards Betts's "P. T. Barnum and the Popularization of Natural History," despite some confusion in its documentation, deserves to be ranked among the very best.

The volume of writing on Barnum continues to swell at such a pace that no bibliography can reasonably lay claim to being up-to-date. Werner, Bryan, and Wallace all include useful bibliographies in their works; and Harris, besides providing his readers with a discriminating bibliographic essay, supplies twenty-four pages of notes in which may be found references to a good many manuscripts, newspapers, and periodicals. Among purely bibliographic works, there is a fine "Historical Summary" and "Survey of Sources" at the head of the chapter on "The Dime Museum and P. T. Barnum" in Don B. Wilmeth's *Variety Entertainment and Outdoor Amusements: A Reference Guide* (1982). The same chapter contains a six-page list of pertinent titles, many of them relating to Barnum and his enterprises; a few additional references are located elsewhere in the volume. Nelle Neafie's very incomplete *A P. T. Barnum Bibliography*, privately published in 1965 as a project toward the compiler's degree in library science, includes a section on Barnum manuscripts in the Bridgeport Public Library and is primarily of use for indicating some of the holdings at that institution. Needless to say, the library's Barnum Collection, which is unquestionably one of the finest and most complete in the world, has grown considerably since Neafie's publication. On the subject of Barnum manuscripts, both the *National Union Catalogue of Manuscript Collections* and *American Literary Manuscripts* list numerous locations for such documents. Additional sources and suggestions for their discovery may be found in the "Note on Sources" appended to my edition of the showman's letters.

Still the most useful and authoritative bibliography is that compiled by the eminent English bibliographer R. Toole-Stott, the first volume of whose *Circus and Allied Arts: A World Bibliography* includes a separate section on Barnum, listing, frequently with annotations, over two hundred titles. As Mr. Toole-Stott continued to work on his bibliography (a truly monumental labor that spanned nearly half a century, incidentally, and was carried out entirely at his own expense), he naturally discovered many additional Barnum-related titles. These were included in subsequent volumes and may be traced through the indices at the ends of Volumes 3 and 4. At the time of his death in 1982, the compiler had just finished working on a fifth volume, based in large part on holdings in American libraries and collections, to which this writer sometimes had the privilege of accompanying him. The typescript reposes today in the library of the University of

California at Santa Barbara, where his fine collections of books on the circus and on Somerset Maugham also went. In early 1988 the International Association of Libraries and Museums of the Performing Arts/Société Internationale des Bibliothèques et des Musées des Arts du Spectacle (SIBMAS) announced it had acquired the copyright to this and to the four previous volumes, and that it planned to publish the final volume "in the form of a photofacsimile of the author's corrected typescript" provided a minimum of 150 subscriptions were received in advance.

I have myself prepared a book-length work entitled "Barnumiana: A Select, Annotated Bibliography of Works by or Relating to P. T. Barnum"—including separate sections on "Original Art Works," "Dramatic Representations," "Major Collections of Barnumiana," etc.—which I hope to publish before long.

Manuscripts

Although manuscripts and their locations are generally described in the text or notes, the following items are singled out for particular attention on account of their recurring value in the preparation of this work.

Barnum, Caroline. "Diary, July 5–Aug. 11, 1848: Trip Across New York State, to Montreal and Quebec, and Return to Bridgeport." Unpaginated notebook in the Bridgeport Public Library, by Barnum's eldest daughter, with corrections in Barnum's hand.
—— Diary of Caroline Barnum During the Jenny Lind Tour, 4 December 1850–7 April 1851. Untitled, unpaginated notebook, also in the BPL.
Barnum, P. T. Ledger, referred to in text as "Bethel ledger." A large, leather-bound volume, donated to the BPL in 1944, sporadically covering Barnum's various business enterprises from c. 1831 to the 1860s, but concentrating on 1832, when he was running his store in Bethel. Iranistan and East Bridgeport expenses and affairs, the American Museum, Barnum's "Asiatic Caravan," livestock owned by the showman, etc. are also touched on at various places.
—— Memorandum Books. These small books, several of which, for the last few years of Barnum's life, are in the BPL, are actually appointment or engagement books, although the showman did not always enter items under the dates he performed them. Often, too, as noted in connection with his *Funny Stories*, he simply used them as notebooks, jotting down in them addresses, recipes, sums of money he owed, lists of vacation and other expenses, references to his will and codicils, etc.
Bowser, Henry E. Office Diaries. Separate, annual volumes kept by Bowser during the years 1880 through 1895, now in the Fred D. Pfening III Collection. Primarily business records, especially relating to Barnum's real-estate transactions in Bridgeport, but also containing some personal information on Bowser and his wife, Jennie; notes on Barnum's circus and its daily location; copies of letters by and to Barnum; frequent mention of the comings and goings of Barnum and members of his family and of visits to Bridgeport by the showman's friends and business associates; etc. Entries are occasionally in an elementary cipher.
"Salmagundi" Ledger. This fairly large volume, also in the BPL, appears to be the same Bowser several times refers to in the Office Diaries as the "Salmagundi" book; hence the use of the term in the present work. It is in fact a kind of master ledger, containing contracts between Barnum and his circus partners; copies of letters by and to him; the plan of Barnum's vault (drawn up by Brothwell) at Mountain Grove Cemetery; the receipts and sometimes routes of his various shows and circuses; records of Barnum's dealings with various individuals, including family members and his father-in-law John Fish; property transactions in Bridgeport and elsewhere around the country; lists of curiosities ordered from Japan; etc. Most of this material dates from c. 1877 to 1890. By far the most significant and engrossing collection of MS materials relating to Barnum I have seen to date, the volume was discovered in a

pile of waste paper in a Bridgeport building and salvaged by a curious citizen before it was thrown out!

Books and Articles

Ames, Mary Clemmer. *A Memorial of Alice and Phoebe Cary, with Some of Their Later Poems.* New York: Hurd and Houghton, 1873.

Appleton, William W. "The Marvellous Museum of P. T. Barnum." In *Le Merveilleux et les Arts du Spectacle*, pp. 57–62. Actes du IIIe Congrès International d'Histoire du Théâtre, 26 June–2 July 1961. Paris: Société d'Histoire du Théâtre, 1963.

Auto-Biography of Barnum; or, The Opening of the Oyster. Danbury, Conn.: n.p., 1889. Miniature, illustrated book of only 16 pp., with very little in the way of text.

The Autobiography of Petite Bunkum, the Showman; Showing His Birth, Education, and Bringing Up; His Astonishing Adventures by Sea and Land; His Connection with Tom Thumb, Judy Heath, the Woolly Horse, the Fudge Mermaid, and the Swedish Nightingale . . . Written by Himself. New York: P. F. Harris, 1855. 64 pp.

Bailey, Chris H. *From Rags to Riches to Rags: The Story of Chauncey Jerome.* Supplement to the *Bulletin* of the National Assn. of Watch and Clock Collectors, No. 15 (Winter 1986). Columbia, Pa.

Bailey, James Montgomery. *History of Danbury, Conn., 1684–1896, from Notes and Manuscript Left by James Montgomery Bailey.* Compiled with additions by Susan Benedict Hill. New York: Burr Printing House, 1896.

Ball, Thomas. *My Threescore Years and Ten: An Autobiography.* Boston: Roberts Brothers, 1891.

Barber, Lynn. *The Heyday of Natural History, 1820–1870.* New York: Doubleday, 1980.

Barbey d'Aurevilly, J. *Mémoires historiques et littéraires.* Paris: Alphonse Lemerre, 1893.

Barnum, Eben Lewis, and Francis Barnum. *Genealogical Record of the Barnum Family, Presenting a Conspectus of the Male Descendants of Thomas Barnum, 1625–1695.* Gardner, Mass.: Meals Printing Co., 1912.

Barnum, Nancy. *"The Last Chapter": In Memoriam, P. T. Barnum.* New York: press of J. J. Little, 1893. 19 pp.

Barnum, P. T. "The Art of Money-Getting." First published in the 1869 edition of Barnum's autobiography (see below), pp. 457–500, then in subsequent editions. (By the time this lecture was finally published, as the showman acknowledges in the autobiography, it had been considerably adapted to the taste of American audiences.)

—— "The First Jenny Lind Ticket," *Cosmopolitan*, October 1887, pp. 107–9.

—— *Funny Stories Told by Phineas T. Barnum.* New York and London: George Routledge and Sons, 1890.

—— *The Humbugs of the World: An Account of Humbugs, Delusions, Impositions, Quackeries, Deceits and Deceivers Generally, in All Ages.* New York: Carleton, 1865. Most extant copies seen by the author bear an 1866 imprint.

—— "I Thus Address the World." Cylinder recording of Barnum's voice made toward the end of his visit to London during the winter of 1889–90. For a transcription and note on reissues in the present century, see *Selected Letters*, p. 335.

◆

—— *The Life of P. T. Barnum, Written by Himself.* New York: Redfield, 1855. 404 pp. The original edition of the autobiography, with preface, dedication, and copyright all dated 1854 and officially published in December of the same year.

—— *Struggles and Triumphs; or, Forty Years' Recollections of P. T. Barnum, Written by Himself.* Hartford, Conn.: J. B. Burr, 1869. 780 pp. The second, greatly expanded, modified edition of the autobiography, which was abridged in 1876 but which Barnum continued to supplement and revise until nearly the end of his life.

—— *Struggles and Triumphs; or, Sixty Years' Recollections of P. T. Barnum, Including His Golden Rules for Money-Making, Illustrated and Brought Up to 1889, Written by Himself.* Buffalo, N.Y.: Courier Co., 1889. 360 pp., including a 3-page "Appendix" dated September 1889. The final edition of the abridged version published during Barnum's lifetime.

—— *Struggles and Triumphs; or, The Life of P. T. Barnum, Written by Himself.* Ed. and intro. by George S. Bryan. 2 vols. with consecutive pagination. New York: Alfred A. Knopf, 1927. The best and most desirable modern edition.

In addition to the above, the following editions have been found useful in the preparation of the present work, primarily on account of the appended material they contain:

—— *Struggles and Triumphs; or, Forty Years' Recollections of P. T. Barnum, Written by Himself.* Author's Edition. Buffalo, N.Y.: Warren, Johnson, 1872. Described on its title page as "complete to April, 1872," copy used includes the first "Appendix" to the 1869 edition (pp. 845–64), the "Conclusion" to same (pp. 865–70), as well as "Appendix II" (pp. 871–80), written and dated by Barnum in February 1873 and continuing the history down to that time. Although the plates employed for the main body of the text were the same as for the 1869 Burr edition, Barnum or his publisher had decided that edition, taking into account its unpaginated illustrations, actually ran to 844 pages. Hence the above pagination of the appended material.

—— *Struggles and Triumphs; or, Forty Years' Recollections of P. T. Barnum, Written by Himself.* Author's Edition. Buffalo, N.Y.: Warren, Johnson, 1873. Containing "Appendix III" (pp. 839–47), dated at London on 28 February 1874. Although this edition, too, was printed largely from the 1869 plates, Chapter 41 ("Bennett and the Herald") has been slightly abridged and Chapter 45 ("A Story-Chapter"), containing a rambling collection of anecdotes, has been entirely excised. Consequently, the book has been repaginated from the former chapter on. Also contains, at its end, an unpaginated 2-page endorsement of "The Climate of Colorado" by Barnum's son-in-law Dr. William H. Buchtel, dated at Denver in February 1873. (By this date Barnum was becoming involved in his Colorado real-estate speculations.)

—— *Struggles and Triumphs; or, Forty Years' Recollections of P. T. Barnum, Written by Himself.* Author's Edition. Buffalo, N.Y.: Courier Co., 1875. Includes a "Card Introductory" and brief "Second Preface," both dated 1875, as well as "Appendix IV" (pp. 849–63), dated at Bridgeport on 25 July 1874; a poem celebrating Waldemere (p. 864); "Appendix V" (pp. 865–70), dated 2 April 1875; together with a few recent magazine and newspaper extracts on Barnum and his enterprises (pp. 871–75). All of this material may also be found in some copies of the 1874 Author's Edition published by the same firm. In 1876 the first drastic abridgment of the autobiography appeared.

—— *Struggles and Triumphs; or, Fifty Years' Recollections of P. T. Barnum, Written by Himself.* Author's Edition. Buffalo, N.Y.: Courier Co., 1884. Containing an "Appendix" (pp. 338–46) dated 1884 at Waldemere.

————◆————

—— *The Liquor Business: Its Effects Upon the Minds, Morals, and Pockets of Our People.* No. 4 in The Whole World's Temperance Tracts. New York: Fowlers and Wells, 1854. 12 pp.

—— *Selected Letters of P. T. Barnum.* Ed. and intro. by A. H. Saxon. New York: Columbia Univ. Press, 1983. Trans. by L.-R. Dauven as *Barnum par lui-même* and published, with corrections and additional illustrations, by Editions de la Gardine, Sorvilier, Switzerland, in 1986.

—— *Why I Am a Universalist.* Boston and Chicago: Universalist Publishing House, n.d. 12 pp. Not to be confused with the considerably abridged version that continued to be published until recently.

—— *Will & Codicils of Phineas Taylor Barnum, Admitted to Probate April 11th, 1891.* Bridgeport, Conn.: Standard Assn., 1891. 53 pp.

Bartlett, A. D. *Wild Animals in Captivity: Being an Account of the Habits, Food, Management and Treatment of the Beasts and Birds at the "Zoo," with Reminiscences and Anecdotes.* Comp. and ed. by Edward Bartlett. 3d ed. London: Chapman and Hall, 1899.

Beebe, Lucius. *The Big Spenders.* Garden City, N.Y.: Doubleday, 1966.

Benton, Joel. *Life of Hon. Phineas T. Barnum, Comprising His Boyhood, Youth, Vicissitudes of Early Years . . . His Genius, Wit, Generosity, Eloquence, Christianity, &c., &c., as Told by Joel Benton, Esq.* Philadelphia: Edgewood, 1891. With the exception of the brief concluding chapter, in fact "told by" Barnum, whose use of the first-person singular pronoun has been transposed by Benton into the third-person singular.

—— "P. T. Barnum, Showman and Humorist," *Century Magazine,* August 1902, pp. 580–92.

Betts, John Rickards. "P. T. Barnum and the Popularization of Natural History," *Journal of the History of Ideas,* 20 (1959), 353–68.

Bleeker, Sylvester. *Gen. Tom Thumb's Three Years' Tour Around the World, Accompanied by His Wife—Lavinia Warren Stratton, Commodore Nutt, Minnie Warren, and Party.* New York: S. Booth, 1872.

Bogdan, Robert. *Freak Show: Presenting Human Oddities for Amusement and Profit.* Chicago: Univ. of Chicago Press, 1988.

Bradford, Gamaliel. *Damaged Souls.* Boston: Houghton Mifflin, 1923.

Brown, T. Allston. *History of the American Stage, Containing Biographical Sketches of Nearly Every Member of the Profession That Has Appeared on the American Stage from 1733 to 1870.* 1870; rpt. New York: Benjamin Blom, 1969.

Bulman, Joan. *Jenny Lind: A Biography.* London: James Barrie, 1956.

Bunn, Alfred. *Old England and New England, in a Series of Views Taken on the Spot.* 1853; rpt. New York: Benjamin Blom, 1969.

[Butler, William Allen.] *Barnum's Parnassus: Being Confidential Disclosures of the Prize Committee on the Jenny Lind Song, with Specimens of the Leading American Poets in the Happiest Effulgence of Their Genius, Respectfully Dedicated to the American Eagle.* New York: D. Appleton, 1850. 52 pp.

Complimentary Banquet to P. T. Barnum, from Citizens of Bridgeport, Conn., Atlantic House, June 25th, 1874. Bridgeport, Conn.: Standard Assn., 1874.

Conklin, George. *The Ways of the Circus, Being the Memories and Adventures of George Conklin, Tamer of Lions.* Set down by Harvey W. Root. New York: Harper & Bros., 1921.

Conover, Richard E. *The Affairs of James A. Bailey: New Revelations on the Career of the World's Most Successful Showman.* Xenia, Ohio: by the author, 1957. 17 pp.

—— "William Cameron Coup of Delavan." In the same author's *The Circus: Wisconsin's Unique Heritage,* pp. 20–25. Baraboo, Wisc.: State Historical Society of Wisconsin and The Circus World Museum, 1967.

Coup, W. C. *Sawdust & Spangles: Stories & Secrets of the Circus.* 1901; rpt. Washington, D.C.: Paul A. Ruddell, 1961. From "notes" left by Coup and edited by Forrest Crissey.

Dahlinger, Fred, Jr. "The Development of the Railroad Circus," *Bandwagon,* 27, No. 6 (1983), 6–11; 28, No. 1 (1984), 16–27; 28, No. 2 (1984), 28–36; 28, No. 3 (1984), 29–36. (Four parts in all.)

Deems, Charles F. "Alice and Phoebe Cary: Their Home and Friends," *Packard's Monthly,* N.S., 3, No. 2 (February 1870), 49–52.

Desmond, Alice Curtis. *Barnum Presents General Tom Thumb.* New York: Macmillan, 1954.

Durant, John, and Alice Durant. *Pictorial History of the American Circus.* New York: A. S. Barnes, 1957.

Emerson, George H. "The Barnums," *The Repository: A Magazine for the Christian Home,* March 1874, pp. 215–20.

Ezell, John Samuel. *Fortune's Merry Wheel: The Lottery in America.* Cambridge, Mass.: Harvard Univ. Press, 1960.

Fellows, Dexter W., and Andrew A. Freeman. *This Way to the Big Show: The Life of Dexter Fellows.* New York: Halcyon House, 1936.

Fisher, L. B. "Recollections of P. T. Barnum," *Christian Leader,* 16 November 1929, pp. 1457–58. First published in 1894 in the *Laurentian* of St. Lawrence University.

Fisk, T. *The Nation's Bulwark: An Oration on the Freedom of the Press, Delivered at the Court House in Danbury, Con.* [sic], *Wednesday, Dec. 5, 1832, on the Liberation of P. T. Barnum, Esq., Editor of the Herald of Freedom, from Imprisonment for an Alledged* [sic] *Libel. To Which Is Appended an Account of the Proceedings on That Occasion, Together with a Letter Addressed to Him While in Prison.* New Haven: at the office of the *Examiner* and *Watchtower of Freedom,* [1832].

Fitzsimons, Raymund. *Barnum in London.* New York: St. Martin's Press, 1970.

Fox, Charles Philip, and Tom Parkinson. *The Circus in America.* Waukesha, Wisc.: Country Beautiful, 1969.

Franco, Barbara. *The Cardiff Giant: A Hundred Year Old Hoax.* Cooperstown, N.Y.: New York State Historical Society, 1969. Reprinted from the October 1969 issue of *New York History.*

Funeral of Mrs. Charity Barnum, Wife of P. T. Barnum, Born in Fairfield, CT., Oct. 28th, 1808, Died in New York City, Nov. 19th, 1873. No place: n.p. [1874]. 20 pp.

Garth, Thomas Russell. *The Life of Henry Augustus Buchtel.* Denver, Colo.: Peerless Printing Co., 1937.

Goldfarb, Alvin. "Gigantic and Miniscule Actors on the Nineteenth-Century American Stage," *Journal of Popular Culture,* 10 (1976), 267–79.

Grimaldi, Lennie. *Only in Bridgeport: An Illustrated History of the Park City.* Northridge, Calif.: Windsor, 1986.

Haberly, Loyd. "The American Museum from Baker to Barnum," *New-York Historical Society Quarterly,* 43 (1959), 273–87.

Hagenbeck, Carl. *Von Tieren und Menschen.* Berlin: Vita Deutsches Verlagshaus, 1909.

Harris, Neil. *Humbug: The Art of P. T. Barnum.* Boston: Little, Brown, 1973.

Hersey, Harry Adams. *A History of Music in Tufts College.* Medford, Mass.: Trustees of Tufts College, 1947.

Hoffman, Richard. *Some Musical Recollections of Fifty Years.* New York: Charles Scribner's Sons, 1910.

Holland, Henry Scott, and W. S. Rockstro. *Memoir of Madame Jenny Lind-Goldschmidt: Her Early Art-Life and Dramatic Career, 1820–1851, from Original Documents, Letters, MS. Diaries, &c., Collected by Mr. Otto Goldschmidt.* 2 vols. London: John Murray, 1891.

James, Henry. *A Small Boy and Others.* New York: Charles Scribner's Sons, 1913.

Jerome, Chauncey. *History of the American Clock Business for the Past Sixty Years, and Life of Chauncey Jerome, Written by Himself. Barnum's Connection with the Yankee Clock Business.* New Haven, Conn.: Dayton, 1860.

Jolly, W. P. *Jumbo.* London: Constable, 1976.

Kunzog, John C. *Tanbark and Tinsel: A Galaxy of Glittering Gems from the Dazzling Diadem of Circus History.* Jamestown, N.Y.: by the author, 1970.

Lanigan, Alice Graham. "Mrs. Phineas T. Barnum," *Ladies' Home Journal,* February 1891.

Larrabee, Eric. "The Old Showman's Last Triumph," *American Heritage,* December 1961. A heavily illustrated article based on one of the scrapbooks assembled during Barnum's 1889–90 visit with his circus to London.

Leland, Charles Godfrey. *Memoirs.* 2 vols. London: Wm. Heinemann, 1893.

Lewisohn, Ludwig. *Expression in America.* New York: Harper & Bros., 1932.

Lots About Lots; or, The Great Fair and What Preceded It. "Sold for the Benefit of the Mountain Grove Cemetery." Bridgeport, Conn.: Farmer Office Presses, 1879.

Ludlow, Noah M. *Dramatic Life as I Found It: A Record of Personal Experience, with an Account of the Rise and Progress of the Drama in the West and South, with Anecdotes and Biographical Sketches of the Principal Actors and Actresses Who Have at Times Appeared Upon the Stage in the Mississippi Valley.* Intro. by Francis Hodge. 1880; rpt. New York: Benjamin Blom, 1966.

McGlinchee, Claire. *The First Decade of the Boston Museum.* Boston: Bruce Humphries, 1940.

Maretzek, Max. *Crotchets and Quavers; or, Revelations of an Opera Manager in America.* New York: S. French, 1855.

Miller, Russell E. *The Larger Hope: The First Century of the Universalist Church in America, 1770–1870.* Boston: Unitarian Universalist Assn., 1979.

—— *The Larger Hope: The Second Century of the Universalist Church in America, 1870–1970.* Boston: Unitarian Universalist Assn., 1985.

Morinni, Clara de. "P. T. Barnum's Second Wife," *New Yorker,* 11 April 1936.

Neafie, Nelle. *A P. T. Barnum Bibliography.* 1965. Reproduced typescript, 55 pp., prepared while the compiler was working toward a graduate degree in library science and listing primarily correspondence by Barnum and books either by or about him that were then in the Barnum Museum and the Bridgeport Public Library.

Niven, John. *Connecticut for the Union: The Role of the State in the Civil War.* New Haven, Conn.: Yale Univ. Press, 1965.

O'Higgins, Harvey, and Edward H. Reede. *The American Mind in Action.* New York: Harper & Bros., 1924.

Orcutt, Samuel. *A History of the Old Town of Stratford and the City of Bridgeport, Connecticut.* 2 vols. with consecutive pagination. New Haven: Tuttle, Morehouse & Taylor for the Fairfield County Historical Society, 1886.

Ordway, Wendell H. *Olympia Gleanings: A Review of the Winter Season of 1889–90 in London, England, with P. T. Barnum's Greatest Show on Earth.* London: Walter Hill, 1890. 80 pp.

Palmquist, David W. *Bridgeport: A Pictorial History.* Rev. ed. Norfolk, Va.: Donning, 1985.

Pond, J. B. *Eccentricities of Genius: Memories of Famous Men and Women of the Platform and Stage.* New York: G. W. Dillingham, 1900.

Presbrey, Frank. *The History and Development of Advertising.* Garden City, N.Y.: Doubleday, Doran, 1929.

Proceedings of the [Bridgeport] *Common Council of 1875–76.* Bridgeport, Conn.: Standard and Farmer Offices, n.d.

Prospectus of Barnum's Museum Company. New York: printed by Kilbourne Tompkins, n.d. A copy of this 8-page pamphlet, for Barnum's grandiose scheme of 1880, is in the Museum of the City of New York's Theatre Collection.

Pulsifer, Janice Goldsmith. "Alice and Phoebe Cary, Whittier's Sweet Singers of the West," *Essex Institute Historical Collections,* 109 (1973), 9–59.

Reports of the Fairfield County Historical Society, Bridgeport, Conn., for 1893–5. No place: by the Society, 1895. Includes descriptions of ceremonies at the opening of the Barnum Institute of Science and History in 1893, an obituary of William H. Noble, etc.

Romaine, Mertie E. *General Tom Thumb and His Lady.* Taunton, Mass.: William S. Sullwold, 1976.

Root, Harvey W. *The Unknown Barnum.* New York: Harper & Bros., 1927.

Rosenberg, C. G. *Jenny Lind in America.* New York: Stringer & Townsend, 1851.

Rourke, Constance Mayfield. *Trumpets of Jubilee: Henry Ward Beecher, Harriet Beecher Stowe, Lyman Beecher, Horace Greeley, P. T. Barnum.* New York: Harcourt, Brace, 1927.

"Route Books." These are nearly always annual volumes—containing a day-by-day record of where a show played; the miles traveled to get there and the number of spectators attending; accidents, deaths, and other notable events; together with lists of performers and the personnel in various "departments"; etc.—that were generally compiled by someone traveling with the show and published at the end of each season as a kind of souvenir. At one time such books—usually pamphlets, but sometimes fairly extensive and bound in hard covers—were produced in connection with most major American circuses. The Bridgeport Public Library possesses route books for most of the years Barnum was in circus management. The Ordway work cited above is an example of such a book for the 1889–90 London season.

Sanger, George. *Seventy Years a Showman*. London: J. M. Dent, 1938.

Saxon, A. H. "Barnum à Bridgeport," *Cirque dans l'Univers*, No. 83 (4ᵉ trimestre 1971), pp. 25–30.

—— "Barnum, Nineteenth-Century Science, and Some 'Unnatural' History," *Discovery* (magazine of Yale University's Peabody Museum of Natural History), 21, No. 1 (1988), 28–35.

—— "Le Cirque Américain." Chapter 17 in *Le Grand Livre du cirque*. Ed. by Monica J. Renevey. 2 vols. Geneva, Switzerland: Edito-Service, 1977.

—— "A Franconi in America: The New York Hippodrome of 1853," *Bandwagon*, 19, No. 5 (1975), 13–17.

—— "Jumbo: Vita, morte e resurrezione," *Circo*, 17, No. 9 (1985), 18–20; 17, No. 10 (1985), 18–20.

—— *Letters I Wish P. T. Barnum Had Written*. Fairfield, Conn.: by the author, 1983. Limited to 25 copies. An 8-page pamphlet containing forgeries by the author, who was tempted to include them in his edition of Barnum's letters, but didn't. Copies have been deposited in the American Philosophical Society's library, the Bridgeport Public Library, the Library of Congress Manuscript Division, the Circus World Museum in Baraboo, Wisconsin, the British Library, Tufts University, the New-York Historical Society, the Boston Athenaeum, and Yale University.

—— *The Life and Art of Andrew Ducrow & The Romantic Age of the English Circus*. Hamden, Conn.: Archon Books, 1978.

—— "Olympia Brown in Bridgeport: 'Acts of Injustice' or a Failed Ministry?" *Proceedings of the Unitarian Universalist Historical Society*, 21, Pt. 1 (1987–88), 55–65.

—— "P. T. Barnum and the Great Sea Serpent," *Bandwagon*, 27, No. 1 (1983), 20–22.

—— "P. T. Barnum, der Meister der Showmen." In *Kassette 9: Rock, Pop, Schlager, Revue, Zirkus, Kabarett, Magie—ein Almanach*, pp. 125–34. Berlin: Henschelverlag, 1986.

—— "P. T. Barnum: Universalism's Surprising 'Prince of Humbugs,'" *The World* (journal of the Unitarian Universalist Assn.), 2, No. 3 (1988), 4–7, 50.

—— "P. T. Barnum's American Museum," *Seaport*, 20, No. 3 (Winter 1986–87), 27–33.

—— "Phinéas T. Barnum Vu à Travers Sa Correspondance," *Cirque dans l'Univers*, No. 124 (1ᵉʳ trimestre 1982), pp. 3–8.

—— "'There's a Sucker Born Every Minute' (But None of Them Ever Die)," *Bandwagon*, 31, No. 2 (1987), 34–35.

—— "La Vie et l'Enigme du 'Général' Tom Pouce," *Cirque dans l'Univers*, No. 141 (2ᵉ trimestre 1986), pp. 3–7.

Scott, Matthew. *Autobiography of Matthew Scott, Jumbo's Keeper, Formerly of the Zoological Society's Gardens, London, and Receiver of Sir Edwin Landseer Medal in 1866. Also Jumbo's Biography, by the Same Author*. Bridgeport: Trow's Printing and Bookbinding of New York, 1885. Not really by Scott, although obviously based on his recollections, but presumably by the author Thomas E. Lowe.

Seaburg, Alan. "Remembering Publishing History: Universalist Periodicals," *Unitarian Universalist World*, 15 April 1971.

Sellers, Charles Coleman. *Mr. Peale's Museum: Charles Willson Peale and the First Popular Museum of Natural Science and Art*. New York: W. W. Norton, 1980.

Shultz, Gladys Denny. *Jenny Lind: The Swedish Nightingale*. Philadelphia: J. B. Lippincott, 1962.

Skinner, Otis. *Footlights and Spotlights: Recollections of My Life on the Stage*. Indianapolis, Ind.: Bobbs-Merrill, 1924.

Smith, Albert. "A Go-A-Head Day with Barnum," *Bentley's Miscellany*, 21 (1847), 522–27, 623–28.

Smith, Sol. *The Theatrical Journey-Work and Anecdotal Recollections of Sol. Smith, Co-median, Attorney at Law, Etc., Etc., Comprising a Sketch of the Second Seven Years of His Professional Life, Together with Sketches of Adventure* [sic] *in After Years.* Philadelphia: T. B. Peterson, 1854. Dedication to Barnum, pp. 7–10.

—— *Theatrical Management in the West and South for Thirty Years.* Intro. by Arthur Thomas Tees. 1868; rpt. New York: Benjamin Blom, 1968.

Speaight, George. *A History of the Circus.* London: Tantivy, 1980.

Sterling, Julian H. "Bridgeport—A Story of Progress," *Connecticut Magazine,* 8 (1903–4), 785–802; 9 (1905), 349–83.

—— *Space, with Historical Memoirs and Other Writings.* Bridgeport, Conn.: Marigold-Foster Printing Co., 1904.

Stott. *See* Toole-Stott, Raymond.

Strong, George Templeton. *The Diary of George Templeton Strong.* Ed. by Allan Nevins and Milton Halsey Thomas. 4 vols. New York: Macmillan, 1952.

Thayer, Stuart. *Annals of the American Circus, 1793–1829.* Manchester, Mich.: Rymack Printing Co., 1976.

—— *Annals of the American Circus, 1830–1847.* Seattle, Wash.: Peanut Butter Publishing, 1986.

Thumb, Mrs. Tom. *The Autobiography of Mrs. Tom Thumb (Some of My Life Experiences).* Ed. and intro. by A. H. Saxon. Hamden, Conn.: Archon Books, 1979.

Toole-Stott, Raymond. *Circus and Allied Arts: A World Bibliography.* 4 vols (with a fifth in typescript at the Univ. of California at Santa Barbara). Derby, Eng.: Harpur & Sons, 1958–71. (Note that the compiler was never very consistent in the hyphenating of his name. He had abandoned the hyphen by the time he came to publish the fourth volume of the present work, and did not reuse it in his later 2-vol. bibliography of conjuring.)

Tupper, Edith Sessions. "P. T. Barnum at Home," *New York World,* 15 March 1891.

Turner, Gregg M., and Melancthon W. Jacobus. *Connecticut Railroads . . . An Illustrated History: One Hundred Fifty Years of Railroad History.* Hartford, Conn.: Connecticut Historical Society, 1986.

Twain, Mark. *Mark Twain's Travels with Mr. Brown, Being Heretofore Uncollected Sketches Written by Mark Twain for the San Francisco* Alta California *in 1866 & 1867, Describing the Adventures of the Author and His Irrepressible Companion in Nicaragua, Hannibal, New York, and Other Spots on Their Way to Europe.* Ed. by Franklin Walker and G. Ezra Dane. New York: Alfred A. Knopf, 1940.

Vail, R. W. G. *Random Notes on the History of the Early American Circus.* Barre, Mass.: Barre Gazette, 1956.

Wallace, Irving. *The Fabulous Showman: The Life and Times of P. T. Barnum.* New York: Alfred A. Knopf, 1959.

Ward, Henry A. *The Life and Death of Jumbo: An Illustrated History of the Greatest, Gentlest and Most Famous and Heroic Beast That Ever Lived.* Philadelphia: n.p., 1886. 15 pp.

Ware, W. Porter, and Thaddeus C. Lockard Jr. *P. T. Barnum Presents Jenny Lind: The American Tour of the Swedish Nightingale.* Baton Rouge, La.: Louisiana State Univ. Press, 1980.

Welles, Gordon, and William Proios. *Port Jefferson: Story of a Village.* Port Jefferson, N.Y.: Historical Society of Greater Port Jefferson, 1977.

Werner, M. R. *Barnum.* New York: Harcourt, Brace, 1923.

Willis, N. P. *Famous Persons and Famous Places.* London: Ward and Lock, 1854.

Wilmeth, Don B. *Variety Entertainment and Outdoor Amusements: A Reference Guide.* Westport, Conn.: Greenwood Press, 1982.

ACKNOWLEDGMENTS

I am indebted to so many people who have aided me in my Barnum research over the past decade that I hardly know where to begin. The late Mrs. Mildred Breul and her son Alvin C. Breul, Esq., also now deceased, were the first of the Barnum descendants to start me on my quest, and it was largely through the latter that I was introduced to, and received the generous support of, other heirs and descendants: in particular Miss Mary D. Upton and her late mother Mrs. John D. Upton, Mrs. Herbert Barnum Seeley Jr., Mrs. Augustine W. Tucker Jr., and the late Mr. Paul T. Rennell.

The hundreds of librarians and curators with whom I have been in contact over this same period have also been of the greatest assistance, and I have already mentioned many of them by name in my edition of Barnum's letters. For their continued support and various favors while the present work was in progress, I wish to express my special gratitude to Mr. David W. Palmquist, former Head of Historical Collections at the Bridgeport Public Library; Mr. Robert Johnson-Lally, Associate Archivist at Tufts University; Mr. Thomas Dunnings, of the New-York Historical Society; Mr. Karl Kabelac, Manuscripts Librarian at the University of Rochester; Mr. Chris H. Bailey, former Managing Director of the American Clock & Watch Museum; Miss Jane Langton, Registrar of the Royal Archives at Windsor Castle; Mr. John D. Cushing, Librarian at the Massachusetts Historical Society; Mr. Greg Parkinson, Director of the Circus World Museum; Mr. Benjamin Ortiz, of the Barnum Museum in Bridgeport; and above all to the Curator of the last-named institution, my good friend Mr. Robert S. Pelton, who has always granted me free access to all the treasures in his keeping, besides encouraging me at several critical junctures.

In Barnum's hometown of Bethel, once part of Danbury, I was assisted by the Reverend Michael S. Strah, Pastor of the First Congregational Church, and Mr. Eugene Reed, of the church's cemetery association; Mr. Thaddeus E. Carzasty, the Bethel Tax Assessor; Mr. George Grumman, of the Bethel Public Library and Historical Society; Mr. and Mrs. George C. Reimers, the onetime owners of Barnum's birthplace; the local historian, Mr. Edward J. Gallagher; and Mrs. Dorothy T. Schling, formerly Director of the Scott-Fanton Museum in Danbury. In Bridgeport and its vicinity I have been materially helped by the Reverend Albert F. Ciarcia, of the Unitarian Universalist Church of Greater Bridgeport; Mr. Charles Brilvitch, architectural historian, who supplied several items of information pertaining to Barnum's real estate and homes; the late Mr. Lou Corbit, photographer; Mr. Armand Chevrette and his staff at Mountain Grove Cemetery; the Honorable Leonard S. Paoletta, former Mayor of Bridgeport; Mr. Lennie Grimaldi; Jerry Davidoff, Esq.; Mr. Eric Saxon; and Mr. Charles H. Parks, who provided information on Barnum's second Fairfield mansion, Lindencroft. Indeed, I am indebted to so many Bridgeporters and former Bridgeporters for stray bits of information that I might almost be pardoned for thanking the entire population of that much maligned city.

Elsewhere I have been aided by the Reverend Bruce Southworth and Mr. David Dunlop, of New York City; Mr. Bill McWilliams, of the Unitarian Universalist Society of Northern Fairfield County; Mr. Alexander P. Clark, of Princeton; Mr. Justin Kaplan, the noted biographer; Messrs. David and Robert Mathisen; Mrs. Helen W. Smith, of the

Newtown Bee; Mr. Ralph L. Emerson Jr.; Mr. Robin Kincaid; Mr. Kenneth B. Holmes, the retired Curator of the Barnum Museum; Mrs. Robert R. Parrish; Messrs. Seth H. Moseley 2d and Bernard Drew; Mrs. Susan C. S. Edwards, of the Berkshire County Historical Society; Mr. Charles Hamilton, the celebrated autograph expert; Dr. Christopher P. Bickford, Director of the Connecticut Historical Society; Mrs. Harriet H. Stickney, of the Little People of America; Mrs. Leslie P. Symington; Messrs. Fred Nathans and his brother, John Avery Nathans; Mr. Merton L. Curtis; Mr. Fred Dahlinger Jr.; Professors Laurence Senelick and Don B. Wilmeth; Mr. Ricky Jay; Mr. Ralph Wilcoxen; Mr. Cor Videler, of Saugatuck Photolab of Westport; Mrs. Florence S. Oliver, Town Historian of Somers, New York; and especially Mr. Manson Whitlock, who kept me at my typewriter on more than one occasion and provided me a place to "hang out" while on my frequent jaunts to New Haven.

Certain other individuals have been more than generous with their time, patience, and friendship over the years, and here I wish to single out Mr. Stuart Thayer, historian of the American circus and past President of the Circus Historical Society; Cyril B. Mills, Esq., author and onetime owner of England's famed Bertram Mills Circus; Messrs. Fred D. Pfening Jr. and Fred D. Pfening III, the latter currently the President of the Circus Historical Society, who have unfailingly granted me access to their private circus collection, undoubtedly the finest and most extensive of its kind in America; and to my dear friend M. L.-R. Dauven, President of the Club du Cirque and Editor, for more years than he probably cares to remember, of its distinguished journal, *Le Cirque dans l'Univers*. Above all, I am indebted to the Reverend Alan Seaburg, poet, Curator of Manuscripts at the Harvard Divinity School, and one of the last, if not the oldest, surviving Universalists in America, who read this book in its preliminary drafts and offered, in his uniquely tolerant way, many invaluable suggestions.

My initial research on Barnum was done under a fellowship provided by the John Simon Guggenheim Memorial Foundation, whose generous financial support, as in the case of my earlier biography of the English equestrian Andrew Ducrow, is gratefully acknowledged. The late President of the Foundation, Mr. Gordon N. Ray, as other fellows can testify, was always equally lavish with moral support, of which authors like myself, in their lonely profession, often stand in need. The Foundation has additionally provided a handsome subvention for the present book's color plates.

A number of topics addressed in this book were previewed in such journals and magazines as *Le Cirque dans l'Univers, Bandwagon, Circo, Seaport*, the Unitarian Universalist *World, Discovery*, the UNESCO *Courier*, and the East German annual *Kassette*. The welcome encouragement of the editors of those publications is also hereby acknowledged. Finally, it gives me great pleasure to pay tribute to the expert and sympathetic assistance I have received these many years from the staff at Columbia University Press, in particular from Mr. William F. Bernhardt, retired Executive Editor, who not only offered me the contracts for this and my earlier volume of Barnum's letters but who also volunteered to serve as editor of the present work; and from Miss Joan McQuary, Managing Editor, who personally did the same for the letters volume.

INDEX OF PERSONS